Eating Disorders

An Encyclopedia of Causes, Treatment, and Prevention

JUSTINE J. REEL, PHD, LPC, CC-AASP,
Editor

GREENWOOD

AN IMPRINT OF ABC-CLIO, LLC
Santa Barbara, California • Denver, Colorado • Oxford, England

Library of Congress Cataloging-in-Publication Data

Eating disorders : an encyclopedia of causes, treatment, and prevention /Justine J. Reel, editor.
   p. cm.
  Includes bibliographical references and index.
  ISBN 978-1-4408-0058-0 (hardback) — ISBN 978-1-4408-0059-7 (ebook)
1. Eating disorders—Encyclopedias. I. Reel, Justine J.
  RC552.E18E28216 2013
  616.85'26003—dc23   2012029948

ISBN: 978-1-4408-0058-0
EISBN: 978-1-4408-0059-7

17 16 15 14 13   2 3 4 5

This book is also available on the World Wide Web as an eBook.
Visit www.abc-clio.com for details.

Greenwood
An Imprint of ABC-CLIO, LLC

ABC-CLIO, LLC
130 Cremona Drive, P.O. Box 1911
Santa Barbara, California 93116-1911

This book is printed on acid-free paper ∞

Manufactured in the United States of America

Contents

Introduction

My fascination with eating disorders and body image began in the 1980s and came into focus when Karen Carpenter died from an eating disorder in 1983. As a teenager, I had not recognized any drawbacks associated with being too thin or being overly disciplined with regard to one's diet. In fact, the term "anorexia nervosa" was new to me, as eating disorders were not discussed in health classes or in blogs. Pro-ana websites did not exist. I understood the emotions and the psyche linked to striving for a different body and wanting to be smaller, blonder, and more attractive to the opposite sex. In high school, I endured lunches consisting of an apple and a slice of diet bread following demoralizing cheerleading practices spent comparing the body weight of squad members to determine who was lightest and most worthy of being on the top of the pyramid. On my way to college I was given a concrete weight goal in the form of an invitation letter from a university cheerleading coach. The coach stated that there was a weight requirement to try out for the squad and I realized with horror that I was 30 pounds heavier than the limit. My newfound motivation helped me engage in exercise beyond exhaustion, running in the rain and snow and continuing to exercise despite being sick, sore, or on vacation. I limited my intake of animal products and instead consumed Fruit Loops and Mountain Dew for energy. Once I started noticing weight loss, my discipline was instantly reinforced, and I was rewarded with compliments from my fellow classmates and teammates. I began scoring the flyer position on the cheerleading squad as I was tossed by my now heavier squad members. Despite the euphoria I felt knowing that I was lighter and my clothing was baggy, I felt incredibly fatigued. My senior year was riddled with absences for sick days when I did not have the energy to go to school. I displayed symptoms of chronic fatigue syndrome before it was identified as a recognized medical condition. My hair was falling out, my temperature was thrown off, and I had headaches and stomachaches constantly. My French teacher asked me if I was taking drugs because I was acting spacey. My obsession with dieting, food, and exercise followed me into the dorms of Clemson University. I ran before class, after class, and between classes when I was not swimming laps for hours. I attended aerobics classes and worked out through exhaustion and hunger. I would binge on my roommate's granola bars and then experience tremendous guilt, which cycled back to a variety of purging methods while suffering in silence. Throughout these two years, no one ever accused me of having an eating disorder. In fact, I was envied for my "perseverance" in exercising regularly and my high school boyfriend wrote in my yearbook that I "looked good now that I had lost all this weight."

x INTRODUCTION

You may wonder how this story ends. Fortunately in my case, I was able to slowly rehabilitate myself from destructive patterns of food and exercise. During my sophomore year in college, I began to reintroduce meat and other restricted foods back into my diet and take a more balanced approach to eating and exercise. I had the opportunity to cheer for a professional cheerleading squad and swim for a water polo club, which boosted my self-confidence and gave me a more structured way to exercise. I received some general counseling for grief/loss issues and relationships, but there were no eating disorder–specific treatment options available at that time in the Carolinas. I read books and learned more about the secretive nature of eating disorders. As an undergraduate student, I vowed to help others with eating and body image struggles as part of my career and life's work. I am a testament to the possibility of achieving "recovered status" from an eating disorder, which I have enjoyed for over 20 years without a scale or calorie counter.

As a master's student, my thesis topic was already identified before I started graduate school. My goal was to study weight pressures associated with high school and college cheerleaders that can contribute to body dissatisfaction and disordered eating behaviors. At the time of this publication, I have studied weight pressures among female and male athletes across sports and dance for the past 19 years as a researcher. I have also investigated the influences of age, race/ethnicity, and gender on body image across general populations.

As a Licensed Professional Counselor in the state of Utah, I have observed eating disorders from the other side of the office working in residential, inpatient, and outpatient settings. I had the opportunity to help develop the first eating disorder residential treatment program in Salt Lake City and created an exercise education component as part of the treatment and recovery process to address exercise dependence. As a primary therapist, I observed clients who lost their jobs, families, dropped out of school, and were hospitalized due to dangerously low potassium levels. I realized that the treatment process resembled a rollercoaster, with some clients improving in the residential setting and showing symptom reduction only to slip when they transitioned to an outpatient level of care. Other clients surprisingly would begin to develop self-harming behaviors once their eating disorder behaviors subsided.

Being an eating disorder treatment provider is extremely rewarding; however, more recently, I have been focusing on prevention by integrating eating disorder and obesity prevention efforts in programming for adolescents and their parents. I started a student organization 10 years ago called Students Promoting Eating Disorder Awareness and Knowledge to increase awareness about eating disorders and to promote positive body image. Although societal awareness has improved exponentially since Karen Carpenter's death, over 10 million individuals suffer from eating disorders in the United States. Many cases go undiagnosed for years and many individuals are overlooked because they do not meet the traditional stereotype of having an eating disorder—being young, white, thin, and female. It is estimated that 10–25 percent of eating disorder cases are males who have severely deteriorated when they finally present for treatment.

Fortunately, treatment options have improved since my high school years and now include eating disorder treatment facilities in most states. Treatment continues to be expensive and can run upward of $1000/day with limited or no insurance support. Families struggle to make decisions on what is affordable versus what is necessary for their daughter's or son's health and survival. Exceptions such as Eating Disorder Anonymous and Overeaters Anonymous provide free support groups in communities across the country.

Eating disorders are often misunderstood as being about eating and food. However, the disorder comes from the emotions underlying a dysfunctional relationship with food, exercise, and the self. Individuals with eating disorders express poor self-esteem, perfectionism, and intense body dissatisfaction. This strong fear of gaining weight can lead to behaviors such as restricting, purging (e.g., self-induced vomiting, laxatives) or binge eating episodes. The categories of eating disorders (Anorexia Nervosa, Bulimia Nervosa and Eating Disorder Not Otherwise Specified) seek to classify disorders by symptoms largely for insurance purposes. However, disordered eating behaviors can exist along a spectrum, and it is important to recognize that the underlying psychological characteristics and emotions can be interconnected for binge eating and restricting. Therefore, programs that target the country's obesity epidemic should be careful to address emotional eating; adequate emphasis should be placed on developing a more positive relationship with food and with one's body. In this volume you will read about a few prevention programs, such as Healthy Buddies and Full of Ourselves, which seek to promote health and prevent eating disorders.

Finally, the volume includes information about how to refer someone who is suspected of having an eating disorder. Being a friend or family member can be extremely difficult; in order to help them eating disorder resources are provided as well as specific entries on treatment modalities (e.g., nutritional treatment approaches). Case studies are presented to illuminate the intricacies associated with various presentations of eating disorders. It should be noted that although patterns exist across individuals with eating disorder symptoms, each person is and should be treated as an individual and unique case.

In sum, as a voice of recovery, an eating disorder researcher, an eating disorder therapist, and the editor of this encyclopedia about the causes, treatment and prevention of eating disorders, I hope that you will use this volume for your own personal and professional needs. If you are writing a research paper you will find the necessary background information here. You will also be able to locate valuable resources and information about how best to support someone with an eating disorder. If you are struggling with an eating disorder you may even see yourself on these pages.

Justine J. Reel, PhD, LPC, CC-AASP

Timeline

1300s	A female saint, Catherine of Siena (1347–1380), was said to eat "only a handful of herbs each day," representing food refusal and prolonged fasting common among female and male saints from 1200 to 1500.
1686	First medically diagnosed case of anorexia nervosa, a 20-year-old female, termed by Richard Morton as "nervous atrophy" and described as "a skeleton only clad with skin."
1865	Dunglison's dictionary defined anorexia as "absence of appetite."
1874	British Physician Sir William Gull formally used the term "anorexia nervosa" (lack of desire to eat due to a mental condition).
1903	Psychiatrist Pierre Janet describes "mixed" eating disorder case of Nadja and emphasizes the obsession with thinness, refusal of food, and secret binges leading to medical term "bulimia" (derived from Latin meaning "hunger of an ox").
1950s	Binge eating was observed and reported in obesity studies by Dr. Albert Stunkard of the University of Pennsylvania; clients referred to as "compulsive overeaters."
1952	Anorexia nervosa was included in the original *Diagnostic and Statistical Manual of Mental Disorders* as a "psychophysiological reaction."
January 1960	Overeaters Anonymous (OA) founded by Rozanne S. and two women to provide a twelve-step group that addressed issues related to food.
1968	Anorexia nervosa was listed under special symptoms/feeding disturbances in the *Diagnostic and Statistical Manual of Mental Disorders 2nd Edition (DSM-II)*
1978	Hilde Bruch published *The Golden Cage* to depict anorexia nervosa for lay audiences.
1980	First classification of eating disorders as a separate section; bulimia nervosa received first mention as a psychiatric disorder in *Diagnostic and Statistical Manual of Mental Disorder 3rd Edition (DSM-III)*.

1981	First scientific journal for eating disorders, *International Journal of Eating Disorders,* published first volume.
February 1983	Karen Carpenter died of heart failure associated with anorexia nervosa at age 32.
1985	The Renfrew Center, the first freestanding eating disorder treatment facility, opened its doors in Philadelphia, Pennsylvania.
1985	*International Association of Eating Disorder Professionals (IAEDP)* formed to provide training to eating disorder providers.
1987	Term "exercise dependence" introduced by Veale and described as a negative mood state experienced in the absence of exercise.
1992	The term "binge eating disorder" was formally introduced in the scientific literature by Robert Spitzer in the *International Journal of Eating Disorders.*
1992	Christy Henrich, an Olympic gymnast, died from complications due to an eating disorder.
1993	Professional organization *Academy for Eating Disorders (AED)* hosted its first meeting of 33 clinicians and researchers in Tulsa, Oklahoma.
1994	Binge Eating Disorder (BED) was included in the research criteria for the *Diagnostic and Statistical Manual of Mental Disorders (DSM-IV).*
1997	Heidi Guenther, a professional ballet dancer from the Boston Ballet Company, dies from an eating disorder.
2000	Eating Disorders Anonymous (EDA) was formed by Alcoholics Anonymous members in Phoenix, Arizona, to offer a twelve-step group for eating disorders.
2001	National Eating Disorder Association, a nonprofit eating disorder organization, was formed to help families.
May 2002	Students Promoting Eating Disorder Awareness and Knowledge founded at University of Utah to conduct eating disorder research and outreach.

A

ACADEMY FOR EATING DISORDERS

The Academy for Eating Disorders (AED) was founded in 1993 by Dr. Craig Johnson in Tulsa, Oklahoma, USA. The first AED conference, which included 33 eating disorder professionals who treated individuals with eating disorders or conducted research on the topic, met to discuss challenges associated with eating disorder treatment including insurance practices and managed care. Currently, AED meets annually and represents an international membership of over 1,000 physicians, psychologists, nurses, social workers, dietitians, and researchers from a variety of fields.

As stated on the Academy for Eating Disorders website, AED is "a global professional association committed to leadership in eating disorders through research, education, treatment and prevention." AED identified objectives for the organization that were related to advancing knowledge about eating disorder treatment and prevention, supporting research efforts, and developing guidelines for evidence-based practice. AED currently supports 23 special interest groups that focus on topics ranging from bariatric surgery and eating disorders to males and eating disorders. In a position paper published in 2009, AED emphasized that eating disorders are serious mental illnesses that warrant the same level of health care coverage as other mental disorders.

JUSTINE J. REEL

See also: Bariatric Surgery.

Bibliography

www.aedweb.org. Retrieved May 31, 2011.
Klump, Kelly L., Cynthia M. Bulik, Walter H. Kaye, Janet Treasure, and Edward Tyson. Academy for Eating Disorders Position Paper: "Eating Disorders Are Serious Mental Illnesses." *International Journal of Eating Disorders* 42, no. 2 (2009): 97–103.

ADOLESCENT DEVELOPMENT

Adolescence refers to the developmental transition from childhood (i.e., 10 to 13 years of age) to adulthood (i.e., 18 to 22 years of age). Adolescence can be a challenging time for both boys and girls, even when development is occurring at a natural and healthy rate. Developmental processes include physical, cognitive, moral, social, and self-identity.

Physical Development

The beginning of adolescence is marked by the onset of puberty (i.e., the process leading to physical, sexual, and psychosocial maturation). From a biological perspective, puberty is the process of maturation of the reproductive system, after which the individual is able to bear children. The physical changes associated with puberty are triggered by hormonal changes (e.g., increased release of androgens and estrogens that lead to increased physical changes in height, weight, body shape, and genital development).

A body-related physical change during puberty is increased height and weight that begins in early adolescence. This growth spurt for girls occurs at approximately 9 years of age, with the peak of pubertal change occurring at 11.5 years. During this time, girls increase in height by approximately 3.5 inches per year. By the time they reach their peak height at approximately 12 years, girls have gained an average of 18 pounds. In addition to an increase in height and weight, girls' hips widen, and this is associated with an increase in estrogen. Unlike girls, boys typically begin puberty a year or two later, at 11 or 12 years of age. A boy's peak growth spurt occurs mid-puberty when his testosterone levels are increasing at a rapid pace. The peak growth spurt for boys is generally between 14 and 15 years with an increase of 11 to 12 inches in height as well as an increase in strength. The change in body composition (i.e., redistribution of fat and increase in muscles) is related to males having more and larger muscle cells than females. In fact, boys have 1.5 times the lean body mass and bone mass of girls, and girls have twice as much body fat as boys.

Adrenarche refers to the earliest phase of puberty when the adrenal glands are activated. It usually begins between the ages of 6 and 9 in girls, and approximately one year later in boys. This early part of puberty is usually characterized by external physical signs (e.g., adult body odor, axillary hair growth, breast buds). Gonadarche is the second phase of puberty which is characterized by the maturation of the primary sexual characteristics (ovaries and testes) and full development of the secondary sexual characteristics (pubic hair, breast and genital development). Gonadarche usually begins at age 9 or 10 in girls and appears a year later in boys. Certainly, the appearance of these bodily characteristics contributes to increased attention from the opposite sex and often leads to heightened feelings of self-consciousness about one's body.

For girls, sexual development includes breast development, enlargement of ovaries, and appearance of pubic hair. Usually the first sign of puberty for boys is testicular enlargement, which is followed by the development of pubic hair and growth of the penis. Within these reproductive changes, menarche occurs during the late-gonadarche phase. Menarche—or the onset of menses in girls—is the most common sign of sexual maturation in girls. It usually occurs at an average age of 12.8 years (range 11–13 years) in the general U.S. adolescent population. For boys, the clearest sign of puberty during gonadarche is spermarche, the onset of nocturnal emission, generally occurring at 13.5 or 14 years. In addition to sexual maturation and physical changes, other dimensions of pubertal maturation include changes in self-perception, social interactions, and perceptions by peers. Therefore, this maturational process has a profound influence on the cognitive functioning of adolescents.

Cognitive Development

In recent years, researchers have been trying to understand the changes that occur in the brain during adolescence. Structural brain imaging studies over the past decade have challenged the belief that structural brain development ends in early childhood, revealing that changes occur through early adulthood. In addition, these studies provide an insight into the biological basis for understanding adolescent thinking and behavior. For example, the ventromedial prefrontal cortex of the brain is responsible for evaluating risk and reward to help guide the person to make a decision. Imaging studies have shown that this part of the brain is the last to mature in adolescents, which supports behavioral studies that show adolescents take greater risks than adults in activities such as substance abuse. Adolescents tend to engage in more reckless behaviors because the area of the brain that assesses risk and benefits has not completely developed yet. These findings, along with other studies examining the maturation of other regions of the prefrontal cortex during adolescence, suggest that the spontaneity, short-sightedness, and risk-taking behaviors associated with adolescence could be partially biological in nature.

According to Jean Piaget's theory of cognitive development, adolescents begin to shift from the rule-bound and concrete styles of problem solving that occur during childhood to gain a greater capacity for abstract and flexible problem-solving skills during adolescence. Concrete operational thoughts occur approximately between the ages of 7 and 11 in which individuals can engage in mental actions that are reversible (e.g., mentally reverse liquid from one jar to another jar of different height or width) and divide things into sets and reason about their interrelations. Logical reasoning replaces intuitive thoughts as long as the principles can be applied to concrete examples. However, it is not until the formal operational stage starting at age 12 that individuals begin to think more abstractly than individuals in the concrete operational stage. They can think hypothetically and generalize from observations that will aid them in future decision making.

Individuals in the operational stage can manage problems with many factors. For example, they can accurately display sticks by color and length of the stick. They can also think in many possibilities. In other words, adolescents at this stage can generate multiple possibilities for any given situation. Therefore, they can assess a problem, generate all the possible hypothetical outcomes, and then test the hypotheses one at a time.

One mechanism that causes cognitive change during adolescence is biological maturation. As children grow physically, they encounter new possibilities for development. Just as biological development is salient to cognitive growth, experience with the physical world and the social environment also influence cognitive development. The quality of the experiences and the social context (home and school) affect the rate at which individuals move from one cognitive stage to the next. Providing new experiences and a comfortable environment to practice the new skills facilitates cognitive development. According to Piagetian perspective, cognitive conflict is the main mechanism of cognitive change. For example, arguing about the rules of the game with peers stimulates cognitive conflict, helping individuals move from one cognitive stage to the next. In addition, Piaget believed that cognitive conflict was important for moral development.

Moral Development

Although the debate on moral development continues, it is clear that cognitive, social, and emotional growth in adolescence underpin the changes in moral reasoning that help build a foundation to guide adolescents through adulthood. Lawrence Kohlberg interviewed many people across the life span regarding moral dilemmas and described six stages of moral development. At the preconventional level, children younger than age 9 have an individualistic perspective where they follow rules to avoid punishment for personal reasons. During adolescence, girls and boys move from preconventional to conventional level of moral reasoning where they are guided by their interpersonal relationships and place in society. Adolescents in this conventional level are concerned with helping and pleasing others, being a "good boy" or "good girl." The shift from preconventional to conventional level is also connected to cognitive and social development. Abstract thinking, ability to take another's perspective, and concern for others are prerequisites to be in the conventional level.

Social Development

Parent-Adolescent Relationship

The parent-adolescent relationship has been studied extensively in the adolescent development research. Studies examining family dynamics during adolescence have mainly focused on the parent-adolescent conflict (i.e., frequency and content of conflict). Parents and teenagers tend to experience arguments without knowing why there is a breakdown in communication. In addition, when there is more fighting among parents and teenagers, closeness (i.e., the amount of time spent with parents) declines. Subsequently, there could be mental health implications for the parents and psychological maladjustment for the teenagers. For example, parents have reported having a difficult time adjusting to their adolescents' desire to be autonomous, and adolescents can develop aggression, depression, and hostility. As a result, teenagers can engage in unhealthy behaviors such as dieting or purging as a way to cope or to attempt to be in control.

According to the separation-individuation theory, parent-child conflicts facilitate the increase in the adolescent's development of autonomy and independence. The distance in relationship is needed to redefine the parent-adolescent relationship under conditions where the teenager still feels loved. As a result of this process, adolescents gain more power and parents become more egalitarian. Furthermore, attachment theory emphasizes that parents who share activities and have emotional connections with their teenagers show support, and in turn, provide space for adolescents to explore the world outside of the family and form new relationships.

The amount of parental support (intimacy and warmth) declines from early to middle adolescence, and then stabilizes in late adolescence. There seems to be a consensus that conflict becomes more intense during early adolescence and less intense during middle to late adolescence. An explanation for an increase in conflict intensity during early adolescence is the biological and psychological changes that accompany puberty.

Boys and girls receive the same amount of support from parents during early adolescence; however, there is an increase in bonding between mothers and daughters from middle to late adolescence. Girls have more conflict with parents than boys, and girls have more conflicts (frequency and intensity) with mothers than fathers. Girls tend to be more autonomous than boys in early adolescence, but this difference disappears later in adolescence. A possible reason for these findings is that girls have an earlier pubertal development than boys. In addition, daughters and mothers argue over everyday issues because mothers are typically more involved than fathers. Recent results from a longitudinal study show that the development of relationships with both parents is similar for girls and boys: (1) conflict is more intense during middle adolescence, (2) support from parents temporarily declines, and (3) conflict with parents temporarily increases. Thus, parent-adolescent relationships do become more equal over time, confirming that adolescents do develop more independence and autonomy over time.

Relationships with Peers

As adolescents develop more autonomy and independence, they are spending more time alone and with their friends. Adolescents bring many qualities they have learned from spending time with their family to their peer relationships. Adolescents from warm and supportive families are more socially competent and have more positive friendships.

There are several findings on how peers influence adolescent development. First, peers have a positive and negative impact on adolescents. Peers influence academic performance and prosocial behaviors but also unhealthy behaviors such as smoking and drinking alcohol. Second, adolescents follow their peers because they admire them and respect their opinions, and not due to peer pressure. Third, adolescents choose friends who are similar to them in cognitions, attitudes, behaviors, and identities. Fourth, adolescents are most influenced by peers during middle adolescence compared to early and late adolescence.

Relationships with peers have become more appealing during their teenage years because their peers are less controlling, fairer, and less judgmental than adults. Thus, adolescents spend twice as much time with peers than parents, and they rely less on their parents to help them resolve problems. Adolescents want to be accepted by their peers. Being accepted by peers provides them with a sense of belonging in the peer group. It is also crucial for social and cognitive development. In contrast, being rejected by peers has detrimental effects on the social, psychological, and emotional development of adolescents. While popular adolescents report having closer friendships and tend to be outgoing, humorous, and friendly, rejected adolescents tend to display characteristics of being aggressive, withdrawn, anxious, and socially awkward. Rejected adolescents may also be lonely, have low self-esteem, suffer from depression, and be vulnerable to teasing, bullying, and victimization by their peers. Some of the teasing surrounds weight, body size and shape, resulting in fat bias. Peer victimization can lead to development of poor self-image. However, rejected adolescents in middle school can become more popular and accepted in later adolescence, as adolescents become less strict in defining what is normal behavior and more tolerant of individual differences.

Friendships become more intimate during adolescence. More than half of U.S. adolescents reported having had a romantic relationship in the past 18 months. By middle adolescence, most individuals have been involved in at least one romantic relationship. Research conducted prior to 1999 on romantic relationships during adolescence has been purely descriptive. More recent work has focused on the quality of relationships and their potential positive and negative implications.

Adolescents with positive romantic experiences have higher self-esteem, self-confidence, and social competence. In contrast, teenagers who worry about saving a relationship often suppress their thoughts and opinions (self-silencing) out of fear of losing their intimate partner and relationship. Self-silencing leads to poorer communication skills with partners, higher levels of depression, and greater sensitivity to rejection from the partner. This in turn can cause adolescents to partake in alcohol and drug use, do poorly in school, and have poorer emotional health. Romantic experiences during adolescence have been found to have qualities similar to romantic relationships in later life.

Development of the Self

Adolescence has been characterized as a period of time of self-exploration for adolescents to determine who they are and how they fit in the world. For many years, studies have supported Erikson's theory that adolescent identity is formed in early adolescence, but recent work has shown that identity formation occurs in late adolescence and even extends into young adulthood. Thus, the focus of research has been on the development of self-conceptions.

As mentioned earlier, individuals begin to develop more abstract thinking and self concepts become more differentiated and better organized in moving from childhood to adolescence. Harter in 1998 expressed that adolescents begin to view themselves based on personal beliefs and standards instead of comparing themselves to others. During middle adolescence, individuals can view themselves in different ways depending on the situation (e.g., shy with classmates and outgoing with family members), but the discrepancies decline over time with adolescents forming a more constant view of themselves in late adolescence. They are able to view themselves in a variety of domains including academics, athletics, appearance, and morality. For example, if adolescents, especially girls, have high perceptions of their appearance, then they have high self-esteem. In addition, adolescents who do not act their true self because they devalue their true self develop depression. On the other hand, if they engage in false-self behaviors to please others, then they most likely will not have depression.

Conclusion

Many factors influence the development of self during adolescence. Numerous studies have examined the impact of early, late, or on-time physical development on self-esteem and self-concept. The deviance hypothesis states that being off time of puberty (late or early) causes difficult times for the adolescent because it places the individual in a socially deviant category. Adolescents who are different from their peers may not adjust well to being different, especially when they have not yet formed their identity. According to the developmental stage termination hypothesis, early maturers are more at risk for developmental difficulties because they do not have the skills to cope with it. For example, girls who mature faster tend to have lower self-esteem and body image. A possible reason is that girls physically develop two years earlier than boys, drawing them more attention from peers and adults. However, for boys, earlier maturers tend to have higher self-esteem because they are taller and have more muscles—qualities that society deems attractive.

SONYA SOOHOO

See also: Puberty and Body Image.

Bibliography

Carver, Karen, Kara Joyner, and J. Richard Udry. "National Estimates of Adolescent Romantic Relationships." In *Adolescent Romantic Relationships and Sexual Behavior: Theory, Research, and Practical Implications,* edited by Peter Florsheim, 291–329. New York: Cambridge University Press, 2003.

Collins, W. Andrew, and Brett Laursen. "Parent-Adolescent Relationships and Influences." In *Handbook of Adolescent Psychology,* edited by Richard M. Lerner and Lawrence D. Steinberg, 331–61. Hoboken, NJ: Wiley, 2004.

Collins, W. Andrew, Deborah P. Welsh, and Wyndol Furman. "Adolescent Romantic Relationships." *Annual Review of Psychology* 60 (2009): 631–52.

De Goede, Irene H. A., Susan J. T. Branje, and Wim H. J. Meeus. "Developmental Changes in Adolescents' Perceptions of Relationships with Their Parents." *Journal of Youth Adolescence* 38, no. 1 (2009): 75–88.

Dorn, Lorah D., Ronald E. Dahl, Hermi R. Woodward, and Frank Biro. "Defining the Boundaries of Early Adolescence: A User's Guide to Assessing Puberty Status and Pubertal Timing in Research with Adolescents." *Applied Developmental Science* 39 (2006): 625–26.

Furman, Wyndol and W. Andrew Collins. "Adolescent Romantic Relationships and Experiences." In *Handbook of Peer Interactions, Relationships, and Groups,* edited by Kenneth H. Rubin, William M. Bukowski, and Brett Laursen. New York: Guilford, 2008.

Harter, Susan. "The Development of Self-Representations during Childhood and Adolescence." In *Handbook of Self and Identity,* edited by Mark R. Leary and June P. Tangney, 610–42. New York: The Guilford Press, 2003.

Hazen, Eric, Steven Schlozman, and Eugene Beresin. "Adolescent Psychological Development: A Review." *Pediatric Review* (2008): 161–67.

Kronenberg, Henry M., Shlomo Melmed, Kenneth S. Polonsky, Larsen P. Reed. *Williams Textbook of Endocrinology, 11th ed.* New York: Elsevier, 2007.

Meeus, Wim, Jurjen Iedema, Gerard Maassen, and Rutger Engels. "Separation-Individuation Revisited: On the Interplay of Parent-Adolescent Relations, Identity and Emotional Adjustment in Adolescence." *Journal of Adolescence* 28 (2005): 89–106.

Pinyerd, Belinda, and William B. Zipf. "Puberty-Timing Is Everything!" *Journal of Pediatric Nursing* 20 (2005): 75–82.

Santrock, John W. *Adolescence.* New York: McGraw-Hill, 2009.

Shanahan, Lilly, Susan M. McHale, Ann C. Crouter, and D. Wayne Osgood. "Warmth with Mothers and Fathers from Middle Childhood to Late Adolescence: Within- and between-Families Comparisons." *Developmental Psychology* 43 (2007): 551–63.

Steinberg, Lawrence, and Amanda S. Morris. "Adolescent Development." *Annual Review of Psychology* 52 (2001): 83–110.

AEROBICS

The term "aerobics" was first coined by Dr. Kenneth Cooper in 1968 to represent a system of exercise to prevent coronary artery disease. Jackie Sorenson developed aerobic dance (i.e., a series of dance routines to improve cardiovascular fitness) a year later. The aerobic dance movement spread throughout the United States and into other countries in the 1970s and 1980s. In 1983, "sportaerobics" was developed by the Sport Fitness International (SFI) organization to host the first national U.S. aerobics championship. Since then, world aerobics competitions have continued with aerobics becoming a global phenomenon. Although the competition aspect of aerobics is important, aerobic dance classes are available in almost every fitness center across the United States. Female and male aerobics class participants exercise in group classes with a variety of motives.

Body Image and Aerobics

Aerobics classes are not just a means to get fit within a 60 minute session; they can also become a culture of their own. Group exercise classes present some body image concerns and opportunities for scrutiny. Similar to dancers, aerobics class participants generally face a mirror while they jump around and participate in aerobics routines. Participants may experience dissatisfaction with the image in the mirror, or they may feel pressure to wear a particular outfit to fit in with the other participants or to dress up for the mirror. Exercise attire may be form-fitting or revealing and this can contribute to body consciousness. Aerobics class participants may also compare their bodies to that of other participants or the group leader. Aerobics participants have reported that they will stay in a class as long as they are not the heaviest person in the room.

Although aerobics participants are most likely to compare their bodies with their peers, it is interesting to note that aerobics instructors' bodies are on display and serve as models of correct form as well as sources of motivation. Therefore, it is expected that there will be certain expectations for aerobics class instructors regarding size, shape, and appearance. In fact, it was reported in 2002 that the Jazzercise company did not hire a 5-foot-8-inch-tall, 240-pound female to teach aerobics class because her size, stature, and physique did not represent the body ideal of a fitness leader.

In one study, 171 aerobics participants were surveyed about the ideal characteristics of aerobics instructors. Interestingly, appearance, age, or body type were less frequently cited characteristics than physical fitness, enthusiasm, motivation, the ability to lead a group exercise class, strong cue skills and demonstration of proper technique. Only 6 percent of participants stated that "being thin" was an important quality for instructors and being "under age 40" was even less important (5 percent of participants).

Aerobics Instructors and Eating Disorders

Well-known aerobics instructors who have admitted to having a struggle with eating disorders include Jane Fonda and Richard Simmons. Research studies about eating disorder rates among aerobics and fitness instructors have yielded mixed results. For one Swedish study, 27 percent of female fitness instructors admitted to having a previous history with anorexia nervosa and/or bulimia nervosa. In a follow-up study with a similar population of Swedish fitness instructors, 30 percent of instructors reported binge eating episodes and uncontrollable eating, 15 percent reported restricted eating, and 72 percent were dissatisfied with their body weight. Additionally, 35 percent of these instructors reported a history of eating disorders with 11 percent admitting to having a current eating disorder. Exercise dependence characteristics were present among these fitness instructors with 71 percent continuing to exercise despite

Actress Jane Fonda released 23 workout videos from 1982 to 1995. (Photofest)

suffering from a cold or illness. For a study looking at 30 U.S. aerobics instructors, 40 percent of instructors reported having an eating disorder history with 23 percent identifying bulimia nervosa and 17 percent indicating a history of anorexia nervosa. The instructors appeared to have greater preoccupation with body weight, higher body dissatisfaction, more perfectionism, and greater drive for thinness, predictive of being more at risk for developing and maintaining disordered eating behaviors or clinical eating disorders.

In contrast to the Swedish and American studies, a separate study of 286 Canadian female aerobics instructors determined that the instructors did not score higher on commitment to exercise, drive for thinness, body dissatisfaction, bulimia or other eating disorder predictors compared to high-exercising populations or the general population. Therefore, more research is needed to better understand which aerobics instructors may be at increased risk for body image disturbances and eating disorders.

Conclusion

Aerobics group exercise classes play a significant role in the lives of many exercisers who belong to a gym or fitness center. Although class participants and their instructor may not compete in sportaerobics, they may still face body image pressures to look a particular way within the aerobics environment. Furthermore, class participants may scrutinize their bodies in the mirror and compare their bodies to that of their peers or the aerobics group leader. Several studies have examined the tendency of aerobics instructors toward eating disorders, with inconclusive findings.

JUSTINE J. REEL

See also: Dancers.

Bibliography

Evans, Retta R., Ellen M. Cotter, and Jane L. Roy. "Preferred Body Type of Fitness Instructors among University Students in Exercise Classes." *Perceptual and Motor Skills* 101 (2005): 257–66.

Fonda, Jane. *My Life So Far.* New York, NY: Random House, 2005.

Hoglund, K. and L. Normen. "A High Exercise Load is Linked to Pathological Weight Control Behavior and Eating Disorders in Female Fitness Instructors." *Scandinavian Journal of Medicine & Science in Sports* 12 (2002): 261–75.

Manley, Ronald S., Karina M. O'Brien, and Sumerlee Samuels. "Fitness Instructors' Recognition of Eating Disorders and Attendant Ethical/Liability Issues." *Eating Disorders* 16 (2008): 103–116. doi: 10.1080/10640260801887162.

Martin, Kathleen A., and Heather A. Hausenblas. "Psychological Commitment to Exercise and Eating Disorder Symptomatology among Female Aerobic Instructors." *The Sport Psychologist* 12, no. 2 (1998): 180–90.

Olson, Michele S., Henry N. Williford, Leigh Anne Richards, Jennifer A. Brown, and Steven Pugh. "Self-reports on the Eating Disorder Inventory by Female Aerobic Instructors." *Perceptual and Motor Skills* 82 (1996): 1051–1058.

Thogersen-Ntoumani, Cecilie, and Nikos Ntoumanis. "A Self-determination Theory Approach to the Study of Body Image Concerns, Self-presentation and Self-perceptions in a Sample of Aerobics Instructors." *Journal of Health Psychology* 12, no. 2 (2007): 301–315. doi: 10.1177/1359105307074267.

AESTHETIC SPORTS

The term "aesthetic" generally refers to beauty or art that we judge by what is pleasing to the eye. Sports have often been classified into categories such as aesthetic, endurance, ball, or team sports to distinguish their various demands. Aesthetic sports represent those sports in which successful athletic performance is dependent upon a certain look or specific standard of physical appearance. Often, aesthetic sports consider leanness, low body weight, and/or a petite body size to be beautiful, artful, and an indicator of optimal athletic performance. Sports that fall into the aesthetic category include gymnastics, figure skating, dance, diving, bodybuilding, and cheerleading.

Examples of Aesthetic Sports

The success of rhythmic gymnastics routines is highly dependent on both technical and artistic components. More specifically, flexibility (e.g., 180 degree splits), detailed choreography, disciplined execution of movements (e.g., pointed toes), careful control of an apparatus (i.e., hoop, ball, rope, clubs, or ribbon), and the purposeful incorporation of music are emphasized. Figure skaters are also judged based on both technical and artistic elements of the program. The skater's choreography, expression, and style of skating are just as important as successful completion of jumps, spins, and footwork sequences. For competitive dancers, performances are often evaluated based on the appropriateness of the music and dance costume in addition to advanced technical skills. Each of these aesthetic sports tends to favor a graceful exterior as well as long and lean body lines. In contrast, bodybuilders are judged on muscularity, skeletal structure, body proportion, balance, and symmetry, while cheerleading has been associated with sex appeal and audience entertainment.

Some aesthetic sports (e.g., diving, gymnastics, pairs skating) demand prepubescent body shapes with long lines and minimal curvature to not only meet specific standards of physical appearance, but to also allow for maximum flexibility, movement, or flight. This is especially true for those aesthetic sports that involve difficult lifts, such as pairs skating and cheerleading. Lighter and leaner athletes are far easier to lift and maneuver in the air, thereby allowing for successful and potentially more competitive athletic performances.

Aesthetic Sports, Body Image Concerns, and Disordered Eating

Research shows that due to the emphasis on weight, shape, and physical appearance, athletes involved in aesthetic sports are at greater risk for disordered eating as compared to non-aesthetic sport athletes (e.g., ball sport participants like soft-ball or soccer players) and non-athletes. This trend has been demonstrated in meta-analyses of the literature, or in other words, summaries of findings across many studies. Unfortunately, aesthetic sport participants (i.e., dancers, gymnasts, cheerleaders, baton twirlers, swimmers, aerobics participants, and figure skaters) as young as five or seven years of age have been shown to experience significantly greater weight concerns than non-aesthetic sport participants (i.e., volleyball, soccer, basketball, softball, hockey, and tennis players as well as martial arts participants and track athletes) and non-athletes.

Other studies examining the presence of body image concerns and disordered eating in aesthetic sports alone have produced astounding statistics. The prevalence of eating disorders among female aesthetic sport athletes at the elite level have been reported at 42 percent. In a study of 35 ballet dancers, 41 percent met criteria for a clinical or subclinical eating disorder. The lifetime prevalence rate of developing an eating disorder as a professional dancer has been found to be as high as 50 percent. Another study of 215 collegiate female gymnasts showed that over 60 percent met criteria for a moderate form of disordered eating, and only 22 percent were categorized as having normal eating habits. In an examination of 42 collegiate female gymnasts, 100 percent reported dieting and over 60 percent reported that they were using at least one pathogenic weight control behavior (e.g., self-induced vomiting, use of diet pills, laxatives, or diuretics). Similar trends have been demonstrated in figure skaters. For example, in a study of 40 male and female national-level figure skaters, 48 percent reported symptoms indicative of an eating disorder.

Females involved in aesthetic sports may also be more vulnerable to negative self-perceptions and low perceived competence, especially during puberty. The physical changes associated with puberty can include breast development and fat gain in girls, greater muscle mass in boys, rapid growth spurts, and weight increases. Each of these changes may not only influence athletic performance by altering balance, stability, speed, and coordination, but also negatively affect body image. In short, aesthetic sport athletes may begin to perceive themselves poorly relative to both the technical and appearance-based aspects of their sport as they experience natural pubertal changes.

Role of Coaches

Scholars believe that pressures from the athletic environment influence athletes' thoughts, beliefs, and attitudes toward weight, shape, appearance, eating, and exercise. The role of coaches in the onset of body image disturbances and disordered eating in aesthetic sport athletes has been a primary area of concern. Among 603 elite female athletes, 67 percent of those who met criteria for a clinical eating disorder were told by a coach to diet. Another study revealed that nearly 70 percent of 42 collegiate female gymnasts reported that their coaches told them they were too heavy. Seventy-five percent of those who received a disparaging comment from their coach reported resorting to a pathogenic weight control behavior. Similar findings have been shown in figure skaters, where the greatest reported pressure to lose or maintain weight is the skaters themselves, followed by their coaches.

Coaches are believed to be powerful, key figures in the lives of their athletes. Athletes may therefore take extreme measures to meet the expectations of their coaches when it comes to appearance, weight, shape, and body size. Unfortunately, coaches tend to make comments about weight based on subjective evaluations of appearance rather than objective measurements and evidence-based practice to improve performance. Therefore, athletes' efforts to lose and maintain weight are often both unstructured and unhealthy.

Due to the strong influence of coaches, the National Collegiate Athletic Association (NCAA) has taken strides to protect aesthetic sport athletes by providing educational materials to coaches regarding the topic. However, much more can and should be done to increase coaches' awareness of their influence on the weight management practices of their athletes. In a study examining collegiate coaches' knowledge of eating disorders, nearly 25 percent of coaches scored between 60 and 69.5 percent, and only 4.3 percent of coaches scored a 90 percent or greater. Nearly 40 percent reported that they were unaware of any eating disorder resources offered by their athletics department.

Role of Judges

Given the subjective scoring system in aesthetic sports, the role of judges is especially important. Judges' scoring in aesthetic sports can be affected by an athlete's shape; leaner athletes with longer lines tend to receive higher scores. Research demonstrates that the primary reason why many aesthetic sport athletes engage in dieting and weight management techniques is because they believe that such practices will help them to achieve athletic success by improving both their performance and appearance. For example, in a study of 28 elite and non-elite gymnasts, 32 percent expressed the need to look good in their leotard, 25 percent believed that being thin would improve their performance, and a substantial number reported being concerned about weight because of the emphasis on appearance (18 percent) and being continuously judged (18 percent). Unfortunately, the dieting and weight management practices associated with the demands of aesthetic sports may evolve into more severe disordered eating attitudes and behaviors or a clinical eating disorder, such as anorexia nervosa or bulimia nervosa. A tragic example of this tendency of an athlete to engage in harmful eating practices is Christy Heinrich, an Olympic gymnast who was told by a judge to lose weight. Her long-standing battle with an eating disorder resulted in a rapid performance decline and eventual death.

Role of Teammates and Parents

Although weight pressures from coaches and judges appear to be a primary concern, teammates and parents are also a reported source of pressure among aesthetic sport athletes. For example, of 28 female collegiate gymnasts, 17 percent reported experiencing pressure from other gymnasts to lose weight. In a study of 32 female figure skaters, parents were the third-most significant source of pressure to lose or maintain weight, followed by the skaters themselves and coaches. Male skating partners have also been shown to be a source of pressure to lose or maintain weight among ice dancers and pairs skaters because of the difficult lifts and flight patterns necessary to succeed in these particular skating disciplines.

Males in Aesthetic Sports

Popular belief suggests that the relationship between aesthetic sport participation and the risk for disordered eating and body image distortions is only evident in females. Although more research is needed, preliminary evidence indicates that males in aesthetic sports may also be vulnerable to pressures associated with the demands to maintain a certain weight, shape, and appearance to succeed in their sport. This has most recently been shown in male dancers who were equally at risk for an eating disorder as females, and where self-evaluative perfectionism (e.g., perceived pressure from others) and conscientious perfectionism (e.g., striving for excellence) were predictive of disordered eating patterns. College male cheerleaders reported similar weight pressures—including coaches, weight requirements to try-out, and uniform—as their female counterparts. However, in contrast to many females, male cheerleaders and other male athletes are expected to gain weight throughout the competitive season while maintaining low body composition and a lean physique.

Benefits of Aesthetic Sport Participation

Although participation in aesthetic sports has been found to be associated with negative struggles for some athletes relative to eating behaviors and body image, it is important to remember that these types of sports are not all bad. In fact, aesthetic sports offer a unique combination of artistic expression and technical skills that define athleticism in new and interesting ways that are unlike any other sport type. Many scholars have noted that the aesthetic appeal of sports in general is one reason why we both appreciate and continue to participate in sports as athletes, coaches, spectators, and sponsors.

Moreover, many aesthetic sport athletes at the youth, high school, collegiate, and elite levels demonstrate positive outcomes. For example, the development of important life skills across sport types has been well documented in literature and can include learning of important values, behaviors, and interpersonal skills. To maximize these benefits and minimize the risks associated with aesthetic sport participation, much should be done to prevent disordered eating and body image disturbances in this unique population of athletes. In an effort to achieve this goal, many governing bodies of aesthetic sports offer educational resources on proper nutrition for optimal performance, healthy body image, and eating disorder prevention available to athletes, coaches, and parents.

Conclusion

To buffer the pressures associated with aesthetic sport participation, social support from parents, coaches, teammates, and peers is also imperative, especially during puberty. In fact, aesthetic sport athletes may do well to be educated on ways to embrace and accept their physical changes rather than reject them. Some experts recommend that important others in the athletes' environment also learn to recognize the signs and symptoms of disordered eating, be role models for healthy eating and exercise behaviors, focus less on weight and more on health, and provide a supportive environment to facilitate ongoing and open communication.

DANA K. VOELKER

See also: Bodybuilding; Cheerleading; Dancers; Figure Skating; Gymnastics.

Bibliography

Galli, N., and Justine J. Reel. "Adonis or Hephaestus? Exploring Body Image in Male Athletes." *Psychology of Men and Masculinity* 10 (2009): 95–108. doi: 10.1037/a0014005.

Hausenblas, Heather A., and Albert V. Carron. "Eating Disorder Indices and Athletes: An Integration." *Journal of Sport & Exercise Psychology* 21 (1999): 230–58.

Neumark-Sztainer, Dianne. "Preventing the Broad Spectrum of Weight-Related Problems: Working with Parents to Help Teens Achieve a Healthy Weight and a Positive Body Image." *Journal of Nutrition Education & Behavior* 37 (2005): S133–S139. doi: 10.1016/S1499-4046(06)60214-5.

Sundgot-Borgen, Jorunn. "Risk and Trigger Factors for the Development of Eating Disorders in Female Elite Athletes." *Medicine and Science in Sports and Exercise* 26 (1994): 414–19.

Sundgot-Borgen, Jorunn, and Monica Klungland Torstveit. "Prevalence of Eating Disorders in Elite Athletes is Higher than in the General Population." *Clinical Journal of Sports Medicine* 14 (2004): 25–32.

Thompson, Ron A., and Roberta Trattner Sherman. *Helping Athletes with Eating Disorders.* Champaign, IL: Human Kinetics, 1993.

Turk, Joanne C., William E. Prentice, Susan Chappell, and Edgar W. Shields. "Collegiate Coaches' Knowledge of Eating Disorders." *Journal of Athletic Training* 34 (1999): 19–24.

AGING AND BODY IMAGE

Although most of the publicity surrounding eating disorders and body image disturbances targets adolescent and college females, it is important to consider what happens to body-related and appearance concerns as people age. A youthful appearance has been equated with beauty and social status which in turn has generated a billion dollar industry for anti-aging products that claim to reduce cellulite, eliminate wrinkles, and wash away gray hairs. In addition to these anti-aging products many males and females have resorted to more drastic measures such as cosmetic surgery in an attempt to stall time and to change their appearance. According to the American Society of Plastic Surgeons, 9.9 million females undergo cosmetic procedures annually and the majority of women are older than

40 years of age. Specifically, 45 percent of women in the age group of 40–50 years, 26 percent of women aged 50 years and over, 19 percent of women in the age group of 30–39 years, and 7 percent of women in the age group of 20–29 years underwent cosmetic surgical (i.e., liposuction, breast augmentation, eyelid surgery) and/or minimally-invasive procedures (i.e., Botox, chemical peels). Men are also seeking cosmetic surgery to enhance body parts, including pectoral implants for a more defined chest and calf implants. Beyond monetary issues, combating natural changes that occur with age (e.g., wrinkles, thinning or graying hair, decreased skin elasticity and sagging skin) can contribute to body dissatisfaction and disordered eating among individuals in their thirties, forties, fifties and beyond.

Body Image and the Media

Youthfulness symbolizes being beautiful and desirable, while aging (i.e., sagging, wrinkles, skin discoloration, weight gain, declining agility) has become something that should be avoided by exercising, restricting certain foods, undergoing cosmetic surgery or using products marketed by the media. Studies that analyzed the media trends found that models in magazines did not represent the age or

Kelli Smith, 39, walks along the Atlantic Ocean, Thursday, July 5, 2007, in Brant Beach on Long Beach Island, New Jersey. Smith went into a residential treatment center for anorexia at age 31. Now, she is doing better and is trying to keep herself healthy. Health professionals and psychiatrists say there are a growing number of women in their 30s, 40s and 50s who are being treated for eating disorders, which can no longer be thought of as a teenage disease. (Mel Evans/AP/Wide World Photos)

size of their readership. Researchers have discovered that models aged 25–34 years were overrepresented in the over-35 magazines (e.g., *Country Living, Martha Stewart,* etc.), models were even younger (18–24 years) in the under-35 magazines (e.g., *Cosmopolitan*), and younger models were thinner. This underrepresentation of older female images and celebration of youthful appearance qualities can reinforce body dissatisfaction.

Originally, it was assumed that adolescent females would be most at risk for body image disturbances and disordered eating disorders due to developmental concerns (e.g., puberty and peer pressures). However, several studies have found no age-related differences in body image and some have found the mid-life group (usually 39–59 years) to show higher body dissatisfaction than younger and older females. These results suggest that women of all ages may feel dissatisfied with their bodies and serve as a caution that individuals do not simply grow out of eating disorders at a certain age. Although aging and males has often been associated with looking more distinguished or wise, 63-year-old former bodybuilder and ex-governor, Arnold Schwarzenegger, admitted during a 2011 interview that he has developed poor body image as a result of age-related bodily changes: http://news.yahoo.com/s/yblog_theticket/20110418/ts_yblog_theticket/arnold-schwarzenegger-is-sad-that-hes-not-young-anymore.

Eating Disorders

Eating disorders have been recognized as psychological disorders that primarily afflict adolescent girls and young women. Although traditionally researchers have argued that the onset of eating disorders is less common later in adulthood, recent research has revealed an increase in the prevalence of eating disorders among older women and also case studies involving mid-life and late onset. It is difficult to know how many women in mid-life and beyond suffer from eating disorders because the disorder may go underdiagnosed or females with eating disorders or disordered eating may refuse to seek treatment. Across studies, middle-aged women report wanting to be thinner, engaging in unhealthy weight loss methods (e.g., self-induced vomiting), and being more aware of the sensations of hunger and satiety than the elderly group. Middle-aged women were also at a higher risk for an eating disorder and endorsed a stronger fear of aging than their older counterparts. Elderly women displayed similar levels of body dissatisfaction as the younger groups, and recently the phenomenon of late-life and late-onset eating disorders has received more attention in treatment settings.

Forman and Davis (2005) investigated eating attitudes and body image in young and mid-life adults and found that women over 35 years of age with eating disorders had similar desires and feelings (wanting to be thin, body image dissatisfaction, perfectionism, feeling of general inadequacy) as younger women with eating disorders. In addition, another study suggested that young women (18–31 years old) and elderly women (60–78 years old) have similar dieting restraints and eating attitudes. Although older women are concerned about their physical appearance as are younger women, the factors (e.g., pregnancy) that can lead older women to develop bodily concerns and disordered eating may be different.

Toward a Thin Ideal

The literature on risk factors of body image concerns and eating disorders in girls and young women has focused on young women and has generally overlooked older populations. This research suggests that a thin ideal is conveyed and reinforced by many sociocultural factors including family, peers, schools, sports, and most significantly, the media. Flashy images of an extremely slim body promoted ubiquitously in magazines, television advertisements, reality shows, and movies may cause people to infer and internalize the idea that a female's body is her most salient attribute. Women are socialized to view their bodies as objects to be scrutinized for flaws and work to sculpt closer to the advertised body ideal. Women who view themselves as objects and conform to societal pressure by comparing themselves to other people and societal ideals may internalize observers' perspectives, feel shame and anxiety, and also experience emotional and behavioral body image disturbances that are closely tied to the natural processes of aging.

Developmental Adulthood Milestones

Several developmental milestones that occur for women as they age may contribute to changes in body image and eating behaviors. Pregnancy represents body changes that are outside of a female's control. Although viewed as the healthy growth of a fetus, weight is often highly monitored and difficult to control during this phase of a woman's life. Menopause is associated with biological changes (e.g., weight gain, slowed metabolism) and may contribute to negative body image. Other life transitions may occur as women age, such as experiencing loss, divorce, or empty nest syndrome, all of which can play a role in the development of eating disorders in older women. Women may engage in appearance-sculpting strategies (e.g., overexercise, cosmetic surgery) as a way to cope or may engage in emotional eating (i.e., overeating or restricting).

Conclusion

Although the prevalence of eating disorders is greater among younger than older people, it is clear that body image concerns can affect individuals of all ages. To date, most research studies have focused primarily on the body image concerns of young women. Clearly, there are unique body image issues and developmental milestones that may influence the self-perceptions of older individuals. One of the key shortcomings of body image research with older participants is the use of cross-sectional designs that directly compare the body image of younger women to that of older women at one moment in time. It is possible that body image for women who grew up during the time of curvy ideal Marilyn Monroe may differ from that of women who grew up during other eras such as the time when the cultural ideal was extremely slender. Additional differences between older and younger adults may occur simply because of the frequency and manner in which they are depicted in the media. Media images of older women's bodies tend to be larger than those of younger women. It is important to tease out whether body image disturbances and/or eating disorders begin during mid-life due to the aging process or whether these disordered behaviors have been present since early adulthood or even adolescence.

JUSTINE J. REEL

See also: Late life and Late-Onset Eating Disorders; Menopause and Body Image; Pregnancy and Body Image; Puberty and Body Image.

Bibliography

American Society of Plastic Surgeons. "2006 Gender Quick Facts: Cosmetic plastic surgery." (2007). Retrieved on January 7, 2008 from http://www.plasticsurgery.org/media/statistics/loader.cfm?url=/commonspot/security/getfile.cfm&PageID=23626

Bailey, Holly. "Arnold Schwarzenegger is Sad He's Not Young Anymore." *The Ticket.* (2011). Retrieved on June 1, 2011 from http://news.yahoo.com/s/yblog_theticket/20110418/ts_yblog_theticket/arnold-schwarzenegger-is-sad-that-hes-not-young-anymore

Bedford, Jennifer L., and Shanthi C. Johnson. "Societal Influences on Body Image Dissatisfaction in Younger and Older Women." *Journal of Women and Aging* 18 (2006): 41–55.

Bessenoff, Gayle R., and Regan Del Priore. "Women, Weight, Age: Social Comparison to Magazine Images across the Lifespan." *Sex Roles* 56 (2007): 215–22. doi: 10.1007/s11199-006-9164-2.

Bordo, Susan. *Unbearable Weight: Feminism, Western Culture, and the Body.* Berkeley, CA: University of California Press, 1993.

Brandsma, Lynn. "Eating Disorders across the Life Span." *Journal of Women & Aging* 19 (2007): 155–72. doi: 10.1300/J074v19n01_10

Cumella, Edward J., and Zina Kally. "Profile of 50 Women with Midlife-Onset Eating Disorders." *Eating Disorders* 16 (2008): 193–203. doi: 10.1080/10640260802016670

Deeks, Amanda A., and Marita P. McCabe. "Menopausal Stage and Age and Perceptions of Body Image. *Psychology and Health* 16 (2001): 367–79.

Ferraro, F. Richard, Jennifer J. Muehlenkamp, Ashley Paintner, Kayla Wasson, Tracy Hager and Fallon Hoverson. "Aging, Body Image, and Body Shape." *The Journal of General Psychology,* 135, no. 4 (2008): 379–92.

Forman, Maryelizabeth and William N. Davis. "Characteristics of Middle-aged Women in Inpatient Treatment for Eating Disorders." *Eating Disorders: Journal of Treatment and Prevention* 13 (2005): 41–48.

Kearney-Cooke, Ann, and Florence Isaacs. *Change Your Mind, Change Your Body: Feeling Good about Your Body and Self after 40.* New York: Atria, 2004.

Lapid, Maria I., Maria C. Prom, M. Caroline Burton, Donald E. McAlpine, Bruce Sutor, and Teresa A. Rummans. "Eating Disorders in the Elderly." *International Psychogeriatrics* 22, no. 4 (2010): 523–36.

Lewis, Diane M., and Fary M. Cachelin. "Body Image, Body Dissatisfaction, and Eating Attitudes in Mid-life and Elderly Women." *Eating Disorders* 9 (2001): 29–39.

Mangweth-Matzek, Barbara., Claudia I. Rupp, Armand Hausmann, Karin Assmayr, Edith Mariacher, Georg Kemmler, Alexandra B. Whitworth, and Wilfried Biebl. "Never Too Late for Eating Disorders or Body Dissatisfaction: A Community Study of Elderly Women." *International Journal of Eating Disorders* 39 (2006): 583–86.

Midlarsky, Elizabeth and George Nitzburg. "Eating Disorders in Middle-aged Women." *The Journal of General Psychology* 135, no. 4 (2008): 393–407.

Patrick, Julie H. and Sarah T. Stahl. "Understanding Disordered Eating at Midlife and Late Life." *The Journal of General Psychology* 136, no. 1 (2008): 5–20.

Peat, Christine M., Naomi L. Peyerl, and Jennifer J. Muehlenkamp. "Body Image and Eating Disorders in Older Adults: A Review." *The Journal of General Psychology* 135, no. 4 (2008): 343–58.

Reel, Justine J. "Body Image and Physical Self-perceptions among African-American and Caucasian Women across the Adult Life Span." *Dissertation Abstracts International:* 61(5-B), 2000.

Reel, Justine J., Sonya SooHoo, Franklin Summerhays, and Diane L. Gill. "Age before Beauty: An Exploration of Body Image Concerns among African-American and Caucasian Women." *Journal of Gender Studies* 17, no. 4 (2008): 321–30.

Scholtz, Samantha, Laura S. Hill, and Hubert Lacy. "Eating Disorders in Older Women: Does Late Onset Anorexia Nervosa Exist?" *International Journal of Eating Disorders* 43, no. 5 (2010): 393–97.

SooHoo, Sonya, Justine J. Reel, and Judy Van Raalte. "Chasing the 'Fountain of Youth': Body Image and Eating Disorders among 'Older' Women." In *The Hidden Faces of Eating Disorders and Body Image,* edited by Justine J. Reel and Katherine A. Beals. Reston, VA: NAGWS/AAHPERD, 2009.

Today Show. Midlife Women with Eating Disorders, 2011. Retrieved May 27, 2011 from http://today.msnbc.msn.com/id/26184891/vp/43032860#43032860.

Zerbe, Kathyrn J. "Eating Disorders in Middle and Late Life: A Neglected Problem. *Primary Psychiatry* 10 (2003): 80–82.

AIRBRUSHING

Airbrushing refers to a process of retouching or altering photographs used in advertising numerous products. The media's frequent use of airbrushing has recently come under heat due to the evidence that digitally altered images contribute to negative body esteem among female adolescent and can trigger disordered eating.

History of Airbrushing

An airbrush is a small, air-operated tool that sprays ink, dye, and paint. Airbrushing has been used to alter photographs in the predigital era. The photograph could be extensively retouched or doctored to result in removing an entire person or surrounding objects, or to change the characteristics of the model. The first airbrush was developed and patented in 1876 by the makers of the Stanley Steamer. The first airbrush instruments were used for painting watercolors and for artistic purposes. Since the inception of airbrush technology, commercial artists and illustrators have used airbrushes to create and alter images for advertising, book covers, comic books, and graphic novels. One of the earliest manipulated photos is a famous image of President Lincoln which is actually a composite of Lincoln's head on another politician's body.

Body Image and Airbrushing

Currently the term "airbrushed" often refers to glamour photos (e.g., magazines) in which the models' imperfections (e.g., moles, scars) have been removed or body parts have been enhanced or altered (e.g., increased breasts, decreased waist). The resulting image represents a socially constructed standard of beauty and the perfection appears as a better version of the model. Some actresses (e.g., Jamie Lee Curtis in *More* magazine) have openly posed for photos showing before and after effects of intensive hair and make-up sessions. In 2010, Britney Spears released un-airbrushed images of herself next to the digitally-altered versions from a Candie's advertisement. It was determined that the resulting photos depicted an image of a female with a smaller waist, slimmer thighs, smaller bottom, and bruises, cellulite, and tattoo removed.

Airbrushing Regulations

The increased airbrushing has led to controversy and both magazines and models have been criticized for digitally enhanced photos (e.g., Kate Winslet in *GQ* magazine). More recently, L'Oreal makeup advertisements featuring airbrushed models Julia Roberts and Christy Turlington were banned in the UK because of their controversial use of airbrushing: http://articles.cnn.com/2011-07-28/world/airbrushed.advertisements.ban_1_julia-roberts-ad-image-tv-advertisement?_s=PM:WORLD. Similar to UK's strictly regulated use of airbrushing, an Arizona lawmaker introduced a bill in February 2012 that would require advertisers to provide a disclaimer for a photograph that has been altered or enhanced: http://www.dailymail.co.uk/news/article-2101915/Arizona-lawmakers-mull-outlaw-airbrushing-Photo-Shopping-ads.html.

Conclusion

Airbrushing has been used in artistic illustrations and photographs for over a century. While the current trend in advertisements has been airbrushing and digital enhancement of photographs that sometimes drastically change the image of the model pictured on a magazine or advertisement, there is recognition that these unrealistic images negatively impact body image and can contribute to disordered eating and eating disorders. Therefore, some groups such as the British Fashion Council are taking steps to ban advertisements that blatantly use airbrushing for products that proclaim to have anti-aging properties.

JUSTINE J. REEL

Bibliography

Brooks, Karen. "Body Image Airbrushing Reality." Last modified May 4, 2010. http://www.ts-si.org/guest-columns/24799-body-image-airbrushing-reality.
Daily Mail Reporter. "Britney Spears Bravely Agrees to Release Un-Airbrushed Images of Herself Next to the Digitally-Altered Versions." Dailymail.co.uk. Last modified April 14, 2010. http://www.dailymail.co.uk/tvshowbiz/article-1265676/Britney-Spears-releases-airbrushed-images-digitally-altered-versions.html#ixzz1VQHB9SqO.
"Campaign for Body Image and Airbrushing in Magazines." Facebook.com. Accessed August 4, 2011. http://www.facebook.com/pages/Campaign-for-Body-Image-and-Airbrushing-in-Magazines/268441480997.

"Crisis of Body Image." Wordpress.com. Last modified July 17, 2007. http://redsquirrel. wordpress.com/2007/07/17/the-crisis-of-body-image/.

Daily Mail Reporter. "Arizona Lawmakers Mull Bill to Outlaw Airbrushing and Photo-Shopping in Ads." Dailymail.co.uk. Last Modified February 16, 2012. http://www. dailymail.co.uk/news/article-2101915/Arizona-lawmakers-mull-outlaw-airbrushing-Photo-Shopping-ads.html.

Jones, Bryony. "Britain Bans Airbrushed Julia Roberts Make-up Ad." CNN.com. Last modified July 28, 2011. http://articles.cnn.com/2011-07-28/world/airbrushed.advertisements. ban_1_julia-roberts-ad-image-tv-advertisement?_s=PM:WORLD.

Martin, Charlotte. "Airbrushed Pictures of Celebs Put Pressure on My 14-Year-Old Daughter to Look Perfect." *The Sun*. Last modified November 11, 2009. http://www.thesun. co.uk/sol/homepage/woman/2723569/Mums-and-teen-girls-on-body-image-and-airbrushing.html.

Tartakovsky, Margartia. "The Art of Airbrushing." Psychcentral.com. Last Modified December 10, 2008. http://psychcentral.com/blog/archives/2008/12/09/the-art-of-airbrushing/.

Womack, Sarah. "Magazines Criticised for Airbrushing Models." *The Telegraph*. Last modified December 21, 2007. http://www.telegraph.co.uk/news/uknews/1573295/ Magazines-criticised-for-airbrushing-models.html.

ALEXITHYMIA

Alexithymia is defined as the inability to identify and describe one's feelings. Alexithymia is a common feature across both depression and eating disorders. Having alexithymic characteristics undermines an individual's ability to form healthy connections and to develop empathy and sensitivity toward others. Children who feel physically and emotionally insecure and are discouraged from expressing their emotions have difficulties identifying and expressing varied emotions as adults. Alexithymia can be related to low self-esteem and the inability to be assertive for individuals with anorexia nervosa or bulimia nervosa and can disrupt successful eating disorder treatment. Therefore, treatment of eating disorders needs to incorporate multidimensional approaches including assertiveness training and self-esteem enhancement as part of a broader cognitive-behavioral therapy (CBT) model to address alexithymic characteristics when present. The Toronto Alexithymia Scale (TAS-20), a 20-item questionnaire, was validated in 1994 by Bagby and colleagues to assess the degree of alexithymia.

JUSTINE J. REEL

See also: Assertiveness Training.

Bibliography

Bekker, Marrie H., Marcel A. Croon, Esther G. van Balkom, and Jennifer B. Vermee. "Predicting Individual Differences in Autonomy-Connectedness: The Role of Body Awareness, Alexithymia and Assertiveness." *Journal of Clinical Psychology* 64, no. 6 (2008): 747–65.

Shina, Akihiro, Michiko Nakazato, Makoto Mitsumori, Hiroki Koizumi, Eui Shimizu, Mihisa Fujisaki, and Masaomi Iyo. "An Open Trial of Outpatient Group Therapy for

Bulimic Disorders: Combination Program of Cognitive Behavioral Therapy with Assertive Training and Self-Esteem Enhancement." *Psychiatry and Clinical Neurosciences* 59 (2005): 690–96.

AMENORRHEA

Amenorrhea refers to a condition in which a female experiences a delayed start to her menstrual cycle or the absence of a period. When a female with secondary sex characteristics has failed to start her period by the age of 15 years it is known as primary amenorrhea. Secondary amenorrhea is defined by the absence of three consecutive menstrual periods after menses has begun. Amenorrhea has been used as one of the ways to diagnose a female with anorexia nervosa in the current *Diagnostic Manual of Mental Disorders, 4th Edition,* but the proposed DSM-5 definition of anorexia nervosa removes lack of menstrual cycle as a criterion so as to be more inclusive of males and postmenopausal females. It is also important to note that the loss of a female's menstrual cycle may occur for other eating disturbances (e.g., bulimia nervosa) as well as in non-eating disordered individuals with exercise dependence as a result of restrictive eating behavior or excessive exercise that leads to an energy deficit.

Causes of Amenorrhea

Scientists initially believed that having a low percentage of body fat led to disruptions in the menstrual cycle. However, recent studies suggest that having low energy availability (i.e., the amount of dietary energy remaining for other physiological functions after exercise) may be the real culprit causing menstrual disturbances. Specifically, when energy availability decreases to a certain threshold, the body compensates by slowing one's metabolism and reducing the amount of energy used for reproductive functioning.

Health Consequences

Low energy availability and estrogen deficiency can slow the rate of increasing bone mass that occurs in adolescence and lead to bone loss, which can impede the attainment of peak bone mass. This can result in lower bone mineral density than women who are the same age, and result in more fragile bone tissue thus increasing the risk for skeletal fractures. Loss in bone mineral density has been observed to occur at an average rate of 2.5 percent per year in women with anorexia nervosa who do not resume menses. Decreased dilation of blood vessels, which is an indicator of premature cardiovascular disease, and infertility are additional consequences of amenorrhea.

Amenorrhea in Athletes

The athletic population is a high risk group for amenorrhea as sport-specific risk factors for disordered eating in addition to high exercise training loads increase the susceptibility to energy deficits. The interrelationship between energy availability, menstrual function, and bone mineral density is termed "The Female Athlete Triad." Each component of the triad exists along a spectrum with amenorrhea as the most severe menstrual cycle disturbance.

Management of Amenorrhea

Hormonal treatments in women with anorexia nervosa, such as estrogen therapies, have not been very effective in restoring bone mass and do not address the nutritional aspects of bone health. Increasing caloric intake and/or reducing exercise can help to restore lost weight and combat the energy deficit and are recommended to reduce the risk for poor bone health. The most significant improvements in bone mineral density have been noted in individuals who adequately restore energy balance and are able to return to having regular menstrual cycles. Anorexia nervosa clients who have resumed menstruation have been shown to have higher metabolic rates and increased levels of reproductive hormones compared with weight-recovered non-menstruating clients. Thus, it may be beneficial to monitor estrogen status and assess energy availability as indicators of sufficient caloric intake for reproductive function.

HOLLY E. DOETSCH

See also: Female Athlete Triad.

Bibliography

Fenichel, Rebecca M., and Michelle P. Warren. "Anorexia, Bulimia, and the Athletic Triad: Evaluation and Management." *Current Osteoporosis Reports* 5, no. 4 (2007): 160–64.

Hoch, Anne Z, Sophia Lal, Jason W. Jurva, and David D. Gutterman. "The Female Athlete Triad and Cardiovascular Dysfunction." *Physical Medicine and Rehabilitation Clinics of North America* 18, no. 3 (2007): 385–400.

Loucks, Anne B. "Energy Availability and Infertility." *Current Opinion in Endocrinology, Diabetes, and Obesity* 14, no. 6 (2007): 470–74.

Loucks, Anne B., and Jean R. Thuma. "Luteinizing Hormone Pulsatility Is Disrupted at a Threshold of Energy Availability in Regularly Menstruating Women." *Journal of Clinical Endocrinology and Metabolism* 88, no. 1 (2003): 297–311.

Miller, Karen K., Ellen E. Lee, Elizabeth A. Lawson, Madhusmita Misra, Jennifer Minihan, Steven K. Grinspoon, Suzanne Gleysteen, Diane Mickley, David Herzog, and Anne Klibanski. "Determinants of Skeletal Loss and Recovery in Anorexia Nervosa." *Journal of Clinical Endocrinology and Metabolism* 91, no. 8 (2006): 2931–2937.

Nattiv, Aurelia, Anne B. Loucks, Melinda M. Manore, Charlotte F. Sanborn, Jorunn Sundgot-Borgen, and Michelle P. Warren. "American College of Sports Medicine Position Stand. The Female Athlete Triad." *Medicine and Science in Sports and Exercise* 39, no. 10 (2007): 1867–1882.

Practice Committee of the American Society for Reproductive Medicine. "Current Evaluation of Amenorrhea." *Fertility and Sterility* 82 (2004): 266–72.

Sanborn, Charlotte F., Bruce H. Albrecht, and Wiltz W. Wagner. "Athletic Amenorrhea: Lack of Association with Body Fat." *Medicine and Science in Sports and Exercise* 19, no. 3 (1987): 207–212.

Sim, Leslie A., Lauren McGovern, Mohamed B. Elamin, Brian A. Swiglo, Patricia J. Erwin, and Victor M. Montori. "Effect on Bone Health of Estrogen Preparations in Premenopausal Women with Anorexia Nervosa: A Systematic Review and Meta-analyses."*International Journal of Eating Disorders* 43, no. 3 (2010): 218–25.

Sterling, Wendy M., Neville H. Golden, Marc S. Jacobson, Rollyn M. Ornstein, and Stanley M. Hertz. "Metabolic Assessment of Menstruating and Nonmenstruating Normal Weight Adolescents." *International Journal of Eating Disorders* 42, no. 7 (2009): 658–63.

ANOREXIA ATHLETICA

Anorexia Athletica is a popular term used to refer to athletes with eating disorder symptoms. Although not listed as one of the official eating disorder diagnoses in the *Diagnostic and Statistical Manual of Mental Disorders (DSM-5)*, anorexia athletica is also known as athletic nervosa or compulsive exercise, and is particularly common among athletes who play a sport that emphasizes the importance of having a lean physique, such as ski jumping, cycling, climbing, gymnastics, and long distance running. Athletes with anorexia athletica show slightly different disordered eating symptoms and characteristics compared to non-athletes who have eating disorders. Primarily, anorexia athletica represents reduced energy intake and body mass despite high physical performance among athletes. Athletes who suffer from anorexia athletica do not enjoy exercise or training, but rather feel compelled to engage in work-outs beyond what is required for one's sport. Typically, the athlete tends to be driven more by sport performance than by body shape. By engaging in excessive exercise or training, the athletes attempt to gain confidence and reduce anxiety related to sport performance. These athletes usually prioritize practice schedules over family occasions, social events with friends, or jobs. They will also exercise while injured and in spite of weather or other external barriers.

History of Anorexia Athletica

In the 1990s, the term "Anorexia Athletica" was coined to label athletes who exhibited partial anorexic behaviors but who did not have full-blown eating disorders. Sundgot-Borgen and Torstveit, who introduced the concept of anorexia athletica described disordered eating as a "continuum model ranging from abnormal eating behavior and eating disorder not otherwise specified (EDNOS) to clinical eating disorders." Thus, to some extent, there are overlapping signs that appear across anorexia athletica, disordered eating, and eating disorders. First, an excessive concern about body shape can be seen among athletes who suffer from anorexia athletica when they compare their degree of fatness to that of other, remarkably more successful athletes. Second, frequent weight cycling such as repeated weight loss and regain is commonly used to control weight in some sports such as ski jumping and wrestling. Third, many athletes have lower body weight and percentages of body fat. Lastly, some athletes may engage in risky dietary restriction and/or definitive overexercising to burn calories.

Differences between Anorexia Athletica and Eating Disorders

In contrast, Sudi and his colleagues explained clear distinctions between anorexia athletica and eating disorders. First, the reduction in body mass and/or the loss in body fat mass (considered as an unwarranted burden) associated with anorexia athletic is initiated for performance reasons rather than for appearance or excessive concern about body shape; and the coaches and trainers may initiate dieting or over-exercising. Second, the loss in body mass leads to a lean physique. Third, anorexia athletica should no longer be detectable after the cessation of an athlete's career.

Conclusion

The term anorexia athletica refers to disordered symptoms among athletes often related to performance pressures. If athletes do not decrease training during the off-season, it is a clear sign that the athlete may be struggling with excessive exercise that goes beyond a desire to improve his or her performance. Although some characteristics of anorexia athletica have been clearly identified, there are no empirically-based diagnostic tools yet. Therefore, it is wise to seek professional consultation from a trained sports physician, dietician or therapist who specializes in eating disorders before assuming that an athlete struggles with anorexia athletica.

MAYA MIYAIRI

See also: Dancers; Gymnastics; Ski Jumping; Wrestling.

Bibliography

Beals, Katherine A. *Helping Athletes with Eating Disorders.* Champaign, IL: Human Kinetics, 2004.

Reel, Justine J., and Katherine A. Beals, eds. *The Hidden Faces of Eating Disorders and Body Image.* Reston, VA: AAHPERD, 2009.

Sudi, Karl, Karl Ottl, Doris Payerl, Peter Baumgartl, Tauschmann Klemens, and Wolfram Muller. "Anorexia Athletica." *Nutrition* 20 (2004): 657–61.

Sundgot-Borgen, Jorunn, and Monica K. Torstveit. "Prevalence of Eating Disorders in Elite Athletes Is Higher than in the General Population." *Clinical Journal of Sport Medicine* (2004): 14–25.

ANOREXIA NERVOSA

The *Diagnostic and Statistical Manual of Mental Disorders, Fourth Edition, Text Revision* (DSM-IV-TR) identified three distinct types of clinical eating disorders: (1) Anorexia Nervosa (AN); (2) Bulimia Nervosa (BN); and (3) Eating Disorder Not Otherwise Specified (EDNOS). Anorexia nervosa, which has been dubbed the "self-starvation syndrome," is characterized by extreme weight loss, fasting or restriction of food intake, body image disturbances, and loss of a female's menstrual cycle. Anorexia nervosa is the third most common chronic disease among adolescent females with a prevalence of one percent. However, onset of this disorder rarely occurs in women over age 40. Anorexia nervosa is most prevalent in industrialized nations with citizens who focus on being thin to be considered attractive within one's culture. This eating disorder is most commonly pictured in psychology textbooks and is often visually represented by a female with pale skin and protruding collar bones.

History of Anorexia Nervosa

The first documented case of anorexia nervosa was a 20-year-old female client who was reported in the medical literature in 1686, although the diagnosis was formalized only much later. The term "anorexia" is of Greek origin and translates as "lack of appetite." This translation is inadequate for understanding the pervasive control and self-discipline features related to an anorexic's eating behavior. In fact, individuals with anorexia nervosa report thinking about food 70–85 percent of the time despite feeling hunger pangs and other physical symptoms (e.g., stomach distress) associated with their food restricting and fasting behavior.

The full clinical term "anorexia nervosa" was adopted in 1874 by physician Sir William Gull to describe individuals who refused to eat, exhibited excessive weight loss and amenorrhea (loss of menstrual cycle) and other medical symptoms (e.g., low pulse rate, constipation) that could not be explained by other medical conditions. Gull described the condition as occurring typically in girls aged 16 to 25 who exhibited irritability, high energy despite poor nutritional intake and low weight, and excessive activity. Although Gull reported one fatality associated with anorexia nervosa, he viewed the condition as treatable. A case study of a 14-year-old girl presented in 1945 illustrated a common pattern of self-starvation, "compulsive hopping" (i.e., excessive exercise), and a dysfunctional mother-daughter relationship.

Clinical cases of anorexia nervosa disappeared from medical documentation during the Great Depression and World War II when food security issues (not having adequate available food to subsist) dominated food-related concerns in society. However, post–World War II, with great affluence in the 1960s, more cases were documented in which female adolescents were developing dysfunctional relationships with food and were engaging in emotional eating. The American public was not exposed to anorexia nervosa until the 1970s when articles began to appear in the popular press (e.g., *Reader's Guide to Periodic Literature, Science Digest*) about a "starving disease" that was found in certain young women who showed an aversion to eating.

From a clinical perspective, anorexia nervosa was identified as a separate disorder from bulimia nervosa in 1980, in the *Diagnostic and Statistical Manual of Mental Disorders III*. The disorder came into focus among the mainstream public in 1983 following the death of Karen Carpenter who struggled with it. By 1984, anorexia nervosa was landing in comedic skits such as *Saturday Night Live* which featured jokes about an "anorexic cookbook," and in movies like *Down and Out in Beverly Hills* which was filmed in 1986 with a daughter with anorexia nervosa as one of the characters. Although the stereotype of anorexia nervosa primarily affecting young, affluent women has remained, it is important to recognize that diverse individuals may meet the clinical criteria for this disorder. Many celebrities have been suspected to have or admitted to having anorexia nervosa, including Victoria Beckham, Spice Girls' singer and fashion designer who described her body image obsession and restriction of food intake to only vegetables in the 1990s:

http://www.celebrities-with-diseases.com/celebrities/victoria-beckham-tells-of-eating-disorder-hell-3296.html.

Symptoms of Anorexia Nervosa

Clinical criteria for anorexia nervosa, according to the *Diagnostic and Statistical Manual of Mental Disorders,* require body weight to be at 85 percent of what is expected to be normal for one's height, and a fear of fatness or gaining weight despite being severely underweight. Although not part of the DSM-IV-TR criteria for anorexia nervosa, body composition (percentage of body fat) or Body Mass Index (BMI, a formula determined by height and weight) may be used to determine how much weight loss has occurred and what level of treatment is required. Using weight in kilograms divided by height in meters squared (W/H^2) to calculate BMI, a BMI value between 15.1 and 19.9 is considered to be underweight. In order to achieve weight loss or maintain an unhealthy low weight, individuals with anorexia nervosa engage in severe restricting behavior that resembles an extreme diet. It is common for individuals with anorexia to participate in periods of fasting or to limit their diet to a very narrow selection of foods that are considered safe. Some anorexic individuals will become vegetarians or vegans as a way of justifying their avoidance of meat or dairy products.

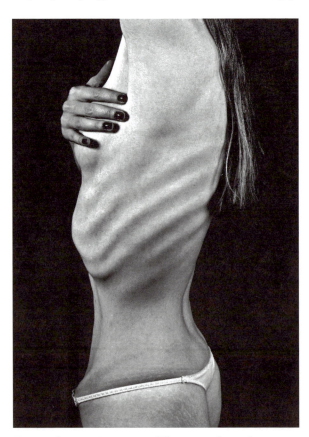

Victim of anorexia nervosa. (Shutterstock.com)

In addition to experiencing weight loss and being severely underweight, anorexic individuals report being obsessed with their body shape, size, and appearance. Anorexic individuals exhibit body dissatisfaction about specific body parts and their overall weight, shape, and size. Body image distortion, in which one's perceived size does not fit with actual measurements, is common among anorexics. Individuals with anorexia nervosa are easy to recognize due to their appearance of being severely underweight that results from severe caloric restriction. Additionally, individuals must have secondary amenorrhea, the absence of a menstrual period for at least three cycles, to be diagnosed with anorexia nervosa; however, this criterion could change in the DSM-5 which is slated to be published in 2013. Using amenorrhea restricts the anorexia nervosa diagnosis from being appropriately used for children or early adolescents who have not yet reached menarche as well as for postmenopausal women who no longer have a period. Additionally, males may fit all of the anorexia nervosa criteria except for amenorrhea. There are currently two types of anorexia nervosa—purging and restricting—listed in the DSM-IV. Anorexia nervosa that is accompanied by occasional purging (e.g., vomiting, misuse of laxatives and diuretics) is classified as the purging type. Anorexic individuals who fit the restricting type have not engaged in either binge or purge behaviors throughout the course of their disorder.

Outcome studies with hospitalized anorexia nervosa populations indicated that 44 percent of clients were able to restore weight and resume menstruation, which was classified as a "good" outcome. However, 24 percent were rated "poor" (unable to restore weight and menstruation), 28 percent were rated between "poor" and "good" and 5 percent had died (premature mortality). Mortality rates reached 20 percent for those anorexia nervosa patients who were followed for more than 20 years. It has been suggested that a poorer prognosis is expected when there is a lower initial body weight, presence of vomiting, or poor familial support.

Personality Characteristics

Psychological characteristics that have been associated with anorexia nervosa include perfectionism, being ego-oriented (i.e., showing strong focus on outcome rather process), and demonstrating strong academic accomplishments or performing well in athletics or other areas. However, clients with anorexia nervosa tend to exhibit low self-esteem. Individuals with anorexia nervosa may appear socially isolated or withdrawn. Anorexic individuals overemphasize weight and size. Body and weight changes are directly connected to one's self-worth. The anorexia nervosa individual may feel rewarded or reinforced for unhealthy restricting behaviors when receiving comments like "you look so thin." Other features of anorexia nervosa include alexithymia (inability to identify and express feelings), a strong need for control, and a lack of assertiveness. Individuals with anorexia may also be diagnosed with personality disorders such as borderline narcissistic obsessive-compulsive disorder (OCD) or dependent personality disorder. They may suffer from other comorbidities such as anxiety disorders or mood disorders and also have a history of trauma.

Health Consequences of Anorexia Nervosa

Sudden cardiac arrest is the leading cause of death in anorexia nervosa. Mortality rates for anorexia nervosa are slightly higher (4 percent) than for bulimia nervosa (3.9 percent). However, there are numerous other health risks and medical complications. Lack of adequate nutrition due to anorexia nervosa results in amenorrhea (loss of period), which places a female at risk for loss of bone mineral density. Bone density loss has been associated with premature development of osteopenia and osteoporosis. Dehydration resulting from lack of fluid intake can cause dry skin, brittle nails, and hair loss. Additionally, lanugo (soft hair) may form on face, back, and arms to protect against the cold due to periods of starvation. Low body temperature leads to eating disordered individuals feeling cold all of the time. Sleep disturbances are common among both anorexia nervosa and bulimia nervosa individuals. Anorexia nervosa individuals are more likely to experience infertility compared to the general female population. Because individuals with anorexia nervosa may require refeeding in order to restore body weight and avoid being medically compromised, they may also experience the risks of refeeding syndrome which include edema (swelling of body tissue). Refeeding syndrome is discussed in more depth in a separate entry.

Anorexia Nervosa among Males

Identification of anorexia nervosa among males has been somewhat controversial since one of the requisite criteria for anorexia is amenorrhea. However, Gull observed this condition in males as well as young girls in the late 1800s, and clinicians documented case studies involving male clients who engaged in restricting, experienced extreme weight loss, and otherwise fit the criteria for anorexia nervosa. A case (Jim) was presented in 1955 that details a 12-year-old male—an only child—who rapidly lost weight, going from 100 pounds to 67 pounds within a matter of months. He refused to eat and exhibited irritability and a dysfunctional relationship with his parents. A description of his medical treatment revealed that he was "forcibly tube-fed, as an imperative lifesaving measure, after emergency medical consultation."

Males reported to be more at risk for developing anorexia nervosa include wrestlers, jockeys, weight class athletes (e.g., lightweight boxers), and ski jumpers who face sport-specific pressures to lose weight or maintain an unhealthy low weight. Bahne Rabe (1963–2011), an Olympic rower who won eight gold medals for West Germany at the 1988 Seoul Olympics, suffered from anorexia nervosa during his competitive career. As a result, he experienced severe weight loss and weakness and eventually died of pneumonia. Similar to athletes, gay males have been found to be overrepresented in cases of males with anorexia nervosa. While it is estimated that only 10–25 percent of eating disorder cases are male, it is suspected that males are less likely to seek treatment or be diagnosed with an eating disorder which has been traditionally considered a "women's disease."

Conclusion

Anorexia nervosa afflicts adolescents and adults and is associated with restriction of food intake and excessive weight loss. Anorexic individuals are terrified of gaining weight and often have a distorted sense of their size when they look in the mirror. Because it leads to extreme weight loss, this disorder is extremely dangerous and requires immediate treatment.

JUSTINE J. REEL

See also: Alexithymia; Amenorrhea; Body Mass Index; Bulimia Nervosa; Carpenter, Karen; Eating Disorder Not Otherwise Specified; Refeeding Syndrome.

Bibliography

Abraham, Suzanne, and Derek Llewellyn-Jones. *Eating Disorders: The Facts.* New York, NY: Oxford University Press, 1995.

American Psychiatric Association. *Diagnostic and Statistical Manual of Mental Disorders, Revised 4th Edition.* Washington, DC: Author, 2000.

Brumberg, Joan Jacobs. *Fasting Girls: The History of Anorexia Nervosa.* New York, NY: Plume, 1989.

Chen, Eunice Yu, Michael S. McCloskey, Sara Michelson, Kathryn H. Gordon, and Emil Coccaro. "Characterizing Eating Disorders in a Personality Disorders Sample." *Psychiatry Research* 185 (2011): 427–32. doi: 10.1016/j.psychres.2010.07.002

Chui, Harold T., Bruce K. Christensen, Robert B. Zipursky, Blake A. Richards, M. Katherine Hanratty, Noor J. Kabani, David J. Mikulis, and Debra K. Katzman. "Cognitive Function and Brain Structure in Females with a History of Adolescent-Onset Anorexia Nervosa." *Pediatrics* 126 (2008): 426–37. doi: 10.1542/peds.2008.0170

Costin, Carolyn. *The Eating Disorder Sourcebook: A Comprehensive Guide to the Causes, Treatments and Prevention of Eating Disorders, Third Edition.* New York, NY: McGraw-Hill, 2007.

Costin, Carolyn. *100 Questions & Answers about Eating Disorders.* Sudbury, MA: Jones and Bartlett, 2007.

Courbasson, Christine, and Jacqueline M. Brunshaw. "The Relationship between Concurrent Substance Use Disorders and Eating Disorders with Personality Disorders." *International Journal of Environmental Research and Public Health* 6 (2009): 2076–2089. doi: 10.3390/ijerph6072076

Falstein, Eugene I., Sherman C. Feinstein and Ilse Judas. "Anorexia Nervosa in the Male Child." *American Journal of Orthopsychiatry* 26, no. 4 (1956): 751–72. doi: 10.1111.j.1939-0025.1956.tb06220.x

Krantz, Mori J., William T. Donahoo, Edward L. Melanson, and Philip S. Mehler. "QT Interval Dispersion and Resting Metabolic Rate in Chronic Anorexia Nervosa." *International Eating Disorders* 37, no. 2 (2005): 166–70.

Lock, James, Daniel Le Grange, W. Stewart Agras, and Christopher Dare. *Treatment Manual for Anorexia Nervosa: A Family-Based Approach.* New York, NY: Guilford Press, 2001.

Mehler, Philip S. "Diagnosis and Care of Patients with Anorexia Nervosa in Primary Care Settings." *Annals of Internal Medicine* 134 (2001): 1048–1059.

Mehler, Philip S., and Mori J. Krantz. "Anorexia Nervosa Medical Issues." *Journal of Women's Health* 12, no. 4 (2003): 331–40.

Mehler, Philip S., and Kenneth L. Weiner. "Use of Total Parenteral Nutrition in the Refeeding of Selected Patients with Severe Anorexia Nervosa." *International Journal of Eating Disorders* 40, no. 3 (2007): 285–87.

Melanson, Edward Louis, William Troy Donahoo, Mori J. Krantz, Paul Poirier, and Philip S. Mehler. "Resting and Ambulatory Heart Rate Variability in Chronic Anorexia Nervosa." *The American Journal of Cardiology* 94 (2004): 1217–1220. doi: 10.1016/j.amjcard.2004.07.103

Reel, Justine J., and Katherine A. Beals, eds. *The Hidden Faces of Eating Disorders and Body Image.* Reston, VA: AAHPERD/NAGWS, 2009.

Sernec, Karin, Martina Tomori, and Bojan Zalar. "Effect of Management of Patients with Anorexia and Bulimia Nervosa on Symptoms and Impulsive Behavior." *Collegium Antropologicum* 34, no. 4 (2010): 1281–1287.
"Victoria Beckham Tells of Her Obsession with Her Body." Celebrities-With-Diseases.com. Last modified February 16, 2010. http://www.celebrities-with-diseases.com/celebrities/victoria-beckham-tells-of-eating-disorder-hell-3296.html.

ANXIETY DISORDERS

Anxiety disorders are mental disorders characterized by a persistent worry or fear that does not subside over time and may interfere with daily life functioning (e.g., school, work). Anxiety disorders were first recognized as psychiatric disorders in the late 19th century. They are generally thought to be caused by a combination of genetic and biological factors— including family history—as well as environmental triggers or stress. The types of anxiety disorders include but are not limited to: generalized anxiety disorder, social phobia and other specific phobias, panic disorder, and obsessive-compulsive disorder (OCD). Generalized anxiety disorder (GAD) is characterized by a persistent worry which is not tied to any particular event or object, and is accompanied by feelings of nervousness and stress beyond what would normally be expected to get through the day. On the other hand, an individual could have a specific phobia which results in an excessive fear of encountering a particular object. Social phobia, or social anxiety disorder, involves worry or fear associated with social interactions. Having a social phobia may result in avoidance of social situations (e.g., parties) and cause an individual to stay at home for risk of perceived embarrassment or scrutiny from others. Individuals with social phobia and specific phobias may also suffer from panic attacks. Panic disorder may accompany a social phobia but is marked by unanticipated panic attacks that may feel like heart attacks and includes several symptoms such as racing heartbeat, dizziness, upset stomach, or sweating. Obsessive-compulsive disorder is characterized by persistent and recurring thoughts and compulsive behaviors. Individuals who suffer from OCD often feel compelled to engage in daily rituals (e.g., hand washing) to satisfy obsessive thoughts and feelings and to feel in control.

Overlap between Anxiety and Eating Disorders

Anxiety disorders are often comorbid with other mental disorders. Approximately 60 percent of individuals with anxiety disorder also suffer from clinical depression. Comorbidity (or the co-occurrence of two mental disorders) between anxiety and eating disorders is incredibly common. Approximately 55–60 percent of anorexic individuals and 57–68 percent of bulimic individuals also experience an anxiety disorder. Although it is suspected that eating disorders and anxiety disorders share a genetic link, anxiety disorders also serve as a risk factor for eating disorders. Having a dual diagnosis creates challenges for treatment as the anxiety disorder may prevent the eating-disordered client from attempting certain social challenges (e.g., trying on clothing, eating out in public) or the fear of panic attacks may be debilitating. However, the treatment team can address the anxiety disorder along with the eating disorder by using treatment approaches that are helpful for both disorders (e.g., psychotropic medications, stress reduction strategies). Psychotherapy that includes a cognitive-behavioral therapy (CBT) approach has produced favorable treatment outcomes and is considered to be effective for addressing both anxiety and eating disorders. Social physique anxiety, which is anxiety specific to one's body or shape, is discussed in a separate entry.

JUSTINE J. REEL

See also: Cognitive Behavioral Therapy (CBT); Depression; Obsessive-Compulsive Disorder; Social Physique Anxiety.

Bibliography

Andrews, Linda Wasmer. *Encyclopedia of Depression, Vol. 1.* California: ABC-CLIO, 2010.

Anestic, Michael D., Jill M. Holm-Denoma, Kathryn H. Gordon, Norman B. Schmidt, and Thomas E. Joiner. "The Role of Anxiety Sensitivity in Eating Pathology." *Cognitive Therapy Research* 32 (2008): 370–85. doi: 10.1007/x10608-006-9085-y

Buckner, Julia D., Jose Sigado, and Peter M. Lewinsohn. "Delineation of Differential Temporal Relations between Specific Eating and Anxiety Disorders." *Journal of Psychiatric Research* 44 (2010): 781–87. doi: 10.1016/j.jpsychires.2010.01.014

Pallister, Emma, and Glenn Waller. "Anxiety in the Eating Disorders: Understanding the Overlap." *Clinical Psychology Review* 28 (2008): 366–86. doi: 10.1016/j.cpr.2007.07.001

Touchette, Evelyn, Adina Henegar, Nathalie T. Godart, Laura Pryor, Bruno Falissard, Richard E. Tremblay, and Sylvana M. Cote. "Subclinical Eating Disorders and Their Comorbidity with Mood and Anxiety Disorders in Adolescent Girls." *Psychiatry Research* 185 (2011): 185–92.

ART THERAPY

Art therapy is a type of therapy that allows for expression without the need to articulate feelings into words. Traditional counseling approaches for eating disorders typically include individual talk therapy, group therapy to address body image issues, and family therapy to confront negative family dynamics, communication, and relationships. Alternative forms of therapy such as art therapy have become increasingly popular as part of a multidisciplinary treatment approach. In fact, many eating disorder residential facilities employ an art therapist or offer a creative arts therapy group as part of the treatment schedule.

Art therapy can be especially effective for clients who have difficulty in identifying or expressing their emotions, which is common for eating disordered individuals. By using clay, pastels, or paint, clients are able to allow repressed feelings to flow without fear of judgment or the need for resistance. This is particularly important for eating-disordered individuals who are often people pleasers and want to be good clients. Art therapy provides a medium for expressing and staying with a previously repressed emotion in that an object (e.g., mask) can be touched, changed, and manipulated with the swipe of a brush. For example, one client with exercise dependence drew herself shackled to a treadmill to represent her emotions of being imprisoned by her feelings of obligation toward exercise.

While artwork can provide a safe mechanism for emotional expression, the act of engaging in art therapy activities can also serve a cathartic purpose. Clients who have been limited in their physical exercise may feel stressed and anxious; however, art can provide a new coping skill for distracting and regulating one's arousal.

Art therapy goals can include nurturance, control, self-esteem and the ability to cope with emotions and identity issues. Initially, art therapy activities are less directed in order to encourage spontaneity and creativity and to avoid having the client attempt to have the perfect picture or art piece. As the client becomes more comfortable with the art therapy process, the trained art therapist gently processes the artwork and the feelings invoked by creating the piece with the client. It is not uncommon for sensitive and difficult issues (e.g., cutting, suicidal thoughts) to arise in an individual or group art therapy session. Therefore, it is important for the art therapist to remain in close communication with the eating-disordered client's primary therapist.

JUSTINE J. REEL

See also: Exercise Dependence.

Bibliography

Beck, Elizabeth H. *Art Therapy with an Eating Disordered Male Population: A Case Study.* Published thesis. Drexel University, 2007.

Frish, Maria J., Debra L. Franko, and David B. Herzog. "Arts-based Therapies in the Treatment of Eating Disorders." *Eating Disorders* 14 (2006): 131–42.

Levens, Mary. "Borderline Aspects of Eating Disorders: Art Therapy's Contribution." *Group Analysis* 23 (1990): 277–84.

Rehavia-Hannauer, Dafna. "Identifying Conflicts of Anorexia Nervosa as Manifested in the Art Therapy Process." *The Arts in Psychotherapy* 30 (2003): 137–49.

ASSERTIVENESS TRAINING

Assertiveness refers to the ability to assert oneself and to say "no" to requests that one does not desire to fulfill. Assertiveness also includes skills that help to maintain healthy boundaries and the ability to express emotions within interpersonal relationships. Individuals with anorexia nervosa and bulimia nervosa feel significantly more controlled by external factors and are less likely to display self-assertion than non-eating disordered comparison groups. Many individuals with eating disorders lack social skills and have difficulty with assertiveness or display social inhibition. Therefore, assertiveness training that teaches social skills should be included as part of a broader eating disorder treatment.

Assertiveness Training

Assertiveness training is designed to help individuals express thoughts and emotions effectively, change self-perceptions, and build self confidence across situations.

Common strategies include demonstrations of healthy assertion behaviors, role playing to practice with feedback, relaxation exercises, and homework. Although assertiveness training can be introduced in individual psychotherapy sessions, researchers suggest that a group approach to assertiveness training is superior because it allows for additional practice with peers and opportunities for more feedback. Assertiveness training as part of a cognitive-behavioral treatment (CBT) group can be used for coping with interpersonal problems, social skills training, and self-esteem enhancement. Additionally, alexithymia can be addressed as part of assertiveness training using role play.

Role play allows for an individual to spontaneously respond to a situation that is simulated to create a challenge. The client has to respond using one's own thoughts, perceptions, feelings, and individual tendencies. Group members can provide feedback and offer suggestions on how to change one's behaviors. Therefore, such role play forces individuals with alexithymic characteristics and lack of assertiveness to recognize their emotions and express those emotions to their group members through their attitude and speech patterns (which should be congruent with how they feel).

JUSTINE J. REEL

See also: Alexithymia.

Bibliography

Bekker, Marrie H., Marcel A. Croon, Esther G. van Balkom, and Jennifer B. Vermee. "Predicting Individual Differences in Autonomy-Connectedness: The Role of Body Awareness, Alexithymia and Assertiveness." *Journal of Clinical Psychology* 64, no. 6 (2008): 747–65.

Hayakawa, Masaya. "How Repeated 15-Minute Assertiveness Training Sessions Reduce Wrist Cutting in Patients with Borderline Personality Disorder." *American Journal of Psychotherapy* 63, no. 1 (2009): 41–51.

Lin, Yen-Ru, Mei-Hsuen Wu, Cheng-I Yang, Tsai-Hwei Chen, Chen-Chuan Hus, Yue-Cune Chang, Wen-Chii Tzeng, Yuan-Hwa Chou, and Kuei-Ru Chou. "Evaluation of Assertiveness Training for Psychiatric Patients." *Journal of Clinical Nursing* 17 (2008): 2875–2883.

Shina, Akihiro, Michiko Nakazato, Makoto Mitsumori, Hiroki Koizumi, Eui Shimizu, Mihisa Fujisaki, and Masaomi Iyo. "An Open Trial of Outpatient Group Therapy for Bulimic Disorders: Combination Program of Cognitive Behavioral Therapy with Assertive Training and Self-Esteem Enhancement." *Psychiatry and Clinical Neurosciences* 59 (2005): 690–96.

Vagos, Paula and Anabela Pereira. "A Proposal for Evaluating Cognition in Assertiveness." *Psychological Assessment* 22, no. 3 (2010): 657–65.

ASSESSMENT

Assessment refers to the process of identifying whether symptoms are present for the purpose of making a clinical diagnosis and prescribing appropriate treatment. An assessment may be conducted for research or clinical purposes, but a research-based assessment will probably look quite different when compared to an assessment conducted for the purpose of informing treatment decisions. The context in which the assessment is conducted also bears on the nature of the assessment itself. For research assessments, individuals may respond to an anonymous questionnaire without having further interaction with the researcher. Clinical assessments are more common and they may take place in inpatient hospitals, residential treatment facilities, or in outpatient settings (e.g., college counseling center).

Who Assesses for Eating Disorders?

Because eating disorder assessments occur in numerous settings, it is recommended that a multidisciplinary approach be employed. Therefore, the individual should be examined by a medical professional for vital signs and health status, by a mental health professional, and by a registered dietitian who can assess psychological states and nutritional behaviors. Data should be gathered from close family members with client consent along with that of the adolescent or adult suspected of having an eating disorder, because family members can provide an invaluable perspective regarding the duration and severity of the eating disorder.

What Are the Eating Disorder Criteria?

Eating disorders, as of this writing, can be classified based on DSM-IV-TR (*Diagnostic and Statistical Manual of Mental Disorders, 4th Edition, Text Revision*) criteria. In 2013, the newest version of the DSM, DSM-5, will be published. It is likely to contain significant changes to diagnostic criteria for eating disorders, including the name of the category itself which will be changed to "Feeding and Eating Disorders." Under the DSM-IV-TR classification system there are three eating disorders: Anorexia Nervosa, Bulimia Nervosa, and Eating Disorder Not Otherwise Specified (EDNOS). Each disorder will be briefly discussed here along with some of the proposed changes for DSM-5.

Anorexia nervosa is currently characterized by being underweight for one's age and height, the absence of menses (at least 3 consecutive months), an intense fear of gaining weight or becoming fat, and a distorted body image. Although the DSM-IV-TR specifies that being underweight refers to weighing less than 85 percent of what would be expected for one's age and height, the DSM-5 will remove the actual percentage as it is possible for an individual to be significantly below expected weight at a percentage greater than 85 percent. Moreover, the phrase "refusal to maintain body weight" in the DSM-IV-TR is deemed to be derogatory and will be replaced by "restriction of energy intake." A criterion that will be removed altogether is the criterion related to menses since it cannot be applied to premenarchial females, postmenopausal females, and males.

Bulimia nervosa under DSM-IV-TR is characterized by binge episodes and also by behaviors designed to get rid of the food consumed or to offset the binge. A binge is characterized by the consumption of a large quantity of food within a brief period by an individual. The food consumed during a binge is more than a typical person would eat given the circumstances. For example, it is not that unusual for individuals in the United States to consume large quantities of food on the Thanksgiving Day holiday. To meet the criteria, however, binge episodes would have to occur on a more regular basis for at least several months and the binge episode should be accompanied by a sense of loss of control over one's eating. In bulimia nervosa, the individual will typically engage in "recurrent inappropriate compensatory behavior" designed specifically to prevent weight gain. These behaviors can include self-induced vomiting, abuse of laxatives, diuretics or syrup of ipecac, fasting, and excessive exercise. Finally, when considering oneself the individual will place a great deal of emphasis on the shape and weight of the body. The DSM-5 will retain the aforementioned criteria for bulimia nervosa.

The third eating disorder category in the DSM-IV-TR, Eating Disorder Not Otherwise Specified (EDNOS), refers to eating disorders that do not meet the criteria for either anorexia nervosa or bulimia nervosa. For example, an individual may meet all of the anorexia nervosa criteria except for amenorrhea. Binge Eating Disorder, widely recognized as a separate eating disorder, has been diagnosed as EDNOS, but will receive a separate classification in the DSM-5. Binge Eating Disorder (BED) will use the same definition for a binge episode as bulimia nervosa and will describe characteristics of eating rapidly, feeling uncomfortably full, eating a lot even when not hungry, feeling disgusted/depressed/ guilty, or eating alone due to embarrassment. The EDNOS category will be eliminated by name in the DSM-5 and will be replaced with "Feeding and Eating Conditions Not Elsewhere Classified." Some of the proposed conditions in this category include: Atypical Anorexia Nervosa, Subthreshold Bulimia Nervosa, Subthreshold Binge Eating Disorder, and Purging Disorder. Authors of this section

Eating disorders include anorexia nervosa, bulimia nervosa, and binge eating. Research shows that more than 90 percent of those who have eating disorders are women between the ages of 12 and 25. (PhotoDisc, Inc.)

of the DSM-5 indicated that additional research is required in order to determine whether or not these disorders are distinct disorders that may stand alone in future revisions of the DSM.

Assessment Methods

There are a variety of methods that can be used to determine whether or not a particular client has an eating disorder. These include self-report measures, structured instruments, and diagnostic interviewing. Self-report measures allow the client to indicate what behaviors she may be experiencing. Although many of these instruments have good psychometric properties and are often inexpensive to use, they are limited in part by the degree to which the information provided by the client is accurate. Self-report measures include the Eating Disorder Examination-Questionnaire (EDE-Q) and the Eating Disorder Diagnostic Scale (EDDS).

Structured measures provide the professional with a set of specific items to address with the client. Each of these measurement tools is designed to gather a specific type of information (e.g., eating disorder-related behavior) and generally do not allow the assessor to ad lib questions. Some tools in this category are referred to as "semistructured." These tools require specific items to be addressed by the assessor while allowing the assessor to ask follow-up questions as needed. Structured measures include the Eating Disorder Examination (EDE) and the Structured Interview for Anorexic and Bulimic Syndromes for DSM-IV and ICD-10.

The clinical interview is helpful in eliciting information from the client and also in terms of establishing a rapport with the client. Establishing a rapport is not only critical for an ongoing therapeutic relationship but also helps to ensure that the information provided by the client will be as accurate as possible. Clinical interviews can be unstructured, semistructured, or structured in nature. The use of one type over another will depend on things such as time needed, type of information needed, and the assessment clinician's familiarity with the tool. Examples of diagnostic interviews include the Eating Disorder Examination and Structured Clinical Interview for DSM-IV.

All of the different types of assessment tools mentioned are only as accurate as the information provided by the patient as well as the assessor's ability to communicate to the client the purpose and importance of the assessment. Therefore, all results should be interpreted in light of the limitations of the tool itself and the data gathered. Professionals, patients, and family members are encouraged to read more about eating disorder assessment tools in order to learn about their purpose and reported effectiveness.

Regardless of the method used, thorough and accurate assessment of eating disorders is important for the appropriate diagnosis so that an individual can receive the proper treatment for his or her level of care. To help providers determine the appropriate level of care for a particular patient the American Psychiatric Association (APA) has published a set of practice guidelines that include recommendations for this type of assessment. The APA notes that there are five levels of care ranging from outpatient treatment to inpatient hospitalization. The degree of treatment required is determined by assessing the severity of symptoms, including but not limited to medical stability, suicidal thoughts, weight, motivation, co-occurring disorders, environmental stressors, and geographical availability of treatment. The appropriateness of using a client's weight to determine his or her level of wellness or illness has received considerable attention. The APA notes that the weight percentages listed in its table are to be considered guidelines and that an appropriate weight for any patient should be considered on a case-by-case basis.

Although typically the purpose of an assessment for an eating disorder is not to determine what kind of insurance coverage a patient will receive, payment for treatment is certainly a point of consideration. Insurance companies will often require a diagnosis from the treating physician or mental health professional; however, the label is less important than understanding the way in which the disorder is impacting the individual. Conducting an assessment to determine whether a particular eating disorder is present may mean that equally serious but not textbook cases may be overlooked. Assessments should be conducted for the purpose of identifying and evaluating particular symptoms. This will help to inform the decision regarding the method of treatment needed on an individualized basis. Moreover, a focus on symptoms rather than diagnostic categories or labels will foster a more supportive climate for both the eating disordered individual and his family so that treatment options can be addressed.

It is important to note that although eating disorders are still heavily associated with adolescent or young adult white females and the majority of cases still fit in this demographic category, the reality is that males, children, adults, and all ethnic minorities can also be at risk for an eating disorder. Therefore, the decision to encourage someone to get assessed for an eating disorder should not be influenced by the age, gender, or race/ethnicity of the individual. Relying on demographics alone is likely to result in a delay in the identification of an eating disorder, or in unidentified cases.

Assessment of Eating Behaviors

Identifying and understanding a client's eating behaviors will not only assist in determining an accurate diagnosis but also help to inform treatment decisions. Eating disorder-related behaviors can include limiting how much food is consumed, overeating, limiting the types of foods eaten, and eating only under certain circumstances or in certain environments. The more behaviors a client identifies, the greater the likelihood that he or she is struggling with an eating disorder.

Depending on the purpose of the assessment, it may be important to differentiate between actual eating behaviors and a client's perception of his or her eating behaviors. For example, the terms "objective binge" and "subjective binge" have been used to differentiate between a binge as defined by the Diagnostic and Statistical Manual of Mental Disorders and a binge as defined by the client herself, which may not meet the diagnostic criteria for a binge. Verifying the objective or subjective nature of what a client reports can also be important for treatment purposes. A client who engages in objective binges will need assistance in eliminating this behavior, whereas a client who engages in a subjective binge (i.e., it *feels* like a binge but technically is not a binge) may benefit from cognitive restructuring and psychoeducation about what constitutes "too much" or "too little" food.

Assessing the quantity of food consumed in a typical day is also an important facet of assessment. Having this information will help providers estimate weight loss or weight gain and extent of dietary restriction. This element of assessment can be elusive. Although individuals with eating disorders will seemingly know a great deal about calories, fat, and carbohydrate content for a wide variety of foods, they are not usually very accurate in estimating how much they consume in a typical day. This does not mean that the amount consumed should not be assessed, but it does suggest that the assessor should not assume that the information he or she has received is accurate. Independent verification of the patient's self-report by someone who witnesses the patient's eating behaviors may be necessary.

Assessment of Physical/Medical Symptoms

Determining the type and level of care needed for a particular patient can be aided by knowing a client's current medical status. This can be ascertained by a medical provider who is able to perform assessments designed to target specific systems in the body (e.g., vital signs, gastrointestinal, cardiovascular, and neurological functioning, bone health). An indicator that one or more of a client's bodily systems may be compromised is the client's current weight and weight history. This may be especially true for individuals diagnosed with or suspected of having anorexia nervosa. Specific and serious medical issues (e.g., heart arrhythmias) are associated with having a severely low weight for one's age, gender, and height, and in comparison to their weight history. Therefore, when a client is identified to have a seriously low weight (as assessed by an eating disorder expert applying current DSM criteria) it is paramount that weight restoration is the first order of treatment. It is important to note, however, that weight alone is not an effective indicator of the health (or lack thereof) of a client. Clients who can be classified as being in a normal weight range may also be seriously medically compromised.

Related to a female client's weight is the issue of whether or not she is menstruating regularly or at all. Although primary amenorrhea (missing three consecutive menstrual cycles in a postmenarchial female) and secondary amenorrhea (delayed onset of menses) are currently a part of the symptom constellation of anorexia nervosa as defined by the DSM-IV-TR, these symptoms are likely to be removed in the upcoming DSM-5. Regardless of the diagnostic status of these symptoms, any significant change in a female's menstrual cycle, or a significant delay in the onset of menses for a pre-adolescent or adolescent female, may indicate that she has not maintained or achieved a sufficient weight to support this physiological function.

In addition to compromised reproductive functioning, an absent or irregular menstrual cycle can result in poor bone health. Osteopenia, mild loss of bone density, is the precursor to osteoporosis or severe loss of bone density which can result in bone fractures or breaks. Therefore, assessing an individual's bone density (assessed by a medical professional ideally using a DXA scan) can confirm any evidence of bone deterioration. It is important to note that clients with menstrual irregularity who regularly engage in high impact/weight bearing activities should have an assessment that measures bone density on a non-weight-bearing location (e.g., lumbar spine). Weight bearing joints in athletes and regular exercisers are likely to be particularly strong and may not be accurate indicators of what is occurring throughout the rest of the skeleton.

Although it is common to associate serious medical problems with anorexia nervosa due in large part to the low weight that many patients reach, patients with bulimia nervosa are also at risk for a host of serious medical problems involving the gastrointestinal system (e.g., esophageal rupture). They are also at risk for cardiac problems (e.g., arrhythmias), oral and dental problems (e.g., gum recession), and reproductive issues (e.g., infertility). Therefore, it is important to assess for the frequency of binge episodes as well as accompanying episodes of pathogenic compensatory behaviors (e.g., vomiting, use of laxatives or diuretics, use of syrup of ipecac, excessive exercise). Although the binge/purge cycle is typically associated with bulimia nervosa, patients with anorexia nervosa can also engage in these behaviors and therefore should be assessed accordingly.

Assessment of Cognitions

The beliefs and attitudes held by clients with eating disorders are typically rigid, affect nearly all aspects of the client's life, and often linger far beyond the stabilization and elimination of eating disorder-related behaviors and their accompanying medical consequences. Therefore, an important element of the assessment process is to identify the nature of a client's thought processes. It is also important to look into the client's awareness of and thoughts about these cognitions, and to identify the reinforcing forces that maintain these cognitions.

It is common for clients to spend a great deal of mental energy on attitudes and beliefs surrounding weight, body shape and size, and self-worth. Often, a client's self-worth is directly tied to their belief about what their current weight means and their degree of body satisfaction. Many clients' belief systems are heavily influenced by media images and messages (i.e., "thin ideal" for females and "muscular ideal" for males), friends and family who hold specific ideas about how one ought to look, and the beliefs of important others including dating partners or athletic coaches. Knowing the influences on a client's belief system has a direct impact on treatment. Interventions can be designed to target specific cognitions or to handle the messages the patient hears from those around her.

A related but separate element of a client's belief system which needs to be assessed is the degree to which the client identifies with or values his or her belief system. That is, are the client's beliefs ego-syntonic or ego-dystonic? Ego-syntonic belief systems suggest an investment in these cognitions that will be resistant to intervention. The client will often indicate that there is something that they like about their thought patterns or that it is helpful to them in some way. Clients who report that they do not like their thought patterns or that these patterns are detrimental in some particular way are more likely to respond favorably to interventions designed to alter or eliminate these beliefs.

Assessment of Interpersonal Functioning

It is also important to assess the quality of and any changes in interpersonal relationships. Frequently, eating disordered individuals are secretive about their behaviors due to the shame and guilt they are experiencing, and they may isolate themselves from others. This interpersonal change may be presented by consistently turning down social invitations that they previously would have accepted.

Conclusion

Determining the complexity of issues with which the individual is coping will help inform treatment decisions and can provide a preliminary indication of treatment outcome (i.e., the presence of certain comorbidities can be associated with less favorable outcome). For example, the most common comorbid psychiatric diagnoses include mood disorders and anxiety disorders. Personality disorders (e.g., borderline personality disorder) may also be present and are typically characterized by dramatic, emotional disturbances. Although there are other facets of an individual's cognitions and behaviors that can be assessed, this section was designed to provide a snapshot of common areas of assessment. Overall, it is important for data to be collected from varied sources and on multiple dimensions of functioning.

CHRISTINE L. B. SELBY

See also: Amenorrhea; Binge Eating Disorder.

Bibliography

American Psychiatric Association. *Diagnostic and Statistical Manual of Mental Disorders, 4th Edition, Text Revision.* Washington DC: American Psychiatric Association, 2000.

American Psychiatric Association. "Feeding and Eating Disorders." *American Psychiatric Association: DSM-5 Development.* Last modified October 6, 2010. http://dsm5.org/ProposedRevision/Pages/FeedingandEatingDisorders.aspx.

American Psychiatric Association. *Practice Guideline for the Treatment of Patients with Eating Disorders, 3rd Edition.* June 2006. http://www.psychiatryonline.com/pracGuide/pracGuideChapToc_12.aspx.

Anderson, Drew A., and Andrea D. Murray. "Psychological Assessment of the Eating Disorders." In *The Oxford Handbook of Eating Disorders,* edited by Stewart W. Agras, 249–58. New York: Oxford University Press, 2010.

Anderson, Drew A., Jason M. Lavender, and Kyle P. De Young. "The Assessment Process: Refining the Clinical Evaluation of Patients with Eating Disorders." In *Treatment of Eating*

Disorders: Bridging the Research-Practice Gap, edited by Margo Maine, Beth Hartman, and Douglas W. Bunnell, 71–87. San Diego: Elsevier Academic Press, 2010.

Mitchell, James E. and Carol B. Peterson, eds. *Assessment of Eating Disorders.* New York: The Guilford Press, 2005.

Tyson, Edward P. "Medical Assessment of Eating Disorders." In *Treatment of Eating Disorders: Bridging the Research-Practice Gap,* edited by Margo Maine, Beth Hartman, and Douglas W. Bunnell, 89–110. San Diego: Elsevier Academic Press, 2010.

Yager, Joel. "Assessment and Determination of Initial Treatment Approaches for Patients with Eating Disorders." In *Clinical Manual of Eating Disorders,* edited by Joel Yager and Pauline S. Powers, 31–77. Washington DC: American Psychiatric Publishing, Inc., 2007.

ATHENA

ATHENA, which stands for Athletes Targeting Healthy Exercise and Nutrition Alternatives, refers to a prevention program designed for sports teams to reduce disordered eating and substance abuse among female athletes. ATHENA parallels a program called ATLAS (Adolescents Training and Learning to Avoid Steroids) which was developed for male athletes with the objective of improving nutrition and exercise while decreasing alcohol and illicit and performance enhancement substances. ATHENA, which is a peer-led program, has been implemented in a team setting and 70 percent of the sessions are led by a trained team member. This trained group leader attends a 90-minute orientation in advance of the sessions and is provided with a script to be used when facilitating the lessons. The prevention program consists of eight 45-minute sessions that take place when the athletes are not training or competing and can meet as a group.

Lessons of ATHENA cover topics like depression, self-esteem, healthy norms, and societal pressures to be thin. Interactive sessions include efforts to deconstruct negative media messages that serve to reinforce ultrathin body ideals and glamorize alcohol, cigarettes, or nutritional supplements. Athletes also receive information about healthy strength training and exercise habits. Sports nutrition education is provided, which deals with necessary carbohydrate, protein, fat, and calcium intake. Because ATHENA is geared toward female athletes who are at risk for developing disordered eating, caloric information of foods is not presented and instead the consequences of eating disorders are discussed. In concordance with evidence-based prevention research, the ATHENA program is interactive (rather than strictly didactic), focuses on females-only (rather than mixed-gender grouping), and provides participants with the opportunity to practice skills throughout the program.

Evaluation of the ATHENA program

ATHENA was shown to be feasible to implement by coaches and athletes within the high school and college team sports setting. In one study with female high school athletes, athletes reported decreased disordered eating and body-shaping drug use (e.g., diet pills, steroids, amphetamines) and increased knowledge regarding sports nutrition and eating disorder consequences. Additionally, ATHENA athletes demonstrated healthy nutritional and exercise habits following the program.

Interestingly, participants were less likely to ride in a car with a driver who had consumed alcohol and were more likely to wear seatbelts. For intentions toward future behaviors, athletes reported less intention toward future vomiting to lose weight, use of diet pills, tobacco, or creatine. At the college level, auxiliary dancers (i.e., majorettes, color guard dance teams) from Southeastern universities participated in the ATHENA program and reported increased knowledge of eating disorders and nutrition.

Conclusion

The recently developed ATHENA program which targets female athletes shows promise in terms of promoting healthy attitudes and behaviors among college and high school sports teams. Within peer-led lessons, participating athletes have the opportunity to learn about sports nutrition, exercise, and strength training, as well as the consequences of disordered eating and substance abuse. Although further testing is needed to show short-term and longer-term success for the program in diverse samples, the initial potential for ATHENA is favorable.

JUSTINE J. REEL

Bibliography

Elliot, Diane L., Linn Goldberg, Esther L. Moe, Carol A. DeFrancesco, Melissa B. Durham, and Hollie Hix-Small. "Preventing Substance Use and Disordered Eating: Initial Outcomes of the ATHENA (Athletes Targeting Healthy Exercise and Nutrition Alternatives) Program." *Archives of Pediatric and Adolescent Medicine* 158 (2004), 1043–1049.

Elliot, Diane L., Linn Goldberg, Esther L. Moe, Carol A. DeFrancesco, Melissa B. Durham, and Hollie Hix-Small. "Definition and Outcome of a Curriculum to Prevent Disordered Eating and Body-Shaping Drug Use." *Journal of School Health* 76 (2006): 67–73.

Elliot, Diane L., Linn Goldberg, Esther L. Moe, Carol A. DeFrancesco, Melissa B. Durham, Wendy McGinnis, and Chondra Lockwood. "Long-term Outcomes of the ATHENA (Athletes Targeting Healthy Exercise and Nutrition Alternatives) Program for Female High School Athletes." *Journal of Alcohol and Drug Education* 52, no. 2 (2008): 73–92.

Stice, Eric, Heather Shaw, and Nathan C. Marti. "A Meta-Analytic Review of Eating Disorder Prevention Programs: Encouraging Findings." *Annual Review of Clinical Psychology* 3 (2007): 207–231. doi: 10.1146/annurev.clinpsy.3.022806.091447.

Torres-McGehee, Toni. M., James M. Green, Deidre Leaver-Dunn, James D. Leeper, Phillip A. Bishop, and Mark T. Richardson. "Attitude and Knowledge Changes in Collegiate Dancers Following a Short-Term, Team-Centered Prevention Program on Eating Disorders." *Perceptual and Motor Skills* 112, no. 3 (2011): 711–25.

ATHLETIC TRAINERS

Athletic trainers are in a unique position to help athletes who display disordered eating behaviors because they are both health care providers and part of the extended coaching staff. As health care professionals, athletic trainers focus on the athlete's overall health and well-being in addition to sport performance. Therefore, athletic trainers can identify eating disordered behaviors and can access the coaching staff and other important sports personnel (e.g., team physician) to seek support for the athlete. Athletic trainers serve as the first line of defense and can detect eating, exercise, and body weight changes in athletes when they occur.

Identification of At-Risk Athletes

Early identification of, and intervention with, athletes who exhibit disordered eating behaviors (e.g., restricting foods) increases the probability of treatment success. Interestingly, 2,800 NCAA coaches who were surveyed reported that athletic trainers were often first responders when it came to identifying athletes at-risk for developing eating disorders. Given the potential for athletic trainers to play such an important role in eating disorder identification and treatment referrals, it is necessary for athletic trainers to receive appropriate training. To this end, the National Athletic Trainers' Association (NATA) published a position statement in 2008 discussing the role of athletic trainers in the prevention, detection, and management of athletes with eating disorder-related behaviors.

NATA's position statement provides recommendations including actions items that should take place immediately (e.g., establishing a well-qualified team of professionals), items describing how to detect eating disorder-related behavior, items on how to manage athletes with eating disordered behaviors, and ways to prevent eating disorder-related behaviors. Given these recommendations, NATA concluded that "[c]ertified athletic trainers have the capacity and responsibility to play active roles as integral members of the health care team." NATA also noted that the knowledge base required for athletic trainers to become certified, in conjunction with experience working with athletes with eating disorder-related behaviors, suggests that athletic trainers' overall effectiveness in working with this unique population will hopefully increase in the coming years.

Recent studies have evaluated certified athletic trainers' perceptions of how prepared they are for working with athletes who develop eating disordered behavior. The certified athletic trainers indicated that they do not think they receive adequate preparation (educationally or professionally) in working with athletes with eating disorder-related behaviors. This study also revealed that despite this perceived lack of preparation, athletic trainers still acknowledged that they are responsible for being able to identify and work with this population. The college athletic trainers surveyed in a different study reported that although nearly all participants had worked with a female athlete with eating disorder-related behaviors, just over one quarter said they felt confident that they could identify an eating disorder, and nearly all respondents indicated that more attention needs to be given to this sub-population of athletes. Both studies concluded that there seems to be a need and a desire for continuing education about eating disorders in athletes. Moreover, the study on college athletic trainers recommended that collegiate athletic programs should develop institutional policies on how to handle athletes with eating disorders. By having policies, athletic trainers can be better equipped to identify at-risk athletes and to refer these athletes for treatment.

Treatment of Eating Disorders

The importance of having a multidisciplinary treatment team working with individuals with eating disorders has been well documented. When an athlete is the client in question, members of that athlete's sport-related community may be a part of that team; however, it is more likely that sports personnel (e.g., coaches, athletic trainers) will be part of what Thompson and Sherman have called a "sport management team." Although it may be appropriate for some sports personnel to be formal members of the treatment team—that is, the group of professionals providing treatment interventions—most sports personnel will be more appropriately a part of the "sport management team." This team will ideally have contact with the treatment team to ensure an expedient recovery for the athlete. Athletic trainers will usually be a part of an athlete's sport management team.

Conclusion

Athletic trainers are important members of an athlete's sport performance team. When the athlete in question is suspected of having an eating disorder, the athletic trainer can be pivotal in detecting the eating disorder and ensuring that the athlete gets the help she needs as quickly as possible. Given this important role, and with findings suggesting that not all athletic trainers feel well prepared to identify and work with athletes who have eating disorders, it is important to ensure that athletic trainers receive adequate and proper training in the prevention, identification, and treatment of eating disorders in athletes.

CHRISTINE L. B. SELBY

Bibliography

Bonci, Christine M, Leslie J. Bonci, Lorita Granger, Craig L. Johnson, Robert M. Malina, Leslie W. Milne, Randa R. Ryan, and Erin M. Vanderbunt. "National Athletic Trainers' Association Position Statement: Preventing, Detecting, and Managing Disordered Eating in Athletes." *Journal of Athletic Training* 43, no. 1 (2008): 80–108.

Sherman, Roberta T, Ron A. Thompson, Denise Dehass, and Mary Wilfert. "NCAA Coaches Survey: The Role of the Coach in Identifying and Managing Athletes with Disordered Eating." *Eating Disorders* 13 (2005): 447–66.

Thompson, Ron A, and Robert T. Sherman. *Eating Disorders in Sport.* New York: Routledge, 2010.

Vaughan, Jennifer L, Keith A. King, and Randall R. Cottrell. "Collegiate Athletic Trainers' Confidence in Helping Female Athletes with Eating Disorders." *Journal of Athletic Training* 39, no. 1 (2004): 71–76.

Whitson, Emily J., Mitchell L. Corova, Timothy J. Demchak, Catherine L. Stemmans, and Keith A. King. "Certified Athletic Trainers' Knowledge and Perception of Professional Preparation Involving Eating Disorders Among Athletes." *Journal of Allied Health* 35, no. 1 (2006): 18–29.

B

BALLET

Ballet, a style of performance dance, dates back to 15th-century Italy where it emerged as a dance interpretation of fencing. Ballet has since spread across Europe and the United States, and numerous professional ballet companies have evolved. In the United States, choreographer George Balanchine choreographed routines in the 1920s and formed his first professional ballet company in 1935. His choreography and techniques had a significant influence on a recognizable ballet body represented by tall dancers who had long limbs to create aesthetically pleasing performance lines. Ballet has been considered an "at risk" activity for development of eating disorders associated with this ultrathin ideal. Recently, a movie featuring actress Natalie Portman entitled *Black Swan* showed the darker side of eating disorders and the pressure to remain slim for ballerinas.

Body Image and Ballerinas

Thirty-seven percent to eighty-four percent of ballet dancers have reported body dissatisfaction and over half (58%) of ballet dancers are preoccupied with body weight and food compared to thirty-eight percent of nondancers. Ballet schools and professional ballet companies place a strong emphasis on body shape, weight, and the appearance of the body during movement. However, unlike cheerleading, ballet schools do not rely on weight requirements but rather on the aesthetic of the body shape, length, and slenderness of body parts. Therefore, young dancers who develop less ideal body shapes as a result of puberty or genetics are often asked to leave or change to another style of dance (e.g., modern dance which allows for a more forgiving body ideal). Within the most elite ballet schools in the United States, only five percent of eight-year-old ballet dancers complete the program. Similar to figure skating, ballet dancers have a small window in which to excel and perform in a professional dance company. Ballet dancers who are competing for limited spots may experience pressure to meet a particular "ballet body" from many sources, including dance teachers, choreographers, the dancers themselves, and other dancers. Because of the separation of gender roles in ballet, female ballerinas are expected to be feminine and dainty. Strong and muscular male ballet dancers must lift female dancers to display lines and beauty. Dancers' bodies are constantly monitored by teachers and choreographers. However, the mirror serves as a constant reminder of one's body size, shape, and appearance during long training. Once a ballet dancer lands a professional role, the body-related evaluation is not over. In one case, a critic made disparaging remarks about a ballet dancer who had an eating disorder history: http://www.telegraph.co.uk/news/worldnews/northamerica/usa/8202087/Sugar-Plump-Fairy-ballet-dancer-says-she-suffered-from-eating-disorders.html

Eating Disorders and Ballet

With the numerous pressures associated with ballet to maintain a low weight and thin appearance, it is no surprise that the prevalence of anorexia nervosa is three to six times higher among ballet dancers than the general population. Forty percent of ballet dancers weighed below 85 percent of their ideal body weight and 27 percent to 47 percent of dancers experienced menstrual dysfunction (i.e., irregular menstrual cycle or amenorrhea). Bulimia nervosa rates among ballet dancers range from 2 percent to 12 percent depending on the study, but the use of purging methods including self-induced vomiting and laxatives have been well documented in the ballet population. Other weight loss strategies reported by dancers have included wearing rubber suits, smoking, and excessive exercising beyond dance training. A recent study reported that six percent of adolescent ballet dancers met the criteria for anorexia athletica, demonstrating that excessive exercise was a concern for this population. The tragedy of eating disorders among ballerinas is shown by the 1997 death of Heidi Guenther, who at age 22 died from an eating disorder after being told that she should lose weight or risk losing her role as a principal dancer in the Boston Ballet Company: http://www.people.com/people/archive/article/0,20122756,00.html.

Conclusion

Ballet dancers have been identified as an "at risk" group for eating disorders since the late 1970s. Body image dissatisfaction has been evident among dancers who attempt to achieve the "ballet body" which is described as being feminine, slender, and delicate. Long lines rather than body weight represent the symbol of success for dancers who may have to leave the stage early if their body shape does not meet the artistic image desired by the choreographer. Ballet dancers—like figure skaters—have a short shelf life and may resort to drastic measures to compete for a few spots within a professional dance company.

JUSTINE J. REEL

See also: Amenorrhea; Anorexia Athletica; Anorexia Nervosa; Figure Skating.

Bibliography

Druss, Richard G., and Joseph A. Silverman. "Body Image and Perfectionism of Ballerinas: Comparison and Contrast with Anorexia Nervosa." *General Hospital Psychiatry* 1, no. 2 (1979): 115–21.

Herbrich, Laura, Ernst Pfeiffer, Ulrike Lehmkuhl, and Nora Schneider. "Anorexia Athletica in Pre-Professional Ballet Dancers." *Journal of Sports Sciences* 29 (2011): 1–9. doi: 10/1080/02640414.2011.578147

Hewitt, Bill. "Last Dance: A Desperate Desire to Be Slender May Have Cost 22-Year-Old Ballerina Heidi Guenther Her Life." *People* 48, no. 4 (1997). Last modified on July 28, 1997. http://www.people.com/people/archive/article/0,20122756,00.html

Ravaldi, Claudia, Alfredo Vannacci, Enrica Bolognesi, Stefania Mancini, Carlo Faravelli, and Valdo Ricca. "Gender Role, Eating Disorder Symptoms, and Body Image Concern in Ballet Dancers." *Journal of Psychosomatic Research* 61 (2006): 529–35. doi: 10/1016/j.jpsychores.2006.04.016

Ringham, Rebecca, Kelly Klump, Walter Kaye, David Stone, Steven Libman, Susan Stowe, and Marsha Marcus. "Eating Disorder Symptomatology Among Ballet Dancers." *International Journal of Eating Disorders* 39, no. 6 (2006): 503–508. doi: 10.1002/eat

Swaine, Jon. " 'Sugar Plump Fairy' Ballet Dancer Says She Suffered from Eating Disorders." *The Telegraph*. Last modified December 14, 2010. http://www.telegraph.co.uk/news/worldnews/northamerica/usa/8202087/Sugar-Plump-Fairy-ballet-dancer-says-she-suffered-from-eating-disorders.html.

Thomas, Jennifer J., Pamela K. Keel, and Todd F. Heatherton. "Disordered Eating Attitudes and Behaviors in Ballet Students: Examination of Environmental and Individual Risk Factors." *International Journal of Eating Disorders* 38, no. 3 (2005): 263–68. doi: 10.1002/eat.20185

Toro, Josep, Marta Guerrero, Joan Sentis, Josefina Castro, and Carles Puertolas. "Eating Disorders in Ballet Dancing Students: Problems and Risk Factors." *European Eating Disorders Review* 17 (2009): 40–49.

BARIATRIC SURGERY

Bariatric surgery, a medical weight loss procedure, has been used since the late 1990s to treat morbid obesity (Body Mass Index [BMI] > 40). The most common bariatric procedure in the United States is the Roux-en-Y gastric bypass which represents 88 percent of bariatric surgeries and involves placing three staple lines in a vertical direction resulting in a pouch. The small size of the pouch leads to decreased dietary intake and results in a loss of up to 65 percent of excess body weight in severely obese patients.

Although most weight loss occurs in the short term (within two years) following bariatric surgery, over 50 percent of individuals reported regaining some weight usually between two and five years. Factors that may influence an individual's ability to maintain weight or vulnerability to weight gain include the type of surgery performed, age, presence of binge eating disorders, eating behaviors, depression, sleep patterns, patient adherence to support groups, and BMI before surgery. Gaining weight led clients to report feelings of shame and guilt to their treatment providers. Some clients, following bariatric surgery, reported feeling alone with their new body and their fears and admitted to a history of dysfunctional eating patterns such as binge eating disorder, night eating syndrome, and emotional eating.

Emotional eating is defined as an automatic reaction to unrecognized negative feelings. In eating disordered individuals, emotions are often suppressed (i.e., alexithymia) rather than expressed, and emotional eating becomes a vehicle for coping with stress. Similarly, research has suggested that emotional eating was prevalent among gastric bypass patients before and after gastric surgeries,

Roux-en-Y Gastric Bypass (RNY)

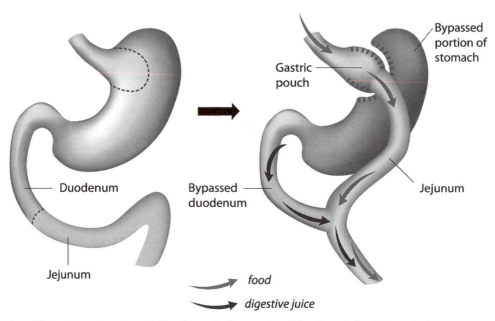

In addition to common complications of all surgeries (bleeding, infection, and adverse reactions to anesthesia), all gastric bypass procedures increase the risk for dehydration, food intolerances, gallstones, hernias, kidney stones, low blood sugar, bleeding stomach ulcers, and vitamin and mineral deficiencies. (Shutterstock.com)

and was accompanied by the belief that food "acts as a sedative." This relationship with food predicted a continuation of disordered eating regardless of initial weight loss. Therefore, it is important to note that individuals are especially vulnerable for developing disordered eating or clinical eating disorders if the thoughts and emotions related to food and body image are not addressed before, during, and after the surgery. It has been argued that individuals suffering from binge eating disorder be treated and stabilized before performing bariatric surgery.

JUSTINE J. REEL

See also: Alexithymia; Binge Eating Disorder; Body Mass Index; Night Eating Syndrome.

Bibliography

Chen, Eunice, Megan Roehrig, Sylvia Herbozo, Michael S. McCloskey, James Roehrig, Hakeemah Cummings, John Alverdy, and Daniel Le Grange. "Compensatory Eating Disorder Behaviors and Gastric Bypass Surgery Outcome." *International Journal of Eating Disorders* 42, no. 4 (2009): 363–66.

Chesler, Betty E., Bernadette G. Harris, and Pamela H. Oestreicher. "Implications of Emotional Eating Beliefs and Reactance to Dietary Advice for the Treatment of Emotional

Eating and Outcome Following Roux-en-Y Gastric Bypass: A Case Report." *Clinical Case Studies* 8 (2009): 277–95.

Kruseman, Maaike, Anik Leimgruber, Flavia Zumbach, and Alain Golay. "Dietary, Weight and Psychological Changes among Patients with Obesity, 8 Years after Gastric Bypass." *Journal of American Dietetic Association* 110 (2010): 527–34. doi: 10.1016/j.jada.2009.12.028

Magro, Daniéla O., Bruno Geloneze, Regis Delfini, Bruna C. Pareja, Francisco Callejas, and José C. Pereja. "Long-Term Weight Regain after Gastric Bypass: A 5-Year Prospective Study." *Obesity Surgery* 18 (2008): 648–51. doi: 10.1007/s11695-007-9265-1

Sarwer, David B., Thomas A. Wadden, Reneé H. Moore, Alexander W. Baker, Lauren M. Gibbons, Steven E. Raper, and Noel N. Williams. "Preoperative Eating Behavior, Postoperative Dietary Adherence and Weight Loss Following Gastric Bypass Surgery." *Surgery Obesity Related Diseases* 4, no. 5 (2008): 640–46. doi: 10.1016/j.soard.2008.04.013.

White, Marney A., Melissa A. Kalarchian, Robin M. Masheb, Marsha D. Marcus, and Carlos M. Grilo. "Loss of Control Over Eating Predicts Outcomes in Bariatric Surgery: A Prospective 24-Month Follow-Up Study." *Journal of Clinical Psychiatry* 71, no. 2 (2010): 175–84. doi: 10.4088/JCP.08m04328blue.

BIGOREXIA

Bigorexia is a condition related to people's perceptions regarding the size and shape of their body. Although the term bigorexia is not typically used as a formal diagnosis, it is believed to be a subtype of Body Dysmorphic Disorder (BDD). BDD is a clinically diagnosable condition in which individuals become preoccupied with a physical defect (e.g., the size of one's nose) that is either minor or imagined. In the case of bigorexia, the defect is a perceived lack of muscularity. Also known as reverse anorexia, and more recently as muscle dysmorphia, bigorexia occurs almost exclusively in male bodybuilders. Bigorexia is characterized by a variety of cognitive and behavioral symptoms. The predominant cognitive symptom of bigorexia is an obsessive preoccupation with the idea that one's body is too small or weak. Preoccupation with the body can lead to inaccurate perceptions of body size and shape, high anxiety, and an inability to focus on other important aspects of their lives. Behavioral symptoms include excessive amounts of time spent lifting weights, monitoring diet, and mirror checking. Although research on bigorexia remains in its infancy, studies have shown that up to 10 percent of male bodybuilders exhibit symptoms of bigorexia, and that the average age of onset is 19.4 years.

Body Image Disturbances and Bigorexia

Although some level of body dissatisfaction is to be expected as individuals enter adolescence, there are several important differences between these normal signs of development and pathological body image concerns associated with bigorexia. First, a person's perception of his body may be severely distorted, leading him to underestimate the total amount of muscle mass he possesses and the size and shape of individual muscles. Second, an individual's sense of self-worth may be highly dependent on the size and shape of his body. Third, efforts to achieve the ideal body are likely to interfere with school, work, and social interactions. Finally, individuals with bigorexia may engage in unhealthy practices such as dietary restrictions, binge eating, or steroid use.

Conclusion

Bigorexia refers to a perceived lack of muscularity. The biopsychosocial model indicates that biological, psychological, and social factors interact to determine risk for bigorexia. Individuals with bigorexia and other forms of BDD may share a genetic predisposition to the condition. From a psychological perspective, bigorexia may be a manifestation of low self-esteem and feelings of inadequate masculinity. Social factors are perhaps the most intriguing with regard to bigorexia. Males learn from the media at a young age that the ideal body for a man is lean and muscular. Similar to females, studies have shown that toys, movies, and magazines play a prominent role in shaping male conceptions of the ideal body.

NICK GALLI

See also: Body Dysmorphic Disorder.

Bibliography

Mosley, Philip E. "Bigorexia: Bodybuilding and Muscle Dysmorphia." *European Eating Disorders Review* 17 (2009): 191–98.

Olivardia, Roberto. "Mirror, Mirror on the Wall, Who's the Largest of Them All? The Features and Phenomenology of Muscle Dysmorphia." *Harvard Review of Psychiatry* 9 (2001): 254–59.

BINGE EATING DISORDER

Binge Eating Disorder (BED) has been described as having recurrent overeating episodes without engaging in a compensatory method of purging (e.g., self-induced vomiting). Although overeating has existed for centuries and was observed among the Romans, the first documented medical case of BED was of Laura in 1949. Binge eating behavior was reported across obesity studies in the 1950s by Dr. Albert Stunkard, and by the 1980s it was determined that bulimia nervosa and binge eating disorder (which was then called "pathological overeating syndrome") should be categorized as separate eating disorders. Likewise, it was important for medical professionals to distinguish between obese clients who engaged in binge eating and those individuals who did not engage in overeating behaviors. In 1992, the term "binge eating disorder" was coined and discussed in the *International Journal of Eating Disorders*. The current *Diagnostic and Statistical Manual of Mental Disorders, 4th Edition* (1994) only identified binge eating episodes associated with bulimia nervosa and included proposed BED research criteria in the appendix. Individuals who presently meet the BED criteria discussed in the next section are diagnosed with "Eating Disorder Not Otherwise Specified." However, it is expected that BED will receive a separate clinical diagnosis in the DSM-5 publication. Although a highly secretive disorder, some celebrities have admitted to struggling with binge eating disorder, including Kara DioGuardi, an *American Idol* judge, Victoria Beckham (Posh Spice from the Spice Girls rock band), and Monica Seles, a tennis star. In 2009, Monica Seles revealed how a violent attack led to a dysfunctional pattern of emotional eating to deal with her overwhelming stress: http://well.blogs.nytimes.com/2009/04/24/monica-seles-talks-about-binge-eating/.

Symptoms of Binge Eating Disorder

The DSM-IV-TR research criteria for Binge Eating Disorder identify recurrent episodes of binge eating as the overarching behavioral component for the disorder. The overeating occurs within a discrete period of time (usually within a two-hour time span) and the binge represents more consumption than would be typical for most people in a similar situation. The binges may last longer than for bulimia nervosa, days rather than hours, for an individual with BED. Additionally, the binges are marked by a sense of feeling out of control over one's eating or how much food is consumed. Binge eating episodes need to include three or more of the following features to meet the criteria for a BED diagnosis: (1) eating more rapidly than normal, (2) eating until feeling uncomfortable—past the point of fullness, (3) eating large amounts of food despite not feeling hungry, (4) eating alone due to embarrassment about how much food one is eating, and (5) feeling disgusted with oneself, experiencing depressed mood or

Eating disorders include anorexia nervosa, bulimia nervosa, and binge eating. People with binge eating disorder often eat an unusually large amount of food and feel out of control during the binges. (PhotoDisc, Inc.)

guilt after the binge eating episode. Individuals with BED report significant distress regarding the binge eating. On average, the binge eating episodes occur at least two days a week for at least six months. It is important to note that this duration is longer than for individuals with bulimia nervosa (i.e., three months). The final criterion for BED requires that binge eating episodes are not accompanied by inappropriate compensatory methods such as vomiting, laxative abuse, and excessive exercise. As a result of the frequent overeating, many individuals with BED struggle with overweight and obesity.

Prevalence of Binge Eating Disorder

Approximately one-fifth to one-third of individuals who seek obesity treatment fit the criteria for BED. Seventy percent of individuals with BED in a community sample were obese and 20 percent of BED individuals had a body mass index over 40. BED is more common than either anorexia nervosa or bulimia nervosa. Approximately 3.5 percent of women and 2 percent of men reported having binge eating disorder at some point in their lives compared with only 0.9 percent of women with anorexia nervosa, 1.5 percent of women with bulimia nervosa or 0.5 percent of men with bulimia nervosa. There is some initial evidence that certain groups (e.g., football players) and minority populations (e.g., African American, Latino/Hispanic, Polynesian groups) may be considered at risk for developing Binge Eating Disorder due to sport demands and cultural traditions (e.g., overeating for family meals).

Personality Characteristics and Coexisting Conditions

BED frequently occurs concurrently with mood and anxiety disorders and substance use. Studies have shown that up to 74 percent of BED individuals reported additional psychiatric disorders. In fact, individuals with BED were significantly more likely to have co-occurring psychiatric disorders than obese clients without BED. One study demonstrated that 60 percent of obese binge eaters met the criteria for one or more psychiatric disorders compared to only 28 percent of non–binge eaters of similar age and weight. Furthermore, binge eaters were more likely to struggle from an affective disorder (e.g., depression) than non–binge eaters with rates of 32 percent and 8 percent respectively. For binge eating individuals, major depressive episodes were often accompanied by weight gain.

Although binge eating individuals were more likely to have psychiatric problems compared to the general population, when examining individuals with anorexia nervosa or bulimia nervosa, individuals with BED were no more likely to have comorbid psychiatric conditions. While studies vary in terms of reported prevalence rates, approximately 36–44 percent of individuals who abused alcohol reported engaging in binge eating episodes.

Health Consequences of BED

Individuals who suffer from BED often experience the same health consequences associated with being overweight or obese. Being overweight or obese carries a higher risk for a number of damaging health conditions such as high blood pressure, high cholesterol, cardiovascular disease, and Type II diabetes. With increased rates of obesity come additional risks of bone and joint problems, respiratory problems, and stroke. Additionally, gall bladder disease is more common among obese individuals, and obese women have twice the rate of bowel or rectal cancer as individuals at a normal weight. Due to binge episodes triggered by psychological states, binge eating individuals experience difficulty in realizing fullness. They may also have difficulty in losing weight and in maintaining a normal or healthy weight for their height and age.

Conclusion

Binge Eating Disorder has become increasingly more recognized as an eating disorder separate from anorexia nervosa and bulimia nervosa. Although BED has been associated with obesity, not all obese individuals meet the clinical criteria for BED which is currently diagnosed as Eating Disorder Not Otherwise Specified. It is expected that BED will receive a separate clinical diagnosis in the next edition of the DSM.

JUSTINE J. REEL

See also: Anorexia Nervosa; Bulimia Nervosa; Eating Disorder Not Otherwise Specified.

Bibliography

Abraham, Suzanne, and Derek Llewellyn-Jones. *Eating Disorders: The Facts.* New York, NY: Oxford University Press, 1995.

American Psychiatric Association. *Diagnostic and Statistical Manual of Mental Disorders, Revised 4th Edition.* Washington, DC: Author, 2000.

Amianto, Federico, Luca Lavagnino, Paolo Leombruni, Filippo Gastaldi, Giovanni Abbate Daga, and Secondo Fassino. "Hypomania across the Binge Eating Spectrum: A Study on Hypomanic Symptoms in Full Criteria and Sub-Threshold Binge Eating Subjects." *Journal of Affective Disorders* (2011): 1–4. doi: 10.1016/j.jad.2011.04.049

Bulik, Cynthia M. *Carve: Why You Binge Eat and How to Stop.* New York, NY: Walker Publishing Company, 2009.

Carrard, I., C. Crépin, P. Rouget, T. Lam, A. Golay, and M. Van der Linden. "Randomised Controlled Trial of a Guided Self-Help Treatment on the Internet for Binge Eating Disorder." *Behavior Research and Therapy* 49 (2011): 482–91. doi: 10.1016/j.brat. 2011.05.004

Castelnuovo, Gianluca, Gian Mauro Manzoni, Valentina Villa, Gian Luca Cesa, and Enrico Molinari. "Brief Strategic Therapy vs. Cognitive Behavior Therapy for Inpatient and Telephone-Based Outpatient Treatment of Binge Eating Disorder: The STRATOB Randomized Controlled Clinical Trial." *Clinical Practice & Epidemiology in Mental Health* 7 (2011): 29–37.

Chen, Eunice Yu, Michael S. McCloskey, Sara Michelson, Kathryn H. Gordon, and Emil Coccaro. "Characterizing Eating Disorders in a Personality Disorders Sample." *Psychiatry Research* 185 (2011): 427–32. doi: 10.1016/j.psychres.2010.07.002

Connolly, Anne M., Elizabeth Rieger, and Ian Caterson. "Binge Eating Tendencies and Anger Coping: Investigating the Confound of Trait Neuroticism in a Non-Clinical Sample." *European Eating Disorders Review* 15 (2007): 479–86. doi: 10.1002/erv.765

Costin, Carolyn. *A Comprehensive Guide to the Causes, Treatments and Prevention of Eating Disorders, Third Edition.* New York, NY: McGraw-Hill, 2007.

Costin, Carolyn. *100 Questions & Answers about Eating Disorders.* Sudbury, MA: Jones and Bartlett, 2007.

Courbasson, Christine, and Jacqueline M. Brunshaw. "The Relationship between Concurrent Substance Use Disorders and Eating Disorders with Personality Disorders." *International Journal of Environmental Research and Public Health* 6 (2009): 2076–2089. doi: 10.3390/ijerph6072076

De Bolle, Marleen, Barbara De Clercq, Alexandra Pham-Scottez, Saskia Meis, Jean-Pierre Rolland, Julien D. Guelfi, Caroline Braet, and Filip De Fruyt. "Personality Pathology Comorbidity in Adult Females with Eating Disorders." *Journal of Health Psychology* 16 (2011): 303–313. doi: 10.1177/1359105310374780

Fairburn, Chris G. *Overcoming Binge Eating.* New York, NY: Guilford Press, 1995.

Grilo, Carlos M., Marney A. White, and Robin M. Masheb. "DSM-IV Psychiatric Disorder Comorbidity and Its Correlates in Binge Eating Disorder." *International Journal of Eating Disorders* 42 (2009): 228–34.

Hall, Lindsey, and Leigh Cohn. *Bulimia: A Guide to Recovery.* Carlsbad, CA: Gurze, 2011.

Harvey, Kate, Francine Rosselli, G. Terence Wilson, Lynn L. DeBar, and Ruth H. Striegel-Moore. "Eating Patterns in Patients with Spectrum Binge-Eating Disorder." *International Journal of Eating Disorders* 44 (2011): 447–51. doi: 10.1002/eat.20839

Hudson, James I., Eva Hiripi, Harrison G. Pope, and Ronald C. Kessler. "The Prevalence and Correlates of Eating Disorders in the National Comorbidity Survey Replication." *Biological Psychiatry* 61, no. 3 (2007): 348–58.

Mehler, Philip S. "Bulimia Nervosa." *The New England Journal of Medicine* 349, no. 9 (2003): 875–82.

Parker-Pope, Tara. "Monica Seles Talks about Binge Eating." *The New York Times,* posted April 24, 2009. http://well.blogs.nytimes.com/2009/04/24/monica-seles-talks-about-binge-eating/

Robinson, Athen Hagler, and Debra L. Safer. "Moderators of Dialectical Behavior Therapy for Binge Eating Disorder: Results from a Randomized Controlled Trial." *International Journal of Eating Disorders* (2011): 1–6. doi: 10.1002/eat.20932

White, Marney A., and Carlos M. Grilo. "Diagnostic Efficiency of DSM-IV Indicators for Binge Eating Episodes." *Journal of Consulting and Clinical Psychology* 79, no. 1 (2011): 75–83.

BODY ALIENATION

Body alienation refers to the condition in which an individual views his or her body as something separate, or alien. The term was first coined by French philosopher and social theorist Simone de Beauvoir in her 1949 book, *Second Sex.* According to de Beauvoir, both girls and boys become alienated from their bodies at a young age. According to her, the alienation process is particularly problematic for girls, as they tend to use their dolls as models for how they should appear. Although dolls represent the body, they also represent the body as something passive and subject to the approval of society. The process of alienation can be further promoted by early sexual abuse or parents who place excessive emphasis on physical appearance. The sense of alienation is only heightened during adolescence when girls' bodies begin to mature. Changes in body shape and size are often confusing to girls, and as a result their body image may become fragmented and described in terms of specific body parts (e.g., breasts, hips) rather than as a whole. A study with teenage boys and girls revealed that while boys described their bodies in terms of physical function (e.g., strong), the girls described their bodies in terms of physical attractiveness (e.g., pretty).

Relationship between Body Alienation and Eating Disorders

Body alienation has recently been linked to low self-esteem and self-harm behaviors such as eating disorders and self-mutilation. With regard to eating disorders and other self-injurious behaviors, the body is viewed as an enemy which must be dealt with. Eating disorders represent an attempt to maintain control over the body and perceive it as a part of the person's entire being. Research has shown that body alienation is related to increased pressure to be thin in adolescent girls. Interviews with women who engaged in self-harming behaviors support the notion that these individuals tend to view their body as an entity separate from themselves. The interviewees often made reference to themselves or their bodies, rather than integrating the two parts. For example, one woman discussed wanting to "kill her body." Other women noted using their body as a tool to manage others and maintain control. Because body alienation has been connected with a variety of negative psychological and behavioral outcomes, it has also been examined in several different at-risk populations, including athletes, nurses, and rheumatoid arthritis patients.

Body Alienation among Athletes

Body alienation may be observed in competitive athletes, as their success is dependent on the speed, strength, and agility of their bodies. Athletes who are alienated from their bodies may spend excessive hours training, attempt to perform despite illness or injury, or engage in disordered eating. Pressure to perform prompts many athletes to become isolated from their body and seek to improve performance by any means necessary. Elite athletes may be encouraged to treat their bodies as high performance cars or strive to turn their bodies into well-oiled machines. Such a view of the body as a machine normalizes and encourages the use of nutritional supplements and performance enhancing drugs as fuel to help the body achieve optimal performance. As Lantz wrote in *The International Journal of Sport Nutrition and Exercise Metabolism*, "[athletes] come to view themselves as machines that, if constantly modified and trained, will be able to achieve maximal force or speed production." Body alienation in sports is closely tied to the ideal that truly dedicated athletes must constantly strive for success, accept risks, and play through pain if they are to be considered a real athlete. There are three components to body alienation in sports: injury tolerance, training through pain, and the use of the body as a tool. Thus, athletes who are alienated from their body will play through injury despite the risk of causing permanent damage to their body, push themselves beyond the boundaries of pain tolerance, and treat their body as if it is a mechanical device designed to help them achieve performance success. A 13-item survey was developed to assess the three components of body alienation in athletes. For example, one question states, "I see myself as a machine designed to perform a specific sport." Although limited research has been conducted on body alienation in athletes, the results of a study on ultramarathoners suggested that runners who identified strongly as exercisers showed more body alienation as indicated by higher injury tolerance than the runners who identified less strongly as exercisers.

Body Alienation in Health Care Settings

For individuals who have a chronic illness such as arthritis, lupus, or bursitis, having a positive view of the body is a challenge. Indeed, it would be easy for an individual with a chronic illness to have the sense that one's body has betrayed them, and is hindering one's ability to live a healthy and happy life. A study with 168 individuals suffering from rheumatoid arthritis showed that feelings of body alienation were related to less self-esteem, and that feelings of harmony with the body were associated with higher self-esteem. Health care professionals who care for sick or injured individuals are also at risk for body alienation. Researchers interviewed seven Brazilian female nurses in critical care units to find out how these women perceive their bodies. Nurses in Brazil work within a rigid hierarchical structure in which they are treated as tools for production. One of the major findings that came from the interviews was that the nurses felt exploited and alienated from their bodies. A nurse discussed her body being used as a tool for production, " . . . and there's that thing, nurses don't get sick, it's just whining, it's not illness . . . you see nurse colleagues who are having a breakdown, who need help, who are anxious . . . they have a lot of issues and aren't worried about it, because apparently it's still working, isn't it? They're working."

Contributing Factors to Body Alienation

A variety of social forces may contribute to body alienation. Some have accused the Western medical profession as being largely responsible for alienating people from their bodies. As Bologh wrote in *Sociology of Health and Illness*, "The medical profession fails to treat its object—the body, as a social body. . . . In the orientation of modern medicine, the curing as well as the illness implicate the body but not as a social body or a body enmeshed in a social environment." Some sociologists argue that a more egalitarian relationship between doctor and patient, in which the patient takes an active role in the treatment process, would lead to a more holistic view of the body, which would then lead to more effective treatment.

Conclusion

Body alienation has been discussed to describe the feeling of being detached from one's body. Body alienation has been observed among athletes and within the health care setting. Alarmingly, by not feeling connected to one's body there could be a higher risk for injury or playing through pain. Therefore, body alienation should be recognized within sports and other settings to provide early intervention using a holistic approach.

NICK GALLI

Bibliography

Albini, Leomar, and Liliana M. Labronici. "Exploitation and Alienation of the Body of the Nurse: A Phenomenological Study." *Acta Paulista de Enfermagem* 20 (2007): 299–304.

Arp, Kristana. "Beauvoir's Concept of Bodily Alienation." In *Feminist Interpretations of Simone de Beauvoir,* edited by Margaret Simons, 161–72. College Park: The Pennsylvania State University Press, 1995.

Bologh, Roslyn W. "Grounding the Alienation of Self and Body." *Sociology of Health and Illness* 3 (1981): 188–206.

Cross, Lisa W. "Body and Self in Feminine Development: Implications for Eating Disorders and Delicate Self-Mutilation." *Bulletin of the Menninger Clinic* 57 (1993): 41–68.

Frederickson, Barbara L., and Tomi-Ann Roberts. "Objectification Theory: Toward Understanding Women's Lived Experiences and Mental Health Risks." *Psychology of Women Quarterly* 21 (1997): 173–206.

Lantz, Christopher D., Deborah J. Rhea, and Karin Mesnier. "Eating Attitudes, Exercise Identity, and Body Alienation in Competitive Ultramarathoners." *International Journal of Sport Nutrition and Exercise Metabolism* 14 (2004): 406–418.

Parent, Mike C., and Bonnie Moradi. "His Biceps Become Him: A Test of Objectification Theory's Application to Drive for Muscularity and Propensity for Steroid Use in College Men." *Journal of Counseling Psychology* 58 (2010): 246–56.

Reinhold, Sandra. "Alienation and Isolation from the Body: A Common Etiology for the Deliberate Self-Harm of Eating Disorders and Self-Mutilation?" PhD dissertation, The Chicago School of Professional Psychology, 2002.

BODY AVOIDANCE

Body avoidance, a behavioral component of body image, refers to the behavior of actively going out of one's way to avoid looking at one's body or in the mirror. In efforts to avoid negative emotions associated with one's body, eating disordered individuals may exhibit avoidance behavior such as not looking in the mirror or wearing baggy clothing to hide one's bodily appearance. The opposite of body avoidance, body checking, represents another behavior associated with negative body image. It is unclear whether these behaviors represent opposite manifestations of body image disturbances or whether they are in fact related to one another. However, checking and avoidance prevent individuals from disconfirming their worst fears about their body shape and weight and serve to maintain dysfunctional attitudes about the body. Avoidance behaviors may also be associated with increased importance being placed on shape and weight.

Treatment of Body Avoidance

Treatment for avoidance behaviors would follow a similar intervention as that aimed to improve body image. Cognitive-behavioral approaches that include a body exposure piece show promise and include systematically increasing one's exposure to observing one's body. Specifically, body image therapy with mirror confrontation has been shown to reduce body dissatisfaction, whereas body image therapy without exposure does not address body avoidance behaviors. By using a full-length mirror or other body exposure techniques (e.g., prescribing client to gradually wear more form-fitting clothing), the body distortion component of body image can also be addressed in treatment. Interestingly, many prevention strategies may encourage individuals to reduce body checking behaviors (e.g., weighing themselves, using the mirror as a form of evaluation) in order to promote decreased attention to appearance or evaluation of one's body and appearance. Therefore, body exposure therapy to reduce body avoidance behaviors should be used with caution so that individuals do not develop excessive body checking behaviors (e.g., looking at oneself in the mirror, weighing or measuring one's body).

Assessment of Body Avoidance

The Body Image Avoidance Questionnaire (BIAQ) was developed by Rosen and colleagues in 1991 to assess behavioral manifestations of body image disturbances. A general score is calculated from 13 items that represent body-related avoidance behaviors (i.e., the tendency to disguise or cover up one's appearance by wearing baggy, nonrevealing clothing, and avoiding social situations in which weight or appearance could be the focus of attention). For example, one item reads, "I wear baggy clothes." This questionnaire includes additional subscales (e.g., grooming, weighing) that do not measure body avoidance behavior but are associated with body image. When using the BIAQ, eating disordered individuals have scored significantly higher than healthy controls on body-related avoidance behaviors. Therefore, it is important to address this behavioral component of negative body image in eating disorder treatment.

JUSTINE J. REEL

Bibliography

Latner, Janet D. "Body Checking and Avoidance among Behavioral Weight-Loss Participants." *Body Image* 5 (2008): 91–98. doi: 10.1016/j.bodyim.2007.08.001

Vocks, Silja, Joachim Kosfelder, Maike Wucherer, and Alexandra Wachter. "Does Habitual Body Avoidance and Checking Behavior Influence the Decrease of Negative Emotions during Body Exposure in Eating Disorders?" *Psychotherapy Research* 18, no. 4 (2008): 412–19.

BODY CHECKING

Body checking, a behavioral component of body image, refers to the repeated attempts to evaluate or scrutinize one's body shape, size, or appearance. In addition to spending excessive time compulsively checking one's body in the mirror, body checking behaviors also include using the fit of clothing to judge whether one's size has changed and feeling one's body parts for bones or fat. Although this body checking behavior has been observed among individuals with Anorexia Nervosa, Bulimia Nervosa, and Binge Eating Disorder, as well as obese individuals and nonclinical populations, females with eating disorders engage in body checking strategies significantly more often than healthy females. Recent attempts have been made to measure body checking among males, which is believed to be tied to Body Dysmorphic Disorder and Muscle Dysmorphia.

It is not clear as to what the relationship between body checking and body dissatisfaction is, but it is predicted that the overestimation of one's body size will naturally contribute to feelings of body dissatisfaction and this occurs more frequently among eating disordered individuals. In fact, researchers speculate that body checking behavior is likely to be associated with body image distortion and needs to be addressed in eating disorder treatment to avoid a relapse triggered by body checking behaviors.

Individuals who engage in body checking behaviors report using the checking as a way to reduce anxiety or to avoid the discomfort associated with not checking. Individuals who engage in body checking may also claim that keeping tabs on one's size and appearance provides a way to take control of one's weight and eating patterns. Unfortunately, in practice, this body checking behavior brings attention to problem areas, and serves to trigger body image disturbances or feed anxiety related to one's physique. Therefore, body checking should be discouraged and needs to be addressed as part of eating disorder treatment.

Treatment of Body Checking

Cognitive-behavioral therapy that includes a body exposure component shows promise for improving body image disturbances. During a session, a client is instructed to look into a full-length mirror to provide exposure in a systematic way. Because the session provides a safe place for the client to engage in taboo behaviors, the client has the opportunity to experience feelings and express emotions to his or her therapist in the moment. The therapist may encourage exposure coupled with coping skills (e.g., relaxation techniques like deep breathing) to reduce stress. After continuing body exposure to the mirror over a number of sessions, the client becomes less anxious and the behavior becomes more normalized. There is hope that using expose techniques in conjunction with newer virtual reality techniques will allow clinicians to help eating disordered individuals deal with intense body image feelings.

Assessment of Body Checking

The Body Checking Questionnaire (BCQ) was developed in 2002 to assess habitual body-related checking strategies. The BCQ consists of 23 items such as "I check my reflection in glass doors or car windows to see how I look." Studies have found that individuals with eating disorders scored significantly higher on the BCQ than their nonclinical counterparts. More recently, a body checking questionnaire was constructed for use among males. The Male Body Checking Questionnaire (MBCQ) contains 19 items, uses the same format as the BCQ, and adapts questions to meet body image concerns of males. For example, the BCQ focuses on female problem areas (e.g., thighs) and fatness; however, males are more likely to be obsessed with muscularity and leanness.

JUSTINE J. REEL

See also: Muscle Dysmorphia; Virtual Reality.

Bibliography

Haase, Anne M., Victoria Mountford, and Glenn Waller. "Understanding the Link between Body Checking Cognitions and Behaviors: The Role of Social Physique Anxiety." *International Journal of Eating Disorders* 40 (2007): 241–46.

Hadjustavropoulos, Heather, and Brandy Lawrence. "Does Anxiety about Health Influence Eating Patterns and Shape-Related Body Checking Among Females?" *Personality and Individual Differences* 43 (2007): 319–28. doi: 10.1016/j.paid.2006.11.021

Hildebrandt, Tom, D. Catherine Walker, Lauren Alfano, Sherrie Delinsky, and Katie Bannon. "Development and Validation of a Male Specific Body Checking Questionnaire." *International Journal of Eating Disorders* 43 (2010): 77–87.

Latner, Janet D. "Body Checking and Avoidance among Behavioral Weight-loss Participants." *Body Image* 5 (2008): 91–98. doi: 10.1016/j.bodyim.2007.08.001

Shafran, Roz, Michelle Lee, Elizabeth Payne, and Christopher G. Fairburn. "An Experimental Analysis of Body Checking." *Behavior Research and Therapy* 45 (2007): 113–121.

Smeets, Elke, Marika Tiggemann, Eva Kemps, Jennifer S. Mills, Sarah Hollitt, Anne Roefs, and Anita Jansen. "Body Checking Induces an Attentional Bias for Body-Related Cues." *International Journal of Eating Disorders* 44 (2011): 50–57.

Vocks, Silja, Joachim Kosfelder, Maike Wucherer, and Alexandra Wachter. "Does Habitual Body Avoidance and Checking Behavior Influence the Decrease of Negative Emotions during Body Exposure in Eating Disorders?" *Psychotherapy Research* 18, no. 4 (2008): 412–19. doi: 10.1080/10503300701797008

BODY DISTORTION

Body image broadly represents affective, cognitive, behavioral, or perceptual aspects of one's size, shape, or appearance. Body image distortion (or perceptual disturbance) refers to the perceptual component of body image and relates to an individual's ability to accurately perceive one's body size and shape. Eating disordered individuals may perceive themselves as being vastly larger than they are in reality, despite looking in the mirror or being told by other people that they are smaller than they believe. In fact, using objective measures (e.g., scales) to confront these cognitive distortions may be met with skepticism that the scale is not functioning properly or has been tampered with by the medical professional.

Body perceptions should be distinguished from the more widely recognized component of body image, body dissatisfaction, which is defined by the subjective negative evaluation of one's body or body parts. However, both body dissatisfaction and body distortion are predictive of disordered eating and clinical eating disorders and should be considered for assessment and treatment. A concept related to body distortion, muscle dysmorphia, involves individuals who largely underestimate their bodies. Muscle dysmorphia has been described as "reverse anorexia" and is discussed elsewhere.

Measurement of Body Distortion

Clinicians and researchers recognize a strong correlation between eating disorders and perceived body size distortions. Unfortunately, previous body image distortion studies have been limited to using figural drawing scales (e.g., Figure Ratings Scale) to assess perceived body size. These silhouette-based instruments include a series of sex-specific drawings of bodies that range from extremely thin to overweight. An individual is asked to identify the silhouette that most resembles his or her current body, preferred body size, and the figure most attractive to dating others. In order to assess for perceptual disturbances, a subjective rater (the researcher or clinician) may also rate the individual's current body on the silhouette scale. Because the figure ratings scales are largely visual, researchers can survey participants across reading levels. However, figural drawing scales do not allow for a comprehensive measurement of size perceptions and may contain the potential for a memory bias for participants since mirrors are not provided during assessment.

Previous work using nonclinical populations demonstrates that changes to one's body size can influence how participants perceive distance and size. For example, Stefanucci and Geuss (2009) manipulated participants' widths by having them hold their hands out wide, and found that larger participants estimated the width of gaps to be significantly smaller. In addition, an earlier study had large and small participants judge their ability to pass through a horizontal gap without rotating their shoulders. Both large and small participants required the gap to be 16 percent larger than their shoulder width to indicate an ability to pass through. This measure directly tests participants' perceptions of environmental extents because they must compare these extents to their own body size in order to decide whether or not they can pass through. A recent paper showed that participants with anorexia nervosa indicated that they needed wider gap widths in order to pass through. These results suggest that those with anorexia nervosa perceive themselves as larger and this distortion of body size influences what they believe they are capable of performing. The emergence of virtual reality (VR) technology may allow for body distortion measurement to improve along with a means for addressing body distortions in treatment. Currently, cognitive-behavioral approaches with exposure therapy to mirrors or body tracings using art therapy have been the main ways to help a client overcome this debilitating aspect of an eating disorder.

JUSTINE J. REEL

See also: Art Therapy; Figural Rating Scales; Muscle Dysmorphia; Virtual Reality.

Bibliography

Allen, Karina L., Susan M. Byrne, Neil J. McLean, and Elizabeth A. Davis. "Overconcern with Weight and Shape is Not the Same as Body Dissatisfaction: Evidence from a Prospective Study of Pre-Adolescent Boys and Girls." *Body Image* 5 (2008): 261–70. doi: 10.1016/j.bodyim.2008.03.005

Gardner, Rick M., and Dana L. Brown. "Body Image Assessment: A Review of Figural Drawing Scales." *Personality and Individual Differences* 48 (2010): 107–111. doi: 10.1016/j.paid.2009.08.017

Grieve, Frederick G. "A Conceptual Model of Factors Contributing to the Development of Muscle Dysmorphia." *Eating Disorders* 15 (2007): 63–80.

McCabe, Marita P., Kelly Butler, and Christina Watt. "Media Influences on Attitudes and Perceptions toward the Body among Adult Men and Women." *Journal of Applied Biobehavioral Research* 12, no. 2 (2007): 101–118.

O'Riordan, Siobhan S., and Byron L. Zamboanga. "Aspects of the Media and Their Relevance to Bulimic Attitudes and Tendencies among Female College Students." *Eating Behaviors* 9 (2008): 247–50. doi: 10.1016/j.eatbeh.2007.03.004

Stefanucci, Jeanine K., and Michael Geuss. "Big People, Little World: The Body Influences Size Perception." *Perception* 38 (2009): 1782–1795.

BODY DYSMORPHIC DISORDER

Body Dysmorphic Disorder (BDD) refers to a mental disorder that is characterized by an excessive, often irrational, preoccupation with an imagined or very slight defect in physical appearance. Although concerns may be related to body weight or shape, BDD should be distinguished from anorexia nervosa, bulimia nervosa, and binge eating disorder. While any body part can become the focus of preoccupation, the most common body parts are skin, hair, nose, and stomach. Approximately 0.7–2.4 percent of individuals met the diagnostic criteria for BDD with males and females represented. The *Diagnostic and Statistical Manual of Mental Disorders* identified the BDD criteria as (1) preoccupation with an imagined defect; (2) preoccupation causes significant distress or impairment; and (3) preoccupation is not better accounted for by another mental disorder.

For individuals with BDD, concerns about appearance are accompanied by repetitive and time-consuming behaviors associated with camouflaging or enhancing one's appearance. Like eating disordered individuals, persons suffering from BDD commonly resort to body checking and body avoidance behaviors. In one study, 80 percent of individuals with BDD excessively checked their appearance in the mirror, while the other 20 percent avoided mirrors altogether. Furthermore, individuals with BDD were found to engage in excessive grooming (e.g., excessive hair removal), compulsive skin-picking, and concealing of perceived flaws with a beard, baggy clothing, or make-up. Typically, BDD begins during adolescence and may not be diagnosed for many years. It can be related to a higher incidence of rhinoplasty surgery to change the shape of one's nose, other cosmetic surgery, or increased dermatologist visits. BDD is associated with poor functioning in areas of social interaction, school, and work. In one study of 200 individuals who were diagnosed with BDD, 36 percent reported missing a week or more of work in the last month and 11 percent dropped out of school because of a struggle with BDD. In the same study, 25 percent of BDD participants reported at least one prior suicide attempt. Other studies have found the rates of suicidal ideation (thinking about suicide) to be even higher (58–78%).

Treatment Considerations for Body Dysmorphic Disorder

Individuals with BDD have been found to have poor insight into their problem. Instead of recognizing BDD as a mental health concern, clients often seek cosmetic procedures to alter the perceived defect. Unfortunately, many clients with BDD report numerous surgeries on the same body part only to continue to struggle with the same negative and obsessive feelings. Clinicians recognize that individuals who meet the BDD criteria share many similarities with individuals with Obsessive-Compulsive Disorder. Therefore, treatment approaches must address the need to replace compulsive behaviors and rituals as part of the recovery process. Furthermore, because of the high level of suicidal ideations and distress, individuals with BDD may struggle to maintain stability. Like clients with borderline personality disorder, BDD clients could benefit from receiving Dialectical Behavior Therapy and skill-based training to regulate emotions and difficult feelings.

Barriers to treatment should be considered for this unique population of individuals with BDD. One study with over 400 BDD clients found that the majority of BDD clients reported shame (56%) or wanting to handle the problem on one's own (57%) as the biggest deterrents for seeking help. In addition, 51 percent of participants felt that treatment would not alleviate BDD symptoms and 50 percent felt it would be too expensive.

Muscle Dysmorphia

Muscle dysmorphia refers to an obsession with one's muscularity and the feeling of being too small. Often dubbed "reverse anorexia," muscle dysmorphia is considered a subtype of BDD with the perceived defect being musculature. Most frequently males suffer from this condition and bodybuilders are overrepresented. This type of BDD is discussed in more detail in another entry.

Conclusion

Body Dysmorphic Disorder is often confused with eating disorders due to the focus on appearance. Similar to people with other eating disorders, individuals with BDD often engage in body checking or avoidance behaviors or feel a sense of shame associated with their disorder. Alarmingly, individuals with BDD sometimes seek extreme cosmetic procedures in order to fix perceived flaws, experience a low quality of life, and have a high prevalence of suicidal ideations.

JUSTINE J. REEL

See also: Dialectical Behavior Therapy (DBT); Muscle Dysmorphia.

Bibliography

American Psychiatric Association. *Diagnostic and Statistical Manual of Mental Disorders, Revised 4th Edition.* Washington, DC: Author, 2000.

Fang, Angela, and Stefan G. Hofmann. "Relationship between Social Anxiety Disorder and Body Dysmorphic Disorder." *Clinical Psychology Review* 30 (2010): 1040–1048. doi: 10.1016/j.cpr.2010.08.001.

Marques, Luana, Hillary M. Weingarden, Nicole J. LeBlanc, and Sabine Wilhelm. "Treatment Utilization and Barriers to Treatment Engagement among People with Body Dysmorphic Symptoms." *Journal of Psychosomatic Research* 70 (2011): 286–93. doi: 10.1016/j.psychores.2010.10.002.

Picavet, Valerie A., Emmanuel P. Prokopakis, Lutgardis Gabriels, Mark Jorissen, and Peter W. Hellings. "High Prevalence of Body Dysmorphia Disorder Symptoms in Patients Seeking Rhinoplasty." *Plastic Reconstructive Surgery* 128, no. 2 (2011): 509–517. doi: 10.1097/PRS.0b013e31821b631f.

Reese, Hannah E., Richard J. McNally, and Sabine Wilhem. "Reality Monitoring in Patients with Body Dysmorphic Disorder." *Behavior Therapy* 42 (2011): 387–98.

Taillon, Annie, Kieron O'Connor, Gilles Dupuis, and Marc Lavoie. "Inference-Based Therapy for Body Dysmorphic Disorder." *Clinical Psychology and Psychotherapy* (July 25, 2011): doi: 10.1002/epp.767

Wilhelm, Sabine. *Feeling Good About the Way You Look: A Program for Overcoming Body Image Problems.* New York, NY: Guilford Press, 2006.

BODY ESTEEM

Body esteem refers to feelings of self-esteem related to the body's abilities, worth, and appearance. Self-esteem is generally a more global concept that represents confidence in one's overall propensity for achievement in academic, social, and physical domains. Strong self-esteem can reduce anxiety across situations and often results from being positively reinforced by parents, teachers, and other social beings. The U.S. culture values the physical body and athletic prowess. The media acts as a vehicle for portraying body ideals and giving feedback on what types of bodies are most valued and considered attractive. Products and strategies for changing one's body to make it closer to the ideal are advertised so that individuals can take action. There are numerous societal rewards (e.g., increased likelihood of being pursued romantically) for working toward appearance ideals and engaging in self-monitoring behaviors (e.g., checking one's body in the mirror). However, the development of body esteem is a largely internal process and may continue to be low despite eating, exercise, and body-related changes.

Gender Differences in Body Esteem

Body standards for men and women are different. In the media, women are portrayed as tall and thin. Because society is bombarded with these images, women are judged by men according to this standard of physical appearance; therefore, they tend to feel self-conscious about their bodies. Particular areas of focus for women are legs, buttocks, face, chest, and lips. Self-esteem or confidence for men is based

Elisabeth Chappell, right, carries Sarah Leiser, 11, on her back as Payton Stewart, background left, 9, and Tyler Moisely, center background, follow on the Southern Methodist University campus in Dallas, Thursday, April 28, 2005. Nutrition and exercise are key to "Girls in Motion," a program started in 2004 at SMU to promote healthy body images and prevent eating disorders among girls before they enter their teen years. (LM Otero/AP/Wide World Photos)

on their degree of muscularity or strength. Women tend to judge men based on those standards as the media has placed a high value on that type of male body.

Throughout the life span from infancy to childhood, adolescence, and adulthood, our bodies are constantly changing and our body esteem can be influenced as well. For example, during childhood girls are highly influenced by their mothers' preoccupation with beauty and weight. Mothers might criticize their own bodies and express the need to lose weight. As a result, their daughters will observe this body scrutiny, learn to develop similar feelings of body shame, and will report lower body esteem.

Puberty and Body Esteem

Likewise, adolescence and pubertal weight gain may influence body esteem. This natural weight gain can be difficult for adolescents to accept and can lead to a sense of feeling out of control in relation to one's body. Meanwhile, adolescents experience intense comparison with their peers and may be subject to teasing from peers or family members. Unfortunately, adolescents may face lower self-esteem and body esteem and may begin to engage in eating disorder behaviors (e.g., skipping meals, overexercising, restricted eating, overeating followed by vomiting). Body esteem in adolescents has been addressed by programs such as Full of Ourselves which strive to: (1) facilitate candid talk regarding the changes the body undergoes during puberty, (2) identify "weightism" as a prejudice, (3) discuss myths about body fat, and (4) practice body tolerance and self-acceptance.

Pregnancy and Body Esteem

Adults are not immune to experiencing poor body esteem as they continue to feel body dissatisfaction beyond adolescence. One trigger for low body esteem among female adults is pregnancy. The necessary weight gain during pregnancy that fosters a healthy baby can lead to negative body image that persists after birth due to slow or no weight loss. For women with an eating disorder history, the weight gain may reactivate past coping strategies such as food restriction, binge eating, and vomiting in order to return to prepregnancy weight. Breast-feeding allows for the mother and baby to bond by encouraging nurturing qualities. While breastfeeding assists the mother in returning to a healthy weight by burning calories, some women may abuse this opportunity by increasing the amount of calories burned by breastfeeding more often or by pumping and disposing the milk.

Measurement of Body Esteem

The Body Esteem Scale (BES) was originally developed for children in 1982 to measure feelings about the body using a yes/no response format. The original BES has been modified into the current 23-item scale that uses a 5-point Likert scale with responses ranging from "never" to "always" for individuals 12 years and older. Sample questions include "I like what I look like in pictures" and "I'm proud of my body." The BES includes three areas of body esteem: BE-Appearance (general feelings about one's appearance), BE-Weight (satisfaction about one's weight) and BE-Attribution (others' evaluation of one's body and appearance). The BES is a valid and reliable measure for use with adolescents and adults.

Conclusion

Body esteem represents the physical side of one's self-esteem or a way of measuring body image. Body esteem in children and adolescents may be influenced by media images and family interactions (e.g., teasing). In order to measure body esteem, researchers have used the Body Esteem Scale to better understand one's feelings about appearance, weight, and the evaluation of others.

HAILEY E. NIELSON

See also: Full of Ourselves.

Bibliography

Cobelo, Alicia Wisz, Estima de Chermont Prochnik, E. Yoshio Nakano, Aparecida M. Conti, and Taki Athanassios Cordas. "Body Image Dissatisfaction and Eating Symptoms in Mothers of Adolescents with Eating Disorders." *Eating and Weight Disorders* 15, no. 4 (2010): 219–25.

Cousineau, Tara M., Debra L. Franko, Meredith Trant, Diana Rancourt, Jessica Ainscough, Anamika Chaudhuri, and Julie Brevard. "Teaching Adolescents about Changing Bodies: Randomized Controlled Trial of and Internet Puberty Education and Body Dissatisfaction Prevention Program." *Body Image* 7 (2010): 296–300. doi: 10.1016/j.bodyim.2010.06.003.

Franzoi, Stephen L., and Jeffrey R. Klaiber. "Body Use and Reference Group Impact: With Whom Do We Compare Our Bodies?" *Sex Roles* 56 (2007): 205–214. doi: 1007/s11199-006-9162-4.

Goldenberg, Jamie L., Shannon K. McCoy, Tom Pyszczynski, Jeff Greenberg, and Sheldon Solomon. "The Body as a Source of Self-Esteem: The Effect of Mortality Salience on Identification with One's Body, Interest in Sex, and Appearance Monitoring." *Journal of Personality and Social Psychology* 79, no. 1 (2000): 118–30. doi: 10.1037//0022-3514.79.1.118.

Mendelson, Beverley K., Morton Mendelson, and Donna R. White. "Body-Esteem Scale for Adolescents and Adults." *Journal of Personality Assessment* 76 (2001): 90–106.

Spangler, Diane, and Eric Stice. "Validation of the Beliefs about Appearance Scale." *Cognitive Therapy and Research* 25, no. 6 (2001): 813–27. doi:10.1023/A:1012931709434.

Steiner-Adair, Catherine, and Lisa Sjostrom. *Full of Ourselves: A Wellness Program to Advance Girl Power, Health, and Leadership.* New York: Columbia University, 2006.

BODY IMAGE

Body image refers to an individual's positive or negative perception of his or her body shape, measurements, weight, or appearance. While the importance that the individual places on this perception can vary greatly, research studies estimate that 80–90 percent of females report body dissatisfaction and about 33–45 percent of males are dissatisfied with their bodies. When compared with males, females are also more likely to engage in self-loathing about body size and weight and have a greater drive for thinness. Women are also more likely to be uncomfortable about their weight and have higher anxiety about how others perceive their body.

Body Dissatisfaction

The most common component of body image is referred to as body dissatisfaction, which literally means being dissatisfied with the physical appearance of one's body. Body dissatisfaction has been positively correlated with lower self-esteem, decreased self-confidence, dieting, eating disorders, and obesity. Body dissatisfaction is often a motivating factor behind weight loss efforts. When an individual gains weight, his or her body dissatisfaction typically increases as well. Individuals with a higher percentage of body fat are more likely to be dissatisfied with their shape.

Body image (body dissatisfaction) is influenced by environment, experiences, and behaviors, which interact to shape a person's attitude toward and perception of his or her body. The development of negative body image comes from both historical and proximal events. Historical events are experiences in the past that influence the way an individual thinks or feels about her body. These experiences can be molded by cultural socialization, teasing, peer or parental expectations, and the media. These historical events combine with proximal events, which are more immediate body image experiences such as not being able to fit into a pair of old jeans or seeing a friend who is perceived to have a better body. These events are more influenced by social learning and a person's immediate environment.

One's body image vacillates constantly, changing daily or throughout the day for many people. A woman may feel positively toward her body in the morning, negatively toward it by afternoon, and feel positively toward it again by evening. There are many influences that affect body image and reinforce these positive or negative feelings toward the self, including exposure to media images, emotions related to eating and meals, and other events throughout the day.

Body Image Influences

Culturally Defined Beauty

Beauty and ideals in body shape and size are culturally defined, as individuals value the physical ideals of their own society. Different cultures have valued different physical attributes as an aesthetically pleasing physical form. For example, historically in China a woman who had small feet was more likely to achieve prestigious marriage. In that culture, bound feet were seen as a physical ideal and some individuals would attribute value strictly based on that ideal. In the modern United States, many women feel the ideal body shape is tall and very thin. The prominence of cheekbones, application of makeup, fashion styles, teeth and skin color, and fat distribution are all examples of socially desirable ideals. A woman in this culture may assess herself according to that ideal, and her body image could be affected by this assessment. The same holds true for men as they may value similar ideals such as tanned skin and white teeth, but they have ideals of a muscular, athletic body with broad shoulders. These ideals for beauty affect body image when an individual places great importance on obtaining the ideal and is unable to do so. For many people, trying to fit into the ideal formed by society is a frustrating and futile experience. Not measuring up to the ideal may then make a person feel worse about his or her body in comparison, thus contributing to a negative body image.

Media

The ideals of beauty are often perpetuated through the media. Traditionally, in television shows and movies, the central character fits the cultural ideal while the supporting role does not. The thin, beautiful women are happy, successful, and able to find love. With more than half of Americans currently overweight or obese, it is interesting that even the reality shows feature beautiful, handsome, thin, and muscular people. Various research studies have found a woman's perception of her own body to become more negative after watching television shows featuring women who meet the cultural ideal. The same result occurs with movies and magazines. A woman's response to these external images most likely fluctuates depending upon a number of different factors. It is suspected that the same is true for men who experience media with images for the male ideal. The influence of the media on body image appears to start relatively young, as children often model what they observe on television. It is believed that most children gain an understanding of the cultural ideal through their television watching.

Peers and Family

The influence of peers and family also plays a role in body image. A person's family is likely to represent his or her first encounter with perceptions of body shape and size. Young girls are more likely to want to lose weight if their mother is trying to lose weight. Similarly, if a child perceives thinness to be important to her parents, she will most likely carry a similar ideal. Multiple research articles have shown that weight-related issues of parents are commonly passed on to their children. Similarly, siblings can have an influence by modeling behavior that reinforces cultural ideals and through teasing others about nonadherence to these ideals.

Even though body image is an extremely personal experience, it is influenced by one's peers, as people compare themselves to people of their own social group. For example, an overweight woman may feel worse about her body if her social circle includes only underweight and normal weight women, whereas an overweight woman who has many overweight friends and associates may not feel as badly about herself. If a person's social comparisons are unfavorable, body dissatisfaction and unhealthy eating behaviors may increase.

Romantic relationships can also influence body image. Overweight women are less likely to be dating than their healthy weight peers and one study found that having a boyfriend was associated with better body satisfaction. However, being in a relationship can positively or negatively affect body image, as negative comments made by a partner concerning body size or shape can dramatically increase body dissatisfaction, whereas positive comments can increase body satisfaction.

Self-Esteem

While the cultural and family/peer influence is strong, an individual's life experience, which may dictate more accurately the way that a person feels, should not be overlooked . Individuals with higher self-esteem are more likely to have more positive body image, regardless of their actual body shape, size, or attractiveness. Many people experience body image shifts associated with aging that lead to a more accepting view of self and others. Other individuals make a concerted effort to improve their self-esteem and body image through classes, counseling, or other mind-body programs. In addition, nonphysical attributes or experiences can positively or negatively affect one's body image. For example, when a woman finds success in her employment, she may feel more positively toward her body, even while her physical attributes have remained unchanged.

Self-Awareness

Body image contains elements of self-assessment and self-awareness, as an individual works to process the ideals of society and then apply them to his or her own physical body. An incorrect self-assessment may be a sign of body distortion. An example of this would be a normal weight woman who feels badly about her body because she thinks she is obese. Thus, body image is expected to be individual to each person, but largely determined by the person's response to and examination of his or her own body in comparison to societal images. The term "body image investment" has been used to refer to the importance that an individual places on body image and in achieving society-defined ideals.

News and Advertisements

Negative body image affects so many people and has become a frequent headline on entertainment news shows and magazine covers. Numerous celebrities have admitted to struggling from body image disturbance or eating disorders, while other celebrities are accused or suspected of such behavior. Articles on loving your body are plastered next to weight loss ads and liposuction promotions. Many dieting and plastic surgery companies actually prey on negative body image to attract clients. A classic example would be a woman on a television commercial explaining how miserable and unhappy her life was and how badly she hated herself until she lost weight through a certain product. The advertisement then promises the viewer similar results in both weight and body image by taking their product (e.g., Hydroxycut www.hydroxycut.com).

There are multiple reality shows on television in which the sole purpose is to change the physical appearance of the participants. Many of these shows claim high viewership levels and encourage audience members to undergo similar transformations as the television "actors." Shows also promote products available to help people make those changes. Multiple shows and specials have been made highlighting children in beauty pageants where they are made up to look like adults with spray-on tans and perfect teeth and makeup (e.g., Toddlers and Tiaras, Little Miss Perfect). Articles about mothers giving their daughters Botox to help them be successful in beauty pageants have recently filled the newspapers.

Multiple industries use the stereotypical ideals to sell products. The beach body ideal for men, with tanned skin, large muscles, broad shoulders, and rugged good looks, is used to sell everything from lotion to alcohol. These advertisements are aimed not only at selling products, but also at making the viewer feel insufficient or inadequate and in need of the product. Such commercials reinforce the cultural ideal of beauty and can affect a person's body image (e.g., Kim Kardashian and Paris Hilton have both done provocative commercials advertising Carl's Jr hamburgers; several celebrities including Jessica Simpson and Alicia Keys have endorsed Proactive acne solution).

In recent years, stories of underweight models near death from eating disorders have filled newspapers and internet sites. In response, several European countries have made laws requiring that models have a certain height-to-weight ratio in order to work.

Body Image Programs

Many programs have been conducted to help people improve their body image. One of the most widespread public campaigns has been the "Dove Campaign for Real Beauty," which is a worldwide marketing campaign including advertisements, videos, workshops, sleepover events, and a book. Commercials celebrating the natural variation in women's bodies began in 2004. Their goal is to inspire people and help them have confidence in themselves. Dove has also worked with young girls to change the concept of beauty from the ultrathin models with perfect features to making every girl feel positively about herself.

Body Image and Health

Body image issues are often associated with psychological consequences, but recently positive body image has also been associated with improved physical health and healthy eating behaviors. Individuals with higher body dissatisfaction are more likely to engage in counterproductive weight loss behaviors, such as short-term starvation diets followed by binge episodes. Negative body image commonly affects the eating habits of individuals. Either they will diet, often gaining back any weight lost, or they may eat less or more than they should, putting them at risk for eating disorders and obesity.

Individuals with body image concerns are less likely to eat fruits and vegetables and are more likely to consume meat and fast food. Body image can affect whether or not someone will engage in or avoid healthy amounts of physical activity. If an individual feels negatively about himself, he may engage in exercise to improve that appearance and even engage in obligatory exercise. However, if an individual experiences negative body image, he or she may express intense social physique anxiety which could result in avoiding public settings (e.g., pools, fitness centers) for exercise.

Body image can also affect the decision to quit smoking, especially if the individual fears that he will gain weight as a result of cessation. Similarly, body dissatisfaction is associated with higher frequency of cigarette and alcohol use. Given the effects that negative body image can have on health behaviors, more health professionals are identifying negative body image as a serious threat to physical health and well-being.

Conclusion

Body image is a strong predictor of one's tendency to develop disordered eating or a clinical eating disorder. Negative body image is more common among women than men, but both sexes experience dissatisfaction. Although body image can change over time, common triggers for negative body image include media images, comments by others, and culturally defined standards of beauty. Body image programs have been developed to improve perceptions of self and body, including the Dove Campaign and Full of Ourselves.

TeriSue Smith-Jackson

See also: Dove Campaign for Real Beauty; Full of Ourselves; Obligatory Exercise; Social Physique Anxiety.

Bibliography

Aruguete, Mara S., Kurt A. DeBord, Alayne Yates, and Jeanne Edman. "Ethnic and Gender Differences in Eating Attitudes among Black and White College Students." *Eating Behaviors* 6, no. 4 (2005): 328–36.

Cash, Thomas F. "Cognitive-Behavioral Perspectives on Body Image." In *Body Image: A Handbook of Theory, Research and Clinical Practice,* edited by Thomas F. Cash and T. Pruzinsky, 38–46. New York, NY: Guilford Press, 2002.

Chu, Hui-Wen, Barbara Bushman, and Rebecca Woodard. "Social Physique Anxiety, Obligation to Exercise, and Exercise Choices among College Students." *Journal of American College Health* 57, no. 1 (2008): 7–14.

Dove Movement for Self-Esteem. (2010). "About the Movement." Retrieved from http://www.dovemovement.com/movement/about on May 25, 2011.

Forbes, Gordon B., Rebecca L. Jobe, and Raynette M. Richardson. "Associations between Having a Boyfriend and the Body Satisfaction and Self Esteem of College Women: An Extension of the Lin and Kulik Hypothesis." *Journal of Social and Clinical Psychology* 146, no. 3 (2006): 381–84.

Franzoi, Stephen L., and Jeffrey R. Klaiber. "Body Use and Reference Group Impact: With Whom Do We Compare Our Bodies?" *Sex Roles* 56 (2007): 205–214.

Gleeson, Kate, and Hannah Frith. "(De)constructing Body Image." *Journal of Health Psychology* 11, no. 1 (2006): 79–90.

King, Teresa K., Mala Matacin, Kamila S. White, and Bess H. Marcus. "A Prospective Examination of Body Image and Smoking in Women." *Body Image* 2 (2005): 19–28.

Roy, Jane L. P., Gary R. Hunter, and Tamilane E. Blaudeau. "Percent Body Fat is Related to Body-Shape Perception and Dissatisfaction in Students Attending an All Women's College." *Perceptual Motor Skills* 103, no. 3 (2006): 677–84.

Shankar, Padmini, Jennie E. Dilworth, and Diana Cone. "Dietary Intake and Health Behavior among Black and White College Females." *Family and Consumer Science Research Journal* 33, no. 2 (2004): 159–71.

Sheets, Virgil, and Kavita Ajmere. "Are Romantic Partners a Source of College Students' Weight Concern?" *Eating Behaviors* 6, no. 1 (2005): 1–9.

Striegel-Moore, Ruth H., and Debra L. Franko. "Body Image Issues among Girls and Women." In *Body Image: A Handbook of Theory, Research, and Clinical Practice,* edited by T. F. Cash and T. Pruzinsky, 183–191. New York, NY: Guilford Press, 2002.

Trampe, Debra, Diederik A. Stapel, and Frans W. Siero. "On Models and Vases: Body Dissatisfaction and Proneness to Social Comparison Effects." *Journal of Personality and Social Psychology* 92, no. 1 (2007): 106–118.

BODY IMAGE GLOBALLY

Body ideals, appearance norms, and eating patterns around the world are highly specific to the cultural norms of particular groups and countries of origin. When considering body weight expectations and eating behaviors, it is important to consider the access to mainstream media, the role of availability of food sources (food security) and the prosperity of nations. The impact of the media on body image is especially apparent in regions such as Fiji that were not previously exposed to media images of beauty. The Fiji study, which is discussed in a separate entry, demonstrates how the media influence resulted in more negative body image and the initiation of pathological dieting practices that did not exist prior to the media's presence in the country.

Food Availability

In developing countries, food availability is not always predictable. Therefore, the tendency to overeat when food is available becomes a survival strategy for individuals who face food security concerns. By gaining weight an individual who faces periods of involuntary starvation can conserve fat stores and calories for energy during times when food is not available. Generally, a heavy body figure or large size has been desirable in developing countries because having a rotund shape has been associated with wealth. Historically, thinness has been associated with both malnourishment and diseases (e.g., HIV, AIDS, malaria, etc.) that might be stigmatized within developing countries (for example, Sub-Saharan Africa, South Africa, India, Brazil, Philippines). It is important to delineate the difference between eating disorders and malnutrition. Although malnutrition is a health consequence of restrictive behavior associated with eating disorders, malnutrition can also be a result of political instability, droughts and disease; eating disorders, on the other hand, are largely psychological in nature. While it is not possible to cover every country in this entry, certain countries will be highlighted to illustrate unique customs and expectations related to appearance and food intake.

Westernization

The term Westernization refers to other cultures looking to the body image and fashion trends in both the United States and Europe to take on that identity.

Americans and Body Image

Americans spend over $40 billion on dieting and diet-related products each year. What is perhaps even more surprising is that 35 percent of normal dieters progress to pathological dieting and of that 35 percent, 20–25 percent progress to partial or full syndrome eating disorders. The diet mentality has infiltrated the American way of life and not only impacts adults, but also affects children and adolescents. The cultural pressure to be thin or at least prove that one is trying to lose weight is not only promoted among adults, but has also been inadvertently or directly taught to children and adolescents. Researchers discovered that 42 percent of first through third grade girls wanted to be thinner, while 81 percent of 10-year-olds were afraid of being fat. There are many psychological factors that contribute to the development of eating disorders. However, the social and cultural environment also plays an important role during critical developmental stages in the life cycle.

Prevalence of Eating Disorders

In the United States, as many as 10 million people have been diagnosed with an eating disorder. According to the American Psychiatric Association (2000), women and girls account for 90–95 percent of individuals suffering from anorexia nervosa. In addition, 0.5–1.0 percent of women in America have the disorder. Forty percent of all newly identified cases of anorexia nervosa are girls in the age group of 15–19 years. In the same report, it was stated that the incidence of bulimia in women in the age group of 10–39 years tripled between 1988 and 1993. Girls and women make up 80 percent of bulimia nervosa clients. Overall, bulimia nervosa affects 1–2 percent of adolescents and young women. Estimates of the prevalence of binge eating disorder range from 1 percent to 5 percent of the population with 60 percent being female and 40 percent male. Research conducted with diverse populations demonstrates that eating disorders and body image concerns are not occurring only among white, female adolescents.

Etiology

Objectification theory suggests that girls and women are naturally acculturated to internalize a person's observation about their physical features as the foremost view of themselves. This perspective regarding the self can lead to frequent and obsessive body monitoring, which can cause an increase in women's susceptibility to shame and anxiety, reduce motivation, and diminish awareness of internal bodily states. The media can serve as a vehicle for reinforcing these body image concerns and feelings of shame. Accumulations of such experiences may result in dieting behavior and ultimately disordered eating in young females. Eating disorders pose a public health risk and are associated with numerous health consequences. This theory is also pertinent to men, as certain kinds of communication in the media can influence both college-aged men and women to be at risk for weight control, disordered eating, and excessive exercise.

Exposure to images of highly attractive same-sex models rather than unattractive models heightens self-consciousness. This suggests that attractive models in the media are likely to evoke a social comparison process, which is also referred to as the internalization of the thin ideal. To change this internalization of the thin ideal, researchers suggest that a short educational message that counters negative body messages should be given to women. While public service announcements (PSAs) have been the most effective thus far, researchers are now discovering adverse effects due to PSAs addressing the issue of the thin ideal incorrectly by showing too many thin models. This suggests that an intervention without pictures might be more effective.

Both men and women experience body dissatisfaction to different capacities. Both genders being sexually objectified in the media results in body dysmorphic disorder. For women it manifests as the thin ideal, while for males muscularity is perceived to be associated with positive attention. Researchers suggest that an unrealistic comparison of bodies for both genders can be successfully addressed with health messages using Cognitive Behavior Therapy (CBT). The use of narrative therapy in health messaging has been effective, as a philosophy of language proposes that meaning is socially constructed. This therapeutic approach assists persons to begin externalizing the negative body image messages by deconstructing the message in positive language.

Europe and Body Image

In the early 19th century, the Industrial Revolution was taking place in Europe. To illustrate the poverty that came as a result of this, artists would paint pictures of the thin, ill, tanned, and impoverished persons seen on the streets. Thinness and dark skin tone were associated with outside labor and were perceived as undesirable qualities in Europe. Instead, a heavier body ideal was desired and became synonymous with wealth and having a limitless food supply. This more curvaceous ideal was enhanced and sexualized in the late 19th century with the invention of the corset which accentuated female body parts (i.e., hips and breasts). Today, body image dissatisfaction and disordered eating behavior in adolescent and female adults in the United Kingdom has reached the same rate as that in the United States through a similar vehicle, ultrathin models in the media. Similar to those in the United States, girls and women monitor their bodies and experience body shame and disordered eating. Milan has been noted as requiring ultrathin models for the catwalk. In 2006, as a result of the increase in body image disturbances and eating disorders, underweight models were banned on the Milan and Madrid catwalks. Males, on the other hand, experienced negative body image and have reported engaging in excessive exercise in attempts to strive for a more fit-looking physique. While Germany and the Netherlands had the lowest rates of eating disorders, France, Belgium, and Italy report the highest rates within Europe.

Japan and Body Image

Japanese females are stereotyped in the United States as pale-skinned, dark-haired women in extravagant kimonos, that is geishas. This stereotype is far from reality. Japan is the fashion capital of Asia and is heavily influenced by Western models. This celebration of Western models and Caucasians as symbols of beauty has led some Asian women to reject stereotypical facial features. Although many Asian women possess epicanthic (slanted) eyes naturally, they report wanting larger eyes and will resort to cosmetic surgery to create a pronounced crease on their eyelids in order to appear more European. Likewise, Japanese women have elected for nose reconstructive surgery to flatten and widen their noses.

Hair color has also been a symbol of beauty for Japanese women. In order to strive for the more Western blond ideal, Japanese women in the 1990s would lighten their hair color by using juices from flowers and herbs (Chapatsu). Currently, chemicals and dyes are used to lighten the naturally black hair of 80 percent of Asian females in their twenties.

Interestingly, Japanese participants have reported lower body esteem and are likely to desire the Western body ideals of Caucasians. Japanese women's reported Body Mass Index (BMI) ideal is 19.0, while the country average is 20.7. This was significantly lower than the reported BMI ideal of Caucasian females (20.4). Data from Nakamura indicated that rates of anorexia nervosa and bulimia nervosa in Japanese females and males (aged 15–29 years) were 17 out of every 100,000 and 6 out of every 100,000, respectively. Over the past 25 years in Japan, eating disorders have increased sixfold and research regarding potential risk factors for the maintenance and onset of eating disorders is vital.

Nearly 20 percent of 10-year-old boys and girls have dieted in Japan; 30 percent of girls aged 6 showed distorted body image, low body-esteem and body consciousness, and greater social anxiety compared to other countries. In Japan approximately 30–50 percent of individuals are diagnosed and treated for social anxiety (i.e., avoidance of interpersonal relationships) called "Taijin Kyofusho." Having overprotective or overcontrolling parents can lead to the development of negative body image and eating disorders. Prevalence of eating disorders is high due to the inflexible nature of the modern Japanese family. Adolescents are sharing weight concerns and dieting behaviors with their mothers who encourage them to lose weight and stay thin. Comparatively, the influences that yield body dissatisfaction and restrictive dieting in American women are identical to those idealized by Japanese women. The reason is that although the women in Japan today are liberated and have more freedoms, they are relegated to take a backseat and conform to traditional culture that supports male dominance. Assertiveness, a protective factor against eating disorders, is viewed in Japan as selfish, immature, and showing bad manners. Men in Japan have a tendency to want to gain weight, which leads to obsessive exercise to gain muscle. As they gain muscle they feel more positive about their bodies.

China

While advertisements (e.g., Levi's) featuring Western models have bombarded Chinese media, Chinese people have not appeared to be as strongly influenced by them as Japanese individuals. Rather, they are influenced by the advertisements in the Chinese media, which focus on the face more than the body and on selling cosmetics and hair products rather than clothing. Being thin and fragile has been connected to female beauty for centuries and it did not originate from Western ideals portrayed through the media. However, with recent cultural, political, and economic reforms in China, Western media has had the opportunity to be introduced to the people of China as early as 1980. Today, children in China are influenced by Western media more than their parents were. Since AD 970, foot binding was a common practice, as having small feet was considered a sign of beauty, attractiveness, identity, virtue, and womanhood. Foot binding is a two-year process that begins by wrapping binding (silk or cotton bandage) around a three to five year old girl's feet to bend the toes back (minus the big toe). This forces the bones in the foot to break. Sharp objects are inserted in the bandages to be tightened daily, which assist in shrinking the feet and cutting off excess skin. The result was that the girl's feet had toes tucked under permanently meeting the heel. Mothers-in-law would choose their sons' wives based on the appearance of the feet. Foot binding was first banned in 1645 but the ban was later lifted. As a result of lifting of the ban in 1895, anti–foot binding societies arose.

Centuries ago, women would mix dyes from various plants in their kitchen to create a rose color to be applied to their cheeks. Mixing oils to moisturize their skin was also common; however, there was not a concern for anti-aging retinols and SPFs. The cosmetic company Estee Lauder caught wind of the Chinese women's drive for beauty through cosmetics. They strategically placed cosmetic advertisements in the first ever Chinese magazine in 1988. Estee Lauder then opened a store in Shanghai in 1993, which led to great success and demand among Chinese women. The primary consumers of the cosmetics industry in China are those under the age of 50 years. Those older and living in the communist era have mostly rejected the modern beauty ideals of the cosmetics industry. While there is no evidence regarding the degree of influence the Japanese "Hattou Shin" ideal has on Chinese consumers of magazines, there is a high desire to have long legs. Shockingly, women will endure a painful surgical procedure in which the bones in the legs are broken and then fitted with a metal brace that can be adjusted to stretch the tendons while the bone heals, adding one more inch to their height. Similar to Japanese women, Chinese women also desire a crease in their eyelid to resemble the shape of a Caucasian's eye. To fulfill this desire, women can buy beauty products such as glue to assist in the creation of a crease; however, plastic surgery has become the number one choice.

As adolescent girls in the United States and Japan are influenced by their mothers' own body image concerns, so are the Chinese girls. Mothers in China have been known to encourage their daughters to engage in diet (i.e. food restriction) and exercise; and mothers and daughters criticize their bodies together. This is further complicated by the controlling and strict nature of Chinese mothers and the pressure to fulfill their expectations. Young girls define diet, exercise, and body criticism as a healthy mother-daughter relationship that is clearly disturbing and unhealthy. This activity is highly influenced by the 1979 "one child only" law set by the government. This law has weakened family bonds and threatened the traditional understanding of self that is discovered in sibling relationships. It has also limited the opportunities for social comparison of the body and isolated the child from extended family networks, leading them to rely heavily on the media and peers to inform them about ideal body types. This has led to peers teasing and criticizing both male and female bodies. The diet behavior that both males and females glean as a result is food restriction. Interestingly, consuming Western foods is related to one's social standing and wealth, as McDonald's entered the Chinese market in the 1980s. Thus far it has resulted in sedentary work and high-calorie and high-fat diets, leading to a 200 percent increase in obesity.

In Chinese culture, masculinity has been related to a man's character rather than physique and muscularity. About 30 percent of adolescent boys in China viewed themselves as underweight, felt pressure to be underweight, and had a clinical diagnosis of "underweight," suggesting that they are at risk for an eating disorder. Comparatively, overweight males were more likely to participate in exercise that builds muscles due to body ideals seen in magazines.

India and Body Image

India has been exposed to Western media for more than a decade. Asian Indian girls and women are facing increasing pressures in meeting international standards not only in the economic sphere, but also in terms of body image. Girls start comparing their bodies to that of thin models in magazines—with the most popular being Aishwarya Rai and Rani Mukherjee—due to peer teasing, which leads to food restriction and bulimic behavior during adolescent years. In comparison, adult women experience less body teasing than girls and adolescents, but still restrict food intake due to body dissatisfaction.

It is suggested by researchers that the Hindu religion may play a role in the disordered eating attitudes and the desire of women and girls to be thin. A vegetarian diet is frequently promoted in India associated with health beliefs, which has roots in Ayurveda (ancient system of medicine in India), rather than to avoid fat or energy intake. A largely vegetarian lifestyle also supports nonviolence toward animals, a more easily digestible diet, and religious beliefs.

Africa

Ghana

In Ghana, 1.5 percent of female adolescents in two secondary schools were found to be underweight due to self-starvation to achieve perfectionist moral and academic standards. At the same time, they had a low sense of self-efficacy over academic pressures and family conflicts. The girls perceived their weight loss as positive and got the idea from religious fasting. While religious fasting does not cause anorexia nervosa, it can be a risk factor for girls with low self-esteem and those who are experimenting with diets; the short fast might give them the opportunity to enjoy feeling hungry and to discover food restriction as a coping mechanism. To compare, women in Ghana preferred an overweight body size because that meant they were more likely to marry, be successful, and prosper; however, those who were obese were dissatisfied with their body. This illustrates the current generational shift in body image.

Men in Ghana felt that women are attracted to muscular men, and 50 percent reported a desire to become more muscular because Western media shows that muscularity brings prestige; they also believed that muscularity helps to intimidate other males in order to defend themselves and to be better at sports. It should be noted that despite the desire to increase muscle mass, Ghanaian men are generally more muscular than American men.

Senegal

Senegal is in the early stages of being introduced to the Western media. Although men desire women who are overweight in Senegal because a large body size is positively associated with having a good job, enough money, a contented husband, great personality, and eating healthy, 97.3 percent of women wanted to be thinner. Of this 97.3 percent, 12.3 percent were clinically underweight (BMI < 18.5). Women knew that overweight and obesity are associated with heart disease, diabetes, and cancer. This knowledge stems from the influence of Western culture and an awareness of health. The largest impact that Western culture has had in Senegal is the desire for lighter skin, which has led to chemical skin bleaching resulting in skin cancer.

South Africa

African women are thought to be protected from eating disorders because there has historically been less cultural pressure to be thin. Recently, some changes in body image beliefs have been observed as African women in South Africa obtain their pressure to be thin from the increasingly more Westernized media. In South Africa, black female fashion models have a significantly lower BMI than Caucasians. In comparison, magazines in the United States show Caucasian models with a lower BMI than black models. While attractiveness in South Africa is defined as the traditional heavy set person by those living in rural areas, young black affluent people tend to conform with the ideals in the media—which equates a thin body with a low BMI—at a higher rate than the Caucasians. Male African fashion models in both South Africa and the United States have a significantly lower BMI than Caucasian models with the addition of a high muscle mass. Likewise, African men tend to engage in more disordered eating associated with gaining muscle than Caucasian males in the United States.

Meal patterns and food habits change during primary school to include food restriction, while beliefs about increased exercise change from primary school to secondary school to conform to body ideals in the media as discussed with friends. However, individuals who have been exposed to persons diagnosed with HIV/AIDS or tuberculosis (TB) do not want to be thin, as there is a severe societal taboo surrounding HIV/AIDS and TB positive persons that leads to isolation. It is believed by a subset of people in South Africa that if a person is thin they have HIV/AIDS or TB. They will be ignored and isolated from society—it is not considered beautiful.

South America

Brazil is the cosmetic surgery capital of the world, with a reported 629,000 surgical procedures in 2009. Eighty-eight percent of these cosmetic surgeries were performed on women. While 15 percent of the surgeries were performed on adolescents under the age of 18, 38 percent were on individuals between the ages of 19 and 35, and 34 percent were on individuals between the ages of 36 and 50.

Because cosmetic surgery prices are lower in Brazil than in Europe and the United States, many people flock to Brazil for breast enhancement and reduction, liposuction, tummy tuck, eyelid surgery, nose modification, and face-lifts. Two-thirds of individuals who travelled to Brazil for cosmetic surgery self-identified as Caucasian and one-third self-identified as black. In Brazil, the body has always played an important role in culture.

Brazilians have a saying that physical appearance is vital for the construction of "uma identidade nacional brasileira" (a national Brazilian identity). It is believed that a beautiful body will give them hope for a higher social class and eternal youth that always needs improvement. Their body plays a role in economics and is a symbol of wealth. Women do not have cosmetic surgery for their husbands or partners who are opposed to the surgery. Rather, they are going under the knife for themselves to address body dissatisfaction that occurs following one's pregnancy—Reportedly women report that breasts and abdominal area are no longer tight and cosmetic surgery can improve psychological well-being while avoiding exercise and dieting. In summary, women and female adolescents are reporting that they opt for cosmetic surgery to increase their self-esteem, as plastic surgeons in Brazil not only perform the surgery, but also provide psychological counseling to patients.

Mexico

Family relationships play a larger role in body image in Mexico unlike in most other countries where the media plays a big role. While Hispanics are exposed to thin bodies in the media, the family widely rejects that ideal, which leads to persons being less likely to use extreme measures, if any, to obtain a thin body as seen in magazines.

Hispanic girls tend to overestimate their weight, and this has resulted in body dissatisfaction and higher levels of eating disorder symptoms (i.e. fasting [4.2%], diuretics [7.9%] or laxatives [3.5%]) than in non-Hispanic white girls. This illustrates a social shift from the traditional ideal of a heavy body type to a thin body type as in the Western media. Although there is evidence of exposure to and influence of the Western media in Mexico, there is no data on whether or not Hispanic girls in Mexico have internalized the thin Western ideal. However, in one study, low-income Hispanic girls living in Mexico showed a high rate of internalizing the thin ideal portrayed in the media, in addition to wanting to achieve a smaller body size than girls in the United States and Europe. It was unclear if the girls in this study who internalized the thin ideal had strong family relationships—a protective factor in Mexico—or not.

Conclusion

Although food security remains endemic in many developing countries, people there do experience eating disorders. Globally, eating disorders and body image dissatisfaction have been linked to ultrathin models in the Western media and in the particular developing country's local media, which affect children, men, and women. These images affect the viewer's self-esteem and body esteem negatively, leading to various unhealthy self-improvement techniques. It has been shown in some global samples that family rejection or peer rejection of these media images and strong family relationships can prevent eating disorders.

HAILEY E. NIELSON

See also: Fiji Study.

Bibliography

American Psychiatric Association. *Diagnostic and Statistical Manual of Mental Disorders, 4th ed.* Washington, DC: American Psychiatric Association, Inc., 1994.
Amuna, Paul, and Francis B. Zotor. "Epidemiological and Nutrition Transition in Developing Countries: Impact on Human Health and Development." *Proceedings of the Nutrition Society* 67 (2008): 82–90. doi: 10.1017/S0029665108006058.
Austin, Julia L., and Jane E. Smith. "Thin Ideal Internalization of Mexican Girls: A Test of the Sociocultural Model of Eating Disorders." *International Journal of Eating Disorders* 41 (2008): 448–57. doi: 10.1002/eat.20529.
Bennett, Dinah, Michael Sharpe, Chris Freeman, and Alan Carson. "Anorexia Nervosa among Female Secondary School Students in Ghana." *British Journal of Psychiatry* 185 (2004): 312–17.

Calogero, Rachel M. "Objectification Processes and Disordered Eating in British Women and Men." *Journal of Health Psychology* 14 (2009). doi: 10.1177/1359105309102192.

China Economic Review. "China Rises to World's Eighth Largest Beauty Market." *China Economic Review,* 2003.

Chisuwa, Naomi, and Jennifer A. O'Dea. "Body Image and Eating Disorders amongst Japanese Adolescents: A Review of the Literature." *Appetite* 54 (2010): 5–15. doi: 10.1016/j.appet.2009.11.008.

Coetzeek, Vinet, and David I. Perrett. "African and Caucasian Body Ideals in South Africa and the United States." *Eating Behaviors* 12 (2010): 72–74. doi: 10.1016/j.eatbeh.2010.09.006.

Dorneles de Andrade, Daniela. "On Norms and Bodies: Findings from Field Research on Cosmetic Surgery in Rio de Janeiro, Brazil." *Reproductive Health Matters* 18, no. 35 (2010): 74–83.

Duncan, Margaret Carlisle. "The Politics of Women's Body Images and Practices: Foucault, the Panopticon, and Shape Magazine". *Journal of Sport and Social Issues* 18 (1994): 48–65. doi: 10.1177/019372394018001004.

Frederick, David A., Leila Sadhgi-Azar, Martie G. Haselton, Gregory M. Buchana, Letitia A. Peplau, Anna Berezovskaya, and Ryan E. Lipinski. "Desiring the Muscular Ideal: Men's Body Satisfaction in the United States, Ukraine, and Ghana." *Psychology of Men and Muscularity* 8, no. 2 (2007): 103–117.

Fredrickson, Barbara L., and Tomi-Ann Roberts. "Objectification Theory: Toward Understanding Women's Lived Experiences and Mental Health Risks". *Psychology of Women* 21 (1997) 173–206.

Hall-Iijima, Christine. "Asian Eyes: Body Image and Eating Disorders of Asian and Asian American Women." *Eating Disorders* 3 (1995): 5–19.

Hall, Howard K., Andrew P. Hill, Paul R. Appleton, and Stephe A. Kozub. "The Mediating Influence of Unconditional Self-acceptance and Labile Self-Esteem on the Relationship between Multidimensional Perfectionism and Exercise Dependence." *Psychology of Sport and Exercise* 10 (2009) 35–44. doi: 10.1018/j.psychsport.2008.05.003.

Hoek, Hans Wijbrand, and Daphne van Hoeken. "Review of the Prevalence and Incidence of Eating Disorders." *International Journal of Eating Disorders* (2003) 383–96. doi: 101992/eat.10222.

Holdsworth, M., A. Gartner, E. Landais, B. Maire, and F. Delpeuch. "Perceptions of Healthy and Desirable Body Size in Urban Senegalese Women." *International Journal of Obesity* 28, no. 12 (2004): 1561–1568. doi:10.1038/sj.ijo.0802739.

Howden-Chapman, Philippa, and Johan Mackenback. "Poverty and Painting: Representations in 19th Century Europe." *British Medical Journal* 325 (2002): 1502–1505. doi: 10.1136.1502.

Jackson, Todd, and Hong Chen. "Factor Structure of the Sociocultural Attitudes towards Appearance Questionnaire-3 (SATAQ-3) among Adolescent Boys in China." *Body Image* 7, no. 4 (2010): 349–55. doi: 10.1016/j.bodyim.2010.07.003.

Kayano, Mami, Kazuhiro Yoshiuchi, Samir Al-Adawi, Nonna Viernes, Atsu S. Dorvlo, Hiroaki Kumano, Tomifusa Kuboki, and Akira Akabayashi. "Eating Attitudes and Body Dissatisfaction in Adolescents: Cross-Cultural Study." *Psychiatry and Clinical Neurosciences* 62, no. 1 (2008): 17–25. doi: 10.1111/j.1440-1819.2007.01772.x

Kowner, Rotem. "Japanese Body Image: Structure and Esteem Scores in a Cross-Cultural Perspective." *International Journal of Psychology* 37, no. 3 (2002): 149–59. doi:10.1080/0020759014300298.

Leahy, Trisha, and R. Harrigan. "Using Narrative Therapy in Sport Psychology Practice: Application to a Psychoeducational Body Image Program." *The Sport Psychologist* 20 (2006): 480–94.

Long, Clive G., Jenny Smith, Marie Midgley, and Tony Cassidy. "Overexercising in Anorexic and Normal Samples: Behavior and Attitudes." *Journal of Mental Health* 4 (1993): 321. doi: 10.3109/09638239309016967.

Macia, Enguerran, Priscilla Buboz, and Lamine Gueye. "Prevalence of Obesity in Dakar." *Obesity Reviews* 11, no. 10 (2010): 691–94. doi: 10.1111/j.1467-789X.2010.00749.x.

Mao, John. "Foot Binding: Beauty and Torture." *The Internet Journal of Biological Anthropology* 1, no. 2 (2008).

Martinelli, Valentina, Ottavia Colombo, Cristiano Nichini, Ilaria Repossi, Piergiuseppe Vinai, and Anna Tagliabue. "High Frequency of Psychopathology in Subjects Wishing to Lose Weight: An Observational Study in Italian Subjects." *Public Health Nutrition* 14, no. 2 (2010): 373–76. doi: 10.1017/S1368980010001576.

McNutt, Suzanne W., Yuanreng Hu, George B. Schreiber, Patricia B. Crawford, Eva Obarzanek, and Laural Mellin. "A Longitudinal Study of the Dietary Practices of Black and White Girls 9 and 10 Years Old at Enrollment: The NHLBI Growth and Health Study." *Journal of Adolescent Health* (1997): 27–37. doi: 10.1016/S1054-139X(96)00176-0

Mond, Jonathan J., Phillipa J. Hay, Bryan Rodgers, Cathy Owen, and James Mitchell. "Correlates of the Use of Purging and Non-Purging Methods of Weight Control in a Community Sample of Women." *Australian & New Zealand Journal of Psychiatry* 40 (2006): 136–42. doi: 10.1080/j.1440-2006.01760.x.

Mukai, Takayo, Akiko Kambara, and Yuji Sasaki. "Body Dissatisfaction, Need for Social Approval and Eating Disturbances among Japanese and American College Women." *Sex Roles* 39 (1998): 751–63. doi: 0021-9630/94.

Nagaoka, Tomoaki, Solchi Watanabe, Kiyoko Sakurai, Etsuo Kunieda, Satoshi Watanabe, Masao Taki, and Yukio Yamanaka. "Development of Realistic High-Resolution Whole-Body Voxel Models of Japanese Adult Males and Females of Average Height and Weight, and Application of Models to Radio-Frequency Electromagnetic-Field Dosimetry." *Physics in Medicine and Biology* 49 (2004): 1–15. doi: 0031-9155/04/010001+15.

Nakamura, Kei, Kenji Kitanishi, Yuko Miyake, Kazuyuki Hahsimoto, and Mikiko Kubota. "The Neurotic Versus Delusional Subtype of Taijin-Kyofu-sho: Their DSM Diagnoses." *Psychiatry and Clinical Neurosciences* 56, no. 6 (2008): 595–601. doi: 10.1046/j.1440-1819.2002.01061.x.

Park, Sung-Yeon, Jacqueline Hitchon McSweeney, and Gi Woong Yun. "Intervention of Eating Disorder Symptomatology Using Educational Communication Messages." *Communication Research* 36 (5) (2009) 677–97. doi: 10.1177/0093650209338910.

Preti, Antonio, Giovanni de Girolamo, Gemma Vilagut, Jordi Alonso, Ron de Graaf, Ronny Bruffaerts, Koen Demyttenaere, Alejandra Pinto-Meza, Josep Maria Haro, and Piero Morosini. "The Epidemiology of Eating Disorders in Six European Countries: Results of the ESEMeD-WMH Project." *Journal of Psychiatric Research* 43 (2008): 1125–1132. doi: 10.1016/j.jpsychires.2009.04.003.

Puoane, Thandi, Lungiswa Tsolekile, and Nelia Steyn. "Perceptions about Body Image and Sizes among Black African Girls Living in Cape Town." *Ethnicity and Disease* 20, no. 1 (2010): 29–34.

Rosemary, B. Duda, Naana A. Jumah, Joseph Seffah, and Richard Biritwum. "Assessment of the Ideal Body Image of Women in Accra, Ghana." *Tropical Doctor* 37, no. 4 (2007): 241–44.

Shisslak, Catherine M, M. Marjorie Crago, and Linda S. Estes. "The Spectrum of Eating Disturbances." *International Journal of Eating Disorders* 18, no. 3 (1995): 209–219. doi: 10.1002/1098-108X(199511)18:<209::AID EAT2260180303>3.0CO;2-E

Shroff, Hemal, and Kevin J. Thompson. "Body Image and Eating Disturbance in India: Media and Interpersonal Influences." *International Journal of Eating Disorders* 35, no. 2 (2004): 198–203. doi: 10.1002/eat.10229.

Sira, Natalia, and Carmel Parker White. "Individual and Familial Correlates of Body Satisfaction in Male and Female College Students." *Journal of American College Health,* 58, no. 6 (2010): 507–513. doi: 10.1080/07448481003621742.

Smith, Delia E., Marsha D. Marcus, Cora E. Lewis, Marian Fitgibbon, and Pamela Schreiner. "Prevalence of Binge Eating Disorder, Obesity and Depression in a Biracial Cohort of Young Adults." *Annals of Behavioral Medicine* 20 (1998): 227–32. doi: 10.1007/BF02884965.

Swami, Viren, Katia Poulogianni, and Adrian Furnham. "The Influence of Resource Availability on Preferences for Human Body Weight and Non-Human Objects." *Journal of Articles in Support of the Null Hypothesis* 4, no. 1 (2006): 17–28.

Thornton, Bill, and Maurice, Jason. "Physique Contrast Effect: Adverse Impact of Idealized Body Images for Women." *Sex Roles* 37 (1997): 433–39. doi: 10.1023/A:1025609624848.

Victoria, Cesar G., Linda Adair, Caroline Fall, Pedro C. Hallal, Reynaldo Martorell, Linda Richter, and Harshpal Singh Sachdev. "Maternal and Child Undernutrition: Consequences for Adult Health and Human Capitol." *Lancet* 371, no. 26 (2008). doi: 10.1016/501406736(07)61692-4

Xu, Xiaoyan, David Mellor, Melanie Kiehne, Lina A. Ricciardelli, Marita P. McCabe, and Yangana Xu. "Body Dissatisfaction, Engagement in Body Change Behaviors and Sociocultural Influences on Body Image among Chinese Adolescents." *Body Image* 7, no. 2 (2010): 156–64. doi: 10.1016/j.bodyim.2009.11.003.

Yamamiya, Yuko, Hemal Shroff, and Kevin J. Thompson. "The Tripartite Influence Model of Body Image and Eating Disturbance: A Replication with a Japanese Sample." *International Journal of Eating Disorders* 41, no.1 (2008): 88–91. doi: 10.1002/eat.

BODY IMAGE IN MALES

Although it was once believed that only women had body image concerns, researchers and practitioners have more recently become aware of growing body dissatisfaction among men. Most experts before the 1990s dismissed body image concerns among males. In the past 25 years, it has become clear that many boys and men are dissatisfied with their bodies, although this dissatisfaction often stems from sources that are different from those for females. Advances in research have been accompanied by changes in the sociocultural climate that have made body weight, size, and shape increasingly more important to boys and men.

Early Research on Body Image in Males

Increased awareness of the prevalence of anorexia and bulimia nervosa in females in the 1970s and 1980s encouraged a focus on the desire to lose weight in girls and women. Thus, most studies were designed to detect body image concerns related to perceptions of being overweight. In one study, men and women were presented with same-sex drawings that ranged from very thin to obese. The women rated their current body as heavier than their ideal drawing, but the men rated their current body as similar to their ideal drawing. Although most researchers ignored negative body image as a male concern, a nationwide survey of body image in 1986 revealed that 44 percent of men were afraid of becoming fat. Furthermore, eating disorders have been acknowledged in males as far back as the 1600s, indicating that a portion of men do express concerns about their body. Certain subpopulations of males may be more at risk for body image concerns related to weight loss. For example, boys and men who compete in sports in which being lean is believed to give them a performance advantage (e.g., cross country running, diving) or in which there are distinct weight classes (e.g., wrestling) are more likely to engage in unhealthy eating behaviors than males who do not compete in these sports.

Gender Differences for Body Image

Researchers have discovered that body dissatisfaction may be experienced differently for males than for females. In one study, young adult males were nearly equally divided between a desire to lose weight (45%) and a desire to gain weight (40%). Only 5 percent of the men expressed satisfaction with their current weight, which refuted the notion that most men have a positive body image. The findings from studies in the 1980s suggested that body image concerns were not just a problem for women. However, the nature of the concerns (i.e., weight gain vs. weight loss) appeared to differ between men and women. Research on body type preference identified another dimension of body image dissatisfaction in males. One study revealed that although 60 percent of males identified themselves as endomorphs (i.e., a body type characterized by high body fat and a tendency to gain weight easily), 95 percent reported a preference for the mesomorph type (i.e., a body type characterized by an athletic physique and the ability to easily gain or lose weight).

Beyond Weight: Contemporary Body Image Research in Males

Research conducted in the 1990s and 2000s highlighted the role of muscularity in constructing males' body image. Specifically, researchers and practitioners developed a dual-pathway model to depict body image dissatisfaction in boys and men that includes both weight and muscularity for male body image. Western males' drive for muscularity may predict a higher tendency toward the use of body/performance enhancing substances, and enhanced risk for weight-related health conditions such as type 2 diabetes and coronary heart disease.

Muscle Dysmorphia

In extreme cases, the drive for muscularity among males may lead to a body image disturbance known as muscle dysmorphia. Also known as reverse anorexia, or bigorexia, muscle dysmorphia is characterized by a variety of cognitive and be-havioral symptoms related to weight and muscle gain. The predominant cognitive symptom of muscle dysmorphia is an obsessive preoccupation with the idea that one's body is too small or weak. Preoccupation with the body can lead to inaccurate perceptions of body size and shape, high anxiety, and an inability to focus on other important aspects of life. Behavioral symptoms include excessive amounts of time spent lifting weights, monitoring diet, and mirror checking. The condition was first noted by psychiatrist Harrison Pope in a series of studies with male bodybuilders conducted in the late 1980s and early 1990s. In one study published in *Comprehensive Psychiatry* in 1993, Pope and his colleagues conducted clinical interviews with 108 bodybuilders. Although three of the bodybuilders reported formerly suffering from anorexia nervosa, nine bodybuilders reported symptoms of muscle dysmorphia. Of these nine, four noted using steroids because they believed they looked too small, and another four developed muscle dysmorphia symptoms after taking steroids. Pope and colleagues' initial findings sparked a plethora of studies focused on muscle dysmorphia. Researchers have been particularly interested in the factors that lead to body image dissatisfaction and muscle dysmorphia among males.

Causes of Body Image Dissatisfaction in Males

Just as with females, a variety of body biological, psychological, and sociocultural factors contribute to body image dissatisfaction in males. In one study of 434 adolescent boys, two of these factors were related with body modification strategies aimed at weight loss and weight gain, and with the use of food supplements. Specifically, more pubertal growth (a biological factor) was related to increased use of food supplements, and pressure from parents and peers to increase muscle mass, increase weight, and decrease weight (sociocultural factors) were related to greater use of weight and muscle change strategies. In another study, higher self-esteem (a psychological factor) was related to less body image dissatisfaction in men and women across a two-year time period. Thus, it is clear that body image dissatisfaction in males results from numerous sources.

Male Body Image Dissatisfaction and Hegemonic Masculinity

Perhaps the most intriguing influences on male body image dissatisfaction are sociocultural or environmental factors. For many males, muscularity is a powerful symbol of masculinity. Muscularity is just one aspect of hegemonic masculinity. Hegemonic masculinity refers to the dominant conceptions of what it means to be a man. In Western cultures, the hegemonically masculine male is physically and mentally strong, competitive, and willing to take risks. Research findings have supported the link between masculinity and muscularity. In one study, men with more traditional attitudes about masculinity (i.e., men who subscribed to hegemonic masculinity) wanted to be more muscular than men with less traditional attitudes. Thus, body image dissatisfaction associated with muscularity signals simultaneous feelings of low self-worth and insecurity regarding one's masculinity. According to many experts, the most important reason for body image concerns being on the rise for males is that they are exposed to increasingly objectified images of the male body. These images serve as a constant reminder to males of the muscular ideal inherent to hegemonic masculinity (i.e., lean and muscular). Three specific sources appear to be most influential (a) parents and peers, (b) media images, and (c) action figures.

Parents and Peers

Weight- and body-related messages from friends and family are a powerful source of influence for adolescent boys. In one study of boys in the age group of 12–15 years, body feedback from fathers and male friends was influential in the boys' adoption of body change strategies such as the use of food supplements and exercise to add muscle mass. Another study revealed that males rated peers of the opposite sex as most important in evaluating their body. However, peer teasing was not related to a drive for muscularity. Although females generally do report more weight- and body-related parental pressure than males, parents may be less aware of signs of body image dissatisfaction in boys. For example, a vigorous commitment to lifting weights and consuming food supplements by their sons may appear to be quite healthy behaviors to many parents. However, due to the relatively recent awareness of male-specific body image disturbances such as muscle dysmorphia, parents may fail to evaluate their son's body image attitudes and behaviors as carefully as they would a daughter who decided to go on a diet. Thus, potentially dangerous body change strategies may go unnoticed by the parents of boys. Although parental knowledge and awareness of body image concerns in boys is yet to be examined, such research would add to professionals' understanding of parents' role in preventing and/or exacerbating male body image dissatisfaction.

Media Images

Just as females can be negatively influenced by media images of ultrathin women, so too can portrayals of hyperlean and muscular men increase body image dissatisfaction in males. Supporting the idea that body shape changes are more relevant for males than body weight changes, one study showed that popular men's magazines contain a significantly higher ratio of shape advertisements (17) to weight-change advertisements (5). Male models in men's magazines help to shape perceptions of the ideal male body. A recent examination of the depiction of male bodies in men's magazines revealed that sexualized and objectified images of men were commonplace. Further, the magazines included content aimed at helping men to either gain muscle mass or lose weight. Photographs and stories in men's magazines do not go unnoticed by males. There is clear evidence that exposure to male models in men's magazines results in depression, anxiety, drive for muscularity, and body image dissatisfaction in males. Men are not alone in their exposure to idealized body images. White preadolescent boys exposed to video game magazines displayed an increased drive for muscularity over a one-year period. Some researchers have suggested that boys have not been taught to be critical of magazine content as girls have, and that this is a necessary step in protecting them from the influence of objectified media images.

Action Figures

Perhaps the most intriguing source of body image influence are the toy action figures played with by many children. Much information about conceptions of the ideal male body can be learned by simply observing how these toys have changed over time. In one study comparing the scaled body measurements of GI Joe figures from the 1970s to the 1990s, the figures exhibited notable growth in their waist (31.7 to 36.5 inches), chest (44.4 to 54.8 inches), and biceps (12.2 to 26.8 inches). Hypermuscular action figures have a negative influence on males' body image. In one study, young adult men who emulated unrealistically muscular action figures had more body image dissatisfaction than men who emulated more life-like action figures.

Programs to Promote Positive Body Image in Males

Given the multifaceted nature of body image dissatisfaction, programs intended to promote healthy body image in males should focus on both psychological and sociocultural factors. The few systematic programs that have been implemented focused on self-esteem, peer relationships, and acceptance of individual differences. However, the programs have yielded mixed results. Professionals interested in developing a program should consider the following guidelines: (a) as previously stated, include a focus on both psychological and sociocultural factors, (b) target older adolescents (15–18 years), as issues of body weight, shape, and size are likely to be more salient for this group than for younger adolescents, and (c) develop programs for specific at-risk populations (e.g., low self-esteem, poor peer relations) rather than all-in-one programs.

Conclusion

Although it was once believed that only women had body image concerns, researchers and practitioners have more recently become aware of growing body dissatisfaction among boys and men. Researchers and practitioners have come to understand a dual-pathway model of body image dissatisfaction in boys and men. The dual-pathway model indicates that both weight and muscularity are important to consider when evaluating body image in males. In extreme cases, males' drive for muscularity may lead to a body image disturbance known as muscle dysmorphia. Muscle dysmorphia is characterized by an obsessive preoccupation with the idea that one's body is too small or weak, along with behaviors (e.g., excessive weight training, supplement use) aimed at achieving greater muscle size and definition. A variety of body biological, psychological, and sociocultural factors contribute to body image dissatisfaction in males. Personality, comments from parents and peers, media images, and hypermuscular action figures are but a few factors that shape males' body image. Body image programs for males should include a focus on both psychological and sociocultural factors, focus on older adolescents (15–18 years), and target specific at-risk populations.

NICK GALLI

See also: Bigorexia; Bodybuilding; Muscle Dysmorphia; Parents.

Bibliography

Adam Drewnowski, and Doris K. Yee. "Men and Body Image: Are Males Satisfied with Their Body Weight?" *Psychosomatic Medicine,* 49 (1987): 626–34.

Cash, Thomas F. "Body-image Attitudes: Evaluation, Investment, and Affect." *Perceptual & Motor Skills* 78 (1994): 1168.

Cash, Thomas F., Barbara A. Winstead, and Louis H. Janda. "The Great American Shape-up: Body Image Survey Report." *Psychology Today* 20 (1986): 30–37.

Hobza, Cody L., and Aaron B. Rochlen. "Gender Role Conflict, Drive for Muscularity, and the Impact of Ideal Media Portrayals on Men." *Psychology of Men & Masculinity* 10 (2009): 120–30.

Jones, Diane C., and Joy K. Crawford. "Adolescent Boys and Body Image: Weight and Muscularity Concerns as Dual Pathways to Body Dissatisfaction." *Journal of Youth & Adolescence* 34 (2005): 629–36.

Lerner, Richard M., and Sam J. Korn. "The Development of Body-Build Stereotypes in Males." *Child Development* 43 (1972): 908–920.

McCabe, Marita P., and Lina A. Ricciardelli. "Parent, Peer, and Media Influences on Body Image and Strategies to Both Increase and Decrease Body Size among Adolescent Boys and Girls." *Adolescence* 36 (2001): 225–40.

Neumark-Sztainer, Dianne, Melanie M. Wall, Mary Story, and Cheryl L. Perry. "Correlates of Unhealthy Weight-Control Behaviors among Adolescents: Implications for Prevention Programs." *Health Psychology* 22 (2003): 88–98.

Pope, Harrison G., David L. Katz, and James I. Hudson. "Anorexia Nervosa and 'Reverse Anorexia' among 108 Male Bodybuilders." *Comprehensive Psychiatry* 34 (1993): 406–409.

Pope, Harrison G., and Roberto Olivardia. "Evolving Ideals of Male Body Image as Seen through Action Toys." *International Journal of Eating Disorders* 26 (1999): 65–72.

BODY MASS INDEX

Body Mass Index (BMI) has been defined as a way to measure whether one is underweight, healthy weight, overweight, or obese. Approximately two-thirds of U.S. adults and one-fifth of U.S. children were considered overweight or obese based on their BMI scores. BMI is calculated by taking body weight in kilograms and dividing by height in meters squared (i.e., kg/m^2). BMI does not measure one's body fat or take into account the size of one's frame.

History of Body Mass Index

The Body Mass Index, originally referred to as the Quetelet Index, was invented in Belgium between 1830 and 1850 by Adolphe Quetelet. The current term "body mass index" was popularized by Ancel Keys in his 1972 paper discussing obesity. The current U.S. BMI charts indicate that having a BMI greater than or equal to 30 is considered obese and that 25 to 29.9 is defined as overweight for adults. Children are measured for BMI using sex-specific, age-growth charts; children at or above the 95th percentile for sex and age are defined as obese; those with BMI between 85th and 95th percentile were considered overweight. Studies using competitive athletes have helped to illustrate the controversy about the measure of obesity, such as a well-known *Journal of the American Medical Association* study that found that 60 percent of National Football League players were overweight or obese. A separate study with varsity high school football players found that 28 percent of players were at risk of being overweight, 45 percent were over-weight, and 9 percent met the criteria for being morbidly obese. While obesity has become a major societal concern, many researchers are using body composition (percentage of body fat) and waist circumference (distance around the small-est point of the waist) in addition to BMI to determine overweight and obesity.

BMI and Eating Disorders

Although the BMI formula has received more attention for assessing levels of obe-sity, BMI can also be used to determine whether an individual is underweight. Generally, optimal weight has been represented by a BMI score between 20 and 25; however, this varies by country. For example, Hong Kong and Japan have stringent cutoffs for overweight (BMI = 23) and obesity (BMI = 25 and higher). The World Health Organization reported that having a BMI less than 18.5 may in-dicate malnutrition or an eating disorder, with severely underweight indicated by a score of less than 16.0. For eating disorders, consideration of being underweight (BMI < 17.5) is often used by medical professionals as an informal criterion for the diagnosis of anorexia nervosa and/or to determine an individual's appropriate level of care. However, BMI is not formally included in the *Diagnostic and Statistical Manual of Mental Disorders, 4th Edition.* Furthermore, BMI is typically monitored in a hospital or residential eating disorder treatment setting to ensure that adequate weight restoration occurs. If BMI drops below a certain level (as determined by the medical provider on an individual basis), the anorexic client may require tube feeding and is likely to be restricted from physical activity (i.e., advised bed rest).

BMI Report Cards

Using BMI for identifying children who are at risk for weight-related problems has been a controversial practice due to the limitations of BMI and the ability to offer adequate education. Some states (e.g., Texas) have introduced BMI report cards in the schools allowing for parents to receive a notification if their children are overweight or obese. There have been concerns about how the weighing takes place and the possibility that focusing on weight could contribute to dieting and disordered eating. Another concern is whether the parents will become the food police once they receive the BMI report card without having the tools to provide healthy meals in the home. See link for more information about how students receive grades for their weight status: http://www.huffingtonpost.com/2011/04/19/bmi-schools_n_850776.html.

Conclusion

The Body Mass Index formula has been popularized as a way to easily screen for overweight and obesity. However, with the focus on monitoring weight in the schools, there comes the likelihood that students and family members will become increasingly more focused on size and bodies. BMI scores have also been used to diagnose eating disorders and monitor weight restoration and maintenance.

JUSTINE J. REEL

Bibliography

Cole, Tim J., Katherine M. Flegal, Dasha Nicholls, and Alan A. Jackson. "Body Mass Index Cut Offs to Define Thinness in Children and Adolescents: International Survey." *British Medical Journal* 335 (2007): 194–202. doi: 10.1136/bmj.39238.399444.55

Dietz, William H., Mary T. Story, and Laura Leviton. "Introduction to Issues and Implications of Screening, Surveillance, and Reporting of Children's BMI." *Pediatrics* 124 (2009): S1–S2.

Harp, Joyce B., and Lindsay Hecht. "Obesity in the National Football League." *Journal of the American Medical Association* 292, no. 24 (2005): 2999. doi: 10.1001/jama.293.9.1061-b

Khan, Laura K., Kathleen Sobush, Dana Keener, Kenneth Goodman, Amy Lowry, Jakub Kakietek, and Susan Zaro. "Recommended Community Strategies and Measurements to Prevent Obesity in the United States." *Morbidity and Mortality Weekly Report: Recommendations and Reports* 58 (2009): 1–29.

Laurson, Kelly R., and Joey C. Eisenmann. "Prevalence of Overweight among High School Football Linemen." *Journal of the American Medical Association* 297, no. 4 (2007): 363–64. doi: 10.1001/jama.297.4.363

Schocker, Laura. "More Schools Including Weight, BMI on Report Cards." *The Huffington Post.* Last modified April 19, 2011. http://www.huffingtonpost.com/2011/04/19/bmi-schools_n_850776.html.

BODYBUILDING

Bodybuilding has been around for over 100 years, but the sport did not become a part of mainstream culture until the 1960s when personalities such as Arnold Schwarzenegger and Lou Ferrigno became household names. However, bodybuilding has continued to slowly increase its visibility supported by magazines such as *Men's Health* and *Flex*.

Although stone lifting, for example, occurred in ancient Greek and Egyptian societies, it was not primarily for physical display as is the case in bodybuilding. The term bodybuilder refers to someone who trains regularly with free weights or machines in order to increase muscularity and reduce body fat for the main purpose of competing. A person who is into bodybuilding engages in weight training to enhance his physique and appearance. However, he does not compete in the sport of bodybuilding. Competitive bodybuilding is generally divided into natural (with drug testing) and nonnatural (no drug testing) competitions.

There are several reasons why someone might want to become a bodybuilder. For both males and females, self-esteem and empowerment, emulation of a hero figure, health reasons, or even previous participation in sports are all frequently cited reasons. A recent study of male bodybuilders found that previous sport participation and emulation were more important than self-esteem in making the decision to become a bodybuilder.

Bodybuilding and Body Image

Competitive bodybuilding and body image are intertwined; after all, how one's image is perceived on stage determines victory or defeat. Therefore, it is not surprising that many bodybuilders exhibit poor body image. It is a vicious cycle wherein a bodybuilder continues to train but is unable to see the improvements made, or feels these improvements are inadequate. In sum, the bodybuilder is unable to accept his or her physique and there is the perception that a body part can be improved in some way.

Although competitive bodybuilders wear revealing attire while they compete, many do not like to expose their bodies for public inspection outside of their

Professional bodybuilders compete for the judges. In pursuit of the desired physique, some bodybuilders resort to performance enhancing drugs. (Corel)

sport. This physique protection demonstrated by many bodybuilders may lead to them wearing bulky clothing to cover their physique or to appear larger. Conversely, other competitive bodybuilders prefer to expose their muscularity and engage in body checking to monitor progress (e.g., mirror checking). These bodybuilders may also seek attention from the opposite sex and other competitors. They may make social comparisons with other bodybuilders during training and competitions.

Competitive bodybuilders are not the only athletes who experience poor body image perceptions. Athletes who weight-train for physique motives but do not compete as bodybuilders have also been found to exhibit similar behaviors as competitive bodybuilders. What is clear is that a continual focus on one's physique can contribute to a negative body image and other harmful practices.

Bodybuilding and Eating Disorders

It is hardly surprising that a bodybuilder who is so focused on his physique relies heavily on a strict nutritional regimen. In fact, most bodybuilders are very knowledgeable regarding nutrition and supplements and take great care monitoring what they put in their bodies. Due to the restrictive practices that are normative in bodybuilding, many competitive bodybuilders exhibit eating practices that resemble clinical eating disorders. Although many competitive bodybuilders are significantly more conscientious about their nutritional habits than the average person, the more accurate label is usually disordered eating unless the practices continue during the off-season.

Because a bodybuilder goes through a period of competition followed by an off-season, nutritional behaviors usually vary radically. During the off-season, the main aim of the competitor is to build as much muscle as possible through anabolism. This dietary practice requires consuming large quantities of both carbohydrates and protein and the bodybuilder is likely to gain substantial weight. Then, during the pre-season which lasts for approximately six to twelve weeks prior to competition, the bodybuilder begins to restrict his or her diet with the intention of burning off fat while retaining muscle mass. During the competitive season, the bodybuilder aims to continue to burn as much fat as possible while retaining muscle mass.

Although this yo-yo dieting follows strict caloric guidelines, there is little doubt that the method in which this restriction occurs is of serious concern. These radical shifts in diet result in extreme changes in weight, and the pre-season can be extremely painful and dangerous. For example, when preparing for a competition, one bodybuilder experienced extreme pain in the soles of his feet caused by lack of fat in the tissue. He also reportedly suffered from dizziness, shortness of breath, increased heart rate and palpitations, and several psychological disturbances. Immediately following a major competition's close, many bodybuilders will gorge themselves on food, as their body has been craving it for days or even weeks. Weight gain is often very rapid and the cycle of weight gain followed by reduction begins for another season.

Conclusion

Although bodybuilding has existed in some form or other for centuries, only within the last 50 years has it gained recognition as a competitive sport. Bodybuilders train religiously, restrict their diets and monitor their bodies and in the process may be prone to physical and psychological consequences associated with disordered eating or body image disturbances. Although the sport is highly focused on physique as a performance measure, it is important not to generalize that all competitive bodybuilders struggle with negative body image and eating disorders. Likewise, other individuals who engage in bodybuilding but do not compete can also express body dissatisfaction and concerns with their physiques.

TIMOTHY M. BAGHURST

Bibliography

Baghurst, Timothy M., and Cathy Lirgg. "Characteristics of Muscle Dysmorphia in Male Football, Weight Training, and Competitive Natural and Non-natural Bodybuilding Samples." *Body Image* 6 (2009): 221–27.

Chapman, David L. *Sandow the Magnificent: Eugen Sandow and the Beginnings of Bodybuilding.* Urbana, IL: University of Illinois Press, 1994.

Fussell, Samuel W. *Muscle.* New York: Avon Books, 1992.

Klein, Alan M. "Special Issue." *Sport in Society* (2007): 1073–1119.

Lambert, Charles P., Laura L. Frank, and William J. Evans. "Macronutrient Considerations for the Sport of Bodybuilding." *Sports Medicine* 34 (2004): 317–27.

Parish, Anthony, Timothy M. Baghurst, and Ronna Turner. "Becoming Competitive Amateur Bodybuilders: Identification of Contributors." *Psychology of Men & Masculinity* 12 (2010): 152–59.

BODYWORKS

The BodyWorks educational program was developed in 2006 by the Office on Women's Health in the U.S. Department of Health and Human Services to teach parents and caregivers of adolescents about healthy nutrition and exercise habits. Using a social cognitive theoretical framework that focuses on both an individual and his or her environment, the BodyWorks curriculum uses parents as role models for healthy behaviors within the family system. Parents are taught experiential lessons with opportunities for hands-on practice of healthy skills. The parent training is conducted through ten 90-minute sessions each week. Adolescents join the parents for two of the sessions to reinforce the lessons and give teenagers an exposure to healthy nutrition and activity concepts.

The BodyWorks program follows a "train-the-trainer" model in which leaders receive training so that they can teach parents in their community. BodyWorks trainers represent almost all of the 50 states. While receiving the training to run the BodyWorks program may vary in cost, a free toolkit is provided to all trainers and parent participants. Toolkits are available electronically on the website http://www.womenshealth.gov. Each toolkit includes guides for parents, teen females and teen males, quizzes, games, and interviews. Additionally, food and fitness journals allow for tracking of eating and exercise behaviors and a recipe book is provided with quick healthy food selections. A meal planner magnet and shopping list (i.e., a form to help families plan weekly menus before they go to the grocery store) are also included in the BodyWorks toolkits.

The BodyWorks program includes lessons regarding portion sizes of fruits, vegetables, and cheese as well as the benefits of various vitamins in the diet. The significance of breakfast and healthy options (e.g., smoothies) are suggested. Fast food alternatives are provided to parents with quick meal ideals and accompanying recipes. Many programs will allow program participants to practice preparing a healthy snack (e.g., fruit kabobs) during the lesson to increase confidence and the likelihood that nutritional choices will be replicated in the home environment. Strategies for increasing the physical activity of teens (e.g., limits on TV times) are also covered to educate parents about obesity prevention.

Implementation of BodyWorks

The BodyWorks program has been implemented in English and Spanish through community-based organizations, state health agencies, nonprofit organizations, health clinics, hospitals, health care systems, and insurance wellness programs. The actual BodyWorks curriculum about nutrition and physical activity is evidence-based; however, more evaluation of individual programs is needed. To date, very little data has been published about the efficacy of the program for changing parent and teen health behaviors.

Conclusion

With the focus on the obesity epidemic in the United States, educational programs have emerged to teach healthy nutritional habits and increase physical activity. The BodyWorks program was designed to train parents about how to create healthier food choices and more access to an active lifestyle so they can serve as role models for their male and female teenagers. Although BodyWorks does not address eating disorders directly, the program promotes a healthy lifestyle rather than using a weight loss approach for addressing the overweight and obesity problem.

JUSTINE J. REEL

Bibliography

"A Project of the U.S. Department of Health and Human Services Office on Women's Health." Womenshealth.gov. Last modified August 22, 2011. http://www.womenshealth.gov.

"BodyWorks." Womenshealth.gov. Last Modified August 22, 2011. http://www.womenshealth.gov/bodyworks/.

Reel, Justine J., Carlie Ashcraft, Rachel Lacy, Robert A. Bucciere, Sonya SooHoo, Donna Richards, and Nicole Mihalopoulos. "Full of Ourselves PLUS: Lessons Learned from an Obesity and Eating Disorder Intervention." *Journal of Sport Psychology in Action* 3, no. 1 (2011): 109–117.

Utz, Rebecca, Darrin Cottle, Kori Fitschen, Julie Metos, Justine Reel, and Nicole Mihalopoulos. "Eat & Live Well: Lessons Learned from an After School Weight Management Program." *Utah's Health: An Annual Review* 13 (2008): 81–88.

BULIMIA NERVOSA

Bulimia Nervosa is a clinical eating disorder that is characterized by cycles of overeating binges followed by purging behavior such as vomiting, laxative abuse, or obligatory exercise. "Bulimia" is a Latin word meaning "hunger of an ox." The practice of overeating and then vomiting was a Roman practice. However, this binge-purge behavior was first documented as a medical case in 1903 by psychiatrist Pierre Janet. Initially, bulimia was considered part of anorexia nervosa and was therefore dubbed as "bulimarexia." However, bulimia nervosa was included as a separate diagnosis in the *Diagnostic and Statistical Manual of Mental Disorders* beginning with the 1980 edition. Many famous celebrities have admitted to suffering from bulimia nervosa including singer Paula Abdul, actress Justine Bateman, and *American Idol* winner Kelly Clarkson. Lady Gaga and Elton John have both discussed their histories with bulimia nervosa. Sharon Osbourne, a television co-host and wife of Ozzy Osbourne, admitted to a 35-year struggle with bulimia nervosa despite having had gastric bypass surgery. Well-known actress and fitness expert, Jane Fonda, discussed being a secret bulimic beginning at age 12 and having an eating disorder for 30 years.

Symptoms of Bulimia Nervosa

In order to be diagnosed as having bulimia nervosa using the *Diagnostic and Statistical Manual of Mental Disorders, 4th Edition, Text Revision* (2000) criteria, individuals must engage in both binge eating episodes and inappropriate compensatory methods. Recurrent binge episodes are described as secretively eating large amounts of food often within a short period of time (usually within a two-hour period). However, binges may last anywhere from 15 minutes to several weeks in duration. Although the binge may start at any time of the day and occur on weekdays or weekends, individuals with bulimia nervosa tend to report having certain days and times of increased vulnerability to binge behavior. A binge is represented by 3 to 30 times the amount of food usually consumed on a typical day. The person experiences a lack of control during the binge episodes, continuing to eat despite feeling full and having a desire to stop eating. Typically, binge foods consist of trigger foods that may be high in calorie, sugar, or fat content such as potato chips, cookies, or ice cream. In fact, individuals may consume thousands of calories (30,000+) in one binge. Individuals may purchase binge foods from multiple drive-through fast food restaurants, contributing to financial strain. Interestingly, the initial motivation behind the binge behavior is the desire to calm emotions, reduce anxiety, or numb uncomfortable feelings. However, following the binge episode, the individual with bulimia nervosa feels intense shame and guilt. In between binge episodes, the individual with bulimia nervosa typically engages in dieting behavior and may restrict forbidden binge foods.

In efforts to prevent weight gain and to dampen feelings of guilt, the food is purged using a compensatory method of choice. Self-induced vomiting may be used, or the individual may misuse laxatives, diuretics, or enemas, or engage in excessive exercise to burn calories. Usually the individual with bulimia nervosa has a preferred method of purging. However, he or she may use different methods depending on

Purging behavior for individuals with bulimia nervosa includes self-induced vomiting. (iStockPhoto)

the setting (e.g., dorm room, home). The binge-purge cycle occurs at least twice a week for at least three months to receive a bulimia nervosa diagnosis. In the current version of the DSM-IV-TR, individuals with bulimia nervosa are separated into purging type and nonpurging type. The purging type is defined as regularly engaging in self-induced vomiting, laxatives, diuretics, or enemas during the current episode of bulimia nervosa. The nonpurging type refers to those using inappropriate compensatory behaviors for the binge such as excessive exercise or fasting without regularly engaging in self-induced vomiting, laxatives, diuretics, or enemas. It is expected that these types within the bulimia nervosa diagnosis will be removed in the next edition of the *Diagnostic and Statistical Manual of Mental Disorders* (DSM-5).

It is important to consider that bulimia nervosa is not solely about eating too much food and feeling compelled to eliminate it afterward. Like anorexia nervosa, individuals with bulimia nervosa express deep concern about body shape, size, and appearance. Body checking (e.g., weighing) and avoidance behaviors (e.g., wearing baggy clothing) are common for individuals with bulimia nervosa. Individuals with bulimia nervosa may appear to be at a normal or slightly-above-normal weight which results in less detection based on weight changes. Individuals with bulimia nervosa struggle with intense body dissatisfaction internally and may feel that they do not deserve to be in eating disorder treatment because they are not thin or sick enough.

Prevalence of Bulimia Nervosa

Because individuals who suffer from bulimia nervosa are secretive about their disorder, the problem may go undetected for many years and it is suspected that the overall prevalence is under-reported. It is estimated that at least 1.0–1.8 percent of college women meet the bulimia nervosa criteria with another 2.6–3.3 percent having characteristics of bulimia nervosa at subclinical levels (disordered eating). Studies vary widely, but generally more adult females (1.5%) than males (0.5%) have bulimia nervosa. In some high school samples, bulimia nervosa rates are reported as much higher (15%) than the adult population. Onset is most commonly during the adolescent and early adulthood years. Recently, however, treatment centers are reporting an insurgence of women in their midlife years with eating disorders triggered by life events (e.g., divorce, menopause).

Personality Characteristics and Coexisting Conditions

Most individuals with bulimia nervosa also suffer from an anxiety disorder or mood disorder (e.g., depression). A relationship has been found between bulimia nervosa and substance abuse as well as sexual promiscuity. As with other eating disorders, individuals with bulimia nervosa may have a history of sexual trauma and in some cases, a traumatic event (e.g., an accident, abuse, divorce) may trigger the onset of binge-purge episodes. Figures for bulimic individuals who report sexual abuse range from 7–70 percent depending on the study. Some individuals with bulimia nervosa also have personality disorders such as borderline, narcissistic, and obsessive-compulsive disorders. Characteristics of being impulsive and compulsive may put individuals with bulimia nervosa at risk for other addictive behaviors (e.g., shopping, gambling, excessive exercise). Therefore, it remains important to teach adaptive coping strategies as part of the treatment process so that individuals with bulimia nervosa do not develop a new addiction. Likewise, body image concerns should be addressed in therapy so that the binge-purge behavior does not evolve into a different type of eating disorder (anorexia nervosa or binge eating disorder).

Health Consequences

Although medical complications will be addressed in more depth in a separate entry, it is important to note that there are numerous medical complications resulting from bulimia nervosa. In addition to mortality, individuals with bulimia nervosa may experience electrolyte imbalances, gastrointestinal difficulties (e.g., constipation, diarrhea), and other symptoms like severe acid reflux, bloating, and dehydration. Oral problems including erosion of tooth enamel, cavities, loss of teeth, gum inflammation, sore throat, and dry mouth frequently occur. Individuals with bulimia nervosa report having cold hands and feet as well as calluses on the back of their hand from vomiting. Additional complications associated with bulimia nervosa include, but are not limited to, internal bleeding, pancreatitis, impaired fertility, compromised bone health leading to osteoporosis, and brain changes. Although less common, some individuals with bulimia nervosa use syrup of ipecac, detergents, or foreign objects to induce vomiting (as a purging method). Abuse of ipecac, a dreadful tasting liquid, can lead to muscle weakness and cardiac arrest.

Conclusion

Bulimia nervosa affects males and females and is considered a separate eating disorder from anorexia nervosa. Specific criteria require both binge and purge episodes to qualify for the bulimia nervosa diagnosis. Because medical complications and health consequences are numerous, it is important for an individual with bulimia nervosa to receive appropriate treatment.

JUSTINE J. REEL

See also: Dehydration; Medical and Health Consequences; Mortality Rates.

Bibliography

Abraham, Suzanne, and Derek Llewellyn-Jones. *Eating Disorders: The Facts.* New York, NY: Oxford University Press, 1995.

American Psychiatric Association. *Diagnostic and Statistical Manual of Mental Disorders, Revised 4th Edition.* Washington, DC: Author, 2000.

Chen, Eunice Yu, Michael S. McCloskey, Sara Michelson, Kathryn H. Gordon, and Emil Coccaro. "Characterizing Eating Disorders in a Personality Disorders Sample." *Psychiatry Research* 185 (2011): 427–32. doi: 10.1016/j.psychres.2010.07.002

Connolly, Anne M., Elizabeth Rieger, and Ian Caterson. "Binge Eating Tendencies and Anger Coping: Investigating the Confound of Trait Neuroticism in a Non-Clinical Sample." *European Eating Disorders Review* 15 (2007): 479–86. doi: 10.1002/erv.765

Costin, Carolyn. *A Comprehensive Guide to the Causes, Treatments and Prevention of Eating Disorders, Third Edition.* New York, NY: McGraw-Hill, 2007.

Costin, Carolyn. *100 Questions & Answers about Eating Disorders.* Sudbury, MA: Jones and Bartlett, 2007.

Courbasson, Christine, and Jacqueline M. Brunshaw. "The Relationship between Concurrent Substance Use Disorders and Eating Disorders with Personality Disorders." *International Journal of Environmental Research and Public Health* 6 (2009): 2076–2089. doi: 10.3390/ijerph6072076

De Bolle, Marleen, Barbara De Clercq, Alexandra Pham-Scottez, Saskia Meis, Jean-Pierre Rolland, Julien D. Guelfi, Caroline Braet, and Filip De Fruyt. "Personality Pathology Comorbidity in Adult Females with Eating Disorders." *Journal of Health Psychology* 16 (2011): 303–313. doi: 10.1177/1359105310374780

Hall, Lindsey, and Leigh Cohn. *Bulimia: A Guide to Recovery.* Carlsbad, CA: Gurze, 2011.

Mehler, Philip S. "Bulimia Nervosa." *The New England Journal of Medicine* 349, no. 9 (2003): 875–82.

Mehler, Philip S., Allison L. Sabel, Tureka Watson, and Arnold E. Andersen. "High Risk of Osteoporosis in Male Patients with Eating Disorders." *International Journal of Eating Disorders* 41, no. 7 (2008): 666–72.

Rowe, Sarah L., Jenny Jordan, Virginia V. W. McIntosh, Frances A. Carter, Chris Frampton, Cynthia M. Bulik, and Peter R. Joyce. "Complex Personality Disorder in Bulimia Nervosa." *Comprehensive Psychiatry* 51 (2010): 592–98.

Sernec, Karin, Martina Tomori, and Bojan Zalar. "Effect of Management of Patients with Anorexia and Bulimia Nervosa on Symptoms and Impulsive Behavior." *Collegium Antropologicum* 34, no. 4 (2010): 1281–1287.

Williams, Kim D., Tracey Dobney, and Josie Geller. "Setting the Eating Disorder Aside: An Alternative Model of Care." *European Eating Disorders Review* 18 (2010): 90–96. doi: 10.1002/erv.989

C

CARPENTER, KAREN

History of Karen Carpenter

Karen Carpenter was a lead singer for the Carpenters, a vocal and instrumental duo in the 1970s. She shocked the world when she died at age 32 from cardiac arrest due to complications associated with anorexia nervosa. During the 1970s hard rock was in great demand, but Karen and her brother Richard Carpenter produced an alternative soft rock musical style and recorded 11 albums during their 14-year career. Karen, who was born in 1950, was identified for her musical talent while still a teenager. In 1966, she sang at a demo session where a trumpet player was auditioning for a part. Los Angeles bassist Joe Osborn stated, "Never mind the trumpet player, this chubby little girl can sing." Some of the Carpenters' hits include "Ticket to Ride" (1969), "Close to You" (1970), and "Rainy Days and Mondays" (1971).

Karen Carpenter and Eating Disorders

Karen's dieting was first observed in 1967 when her doctor placed her on a water diet resulting in marked weight loss over a short period of time. As she continued to drop weight, she was reportedly complimented by others for her appearance. However, by the fall of 1975, Karen's weight had dipped to below 80 pounds and she was abusing thyroid pills, vomiting, and abusing laxatives. Apparently, Karen continued to perform, but was forced to lie down between shows due to her body's weakness. In 1975, Karen collapsed on stage in Las Vegas while performing "Top of the World." When she was hospitalized it was determined that she was 35 pounds underweight and she had an eating disorder. Although she sought treatment for her disorder, she died on February 4, 1983, of a cardiac arrest caused by the strain that anorexia nervosa had placed on her heart. She was 32 years old, 5'4" tall, and weighed 108 pounds.

Her death was significant for raising public awareness regarding anorexia nervosa and advancing eating disorder treatment approaches. Prior to her death, dieting and disordered eating had been seen as normative behavior for teenage girls without cause for alarm or health consequences. The secretive nature of the disorder had kept many individuals feeling that they were struggling alone from the disorder. Following Karen's death, television actress Tracey Gold and Princess

The Carpenters, Richard and Karen, pose with their Grammy during the 13th annual 1970 Grammy Awards in Los Angeles on March 17, 1971. The brother-sister duo was named best new artist of the year and also won as the best contemporary duo. (AP/Wide World Photos)

Diana of Wales revealed that they too had struggled from eating disorders. Eating disorder treatment facilities began to spring up in the 1980s. In June 1985 the country's first residential facility for the treatment of women with eating disorders, the Renfrew Center of Philadelphia Eating Disorders, opened its doors for business.

Conclusion

Many individuals have been secretly struggling from eating disorders and medical cases of anorexia nervosa have been documented over the past century. However, Karen Carpenter's death from an eating disorder brought eating disorders to the attention of the public and medical community. She is a metaphor for the dangerous nature of these disorders and the potential for mortality. Her death helped raise awareness regarding the need for stronger treatment and prevention efforts.

JUSTINE J. REEL

See also: Anorexia Nervosa.

Bibliography

"Anorexia Bulimia Eating Disorder Treatment." Renfrewcenter.com. Accessed August 18, 2011. www.renfrewcenter.com.
"Battling Anorexia: The Story of Karen Carpenter." Think Quest: Library. Accessed August 4, 2011. http://library.thinkquest.org/2129/Mind&Body/Carpenter.html.
"Karen Carpenter Anorexia: The Carpenters; Tragic Loss of Celebrities with Eating Disorders." Anorexia Reflections. Accessed August 4, 2011. http://www.anorexia-reflections.com/karen-carpenter-anorexia.html.
"Karen Carpenter Story." Eating Disorders 411. Accessed August 4, 2011. http://www.eatingdisorders411.com/karen-carpenter-story.html.
Schmidt, Randy L. *Little Girl Blue: The Life of Karen Carpenter.* Chicago, IL: Chicago Reviewer Press, 2010.

CAUSES

The causes of eating disorders are multifaceted and usually include a combination of psychological, familial, sociocultural, and biological or genetic factors rather than a sole determinant of the disorder. Furthermore, not all individuals who possess a genetic predisposition or certain biological factors will develop clinical eating disorders. On the other hand, other individuals who have no family history of anorexia, bulimia nervosa, or substance abuse can still suffer from disordered eating or clinical eating disorders.

Given the difficulties of identifying causal factors at the epidemiological or individual level, some researchers have suggested that identifying the cause may not be nearly as important as identifying the maintaining factors of an eating disorder. One researcher noted that "what starts a disorder may not be what maintains it, and the latter may be of greater practical importance." If the maintaining factors replace the causal factors, the treatment of an eating disorder must focus on what keeps the eating disorder behaviors going. What follows is a brief summary of various factors thought to contribute to the development of eating disorders.

Psychological Factors

Individual factors thought to contribute to the development of an eating disorder can be categorized in terms of cognitive factors, interpersonal experiences, emotions, and degree of body dissatisfaction. With respect to cognitive factors, research findings consistently point to cognitive patterns that are often associated with eating disorders. These patterns can include having obsessive thoughts (a comorbid diagnosis of obsessive-compulsive disorder with anorexia nervosa is not uncommon with lifetime prevalence rates ranging from 9.5% to 62%) about which most clients report feeling frustrated; they also report having attempted to decrease the obsessive thinking. Some clients, however, report a strong identification with these thought patterns and are therefore not invested in making them diminish or disappear. Cognitive patterns associated with eating disorders can also involve perfectionistic thinking which will drive perfectionistic behaviors (e.g., behaviors related to the eating disorder itself or other pursuits such as academics or sport). Some studies have demonstrated that despite being weight restored, individuals with anorexia nervosa will continue to score high on measures of perfectionism. This finding has led some to conclude that perfectionism should be considered as an antecedent of anorexia nervosa and therefore is a causative factor.

Interpersonal experiences that have been consistently linked to eating disorders include trauma, abuse, and teasing. Typically, in the context of eating disorders, the teasing that some individuals experience is focused on weight, and body shape and size. Thus, in an effort to end the teasing, the individual may engage in behaviors intended to change one's weight, body shape, or size, which for some may mean that they engage in eating disorder related behaviors. Some professionals have suggested that the presence of sexual abuse or other forms of abuse and trauma is overestimated in the eating disorder population. However, there is evidence to suggest that the presence of trauma and abuse is associated with eating disorders.

The connection between emotions and eating disorders typically involves the regulation of emotions. Eating disorder related behaviors are often linked to the individual being aware of an unpleasant emotional experience, becoming overwhelmed by his or her feelings, and using eating disorder behaviors as a way to cope with the uncomfortable feelings. Eating disorders can serve as a way to cope with overwhelming emotional experiences (e.g., restricting) and to feel numb to those feelings.

Finally, body dissatisfaction has been strongly linked to eating disorder behaviors and it is included in the diagnostic classification of eating disorders. Some have suggested that body dissatisfaction can be linked to nearly all other potential causative factors. For example, if an individual is teased about her body weight/shape/size and she is dissatisfied with her body an eating disorder may develop. Additionally, an individual who is dissatisfied with his or her body may be more detrimentally affected by media images illustrating the perfect body for his or her sex. Some researchers have also suggested that body dissatisfaction is directly tied to one's sense of self or one's identity. If an individual is dissatisfied with who she is as a person and she remains unclear about how to become more satisfied with herself, she may very well focus her efforts (cognitive, behavioral, interpersonal) on manipulating how she looks if she also has a high degree of body dissatisfaction. Engaging in eating disorder related behaviors, therefore, can be seen as an unhealthy solution to a problem concerning one's identity. If the dissatisfied person can become the one with self-control, or the skinny one or the muscular one, then he or she is likely to experience a sense of purpose and ultimately a sense of self. This identity, of course, is tenuous at best.

Sociocultural Factors

There are a multitude of sociocultural factors that have been linked to eating disorders. One such factor involves living in a culture where food resources are abundant. In such cultures there is a corresponding valuation of thinness as the preferred physique for females, whereas in cultures where food is scarce, a larger female body type tends to be idealized. This idealization of a specific physique is often discussed in terms of the "thin ideal" for females; however, recently there has been recognition that the "muscular ideal" is the standard to which males in abundant cultures are typically held. Regardless of the particular standard, many studies have pointed to the importance of Western cultures as being contributing factors to the development of eating disorders.

Another sociocultural factor involves media influences. Numerous studies have been conducted to examine the effect of various media on self-esteem and self-worth, cognitions around the desire to achieve the ideal standard, etc. Typically, media images often portray unrealistic images of both males and females. Those individuals portrayed often represent a statistical minority or are engaged in extraordinary (and potentially harmful) behaviors to achieve this ideal body type.

The above findings are tempered by a recent meta-analysis of studies examining the influence of cultural factors on the development of eating disorders. The findings from this study suggested that eating disorders *may* be culture-bound syndromes. This depends in part on which eating disorder is being considered and how an eating disorder is defined (not all researchers faithfully follow DSM diagnostic criteria or apply the criteria in the same way). Therefore, while culture may have the types of influences noted above, it is best and probably more accurate to take into account the myriad other potential factors that will be briefly discussed below in this section and the sections that follow.

The effect of one's peers on various maladaptive behaviors has been studied widely and has included eating disorders. Researchers indicate that individuals with eating disorders can learn or perfect their pathogenic eating-related behaviors from peers. Additionally, they may share similar attitudes and beliefs with respect to a desire to achieve a specific body type which will probably result in the entrenching of these attitudes and beliefs. While changing peer groups will not necessarily prevent an eating disorder from developing, the evidence does suggest that the peers with whom one associates can be potentially harmful.

Although the sociocultural factors discussed above demonstrate converging evidence for their impact on the development and maintenance of eating disorders, Polivy and Herman (2002) remind us that these influences are "so broad and pervasive that [they] ought to cause more pathology than actually occurs." The fact remains that eating disorders only exist in a small minority of individuals exposed to these factors. Therefore if these factors were causative in the way that many believe they are, we would see a much higher incidence of eating disorders.

Familial Factors

Historically, familial factors were blamed for causing eating disorders. To date, there are numerous studies documenting familial influences on eating disorders, including the encouragement of eating disorder related behavior by family members. For example, family members may reinforce efforts to lose weight or express envy about the individual's slimness or ability to exhibit self-control. Additionally, other studies have pointed to certain family dynamics (e.g., being highly critical, intrusive, hostile, emotionally dismissive) as breeding grounds for eating disorders. Evidence has also been reported that daughters of mothers with eating disorders can be particularly negatively influenced by their mothers' own struggles with these disorders and as a result can develop their own eating disorder.

Few research studies examining the impact of the family on the development of eating disorders are experimental in nature, which means that the findings reported above are correlational. Thus, the dysfunctional family dynamics often reported when a family member has an eating disorder may mean that the presence of the eating disorder itself may be a causal factor in the dysfunction and not the other way round. Moreover, individuals with eating disorders can also be found in families where dysfunctional family dynamics do not exist. Thus, many have declared that it is no longer appropriate to consider families as causal agents of eating disorders. In fact, the Academy for Eating Disorders (AED) has published a position statement asserting "whereas family factors can play a role in the genesis and maintenance of eating disorders, current knowledge refutes the idea that they are either the exclusive or even the primary mechanisms that underlie risk." AED continued by stating that the organization "condemns generalizing statements that imply families are to blame for their child's illness." Therefore, as is the case with sociocultural factors, to the extent that families have any impact on the development of eating disorders it is clear that the emergence of an eating disorder is dependent on factors apart from familial factors.

Genetic Factors

Genetic studies (i.e., studies on factors that are inherited from one's biological relatives) usually involve investigating families and twins of individuals with eating disorders. Historically, reports of eating disorders running in families have relied on imprecise data collection methods and definitions of the disorders, anecdotal reports, and other nonrigorous methods. Contemporary studies of family transmission processes are well designed and have the benefit of a diagnostic classification system that can help make identifying individuals with various forms of eating disorders more accurate. Thus, these studies have revealed that eating disorders are much more common in families that have biological relatives with eating disorders in comparison to the population at large. This in part supports the notion that genetics plays a role in the presence of an eating disorder.

Twin studies help to parcel out the question of whether or not the findings revealed in family studies reflect the intergenerational transmission of genetic material or environmental influences. Studies examining monozygotic and dizygotic twins indicate that monozygotic twins are more likely to show both individuals of the twin dyad with an eating disorder than dizygotic twins. This finding provides additional evidence for the genetic transmission of eating disorders. Genetic researchers caution, however, that it is important to consider all possible causes for the development of eating disorders. It has been suggested that "[t]he search for etiological processes must, however, retain its broad perspective, because the pathways to symptom formation are multiple and interactive."

Conclusion

In conclusion, there is no single factor identified as the primary causative agent in the development of eating disorders. Rather there are a multitude of factors involving the individual himself or herself, the environment in which he or she exists, and physiological and genetic processes. When these combine in the right way for a particular individual then an eating disorder can emerge; however, predicting what the right conditions are for any one person is probably an impossibility.

CHRISTINE L. B. SELBY

Bibliography

Collier, David A., and Janet L. Treasure. "The Aetiology of Eating Disorders." *British Journal of Psychiatry* 185, no. 5 (2004): 363–65.

Godart, Nathalie T., M. F. Flament, F. Perdereau, and P. Jeammet. "Comorbidity between Eating Disorders and Anxiety Disorders: A Review." *International Journal of Eating Disorders* 32, no. 3 (2002): 253–70.

Keel, Pamela K., and Kelly L. Klump. "Are Eating Disorders Culture-Bound Syndromes? Implications for Conceptualizing Their Etiology." *Psychological Bulletin* 129, no. 5 (2003): 747–69.

le Grange, Daniel, James Lock, Katharine Loeb, and Dasha Nicholls. "Academy for Eating Disorders Position Paper: The Role of the Family in Eating Disorders." *International Journal of Eating Disorders* 43, no. 1 (2010): 1–5.

Palmer, Bob. "Causes of Eating Disorders." In *ABC of Eating Disorders,* edited by Jane Morris, 5–8. Williston, VT: Wiley-Blackwell Publishing, 2008.

Polivy, Janet, and C. Peter Herman. "Causes of Eating Disorders." *Annual Review of Psychology* 53 (2002): 187–213.

Schmidt, Ulrike. "Aetiology of Eating Disorders in the 21st Century: New Answers to Old Questions." *European Child & Adolescent Psychiatry [Suppl 1]* 12 (2003): 30–37.

Strober, Michael, and Cynthia M. Bulik. "Genetic Epidemiology of Eating Disorders." In *Eating Disorders and Obesity: A Comprehensive Handbook,* edited by Christopher G. Fairburn and Kelly D. Brownell, 238–42. New York: The Guilford Press, 2002.

CHEERLEADING

History of Cheering

More than three million individuals compete in cheerleading across the United States. Although cheerleaders are often stereotyped as blonde, bubbly, and beautiful women, the first cheerleaders were male yell leaders in the 1890s. Beginning in the 1920s, all-male squads comprised of highly masculine members who performed stunts and gymnastics to the delight of the crowds at college football games. Females were restricted from cheerleading participation due to fear of masculinization associated with raising and deepening one's voice and participating in a highly athletic endeavor. However, despite numerous female bans from cheerleading that were documented in both high schools and colleges into the 1950s, females entered the sport during World War II and were there to stay. Cheerleading grew more competitive and formalized in the 1980s, and ESPN televised the first national high school competition in 1981. The majority of today's cheerleaders are affiliated with junior highs, high schools, and colleges, but the squads may compete in national competitions. In the 1990s, all-star cheerleading competition squads emerged with the sole purpose of training and competing in local, regional, and national competitions without cheering for any particular team. Interestingly, when females entered the sport, cheerleading became regarded as a highly feminine endeavor despite the fact that males continued to participate. With increased opportunity to participate in competitions, difficulty levels have increased and led the way for stringent weight requirements.

Body Image and Cheerleading

In addition to gymnastics and figure skating, cheerleading is considered an aesthetic sport that values appearance as a successful component of performance. In cheerleading, being lighter has generally been associated with more opportunity to become a flyer (the most desirable cheerleading position due to higher visibility than the base position) and more difficult partner stunts. The gymnastic elements of cheerleading also promote a lean physique with the perception that it improves the ability to perform flips and handsprings.

Few studies examining female athletes and body image have included cheerleaders. However, one study found that 70 percent of high school female cheerleaders were dissatisfied with their bodies. In another study, 34 percent of cheerleaders admitted to fasting to lose weight and another 30 percent reported vomiting to control weight. A researcher at University of South Carolina estimated eating disorder risk for college cheerleaders at 33 percent and found that flyers (i.e., cheerleaders who are thrown in the air during stunts) were more at risk for disordered eating and body image dissatisfaction than other cheerleading positions (e.g., base). In a separate 1996 study that included both college and high school cheerleaders, Reel and Gill found that of 157 high school and college cheerleaders, 84 percent reported feeling pressured due to cheerleading to lose weight or maintain an unhealthy weight. In this study, weight pressures specific to the sport of cheerleading were identified.

Weight Pressures

Cheerleaders at the college level reported significantly more sport-specific weight pressures than high school cheerleaders. Conversely, high school cheerleaders were more likely to report stronger body dissatisfaction, social physique anxiety, and eating disorder tendencies. Overall the most frequently reported weight pressure (58%) for competitive cheerleaders was the revealing team uniform. However, other sport-specific pressures included peers, stunt partner, coaches, a perceived performance advantage, and weight requirements for the sport including weigh-ins.

Uniform

The majority of high school (61%) and college (54%) female cheerleaders felt the team uniform contributed to pressure to lose weight or control eating to maintain an unhealthy size as compared with 41% of male cheerleaders. Over the decades cheerleading uniforms have become more revealing and tighter fitting. Cheerleaders experienced the greatest body image dissatisfaction when wearing their most revealing uniforms that displayed midriffs. Interviews with adolescent competitive cheerleaders aged 10 to 17 years demonstrated that uniforms often contributed to self-conscious feelings due to lack of coverage. One 16-year-old cheerleader explained, "it [the uniform] makes it hard sometimes because of the things we wear with the short skirts and tight shirts . . . everyone is looking at you . . . things bother me when I wear my uniform." The increasingly more revealing uniforms have sparked some controversy in the news. The conservative fans and alumni at University of Idaho protested the short skirts and skimpy tops when the new cheerleading coach released an updated uniform, and this resulted in the team ordering more modest replacement uniforms: http://www.foxnews.com/story/0,2933,426270,00.html.

Coach and Other Pressures

Another noteworthy pressure among competitive cheerleaders and other athletes is the coach. In cheerleading, 70 percent of female college cheerleaders, 88 percent of male college cheerleaders, and 25 percent of high school cheerleaders felt that weight was important to their coaches. Furthermore, 49 percent of female and 65 percent of male college cheerleaders were subjected to a weight limit to try out and 40 percent of college cheerleaders had weigh-ins throughout the season to monitor body weight for their current cheerleading squad.

Being the flyer on the squad was associated with more pressure to stay light and more risk for disordered eating. Having different weight expectations by position (flyer versus base) meant comparison with other teammates to determine who would score the prestigious flyer role.

Stunt partners who lifted and threw other cheerleaders noticed when flyers gained weight. Therefore, 42 percent of high school and 30 percent of college cheerleaders reported the stunt partner as a weight pressure. It is likely that the ability to execute difficult stunts resulted in a perceived performance advantage with lower weight, which was expressed by 43 percent of college and 38 percent of high school cheerleaders.

Conclusion

Celebrities Paula Abdul and Nicole "Snooki" Polizzi, who were both former cheerleaders, have disclosed their eating disorder histories. Snooki from the television show *Jersey Shore* admitted that her eating disorder started in high school because she was worried about being replaced on the cheerleading squad by thinner and younger freshmen females. Cheerleading is a unique sport that combines appearance expectations with gymnastic and stunting skills designed to entertain a crowd. Body image concerns among college cheerleaders have included pressures to lose weight and maintain low weights for females and pressures to gain weight, strength, and muscles for males. Competitive cheerleaders report the revealing team uniforms, coaches, position type, and weight requirements most frequently as sport-specific pressures.

JUSTINE J. REEL

See also: Aesthetic Sports; Body Dissatisfaction; Coaches; Figure Skating; Gymnastics; Social Physique Anxiety.

Bibliography

Associated Press. "Cheerleaders Ditch Skimpy Uniforms after Complaints from Fans." FOXNEWS.com. Last modified September 23, 2008. http://www.foxnews.com/story/0,2933,426270,00.html

Lundholm, Jean K., and John M. Litrell. "Desire for Thinness among High School Cheerleaders: Relationship to Disordered Eating and Weight Control Behaviors." *Adolescence* 83 (1986): 573–79.

Reel, Justine J., and Diane L. Gill. "Psychosocial Factors Related to Eating Disorders among High School and College Female Cheerleaders." *The Sport Psychologist* 10 (1996): 195–206.

Reel, Justine J., and Diane L. Gill. "Weight Concerns and Disordered Eating Attitudes among Male and Female College Cheerleaders." *Women in Sport and Physical Activity* 7, no. 2 (1998): 79–94.

SooHoo, Sonya. "Social Construction of Body Image among Female Adolescent Cheerleaders." PhD Dissertation, University of Utah, 2008.

Taub, Diane E., and Blinde, Elaine M. "Disordered Eating and Weight Control among Adolescent Female Athletes and Performance Squad Members." *Journal of Adolescent Research* 9 (1994): 483–97.

Torres-McGehee, Toni. "Eating Disorder Risk and the Role of Clothing on Body Image in College Cheerleaders." *Journal of Athletic Training* 45, no. 5 (2012): In Press.

CHILDREN AND ADOLESCENTS

Introduction and Prevalence of Eating Disorders

Historically, eating disorders have been most commonly associated with females in their late teens and early twenties. Individuals beyond the college years were assumed to outgrow eating disorders and body issues. Children and early adolescent boys and girls were thought to be too young to think about dieting or engage in disordered eating. However, a recent news story discussed young children aged five to seven years who were already showing signs of eating disorders: http://parentables.howstuffworks.com/health-wellness/study-finds-5-year-olds-being-treated-eating-disorders.html.

Alarmingly, the American Academy of Pediatrics issued a 2010 report that brought attention to the increased prevalence of eating disorders in children and adolescents. Specifically, hospitalizations for eating disorders rose 119 percent between 1999 and 2006 for children younger than 12 years of age. Eating disorders represent the most common psychiatric problem among adolescents, and mortality rates for anorexia nervosa are among the highest for any psychiatric disorder. It is estimated that less than 1 percent of adolescent girls in the United States meet the criteria for anorexia nervosa, 1.0–3.0 percent for bulimia nervosa, and 0.8–14.0 percent fall into the Eating Disorder Not Otherwise Specified category. In a Canadian study, it was found that the incidence of restrictive eating disorders among children was two times greater than the incidence of type 2 diabetes among all children younger than 18 years of age. Similar to other health problems, pediatricians often serve as the first line of defense for eating disorder detection. Unfortunately, although the eating disorders have the potential to cause health problems and medical complications in children and adolescents, treatment for this population has often been ineffective in addressing restrictive behaviors and eating disorders.

Barriers to Treatment of Children and Adolescents

There are many barriers associated with children and adolescents receiving treatment for eating disorders. Firstly, many individuals under 18 years of age seek treatment on an involuntary basis rather than making the choice to enter therapy. Clients who feel they have been pushed into treatment may not feel ready or motivated to change their behaviors or discard their eating disorder identity. Furthermore, children and adolescents may discover that treatment is usually centered around individual therapy and participating in group therapy with other adults. Younger individuals may lack the cognitive development to process their thoughts and feelings related to their disorder. Additionally, children and adolescents often learn the disordered eating behaviors from their peers and such behavior is often part of their normative culture. If children and adolescents receive treatment in a residential or inpatient setting, they will return to a system (e.g., family and peers) that represents the same pressures and dynamics that contributed to the eating disorder in the first place. Family members may lack the insight to manage or support the child or adolescent when he or she returns to the home.

Treatment Recommendations for Children and Adolescents

Adolescents and children who can be treated in outpatient and inpatient settings should receive care from a physician, dietitian, and mental health therapist. The family pediatrician may refer the client to a physician or psychiatrist who specializes in monitoring and managing eating disorders. It is important for these treatment professionals to collaborate with one another to form an outpatient treatment team. Medical stabilization and developing healthy eating will be important goals for the initial phase of treatment. However, addressing mental health concerns and psychological factors that contributed to the eating disorder will require ongoing care. Mental health professionals may find that everything from alternative forms of therapy such as art therapy, equine therapy and yoga therapy to the traditional "talk therapy" are needed to reach the younger client. It is generally recommended that family members receive education and be part of the treatment plan. A popular approach for family therapy, the Maudsley approach, is discussed in detail in another entry.

Conclusion

Although eating disorders represent the most common psychiatric disorders among adolescents, most treatment approaches for eating disorders have been developed for adults. Prevalence rates among children and adolescents have increased and it is important to have early detection and treatment for these individuals. Barriers to treatment include involuntary participation and family dynamics which may exacerbate the eating disorder. Treatment for this younger population should include a variety of treatment professionals and needs to involve an education and therapy component for family members.

JUSTINE J. REEL

See also: Art Therapy; Equine Therapy; Maudsley Family Therapy; Yoga.

Bibliography

Copeland, Blythe. "Study Finds 5-Year-Olds Being Treated for Eating Disorders." *Parentables.* Last modified August 5, 2011. http://parentables.howstuffworks.com/health-well ness/study-finds-5-year-olds-being-treated-eating-disorders.html.

Eddy, Kamryn T., Daniel le Grange, Ross D. Crosby, Renee Rienecke Hoste, Angela Celio Doyle, Angela Smyth, and David B. Herzog. "Diagnostic Classification of Eating Disorders in Children and Adolescents: How Does DSM-IV-TR Compare to Empirically-Derived Categories?" *Journal of American Academy of Child and Adolescent Psychiatry* 49, no. 3 (2010): 277–93.

Lock James, and Kathleen Kara Fitzpatrick. "Advances in Psychotherapy for Children and Adolescents with Eating Disorders." *American Journal of Psychotherapy* 63, no. 4 (2009): 287–303.

Lock, James. "Treatment of Adolescent Eating Disorders: Progress and Challenges." *Minerva Psichiatrica* 51, no. 3 (2010): 207–216.

Loeb, Katharine L., Diel Le Grange, Tom Hildebrandt, Rebecca Greif, James Lock, and Lauren Alfano. "Eating Disorders in Youth: Diagnostic Variability and Predictive Validity." *International Journal of Eating Disorders* 44 (2010): 1–11.

Pinhas, Leora, Anne Morris, Ross D. Crosby, and Debra K. Katzman. "Incidence and Age-Specific Presentation of Restrictive Eating Disorders in Children." *Archives of Pediatric Adolescent Medicine* 165, no. 10 (2011): 895–99.

Rosen, David S. "Identification and Management of Eating Disorders in Children and Adolescents." *Pediatrics* 126 (2010): 1240–1253.

Sinton, Meghan M., Andrea B. Goldschmidt, Vandana Aspen, Kelly R. Theim, Richard L. Stein, Brian E. Saeiens, Leonard H. Epstein, and Denise E. Wilfley. "Psychosocial Correlates of Shape and Weight Concerns in Overweight Pre-Adolescents." *Journal of Youth Adolescence* Online June 22 (2011): 1–9. doi: 10.1007/s10964-011-9686-y.

COACHES

Coaches of sports teams are employed to teach sports skills, devise strategies, and improve the performance of athletes of all ages and competitive levels. Coaches are viewed as experts regarding the sport-specific demands, nutrition, strength and conditioning, and injury concerns. As a result, many athletes unconditionally accept the coaching recommendations with hopes of achieving a competitive edge despite the potential for short- and long-term consequences (e.g., injuries). Some coaching recommendations are related to size, weight, and appearance and have been linked to pathogenic weight control methods and severe health concerns (e.g., eating disorders).

Weight-Related Coach Pressure

Athletes may experience pressure from their coaches to lose weight or maintain a low body weight in the pursuit of improved sport performance. Moreover, weight-related coach pressure may be reinforced by the use of weekly weigh-ins or weight-related tryout requirements. Coaches may also directly state weight-related goals for an athlete or team or may engage in teasing athletes about their weight, shape, or size. In one study, 50–70 percent of cheerleaders believed that weight was important to their coach and almost 20 percent reported having coaches who openly encouraged weight loss.

Consequently, athletes who hear of weight concerns from coaches and others are almost three times more likely to develop unhealthy eating patterns (e.g., eating disorders and disordered eating). In one study, nearly half of the athletes who reported experiencing past coach comments to lose weight or maintain a low body weight felt upset and more self-conscious as a result of those comments. Unfortunately, the negative impact of coach comments regarding weight increases as the frequency and severity of those comments increases, leaving the athlete feeling more upset and more self-conscious.

As a coach's job is to make athletes better—to win—coaches may notice what they perceive to be excessive weight on an athlete and recommend weight loss with the intention to help an athlete improve his or her performance. It should be noted that many coaches probably give this advice based on the misguided belief that reduced weight improves performance rather than on scientific evidence. Although some coaches may encourage their athletes to lose weight inadvertently through public weigh-ins, uniform choice, or weight requirements, other coaches may bench athletes or cut athletes from the team if they do not "make weight." If the athlete feels that the coaching recommendations are credible and he or she wants to avoid consequences (e.g., public humiliation, being benched), disordered eating behaviors (e.g., restricting calories or certain foods) may seem like the logical choice. Likewise, if the athlete experiences initial performance improvement after losing some initial weight, he or she may be more motivated to continue disordered eating behaviors to lose additional weight.

Sources of Weight-Related Coach Pressure

Whether or not athletes perceive pressure from their coaches to lose weight or maintain a low body weight through direct instructions to lose weight, athletes who perceive weight-related pressure tend to believe that they *need* to lose weight, exhibit more disordered eating behaviors, and are diagnosed with eating disorders more often than athletes who have not experienced similar weight-related coach pressures. Research has even indicated that perceived weight-related coach pressure can have a stronger effect on elite athletes' dietary patterns than their previous perceptions about their bodies.

Coach-Athlete Relationship

Experienced coaches understand that the coach-athlete relationship has a large impact on the athlete's entire life. Athletes who report a strong relationship with their coaches feel more support and less conflict than athletes who report having a weak coach-athlete relationship. Although research on coach-athlete relationships and eating disorders is sparse, one study indicated that the coach-athlete relationship predicted 25 percent of disordered eating behaviors in youth athletes. That is, weak coach-athlete relationships were associated with disordered eating behaviors such that they accounted for 25 percent of the difference in disordered eating scores; they did not explain the other 75 percent of the difference in disordered eating behavior scores.

Conclusion

Although coaches are not the only contributing factor associated with the development of eating disorders and disordered eating patterns, coaches play an influential role in determining the importance of weight, size, and shape for athletes. Many factors contribute to the development of eating disorders and disordered eating patterns in athletes, but when an athlete becomes invested in the coach's suggestion to lose weight, dieting and disordered eating behaviors may be the unfortunate result.

ASHLEY M. COKER-CRANNEY

Bibliography

Berry, Tanya R., and Bruce L. Howe. "Risk Factors for Disordered Eating in Female University Athletes." *Journal of Sport Behavior* 23 (2000): 207–218.

de Bruin, A. P. (Karin), Raoul R. D. Oudejans, and Frank C. Bakker. "Dieting and Body Image in Aesthetic Sports: A Comparison of Dutch Female Gymnasts and Non-Aesthetic Sport Participants." *Psychology of Sport and Exercise* 8 (2007): 507–520.

Harris, Mary B, and Debbie Greco. "Weight Control and Weight Concern in Competitive Female Gymnasts." *Journal of Sport & Exercise Psychology* 12 (1990): 427–33.

Jowett, Sophia, and Duncan Cramer. "The Prediction of Young Athletes' Physical Self from Perceptions of Relationships with Parents and Coaches." *Psychology of Sport and Exercise* 11 (2010): 140–47.

Kerr, Gretchen, Erica Berman, and Mary Jane De Souza. "Disordered Eating in Women's Gymnastics: Perspectives of Athletes, Coaches, Parents, and Judges." *Journal of Applied Sport Psychology* 18 (2006): 28–43.

Muscat, Anne C., and Bonita C. Long. "Critical Comments About Body Shape and Weight: Disordered Eating of Female Athletes and Sport Participants." *Journal of Applied Sport Psychology* 20 (2005): 1–24.

Reel, Justine J., and Diane L. Gill. "Psychosocial Factors Related to Eating Disorders among High School and College Female Cheerleaders." *The Sport Psychologist* 10 (1996): 195–206.

Reel, Justine J., Sonya SooHoo, Trent A. Petrie, Christie Greenleaf, and Jennifer E. Carter. "Slimming Down for Sport: Developing a Weight Pressures in Sport Measure for Female Athletes." *Journal of Clinical Psychology* 4 (2010): 99–111.

Thompson, Ron A., and Roberta Trattner Sherman. *Eating Disorders in Sport.* New York: Routledge, 2010.

Waldron, Jennifer J., and Vikki Krane. "Whatever It Takes: Health Compromising Behaviors in Female Athletes." *QUEST* 57 (2000): 315–29.

Williams, Patti L., Roger G. Sargent, and Larry J. Durstine. "Prevalence of Subclinical Eating Disorders in Collegiate Female Athletes." *Women in Sport & Physical Activity Journal* 12 (2003): 127–45.

COGNITIVE BEHAVIORAL THERAPY (CBT)

Definition

Cognitive behavioral therapy (CBT) is a psychotherapeutic approach that addresses dysfunctional emotions, behaviors, and cognitions through a goal-oriented procedure. CBT has been used as an umbrella term to refer to therapies that share a foundation in behavior learning theory and cognitive psychology. The goals of CBT are to challenge the thoughts about troubling personal situations by identifying the cognitive traps, and to help the client identify less disturbing thoughts and behaviors which can then be tested in real life situations.

CBT is an evidence-based treatment for a variety of mental disorders including mood disorders, anxiety disorders, personality disorders, eating disorders, substance abuse disorders, and psychotic disorders. CBT is often brief and time-limited and is used in both individual therapy and group settings. CBT techniques can also be adapted for self-help applications, such as replacing destructive thoughts with verbal personal compliments while looking in the mirror. CBT therapists identify and monitor thoughts, assumptions, beliefs, and behaviors that are related to and accompanied by debilitating negative emotions. The therapist guides the client to replace or transcend inaccurate or unhelpful emotions with realistic and useful cognitive and behavioral tools.

History

The infancy of CBT can be traced back to the development of behavior therapy in the early 20th century, the development of cognitive therapy in the 1960s, and the subsequent merging of the two. Behavioral approaches appeared as early as 1924, with Mary Cover Jones's work on the unlearning of fears in children. However, between 1950 and 1970, the field emerged with researchers who were inspired by the behaviorist learning theories of Ivan Pavlov, John Watson, and Clark Hull. Psychologists also began applying the radical behaviorism of B.F. Skinner to clinical use.

CBT was primarily developed through a merging of behavior therapy with cognitive therapy during the late 1980s and early 1990s. While rooted in rather different theories, cognitive and behavioral therapies found common ground in focusing on the "here and now" and symptom removal. Many CBT treatment programs have since been developed to address symptoms of specific disorders such as depression, anxiety, and eating disorders. The health care trend of evidence-based treatment has favored CBT over other approaches such as psychodynamic treatments. For example, in the United Kingdom, the National Institute of Health and Clinical Excellence recommends CBT as the treatment of choice for bulimia nervosa.

In the 1960s, cognitive therapy rapidly became a frequently used intervention based on the work of Albert Ellis who developed Rational Emotive Behavior Therapy in the early 1950s. Aaron Beck, inspired by Ellis, became known as the father of cognitive therapy and the inventor of the widely used Beck Scales. Beck also distinguished three levels of cognition that cause and maintain psychopathology: (1) schemas/core beliefs, which are internal models of the self and the world that develop over the course of experiences beginning early in life. Schemas may lie dormant until they are activated by conditions similar to those under which they originally developed; (2) maladaptive assumptions, which include "must/should" and "if-then" statements; and (3) automatic thoughts, which include negative view of self, negative view of the future, and negative view of the world. During the 1980s and 1990s, cognitive and behavioral techniques were merged into cognitive behavioral therapy. Core beliefs often fuel the development of eating disorders. Maladaptive assumptions and automatic thoughts contribute to the maintenance of eating disorder symptoms, including a negative view of the inner self and a negative image of the physical body. As such, addressing the three levels of cognition assists the eating disorder client to achieve relief from symptoms and to begin healing.

Techniques

CBT techniques commonly include: (1) keeping a diary of significant events and associated feelings, thoughts, and behaviors; (2) questioning and testing cognitions, assumptions, evaluations, and beliefs that might be unhelpful and unrealistic; (3) gradually facing activities which may have been avoided; and (4) trying out new ways of behaving and reacting. Relaxation, mindfulness, and distraction techniques are also commonly used. More specific to keeping a diary is maintaining a dysfunctional thought record, which is used to identify, evaluate, and change automatic thoughts. A thought record has columns for objectively describing triggering situations and associated automatic thoughts and emotions, and alternative, self-enhancing responses.

Eating Disorders

CBT as a therapeutic approach can treat all eating disorders regardless of actual diagnosis. Diaries of events, for example, can be useful for binge eaters to track the time, the amount of food consumed, and emotional triggers of a binge over a certain period. Patterns can then be identified, and unhelpful thoughts are recorded in thought records along with healthy thought substitutes. Additionally, individuals who suffer from anorexia nervosa can try eating a forbidden food at a restaurant with a support person. Someone with bulimia nervosa may be challenged to take a walk or write in a journal for 45 minutes following a meal or until the urge to purge abates.

Furthermore, CBT for anorexia nervosa employs behavioral strategies including the establishment of a regular pattern of eating and systematic exposure to several forbidden foods, while simultaneously addressing cognitive aspects of the disorder such as motivation for change and the disturbance in the experience of shape and weight. Specifically, what are the client's reasons for seeking treatment? Is motivation internal? How does the individual view the physical body and what are the automatic thoughts associated with examining the body in a mirror or other reflection? CBT challenges schema-level core beliefs and the inextricable tie between personal identity, body image, and the eating disorder. Healing is facilitated, for example, by a change in core beliefs about the value of the self from the inside out, thus reducing the desire to control the physical weight or appearance. CBT has also become a leading treatment for bulimia nervosa. For instance, a thought record can be used to track automatic thoughts that occur prior to, during, and after a binge. Helpful thoughts are suggested to replace automatic thoughts and the client is encouraged keep a written record of results. Additionally, replacement behaviors (walks, journaling, visiting with supportive friends) are recommended following meals to help the client avoid purging until the feeling passes. A similar thought record can be used for binge eating disorder. Food diaries can be coupled with thought records to help the client identify the pattern of binge behaviors and the amount of food consumed during binges. Behaviors to replace binge episodes are suggested. Automatic thoughts and feelings associated with new behaviors are monitored and replacement thoughts are suggested. Ideally, the replacement thoughts become the automatic thoughts as the client ventures into emotional health and well-being.

Obstacles

Obstacles to using CBT in early intervention include excessive avoidance, dissociation, anger, grief, extreme anxiety, catastrophic beliefs, prior trauma, comorbidity (specifically borderline personality disorder and psychotic disorders), substance abuse, depression and suicide risk, poor motivation, ongoing stressors, and certain cultural issues. Dissociation, for example, occurs when an individual detaches from the present or escapes to a safe emotional place because present thoughts or feelings remind him or her of a traumatic past event and are too painful to endure. The detachment can interfere with the person's ability to focus on the here-and-now, a premise of CBT. Dissociation is often seen in other disorders such as borderline personality disorder and schizophrenia. Therefore, having more than one diagnosis can impair a client's ability to positively respond to CBT. Substance abuse, for instance, chemically removes the client from here-and-now reality and thus reduces the effectiveness of CBT.

Conclusion

In summary, CBT is an evidence-based treatment for many mental disorders including mood disorders, anxiety disorders, personality disorders, eating disorders, substance abuse disorders, and psychotic disorders. CBT was developed through a merging of behavior therapy with cognitive therapy during the late 1980s and early 1990s and is now widely used in the treatment of eating disorders. Common behavioral strategies include the establishment of regular eating patterns and exposure to forbidden foods. Cognitive aspects simultaneously address issues such as motivation for change and the disturbance in the experience of body shape and weight. Although obstacles to treatment exist, CBT remains a primary intervention for the management of eating disorders.

JULIANN M. COOK

Bibliography

Alford, Brad, and Aaron Beck. *The Integrative Power of Cognitive Therapy.* New York: The Guilford Press, 1998.

Beck, Aaron T. *Cognitive Therapy and Emotional Disorders.* International Universities Press Inc., 1975.

Beck, Aaron T., John A. Rush, Brian F. Shaw, and Gary Emery. *Cognitive Therapy of Depression.* New York: The Guilford Press, 1979.

Fairburn, Christopher G., Zafra Cooper, and Roz Shafran. "Enhanced Cognitive Behavior Therapy for Eating Disorders (CBT-E): An Overview." *Cognitive Behavior Therapy and Eating Disorders.* New York: Guilford, 2008.

Halmi, Katherine A., W. Stewart Agras, Scott Crow, James Mitchell, G. Terrance Wilson, Susan W. Bryson, and Helena C. Kraemer. "Predictors of Treatment Acceptance and Completion in Anorexia Nervosa: Implications for Future Study Designs." *Archives of General Psychiatry* 62, no. 7 (2005): 776–81.

COMORBIDITY

Comorbidity is defined as the co-occurrence of more than one mental disorder and is sometimes referred to as a dual diagnosis. Eating disorders have high rates of coexisting with other mental illnesses. In fact, mood disorders, which represent the most common comorbid condition, are usually estimated to coexist with eating disorders at 50 percent. However, one study that separated participants by type of eating disorder diagnosis found that mood disorders are present in 64.1–96.0 percent of clients with anorexia nervosa, and in 50–90 percent of clients with bulimia nervosa.

It is important to consider any comorbid conditions with eating disorders for treatment planning in order to maximize successful treatment outcomes and increase the chances of recovery. In addition to depression, it is common for individuals with eating disorders to concurrently be diagnosed with an anxiety disorder or obsessive-compulsive disorder (OCD). Additionally, eating disordered clients may also present with bipolar disorder (i.e., a mood disorder with periods of mania and depression), substance abuse, personality disorders, a history of trauma, or self-harming behaviors. These conditions are discussed in separate entries of this volume.

Clients should be assessed for the potential for overlap in psychiatric conditions and treated accordingly. For example, clients who are diagnosed with depression and eating disorders may receive psychotropic medications which may help lessen the intensity of emotional triggers to engage in eating disorders as well as improve overall mood. The client with comorbid conditions may appear more resistant to treatment recommendations. However, it is important to establish which diagnosis should receive primary diagnosis status and match treatment accordingly. For example, individuals who have both a substance abuse issue and an eating disorder should be assessed carefully for placement in an eating disorder specialty or substance abuse treatment center for appropriate care. On a positive note, many eating disorder facilities have recognized the high prevalence of comorbidity and offer dual diagnosis treatment.

Conclusion

Comorbidity refers to the co-occurrence of mental disorders. Individuals with eating disorders may also receive a diagnosis for another mental disorder such as a mood or anxiety disorder, OCD, or substance abuse. These comorbid conditions are considered during assessment to inform appropriate level of care and treatment recommendations.

JUSTINE J. REEL

See also: Levels of Care.

Bibliography

Bardone-Cone, Anna M., Megan B. Harney, Christine R. Maldonado, Melissa A. Lawson, D. Paul Robinson, Roma Smith, and Aneesh Tosh. "Defining Recovery from an Eating Disorder: Conceptualization, Validation, and Examination of Psychosocial Functioning and Psychiatric Comorbidity." *Behaviour Research and Therapy* 48, no. 3 (2010): 194–202. doi: 10.1016/j.brat.2009.11.001.

Jordan, Jennifer, Peter R. Joyce, Frances A. Carter, Jacqueline Horn, Virginia V. W. McIntosh, Suzanne E. Luty, Janice M. McKenzie, Christopher M. A. Frampton, Roger T. Mulder, and Cynthia M. Bulik. "Specific and Nonspecific Comorbidity in Anorexia Nervosa." *International Journal of Eating Disorders* 41, no. 1 (2008): 47–56. doi: 10.1002/eat.

McElroy, Susan L., Renu Kotwal, and Paul E. Keck. "Comorbidity of Eating Disorders and Bipolar Disorder and Treatment Implications." *Bipolar Disorders* 8 (2006): 686–95.

Mischoulon, David, Kamry T. Eddy, Aparna Keshaviah, Diana Dinescu, Stephanie L. Ross, Andrea E. Kass, Debra L. Franko, and David B. Herzog. "Depression and Eating Disorders: Treatment and Course." *Journal of Affective Disorders* 130 (2011): 470–77. doi: 10.1016/j.jad.2010.10.043.

D

DANCERS

Dance has been used for ceremony, rituals, and entertainment since the earliest days of human civilization. Although ballet was formalized in 18th-century Italy and France (e.g., Paris Opera), other forms of dance (e.g., modern dance) emerged a few centuries later. Relative to body image and eating disorder concerns, ballet (which is typically represented by thin and feminine dancers) has received the most notoriety in the media and in research. However, other forms of dance (e.g., modern and belly dance) have important implications for body identity and health and will be discussed in this entry. Modern dance is particularly salient to cover because some dancers who are trained in classical ballet are encouraged to change to modern dance if their body does not fit the ballet ideal.

Modern Dance

Modern dance, which was later dubbed as contemporary dance, emerged in the early 20th century. Modern dance is typically perceived as a more forgiving form of dance than ballet. For example, unlike ballerinas who traditionally wear black leotards and pink tights to train, modern dancers are given more flexibility to choose training attire and sometimes costumes. However, in body image studies, modern dancers tend to report body dissatisfaction equivalent to those of ballet dancers and high levels of social physique anxiety (i.e., anxiety surrounding one's physique or body shape).

Body Image

Modern dancers in university dance programs revealed that they experienced significant weight pressures associated with preparing to become professional dancers. Despite the stereotypes of modern dance being more forgiving of body type, dancers felt constrained by the desires of various choreographers who would be making hiring decisions for the next dancers in their company. Modern dancers reported that choreographers had distinct preferences in height, size, and appearance of dancers based upon the aesthetic being created in the performance. In some cases, the decision of which dancer was hired came down to who could fit into the last dancer's costume. Most frequently reported weight pressures for college modern dancers included mirrors (100%), costumes (99%), performance advantages (97%), other dancers (83%), and the audience (70%). Like their ballet counterparts, modern dancers felt that weight was not the sole feature of the ideal dancer's body. However, the majority (65%) of dancers stated that they would perform better if they lost five pounds.

Eating Disorders

Modern dancers in university settings have reported strong body dissatisfaction and pressure to lose weight; however, they have shown lower rates of disordered eating and clinical eating disorders than ballet samples. In one study, college modern dancers reported controlling their weight by excessively exercising (39%), fasting (38%), restricting fat or calories (29%), and vomiting (26%). Another 29 percent of dancers reported using fad diets and 14 percent wore plastic clothing to maintain low body weight or lose weight. Interestingly, 23 percent of dancers admitted to smoking cigarettes to control their weight, underscoring the health risk associated with the weight-focused nature of the dance culture.

Belly Dance

History and Costumes of Belly Dance

Belly dance, the Western label for traditional Middle Eastern dance or Arabic dance, has roots in the Middle East and North Africa. Belly dancing originated as a dance dedicated to the goddess of fertility and for entertainment purposes. In the United States, belly dancing first received attention in the late 19th century at the Chicago World Fair. During the 1960s and 1970s, belly dancing in the United States grew as a performance and participatory activity and has recently been valued as a form of exercise.

Belly dance, which is in Egypt, Lebanon, Turkey, the United States, and Canada, has different costume variations depending on the country. In Egypt, women have been prohibited from baring their midriffs or showing excessive skin since the 1950s. The Egyptian belly dance costume typically consists of a long, form-fitting, one-piece Lycra gown with sheer body stocking to cover the midsection. By contrast, in Lebanon and Turkey belly dancers wear bedleh style costumes which have shorter skirts and more sheer material with midriff showing. American belly dancers' costumes resemble those from Egypt or Turkey but also include a headband with fringe instead of a veil. Women may choose to wear harem pants or a skirt rather than the Egyptian Lycra gown.

Body Image of Belly Dance

The costume for belly dance is widely recognized for its revealing characteristics and decorative flourishes that may leave a bare midriff and plunging neckline. However, compared to other forms of dance, belly dance tends to use costuming as a way to accentuate the female form. Belly dancers also report less body dissatisfaction or desire to change their bodies than modern dancers and ballet dancers. Only 18 percent of female belly dance participants were dissatisfied with their bodies in one study. This percentage is considerably lower than dancer or nondance populations of females. Likewise, belly dancers did not experience the same types of weight pressures (e.g., choreographer, other dancers, performance advantage) reported by modern dancers. Audience scrutiny (40%) was the sole pressure reported by belly dancers who as a whole reported a supportive, body-accepting community of dancers. Curves were celebrated and belly dance seemed to play a positive role in promoting positive body image and health.

Other Types of Dance

Similar to belly dance, street dancers have reported being more satisfied with their bodies than other dancers or nondancers. Street dance became popularized in the 1970s with the Jackson 5 and the television show *Soul Train*. Meanwhile, hip-hop dance from Jamaica emerged in the United States in 1967, with b-boys and b-girls performing breakdancing movements on the streets. These dance styles (e.g., breakdancing, locking, krumping, popping) have evolved outside of formal settings and have typically been improvisational and social in nature. More recently, these dance trends have expanded to exercise settings (e.g., cardio funk or hip-hop aerobics classes) and televised reality show competitions (e.g., *So You Think You Can Dance?*). In a rare study of 83 female street dancers, it was discovered that street dancers reported higher body appreciation than nondancers, reflecting a higher tendency toward body acceptance. More body image research is needed to investigate specific body image concerns and disordered eating rates within street dance as well as other types of dance such as folk dance, ballroom dance, and jazz dance.

Conclusion

Dance involves the display of one's body for performance and entertainment. Although ballet has been associated with eating disorders in movies like *Black Swan* and the death of Heidi Guenther, other kinds of dancers may not experience the same types of body-related pressures. In fact, belly dance seemed to have a positive influence on body image due to the accepting nature of the dancing community.

JUSTINE J. REEL

See also: Ballet; Social Physique Anxiety; Weight Pressures in Sport.

Bibliography

Clabaugh, Alison, and Beth Morling. "Stereotype Accuracy of Ballet and Modern Dancers." *The Journal of Social Psychology* 144, no. 1 (2004): 31–48.

Downey, Dennis J., Justine J. Reel, Sonya SooHoo, and Sandrine Zerbib. "Body Image in Belly Dance: Integrating Norms into Collective Identity." *Journal of Gender Studies* 19, no. 4 (2010): 377–93. doi: 10.1080/09589236.2010.514209

Langdon, Susan W., and Gina Petracca. "Tiny Dancer: Body Image and Dancer Identity in Female Modern Dancers." *Body Image* 7 (2010): 360–63. doi: 10.1016/j.bodyim.2010.06.005.

Reel, Justine J., Sonya SooHoo, Katherine M. Jamieson, and Diane L. Gill. "Femininity to the Extreme: Body Image Concerns among College Female Dancers." *Women in Sport and Physical Activity Journal* 14, no. 1 (2005): 39–51.

Swami, Viren, and Martin J. Tovee. "A Comparison of Actual-Ideal Weight Discrepancy, Body Appreciation, and Media Influence between Street-Dancers and Non-Dancers." *Body Image* 6 (2009): 304–307.

Tiggemann, Marika, and Amy Slater. "A Test of Objectification Theory in Former Dancers and Non-Dancers." *Psychology of Women Quarterly* 25 (2001): 57–64. doi: 10.111j/1471-6402.00007

Wright, Jan, and Shoshana Dreyfus. "Belly Dancing: A Feminist Project?" *Women in Sport and Physical Activity Journal* 7, no. 2 (1998): 95–114.

DEHYDRATION

Dehydration occurs when the body receives inadequate fluid intake to maintain bodily systems. Six to ten cups of noncaffeinated, nonalcoholic beverages daily are required to maintain fluid balance in the body. Fluid requirements increase with exercise, and consuming six to eight ounces of fluid every 15 minutes during exercise is necessary to maintain proper hydration status.

Eating Disorders and Dehydration

Individuals with eating disorders may experience dehydration resulting from self-induced vomiting, diuretic abuse, and laxative use behaviors. An eating disordered individual may also avoid drinking fluids due to fear of weight gain, leading to liquid restriction, including water. Individuals who abuse laxatives and diuretics are often motivated to lose a large amount of weight in a short period of time. However, most of the weight loss from these purging methods is from water loss and dehydration. Therefore, these pounds will be regained once an individual's hydration status is returned to normal. Severe dehydration can lead to alterations in electrolytes and cause kidney failure and cardiac problems.

Laboratory tests help confirm dehydration in eating disordered individuals. Blood tests may show high blood urea nitrogen and fluctuations in serum sodium. A urinalysis may show an elevation in an individual's urine specific gravity. In individuals who purge, lab results may reveal a metabolic alkalosis (increased serum bicarbonate). In addition to dehydration, eating disordered individuals who purge can also experience electrolyte abnormalities, including hypokalemia (low serum potassium), hyponatremia (low serum sodium), hypomagnesemia (low serum magnesium), and hypercalcemia (low calcium). Dehydration triggers the body's rennin-angiotensin system, which results in secretion of high levels of the hormone aldosterone from the adrenal cortex. This occurs to prevent low blood pressure and fainting in the presence of ongoing purging behaviors or fluid restriction.

Clinical Manifestations

An individual who is dehydrated may experience constipation, dizziness, light-headedness, and weakness. The individual may also complain of headache, dry mouth, dry skin, and muscle cramps. Decreased urine output, low blood pressure, and tachycardia (high heart rate) may also occur. In severe cases of dehydration, confusion, breathing difficulty, seizures, kidney damage, and death is possible.

Orthostatic Hypotension

It is not unusual for a dehydrated individual to experience orthostatic hypotension. This is a form of hypotension in which the individual's blood pressure suddenly falls when he or she shifts from a sitting to a standing position. The most common symptom of orthostatic hypotension is a feeling of dizziness on standing up. However, this marked drop in blood pressure can cause fainting, blurred vision, confusion, and nausea.

Treatment

Dehydrated individuals are treated with aggressive oral hydration, or in severe cases, intravenous infusions of sodium chloride saline in order to shut off the renin-angiotensin system and stop aldosterone production. Individuals who are being rehydrated need to be carefully monitored for electrolyte imbalances. In hypokalemic individuals, high levels of aldosterone will continue to cause potassium loss if dehydration is not treated first. In eating disordered individuals who have significant hyponatremia (low sodium), saline solutions should be run slowly to prevent the development of a neurological complication called central pontine myelinolysis. Rapid infusions may cause edema in some individuals. Doctors need to reassure these individuals that edema will resolve with continuing treatment and avoiding eating disorder behaviors.

Conclusion

Dehydration can occur when the body receives inadequate fluid intake to maintain body functioning. Eating disordered individuals often become dehydrated due to inconsistent eating and drinking patterns as well as use of laxatives and diuretics. Dehydration should be avoided due to medical complications and may require oral hydration treatment.

SHELLY GUILLORY

Bibliography

Brunzell, Carol, and Mary Hendrickson-Nelson. "An Overview of Nutrition." In *The Outpatient Treatment of Eating Disorder: A Guide for Therapists, Dietitians, and Physicians,* edited by James E. Mitchell, 222–23. Minneapolis: University of Minnesota Press, 2001.

"Dehydration." MayoClinic.com. Last modified in November 2011. Accessed May 20, 2011. http://www.mayoclinic.com/health/dehydration/DS00561.

Mehler, Philip S, and Arnold E. Anderson. "Evaluation and Treatment of Electrolyte Abnormalities." *Eating Disorders: A Guide to Medical Care and Complications, 2nd ed.,* 97–107. Baltimore: Johns Hopkins University Press, 2010.

Miller, Karen K., Steven K. Grinspoon, Julia Ciampa, Joan Hier, David Herzog, and Ajnne Klibanski. "Medical Findings of Outpatients with Eating Disorders." *Archives of Internal Medicine* 135, no. 5. (2005): 561–66. http://archinte.ama-assn.org/cgi/re print/165/5/561.

"Orthostatic Hypotension." MayoClinic.com. Last modified in July 2009. Accessed May 20, 2011. http://www.mayoclinic.com/health/orthostatic-hypotension/DS00997

DEPRESSION

Depression is a type of affective or mood disorder that is characterized by depressed mood, sadness, low energy, fatigue, and feelings of hopelessness. Depression in the form of Major Depressive Disorder or another type of mood disorder commonly exists among individuals who have an eating disorder. Over half of clients with eating disorders are thought to have a mood disorder, but some studies have found even higher rates when considering age, type of eating disorder, and level of care. For example, one study found that the prevalence of mood disorders varied between 64.1 percent and 96 percent for individuals, whereas a more recent study found the comorbidity rate to be between 12.7 percent and 68 percent for anorexia nervosa. By contrast, 50–90 percent of individuals with bulimia nervosa were reported to suffer from a mood disorder compared to a current comorbidity rate of 40 percent.

Explanations for Overlap between Depression and Eating Disorders

Although it is difficult to come to a clear conclusion regarding whether depression causes the eating disorder or the other way round, there have been several theories forwarded to explain the coexistence of depression and eating disorders. One theory is that depression might pave the way for an eating disorder since the depressed mood may contribute to reduced sleep and increased vulnerability to stress and dysfunctional coping strategies. A second explanation is that both disorders may be the outgrowth of a common foundation. Genetic factors are related for depression and eating disorders, and it is common for individuals with eating disorders to have a family history of depression. Another possible explanation for the co-occurrence of depression and eating disorders is that the eating disorder may lead to increased vulnerability for depression. A further complication is that starvation can produce physiological and psychological symptoms that resemble depression diagnostic criteria.

Conclusion

Depression represents the highest comorbidity with eating disorders. Although prevalence rates vary for co-occurrence, it is generally believed that 50 percent of eating disorder clients suffer from depression. It is difficult to determine whether eating disorders lead to depression, whether depression causes the eating disorder, or whether both conditions arise from a shared causal foundation (e.g., genetic, psychological).

JUSTINE J. REEL

Bibliography

Casper, Regina C. "Depression and Eating Disorders." *Depression and Anxiety* 8, no. 1 (1998): 96–104.

Ferreiro, Tatima, Gloria Seoane, and Carmen Senra. "A Prospective Study of Risk Factors for the Development of Depression and Disordered Eating in Adolescents." *Journal of Clinical Child & Adolescent Psychology* 40, no. 3 (2011): 500–505.

Giovanni, Abbate-Daga, Carla Gramaglia Carla, Enrica Marzola, Federico Amianto, Maria Zuccolin, and Secondo Fassino. "Eating Disorders and Major Depression: Role of Anger and Personality." *Depression Research and Treatment* (2011): 1–7. doi: 10.1155/2011/194732.

Mischoulon, David, Kamry T. Eddy, Aparna Keshaviah, Diana Dinescu, Stephanie L. Ross, Andrea E. Kass, Debra L. Franko, and David B. Herzog. "Depression and Eating Disorders: Treatment and Course." *Journal of Affective Disorders* 130 (2011): 470–77. doi: 10.1016/j.jad.2010.10.043.

Touchett, Evelyne, Adina Henegar, Nathalie T. Godart, Laura Pryor, Bruno Falissard, Richard E. Tremblay, and Sylvana M. Cote. "Subclinical Eating Disorders and Their Comorbidity with Mood and Anxiety Disorders in Adolescent Girls." *Psychiatry Research* 185 (2011): 185–92. doi: 10.1016/j.psychres.2010.04.005.

DIABETES

Individuals with type 1 diabetes, an autoimmune disease in which the pancreas ceases to produce insulin, represent a high risk group for eating disorders and subclinical eating disorders. This is often referred to as diabulimia. Insulin is a hormone that helps regulate blood glucose levels. Type 1 diabetes is managed by routinely self-administering insulin, checking blood glucose levels, and monitoring the dietary intake of carbohydrate, which increases blood sugar levels. Although overexercising, binge eating, purging, dietary restriction, and laxative abuse are disordered eating behaviors present among the general population, insulin omission is a weight control behavior unique to eating disordered individuals with type 1 diabetes. Neglecting to take one's prescribed insulin has been identified as an alternative method of purging. Missing insulin doses or taking less insulin than required can cause blood sugar levels to rise and the kidneys must then work to rid the body of excess blood sugar, which results in rapid weight loss.

Rates of diagnosable eating disorders and subclinical eating disturbances among the diabetic population have varied across studies, depending on how eating disorders were defined. According to the results of many research studies, the prevalence of bulimia nervosa, but not anorexia nervosa, has been found to be higher in female adolescents and adults with type 1 diabetes compared to age-matched peers. A higher prevalence of subclinical eating disorders among females with type 1 diabetes is also a common finding, especially when insulin omission is included as a weight loss method. The prevalence of eating disorders among males who have type 1 diabetes and individuals with type 2 diabetes is unknown.

Risk Factors

Similar to eating disorders among the general population, psychological, physical, and family factors have been associated with eating disorders among individuals with type 1 diabetes. These include low self-esteem, depression, perfectionism and borderline personality characteristics, negative and avoidant coping styles, body dissatisfaction, a higher BMI and being overweight, parental dieting behaviors and negative eating attitudes, infrequent family meals, and impaired family functioning. There may also be specific aspects of diabetes management, which may increase risk for developing eating disorders.

Diabetes Care and Weight Gain

Weight loss is a common symptom of new onset type 1 diabetes; consequently, once an insulin regimen is established to manage blood sugar levels, weight gain occurs. The fear of excessive weight gain with improved blood glucose may lead some individuals to omit insulin as a weight loss method. Weight-related concerns may also stem from experiencing hypoglycemia (i.e., low blood sugar levels) in that additional calories must be consumed in order to normalize levels or that they will be triggered to overeat. Interestingly, some individuals with both type 1 diabetes and eating disorders initially restricted insulin to avoid hypoglycemia or other issues that impact one's adherence to diabetes management. When they noticed the resulting weight loss from not taking their medicine, they were motivated to continue the disordered behavior.

Preoccupation with Food

Dietary management of type 1 diabetes involves monitoring carbohydrate intake. Although current dietary regimens allow considerably more flexibility than traditional meal planning for diabetes in terms of how strict limits on the types and amounts of food are no longer promoted, it has been suggested that constant awareness of food portions and carbohydrate content could reinforce perfectionism, rigid thinking about food, and dietary restraint in individuals who are already at risk for eating disorders. Dietary restraint may lead to hypoglycemia and binge eating episodes, which, in turn, may lead to insulin omission to avoid weight gain.

Stressors Related to Diabetes Management

The strict regimen required for diabetes management may trigger feelings of having a low sense of control over one's life. The pubertal years, in particular, are a time when individuals strive for more autonomy and control over their lives. However, due to rapid growth and development, insulin requirements are greater and glycemic control may be more difficult to achieve during adolescence. The increased responsibilities and changes associated with diabetes management during adolescence may adversely impact one's sense of control and engaging in disordered eating behaviors may be a resultant coping strategy. Promoting an environment of autonomy in conjunction with addressing the challenges of diabetes management can be difficult for families to balance. Individuals with diabetes may feel a loss of independence if family members are overprotective or anxious with regard to their health and diabetes regimen. On the other hand, the lack of familial support and validation may contribute to feelings of helplessness and ineffectiveness in individuals with diabetes. Similarly, the perceived lack of support from health professionals has been described by people with concurrent type 1 diabetes and eating disorders. Those who adhere to a diabetes care regimen and yet are unable to achieve the standards placed for them by health professionals may experience feelings of hopelessness and depression, especially if they are receiving consistent disapproval from their provider as well as family.

Health Consequences

The combination of type 1 diabetes and eating disorder behaviors is associated with poor blood sugar control. Thus, individuals face an increased risk for diabetes-related medical complications, including diabetic ketoacidosis, an acute life-threatening complication in which a shortage of insulin in the body promotes high blood sugar levels. Because the body cannot use blood glucose for energy without insulin, there is an increased breakdown of fat for energy, and the production of acidic ketone bodies. This condition leads to dehydration and electrolyte imbalances; symptoms include nausea, vomiting, abdominal pain, confusion, and, if not treated quickly, loss of consciousness, fluid swelling in the brain, and even death. Treatment requires hospitalization. Health consequences of having both type 1 diabetes and eating disorders also include an increased risk for diseases of the smallest arteries of the body, particularly damage to the eye (diabetic retinopathy), which can lead to blindness, kidney disease (nephropathy), and nerve damage (neuropathy), which can affect many organ systems. Furthermore, higher mortality rates have been reported among clients with both eating disorders and diabetes than either diagnosis by itself.

Management of Diabetes

Routine use of an effective and efficient screening tool that considers diabetes-related risk factors for disordered eating is important for early detection and intervention. A multidisciplinary team approach that includes, but is not limited to, an endocrinologist (a physician who specializes in treating hormonal diseases) to assist clients with developing an appropriate insulin regimen, diabetes nurse educator (nurses who maintain a special certification in diabetes) to provide education on various aspects of diabetes management as needed, such as how to correctly monitor blood sugar levels and provide insulin injections, a registered dietitian to provide dietary education and counseling, and a psychotherapist to provide mental health counseling and address the underlying thoughts and feelings that contribute to disordered eating is the standard of care for addressing various aspects of treatment for concurrent eating disorders and type 1 diabetes. Established treatments for eating disorders may be implemented, but should be modified to address insulin omission, glycemic control, and diabetes-related risk factors.

It is suggested that small, gradual goals can be negotiated with the client to improve diabetes care and eating disorder recovery and to decrease the risk of relapse. For example, instead of the fully prescribed amount of multiple insulin injections per day, clients may start with twice per day insulin injections as a manageable first step. It is important to discuss fears related to diabetes management (e.g., weight gain with insulin restart, hypoglycemia). The treatment provider should also offer education and coping skills to help reduce stress and discomfort with the treatment plan. Family therapy may also be beneficial in terms of fostering communication and support among family members.

Conclusion

Diabulimia refers to a subgroup of eating disordered individuals who also suffer from type 1 diabetes. As part of their disordered eating behaviors, they neglect to take their prescribed insulin resulting in weight loss. However, medical consequences of forgoing insulin are severe and it is important to properly treat and manage diabetes as a first step in addressing eating disorder concerns.

HOLLY E. DOETSCH

See also: Dietary Restraint.

Bibliography

Daneman, Denis, Gary Rodin, Jennifer Jones, Patricia Colton, Anne Rydall, Sherry Maharaj, and Marion Olmsted. "Eating Disorders in Adolescent Girls and Young Adult Women with Type 1 Diabetes." *Diabetes Spectrum* 15, no. 2 (2002): 83–105.

Goebel-Fabbri, Ann E. "Disturbed Eating Behaviors and Eating Disorders in Type 1 Diabetes: Clinical Significance and Treatment Recommendations." *Current Diabetes Reports* 9 (2009): 133–39.

Hillege, Sharon, Barbara Beale, and Rose McMaster. "The Impact of Type 1 Diabetes and Eating Disorders: The Perspective of Individuals." *Journal of Clinical Nursing* 17, no. 7B (2008): 169–76.

Jones, Jennifer M., Margaret L. Lawson, Denis Daneman, Marion P. Olmsted, and Gary Rodin. "Eating Disorders in Adolescent Females with and without Type 1 Diabetes: Cross Sectional Study." *British Medical Journal* 320, no. 7249 (2000): 1563–1566.

Maharaj, Sherry I., Gary M. Rodin, Marion P. Olmsted, and Denis Daneman. "Eating Disturbances, Diabetes, and the Family: An Empirical Study." *Journal of Psychosomatic Research* 44, no. 3–4 (1998): 479–90.

Maharaj, Sherry I., Gary M. Rodin, Marion P. Olmsted, Jennifer A. Connolly, and Denis Daneman. "Eating Disturbances in Girls with Diabetes: The Contribution of Adolescent

Self-Concept, Maternal Weight and Shape Concerns and Mother-Daughter Relationships." *Psychological Medicine* 33, no. 3 (2003): 525–39.

Mannucci, Edoardo, Francesco Rotella, Valdo Ricca, Sandra Moretti, Gian F. Placidi, and Carlo M. Rotella. "Eating Disorders in Patients with Type 1 Diabetes: A Meta-analysis." *Journal of Endocrinological Investigation* 28 (2005): 417–19.

Markowitz, Jessica T., Michael R. Lowe, Lisa K. Volkening, and Lori M. B. Laffel. "Self-reported History of Overweight and its Relationship to Disordered Eating in Adolescent Girls with Type 1 Diabetes." *Diabetic Medicine* 26, no. 11 (2009): 1165–1171.

Mellin, Allison E., Dianne Neumark-Sztainer, Joan Patterson, and Joseph Sockalosky. "Unhealthy Weight Management Behavior among Adolescent Girls with Type 1 Diabetes Mellitus: The Role of Familial Eating Patterns and Weight-Related Concerns." *Journal of Adolescent Health* 35, no. 4 (2004): 278–89.

Nielsen, Soren. "Eating Disorders in Females with Type 1 Diabetes: An Update of a Meta-analysis." *European Eating Disorders Review* 10, no. 4 (2002): 241–54.

Nielsen, Soren, Charlotte Emborg, and Anne-Grethe Molbak. "Mortality in Concurrent Type 1 Diabetes and Anorexia Nervosa." *Diabetes Care* 25 (2002): 309–312.

Olmsted, Marion P., Patricia A. Colton, Denis Daneman, Anne C. Rydall, and Gary M. Rodin. "Prediction of the Onset of Disturbed Eating Behavior in Adolescent Girls with Type 1 Diabetes." *Diabetes Care* 31, no. 10 (2008): 1978–1982.

Peveler, Robert C., Kathryn S. Bryden, H. Andrew W. Neil, Christopher G. Fairburn, Richard A. Mayou, David B. Dunger, and Hannah M. Turner. "The Relationship of Disordered Eating Habits and Attitudes to Clinical Outcomes in Young Adult Females with Type 1 Diabetes." *Diabetes Care* 28 (2005): 84–88.

Pollock-BarZiv, Stacey M., and Caroline Davis. "Personality Factors and Disordered Eating in Young Women with Type 1 Diabetes Mellitus." *Psychosomatics* 46 (2005): 11–18.

Rydall, Anne C., Gary M. Rodin, Marion P. Olmsted, Robert G. Devenyi, and Denis Daneman. "Disordered Eating Behavior and Microvascular Complications in Young Women with Insulin-Dependent Diabetes Mellitus." *New England Journal of Medicine* 336 (1997): 1849–1854.

Steel, Judith M., Robert J. Young, Geoffrey G. Lloyd, and Basil F. Clarke. "Clinically Apparent Eating Disorders in Young Diabetic Women: Associations with Painful Neuropathy and other Complications." *British Medical Journal* 294, no. 6576 (1987): 859–62.

Walker, James D., Robert J. Young, Jill Little, and Judith M. Steel. "Mortality in Concurrent Type 1 Diabetes and Anorexia Nervosa." *Diabetes Care* 25 (2002): 1664–1665.

Young-Hyman, Deborah L., and Catherine L. Davis. "Disordered Eating Behavior in Individuals with Diabetes." *Diabetes Care* 33, no. 3 (2010): 683–89.

DIAGNOSTIC INTERVIEW

The diagnostic interview, which is commonly referred to as the clinical interview, is a well-established way to assess for eating disorders in both clinical and research settings. Used in a clinical setting, a diagnostic interview can provide valuable information to guide the treatment planning process and can help to establish rapport and "buy in" for treatment. It is necessary to identify symptoms and formulate an accurate diagnosis (e.g., anorexia nervosa, bulimia nervosa, eating disorder not otherwise specified) to develop treatment approach and facilitate health insurance support for payment if relevant.

The advantage of using a diagnostic interview rather than a standardized questionnaire is that clients can respond in their own words to key questions. Clinicians who can begin to build trust with clients can also read nonverbal cues allowing for follow-up questions to gather more in-depth information. Like other forms of assessment (e.g., eating disorder questionnaires), the information provided in a diagnostic interview is self-report. Therefore, the challenge is whether the client feels comfortable enough to share the level and intensity of the problem and whether memory creates a bias in what information is reported. It is not uncommon for eating disordered individuals to minimize their symptoms or normalize their eating behaviors during a diagnostic interview.

Topics Covered during a Diagnostic Interview

In order to understand the complexity of an eating disorder case and to provide an individualized treatment approach, questions should be asked about all possible types of disordered eating symptoms ranging from binge eating episodes to restricting and purging behaviors. If a client admits to engaging in a particular behavior, it is critical to gauge the intensity and frequency of its occurrence. For example, an interviewer should ask, "How often did you binge in the last week?" and "Can you tell me more specifically what you ate during your last binge?" In addition to eating patterns, the interviewer should ask about body weight, body image and dissatisfaction, and overall self-worth. In order to understand a client's level of body preoccupation, the interviewer will ask about body checking and body avoidance behaviors. Finally, clinicians will attempt to ascertain whether any comorbid conditions are present, such as substance abuse, depression, anxiety, or personality disorders.

Conclusion

The diagnostic interview is considered the gold standard for eating disorder assessment in both research and clinical settings. Diagnostic interviews can inform diagnostic decisions, treatment planning, and prognosis. Allowing for a more guided approach, the interviewer can cover a greater depth and breadth of questions while establishing a rapport with the eating disordered individual. Like other self-report measures, it is important to consider the potential of an individual to minimize symptoms. Therefore, whenever possible, follow-up questions can be asked to allow for increased specificity of responses and improve accuracy of information.

JUSTINE J. REEL

See also: Body Avoidance; Body Checking.

Bibliography

Cooper, Zafra, and Christopher Fairburn. "The Eating Disorder Examination: A Semi-structured Interview for the Assessment of the Specific Psychopathology of Eating Disorders." *International Journal of Eating Disorders* 6, no. 1 (1987): 1–8.

Goldfein, Juli A., Michael J. Devlin, and Claudia Kamenetz. "Eating Disorder Examination-Questionnaire with and without Instruction to Assess Binge Eating in Patients with Binge Eating Disorder." *International Journal of Eating Disorders* 37, no. 2 (2005): 107–111. doi: 10.1002/eat.20075.

Mitchell, James E., and Carol B. Peterson. *Assessment of Eating Disorders.* New York, NY: Guilford Press, 2005.

Mond, Jonathan M., Phillipa J. Hay, Bryan Rodgers, Cathy Owen, and Pierre J. V. Beumont. "Temporal Stability of the Eating Disorder Examination Questionnaire." *International Journal of Eating Disorders* 36 (2004): 195–203. doi: 10.1002/eat.2007.

Sysko, Robyn, B. Timothy Walsh, and Christopher Fairburn. "Eating Disorder Examination-Questionnaire as a Measure of Change in Patients with Bulimia Nervosa." *International Journal of Eating Disorders* 37 (2005): 100–106.

Wolk, Sara L., Katharine L. Loeb, and B. Timothy Walsh. "Assessment of Patients with Anorexia Nervosa: Interview Versus Self-Report." *International Journal of Eating Disorders* 47 (2005): 92–99. doi: 10.1002/eat.20076.

DIALECTICAL BEHAVIOR THERAPY (DBT)

Dialectical behavior therapy (DBT) was first developed as a targeted treatment for chronically parasuicidal women and was introduced to the scientific community in 1987. The treatment was designed by Marsha Linehan to treat individuals with borderline personality disorder (a personality disorder listed in the *Diagnostic and Statistical Manual of Mental Disorders*) who had usually remained resistant to traditional forms of therapy and exhibited a poor prognosis for improvement. DBT, which is a skills-based form of cognitive behavioral therapy (CBT), addresses the key tenets of acceptance and change. Used in both inpatient and outpatient settings with clients diagnosed with borderline personality disorder, DBT targets suicidal behaviors, self-injury, treatment interfering behaviors, and behaviors that prolong hospitalization. Ever since its development, this treatment approach has been helpful for individuals suffering from other mental disorders including substance abuse, eating disorders, and depression.

Description of DBT

DBT is often implemented in a group setting with multiple sessions varying from 50 minutes to 2.5 hours in length. Most eating disorder clients also participate in individual therapy, and if a substance abuse issue is present, they may also attend twelve-step groups. In one treatment program that reported success with bulimia nervosa and binge eating disordered clients, treatment involved 20 sessions of weekly 50-minute meetings to teach emotional regulation skills to specifically address the eating disorder.

Within the first two sessions, the client is usually introduced to the concept that there is a relationship between disordered eating behaviors and emotions. Clients are asked to pick a recent episode of purging or binge eating and to report the circumstances and emotions that came before the event. Clients receive a diary card to record frequency of targeted behaviors (e.g., vomiting), to rate the intensity of emotions, and to note the skills that were practiced each day. Clients begin to brainstorm about more healthy behaviors (e.g., singing, knitting) that can replace the problematic behaviors. Within DBT, mindfulness is taught as a way to increase the client's awareness of his or her emotions before reacting to them. Clients are taught to observe emotions in a nonjudgmental way so that they can describe and analyze their feelings and behaviors. Clients are encouraged to engage in mindful eating so that they can consume food with a higher degree of awareness of bodily cues of hunger and fullness as well as the taste of food.

Clients who participate in DBT also learn about how to manage their emotions more effectively by identifying triggers, reducing vulnerability to intense emotions, and changing emotional experiences. Clients practice distress tolerance skills to gain strength to cope with painful emotions that accompany stressful situations. Some of these survival strategies include distracting (e.g., going for a walk), self-soothing (e.g., taking a bubble bath), and visualization (e.g., imagining a relaxing setting like the beach). Throughout, the sessions continue to practice and apply the skills to eating disordered behaviors.

DBT as Eating Disorder Treatment

DBT has been used with eating disordered clients for over a decade. It is important to consider that many eating disordered clients are diagnosed with comorbid mental health conditions (e.g., substance abuse, borderline personality disorder) that add to the complexity of treatment needs and serve as an additional barrier for recovery. It has been estimated that at least one-third of those eating disordered clients who did not respond to traditional cognitive behavioral therapies could be concurrently diagnosed with borderline personality disorder. DBT, which has been demonstrated as being the most established treatment with borderline personality disorder, shows much promise for individuals with anorexia nervosa, bulimia nervosa, and binge eating disorder who engage in impulsive behaviors (e.g., cutting) or struggle to manage emotions in a healthy way. DBT focuses on helping clients develop self-awareness of problems, impulsivity, and emotional dysfunction. Clients are able to receive training and practice for emotional regulation strategies and for increasing coping skills (e.g., mindfulness meditation).

Comorbidities with Eating Disorders

When DBT was applied to individuals who were diagnosed with both eating disorder and borderline personality disorder, reductions in both self-harm behaviors and eating disorder behaviors were observed. In a separate study of 25 clients who had an eating disorder and substance abuse issue, DBT was helpful in reducing binge eating episodes, bulimic or restricting tendencies, and weight concerns as well as reducing substance abuse. A greater retention rate for treatment was observed for the DBT group versus traditional therapy and clients reported positive feedback about receiving mindfulness training. Furthermore, several clients expressed feeling validated and more motivated for change after participating in a treatment that they felt addressed both of their problems simultaneously; they reported feeling that they were empowered to recover.

Binge Eating Disorder and Bulimia Nervosa

Even among eating disordered individuals without personality disorders and other comorbid conditions, DBT has been an effective form of treatment. Eighty nine percent of clients with binge eating disorder who participated in a DBT skills group were able to eliminate binge eating episodes compared with only 13 percent in the control group. In a separate study with bulimia nervosa, 29 percent of clients were able to abstain from purging or binge eating behaviors after completing DBT compared with none of the participants in the control group. A case study report of a 36-year-old bulimia female who participated in 20 DBT sessions yielded positive feedback regarding the skills provided to address eating disorders. The client felt she was better equipped to handle inevitable stressful situations in a healthy way rather than sliding back into disordered eating behaviors. This client was able to maintain a healthy weight and experience higher levels of body satisfaction following treatment.

Conclusion

Although DBT was originally designed to treat individuals with borderline personality disorder, it has been shown to be effective in treating individuals who suffer from comorbid conditions such as eating disorders, personality disorders, substance abuse, and depression that cause traditional forms of therapy to be undermined. Clients with eating disorders have been shown to reduce both binge eating and purging behaviors after participating in DBT-based skills groups; they have been shown to feel confident to approach difficult situations in a more functional way.

JUSTINE J. REEL AND ROBERT A. BUCCIERE

See also: Cognitive Behavioral Therapy.

Bibliography

Ben-Porath, Denise D., Lucene Wisniewski, and Mark Warren. "Differential Treatment Response for Eating Disordered Patients with and without a Comorbid Borderline Personality Diagnosis Using a Dialectial Behavior Therapy (DBT)-Informed Approach." *Eating Disorders* 17 (2009): 225–41. doi: 10.1080/10640260902848576.

Chen, Eunice Y., Lauren Matthews, Charese Allen, Janice R. Kuo, and Marsha M. Linehan. "Dialectical Behavior Therapy for Clients with Binge Eating Disorder or Bulimia Nervosa and Borderline Personality Disorder." *International Journal of Eating Disorders* 41 (2008): 505–512. doi: 10.1002/eat.20522.

Courbasson, Christine, Yasunori Nishikawa, and Lauren Dixon. "Outcome of Dialectical Behavior Therapy for Concurrent Eating and Substance Use Disorders." *Clinical Psychology and Psychotherapy* (2011): 1–16. doi: 10.1002/cpp.748.

Kroger, Christoph, Ulrich Schweiger, Valerija Sipos, Soren Kliem, Ruediger Arnold, Tanja Schunert, and Hans Reinecker. "Dialectical Behaviour Therapy and An Added Cognitive Behavioral Treatment Module for Eating Disorders in Women with Borderline Personality Disorder and Anorexia Nervosa or Bulimia Nervosa Who Failed to Respond to Previous Treatments. An Open Trial with a 15-month Follow-up." *Journal of Behavioral Therapy and Experimental Psychiatry* 41 (2010): 381–88. doi: 10.1016/j.jbtep.2010.04.001.

Palmer, Robert L., Helen Birchall, Sadhana Damani, Nicholas Gatward, Lesley McGrain, and Lorraine Parker. "A Dialectical Behavior Therapy Program for People with an Eating Disorder and Borderline Personality Disorder—Description and Outcome." *International Journal of Eating Disorders* 33 (2003): 281–86.

Safer, Debra L., Christy F. Telch, and W. Stewart Agras. "Dialectical Behavior Therapy Adapted for Bulimia: A Case Report." *International Journal of Eating Disorders* 30 (2001): 101–106.

Telch Christy F., W. Stewart Agras, and Marsha M. Linehan. "Group Dialectical Behavior Therapy for Binge Eating Disorder: A Preliminary, Uncontrolled Trial." *Behavior Therapy* 31 (2000): 569–82.

DIETARY RESTRAINT

Dietary restraint is a psychological concept that refers to one's intention to restrict food intake due to concern with weight. The concept of restrained eating was introduced by researchers in the 1970s to describe a condition of chronic dieting. Restrained eating can range from restricting certain foods or meals to intense caloric restriction that resembles anorexic behavior. Restrained eaters report successful dieting when they believe that they have exerted self-discipline and feel control over eating by ignoring physiological cues of hunger. These periods of dietary restraint predictably become undermined by disinhibiting events. Disinhibiting eating is said to occur when the restrained eater engages in excessive eating or overeating in response to a triggering event. Most commonly reported disinhibiting events include alcohol consumption which decreases sensitivity to eating cues, negative emotional states (e.g., stress), and consumption of forbidden foods.

Characteristics of Restrained Eaters

Restrained eating has been associated with clinical eating disorders, disordered eating, and obesity. With regard to personality characteristics, restrained eaters have been described as narcissistic, perfectionistic, and highly impulsive. Research studies have shown that while restrained eaters tend to report negative body image, they also tend to have high self-esteem when compared with eating disordered clients. In a study of 1,470 middle-aged women, eating behavior beyond hunger (disinhibition) was related to higher weight and larger size for restrained eaters. Individuals who reported high dietary restraint were not significantly thinner or lighter than nonrestrained eaters, showing that restrained eating is often counterproductive.

A well-known ice cream study conducted in the 1980s with 48 female under-graduates observed eating behavior in a blinded taste test scenario. College students arrived to sample bowls of vanilla, strawberry, and chocolate ice cream. However, the researcher left the subjects alone for 15 minutes and instructed them to eat whatever amount they desired before throwing out the containers. The amount consumed was correlated with tendency toward dietary restraint. The most noteworthy finding from the study was that measurement of dietary restraint (how it was labeled) was most important. Several surveys have been developed to measure dietary restraint.

Measurement of Dietary Restraint

The most commonly used instrument for measuring dietary restraint has been the Revised Restraint Scale (RS), a 10-item self-report questionnaire created in 1975 to assess cognitive components of self-control inherent in people's attempts to restrict food intake and lose weight. A sample item of the RS is "Do you eat sensibly in front of others and splurge alone?" In attempts to address the disinhibition quality of restrained eaters, the Three Factor Eating Questionnaire (TFEQ) was developed in 1985 by Stunkard and Messick. The TFEQ, a 51-item self-report scale, measures dietary restraint, disinhibition, and hunger. Dietary restraint refers to control over food intake in order to influence body weight and shape. Disinhibition represents episodes experienced by restrained eaters that involve a loss of control over eating. Finally, the hunger items assess subjective feelings of hunger and food cravings.

Another popular instrument for measuring dietary restraint is the Dutch Eating Behavior Questionnaire (DEBQ). The 33-item DEBQ was developed to measure several aspects of eating behaviors represented by several subscales: restrained eating, emotional eating, and external eating. Restrained eating is demonstrated by items like, "do you try to eat less at mealtimes than you would like to eat?" Emotional eating asks participants questions like "do you have a desire to eat when you are irritated?" External eating measures responses to environmental cues and a sample item is "if you walk past the bakery do you have the desire to buy something delicious?"

Conclusion

Dietary restraint was conceptualized in the 1970s and has been linked to both eating disorders and obesity. In addition to food restriction to control one's weight, restrained eaters lose control during disinhibiting events and tend to overeat. Hunger cues are often denied and emotional eating may be observed. Measurement of dietary restraint to include these multiple dimensions is important for understanding how to treat restrained eaters and preventing dietary restraint when dieting has become the societal norm.

JUSTINE J. REEL

Bibliography

Atlas, Jana G., Gregory T. Smith, Leigh Anne Hohlstein, Denis M. McCarthy and Larry S. Kroll. "Similarities and Differences between Caucasian and African American College Women on Eating and Dieting Expectancies, Bulimic Symptoms, Dietary Restraint, and Disinhibition." *International Journal of Eating Disorders* 32 (2002): 326–34.

Dykes, J., E. J. Brunner, P. T. Martikainen and J. Wardle. "Socioeconomic Gradient in Body Size and Obesity among Women: The Role of Dietary Restraint, Disinhibition and Hunger in the Whitehall II Study." *International Journal of Obesity* 28 (2004): 262–68.

Goldfield, Gary S., and Andrew Lumb. "Effects of Dietary Restraint and Body Mass Index on the Relative Reinforcing Value of Snack Food." *Eating Disorders* 17 (2009): 46–62.

Lejeune, M.P.G.M, D.P.C van Aggel-Leijssen, M. A. van Baak, and M. S. Westerterp-Plantenga. "Effects of Dietary Restraint vs. Exercise during Weight Maintenance in Obese Men." *European Journal of Clinical Nutrition* 57 (2003): 1338–1344.

Safer, Debra L., Stewart Agras, Michael R. Lowe, and Susan Bryson. "Comparing Two Measures of Eating Restraint in Bulimic Women Treated with Cognitive-Behavioral Therapy." *International Journal of Eating Disorders* 36 (2004): 83–88.

Stein, David M. "The Scaling of Restraint and the Prediction of Eating." *International Journal of Eating Disorders* 7, no. 5 (1988): 713–17.

Yeomans, M. R., H. M. Tovey, E. M. Tinley, and C. J. Haynes. "Effects of Manipulated Palatability on Appetite Depend on Restraint and Disinhibition Scores from the Three-Factor Eating Questionnaire." *International Journal of Obesity* 28 (2004): 144–51.

DISORDERED EATING

Disordered eating refers to destructive weight control patterns that are unhealthy and may lead to a full-blown clinical eating disorder (e.g., anorexia nervosa or bulimia nervosa) if left untreated. Individuals who engage in disordered eating may present with a variety of symptoms including, but not limited to, restricting overall food intake or certain types of foods (e.g., those with high fat or caloric content), occasional purging (e.g., vomiting, laxatives), frequent weighing, secretive eating or excessive exercise to lose weight or to compensate for a meal.

The term disordered eating was used by the American College of Sports Medicine (ACSM) to refer to dysfunctional eating patterns that were associated with the female athlete triad. In ACSM's original position stand disordered eating was defined as "a wide spectrum of harmful and ineffective eating behaviors used in attempts to lose weight or achieve a lean appearance. The spectrum ranges in severity from restricting food intake, to binging and purging, to the DSM-IV defined disorders of anorexia nervosa and bulimia nervosa" (American College of Sports Medicine, 1997, p. i.). In a recent update to ACSM's position stand the term disordered eating was replaced with energy availability.

Disordered Eating versus Clinical Eating Disorders

Disordered eating has been commonly used to identify dysfunctional eating behaviors that may result in health consequences (e.g., menstrual and bone complications) but may not be severe enough to meet the entire clinical criteria for either anorexia nervosa or bulimia nervosa. By recognizing a problem before an individual has a full-blown eating disorder, earlier intervention can take place. Furthermore, disordered eating is much more common among athletes and the general population and can be addressed as part of prevention programs. Studies found that 18.2 percent of high school athletes, 26.1 percent of college athletes, and 46.2 percent of elite athletes engaged in disordered eating practices.

Conclusion

Disordered eating has been used to refer to a spectrum of dysfunctional eating patterns that can cause medical consequences and health problems but may not be diagnosed as a clinical eating disorder. Used frequently in association with the athletic population, disordered eating was part of the original ACSM position stand on the female athlete triad.

JUSTINE J. REEL

See also: Energy Availability; Female Athlete Triad.

Bibliography

American College of Sports Medicine (ACSM). "Position Stand: The Female Athlete Triad." *Medicine & Science in Sport & Exercise* 29 (1997): i–ix.

American College of Sports Medicine. "Disordered Eating Patterns May Lead to Eating Disorders." ACSM.org. Last Modified May 2, 2002. http://www.acsm.org/AM/Template.cfm?Section=Home_Page&CONTENTID=4275&TEMPLATE=/CM/ContentDisplay.cfm.

Beals, Katherine A. *Disordered Eating among Athletes: A Comprehensive Guide for Health Professionals.* Champaign, IL: Human Kinetics, 2004.

Nichols, Jeanne F., Mitchell J. Rauh, Mandra J. Lawson, Ming Ji, and Hava-Shoshana Barkai. "Prevalence of Female Athlete Triad Symptoms among High School Athletes." *Archives of Pediatric and Adolescent Medicine* 160 (2006): 137–42.

Reel, Justine J., Sonya SooHoo, Holly Doetsch, Jennifer Carter, and Trent Petrie. "The Female Athlete Triad: Is the Triad a Problem for Division I College Female Athletes?" *Journal of Clinical Sport Psychology* 1 (2007): 358–70.

Thompson, Ron A., and Roberta Trattner Sherman. *Eating Disorders in Sport.* New York, NY: Routledge, 2010.

Torstveit, Monica K., Jan H. Rosenvinge, and Jorunn Sundgot-Borgen. "Prevalence of Eating Disorders and Predictive Power of Risk Models in Female Elite Athletes: A Controlled Study." *Scandinavian Journal of Medicine & Science in Sports* 18 (2008): 108–118.

DISTANCE RUNNING

The ability to run was developed about four and a half million years ago as a means to hunt animals in an upright position. Competitive running emerged from religious festivals in Greece, Egypt, Asia, and Africa. The Tailteann Games, an Irish sports festival to honor goddess Tailtiu, represents one of the earliest records (i.e., 1829 BC) of competitive running. Distance running competitions between males were quite the spectacle during the original Greek Olympics of 776 BC in which the competitors are believed to have competed in the buff. The rules and traditions of cross-country running were formalized in Britain with the first English National Competition in 1876 and the International Cross Country Championships in 1903.

Distance Running and Eating Disorders

Distance running, which represents marathon runners and cross-country athletes, has been identified as an endurance sport that is at risk for disordered eating and eating disorders. As early as the late 1980s, researchers found that almost half (48%) of female runners and 24 percent of male runners were preoccupied with becoming thinner. Within the same study, 48 percent of female runners and 20 percent of male runners feared gaining weight and 57 percent of females and 37 percent of males were dissatisfied with their body weight, size, or appearance. Another study in the 1980s found that half of runners were engaging in at least one pathogenic weight control method.

A female athlete competes in the Great Scottish Run half marathon, passing through Bellahouston Park in Glasgow, Scotland. (iStockPhoto)

A more recent study with elite women runners in the United Kingdom revealed that 16 percent of athletes had an eating disorder at the time of the study and additional participants reported having an eating disorder history. Runners with eating disorders were found to be significantly less satisfied with their physical appearance, increased dieting, and reported poorer psychological health than nondisordered runners. This eating disorder prevalence was higher than the general population, but was consistent with other studies using distance runners. For example, in a separate study, 24 percent of female runners and 8 percent of male runners admitted to having eating disorder symptoms. Runners have been found to experience overuse injuries, body image distortion, and excessive weight concerns as a group.

Weight Pressures in Distance Running

Distance runners face unique performance demands associated with their sport. The perception that losing weight will improve performance is rampant. Although performance may initially increase, once an athlete faces an energy deficit, his or her performance drops sharply. Cross-country runners have reported revealing team attire (e.g., short shorts) as contributing to feelings of body dissatisfaction. Likewise, coaches often promoted weight loss and dieting behaviors. Stereotypes were associated with a larger runner being labeled as slow or lazy and thinner runners receiving more positive comments and extra attention from the coaching staff. Pressure to be the thinnest runner was present with intense comparisons of body sizes occurring at high school and college ranks for distance runners.

Conclusion

Distance runners have been found to experience disordered eating and eating disorders at a higher rate than the general population and are considered an at-risk group of athletes. Distance runners experience many weight-related pressures including perceived performance advantages, racing attire, coach comments, and comparison with teammates. Both male and female athletes who participate in cross-country races and in marathons should be monitored for healthy nutrition so that they receive adequate energy intake to meet the demands of their sport and to prevent overuse injuries.

JUSTINE J. REEL

See also: Endurance Sports.

Bibliography

Barrack, Michelle T., Mitchell J. Rauh, Hava-Shoshana Barkai, and Jeanne F. Nichols. "Dietary Restraint and Low Bone Mass in Female Adolescent Endurance Runners." *American Journal of Clinical Nutrition* 87 (2008): 36–43.

Baum, Antonia. "Eating Disorders in the Male Athlete." *Sports Medicine* 36, no. 1 (2006): 1–6.

Hulley, Angela J., and Andrew J. Hill. "Eating Disorders and Health in Elite Women Distance Runners." *International Journal of Eating Disorders* 30 (2001): 312–17.

Karlson, Kristine A., Carolyn Black Becker, and Amanda Merkur. "Prevalence of Eating Disordered Behavior in Collegiate Lightweight Rowers and Distance Runners." *Clinical Journal of Sport Medicine* 11 (2001): 32–37.

Tenforde, Adam S., Lauren C. Sayres, Mary L. McCurdy, Herve Collado, Kristin L. Sainani, and Michael Fredericson. "Overuse Injuries in High School Runners: Lifetime Prevalence and Prevention Strategies." *America Academy of Physical Medicine and Rehabilitation* 3 (2011): 123–31.

Wilmore, Jack H., C. Harmon Brown, and James A. Davis. "Body Physique and Composition of the Female Distance Runner." *Annals of the New York Academy of Sciences* 301 (1977): 764–76. doi: 10.1111/j.1749-6632.1977.tb38245.x.

DIURETICS

Diuretics refer to medications that cause the kidneys to get rid of water and salt from the tissues and the bloodstream through urination. Diuretics are sometimes prescribed to help control blood pressure, heart problems, and other medical conditions. However, abusing diuretics may represent a purging method by an eating disordered individual in an effort to lose weight in a short amount of time. The weight that is lost from diuretic use is regained quickly once the individual rehydrates by consuming water in foods and fluids.

Types of Diuretics

A study in the April 2011 edition of *International Journal of Eating Disorders* reported that thiazide, loop, and potassium-sparing diuretics are the most commonly abused diuretics. Thiazide diuretics inhibit sodium chloride reabsorption in the distal renal tubule of the kidney, which causes the excretion of sodium in the urine via the kidneys. The excretion of sodium and water decreases plasma volume and reduces edema in individuals with complications from fluid retention. Sodium and water loss can also stimulate the renin-angiotensin system, which can lead to hypokalemia (low serum potassium) and metabolic alkalosis (high serum bicarbonate).

Loop diuretics work on the kidney by inhibiting the reabsorption of sodium by blocking the sodium-chloride-potassium-chloride cotransporter. Loop diuretics also cause the activation of the renin-angiotensin system. Using loop diuretics can also result in hypokalemia and metabolic alkalosis. Hypomagnesemia (low serum magnesium), hypocalcemia (low serum calcium) and hyperuricemia (high uric acid) can also occur.

Potassium-sparing diuretics act on epithelial sodium channels. This class of medication causes sodium and water loss, but does not cause a loss of potassium. In contrast to thiazide and loop diuretics, potassium-sparing diuretics put individuals at risk for hyperkalemia (high serum potassium) and metabolic acidosis (low serum bicarbonate).

Diuretic Abuse

In an effort to prevent dehydration due to ongoing diuretic abuse, the body's renin-angiotensin system is activated. A high level of the hormone aldosterone is secreted, which increases sodium and bicarbonate reabsorption in the kidney in exchange for potassium and hydrogen. This system is further potentiated by dehydration. According to *Eating Disorders: A Guide to Medical Care and Complications,* the metabolic alkalosis seen in individuals who abuse diuretics is milder than that found in individuals who induce vomiting. But because electrolyte imbalances and metabolic acidosis are rarely seen in anorexia nervosa, high or low bicarbonate levels and other electrolyte abnormalities present in laboratory results of individuals with anorexia nervosa who deny purging can be useful to physicians who suspect purging behaviors.

Clinical Manifestations

Eating disordered individuals with electrolyte abnormalities may complain about vague symptoms, including weakness, fatigue, constipation, dizziness, and depression. Hypokalemia can cause serious, life-threatening cardiac arrhythmias that lead to sudden death. Cardiac complications can be diagnosed by performing an electrocardiogram. Although hypomagnesemia and hypocalcemia (low serum calcium) are not common in individuals with bulimia, hypomagnesemia should always be assessed in eating disordered individuals who purge using diuretics. Hypomagnesemia and hypocalcemia can contribute to cardiac arrhythmias and can cause tetany, an involuntary contraction of the muscles.

Pseudo-Bartter Syndrome

According to an article published in the *International Journal of Eating Disorders,* pseudo-Bartter syndrome is widely recognized in eating disordered individuals who abuse diuretics. Bartter syndrome is characterized by hypokalemia, metabolic alkalosis, hyperaldosteronism (high aldosterone), and normal blood pressure. There is also hyperplasia of the juxtaglomerular apparatus in the kidney. The juxtaglomerular cells stimulate the secretion of the adrenal hormone aldosterone which causes sodium and bicarbonate reabsorption. The article further reports that unlike Bartter syndrome, in pseudo-Bartter syndrome there is a lack of intrinsic pathology in the renal tubules and a normal urinary chloride level. Once the purging is eliminated, pseudo-Bartter syndrome resolves.

Treatment

When treating individuals with electrolyte imbalances and dehydration from diuretic use, hydration status must be restored before treating the resulting electrolyte abnormalities. Because dehydration stimulates aldosterone production, hydration status must be corrected first to shut off the renin-angiotensin system and stop the loss of potassium in the urine. Normalizing aldosterone levels may take from one to two weeks after the individual has ceased purging behaviors. Rapid, intravenous infusions of normal saline can cause further sodium and water retention, and the resulting edema may cause individuals with bulimia to be reluctant to give up using diuretics or other purging methods. Eating disordered individuals should be reassured that edema will cease with continued treatment. *Eating Disorders: Guide to Medical Care and Complications* recommends dietary salt restriction, elevation of legs for 10 to 15 minutes a few times each day, and a slow infusion of saline to help prevent edema. In some cases, a low dose of spironolactone, a potassium-sparing diuretic that inhibits the action of aldosterone and aids in hypokalemia correction, is given daily to prevent or treat edema.

Conclusion

Individuals with bulimia nervosa may engage in a variety of purging methods following an uncontrollable binge. While the most common types of purging are vomiting and laxative abuse, diuretic use is another way by which individuals have experienced rapid weight loss. Unfortunately, weight is restored when an individual consumes fluids and diuretic use can result in a number of medical complications related to dehydration. Therefore, it is important to inform individuals of the risks associated with diuretic use.

SHELLY GUILLORY

Bibliography

Mascolo, Margherita, Eugene S. Chu, and Philip S. Mehler. "Abuse and Clinical Value of Diuretics in Eating Disorders Therapeutic Applications." *International Journal of Eating Disorders* 44, no. 3 (2011): 200–202. Accessed May 15, 2011. doi: 10.1002/eat.20814

Mehler, Philip S., and Arnold E. Anderson. "Evaluation and Treatment of Electrolyte Abnormalities." *Eating Disorders: A Guide to Medical Care and Complications, 2nd ed.,* 96–107. Baltimore: Johns Hopkins University Press, 2010.

Mitchell, James E., Claire Pomroy, Marvin Seppala, and Marguerite Huber. "Pseudo-Bartter's Syndrome, Diuretic abuse, Idiopathic Edema, and Eating Disorders." *International Journal of Eating Disorders* 7, no. 2 (1988): 225–37. Accessed May 15, 2011. doi: 10.1002/1098-108X (198803)7:2<225:AID-EAT2260070209>3.0.CO;2-2

DOLLS

Dolls and action figures have been around for centuries and they represent a multibillion dollar industry every year. However, only in the last several decades have we begun to consider the way that dolls might influence or shape a child's perceptions of body image. This is in part due to the emergence of plastic figures in the late 1950s with Barbie and early 1960s with G. I. Joe. The transition to plastic allowed manufacturers to better manipulate the figures to resemble a particular person or physique, modeling societal trends of the time.

Barbie and Body Image

There has been extensive research focusing on the unrealistic physical proportions of toys and action figures. Most of this research has focused on dolls such as Barbie. Barbie is often viewed as an icon of female beauty. For example, it has been reported that preadolescent girls viewed Barbie as perfect, and that adult social scripts can be enacted by playing with Barbie. In one study, the Barbie doll was scaled to the same height as another female doll—Army Norma—that was based on female army recruits. They found that if Barbie was five feet four inches, her physical measurements would be 32x17x28 inches, representing an anorexic physique.

There has been some media and parental concern about the extreme figure that is portrayed by dolls such as Barbie. In response to these body image concerns, Mattel, the makers of Barbie, have altered some Barbie dolls by increasing waist and hip circumferences and decreasing breast size. However, these dolls may still reinforce unrealistic expectations of a woman's body shape. In another study, girls who played with Barbie dolls showed greater desire for thinness and lowest self-esteem compared to preadolescents who played with an Emme doll or no doll at all. The researchers concluded that such figures could lead to future body image concerns including weight cycling and disordered eating.

A contemporary version of the Barbie doll, right, stands next to the original 1959 doll. The Barbie doll was introduced on March 9, 1959. (Chris Pizzello/AP/Wide World Photos)

Action Figures and Body Image

Although the majority of research focuses on gender-based female dolls and toys, action figures are an important part of a boy's socialization. Boys tend to prefer action figures to other male figures as they represent masculinity, strength, and invincibility. An action figure differs from a doll such as Barbie in several ways. Typically, the figure is a superhero made of plastic that is capable of bending at the limbs and standing on its own. It is distinguished from other figures primarily because it is designed for boys. G. I. Joe is considered to be the first action figure appearing in the US market in the mid-1960s.

Although action figures are socially acceptable for boys, some researchers question the violent symbolisms behind action figures. In addition, action figures represent unrealistic and unattainable physiques for the average male. Baghurst and colleagues compared the physical dimensions of original action figures to today's version. They found that the current action figures have much larger measurements for the neck, chest, arms, forearms, thighs, and calves. In one study, these action figures were presented to a group of adolescent boys to determine their opinions about the figures. The boys overwhelmingly preferred the current action figure due to its larger size and increased muscularity.

Body Image

Every toy is educational and sends an intended or unintended message. Thus, it is important to understand that dolls and action figures may influence the body image of males and females. Viewing dolls (e.g. Barbie or G. I. Joe) as having a desirable appearance may lead to internalizing larger societal expectations. Seeking a physique that is disproportionate to real life could lead to unattainable and unhealthy body image ideals. Simply playing with a toy can influence one's body-esteem. Interestingly, even adults who emulate a figure may be affected and body esteem may be lowered a result.

Conclusion

Unfortunately, as dolls and action figures have continued to be improved by technological advancements, the lessons they teach with respect to body image may contribute to increased concerns, as toys influence behavior. For example, toys such as action figures or dolls have roles, characters, friends, enemies, and life struggles. A toy is designed to portray information and ask questions concerning its type, how it is played with, and the modes of self-expression it can provide. It is important to understand that a doll can be interpreted positively, and this may hold true to body image. Some research has found that children previously unaccustomed to playing with a doll can learn positive social roles if they are educated on those specific roles. However, with respect to body image, the propensity for encouraging poor body-esteem in children is a strong possibility.

TIMOTHY M. BAGHURST

Bibliography

Baghurst, Timothy M., Dan B. Hollander, Beth Nardella, and G. Gregory Haff. "Change in Sociocultural Ideal Male Physique: An Examination of Past and Present Action Figures." *Body Image* 3 (2006): 87–91.

Baghurst, Timothy M., David Carlston, Julie Wood, and Frank Wyatt. "Preadolescent Male Perceptions of Action Figure Physiques." *Journal of Adolescent Health* 41 (2007): 613–15.

Barlett, Chris, Richard Harris, Scott Smith, and J. Bonds-Raake. "Action Figures and Men." *Sex Roles* 53 (2005): 877–85.

Kline, Steven. "Toys as Media: The Role of Toy Design, Promotional TV and Mother's Reinforcement in Young Males (3–6) Acquisition of Pro-social Play Scripts for Rescue Hero Action Toys." Presentation at the International Toy Research Association Conference, Halmstadt, Sweden, June 18, 1999.

Kuther, Tara L., and Erin McDonald. "Early Adolescents' Experiences with and Views of Barbie." *Adolescence* 39 (2004): 39–51.

McCreary, Donald R., and Doris K. Sasse. "An Exploration of the Drive for Muscularity in Adolescent Boys and Girls." *Journal of American College Health* 48 (2000): 297–304.

Thomas, Jeannie B. *Naked Barbies, Warrior Joes, & Other Forms of Visible Gender.* Urbana, IL: University of Illinois Press, 2003.

Urla, Jacqueline., and Alan C. Swedlund. "The Anthropometry of Barbie: Unsettling Ideals of the Feminine Body in Popular Culture." In *Deviant Bodies: Critical Perspectives in Science and Popular Culture,* edited by Jennifer Terry and Jacqueline Urla, 277–313. Bloomington, IN: Indiana University Press, 2004.

DOVE CAMPAIGN FOR REAL BEAUTY

The Dove Campaign for Real Beauty was a global effort launched in 2004 to serve as a starting point for widening the definition and discussion of beauty and to celebrate diverse and healthy body shapes. The campaign included videos, advertisements, workshops, sleepover events, a book, and a play production to improve self-esteem in girls and women of all ages. It is currently available in 30 different countries. Dove has released marketing campaigns in video formats that reveal the truth behind the media images with the following mission as stated on their website: "Dove is committed to building positive self-esteem and inspiring all women and girls to reach their full potential."

"Evolution of Beauty" Video

The "Evolution of Beauty" video takes the viewer through a visual journey of the harsh world of modeling. At the beginning of the video a female model is seen plainly dressed with hair that has not been styled; and she is not wearing makeup. Professional hair and makeup artists go to work to mold her into a more desirable media-ready photograph by styling her hair and layering on makeup. The photographer manipulates the lighting on set to make her look thinner than she is in person. After the photographs have been meticulously shot from various eye-pleasing angles, they are transferred to a computer for digital enhancement. Enhancements or changes that are made to the model's body might include changing her eye color, eyebrow shape, eye size, and face shape (to make it thinner and longer). They may also involve enlarging her lips, moving her cheekbones, elongating her neck, and removing fat from her body. All the aforementioned changes made to the models' bodies are unrealistic. The emerging image of the model does not resemble her original appearance, and her beauty transformation can be viewed at http://www.youtube.com/watch?v=iYhCn0jf46U.

Dove Advertisements

Dove has thoughtfully placed advertisements of their products through magazines using women of all sizes rather than models. Their appearances, unlike in most other advertisements, have not been digitally enhanced or changed in any way. The model's body seen in the Dove advertisements in magazines will look the same when placed next to the model in person. This real form of advertisement is to teach girls and women of all ages that they are beautiful regardless of their body shape, size, height, or color. Emphasizing a positive body image message is refreshing, as it is easy to criticize one's body after viewing ultrathin models in magazine advertisements. This advertisement can be viewed at http://www.dove.us/Social-Mission/campaign-for-real-beauty.aspx.

Gina Crisanti leans against a billboard Tuesday, July 26, 2005, in downtown Chicago, where she and five other women posed for in their underwear for an ad campaign to sell Dove Beauty products. The ads, featuring "real" women and not models, are a hot topic of conversation. (Nam Y. Huh/AP/Wide World Photos)

Dove Workshops

The Dove Campaign for Real Beauty offers free workshops throughout the world. These workshops can be conducted by any person willing to learn and teach the curriculum. To obtain the curriculum go to the Dove website: http://www.dove. us/Social-Mission/Self-Esteem-Toolkit-And-Resources/. Curriculum lesson plans include assertiveness training, media literacy, and self-esteem training. Media literacy involves being able to critically analyze manipulated and negative media images and advertisements. Dove also offers online workshops for parents and daughters. One workshop activity involves building a "self-esteem bubble" by dragging names and images that evoke feelings of happiness into a bubble shape and printing it out. The "Playing with Beauty" activity shows what the proportions of a Barbie doll would look like if the doll's measurements were extrapolated into a human being's size and height. The "True You for Mothers and Daughters" workbook, which aims to strengthen the mother-daughter relationship, is also available online as a resource and serves to build body image and self-esteem.

Conclusion

The Dove Campaign has represented an effort on the part of a business to use the media to positively influence body image. By showing models of diverse sizes in commercials and using positive messages about body image, self-acceptance is promoted. Videos showing the transformation of a model for a photograph have made a strong impact on teen girls striving for magazine perfection.

HAILEY E. NIELSON

Bibliography

"Dove Campaign for Real Beauty." http://www.dove.us/Social-Mission/Self-Esteem-Toolkit-And-Resources/. Last modified in 2011.

Dove Movement for Self-Esteem (2010). "About the Movement." Retrieved from http://www.dovemovement.com/movement/about on May 25, 2011.

Falcione, Olivia, and Laura Henderson. "The Dove Campaign for Real Beauty Case Study." *The Dove Campaign* (2009).

DRILL TEAM/DANCE TEAM

Historically, the term "drill teams" referred to squads of individuals (typically females) who performed line dances and high kick and jazz routines often in association with their school's marching band. The Universal Dance Association (UDA) was founded in 1980 as Universal Dance Camps with the intent to educate dancers about proper techniques and fitness. UDA changed the name from "drill teams" to "dance teams" to better represent the fitness associated with the activity. To date, there are numerous dance championships across the United States.

Athletes and dancers have been identified as being at risk for body image disturbances, disordered eating, and clinical disorders due to the weight-focused nature of the training and the competitive environment. Dance squads and drill teams perform separately from cheerleaders and other athletes and have been largely ignored in large-scale eating disorder studies with athletes. However, the training and performance schedules are stringent and the practice of difficult choreography and skills is rigorous, and like in cheerleading and ballet a certain body type may be selected or valued by choreographers and dance team coaches.

Body Image and Eating Disorders in Auxiliary Team Members

Although auxiliary units (e.g., dance team squad members, majorettes) have been overlooked in most athlete studies, they may experience physical and psychological pressures associated with their participation. Expectations to be feminine and pretty to fit into the stereotype of dance performers—apart from types of uniforms and choreographers—may contribute to pressure to maintain a low body weight or size. Dance teams may wear tight stretch pants, short hot pants, short skirts, and tops that display midriffs. Similar to cheerleaders, there may be weight requirements associated with trying out for a dance team and dancers may be told to lose weight to fit the appearance desired for the squad. Naturally, majorettes are the central focus of a marching band and are scrutinized for their appearance and beauty.

A rare study of 101 female auxiliary unit members representing three National Collegiate Athletic Association Division I universities found that approximately 30 percent of women were at risk for eating disorders with 31 percent of color guard members, 26 percent of dance line members, and 37 percent of majorettes displaying disordered eating risk factors. Color guard members reported the highest frequency for binge eating (20%) compared to 15 percent for the whole sample. Vomiting to lose weight (14%) was also higher in color guards than the entire sample (10%). However, majorettes were more likely to admit laxative abuse, diet pills, or diuretics (26%) than the rate for all participants (19%).

Conclusion

Auxiliary team members may be overlooked in studies that examine disordered eating behaviors and risk for eating disorders in athletic populations. However, some initial research indicates that dance team members and majorettes also face pressures associated with their body weight, size, and appearance. When considering the revealing team uniforms and the focus on appearance associated with performing, it is important to examine this potentially at-risk group.

JUSTINE J. REEL

See also: Ballet; Cheerleading.

Bibliography

Black, David R., Laurie J. S. Larkin, Daniel C. Coster, Larry J. Leverenz, and Doris A. Abood. "Physiologic Screening Test for Eating Disorders/Disordered Eating among Female Collegiate Athletes." *Journal of Athletic Training* 38, no. 4 (2003): 286–97.

Kurtzman, Felice D., John Landsverk, Diane C. Bodurka. "Eating Disorders among Selected Female Student Populations at UCLA." *Journal of the American Dietetic Association* 89, no. 1 (1989): 45–53.

Torres-McGehee, Toni M., James M. Green, James D. Leeper, Deidre Leaver-Dunn, Mark T. Richardson, and Phillip A. Bishop. "Body Image, Anthropometric Measures, and Eating-Disorder Prevalence in Auxiliary Unit Members." *Journal of Athletic Training* 44, no. 4 (2009): 418–26.

Torres-McGehee, Toni M., James M. Green, Deidre Leaver-Dunn, James D. Leeper, Phillip A. Bishop, and Mark T. Richardson. "Attitude and Knowledge Changes in Collegiate Dancers Following a Short-Term, Team-Centered Prevention Program on Eating Disorders." *Perceptual and Motor Skills* 112, no. 3 (2011): 711–25. doi: 10.2466/06.PMS.112.3.711-725.

"Universal Dance Association." Varsity.com. Accessed August 22, 2011. http://uda.varsity.com/default.aspx.

DRIVE FOR MUSCULARITY

Drive for muscularity (DM) is the tendency of some individuals in Western society to strive for a body that is lean and muscular. Drive for muscularity was first introduced in a 2000 issue of the *Journal of American College Health* by researcher

Donald McCreary. McCreary noted that although males tend to have a low drive for thinness, they do display a desire for increased body size and muscularity. For example, 40 percent of college men in one study desired to gain weight. In another study, 95 percent of adult males preferred to be a mesomorph, a body type characterized by an athletic physique and the ability to easily gain or lose weight. According to McCreary, DM has two components: (1) muscularity-oriented body image (e.g., wanting to be more muscular), and (2) muscularity behavior (e.g., lifting weight to build more muscle). DM parallels the drive for thinness so pervasive in females of all ages. Just as many women perceive themselves to be larger and heavier than their actual size, many men see themselves as smaller and skinnier than they actually are. As a result, a substantial number of normal weight adolescent boys seek to gain weight, primarily through increasing muscle mass.

Although the prevalence of DM is unknown, a 2010 study of 235 college men and women revealed that 41 percent of the participants scored above the median on a paper-and-pencil measure of DM. Calculating an exact prevalence of DM may be problematic, as the concept is currently viewed as existing on a continuum rather than as a discrete condition. Thus, individuals may be classified as "high" or "low" on DM, but specific criteria for pronouncing someone as "having" or "not having" DM do not yet exist.

Assessment of Drive for Muscularity

The systematic assessment of male body image to measure DM has only recently been addressed by researchers. Both perceptual tests, which use photos and videos to measure an individual's ability to correctly estimate one's body measurements, and subjective tests, which use paper-and-pencil surveys and drawings to measure an individual's thoughts and feelings about one's body, have been used to assess DM. Most perceptual tests are focused on body size and weight without consideration for muscularity, and are thus ill equipped to assess DM. However, several subjective tests show promise in assessing DM. Most subjective assessments are in the form of paper-and-pencil surveys scored using Likert rating scales (e.g., 0 = strongly disagree to 5 = strongly agree) to assess individuals' attitudes about muscularity (e.g., "I think I have too little muscle on my body"). An abundance of paper-and-pencil tests specifically focused on DM have been developed in the past 10 years. These tests include the Drive for Muscularity Scale (DMS), the Male Body Attitudes Scale (MBAS), the Muscle Appearance Satisfaction Scale (MASS), and the Drive for Muscularity Attitudes Questionnaire (DMAQ). The DMS was the first test created, and is by far the most widely used of the paper-and-pencil subjective assessments. Example items from the 15-item DMS include "I wish that I were more muscular," and "I drink weight-gain or protein shakes."

Less used to subjectively assess DM than paper-and-pencil tests are contour-drawn silhouette scales. Assessment using silhouette scales involves presenting individuals with a series of same-sex body figures ranging from very large to very small. Individuals are asked to select the figure that most accurately portrays their own body, as well as the figure that represents the body they would most like to have. Early silhouette scales were characterized by figures that ranged from low to high adiposity, and did a poor job of assessing DM. However, the somatomorphic matrix (SM) consists of a 10 x 10 matrix of 100 figures that vary in terms of both muscularity and body fat. Because it portrays figures based on both muscularity and body fat, the SM is the most valid silhouette scale assessment of DM.

Gender Differences in Drive for Muscularity

Although girls and women do exhibit DM, the drive for muscularity is generally higher in males. Further, DM seems to be more relevant for the mental and physical health of males than the health of females. Regardless of gender, excessive DM can lead to a variety of negative consequences, including binge eating, the use of body/performance enhancing substances, the development of body image disturbances such as muscle dysmorphia, and enhanced risk for weight-related health conditions such as type 2 diabetes and coronary heart disease.

Although males do tend to report higher DM than females, DM should not be ignored among girls and women. DM in females centers more on a lean and toned physique rather than a big and muscular physique. One study did reveal that differences between men and women on DM disappeared when the focus was on muscle tone instead of muscle mass. The same study also showed that DM was related to similar behaviors (e.g., physical activity, diet) in men and women. Thus, efforts to build muscle in those high on DM are similar regardless of one's gender.

Sexuality and Drive for Muscularity

In addition to gender, sexuality can influence a person's tendency to experience drive for muscularity. Researchers have determined that gay males as a group may be at increased risk for body dissatisfaction and DM, as the quest for a muscular body may represent a vehicle for overcoming years of teasing and questions related to their masculinity. In one study, gay males perceived themselves to be less muscular and reported more body dissatisfaction specific to their muscles than heterosexual men. Another study compared DM between 70 gay and 71 heterosexual men. The gay males reported more awareness and internalization of a lean and muscular ideal than the heterosexual men. Thus, due at least partially to the stigma associated with being gay, gay males are a subpopulation that may be particularly at risk for high DM.

Race and Ethnicity

Unfortunately, very few researchers have examined racial and ethnic differences for DM. A study comparing muscularity satisfaction between college men in the United States and those in Hong Kong revealed that the Hong Kong men were significantly more satisfied with their muscularity than their U.S. counterparts.

Western conceptions of masculinity and the muscular ideal remain largely rejected by males in Hong Kong, as they conflict with the traditional Chinese notion of a more well-rounded masculinity which may include either physical *or* scholarly traits. The lone study focused on DM in African American men showed that muscularity was an important component of their racial/ethnic identity.

Athletes and Drive for Muscularity

Competitive athletes are a subpopulation of interest when considering DM. Not only do athletes face the same pressures as non-athletes to conform to societal body ideals of muscularity, but they also encounter pressures from coaches and teammates to achieve sufficient muscularity for their sport. Male and female athletes in team and individual sports have reported a strong DM. In support of a dual pathway of body image dissatisfaction, one study of college-aged male athletes showed that the participants reported a desire to gain an average of 3.2 pounds while at the same time *lose* an average of 5.1 percent body fat. In another study, 100 percent of college male athletes reported a desire to be muscular. Female athletes also express DM, although at lower levels than male athletes. In a recent study, college female athletes expressed a significantly stronger DM than female non-athletes. In the same study, the 84 percent of female athletes who wanted to be muscular reported that muscularity was important for several reasons, including functionality (i.e., sport performance), health, external gratification (i.e., sex appeal), and internal gratification (i.e., self-esteem).

Other Characteristics Associated with Drive for Muscularity

A variety of factors have been suggested as leading to DM, including biology, personality, physical attributes, gender role perceptions, and social environment. The results of one study showed that prenatal testosterone exposure was related to higher DM in adult males. In terms of personality, men with high DM may also be anxious, perfectionistic, and strongly focused on their fitness and appearance. Surprisingly, the only physical measure related to DM is circumference of the biceps. Thus, body mass index (BMI), body fat percentage, and other anthropometric measures have not shown a relationship with DM.

In comparison to biology, personality, and physical attributes, much more research has focused on the influence of gender roles and social environment on DM. In Western society, muscularity is often equated with masculinity and individuals who identify as more masculine tend to show higher DM. Men who endorse more traditional views of masculinity such as the taking of risks, being physically strong and tough, and controlling one's emotions, are also more likely to have a stronger DM.

The social environment is believed to have a strong influence on men's conceptions of masculinity, and what it means to have a masculine body. Images of the ideal male body have evolved from the strong and burly John Wayne in the 1950s and 1960s—http://cache2.allpostersimages.com/p/LRG/21/2115/UG4ED00Z/posters/

john-wayne.jpg—to the tanned, ripped, and muscular action heroes of the 2000s and 2010s—http://images.hitfix.com/photos/689885/Vin-Diesel-in-Fast-Five_gallery_primary.JPG. Arnold Schwarzenegger is largely credited for bringing bodybuilding to the mainstream with his 1977 documentary, *Pumping Iron*—http://www.youtube.com/watch?v=IjH9lJVofh0. *Pumping Iron* made lifting weights socially acceptable for boys and men, and signaled a shift in the body ideal for boys and men.

Movies are not the only media source to help normalize hypermuscularity in males. Male models in health and fitness magazines tend to have less fat and more muscle mass today than they did in the 1970s and 1980s. Changes to the design of action figures have ensured that boys are exposed to the muscular ideal at a young age. Whereas action figures from the 1970s and early 1980s depicted men's bodies as relatively skinny— http://nsidecollectibles.com/catalog/images/vintagesolo.jpg—the same characters portrayed in the 1990s showed marked upper body development—http://home.comcast.net/˜smpratt/HTMLfiles/Solo/JabbaBeastPack.JPG. Video games and gaming magazines are another source of information for boys about the type of body they should strive to attain. Many researchers believe that changes to the portrayal of the male body have had the strongest influence on DM in boys and men today. Research supports this link, as numerous studies have shown that exposure to muscular male models in magazines leads to worsened mood and increased body dissatisfaction, depression, and DM in males.

Conclusion

Research conducted on body image dissatisfaction over the past 25 years has revealed that in addition to a drive for thinness, many individuals express a drive for muscularity. Although both males and females may report DM, males have generally received more pressure and reinforcement for being more muscular and masculine than females. DM assessment may include tests designed to measure individuals' attitudes and/or perceptions regarding muscularity. Research studies have shown that biological, psychological, and social factors all play a role in DM. DM is related to anxiety and perfectionism in males. Further, media images and action figures can contribute to a person's desire to be larger and more muscular.

NICK GALLI

Bibliography

Cafri, Guy, and Kevin J. Thompson. "Measuring Male Body Image: A Review of the Current Methodology." *Psychology of Men and Masculinity* 1 (2004): 18–29.

Davis, Caroline, Kristina Karvinen, and Donald R. McCreary. "Personality Correlates of a Drive for Muscularity in Young Men." *Personality & Individual Differences* 39 (2005): 349–59.

Drewnowski, Adam, and Doris K. Yee. "Men and Body Image: Are Males Satisfied with Their Body Weight?" *Psychosomatic Medicine* 49 (1987): 626–34.

Galli, Nick, and Justine J. Reel. "Adonis or Hephaestus? Exploring Body Image in Male Athletes." *Psychology of Men and Masculinity* 10 (2009): 95–108.

Giles, David C., and Jessica Close. "Exposure to 'Lad Magazines' and Drive for Muscularity in Dating and Non-dating Young Men." *Personality & Individual Differences* 44 (2008): 1610–1616.

"Han Solo 1970s Action Figure." Northside Collectibles, accessed May 30, 2011, http://nsidecollectibles.com/catalog/images/vintagesolo.jpg.

"Han Solo 1990s Action Figure." Home.Comcast.net, accessed May 30, 2011, http://home.comcast.net/~smpratt/HTMLfiles/Solo/JabbaBeastPack.JPG

Harrison, Kristen, and Bradley J. Bond. "Gaming Magazines and the Drive for Muscularity in Preadolescent Boys: A Longitudinal Examination." *Body Image* 4 (2007): 269–77.

"John Wayne." Allposters.com, accessed May 30, 2011, http://cache2.allpostersimages.com/p/LRG/21/2115/UG4ED00Z/posters/john-wayne.jpg.

Jung, Jaehee, Gordon B. Forbes, and Priscilla Chan. "Global Body and Muscle Satisfaction among College Men in the United States and Hong Kong-China." *Sex Roles* 63 (2010): 104–17.

Kelley, Courtney C., Jennie M. Neufeld, and Dara R. Musher-Eizenman. "Drive for Thinness and Drive for Muscularity: Opposite Ends of the Continuum or Separate Constructs?" *Body Image* 7: 74–77.

Kyretjo, Jacob W., Amber D. Mosewich, Kent C. Kowalski, Diane E. Mack, and Peter R. E. Crocker. "Men's and Women's Drive for Muscularity: Gender Differences and Cognitive and Behavioral Correlates." *International Journal of Sport and Exercise Psychology* 6 (2008): 69–84.

Lerner, Richard M., and Sam J. Korn. "The Development of Body-Build Stereotypes in Males." *Child Development* 43 (1972): 908–920.

McCreary, Donald R., and Doris K. Sasse. "An Exploration of the Drive for Muscularity in Adolescent Boys and Girls." *Journal of American College Health* 48 (2000): 297–304.

McCreary, Donald R., Deborah M. Saucier, and Will H. Courtenay. "The Drive for Muscularity and Masculinity: Testing the Associations among Gender-role Traits, Behaviors, Attitudes, and Conflict." *Psychology of Men and Masculinity* 5 (2005): 83–94.

Pope Jr., Harrison G., Katharine A. Phillips, and Robert Olivardia. *The Adonis Complex: The Secret Crisis of Male Body Obsession.* New York: Free Press, 2000.

Pumping Iron. YouTube.com, accessed May 30, 2011, http://www.youtube.com/watch?v=IjH9lJVofh0.

Smith, April R., Sean E. Hawkeswood, and Thomas E. Joiner. "The Measure of a Man: Associations Between Digit Ratio and Disordered Eating in Males." *International Journal of Eating Disorders* 43 (2010): 543–48.

Steinfeldt, Jesse A., Hailee Carter, Emily Benton, and Matthew C. Steinfeldt. "Muscularity Beliefs of Female College Athletes." *Sex Roles* 64 (2011): 543–54.

Tiggemann, Marika, Yolanda Martins, and Alana Kirkbride. "Oh to be Lean and Muscular: Body Image Ideals in Gay and Heterosexual Men." *Psychology of Men and Masculinity* 8 (2007): 15–24.

"Vin Diesel." Hitfix.com, accessed May 30, 2011, http://images.hitfix.com/photos/689885/Vin-Diesel-in-Fast-Five_gallery_primary.JPG.

E

EATING DISORDER NOT OTHERWISE SPECIFIED

The fourth edition of the *Diagnostic and Statistical Manual of Mental Disorders* identifies three categories of eating disorders: Anorexia Nervosa, Bulimia Nervosa, and Eating Disorder Not Otherwise Specified (EDNOS). EDNOS is diagnosed when an individual with an eating disorder does not meet the full criteria for anorexia nervosa or bulimia nervosa. EDNOS has been labeled the "garbage can" for eating disorder diagnoses because it is used when an individual presents with eating-related syndromes that are not yet covered by the DSM-IV-TR such as binge eating disorder, night eating syndrome, selective eating disorder, and orthorexia. In the DSM-5, it is expected that binge eating disorder and some of the other syndromes will be identified by name and will likely receive separate classification categories.

Examples of EDNOS Diagnoses

Individuals who are considered subclinical cases—that is, they present with disordered eating that is not as severe as full-blown eating disorder—and show potential to develop into clinical eating disorders may receive the EDNOS diagnosis. Even individuals who display disordered eating behaviors face the same risk for medical complications as individuals with full-fledged clinical eating disorders.

EDNOS is also given as a diagnosis when an individual with a severe eating disorder does not quite fit into the category for anorexia nervosa (e.g., everything except for amenorrhea) or bulimia nervosa (e.g., frequency less than twice a week or duration less than three months). Additionally, individuals who exhibit what has been dubbed as bulimiarexia, a disorder in which they alternate between restricting and binge/purge behaviors usually receive the EDNOS diagnosis. As mentioned above, individuals with binge eating disorder have received the EDNOS diagnosis to date, but BED should have a separate clinical category when the DSM-5 manual is published.

Conclusion

Although the EDNOS category has represented a "catch all" eating disorder category, it has been important in providing a diagnosis for subclinical cases as well as binge eating disorder and other syndromes not covered in the DSM-IV-TR. It is expected that this popular diagnosis will be replaced with more specific categories in DSM-5.

JUSTINE J. REEL

Bibliography

American Psychiatric Association. *Diagnostic and Statistical Manual of Mental Disorders, 4th Edition, Text Revision.* Washington, DC: American Psychiatric Association, 2000.

"DSM-5: The Future of Psychiatric Diagnosis." Dsm5.org. Accessed October 12, 2011. http://www.dsm5.org/ProposedRevision/Pages/FeedingandEatingDisorders.aspx.

"Eating Disorder Not Otherwise Specified (EDNOS)." Nami.org. Accessed October 12, 2011. http://www.nami.org/Template.cfm?Section=By_Illness&template=/ContentManagement /ContentDisplay.cfm&ContentID=65849.

EATING DISORDERS ANONYMOUS

Eating Disorders Anonymous (EDA) was formed in 2000 by Alcoholics Anonymous members in Phoenix to bring together individuals who were struggling with eating disorders and could share their common experience in a support group. Until that time, individuals with eating disorders would either attend Overeater's Anonymous (OA) or other twelve-step groups as part of their treatment and recovery process. However, individuals with anorexia nervosa and bulimia nervosa did not always feel like their experience fit with the other anonymous types of groups.

Unlike other eating disorder associations (e.g., National Eating Disorder Association) which engage in activist work to change societal beliefs and combat harmful media messages, EDA self-identifies as not wanting to participate in controversies or affiliate with any particular sect, denomination, political party, organization, or institution. EDA's primary purpose is "to recover from our eating disorders and to carry this message of recovery to others with eating disorders." Recovery has been defined by EDA as "living without obsessing on food, weight and body image" and making healthy choices in life, regaining trust in self, and practicing self-care. The only requirement for becoming an EDA member is to have the desire for recovery from an eating disorder.

EDA Meetings

EDA meetings function as support groups for males and females of all ages who suffer from an eating disorder. Groups average 8 attendees, but often range from 2 to 20 participants. The EDA's proposed solution parallels the twelve steps and twelve traditions of EDA published in a workbook format. Each meeting begins with a serenity prayer followed by a reading of the twelve steps or traditions. Participants have the opportunity to share their story and members can seek support by relating to other individuals in the group who have a shared experience. Currently, meetings take place as face-to-face, online, or phone meetings in almost all of the states in America, as well as Canada, Ireland, South Africa, and Ukraine.

There is no cost to attend meetings or to join EDA but donations are accepted to support the foundation.

Conclusion

EDA has been providing support groups and meetings using a traditional twelve-step format since 2000. Individuals with eating disorders are welcome to attend free meetings to find solace in hearing about others who struggle from eating disorders. Like other anonymous groups, EDA mentions a "higher power"; however, the group is not affiliated with any particular religion or group. Because eating disorder treatment has traditionally been extremely expensive (sometimes ranging from $1000 to $2000 for a night's stay in a residential facility), EDA offers a free option for receiving support to recover.

JUSTINE J. REEL

See also: National Eating Disorders Association; Twelve-Step Programs.

Bibliography

Eating Disorders Anonymous. Accessed August 18, 2011. www.eatingdisordersanony mous.org.
Overeaters Anonymous. Accessed August 18, 2011. www.oa.org.
The Alliance for Eating Disorders. Accessed August 18, 2011. www.allianceforeatingdis orders.com.

EDEMA

Edema is defined as swelling caused by fluid accumulation between cells. In eating disorder clients, edema most frequently affects the tissue in the lower legs, usually around the feet and ankles. Some cases of edema are described as "pitting," which is the formation of an indentation in the skin when pressure is applied to the area. Many cases of edema are mild, but severe prolonged lower limb edema may result in increasingly painful swelling, leg stiffness, and difficulty walking. For eating disorder clients, the acute, rapid weight gain that edema causes may intensify body image disturbances and reinforce the fear of gaining too much weight or becoming fat, which may trigger a return to eating disordered behaviors.

Causes of Edema

There can be multiple causes of edema and those that impact eating disordered clients are not entirely understood. However, the most commonly proposed causes of edema in eating disordered clients involve (1) the retention of sodium and fluid by the kidneys and (2) the movement of fluid from the blood vessels into the tissues between the cells. However, other causes of edema should not be ruled out, including heart, liver, or kidney failure.

Sodium and Fluid Reabsorption
Purging and Edema

Self-induced vomiting and laxative and diuretic abuse are common purging methods in eating disorder clients and may lead to chronic dehydration. In order to adapt, the body increases the production of aldosterone, a hormone that signals the kidneys to reabsorb more fluid and sodium. When purging behaviors are discontinued abruptly or if an individual undergoes rapid rehydration (e.g., via intravenous administration), aldosterone levels may remain elevated and lead to edema.

Refeeding Edema

Refeeding syndrome is characterized by a myriad of metabolic complications that develop when nutrition is re-introduced, including fluid and electrolyte disturbances (see "Refeeding Syndrome" for the full description). Edema may be one of the first signs of refeeding syndrome. Undernourished clients may have an increased sensitivity to insulin, a hormone which regulates carbohydrate and fat metabolism. The elevation in insulin levels that occurs when carbohydrates are provided in higher amounts and utilized again by the body after a period of starvation may stimulate sodium reabsorption and, thus, fluid retention.

Blood Vessel Permeability
Reproductive Hormones

Menstrual cycle disturbances are a common symptom of malnutrition in which the body's production of sex hormones decreases. During nutrition and weight repletion, these hormone levels increase leading to the return of menses. It is possible that estrogens cause blood vessels to widen, which may cause fluid to leak out of vessels and build up in the surrounding tissues.

Management of Edema

Edema usually resolves on its own over time without any form of treatment. The length of time that it takes for edema to go away varies depending on the situation, but may take a few weeks for some. However, mental health providers should discuss the possibility of edema with the client to help prepare them psychologically for any acute physiological changes when nutrition is reintroduced, or refeeding occurs. For severe edema, leg elevation is helpful in reducing the swelling in some clients. Sometimes, diuretics are prescribed in low doses; however, use of diuretics is closely monitored by a physician to prevent abuse. Edema may also occur less often in clients who consume a low sodium diet during the initial weeks of refeeding to reduce sodium retention. To help prevent or reduce the severity of edema, nutritional rehabilitation should occur gradually in undernourished clients, with a slow increase in caloric intake, close monitoring of electrolyte levels, avoidance of excessive fluid intake, and regular physical examinations.

Conclusion

Edema, the swelling caused by fluid accumulation between cells, frequently occurs among eating disordered individuals. These individuals complain of swelling in their lower legs, feet, and ankles. This medical consequence of disordered eating behaviors may serve as a negative trigger for body image disturbances and reinforce the fear of gaining too much weight. Therefore, the client's reaction to this symptom should be monitored carefully to avoid a potential relapse.

HOLLY E. DOETSCH

See also: Diuretics; Laxative Abuse; Refeeding Syndrome.

Bibliography

Ehrlich, Stefan, Uwe Querfeld, and Ernst Pfeiffer. "Refeeding Oedema: An Important Complication in the Treatment of Anorexia Nervosa." *European Child and Adolescent Psychiatry* 15 (2006): 241–43.

Kalambokis, Georgios N., Agathocles A. Tsatsoulis, and Epameinondas V. Tsianos. "The Edematogenic Properties of Insulin." *American Journal of Kidney Diseases* 44, no. 4 (2004): 575–90.

Mascolo, Marguerita, Eugene S. Chu, and Philip S. Mehler. "Abuse and Clinical Value of Diuretics in Eating Disorders Therapeutic Applications." *International Journal of Eating Disorders* 44 (2011): 200–202.

Rigaud, Daniel, Alain Boulier, Isabelle Tallonneau, Marie Claude Brindisi, and Raymond Rozen. "Body Fluid Retention and Body Weight Change in Anorexia Nervosa Patients during Refeeding." *Clinical Nutrition* 29 (2010): 749–55.

Roerig, James L., Kristine J. Steffen, James E. Mitchell, and Christie Zunker. "Laxative Abuse: Epidemiology, Diagnosis and Management." *Drugs* 70, no. 12 (2010): 1487–1503.

Tey, Hong Liang, Su Chi Lim, and Alison M. Snodgrass. "Refeeding Oedema in Anorexia Nervosa." *Singapore Medical Journal* 46 (2005): 308–310.

Yucel, Basak, Nese Ozbey, Aslihan Polat, and Joel Yager. "Weight Fluctuations during Early Refeeding Period in Anorexia Nervosa: Case Reports." *International Journal of Eating Disorders* 37 (2005): 175–77.

ELECTROCARDIOGRAM

An electrocardiogram, also known as EKG or ECG, is a noninvasive, painless test that measures the heart's electrical activity. During the 10 to 15 minute test, a person is asked to lie flat. Twelve electrodes, called leads, are placed on the arms, legs, and chest. The leads are connected to a machine that records the electrical signals of the heart and produces a graphic tracing of the electrical impulses.

The heart's conduction system is made up of specialized neuromuscular tissue located throughout the heart. The movement of charged ions across the membranes of myocardial cells produces the wave forms on the EKG. EKG results help determine abnormalities in heart rate, heart rhythms, and the strength and timing of the electrical signals as they pass through each part of the heart.

EKG Changes in Anorexia Nervosa

On an EKG, the QT interval reflects the time during which the left and right ventricles of the heart are triggered to contract and then build the potential to contract again. On an EKG reading, the QT interval usually lasts for one third of the heartbeat cycle. This is known as depolarization and repolarization. As the heart rate increases, the depolarization-repolarization must happen more quickly and the QTc, the corrected QT interval, adjusts for this.

It was once thought that a ventricular arrhythmia caused by QT prolongation was responsible for sudden deaths in individuals with anorexia nervosa. Although studies have documented prolonged QT intervals in severely anorexic individuals, this has not been a consistent finding. According to *Eating Disorders: A Guide to Medical Care and Complications,* the prevalence and cause of prolonged QT interval remains controversial. Currently, the assumption is that the QT interval is not inherently prolonged in anorexia nervosa, and it is not the independent cause of sudden death. A 2006 study published in the *International Journal of Cardiology* reported that in individuals with anorexia nervosa, the QT interval is usually normal, but individuals with severe hypokalemia (decreased serum potassium) are at risk for *tosarde de pointe,* a life-threatening arrhythmia. If a person with anorexia nervosa has a prolonged QT interval, electrolyte imbalances should be considered.

In addition to a prolonged QT interval, other EKG changes result from electrolyte abnormalities. Severe hypokalemia can cause T-wave flattening, prominent U waves, and ST segment depression. Low magnesium and low calcium can also cause a prolonged QT interval and T-wave changes. QRS segment depression, ST segment alterations, and T-wave changes on an EKG can also be related to the decreased thickness of the left ventricle wall and cardiac chamber size due to decreased muscle mass from starvation.

QT dispersion on an EKG is another marker for determining arrhythmia risk. The length of the QT interval is usually similar between each of the 12 leads. QT dispersion is the difference between the maximum QT interval and minimum QT interval occurring in any of the 12 leads. A 2005 study in the *International Journal of Eating Disorders* found that when the QT dispersion is increased, the individual may develop ventricular arrhythmias. The reason for an increased QT dispersion in individuals with anorexia nervosa is unknown, but it is hypothesized that a decreased resting metabolic rate and decreased skeletal and cardiac muscles due to starvation increases QT dispersion.

EKG Changes in Bulimia Nervosa

Eating Disorders: A Guide to Medical Care and Complications also reports that normal weight individuals suffering from bulimia nervosa have fewer cardiac complications than those with anorexia nervosa. EKG changes in individuals with bulimia nervosa are usually indicative of electrolyte abnormalities. Low blood levels of potassium and magnesium are a danger to the heart, especially in individuals who purge frequently by vomiting or by taking laxative and diuretics.

EKG Changes and Refeeding

Most of the EKG changes can be reversed with the correction of electrolyte imbalances, hydration, and nutritional status; however, during the refeeding process, electrolytes must be carefully monitored because there may be alterations in phosphorus, magnesium, and potassium which can cause electrolyte abnormalities and EKG changes.

Conclusion

An electrocardiogram or EKG measures heart activity. EKG changes have been observed among individuals with anorexia nervosa, bulimia nervosa, and individuals who are subjected to refeeding. It is important to monitor EKG since cardiovascular complications are a dangerous and sometimes deadly consequence of eating disorders.

SHELLY GUILLORY

Bibliography

Facchini, M., L. Sala, G. Malfatt, R. Bragata, G. Redelli, and C. Invitti. "Low K+ Dependent QT Prolongation and Risk for Ventricular Arrhythmias in Anorexia Nervosa." *International Journal of Cardiology* 106, no. 2 (2006): 170–76. Accessed May 7, 2011. doi: 10.1016/j.ijcrd.2005.01.041

Garner, David M., and Paul E. Garfinkel. "Medical Complications." *Handbook of Treatment for Eating Disorders,* 2nd ed., 387–88. New York: The Guilford Press, 1997.

Krantz, Mori J., William T. Donahoo, Edward L. Melanson, and Philip S. Mehler. "QT Interval Dispersion and Resting Metabolic Rate in Chronic Anorexia Nervosa." *International Journal of Eating Disorders* 37, no. 37 (2005): 166–70. Accessed May 6, 2011. doi: 10.1002/eat.20082.

Lewis, Sharon M., Margaret Heitkemper, and Sharon Dirkson. "Fluid, Electrolyte and Acid-Base Balance." In *Medical-Surgical Nursing: Assessment and Management of Clinical Problems. 5th ed.,* edited by Sally Shrefer, 324–26. St. Louis: Mosby, Inc., 2000.

Mehler, Philip S., and Arnold E. Anderson. "Evaluation and Treatment of Electrolyte Abnormalities." In *Eating Disorders: A Guide to Medical Care and Complications, 2nd ed.,* 96–107. Baltimore: Johns Hopkins University Press, 2010.

National Heart and Blood Institute. "Electrocardiogram." Last revised October 2010. Accessed May 6, 2011. http://www.nhlbi.nih.gov/health/dci/Diseases/ekg/ekg_what.html

Takimoto, Yoshiyuki, et al. "QT Interval and QT Dispersion in Eating Disorders." *Psychotherapy and Psychosomatics* 73, no. 5 (2004): 324–28. Accessed May 7, 2011. doi: 10.1159/000078550

ELECTROLYTE IMBALANCE

Electrolytes are substances whose molecules dissipate or split into ions when placed in water. Ions are electrically charged particles. Positive ions, called cations, include sodium, potassium, calcium, and magnesium. Anions are negatively charged particles. Examples include phosphorous, chloride, and bicarbonate.

Electrolytes are found in blood, urine, and bodily fluids and are used to help regulate nerve and muscle function in the body.

Electrolytes help the body maintain the normal fluid levels within the cells, the space around the cells, and in the blood. The fluid within these three compartments should remain fairly stable; however, how much fluid a compartment contains depends on the concentration of electrolytes. To adjust fluid levels, the body actively moves electrolytes in and out of the cells. If the electrolyte concentration is high, fluid moves into the compartment. If electrolyte concentration is low, fluid moves out of the compartment.

Electrolyte Imbalances and Eating Disorders

Despite significantly low body weight, individuals with anorexia nervosa who do not engage in purging behaviors rarely present with severe electrolyte disturbances. Most electrolyte imbalances are seen in individuals with bulimia nervosa who purge through self-induced vomiting, laxative abuse, and diuretic misuse. According to one study, the most common abnormality seen in individuals with bulimia was elevated serum bicarbonate, but other abnormalities included hypokalemia (low potassium), hypochloremia (high chloride), hyponatremia (low sodium), hypomagnesemia (low magnesium), and decreased serum bicarbonate. A separate study found that hypokalemia and hyponatremia were the most frequently altered electrolytes. Hypomagnesemia and hypokalemia were most commonly discovered in individuals with bulimia who used diuretics to purge.

Metabolic Alkalosis and Metabolic Acidosis

A normal serum bicarbonate level is 22–28 mmol/L. In individuals with bulimia, metabolic alkalosis, which results in an increased serum bicarbonate level, is almost always the result of purging through self-induced emesis or diuretic abuse. An elevated bicarbonate level or other electrolyte imbalances that are not consistent with an individual's self-reported history can help alert doctors when a client denies purging.

Metabolic alkalosis develops from self-induced vomiting because of acid and sodium chloride (NaCl) lost in the vomitus. Lost NaCl causes a state of decreased intravascular volume from dehydration, which stimulates the kidney's renin-angiotensin system. This causes the adrenal cortex to secrete high levels of aldosterone—a hormone that increases salt absorption and bicarbonate reabsorption in the kidney—to prevent low blood pressure and fainting. This sequence of events is the body's normal response to prevent dehydration despite ongoing purging behaviors.

Diuretics cause increased sodium and chloride excretion, which causes decreased intravascular volume depletion and dehydration, which again activates the renin-angiotensin system. The metabolic alkalosis that occurs as a result of diuretic abuse, however, is often not as severe as seen in individuals who engage in self-induced vomiting. Most serum bicarbonate concentrations over 38 mEq/L are almost always the result of self-induced vomiting.

Self-induced vomiting and diuretic abuse cause metabolic alkalosis, but laxative abuse can cause either a metabolic alkalosis or a metabolic acidosis. Acute diarrhea can cause large amounts of bicarbonate to be lost in the stool, causing hyperchloremic (high serum chloride) metabolic acidosis. However, the more common acid-base balance caused by laxative abuse is a metabolic alkalosis with a low serum chloride and low serum potassium. The alkalosis is usually in the mild range of 30–34 mEq/L, but the hypokalemia can be severe.

Clinical Manifestations

Eating disordered individuals with electrolyte imbalances may have complaints of weakness, fatigue, constipation, dizziness, and depression. The normal range for serum potassium concentration is 3.5–5.5 mmol/L. Clinical manifestations of hypokalemia (less than 3.6 mmol/L) include generalized muscle weakness, fatigue, constipation, and heart palpitations. In severe cases of hypokalemia (less than 2.5 mmol/L), the individual is at high risk for cardiac complications and sudden death. Cardiac complications can be seen on the client's EKG and include T-wave changes, ST segment depression, prominent U waves, and QT prolongation. Although it is rare to see cardiac complications in a client with a potassium level greater than 3 mmol/L, complications are increased in clients with co-occurring heart disease who have a potassium level of less than 3.9 mmol/L. A low serum magnesium level can complicate hypokalemia symptoms and further contribute to arrhythmias and sudden death. Hypomagnesemia and hypocalcemia can also cause a prolonged QT interval and T-wave changes.

Electrolyte Abnormalities during Refeeding and Rehydration

The metabolic alkalosis from dehydration must first be reversed before attempting to normalize potassium levels. Aldosterone production must be stopped in order to halt renal potassium excretion. Intravenous sodium chloride is used to treat severe metabolic alkalosis; mild cases can be treated orally with fluids that contain sodium. Treatment of an individual with severe hyponatremia is carried out slowly because rapidly correcting serum sodium can cause a neurological complication called central pontine myelinolysis. Magnesium deficiency can also cause potassium loss. Magnesium deficiency should also be evaluated for individuals who purge using diuretics, as all diuretics cause some loss of magnesium.

Electrolytes should also be monitored frequently during the refeeding process, especially for clients who are at risk for refeeding syndrome—a syndrome consisting of metabolic disturbances that can occur when individuals who are malnourished begin to eat. Refeeding syndrome can be fatal if not recognized or treated properly. Hypokalemia, hypomagnesemia, and high blood sugar can occur, but hypophosphatemia (low serum phosphorus) is the main electrolyte disturbance during refeeding syndrome and it causes significant morbidity and mortality. A dangerous drop in phosphorous can occur within three days of initiating nutrition therapy. According to an article in *Nutrition Reviews,* complications from hypophosphatemia include cardiac failure, muscle weakness, immune dysfunction, and death.

Conclusion

Electrolyte imbalances are often observed among individuals with bulimia nervosa who engage in purging methods (e.g., vomiting, laxative abuse) that disrupt electrolytes in the body. These imbalances should be monitored carefully because they can result in severe medical complications. Electrolyte imbalances are also a potential risk when individuals are undergoing the refeeding process and can be fatal if not treated properly.

SHELLY GUILLORY

Bibliography

"Fluid and Electrolyte Balance." MedlinePlus.com. Last modified May 2011. Accessed May 12, 2011. http://www.nlm.nih.gov/medlineplus/fluidandelectrolytebalance.html

Johnson, Larry E. "Disorders of Nutrition and Metabolism: Minerals and Electrolytes." merckmanuals.com. Last modified August 2008. Accessed May 12, 2011. http://www.merckmanuals.com/home/sec12/ch155/ch155a.html.

Lewis, Sharon M., Margaret Heitkemper, and Sharon Dirkson. "Fluid, Electrolyte and Acid-Base Balance." In *Medical-Surgical Nursing: Assessment and Management of Clinical Problems, 5th ed.,* edited by Sally Shrefer, 324–26. St. Louis: Mosby, Inc., 2000.

Marinella, Mark A. "The Refeeding Syndrome and Hypophophatemia." *Nutrition Reviews* 61, no. 9 (2003): 320–23. Accessed May 24, 2011. doi: 10.1301/nr.2003.sept.320–323.

Mehler, Philip S., and Arnold E. Anderson. "Evaluation and Treatment of Electrolyte Abnormalities." In *Eating Disorders: A Guide to Medical Care and Complications, 2nd ed.,* 96–107. Baltimore: Johns Hopkins University Press, 2010.

Mehler, Philip S. "Diagnosis and Care of Patients with Anorexia Nervosa in Primary Care Settings." *Annals of Internal Medicine* 134, no. 11. (2001): 1048–59. Accessed May 11, 2011. ISSN: 00034819 PMID: 1138881 Accessed May 10 2011. http://web.ebscohost.com.ezproxy.lib.utah.edu/ehost/pdfviewer/pdfviewer?sid=549156cf-0022-4603-9b14-667b2e44c22d%40sessionmgr114&vid=4&hid=126

Miller, Karen K., Steven K. Grinspoon, Julia Ciampa, Joan Hier, David Herzog, and Ajnne Klibanski. "Medical Findings of Outpatients with Eating Disorders." *Archives of Internal Medicine* 135, no. 5. (2005): 561–66. Accessed May 11, 2011. http://archinte.ama-assn.org/cgi/reprint/165/5/561.

Wolfe, Barbara E., Mark E. Rosenberg, James E. Mitchell, and Paul Thuras. "Urine Electrolytes as Markers of Bulimia Nervosa." *International Journal of Eating Disorders* 30, no. 3 (2001): 288–93. Accessed May 12, 2011. doi: 10.1002/eat.1085.

Wolfe, Barbara E., Eran D. Metzger, Jeffery M. Levine, and David C. Jimerson. "Laboratory Screening for Electrolyte Abnormalities and Anemia in Bulimia Nervosa: A Controlled Study." *International Journal of Eating Disorders* 30, no. 3 (2001): 388–93. Accessed May 12, 2011. doi: 10.1002/eat.1086.

EMDR: EYE MOVEMENT DESENSITIZATION AND REPROCESSING

Eye Movement Desensitization and Reprocessing (EMDR) is a therapy developed by Dr. Francine Shapiro to help people work through unresolved traumas. Ten years prior to EMDR's official birth, Shapiro began an extraordinary journey. While working as a teacher and doctoral student, she was diagnosed with cancer. After she was considered cured by her physicians, she was told that the cancer could resurface, but the doctors did not know what to do. Shapiro decided to educate herself in psychoimmunology and the mind-body connection. Soon after, in an effort to benefit mankind, she developed a nonprofit organization, Metadevelopment and Research Institute, to synthesize different areas of learning. In 1987, EMDR was born when Shapiro noticed her own life stress reactions were alleviated when she swept her eyes spontaneously back and forth during her daily walk through the park. She began to experiment and discovered that the process was effective for other people as well.

Overview of EMDR

EMDR entails having an individual recall a stressful past event while thinking about a positive self-chosen belief. Rapid eye movements during this dual thought process serve to actually reprogram the memory and soften the impact that the traumatic or stressful memory has on the individual's ability to thrive. The key element to reprogramming the memory lies in dual stimulation where the client is asked to think or talk about triggers, painful emotions, and memories while focusing on the therapist's moving finger. Other forms of bilateral stimulation can be utilized with similar benefit. Some people respond better to alternating hand taps or listening to a chime that sound back and forth from ear to ear.

At the time that a stressful or traumatic event occurs, strong emotions can interfere with one's ability to process the experience, and the event can then become frozen in time. Recalling the incident may feel as though one is reliving the trauma because the smells, sounds, images, and feelings are still there in a frozen state and can be triggered in the present. When activated, the memories can cause a negative impact on one's daily functioning and can interfere with self-concept and how one relates to others. EMDR therapy seems to directly affect the brain by unfreezing the traumatic memories. The individual then has an opportunity to process the memories, find resolution, and move on.

EMDR and Eating Disorder Treatment

Eating disordered individuals have a tendency to be shaped by traumatic events and fail to establish healthy and secure bonds with others. Although originally applied to the treatment of Post-Traumatic Stress Disorder (PTSD) and other anxiety disorders, EMDR has been found to be quite useful in the treatment of eating disorders because perceived traumatic events and body image disturbance are often at the root of eating disorders. A 2008 study found that eating disorder clients in a residential treatment facility who received EMDR therapy reported less distress about negative body image memories and lower body dissatisfaction at post-treatment, 3-month, and 12-month follow-up, compared to those clients who did not receive EMDR.

EMDR therapy for eating disorder treatment typically includes eight phases. Phase one includes history and treatment planning. The therapist typically does not discuss traumatic events in detail but learns a general timeline of significant events in the client's life. Phase two, preparation, involves teaching the client self-care techniques (e.g., relaxation) to deal with strong emotions that may occur between sessions. Phase three, assessment, establishes the groundwork for the actual EMDR therapy sessions. The client is asked to identify (1) a specific scene or picture, (2) a negative belief, and (3) a positive belief. Beliefs are then rated on a scale of one to seven based on how strongly they are believed to be true. Locations in the body are identified where physical sensations are experienced related to the traumatic event. Phase three is a poignant intervention to help eating disordered clients to begin to make a mind-body connection. In phase four, desensitization, the client concentrates on all of the negative beliefs, disturbing emotions, and bodily sensations that come up as he or she focuses on the target image while following the therapist's finger back and forth. The client takes note of all the reactions to the processing and checks in with the therapist to assess the level of disturbance regarding the target image. Eating disorder clients learn to identify how their perceived traumas are contributing to disordered eating behaviors by understanding how their reactions are supporting the eating disorder. In phase five (installation), the client is asked to focus on the identified positive belief to replace the old negative belief about the trauma while simultaneously tracking the therapist's finger with the eyes. The eating disorder client learns to sense the physical body in a new way. Phase six (body scan) includes checking for any lingering tension or uncomfortable physical sensations, which are then targeted with bilateral stimulation until they are resolved. EMDR is often used in conjunction with other eating disorder therapies (e.g., cognitive behavioral therapy) so that integration occurs between resolution of lingering tension and cessation of disordered behaviors. Phases seven and eight of therapy focus on creating closure and evaluating the client's progress.

Conclusion

Although EMDR was originally developed for the treatment of PTSD, empirical studies have noted that EMDR can be quite effective in the treatment of eating disorders because eating disorder symptoms are often fueled by disturbing thoughts regarding perceived traumatic events, both past and present. The original eight phases of EMDR are currently utilized in conjunction with other therapies for treatment of eating disorders with positive results. Diminishing or eliminating the power that perceived traumatic events have on the eating disordered individual leads to new levels of relief and healing from eating disorders.

JULIANN M. COOK

Bibliography

Bloomgarden, Andrea, and Calogero, Rachel. "A Randomized Experimental Test of the Efficacy of EMDR Treatment on Negative Body Image in Eating Disorder Inpatients." *Eating Disorders* 16, no. 5 (2008): 418–27.

Dziegielewski, Sophia. "Eye Movement Desensitization and Reprocessing (EMDR) as a Time Limited Treatment Intervention for Body Image Disturbance and Self Esteem: A Single Subject Case Design." *Journal of Psychotherapy in Independent Practice* 1 (2000): 1–16.

Shapiro, Francine. *Eye Movement Desensitization and Reprocessing: Basic Principles, Protocols and Procedures.* New York: The Guilford Press, 1995.

Shapiro, Francine. "Eye Movement Desensitization and Reprocessing (EMDR): Evaluation of Controlled PTSD Research." *Journal of Behavior Therapy and Experimental Psychiatry* 27 (1996): 313–17.

Shapiro, Francine. *EMDR as an Integrative Psychotherapy Approach: Experts of Diverse Orientations Explore the Paradigm Prism.* Washington, DC: The American Psychological Association, 2002.

vonRanson, Kristen, and Robinson, Kathleen. "Who Is Providing What Type of Psychotherapy to Eating Disorder Clients? A Survey." *International Journal of Eating Disorders* 39 (2006): 27–34.

EMOTIONAL EATING

Emotional eating is the tendency to eat in response to negative or positive emotions. Rather than listening to biological cues of hunger and fullness, emotional eaters tend to consume more food when they are experiencing anxiety, anger, depression, or elation, or when they are feeling upset. By contrast, individuals who are not emotional eaters may actually lose appetite or forget to eat when they are experiencing similar emotions. Emotional eating has been associated with excessive eating and a greater tendency to indulge in one's trigger foods that are often high in sugar, salt, or fat (e.g., ice cream, cookies).

Emotional Eating and Eating Disorders

Therefore, becoming overweight and obesity may be the natural outcome from a pattern of overeating behavior. Additionally, emotional eating may be associated with dieting and yo-yo weight cycling which can contribute to obesity and eating disorders such as binge eating disorder and bulimia nervosa. In a study of 129 Finnish college students, emotional dieters reported higher body dissatisfaction, perfectionism, drive for thinness, and maturity fears than nondieters, indicating a higher risk for eating disorders among this group. Emotional dieters also had more depression, feelings of inadequacy, poorer body image, and lower self-esteem globally than nondieters. Emotional eaters had some overlap with restrained eaters, showing that emotional eaters have a tendency to fluctuate between periods of excessive food intake and food restriction. Therefore, individuals who have been diagnosed with binge eating disorder or bulimia nervosa often admit to struggling with emotional eating and have often lost a sense of when they are truly hungry (or full).

In the treatment setting, emotional eating should be addressed so that individuals may begin to develop a more biologically-based approach to evaluating one's hunger or fullness. Individuals may benefit from intuitive eating so that they can listen to their bodies and move away from emotional eating patterns.

Conclusion

Emotional eating in response to strong feelings can occur among individuals of any weight or size. Although related to bulimia nervosa and binge eating disorder, emotional eating is strongly related to dieting and weight fluctuations. If emotional eating continues, overweight and obesity may result or disordered eating may become more extreme. Therefore, it is important that emotional eating is addressed as part of treatment and that an individual can begin to adopt an intuitive eating approach.

JUSTINE J. REEL

See also: Intuitive Eating.

Bibliography

Eldredge, Kathleen L., and W. Stewart Agras. "Weight and Shape Overconcern and Emotional Eating in Binge Eating Disorder." *International Journal of Eating Disorders* 19 (1996): 73–82.

Lindeman, Marjaana, and Katarina Stark. "Emotional Eating and Eating Disorder Psychopathology." *Eating Disorders* 9 (2001): 251–59.

Lowe, Michael R., and Edwin B. Fisher, Jr. "Emotional Reactivity, Emotional Eating and Obesity: A Naturalistic Study." *Journal of Behavioral Medicine* 6 (1985): 135–49.

Van Strien, Tatjana, Gerard M. Schippers, and W. Miles Cox. "On the Relationship between Emotional and External Eating Behavior." *Addictive Behaviors* 20 (1995): 585–94.

Waller, Glenn, and Miki Matoba. "Emotional Eating and Eating Psychopathology in Nonclinical Groups: A Cross-cultural Comparison of Women in Japan and the United Kingdom." *International Journal of Eating Disorders* 26 (1999): 333–40.

Waller, Glenn, and Selen Osman. "Emotional Eating and Eating Psychopathology among Non–Eating Disordered Women." *International Journal of Eating Disorders* 23 (1998): 419–24.

ENDURANCE SPORTS

Endurance sports have been defined based on the physiological and competitive requirements that they share. More specifically, endurance sports are classified as those sports that primarily depend on aerobic energy systems (i.e., with oxygen) and require lower intensity training of long duration. Endurance sports can include cross-country and track, cross-country skiing, cycling, swimming, water polo, rowing, and speed skating. Perhaps the most studied endurance sport athlete within the eating disorder area is the endurance runner.

Energy Deficits

Some endurance athletes, especially marathon runners, have difficulty consuming enough calories to sustain their athletic performance and/or other metabolic processes necessary for optimal bodily functioning. These athletes are said to run on an energy deficit, with little dietary energy available for metabolic processes after exercise. But why does this happen? Scholars contend that some endurance athletes may lack a significant biological drive to consume enough calories and counterbalance the amount of energy expended each day. In this case, energy deficits are unintentional. However, others may purposefully restrict their calorie consumption to manage weight or alter body composition for performance purposes. After all, many endurance athletes often strive for a leaner and lighter build simply to facilitate faster race times. Of most concern is the fact that some endurance athletes may compulsively engage in more pathological weight control behaviors, including severe calorie restriction, in an attempt to lose weight or body fat to improve appearance and performance.

Weight Pressures

Pressures to lose or maintain weight are evident in endurance sports. In a study of 62 female collegiate swimmers, the most frequently cited weight pressures were having to wear revealing swimming attire (45.2%), the belief that being lighter improves swimming performance (42%), as well as perceptions that teammates notice their weight (16.1%) and that the spectators scrutinize their body (12.9%). In addition to swimming, some researchers have postulated that rowers may also experience weight pressures because their sport requires them to make a particular weight class. Female lightweight rowers may be especially at risk for disordered eating because of thin ideal standards for women in general and having to maintain a suitable weight for the lightweight category of their sport. Runners and cyclists may also face a unique set of weight pressures, including the belief that thinness means faster times. Although many athletes and coaches believe this to be true, evidence suggests that endurance athletes with the lowest body fat or body mass index (BMI) do not always have the fastest times. For example, in a study of 70 female distance runners, one of the best running performances was from the athlete with the highest percentage of body fat in the sample at 35.8 percent.

Body Image Concerns and Disordered Eating

Unsurprisingly, elite female endurance and aesthetic athletes tend to be leaner and at greater risk for disordered eating; they also have higher training volumes as compared to other sport types, such as technical (e.g., golf) and ball-game sports (e.g., soccer). The prevalence of eating disorders has been reported at 24 percent in elite female endurance athletes and 9 percent in elite male endurance athletes. At the high school level, the prevalence of eating disorders has been reported at 8 percent and 20 percent for male and female endurance athletes, respectively.

Disordered eating has been most extensively studied in swimmers, rowers, and runners as compared to other endurance sports. Unfortunately, the research has not been entirely optimistic. For example, in a study of 487 female and 468 male swimmers in the age group of 9–18 years, 15.4 percent of the girls and 3.6 percent of the boys reported engaging in at least one unhealthy weight control behavior, including fasting, self-induced vomiting, and the consumption of diet pills, laxatives, and diuretics. Binge eating, fasting, and vomiting may be a particular concern in some rowers. Among 162 collegiate rowers (89 males and 73 females), 20 percent of the females and 12.3 percent of the males reported binge eating at least twice a week, 57 percent of males and 25.4 percent of females reported fasting, and 2.5 percent of males and 13.2 percent of females reported vomiting as a means of cutting weight. In a study of 412 high school, university, and track and field athletes, 11.8 percent of middle/long distance athletes and 4.7 percent of sprint athletes reported symptoms indicative of an eating disorder. Together, research conducted with these athletes suggests that although most do not engage in disordered eating behaviors, some do engage in extremely harmful weight control behaviors.

Regardless of the method or the intentions for such behaviors, inadequate caloric intake can lead to a deficiency in important micronutrients (i.e., dietary minerals like iron and potassium) and macronutrients (i.e., major energy sources including fats, proteins, and carbohydrates) critical for optimal athletic performance and everyday functioning. Prolonged energy deficits in the body can place these athletes at risk for developing components of the female athlete triad, including low bone mineral density and menstrual dysfunction. Low bone mineral density is a special concern among athletes in endurance sports like swimming, rowing, and cycling, where there is very little impact loading on the bones to strengthen them and offset the effects of low energy availability and poor calcium intake. For those endurance sports with high impact loading, like running, low bone mineral density can lead to stress fractures, especially when combined with overtraining and inadequate nutrition.

Coaches of endurance athletes could play a major role in the prevention of disordered eating, the female athlete triad, and the associated consequences including stress fractures. Researchers agree that education on proper training and nutrition is imperative. Unfortunately, preliminary evidence suggests that some coaches are limited in their understanding of specific methods of recovery, sports nutrition, and eating disorders. Although resources are available at the more elite levels of sport (e.g., through the United States Olympic Committee and the National Collegiate Athletic Association), such educational tools are scarce in the arena of youth and high school athletics.

Benefits

Although appropriate prevention measures should be taken in light of the risk for inadequate energy intake, unhealthy weight control practices, and components of the female athlete triad, it is critical to remember that endurance sports can also be quite healthy for the body when proper training and nutritional practices are employed. Aerobic exercise training in general has been associated with a number of benefits, including reduced risk for cardiovascular disease and diabetes. In fact, healthy elite endurance-trained athletes have been found to live longer than the general population, probably due to the reduced risk for disease. Other preliminary research suggests that aerobic exercise training is associated with improvements in visuospatial memory and positive emotion in young adults. Education on nutrition and appropriate training for the endurance sport athlete is one important way in which we can minimize the detriments and maximize the benefits of this type of sport participation.

Conclusion

Not all endurance sport athletes will resort to unhealthy weight management practices in an attempt to improve appearance and performance. However, research suggests that some do, which should make prevention efforts a top priority across all levels of participation. Such efforts may include educating athletes, coaches, and parents about overtraining, the importance of rest and recovery, sports nutrition, and signs and symptoms of disordered eating as well as the female athlete triad. Education should also include discussion of the myths associated with endurance sports training, including the misperception that more training and lighter weight is always associated with performance improvements.

DANA K. VOELKER

See also: Coaches; Rowing; Swimming and Synchronized Swimming; Weight Pressures in Sport.

Bibliography

Hausenblas, Heather A., and Kimberly D. McNally. "Eating Disorder Prevalence and Symptoms of Track and Field Athletes and Nonathletes." *Journal of Applied Sport Psychology* 16 (2010): 274–86.

Kellmann, M. "Preventing Overtraining in Athletes in High-Intensity Sports and Stress/Recovery Monitoring." *Scandinavian Journal of Medicine and Science in Sports* 20 (2010): 95–102.

Loucks, Anne B. "Low Energy Availability in the Marathon and Other Endurance Sports." *Sports Medicine* 37 (2007): 348–52.

Reel, Justine J., and Diane L. Gill. "Slim Enough to Swim? Weight Pressures for Competitive Swimmers and Coaching Implications." *The Sport Journal* 4 (2001).

Rosendahl, J., B. Bormann, K. Aschenbrenner, F. Aschenbrenner, and B. Strauss. "Dieting and Disordered Eating in German High School Athletes and Non-Athletes." *Scandinavian Journal of Medicine and Science in Sports* 19 (2009): 731–39. doi: 10.1111/j.1600-0838.2008.00821.x.

Sundgot-Borgen, Jorunn, and Monica Klungland Torstveit. "Prevalence of Eating Disorders in Elite Athletes Is Higher than in the General Population." *Clinical Journal of Sports Medicine* 14 (2004): 25–32.

Thompson, Ron A., and Roberta Trattner Sherman. *Helping Athletes with Eating Disorders.* Champaign, IL: Human Kinetics, 1993.

ENERGY AVAILABILITY

Energy availability is energy that is left or available after energy has been spent during exercise. In other words, energy availability equals dietary energy intake minus energy expenditure. Energy availability can fall within a spectrum ranging from optimal available energy to low energy availability. Low energy availability occurs when a female consumes insufficient food to support her level of physical activity as well as normal growth and development. Having too few calories (i.e., low energy availability) may reflect the presence of disordered eating associated with restrictive behavior and the desire to lose weight. However, low energy availability may also occur when an athlete engages in strenuous training accompanied by inadequate energy intake due to lack of knowledge about how many calories are required. Unfortunately, low energy availability, like disordered eating, can have health consequences and may result in reproductive system disruption to conserve energy resulting in inadequate estrogen production.

In the 2007 female athlete triad position stand, the American College of Sports Medicine (ACSM) replaced disordered eating with energy availability for a component of the female athlete triad. Researchers have suggested that low energy availability is predictive of exercise-induced menstrual dysfunction rather than low body weight or low body fat. Although the prevalence of low energy availability is unknown, one study found that 15 percent of college female athletes and 26 percent of college male athletes consumed insufficient energy in the form of carbohydrates and proteins to meet nutritional needs of athletes.

Conclusion

Low energy availability refers to not meeting the caloric demands of energy expenditure. Athletes tend to be more at risk for low energy availability due to high energy output. However, any physically active individual can suffer the consequences (e.g., menstrual dysfunction) associated with low energy availability. Energy availability has replaced disordered eating as a component of the female athlete triad and is used to identify health concerns within the athletic population.

JUSTINE J. REEL

See also: Female Athlete Triad.

Bibliography

American College of Sports Medicine (ACSM). "Position Stand: The Female Athlete Triad." *Medicine & Science in Sports & Exercise* 39 (2007): 1867–1882.

Hinton, Pamela S., Tiffany C. Sanford, M. Meghan Davidson, Oksana F. Yakushko, and Niels C. Beck. "Nutrient Intakes and Dietary Behaviors of Male and Female Collegiate Female Athletes." *International Journal of Sport Nutrition and Metabolism* 14 (2004): 389–405.

Loucks, Anne B., Bente Kiens, and Hattie H. Wright. "Energy Availability in Athletes." *Journal of Sports Sciences* (2011). doi: 10.1080/02640414.2011.588958.

Loucks, Anne B., Nina S. Stachenfield, and Loretta DiPietro. "The Female Athlete Triad: Do Female Athletes Need to Take Special Care to Avoid Low Energy Availability?" *Medicine & Science in Sports & Exercise* 38 (2006): 1694–1700.

Thompson, Ron A., and Roberta Trattner Sherman. *Eating Disorders in Sport.* New York, NY: Routledge, 2010.

EQUINE THERAPY

Equine therapy is defined as a type of animal-assisted therapy using horses in the treatment of psychological issues. Animals have been used for mental health treatment since before 1792. In fact, ancient Greeks recognized the therapeutic effects of horses and would offer rides to individuals who were believed to have incurable or untreatable illnesses in order to improve their mood and outlook. Pet therapy is considered an evidence-based treatment for addressing a variety of mental disorders including eating disorders.

Equine therapy, which is also referred to as Equine-Assisted Experiential Therapy (EAET) or Equine-facilitated Psychotherapy (EFP), allows individuals to work on communication, trust, and living in the present, and to develop coping skills necessary for healthy recovery from eating disorders. Equine activities include performing daily chores such as caring for the animals; horse grooming can occur as part of a client's daily schedule at a residential facility. Additionally, therapeutic exercises include role-plays to work on psychological issues during individual or group therapy. Equine therapy can provide an effective supplement or an alternative to traditional eating disorder treatment (i.e., talk therapy).

Benefits of Equine Therapy for Eating Disorder Treatment

A stigma remains for individuals who seek traditional mental health services which can serve as a barrier to opening up in therapy in order to achieve sufficient treatment progress. However, the horse seems to act as a normalizing effect allowing many clients to relax and experience a safe environment for expressing emotions spontaneously and taking risks within the therapeutic environment. Additionally, treatment providers (e.g., psychologists) are able to observe their clients outside of the office setting which can provide valuable information about their ability to communicate and set boundaries. Importantly, equine therapy provides the opportunity to explore relevant metaphors regarding the role an eating disorder is playing for a client as well as the recovery process.

An example of the use of equine therapy in an eating disorder setting is described by Jo Christian's case study. Five buckets of feed which are labeled by the client as the five most important aspects of her life (education, ballet, family, friends, and health) are placed along the inside rail of the round arena. Meanwhile, the horses are labeled shame, control, and perfection using sidewalk chalk. The client is able to practice assertiveness by directing the horses to move to the particular buckets. She must use appropriate verbal and nonverbal communication to guide the horses in the right direction. During an equine-assisted exercise, the client's treatment team can observe and provide support and encouragement to the client. After the exercise, the client can process emotions that arose during the real-life enactment of her life.

JUSTINE J. REEL

Bibliography

Bizub, Anne L., Ann Joy, and Larry Davidson. "It's Like Being in another World: Demonstrating the Benefits of Therapeutic Horseback Riding for Individuals with Psychiatric Disability." *Psychiatric Rehabilitation Journal* 26, no. 4 (2003): 377–84.

Christian, Jo Ellen. "All Creatures Great and Small: Utilizing Equine-Assisted Therapy to Treat Eating Disorders." *Journal of Psychology and Christianity* 24, no. 1 (2005): 65–67.

Karol, Jane. "Applying a Traditional Individual Psychotherapy Model to Equine-Facilitated Psychotherapy (EFP): Theory and Method." *Clinical Child Psychology and Psychiatry* 12 (2007): 77–90. doi: 10.1177/1359104507071057

Klontz, Bradley T., Alex Bivens, Deb Leinart, and Ted Klontz. "The Effectiveness of Equine-Assisted Experiential Therapy: Results of an Open Clinical Trial." *Society and Animals* 15 (2007): 257–67. doi: 10.1163/156853007X217195

Rothe, Eugenio Quiroz, Beatriz Jimenez Vega, Rafael Mazo Torres, Silvia Maria Campos Soler, and Rosa Maria Molina Pazos. "From Kids and Horses: Equine Facilitated Psychotherapy for Children." *International Journal of Clinical and Health Psychology* 5, no. 2 (2005): 373–83.

Vidrine, Maureen, Patti Owen-Smith, and Priscilla Faulkner. "Equine-Facilitated Group Psychotherapy: Applications for Therapeutic Vaulting." *Issues in Mental Health Nursing* 23 (2002): 587–603. doi: 10.1080/01612840290052730

EXERCISE

The relationship between exercise and eating disorders can be both positive and negative. On the one hand, if exercise behaviors are taken to the extreme and exercise is used as a purging method as part of an eating disorder, having a dysfunctional relationship with physical movement can be detrimental to treatment and recovery. Dysfunctional exercise has been referred to as activity anorexia, overexercise, exercise addiction, excessive exercise, exercise dependence, exercise abuse, and obligatory exercise. These represent labels for pathological exercise that continues beyond injury and illness and results in an individual missing social, family, and work obligations for exercise sessions.

Conversely, exercise can be a positive coping mechanism for stress and anxiety and has been linked with improved mood, decreased depression, and increased self-confidence. Exercise therapy can be integrated into a comprehensive treatment program for mental health populations such as those with mood disorders, substance abuse, and eating disorders.

History of Exercise and Eating Disorder Treatment

Historically, exercise has been severely limited during eating disorder treatment due to the presence of dysfunctional exercise among many of the clients and the concern that movement would undermine necessary weight restoration goals. The excessive hyperactivity was observed in some of the earliest documented cases of eating disorders. However, in the 1970s, researchers discovered that 25 out of 33 anorexia nervosa clients who were hospitalized for eating disorder treatment over a 10-year period showed symptoms of excessive exercise behaviors. Another research in 1963 discovered that 75 percent of anorexia nervosa clients exhibited excessive exercise (which was referred to as "intense athleticism" in that early study).

Until the 1990s, clients with anorexia nervosa who entered treatment were placed on bed rest with all movement restricted during their stay. Any form of exercise as part of eating disorder treatment was considered controversial despite the fact that 97 percent of clinicians and researchers admitted that physical activity and eating disordered behaviors were related and realized that the benefits of exercise extended beyond health.

Beumont and his colleagues introduced the first structured exercise program into eating disorder treatment in 1994 to include anaerobic exercise (e.g., resistance training). The rationale for the inclusion of exercise was that distorted beliefs surrounding exercise should be addressed and challenged within treatment. The need for exercise education (e.g., how to engage in healthy exercise and expand motivations to exercise) was important and they realized that the total elimination of movement had been ineffective and unrealistic for eating disorder clients.

Benefits of Exercise

In addition to the numerous health benefits associated with physical activity (e.g., disease prevention, increased strength, improved cardiovascular functioning and bone health, etc.), exercise has psychological implications as well. In addition to the well-researched mood benefits of exercise, which include reduction of overall depression and anxiety, eating disorder clinicians and researchers realized that exercise can also help reduce anxiety around meals and can improve program compliance. Additional findings were that exercise increased weight gain and body composition and prevented relapse. Ideally, exercise education can be used along with actual movement to challenge distorted thoughts and feelings about exercise and help clients move away from dysfunctional exercise behaviors and toward a more mindful approach to exercise.

Physical Activity Recommendations for Eating Disorder Treatment

Any movement during eating disorder treatment should be prescribed, supervised, and individualized to the client's needs and preferences whenever possible. Exercise education and a debriefing period to follow movement is optimal as part of the treatment process.

Prescribed

If a client is medically compromised, has a Body Mass Index below 14, or is restricted to bed rest, he or she should wait to participate in exercise and movement sessions until being cleared by his or her physician. Exercise that is provided within an inpatient or residential setting should be deliberate with specific functions. For example, stretching can be helpful for clients who have spent much time sitting and experience back pain. Light lifting or resistance training can be useful to provide impact to improve bone health. Other types of exercise that tend to be associated with playfulness and enjoyment (e.g., Nia, zumba, and yoga) and those that tend to be less likely to be abused by clients are ideal. Generally, running should be avoided during initial stages of treatment due to high caloric demands and potential for injury and stress fractures. Also, running often involves moving despite feeling pain which is the opposite of mindful exercise (i.e., listening to one's body and adapting exercise to what feels good). As a general rule, it is recommended that a treatment program expose clients to a wide variety of movement patterns and types of exercise to deliver the message that there are many forms of activities as exercise.

In an outpatient setting it is recommended that the treatment team include an exercise specialist who is knowledgeable about the specific needs and challenges associated with the eating disorder population. This specialist should work with the physician on the treatment team to prescribe an exercise routine that emphasizes quality over quantity. The client should be encouraged to begin exercise gradually and introduce a variety of types of movement. Generally yoga, resistance training, and other forms of stretching would be recommended over running and intense activities during the initial phases of treatment.

Supervised

Supervising physical activity is much manageable in a residential or inpatient setting. Nonetheless all activity should be monitored throughout the day. Some treatment programs provide specific classes such as yoga, but also have casual walks throughout the day between treatment groups. It is recommended that all exercise and movement be structured (planned) and supervised by staff with exercise qualifications who can gauge intensity of exercise. During exercise classes, the instructor can observe facial expressions to determine whether any clients are abusing exercise or becoming overly intense during the session. The exercise instructor should be trained to change cues to reflect an eating disordered population. The focus should be on enjoyment or health benefits rather than burning fat and calories or looking good. Some yoga postures may need to be modified to avoid competition within the group. Generally mirrors are discouraged in a treatment setting, but if used they should only be a guide for technique rather than a way for clients to monitor weight changes and appearance.

In outpatient settings supervision becomes more difficult. Family members and others can help support the exercise plan so that clients are not engaging in additional activities that lead to too much energy expenditure. Family members and friends may need to receive education that exercise that is prescribed is actually helpful to treatment. Some personal trainers can help monitor exercise routines for outpatient clients; however, few receive training in eating disorder population needs. A client may be encouraged to exercise with a friend who can help set a moderate, less intense pace. It is recommended that the treatment team consider whether the client is able to continue organized sports and other activities that may have contributed to exercise abuse prior to admission for treatment.

Individualized

The amount of exercise and types of movement should ideally be individualized like any other type of prescription medication. For example, individuals with bulimia nervosa and binge eating disorder may be able to engage in aerobic exercise sooner than individuals with anorexia nervosa who are still working on weight restoration. Additionally, client preferences may allow for certain modifications in the types of activities performed. Some clients may feel triggered (i.e., experience negative body image) by participating in yoga and may choose nia or zumba instead. Although individualizing exercise plans can be costly within a residential setting, each client should be provided with an exercise plan as she or he is transitioning to an outpatient setting.

For clients who are in the outpatient setting, individualizing treatment is much more manageable and is only limited by the types of exercise that are available in a client's community. An exercise therapist may not be able to screen every exercise class and may have to work with clients to cope with triggers in the exercise environment as they arise.

Exercise Education

Exercise education should accompany actual movement or exercise sessions so that eating disorder clients can learn about healthy forms of exercise and work toward changing their dysfunctional mindset toward exercise. An important topic to include is motivation to exercise. While clients may enter treatment with the sole motive for exercise being to burn calories or lose weight, it is important to identify the many reasons why people choose to move their bodies. Clients can also work on topics such as improving self-confidence and assertiveness in exercise classes (e.g., martial arts and self-defense).

Debriefing Feelings Following Exercise

Following exercise clients should have the opportunity to process feelings that arise during the exercise session. It is not uncommon for individuals to feel a full range of emotions—such as frustration that their body can actually feel less intense and shorter bouts of movement, and anxiety about not doing enough exercise to burn the calories consumed. It is especially powerful for individuals to process thoughts that occurred during movement such as feeling compulsive or detached from one's body or feeling joy associated with movement.

Types of Exercise

When clients admit for treatment they should be screened for dysfunctional exercise; the activities which they abused before seeking treatment should also be determined. Clients should initially be prescribed new activities that are less aerobic in nature. Throughout treatment clients will have the opportunity to practice many different types of exercise. However, some of the more common forms of exercise available at eating disorder treatment centers include yoga, nia, horseback riding, and stretching. Exercise options are expanding and, depending on the geographical location, clients may be able to engage in water aerobics, hiking, or ice skating. Zumba, which has recently gained in popularity across the United States, shows much promise for eating disorder clients. Similar to dance, Zumba encourages participants to embrace the music and learn steps and routines while moving in a low-impact fashion.

Conclusion

Exercise and eating disorders can be a complicated topic. Although dysfunctional exercise has been associated with eating disorders, it is important to address distorted thinking, feelings, and behaviors while the client is in treatment. Mindful exercise can be taught and prescribed during treatment at any level of care. It is recommended that an exercise specialist should participate in the multidisciplinary treatment team when dysfunctional exercise is identified. Ultimately, whether residential or outpatient, exercise should be prescribed, supervised, and individualized to the client's needs. Exercise education is a vital part of the treatment program and should include an opportunity for clients to debrief about feelings that come up during exercise sessions.

JUSTINE J. REEL

See also: Exercise Dependence; Nia; Obligatory Exercise; Yoga.

Bibliography

Beumont, Peter J. V., Brenden Arthur, Janice D. Russell, and Stephen W. Touyz. "Excessive Physical Activity in Dieting Disorder Patients: Proposals for a Supervised Exercise Program." *International Journal of Eating Disorders* 15, no. 1 (1994): 21–36.

Calogero, Rachel M., and Kelly N. Pedrotty. "The Practice and Process of Healthy Exercise: An Investigation of the Treatment of Exercise Abuse in Women with Eating Disorders." *Eating Disorders* 12 (2004): 273–91.

Calogero, Rachel M., and Kelly N. Pedrotty-Stump. "Incorporating Exercise into Eating Disorder Treatment and Recovery." In *Treatment of Eating Disorders: Bridging the Research to Practice Gap,* edited by Margo Maine, Beth Hartman McGilley, and Doug Bunnell, 425–43. London, UK: Elsevier, 2010.

Hechler, Tanja, Peter Beumont, P. Marks, and Stephen Touyz. "How Do Clinical Specialists Understand the Role of Physical Activity in Eating Disorders?" *European Eating Disorders Review* 13 (2005): 125–32. doi: 10.1002/erv.630.

Thien, Vincent, Alison Thomas, Donna Markin, and Carl Laird Birmingham. "Pilot Study of a Graded Exercise Program for the Treatment of Anorexia Nervosa." *International Journal of Eating Disorders* 28 (2000): 101–106.

Tokumura, Mitsuaki, Shigeki Yoshiba, Tetsuya Tanaka, Selichiro Nanri, and Hisako Watanabe. "Prescribed Exercise Training Improves Exercise Capacity of Convalescent

Children and Adolescents with Anorexia Nervosa." *European Journal of Pediatrics* 162 (2003): 430–31. doi: 10.1007/s00431-003-1203-1.

Touyz, Stephen W., Wolfgang Lennerts, Brenden Arthur, and Peter J.V. Beumont. "Anaerobic Exercise as an Adjunct to Refeeding Patients with Anorexia Nervosa: Does it Compromise Weight Gain?" *European Eating Disorders Review* 1, no. 3 (1993): 177–82.

EXERCISE DEPENDENCE

The "exercise as medicine" movement has largely touted the benefits of exercise including reduced stress and improved cardiovascular function which makes it difficult to view physical activity as a negative habit. However, exercise dependence is defined as engaging in physical activity that is excessive with a dysfunctional psychological mindset. Exercise dependence, also referred to as exercise addiction and excessive exercise, can be identified by the presence of at least three of the following characteristics: tolerance (i.e., a need to increase exercise amount to avoid guilt), withdrawal effects (i.e., experiencing symptoms such as anxiety and fatigue when unable to exercise), intention effects (i.e., exercise is often in larger amounts or over a longer period than was planned), lack of control (i.e., a persistent desire or unsuccessful effort to decrease or control exercise), time (i.e., a great amount of time is spent exercising), reductions in other activities (i.e., exercise is prioritized over social, occupational, or recreational activities), and continuance (i.e., exercising despite injury and illness). Furthermore, individuals who exhibit exercise dependence refuse to incorporate rest days into their workout routines and tend to engage in a rigid routine that does not include a variety of movement activities.

History of Exercise Dependence

The term "exercise dependence" was originally coined by Veale in 1987 and has been described as a negative mood state experienced in the absence of a drug, object, or activity. In other words, exercise is a stimulant that leads to the physiological arousal of the brain and the avoidance of negative feelings. For some individuals, exercise alters the mood in the short term and can occasionally stimulate a state of euphoria popularly referred to as the "runners' high" by competitive and recreational runners beginning in the 1970s. Veale selected the term "exercise dependence" over "runner's high" to allow for a broader application across sports and recreational activities and to capture the negative and compulsive nature of this condition. In recent years, the importance of identifying both an individual's psychological mindset and reasons for exercise have become key for the detection of exercise dependence.

Symptoms of Exercise Dependence

The symptoms of exercise dependence include depressed mood, irritability, fatigue, anxiety, impaired concentration, and sleep disturbances. The negative impact on mood and evidence of depression has been observed among runners identified as having exercise dependence following just one day without exercise. Physical complications associated with exercise dependence include repeated soft tissue injuries and stress fractures, pressure-sores (i.e., damaged skin caused by staying in one position for too long), gastrointestinal blood loss and anemia, myocardial infarction and death. These harmful effects have been documented most comprehensively in long-distance runners since the late 1970s.

Primary versus Secondary Exercise Dependence

The two classifications of exercise dependence are primary and secondary exercise dependence. In primary exercise dependence, exercise is an end in itself, but secondary exercise dependence goes beyond an exercise addiction. Specifically, individuals with secondary exercise dependence engage in excessive exercise as a purging method as part of an eating disorder.

Primary exercise dependence, which is not associated with an eating disorder, is characterized by several symptoms. The most common symptom is preoccupation with exercise. Withdrawal symptoms such as mood swings and irritability are also seen in the absence of exercise. Additionally, the individual with primary exercise dependence experiences distress or impairment in his or her physical, social, occupational, or other important areas of functioning. Additionally, in order to be primary exercise dependence, the individual's preoccupation with exercise is not aimed at another mental disorder (e.g. a means of losing weight or controlling calorie intake as in an eating disorder).

By contrast, individuals with secondary exercise dependence intentionally use exercise as a purging method to control weight as part of an eating disorder. As a typical pattern of secondary exercise dependence, the individual often selects cardiovascular fitness and exercises for a few hours once or more daily. Furthermore, the exercise intensity level and amount become excessively increased with subjective awareness of a compulsion to exercise over the years. The individual with secondary exercise dependency also relies on exercise to cope with the stress or fear of gaining weight and experiences withdrawal symptoms on cessation of exercise schedule. Therefore, the individual with secondary exercise dependence prioritizes exercise over other activities to maintain the exercise schedule.

Secondary Exercise Dependence: Warning Signs

Secondary exercise dependence is commonly identified in eating disorders. Studies have reported secondary exercise dependence as being identified among approximately 80 percent of anorexia nervosa and 55 percent of bulimia nervosa clients. The following warning signs are identified in the secondary exercise dependence:

1. Exercising a couple of times a day, two to five hours total.
2. Counting calories in order to figure out what exercise you need to do to burn them.
3. Rearranging one's day in order to fit exercise in.

4. When one's daily routine or cycle is disrupted by a constant need to exercise above all else; the individual will stop whatever it is he or she is doing, no matter how important, to exercise.
5. Food is viewed as the enemy.
6. Exercise becomes the sole activity and only social outlet.

The causes of exercise dependence are not entirely clear, but the motivation to lose weight or to keep weight low is a significant factor for both disordered eating and excessive exercise behaviors. Psychological characteristics of exercise dependence such as perfectionism, low self-esteem, and negative self-acceptance/self-image also overlap with psychological characteristics associated with eating disorders. Recently, researchers have found a potential link between brain activity and exercise dependence showing evidence that exercise dependence may have addictive qualities similar to substance abuse (e.g., cocaine, morphine).

Conclusion

Assessing for exercise dependence is important in understanding how to best treat the complexity of the eating disorder. In addition to identifying the frequency and duration of exercise, it is also necessary to determine an individual's motivation for exercise and whether he or she feels obligated to engage in a specific and ritualistic exercise routine. Although exercise provides many psychological and physical benefits, excessive exercise that begins to resemble an addiction can yield some dangerous health consequences. When exercise dependence is coupled with an eating disorder, it complicates the treatment process and needs to be addressed as a separate purging method. The good news is that treatment professionals are more aware of the need to promote a healthy relationship with exercise and are beginning to incorporate exercise education as part of a multidisciplinary treatment approach.

MAYA MIYAIRI

Bibliography

Adams, Jeremy, and Robert J. Kirkby. "Excessive Exercise as an Addiction: A Review." *Addiction Research and Theory* 10, no. 5 (2002): 415–37.

American Psychological Association. *Diagnostic and Statistical Manual of Mental Disorder, 4th ed.* Washington, DC: American Psychological Association, 2000.

Bamber, Diane, Ian M. Cockerill, Sue Rodgers, and Doug Caroll. "Diagnostic Criteria for Exercise Dependence in Women." *British Journal of Sports Medicine* 37 (2003): 393–400.

Blaydon, Michelle J., Koenraad J. Linder, and John H. Kerr. "Metamotivational Characteristics of Exercise Dependence and Eating Disorders in Highly Active Amateur Sport Participants." *Personality and Individual Differences* 36 (2004): 1419–1432.

Bratland-Sanda, Solfrid, Jorunn Sundgot-Borgen, Øyvind Rø, Jan H. Rosenvinge, Asle Hoffart, and Egil W. Martinsen. "Physical Activity and Exercise Dependence during Inpatient Treatment of Longstanding Eating Disorders: An Exploratory Study of Excessive and Non-Excessive Exercisers." *International Journal of Eating Disorders* 43, no. 3 (2010): 266–73.

Ferreira, Anthony, Fernando Perez-Diaz, and Charles Cohen-Salmon. "The Relationship between Physical Activity and Cocaine Intake in Mice." *Journal of Clinical Sports Psychology* 3 (2009): 232–43.

Ferreira, Anthony, Fabien Cornilleau, and Fernando Perez-Diaz. "Exercise Dependence and Morphine Addiction: Evidence from Animal Models." *Journal of Clinical Sports Psychology* 2 (2008): 17–24.

Gapin, Jennifer, Jennifer L. Etnier, and Denise Tucker. "The Relationship between Frontal Brain Asymmetry and Exercise Addiction." *Journal of Psychophysiology* 23, no. 3 (2009): 135–42.

Glasser, William. *Positive Addiction.* New York: Harper and Row, 1976.

Hagan, Amy L., and Heather Hausenblas. "The Relationship between Exercise Dependence Symptoms and Perfectionism." *American Journal of Health Studies* 18, no. 213 (2003): 133–37.

Hall, Howard K., Andrew P. Hill, Paul R. Appleton, and Stephen A. Kozub. "The Mediating Influence of Unconditional Self-Acceptance and Labile Self-Esteem on the Relationship between Multidimensional Perfectionism and Exercise Dependence." *Psychology of Sport and Exercise* 10 (2009): 35–44.

Harmon, Kevin Bernard. "Are You an Exercise Addict?" *American Fitness* (2009): 52–53.

Hausenblas, Heather A., and Danielle Downs Symons. "Exercise Dependence: A Systematic Review." *Psychology of Sport and Exercise* 3 (2002): 89–123.

Peñas-Lledó, Eva, Francisco J. Vaz Leal, and Glenn Waller. "Excessive Exercise in Anorexia Nervosa and Bulimia Nervosa: Relation to Eating Characteristics and General Psychopathology." *International Journal of Eating Disorders* 31 (2002): 370–75.

Reel, Justine J., and Katherine A. Beals, eds. *The Hidden Faces of Eating Disorders and Body Image.* Reston, VA: AAHPERD/NAGWS, 2009.

Russell, Michael. "What Is Dependence?" In *Drugs and Drug Dependence,* edited by Griffith Edwards. Lexington, MA: Lexington Books, 1976.

Shroff, Hemal, Lauren Reba, Laura M. Thornton, Federica Tozzi, Kelly L. Klump, Wade H. Berrettini, Harry Brandt, Steven Crawford, Scott Crow, Manfred M. Fichter, David Goldman, Katherine A. Halmi, Craig Johnson, Allan S. Kaplan, Pamela Keel, Maria LaVia, James Mitchell, Alessandro Rotondo, Michael Strober, Janet Treasure, D. Blake Woodside, Walter H. Kaye, and Cynthia M. Bulik. "Features Associated with Excessive Exercise in Women with Eating Disorders." *International Journal of Eating Disorder* 39 (2006): 454–61.

Veale, de Coverley. "Exercise Dependence." *British Journal of Addiction* 82 (1987): 735–40.

F

FAMILY INFLUENCES

In the 1980s, family members and particularly parental styles (i.e., overbearing mother and distant father figure) were solely blamed for causing eating disorders. However, researchers and clinicians have realized that while families can contribute to eating disorders, they also provide the necessary support to foster healthy treatment and recovery from eating disorders. Additionally, families can provide a source of self-esteem and self-worth that can serve as a protective factor against body dissatisfaction and body image disturbances. By contrast, a family's overemphasis on appearance or praise for slenderness can contribute to an environment that values beauty over other qualities (e.g., athletic ability, academic prowess). Furthermore, dieting and restricting certain foods in the home can heighten a mindset of "good" and "bad" foods that may perpetuate disordered thoughts and an unhealthy relationship with food.

Family Dynamics

Family dynamics have been identified as key factors in both the development and perpetuation of eating disorders. Dated studies and case reports of families that had a member with an eating disorder have indicated that the families tended to be intrusive, enmeshed, and hostile. Within the past few years, several studies have suggested that people who suffer from eating disorders seem to have insecure attachments with their family members.

Eating disorder clients have at times described a critical family environment with coercive parental control. Adolescents who report poor family communication and low parental expectations, as well as those who report sexual or physical abuse, seem to be at increased risk for developing eating disorders. Additionally, children who are raised by separated, divorced, or widowed parents are at higher risk and they also tend to engage in solitary eating more often, which has been found to be a contributing factor in the development of eating disorders. Single-parent families may be more likely to lack the ability to educate children regarding food habits and eating patterns, precisely due to the absence of one of the two parents during meals. This parental input is believed to exert a very important role in preventing eating disorders. Clients with bulimia nervosa also report that parents are intrusive, jealous, and competitive, and that privacy is not respected. In contrast, perceived parental encouragement of autonomy is associated with less dieting behavior, which can serve as a protective function against eating disorders.

Maternal Influence

Mothers provide a role model for eating and body image scrutiny for their daughters and sons. Mothers who make disparaging comments about their own bodies may socialize their children to be critical of their body parts and perceived flaws. In some cases, mothers of daughters with eating disorders exhibited eating disorder behaviors themselves, which may have had an influence on their daughters' development of eating disorder pathology. According to one study, mothers with eating disorder symptoms fed their children at irregular times, used food for rewards and punishments, expressed concern about their children's weight as early as age two, and were more dissatisfied with the general functioning of the family system. By age five, these children exhibited greater signs of depression and anxiety than did the offspring of mothers without eating disorders. One study conducted by Lilenfeld, et al. (1998) suggested that 50 percent of children of mothers with eating disorders display symptoms of depression, anxiety, obsessive-compulsive disorder, and eating disorders. Furthermore, the mother's direct comments to her children seem to be more influential than her behavior regarding weight and body image concerns, although even modeling does appear to affect children's weight- and shape-related attitudes and behaviors. Several studies suggest that a mother's critical comments increase the probability of development of eating disorder behaviors in their daughters.

Paternal Influence

Fathers appear to play a significant role in their children's development of eating disorders. A noteworthy study conducted by Canetti, et al. (2008) found that fathers of daughters with anorexia nervosa tend to be less caring and more controlling. According to this study, controlling fathers did not predict the *severity* of their daughter's symptoms, but did contribute to the *onset* and *maintenance* of the eating disorder symptoms. Furthermore, when the daughters viewed the fathers as displaying "affectionless control," the daughters reported increased eating disorder symptoms. In addition, the researchers examined the roles of grandparents in the client's eating disorder development. Fathers who perceived their own mothers (paternal grandmother to client) as less caring had daughters who reported increased eating disorder behaviors. Also, a father's controlling behavior and uncaring attitude toward his children was associated with the controlling behavior of his own father. The father-daughter relationship seemed to have a direct influence on the development of and maintenance of an eating disorder. These findings were consistent with several other studies regarding the influence of parent-child relationships on children's eating disorders. Furthermore, the authors suggested that when considering parent-child relationships, it is often difficult to determine if existing problems contributed to the development of the eating disorder or if the eating disorder contributed to the development of the existing relationship problems. For example, does the eating disorder actually change the parents' behavior so the parents become less caring, or does a real lack of care contribute to the development of an eating disorder? Similarly, does a defiant adolescent have a distorted perception that the parents are controlling, or have the parents adopted a new parental attitude as a result of their effort to cope with the child's self-harming illness?

Sibling Influence

Currently, a paucity of research exists regarding the influence of sibling relationships on body image and disordered eating. In a separate study, researchers suggested that the relationship with one's sister may be the most potent modeling agent of weight concerns within the family environment. Other studies noted that sisters were perceived to communicate equivalent pressures to be thin as both parents combined. As sisters may recognize more modeling cues from each other than either parent, they also engage in high levels of social comparison. The comparison may be more negative if one sister is perceived by societal others as more attractive. One study found that sisters reported similar levels of internalization of the thin-ideal and body image disturbance, especially within a familial subculture of thinness. Another study showed that sisters of clients with eating disorders did not demonstrate a significant disturbance in their perception of their own body image. The authors also found a tendency toward overestimation of body fat in brothers compared to male controls. This finding, together with a higher muscularity overestimation, points toward a potential for more negative body perception in brothers of clients.

Ethnicity

Research has also examined the role of the ethnicity of the family in the development of eating disorders. Caucasian subjects have frequently been found to report greater body dissatisfaction and eating concerns than both Asian and African American subjects. Conversely, one study demonstrated that British Asian individuals showed higher dietary restraint scores than their Caucasian contemporaries and a higher prevalence of eating disorders in Asian than Caucasian girls. Furthermore, a series of studies with New Zealand families from a range of different cultural backgrounds showed vast differences in attitudes about eating. For instance, Maori and Pacific Islands women showed no concerns about their eating and body image/shape. However, Pacific Islander women who were raised in families that identified with Pakeha ways had a high incidence of anorexia and bulimia. Also, one study showed that the introduction of television into the lives of Fijian families resulted in a negative impact upon the adolescent daughters' disordered eating attitudes and behaviors. Many studies have shown that a greater prevalence of eating disorders exists within families from industrialized societies than within families from developing societies.

Conclusion

In summary, earlier research from the 1980s and 1990s blamed the family unit and individual family members (e.g., mother, father, siblings) for the development and maintenance of a family member's eating disorder. Many studies have examined the role of family dynamics, parental influence, and family ethnicity in the development of eating disorders. Because family members can play an important role in the treatment of and recovery from eating disorders, it is critical to consider how to educate families about how to best support someone who is struggling with an eating disorder.

JULIANN M. COOK

Bibliography

Becker, Anne, Rebecca Burwell, David Herzog, Paul Hamburg, and Stephen Gilman. "Eating Behaviors and Attitudes Following Prolonged Exposure to Television among Ethnic Fijian Adolescent Girls." *The British Journal of Psychiatry* 180 (2002): 509–514.

Bennington, Dieter, Nina Tetsch, and Gunter Jantschek. "Patients with Eating Disorders and Their Siblings: An Investigation of Body Image Perceptions." *European Child and Adolescent Psychiatry* 17 (2008): 118–26.

Bulik, Cynthia M., Patrick F. Sullivan, and Kenneth S. Kendler. "Genetic and Environmental Contributions to Obesity and Binge-Eating." *International Journal of Eating Disorders* 33, no. 3 (2003): 293–98.

Canetti, Laura, Kyra Kanyas, Bernard Lerer, Yael Latzer, and Eytan Bachar. "Anorexia Nervosa and Parental Bonding: The Contribution of Parent-Grandparent Relationships to Eating Disorder Psychopathology." *Journal of Clinical Psychology* 64 (2008): 703–716.

Coomber, Kerri, and Ross M. King. "The Role of Sisters in Body Image Dissatisfaction and Disordered Eating." *Sex Roles* 59 (2008): 81–93.

Hodes, Marquis, Saw Timimi, and Patrick Robinson. "Children of Mothers with Eating Disorders: A Preliminary Study." *European Eating Disorders Review* 5 (1997): 11–24.

Lilenfeld, Lisa R., Walter H. Kaye, Catherine G. Greeno, Kathleen R. Merikangas, Katherine Plotnicov, Christine Pollice, Radhika Rao, Michael Strober, Cynthia Bulik, and Linda Nagy. "A Controlled Family Study of Anorexia Nervosa and Bulimia Nervosa: Psychiatric Disorders in First-Degree Relatives and Effects of Proband Comorbidity." *Archives of General Psychiatry* 55 (1998): 603–610.

Strober, Michael, Cloughton Lambert, William Morrell, James Burroughs, and Charles Jacobs. "A Controlled Family Study of Anorexia Nervosa: Evidence of Familial Aggregation and Lack of Shared Transmission with Affective Disorders." *International Journal of Eating Disorders* 9 (1990): 239–53.

FAMILY THERAPY

Family therapy encompasses specific techniques beyond basic psychotherapy that assist families and couples with relationship difficulties. The family therapist typically works with the couple or family at the same time instead of using individual sessions. Change is viewed in terms of the interactions between the couple or the family members. Family therapy is an important component of effective treatment for individuals who suffer from eating disorders. For adolescents who continue to cope with family dynamics in the home, it is a critical piece for relapse prevention as part of a comprehensive eating disorder treatment plan. Family therapy for adult eating disordered clients may be optional and depends on the continued relationship with family members (e.g., parents, siblings) and the need to address unhealthy bonds that serve as triggers for disordered eating.

History of Family Therapy

Family therapy as its own unique professional practice originated in the 19th century with the marriage counseling and child guidance movements. The formal development of family therapy dates back to the 1940s and early 1950s with the formation of the American Association of Marriage Counselors in 1942. Initial influence came from psychoanalysis and social psychiatry, and later from learning theory and behavior therapy. In the early 1950s, Dr. Bateson and his colleagues began to study the communication patterns that his schizophrenic clients had with their families. He believed that the thought processes of the clients emerged out of bizarre communication patterns within the family. The team also observed that if the client improved, the family became destabilized, and resisted or blocked the client's improvement. Essentially, in order for the family system to operate, the client needed to remain sick. Dr. Bateson's team described the family as a system with homeostatic tendencies, hierarchies, boundaries, coalitions, and conflicts between specific members. By the mid-1960s, a number of other distinct schools of family therapy (e.g., Adlerian, Cognitive Behavioral, Experiential, Family Systems, Feminist, Strategic, Structural) had emerged, many of which have become integral parts in the treatment of eating disorders.

Adlerian Family Therapy

Founded by Alfred Adler in the 1920s, this approach examines the client within the family system. Treatment focuses on healing the underlying issues behind the eating disorder and the purposes the eating disorder serves for the individual and his or her family. Adler asserted that people are constantly striving to meet a real or fictional goal in life. With an eating disorder, perceptions are often distorted and can lead to destructive behaviors due to especially high sensitivity levels of eating disorder clients and due to the misinterpretations of events. Adlerian techniques are used to assist the family in understanding each member's role in the development and maintenance of the eating disorder and in reframing interpretations of events and family interactions.

Cognitive Behavioral Family Therapy (CBT)

John Gottman and Albert Ellis originally viewed family problems to be the result of operant conditioning. Operant conditioning in the context of family therapy refers to negative behaviors being reinforced by the family's interpersonal exchanges, which promotes incentives for unhealthy behaviors. Eating disorder symptoms are viewed as unhealthy behaviors that are in response to the client's interpersonal family relationships. The goals of CBT for the family are: (1) to help the family understand how members' maladaptive eating disorder behaviors originate with maladaptive thoughts, then feelings; (2) to help the family identify negative consequences (i.e., the client's eating disorder symptoms) of their behaviors; and (3) to help family members change their thoughts, which changes feelings and then behaviors. Although family members are not to blame for the client's eating disorder, they can certainly play a crucial role in the recovery from an eating disorder.

Experiential Family Therapy

This approach proposes that growth and healing occur through a real-life encounter with a therapist who is intentionally authentic with clients without pretense, often in a playful way, as a means to foster flexibility in the family and promote individuation. Experiential therapy includes, but is not limited to, activities such as family sculpture, role play, yoga, hiking, and art therapy to help family members explore their relationships and connections with one another. The therapist assists the family in enacting past and present emotional climates, giving family members a chance to view their relationships from a different perspective. For instance, a therapist uses family sculpture by having each family member take a position within the therapy room that symbolically represents the nature of their relationships with the other family members. Also, the therapist may have family members role-play, or act out, certain scenarios that happen within the family and may suggest making changes that could result in improved relationships. The goal of experiential therapy in eating disorder treatment is to free the family from the unresolved emotions around their relationships so that they are able to live in the present. Ultimately, self-discovery through resolving the family's emotional conflicts is a vital element for the patient in eating disorder treatment because his or her self-identity has been so entangled in the development and maintenance of the eating disorder.

Family Systems Therapy

Based on the work of Murray Bowen, this approach refers to conceptualizing family members as driven to achieve internal and external balance and often causing anxiety and emotional isolation. Family members become emotionally distanced from each other (internal) and the family unit becomes isolated from society (external). Societal isolation often stems from a lack of communication within the family that is extended to outside relationships. Also, the family may be ashamed of the internal struggles, which can lead to external isolation. Eating disorder symptoms serve a function by absorbing the anxiety in the family system. A major focus of family systems therapy is to activate each individual in the family to develop initiative and to accept responsibility for his or her own actions. At the same time, the therapist must address the forces within the family that may thwart individual motivation. Unresolved emotional issues are addressed, which brings awareness to the anxiety and other emotional processes within the family. Awareness of unfulfilled emotional needs creates room for options that may help the client manage eating disorder behaviors as other family members learn to adapt to the change in relationships that occur as the client becomes well.

Feminist Family Therapy (FFT)

This approach is based on the feminist perspective that eating disorders develop within a social and familial context that views women as nurturers and places emphasis on their conforming to culturally defined norms of physical attraction. Social expectations are identified as being the root of the problems rather than the family system itself. FFT therapists work to model an egalitarian perspective of healthy family relationships (each family member holds equal status within the family) and use a less directive approach than other therapists to explore the way cultural values get expressed in the family. The therapist tends to ask questions and listen rather than give specific instructions to family members so that the family is empowered to take an active role in treatment and recovery. FFT embraces a therapeutic attitude of equality, an opposition to the use of male power against women and a special respect for the emerging individuality and femininity of the female eating disorder client. FFT is particularly powerful in addressing cultural pressures pertaining to the eating disorder patient's body image distortion. The therapist may ask probing questions about the media and other societal pressures to be thin, thus encouraging the client and family to explore and challenge their own maladaptive beliefs.

Strategic Family Therapy

This approach is influenced by the work of Jay Haley (late 1960s) and views an eating disorder as a set of symptoms that are purposeful in maintaining balance in the family hierarchy. The therapist's goal is to discover and disconnect the eating disorder symptoms from the roles that the symptoms play in the family's interactions. The therapist will prescribe specific healthy behaviors for family members and guide the family members as they practice their healthy roles. As family members begin to change their behaviors (e.g., having family meals), the eating disorder symptoms fade from the central role in the family, the family organization shifts, and the client and other family members develop more adaptive ways of functioning.

Structural Family Therapy

The structural family therapy approach is based on Salvador Minuchin's early 1960s conceptualization of the psychosomatic family, which has had a major impact on the treatment of eating disorders. Within this model, family problems are viewed as arising from maladaptive boundaries and subsystems, indirect communication and avoidance of conflict, which are all created within the overall family system of rules and rituals that governs interactions. The focus of structural family therapy is to change the family's interactional patterns, thereby strengthening some bonds (i.e. between the parents), weakening other bonds (i.e. between the mother and the daughter/eating disorder client), and promoting the eating disorder client's autonomy. Essentially, the therapist challenges whatever it is in the family structure that might be contributing to curtailing the client's autonomy and growth. The therapist encourages all family members to speak for themselves and avoid saying how another person thinks or feels. This allows each person in the family system to claim his or her own space, which promotes self-discovery and individuation, which are vital components of eating disorder recovery.

Maudsley Approach or Family-Based Treatment (FBT)

This approach was conceived by a team of child and adolescent psychiatrists and psychologists at the Maudsley Hospital in London during the early 1990s. The Maudsley Approach will be covered in a separate section.

Conclusion

Family therapy for the treatment of eating disorders includes, but is not limited to, Adlerian Family Therapy, Cognitive Behavioral Family Therapy, Experiential Family Therapy, Family Systems Therapy, Feminist Family Therapy, Strategic Family Therapy, Structural Family Therapy and the Maudsley Approach. The main limitation of many theoretical models of family therapy is that the focus tends to be on etiology rather than on an understanding of how families become organized around a potentially life-threatening problem such as an eating disorder. Many family therapists who treat eating disorder clients have thus adopted an eclectic approach in attempts to engage the family, assist the family in challenging the symptoms, explore issues of individual and family development, and help the family formulate future plans.

JULIANN M. COOK

Bibliography

Becvar, Dorothy S., and Raphael J. Becvar. *Family Therapy: A Systemic Approach.* Boston: Allyn and Bacon, 2008.

Eisler, Ivan, Christopher Dare, Marquis Hodes, Gerald Russell, Elizabeth Dodge, and Dominique LeGrange. "Family Therapy for Anorexia Nervosa: The Results of a Controlled Comparison of Two Family Interventions." *Journal of Child Psychology and Psychiatry* 41 (2000): 727–36.

Hare-Mustin, Rachel T. "A Feminist Approach to Family Therapy." *Family Process* 17 (1978): 181–94.

Mayer, Robert D. *Family Therapy in the Treatment of Eating Disorders in General Practice* (dissertation). London: University of London, 1994.

Minuchin, Salvador, Bernice L. Rosman, and Lester Baker. *Psychosomatic Families: Anorexia Nervosa in Context.* Cambridge, MA: Harvard University Press, 1978.

Nichols, Michael P., and Richard C. Schwartz. "Recent Developments in Family Therapy: Integrative Models." *Family Therapy: Concepts and Methods.* Boston: Pearson/Allyn and Bacon, 2006.

Rumney, Avis. *Dying to Please: Anorexia, Treatment and Recovery.* North Carolina: McFarland & Company, Inc. Publishers, 2009.

FAT BIAS/FAT DISCRIMINATION

Fat bias refers to negative judgments of individuals who appear to be overweight or obese. Fat discrimination is often a consequence of fat bias and refers to prejudicial action directed toward overweight and obese individuals. Overweight and obese individuals are often the targets of bias and discrimination. Although large, rotund bodies were thought to be socially ideal in the past (e.g., prior to the 1920s) as they represented wealth and success, today, in Western society, lean, toned and athletic bodies are idealized. These lean body ideals stand in stark contrast to reality as the World Health Organization estimates that 1.5 billion adults are overweight. Yet, a lean and thin body has come to be viewed as the physical display of self-discipline, motivation, and achievement, whereas a large, fat body is viewed as the ultimate failure publicly displayed for all to see and judge. Although there has been little research examining fat bias and discrimination in relationship to eating disorders, the evidence that does exist suggests that experiences of bias and discrimination are associated with a number of unhealthy eating behaviors and negative body image.

Social Influences on Idealized Bodies

Social consciousness and awareness of the body in Western society are shaped and fueled by the booming diet industry, estimated to bring in $40–50 billion each year. The mass media publicizes an ultrathin physique as ideal resulting in increased social value placed on having a lean body. The combination of the current food environment (where food—especially high-calorie, low-nutrition food—is plentiful, accessible, and affordable) and the physical environment (where physical activity has been engineered out of the environment) creates a scenario that is extremely challenging for most people to navigate. The diet industry, playing off the socially constructed body ideal, promotes and advertises that weight loss is easily attainable with enough effort, willpower, and motivation.

Television shows, such as NBC's *Biggest Loser* and Bravo TV's *Thintervention,* emphasize the need for discipline to achieve weight loss while disregarding biological, social, and environmental factors that influence eating and physical activity behaviors associated with weight. Moreover, research has documented that large individuals are rarely shown on television or in the movies, and when they are included, they are often stereotyped as unattractive and unappealing, are the target of jokes, and are shown overeating.

Fat Bias and Discrimination as Acceptable

The assumed inherent value of thinness, where thin = good and fat = bad, contributes to the pervasive nature of fat bias and discrimination. Researchers from the

Yale Rudd Center for Food Policy and Obesity suggest that overweight and obese people constitute one of the last socially acceptable targets of bias and discrimination. While other forms of bias and discrimination, such as gender and race bias and discrimination, have become socially unacceptable and grounds for job dismissal, fat bias and discrimination are still prevalent. Research indicates that about 12 percent of adults experience fat discrimination and that fat discrimination is the fourth most prevalent form of discrimination.

Why is fat bias so pervasive? It is likely that because the body and weight are assumed to be controllable and malleable (as communicated by the diet industry and reinforced via mass media), there is an "ideology of blame," a phrase coined by Crandall in 1994, when it comes to overweight and obesity. Attributions (or perceived causes) for weight are generally internal and controllable; in other words, people believe that an individual's weight is the result of personal eating and activity habits, and thus those who are overweight or obese must lack willpower, be lazy, and be overindulgent. Because the causes of obesity are believed to be within a person's control, individuals who are overweight or obese are thought to be deserving of any and all psychological, social, or physical consequences of their weight—they have only themselves to blame. Experiences of weight loss, though often unsustainable, seem only to strengthen such beliefs.

Experiences of Fat Bias and Discrimination

Overweight and obese individuals report experiencing fat bias and discrimination in a variety of ways, including others' negative assumptions about their abilities, critical comments about their weight and size from children, physical barriers and obstacles in public places, and disparaging comments from doctors and family members. Bias and discrimination are experienced in a number of different settings, including home, work, school, and health environments. Within the home environment, family members are the primary source of stigma, with mothers, spouses, fathers, and siblings rated as the most common sources of negative and critical comments. In the work setting, overweight employees and prospective employees are often perceived as less conscientious, less agreeable, less emotionally stable, and less extroverted than thin employees. Interestingly, although these stereotypes are common, research contradicts these perceptions. Overweight employees do not differ from thin employees when it comes to these personal characteristics. Unfortunately, overweight and obese individuals do face discriminatory hiring practices and tend to be paid lower wages, receive fewer promotions, and are terminated more frequently than thin employees.

Overweight and obese individuals report that health care providers are the second most common source of fat bias and discrimination. Research has documented fat bias among obesity specialists, physicians and medical students, nurses, dieticians, fitness professionals, and physical education teachers. Physicians tend to report that they do not feel confident in their ability to treat weight problems. In fact, some physicians indicate that the treatment of overweight and obesity is useless. Similarly, dieticians have negative perceptions of overweight clients, with common perceptions being that overweight clients lack commitment and motivation, have poor compliance with instruction, and have unrealistic expectations.

Interestingly, fitness pre-professionals and professionals also believe that overweight and obese clients are likely to be lazy, lack willpower, be unattractive. However, fitness professionals, unlike physicians, report feeling competent to prescribe exercise for weight loss and enjoy helping their clients work toward and achieve weight-related goals. Physical educators also report negative attitudes toward overweight students and have lower expectations of them, yet report being motivated to help students develop physical skills and enjoyment of movement.

For young people, school settings are the prime settings in which they experience fat bias and discrimination. Peer teasing is common and research has found that children and adolescents believe that thin people have many friends and are smart, healthy, and happy, whereas fat people have few friends, and are lazy and unhealthy. Moreover, young people are less willing to engage in a variety of activities with overweight and obese peers not only in comparison to average weight peers, but also in comparison to peers in a wheelchair, missing a limb, on crutches, or disfigured. In addition to facing teasing and social rejection from their peers, overweight and obese children and adults also face bias and discrimination from teachers.

Correlates and Consequences of Fat Bias and Discrimination

Negative attitudes directed toward overweight and obese individuals and stereotypes of them can result in negative interpersonal interactions, social rejection and bullying, and discrimination, all of which can have serious effects on physical and psychological health. Experiences of fat bias and discrimination are associated with poor psychological well-being as well as behaviors that can negatively influence physical health.

Psychological Well-Being

To date, few studies have examined the relationship between fat bias and psychological well-being; however, the research that has been completed indicates that depression, poor body image, low self-esteem, and low quality of life are associated with experiences of fat bias and discrimination among adults and children. The serious effects of poor psychological well-being have been well documented: depression is associated with risk of suicidal ideology and actions; low self-esteem is associated with depression; and poor body image is associated with disturbed eating. Thus, although additional research is needed to better understand the mechanisms underlying the relationships between fat bias and discrimination and psychological well-being, there is certainly enough evidence to suggest that the effects are serious and harmful.

Health Behaviors

Unhealthy behaviors associated with experiences of fat bias and discrimination may include the delay and avoidance of health care due to weight-related concerns, physical inactivity, and overeating and binge eating. For example, overweight and obese individuals report fear of being weighed, concerns about not fitting into dressing gowns, and worries about negative weight-related comments associated with delaying health care. Overweight and obese women are less likely than average weight women to seek gynecological health care. Delaying or avoiding health care can negatively impact the physical health of overweight and obese individuals.

Avoiding physical activity is another problematic behavior associated with fat bias and discrimination. Individuals who are overweight or obese may experience embarrassment or shame in physical activity or exercise settings, feel incompetent, and be self-conscious about their body and appearance. Although it has been suggested that some level of dissatisfaction with one's body may serve as motivation to lose weight, the reality seems to be just the opposite—when individuals are made to feel bad about or feel guilty about their bodies and their weight, rather than increasing activity, they may actually become inactive in order to avoid the discomfort and attention.

Similarly, research has indicated that individuals who experience fat bias and discrimination are more likely to binge eat. Indeed, one study documented that eating was one of the most prevalent coping mechanisms for dealing with stigmatizing experiences. Thus, in response to negative attitudes, weight-related teasing, and experiences of bias, overweight and obese individuals may turn to overeating and binge eating in order to comfort themselves and stuff down negative feelings.

Approaches for Reducing Fat Bias and Discrimination

Increasing Awareness

Fat bias may be both conscious and unconscious. Research indicates moderate to low levels of conscious (e.g., implicit) bias, but higher levels of unconscious (e.g., explicit) bias. It is likely that social desirability influences responses to conscious measures of bias. Increasing the levels of awareness of unconscious bias is particularly important as individuals are probably unaware of the degree to which they have internalized and automatized stereotypes of overweight and obese individuals. An online version of the Weight Implicit Associations Test (IAT) allows individuals to assess their unconscious associations by completing a pairing task whereby fat and thin faces are presented in conjunction with words representing personal attributes or characteristics such as motivated/lazy and good/bad (https://implicit.harvard.edu/implicit/demo/selectatest.html). Typically, individuals are faster and more accurate when thin faces are paired with good or positive personal attributes and are slower and less accurate when fat faces are paired with good or positive attributes. The Weight IAT allows individuals to become more aware of their own bias, which is a first step toward reducing the prevalence of fat bias and discrimination.

Challenging Perceived Social Consensus

Perceived social consensus refers to individuals' beliefs about the degree to which others endorse particular beliefs, such as fat people are unattractive and unhealthy. Research indicates that when perceived social consensus is challenged, fat bias is reduced—that is, as individuals come to see that not everyone has negative attitudes toward or negative beliefs about overweight and obese people, they are more likely to challenge their own beliefs and lessen their biased attitudes.

Promoting Empathy

Promoting empathy for and understanding of overweight and obese individuals is another important step in reducing fat bias and discrimination. Although research demonstrating the efficacy of inducing empathy is limited, it is reasonable to expect that developing a sense of understanding of the challenges that overweight and obese individuals face would be beneficial. One way of promoting empathy is providing people, especially professionals who work with overweight and obese individuals, opportunities to gain experience and perspective in simulated situations. The obesity empathy suit (http://www.empathysuit.com/) is a device that may be useful. The obesity empathy suit is designed to simulate the actual weight and bulk of being overweight—while wearing the suit, individuals can experience the challenges of daily living, such as carrying groceries up the stairs, picking up items off the floor, and getting into and out of a car.

Revising Educational Training and Development Models

Educational training and professional development models should be revised in order to address issues of fat bias and discrimination among health professionals and educators. Physicians, nurses, and dieticians need better training in working with overweight and obese clients and need effective strategies for intervention and need to feel comfortable and confident in their ability to work with clients. The Exercise is Medicine initiative by the American College of Sports Medicine (ACSM) provides a number of resources for health professionals who wish to talk with their clients about weight. Moreover, educators need training specifically for dealing with weight-related teasing in bullying.

Resources on Fat Bias and Discrimination

The Yale Rudd Center on Food Policy and Obesity (http://www.yaleruddcenter. org/) is the worldwide leader in research, education, and advocacy on issues related to fat bias and discrimination. The Center's website offers many resources for researchers, health professionals, teachers, parents, employers, youth, and policy makers. The Rudd Center has also produced several videos that highlight the myths and facts of fat bias, and experiences of fat bias and discrimination at home, school, and in health care settings (http://www.yaleruddcenter.org/what_ we_do.aspx?id=254). Additionally, resources for overweight and obese individuals interested in physical activity are available at *Active at Any Size* (http://win.niddk. nih.gov/Publications/active.htm).

Summary

Overweight and obese individuals face a number of physical, social, and psychological challenges. Experiences of fat bias and discrimination are associated with a number of negative outcomes, such as binge eating and avoidance of physical activity. Although many people believe that weight is easily controlled through self-control and will-power, the reality is that for many individuals, attaining and maintaining a healthy weight is complicated and challenging. Eating behaviors are certainly an important part of weight management and being aware of and sensitive to fat bias and discrimination is essential when working with overweight and obese individuals.

CHRISTY GREENLEAF

Bibliography

Ashmore, Jamile A., Kelli E. Friedman, Simona K. Reichmann, and Gerard J. Musante. "Weight-based Stigmatization, Psychological Distress, and Binge Eating Behavior among Obese Treatment-seeking Adults." *Eating Behaviors* 9 (2008): 203–209.

Blaine, Bruce E., Deanne M. DiBlasi, and Jane M. Connor. "The Effect of Weight Loss on Perceptions of Weight Controllability: Implications for Prejudice against Overweight People." *Journal of Applied Biobehavioral Research* 7 (2002): 44–56.

Crandall, Chris S. "Prejudice against Fat People: Ideology and Self-Interest." *Journal of Personality and Social Psychology* 66 (1994): 882–94.

Drury, Christine Aramburu Alegria, and Margaret Louis. "Exploring the Association between Body Weight, Stigma of Obesity, and Health Care Avoidance." *Journal of the American Academy of Nurse Practitioners* 14 (2002): 554–61.

Empathy Suit. "Obesity Empathy Suit." Accessed May 30, 2011. http://www.empathy suit.com/

Faith, Myles S., Mary Ann Leone, Tim S. Ayers, Moonseong Heo, and Angelo Pietrobelli. "Weight Criticism during Physical Activity, Coping Skills, and Reported Physical Activity in Children." *Pediatrics* 110 (2002): e23.

Greenleaf, Christy, Heather Chambliss, Deborah J. Rhea, Scott B. Martin, and James R. Morrow Jr. "Weight Stereotypes and Behavioral Intentions toward Thin and Fat Peers among White and Hispanic Adolescents." *Journal of Adolescent Health* 39 (2006): 546–52.

Greenleaf, Christy, and Karen Weiller. "Perceptions of Youth Obesity among Physical Educators." *Social Psychology of Education* 8 (2005): 407–423.

Latner, Janet D., and Albert J. Stunkard. "Getting Worse: The Stigmatization of Obese Children." *Obesity Research* 11 (2003): 452–56.

National Institute of Diabetes and Digestive and Kidney Diseases of the National Institutes of Health. "Active at Any Size." Accessed May 30, 2011. http://win.niddk.nih.gov/Pub lications/active.htm

O'Brien, Kerry S., Jackie A. Hunter, and M. Banks. "Implicit Anti-Fat Bias in Physical Educators: Physical Attributes, Ideology and Socialization." *International Journal of Obesity* 31 (2007): 308–314.

Project Implicit. "Project Implicit." Accessed May 30, 2011. https://implicit.harvard.edu/implicit/demo/selectatest.html

Puhl, Rebecca M., and Chelsea A. Heuer. "The Stigma of Obesity: A Review and Update." *Obesity* 17 (2009): 940–64.

Puhl, Rebecca M., Corinne A. Moss-Racusin, and Marlene B. Schwartz. "Internalization of Weight Bias: Implications for Binge Eating and Emotional Well-Being." *Obesity* 15 (2007): 19–23.

Puhl, Rebecca M., and Janet D. Latner. "Stigma, Obesity, and the Health of the Nation's Children." *Psychological Bulletin* 133 (2007): 557–80.

Puhl, Rebecca M., and Kelly D. Brownell. "Psychosocial Origins of Obesity Stigma: Toward Changing a Powerful and Pervasive Bias." *Obesity Reviews* 4 (2003): 213–27.

Puhl, Rebecca M., and Kelly D. Brownell. "Confronting and Coping with Weight Stigma: An Investigation of Overweight and Obese Adults." *Obesity* 14 (2006): 1802–1815.

Puhl, Rebecca M., Marlene B. Schwartz, and Kelly D. Brownell. "Impact of Perceived Consensus on Stereotypes about Obese People: A New Approach for Reducing Bias." *Health Psychology* 24 (2005): 517–25.

Puhl, Rebecca M., T. Andreyeva, and Kelly D. Brownell. "Perceptions of Weight Discrimination: Prevalence and Comparison to Race and Gender Discrimination in America." *International Journal of Obesity* 32 (2008): 992–1000.

Vartanian, Lenny R., and Jacqueline G. Shaprow. "Effect of Weight Stigma on Exercise Motivation and Behavior: A Preliminary Investigation among College-aged Females." *Journal of Health Psychology* 13 (2008): 131–38.

World Health Organization. "Obesity and Overweight." Last modified March 2011. http://www.who.int/mediacentre/factsheets/fs311/en/

Yale Rudd Center on Food Policy and Obesity. "Yale Rudd Center on Food Policy and Obesity." Accessed May 30, 2011. http://www.yaleruddcenter.org/

Yale Rudd Center on Food Policy and Obesity. "Videos Exposing Weight Bias." Accessed May 30, 2011. http://www.yaleruddcenter.org/what_we_do.aspx?id=254

FEMALE ATHLETE TRIAD

In 1992, a group of esteemed scholars held a consensus conference called by The Task Force on Women's Issues of the American College of Sports Medicine (ACSM) to discuss the incidence of three interconnected disorders that were observed in female athletes with increasing frequency—disordered eating, amenorrhea, and osteoporosis. Although it was likely that they had been occurring in female athlete populations for decades, increasing attention in the research literature sparked the initiation of a conference specifically designed to address these medical conditions. In 1997, ACSM published a position statement identifying the term "female athlete triad" to describe the interrelationship between disordered eating, amenorrhea, and osteoporosis.

Since then, a growing body of research has informed a more recent ACSM position statement published in 2007 and has improved our understanding of this complex phenomenon. More specifically, the components of the female athlete triad have been redefined as the interrelationship between energy availability, menstrual status, and bone health where each component represents a continuum from a healthy to unhealthy status. This important change is depicted in the following excerpt from ACSM's 2007 position stand:

> Low energy availability (with or without eating disorders), amenorrhea, and osteoporosis, alone or in combination, pose significant health risks to physically active girls and women. The potentially irreversible consequences of these clinical conditions emphasize the critical need for prevention, early diagnosis, and treatment. Each clinical condition is now understood to comprise the pathological end of a spectrum of interrelated subclinical conditions between health and disease.

The development of the female athlete triad follows a progressive pattern that typically begins with low energy availability and can result in more serious disordered eating issues as well as menstrual and/or bone health concerns. Often, each component is linked directly or indirectly to the other. In the most severe case, an athlete may develop a clinical eating disorder, extreme menstrual irregularities like amenorrhea, and a serious bone disease such as osteoporosis. Each component of the female athlete triad is discussed in turn.

Energy Availability

Dietary energy (i.e., energy from food) is necessary to fuel the metabolic processes of the body and sustain life. Energy availability is defined as the amount of energy left for these important metabolic processes after expending energy during exercise. This term is often better explained in the form of a simple equation: Energy Availability (EA; available energy left to use) = Dietary Energy Intake (EI; what you eat)–Exercise Energy Expenditure (EE; what you burn during exercise). When a sufficient amount of energy is available, the body can support healthy reproductive function and facilitate bone formation. However, when energy availability is low, reproductive functioning suffers and bones weaken.

Athletes have low energy availability when their energy expenditure during exercise exceeds their dietary intake. In other words, the amount of energy consumed does not match the energy expended. While some athletes may reach a point of low energy availability inadvertently, other athletes purposefully engage in disordered eating behaviors such as diet restriction in order to lose weight, alter body shape, or change their appearance in an attempt to achieve athletic success. This is especially true for athletes who participate in aesthetic sports (e.g., gymnastics, figure skating) and endurance sports (e.g., running, cycling), which tend to favor lighter and leaner athletes. In addition to conforming to sport-specific pressures, female athletes may also intentionally diet to achieve societal standards of appearance for women. In Western cultures, a long and lean figure or thin ideal is emphasized.

Menstrual Status

Low energy availability can lead to menstrual dysfunction in female athletes. More specifically, low energy availability is believed to deprive the brain of important carbohydrates necessary for proper hormonal secretion and release (e.g., gonadotropin-releasing hormone from the hypothalamus located in the brain and follicle stimulating and luteinizing hormones from the pituitary gland). As a result, the functioning of the ovaries and subsequent production of estrogen and progesterone are disrupted.

Due to improper hormonal release and production, a variety of menstrual dysfunctions can ensue. For example, primary amenorrhea occurs in individuals who either (a) have not developed secondary sex characteristics (e.g., breast development and body hair growth) and have not had their first menstrual cycle by the age of 14; or (b) have experienced normal growth and development of secondary sex characteristics, but have not had their first menstrual cycle by the age of 16. In contrast, secondary amenorrhea occurs in individuals who have had their first menstrual cycle, but have not menstruated for three months or longer. Other menstrual dysfunctions can include luteal suppression (i.e., a shortened luteal phase of the menstrual cycle), anovulation (i.e., absence of ovulation), and oligomenorrhea (i.e., prolonged length of time between cycles). Because of the critical role that hormones play in the menstrual cycle, serious menstrual disturbances may also be a sign that an athlete's bone health is also at risk.

Bone Health

Poor bone health can include a number of disorders ranging from osteopenia (i.e., a condition characterized by lower-than-expected bone thickness or low bone mineral density) to osteoporosis (i.e., a severe disease characterized by skeletal degeneration and loss of bone strength). Poor bone health can occur as a result of low energy availability and inadequate nutrition, as well as menstrual dysfunction.

As discussed previously, when athletes engage in disordered eating behaviors such as restrictive dieting, they tend to consume far less than the recommended number of calories necessary to compensate for the energy expended in their sport. The little energy that is available is believed to be devoted toward survival functions and sport training as opposed to proper growth and maturational processes. Some researchers contend that longitudinal growth (or height) in particular can be permanently or temporarily stunted with inadequate caloric intake.

In addition to the consequences of low energy availability in general, poor calcium intake is of special concern because of its crucial role in bone health, growth, and mass. Peak bone mass is not achieved until approximately 30 years of age and steadily decreases thereafter. Female athletes with poor nutritional habits, low energy availability, and inadequate calcium intake do not accumulate sufficient bone mass early in life and are therefore at risk for poor bone health not only during childhood and adolescence but also throughout adulthood.

Poor bone health can also occur as a direct result of the absence or disruption of the menstrual cycle. Estrogen is a principal hormone for the suppression of cells responsible for breaking down bone (i.e., bone resorption). In other words, estrogen prevents certain cells from eating the bone away. Irregular hormonal release and low estrogen levels due to menstrual dysfunction can lead to an increase in bone resorption and therefore a decline in bone quality. Research demonstrates that missed menstrual cycles are associated with significant and potentially permanent losses in bone mineral density.

Athletes with poor bone health are at increased risk for stress fractures. Stress fractures are partial or complete breaks in the bone often resulting from repetitive weight-bearing impact. The most common areas for stress fractures are the tibia (i.e., the shin), the ankle, and the foot. Weight-bearing exercises can work to strengthen bone. However, individuals with poor nutritional habits, low energy availability, menstrual dysfunction, or some combination of these factors tend to weaken their body's ability to repair injured bones over time. As a result, the wear and tear of everyday activities as well as sport training frequently lead to stress fractures, particularly in runners.

A Fourth Component to the Triad

Some scholars contend that there may be a fourth component to the triad called endothelial dysfunction because of the link between this medical condition, amenorrhea, and low estrogen levels. The endothelium is the inner lining of the blood vessels. Dysfunction of endothelial cells can impair functioning of the heart, reduce exercise capacity and blood flow to important muscles during exercise, and hasten the development of cardiovascular disease and events (e.g., heart attacks). Oral contraceptives and folic acid supplements have been proposed as possible treatments for endothelial dysfunction. Although more research is needed to make strong conclusions about the presence of endothelial dysfunction in female athletes and its link to other components of the triad, these health concerns should certainly be taken seriously.

Prevalence of the Female Athlete Triad

The prevalence of all three components of the triad is relatively small. That is, few female athletes show low energy availability, menstrual dysfunction *and* poor bone health. However, from a physical and performance perspective, signs of even just one component of the triad are cause for concern. Researchers provide prevalence estimates for each triad component suggesting that between 1 percent and 62 percent of female athletes engage in disordered eating, between 6 percent and 79 percent of female athletes experience menstrual dysfunction, and between 22 percent and 50 percent of female athletes have osteopenia. The variability of these statistics is due to differences in how each component of the triad was measured and defined as well as differences in the sample of individuals included in each study. Although determining precise prevalence estimates is difficult, what is certain is that low energy availability, menstrual dysfunction, and poor bone health do exist among female athletes.

Prevention and Treatment of the Female Athlete Triad

The cyclical nature of the female athlete triad and the associated health risks warrant attention and concern. Many scholars have argued for the need to educate audiences about the female athlete triad and methods of prevention. The Female Athlete Triad Coalition is one such resource that works to prevent the triad around the globe. The National Collegiate Athletic Association (NCAA) has published materials specifically designed to inform coaches on how to identify, manage, and prevent the female athlete triad. Coaches are believed to play an integral role in these processes because of the significant amount of interaction they have with athletes as well as their influence as mentors and supportive adults. In addition to coaches, athletes and parents should be educated on the proper nutrition for adolescent and young adult athletes, characteristics of normal versus dysfunctional menstrual cycles, and the importance of accruing bone mass through regular weight-bearing exercise. Because the female athlete triad typically begins with disordered eating, ACSM specifically contends that policies and procedures should be put in place to safeguard against unhealthy and detrimental weight loss practices in female sports.

In addition to educational materials, other scholars contend that a physical screening is necessary prior to sport participation. More specifically, school nurses and medical doctors are in an optimal position to detect and prevent the triad through pre-participation physical exams. Screening for disordered eating as well as menstrual dysfunction in adolescent and college-aged athletes is believed to be an important first step in preventing the development and progression of the triad. For example, if detected, menstrual dysfunction can be reversed with increases in energy availability. Unfortunately, research shows that most high school athletic programs do not adequately screen for these signs and symptoms.

Relative to treatment, scholars and practitioners have long supported a multi-disciplinary team approach that consists of coaches, athletic trainers, team physicians, registered sport dietitians, sport psychologists, and sport administrators. Parents and teammates can also play supportive roles in the treatment process. ACSM contends that increasing energy consumption or reducing energy expenditure is the first important step in the treatment process and may require nutritional counseling, psychotherapy, and/or restriction from training and competition. Pharmacological treatment may include antidepressants, oral contraceptive pills, or hormone replacement therapy. In all cases, social support for the at-risk or affected athlete is essential.

Conclusion

The female athlete triad consists of energy availability, menstrual status, and bone health that range from health to disease. Unfortunately, research indicates that the most severe forms of these conditions, including clinical eating disorders, amenorrhea, and osteoporosis, do occur in female athletes. Although prevalence rates suggest that a relatively small percentage of female athletes have all three medical conditions, the presence of even a single symptom is cause for concern. Experts recommend that prevention of the female athlete triad should begin with making education of athletes, coaches, and parents a top priority. Because the triad often begins with disordered eating, nutrition education as well as policies intended to reduce harmful weight loss techniques in sports are necessary. Should an athlete experience symptoms of one or more components of the female athlete triad, a team approach to treatment is recommended.

DANA K. VOELKER

Bibliography

Beals, Katherine A., and Amanda K. Hill. "The Prevalence of Disordered Eating, Menstrual Dysfunction, and Low Bone Mineral Density among US Collegiate Athletes." *International Journal of Sport Nutrition and Exercise Metabolism* 16 (2006): 1–23.

Beals, Katherine A., and Nanna L. Meyer. "Female Athlete Triad Update." *Clinics in Sports Medicine* 26 (2007): 69–89.

Ireland, Mary Lloyd, and Aurelia Nattiv. *The Female Athlete.* Philadelphia, PA: Saunders, 2002.

Lancer, Erica M., Karie N. Zach, and Anne Z. Hoch. "The Female Athlete Triad and Endothelial Dysfunction." *Physical Medicine and Rehabilitation* 3 (2011): 458–65.

Manore, Melinda M., Lynn Ciadella Kam, and Anne B. Loucks. "The Female Athlete Triad: Components, Nutrition Issues, and Health Consequences." *Journal of Sports Sciences* 25 (2007): S61–S71. doi: 10.1080/02640410701607320.

Nattiv, Aurelia, Anne B. Loucks, Melinda M. Manore, Charlotte F. Sanborn, Jorunn Sundgot-Borgen, and Michelle P. Warran. "The Female Athlete Triad Position Stand." *Medicine and Science in Sports and Exercise* 39 (2007): 1867–1882. doi: 10.1249/mss.0b013e318149f111.

Otis, Carol K., Barbara Drinkwater, Mimi Johnson, Anne Loucks, and Jack Wilmore. "ACSM Position Stand: The Female Athlete Triad." *Medicine and Science in Sports and Exercise* 29 (1997): i–ix.

Thompson, Ron, and Roberta Trattner Sherman. *NCAA Coaches Handbook: Managing the Female Athlete Triad.* Indianapolis, IN: The National Collegiate Athletic Association, 2010.

Yeager, Kimberly K., Rosemary Agostini, Aurelia Nattiv, and Barbara Drinkwater. "The Female Athlete Triad: Disordered Eating, Amenorrhea, Osteoporosis." *Medicine and Science in Sports and Exercise* 25 (1993): 775–77.

Zach, Karie N., Ariane L. Smith Machin, and Anne Z. Hoch. "Advances in Management of the Female Athlete Triad and Eating Disorders." *Clinical Journal of Sports Medicine* 30 (2011): 551–73.

FEMININITY IDEALS

Femininity is a socially constructed phenomenon that includes the roles, behaviors, and attributes that are believed to characterize women and girls. To be considered feminine in Western cultures, women and girls are often expected to fulfill traditional gender roles like housekeeping and childbearing, display passivity, submissiveness, modesty, and nurturance, and invest in improving their physical appearance. Although feminine ideals have drastically changed over the past century, women and girls still face many pressures to conform to culturally defined standards, especially in relation to appearance and beauty.

History of the Ideal Female Body

The definition of beauty and physical perfection for women has dramatically evolved over time. During the Victorian era in the 20th century, fair-skinned women with a rotund or well-rounded figure were considered ideal and desirable by both men and women alike. Drawings by the famous illustrator, Charles Dana Gibson, became popular icons of femininity throughout the early 1900s. His *Gibson Girl* drawings featured women with neatly placed thick hair and an hourglass figure with unimaginably tiny waists. Remaining popular until the end of World War I, the *Gibson Girl* image was considered the first "pin-up girl," so named because of the posters placed in male locker rooms, auto shops, and other venues across the country.

With increased freedom of expression, independence, and the right to vote in the 1920s, many women dressed as "flappers"—a style characterized by short skirts, long legs, and more skin. Also popular was the bob hairstyle, often cut to the ears and curled. Such short hair on women was considered androgynous because it challenged traditional feminine hairstyles and had both masculine and feminine features. With the rise of the film industry in the 1930s, female movie stars such as Carole Lombard and Judy Garland accentuated the long and lean figure desired by most men and women of this time period. During the World War II era, curves became more popular, and Bettie Page became the staple of female beauty. Named the "Best Pin-Up Girl in the World" in 1955, Bettie often posed partially nude and with props to engage audiences. She eventually became known as the "girl with the perfect figure" with curvy lines and long legs.

In the 1950s, actress Marilyn Monroe further popularized the voluptuous figure and, by today's standards, is estimated to have been a size 12. With her fame and good looks, Marilyn was considered the sex symbol of the century. However, although her curvy figure and proportions were applauded and revered in the acting world, models were at the same time becoming much thinner. Twiggy, a supermodel of the 1960s, signified a stick-thin, boyish, and even underdeveloped figure and has often been blamed for promoting an unhealthy body image for women and girls. Figures like that of model Kate Moss and contestants on the popular reality television show, *America's Next Top Model,* demonstrate the ultrathin ideal of today. Recent research has shown that most fashion models are thinner than 98 percent of women in the United States.

Ultrathin Ideal, Body Image Concerns, and Disordered Eating

Both research and the popular press suggest that the ideal image of the female body has continued to become gradually thinner over time. Individuals in Western cultures tend to idolize thin female bodies, which places unrealistic pressures on women and girls in relation to weight, shape, and body size. Exposure to the ultrathin ideal could have major physical and psychological health implications for women and girls attempting to achieve this figure. Interestingly, some experts suggest that the sociocultural demands to achieve and maintain an increasingly thinner female physique is at odds with what is physiologically possible. In other words, most females cannot become as thin as what their culture says they should become.

Unfortunately, evidence suggests that both males and females idolize this unrealistic ideal from childhood through adulthood. Primary school children as young as four years of age perceived that thinner female bodies were more attractive than those perceived to be the norm. Moreover, female children between the ages of five and eight tended to show lower body esteem and greater desire for thinness following exposure to *Barbie,* the doll that has also played a major role in defining the ideal female physique. These perceptions appear to persist well into the adult years and may affect women across race and ethnicity in the United States. For some, early exposure and pressure to achieve the thin ideal can lead to long-term body dissatisfaction, the adoption of unhealthy weight management techniques, or serious clinical eating disorders.

Through an extensive examination of bulimia nervosa, researchers have proposed that families, peers, and the media are the three major sociocultural influences affecting women and girls today and contend that females become driven to achieve the thin ideal either through social reinforcement and a perceived pressure to be thin (e.g., by receiving disparaging comments from important others, being exposed to thin models in magazines) or modeling behavior (e.g., by observing and copying the weight management techniques of others). Women and girls exposed to these pressures are particularly vulnerable to what is known as "internalization," or the acceptance and application of societal values of thinness to one's personal image. Internalization of the thin ideal strongly predicts body image disturbances and disordered eating behaviors.

Femininity Ideals and Athletes

Recent studies have examined femininity ideals in the context of female athletics. Because the world of sports is predominantly masculine, female athletes have often been pressured to prove or demonstrate their femininity to meet the sociocultural standards deemed appropriate for their sex. This is one reason why media portrayals of female athletes tend to promote sex appeal and family-based ideals rather than athletic prowess. For example, famous tennis player, Anna Kournikova, is often portrayed in the media as a sex symbol posing in lingerie and swimsuits rather than as an elite athlete. Despite never winning a WTA (Women's Tennis Association) singles tournament, she is one of the most well-known players because of the attention she receives for her looks off the court.

Some scholars argue that female athletes are continually receiving mixed messages not only about how they should behave, but also about how they are expected to look. For example, although many female athletes are proud of their athleticism and the muscles that allow them to succeed in their sport, muscles that are too big are often perceived as a negative attribute and a detriment to their femininity. Body image disturbances and disordered eating may be a concern for some female athletes attempting to meet the demands of their sport while also striving to achieve societal expectations for their weight, shape, and body size.

Conclusion

Femininity is a term used to describe the roles, behaviors, and attributes expected of women and girls. One of the most salient aspects of femininity is the female body. Over time, the definition of beauty and standards of appearance for women have changed with the values of society. What was considered beautiful in the Victorian era (e.g., a well-rounded figure) is no longer portrayed as the body ideal (a long and lean build is considered beautiful today). Unfortunately, research suggests that young girls are influenced by the ultrathin ideals currently promoted in

Western cultures. Body image disturbances and disordered eating are two potential consequences. Efforts to both change the way our culture views femininity and educate women and girls on how to cope with thin ideal images are critical aspects of eating disorder prevention.

DANA K. VOELKER

Bibliography

Blowers, Lucy C., Natalie J. Loxton, Megan Grady-Flesser, Stefano Occhipinti, and Sharon Dawe. "The Relationship between Sociocultural Pressure to be Thin and Body Dissatisfaction in Preadolescent Girls." *Eating Behaviors* 4 (2003): 229–44. doi:10.1016/S1471-0153(03)00018-7.

Brown, Felicity L., and Virginia Slaughter. "Normal Body, Beautiful Body: Discrepant Perceptions Reveal a Pervasive 'Thin Ideal' from Childhood to Adulthood." *Body Image* 8 (2011): 119–25. doi:10.1016/j.bodyim.2011.02.002.

Brownell, Kelly D. "Dieting and the Search for the Perfect Body: Where Physiology and Culture Collide." *Behavior Therapy* 22 (1991): 1–12. doi:10.1016/S0005-7894(05) 80239-4.

Dittmar, Helga, Suzanne Ive, and Emma Halliwell. "Does Barbie Make Girls Want to be Thin? The Effect of Experimental Exposure to Images of Dolls on the Body Image of 5- to 8-Year Old Girls." *Developmental Psychology* 42 (2006): 283–92. doi: 10.1037/0012-1649.42.2.283.

Grabe, Shelly, Janet Shibley Hyde, and L. Monique Ward. "The Role of the Media in Body Image Concerns among Women: A Meta-Analysis of Experimental and Correlational Studies." *Psychological Bulletin* 134 (2008): 460–76. doi: 10.1037/0033-2909. 134.3.460.

Krane, Vikki. "We Can be Athletic and Feminine, but Do We Want To? Challenging Hegemonic Femininity in Women's Sport." *Quest* 53 (2001): 115–33.

Krane, Vikki, Precilla Y. L. Choi, Shannon M. Baird, Christine M. Aimar, and Kerrie J. Kauer. "Living the Paradox: Female Athletes Negotiate Femininity and Muscularity." *Sex Roles* 50 (2004): 315–29.

Murnen, Sarah K., and Linda Smolak. "Femininity, Masculinity, and Disordered Eating: A Meta-Analytic Review." *International Journal of Eating Disorders* 22 (1997): 231–42. doi: 10.1002/(SICI)1098-108X(199711)22:3<231::AID-EAT2>3.0.CO;2-O.

Stice, Eric, Chris Ziemba, Joy Margolis, and Penny Flick. "The Dual Pathway Model Differentiates Bulimics, Subclinical Bulimics, and Controls: Testing the Continuity Hypothesis." *Behavior Therapy* 27 (1996): 531–49.

Thompson, Kevin J., and Eric Stice. "Thin-Ideal Internalization: Mounting Evidence for a New Risk Factor for Body-Image Disturbance and Eating Pathology." *Current Directions in Psychological Science* 10 (2001): 181–83.

FIGURAL RATING SCALES

Body image assessment has commonly included questionnaires that focus on satisfaction with one's overall shape and body parts and figural rating scales that measure body size satisfaction and discrepancies. The most widely used figural rating scale, the Figure Rating Scale (FRS), was initially developed by Dr. Stunkard in 1983 to examine obesity rates within 3,651 Danish adults who ranged in age from 34 years to 57 years. The FRS and other figural rating scales have been used extensively to measure body image with a variety of international populations since its development and have been widely accepted as a way to assess body-size satisfaction.

Advantages of Figural Rating Scales

Figural rating scales, such as the FRS, include figures that range from extremely thin or emaciated to extremely overweight or obese. The FRS provides nine figures for males and females that should represent current figure, ideal figure, and figure most attractive to the opposite sex. The participant is asked to select the actual silhouette that matches perceptions about size. Interestingly, figural rating scales vary in the number of figures from two to thirteen silhouettes. Most commonly used scales present seven to nine figures in sequential order from thinnest to heaviest in size.

One advantage of the figural rating scale is that because it is a visual instrument, individuals who have minimal education or reading ability can easily and quickly complete the assessment. In fact, the FRS has been used to measure body image with individuals who have an intellectual disability. The silhouette scales show size discrepancies clearly and participants can indicate whether they want to be smaller or larger which provides a representation of the desire to change one's size. Figural rating scales can be used to measure perceptual distortions as well, with an objective researcher assessing current size for comparison with the participant's response.

Disadvantages of Figural Rating Scales

Although figure rating scales provide the benefit of being easy to understand and efficient assessment tools for body image, there have been a few criticisms of this type of instrument. For example, some researchers have argued that the change from one figure to the next does not reflect proportional changes and lacks consistent size graduations. Another drawback of the figural rating scales is that research participants and clients do not always feel like the silhouettes resemble their actual dimensions and sizes.

Because height is not represented in the figures, the standardized silhouettes may represent different proportions (e.g., larger top than bottom). A respondent may indicate that some of her (or his) body parts are reflected by a few of the figures. Figures may not always capture cultural differences either and may appear to have a Caucasian bias. In recent years, various researchers have attempted to develop silhouette scales that reflect different body types to include a muscularity scale (i.e., muscularity rating scale).

Conclusion

Body image may be measured using a variety of questionnaires and silhouette scales. Figures are drawn that reflect very thin to grossly overweight sizes and can be predictive of size satisfaction and desire to gain or lose weight. Despite the advantages of being visual in nature, figural rating scales have received criticism due to the difficulty of creating standardized figures that represent the entire population.

JUSTINE J. REEL

Bibliography

Ambrosi-Randic, Neala, Alessandra Pokrajac-Bulian, and Vladimir Taksic. "Nine, Seven, Five or Three: How Many Figures Do We Need for Assessing Body Image?" *Perceptual and Motor Skills* 100 (2005): 488–92.

Furnham, Adrian, Penny Titman, and Eleanor Sleeman. "Perception of Female Body Shapes as a Form of Exercise." *Journal of Social Behavior and Personality* 9 (1994): 335–52.

Reel, Justine J., Sonya SooHoo, Julia Franklin Summerhays, and Diane L. Gill. "Age Before Beauty: An Exploration of Body Image in African American and Caucasian Adult Women." *Journal of Gender Studies* 17, no. 4 (2008): 321–30.

Stunkard, Albert J., T. Sorenson, and F. Schulsinger. "Use of Danish Adoption Register for the Study of Obesity and Thinness." In *The Genetics of Neurological and Psychiatric Disorder,* edited by S. Kety, 115–20. New York: Raven, 1983.

Swami, Viren, Rosanne Taylor, and Christine Carvalho. "Body Dissatisfaction Assessed by the Photographic Figure Rating Scale is Associated with Sociocultural, Personality and Media Influences." *Scandinavian Journal of Psychology* 52 (2011): 57–63. doi: 10.1111/j.1467-9450.2010.00836x.

Thompson, J. Kevin, Leslie J. Heinberg, Madeline Altabe, and Stacey Tantleff-Dunn. *Exacting Beauty: Theory, Assessment, and Treatment of Body Image Disturbance.* Washington, DC: American Psychological Association, 1999.

FIGURE SKATING

Ice skating was a popular means of transportation on the frozen canals of Nordic countries in the 1400s, became popular with the social elite in England in the 1600s, and became a competitive sport in Europe and the United States in the mid-1800s. The first World Figure Skating Championship was held in 1896 and was open only to male skaters; women were allowed to compete in 1906. The first United States national competition was held in 1914. Today, U.S. Figure Skating, the official governing body of figure skating in the United States, reports having more than 176,000 members.

In the early- to mid-1800s, figure skating took place outdoors and involved creating and tracing intricate figures or patterns on the ice. Thus, the typical attire was mainly geared toward warmth. As figure skating became more athletic, skating attire became more form-fitting and body-revealing. Sonja Henie, 10-time world champion and 3-time Olympic champion in the late 1920s and early 1930s, is credited with making short, leg-revealing skirts popular among female skaters.

Norwegian-born Olympic and world figure skating champion Sonja Henie (shown here in the 1930s). She came to the United States and later became a Hollywood film star. (Library of Congress)

Moreover, as the technical and athletic aspects of figure skating have become more demanding, skaters face pressure to attain and maintain a very thin, lean body shape.

Figure Skating and Eating Disorders

A number of high-level skaters including Nancy Kerrigan, 1992 Olympic bronze medalist and 1994 Olympic silver medalist, and Jamie Silverstein, 2006 Olympic ice dancer, have reported experiencing disordered eating and weight-related pressures. Jenny Kirk, world junior champion and world senior competitor, retired from figure skating in 2005 because of an eating disorder. Prior to the 2010 Winter Olympics, Jenny spoke about her experiences and discussed what she sees as pervasive eating and weight pressures in the world of figure skating: http://www.huffingtonpost.com/ lesleyann-coker/jenny-kirk-on-figure-skat_b_430032.html http://www.huffington post.com/lesleyann-coker/jenny-kirk-on-figure- skat_b_431698.html

Eating disorders and pathogenic eating behaviors and attitudes among figure skaters are considered problematic. Although specific clinical prevalence rates among skaters are unknown, previous research has documented elevated levels of psychological factors associated with eating disorders including drive for thinness and body and weight dissatisfaction. In a study of adolescent female figure skaters, Monsma and Malina (2004) found that 38 percent had elevated drive for thinness, 54 percent had elevated body dissatisfaction, and 8 percent of the skaters had elevated scores on both risk factors. In a separate study, 30 percent of elite female figure skaters reported desiring a thinner physique. Similarly, Ziegler and colleagues (1998) found that 72 percent of female and 39 percent of male competitive skaters wanted to lose weight and that 65 percent of female and 26 percent of male skaters had purposefully dieted to lose weight.

A number of factors contribute to an environment in which unhealthy eating behaviors and attitudes are present, including the physical demands of skating, the evaluative nature of figure skating, and weight-related pressures within figure skating.

Physical Demands of Figure Skating

Like athletes in many sports, figure skaters are motivated to perform at a high level, to be competitive, and to be successful in their sport. Having a thin, lean body is considered to offer a performance edge for skaters. Across the four primary disciplines in figure skating (i.e., singles, pairs, ice dance, and synchronized skating), skaters' bodies are required to perform a variety of complex physical stunts such as multiple rotation jumps, fast spins, and intricate footwork sequences with fast changes of direction. Moreover, in pairs skating, there is even greater pressure for female skaters who are lifted and thrown by their male partners. In a study of female pairs and ice dance skaters, 92.7 percent reported pressure to maintain a low body weight. Synchronized skaters may face unique weight-related pressures as they are expected to present a uniform appearance with their teammates, which may heighten social comparison. In a study of collegiate synchronized skaters, 48.8 percent indicated that they felt pressure to maintain a low body weight.

Because skaters with thin, lean bodies are considered to have a performance advantage, some figure skaters engage in unhealthy behaviors such as caloric restriction, purging, and excessive exercise in order to attain or maintain a body which they believe will allow them to perform at a higher level. For example, in a study of elite skaters, researchers estimated that males consumed only 75 percent and females only 59.1 percent of the calories needed given their level of training. Another study found that 9 percent of male and 26 percent of female skaters used excessive exercise to manage their weight. It is important to note that although there may be an initial performance improvement for figure skaters who have lost weight or maintain a lean, thin physique, there are serious health risks associated with low body weight and inadequate nutritional intake, such as fatigue, amenorrhea, and increased risk of stress fractures.

Figure Skating as a Judged, Aesthetic Sport

In addition to the physical demands of figure skating that contribute to unhealthy eating attitudes and behaviors, the evaluative nature of the sport may also be associated with eating disorders. Figure skating is a judged, aesthetic sport. That is, performance is evaluated by a panel of expert judges who not only rate the skaters' actual technical performance, but also their physical appearance. Skaters are socialized to understand that their appearance will be evaluated and that they will be rewarded for having an attractive physical appearance, long lines (e.g., lean bodies), and graceful movements. In fact, in the International Judging System (IJS) used in competition, judges evaluate posture, style, and even personality. Thus, it is not surprising that in a sport like figure skating, with subjective evaluation, the skaters would be concerned about, and possibly engage in, pathogenic behaviors to maintain a low body weight in order to have the ideal figure skating physique. One study found that 44 percent of male and 77 percent of female skaters were terrified of weight gain.

Sources of Weight Pressures in Figure Skating

Skaters may experience weight-related pressures from a number of sources, including significant others and form-fitting costumes. Skaters have reported that comments from judges, coaches, parents, and peers negatively influence how they feel about their bodies. Some coaches have weigh-ins and require their skaters to turn in food diaries; skaters struggling with their body weight and bodies may respond by taking unhealthy actions to achieve a desired weight in order to gain approval from their coach. Parents may unknowingly reinforce pathogenic weight control behaviors by rewarding and praising improved performance associated with weight loss. Skaters, like other athletes, are likely to engage in social comparison—evaluating their own bodies in relationship to other skaters—which may lead to body dissatisfaction. Form-fitting costumes typically worn in figure skating are another potential source of pressure for skaters. Wearing physique-revealing costumes may increase skaters' awareness of and concerns about their bodies and physical appearance and lead to body dissatisfaction. Because body dissatisfaction is a known precursor to disordered eating, it is important to recognize factors that contribute to skaters being unhappy with their bodies.

Conclusion

Figure skaters face a number of physical demands and pressures to maintain a low body weight, which may put them at increased risk for pathogenic eating attitudes and behaviors. U.S. Figure Skating, the national governing body for figure skating in the United States, has a number of resources available to support healthy eating and nutrition among skaters (http://www.usfigureskating.org/Athletes.asp?id=346) including a guide for coaches.

CHRISTY GREENLEAF

See also: Aesthetic Sports; Amenorrhea.

Bibliography

Coker, Lesleyann. "Jenny Kirk on Figure Skating's Eating Disorder Epidemic (Part I)." Huffingtonpost.com. Last modified January 20, 2010. http://www.huffingtonpost.com/lesleyann-coker/jenny-kirk-on-figure-skat_b_430032.html

Coker, Lesleyann. "Jenny Kirk on Figure Skating's Eating Disorder Epidemic (Part II)." Huffingtonpost.com. Last modified January 21, 2010. http://www.huffingtonpost.com/lesleyann-coker/jenny-kirk-on-figure-skat_b_431698.htmlhttp://www.huffingtonpost.com/lesleyann-coker/jenny-kirk-on-figure-skat_b_430032.html

Greenleaf, Christy. "Weight Pressures and Social Physique Anxiety among Collegiate Synchronized Skaters." *Journal of Sport Behavior* 27 (2004): 260–76.

Jonnalagadda, Jatya S., Paula J. Ziegler, and Judy A. Nelson. "Food Preferences, Dieting Behaviors, and Body Image Perceptions of Elite Figure Skaters." *International Journal of Sport Nutrition and Exercise Metabolism* 14 (2004): 594–606.

Monsma, Eva V., and Robert M. Malina. "Correlates of Eating Disorder Risk among Female Figure Skaters: A Profile of Adolescent Competitors." *Psychology of Sport & Exercise* 5 (2004): 447–60.

Monsma, Eva V., and Robert M. Malina. "Anthropometry and Somatotype of Competitive Female Figure Skaters 11–22 years: Variation by Competitive Level and Discipline." *Journal of Sports Medicine and Physical Fitness* 45 (2005): 491–500.

Taylor, Gail M., and Diane M. Ste-Marie. "Eating Disorder Symptoms in Canadian Female Pair and Dance Figure Skaters." *International Journal of Sport Psychology* 32 (2001): 21–28.

US Figure Skating. "Nutrition." http://www.usfigureskating.org/Athletes.asp?id=346

Ziegler, Paula J., Chor San Khoo, Bonnie Sherr, Judith A. Nelson, Wendy M. Larson, and Adam Drewnowski. "Body Image and Dieting Behaviors among Elite Figure Skaters." *International Journal of Eating Disorders* 24 (1998): 421–27.

Ziegler, Paula J., Srimathi Kannan, Satya S. Jonnalagadda, Ambika Krishnakumar, Sara E. Taksali, and Judith A. Nelson. "Dietary Intake, Body Image Perceptions, and Weight Concerns of Female U.S. International Synchronized Figure Skating." *International Journal of Sport Nutrition and Exercise Metabolism* 15 (2005): 550–66.

FIJI STUDY

The well-known Fiji Study refers to an ethnographic study conducted over a decade (1988 to1998) by Anne Becker, an anthropologist, of the Nahigatoka Village. Becker sought to better understand the interrelationships between cultural identity, body shape, the influence of media, and eating disorders within Fijian society. Becker's study is significant and frequently cited because it represents one of the few opportunities to study a culture before and after Western media was introduced, while looking at a variety of factors. It is noteworthy that societal members who were largely unaware of body shape and expressed neutral feelings about body image seemed to develop negative attitudes toward their bodies and the desire to lose weight after the introduction of Western media, which has been associated with ultrathin models and a strong emphasis on appearance. Furthermore, in a society devoid of eating disorders, dieting behavior has become increasingly more common with the influence of television and evidence of binge eating disorder is present among Fijian women.

Native Fijians have made a strong effort at retaining traditional ceremonies, rituals, and dances and passing them on to their children. (Corel)

Body Image and Fiji

Fiji provided an ideal study site to investigate body image because television was not introduced there until 1995 and moreover, in Fijian culture, robust and larger body types were considered more aesthetically pleasing. Traditional Fiji culture has been associated with feasts, and food was symbolic of social connectivity. The consumption of calorically dense foods with the encouragement to eat heartily has been evident (e.g., *"kana, mo urouro"* meaning "eat, so you will become fat") at meals.

Fiji being a media-naïve culture, Fijian females of all ages reported little desire to change their body shape. However, between 1995 and 1998, Dr. Becker found that 83 percent of Fijian school girls felt that television had influenced attitudes toward body shape and weight. These young females reported wanting to look like television characters and 40 percent felt that they would improve career prospects or become more useful at home if they lost weight or ate less. In addition, 30 percent of interviewees indicated that television characters were powerful role models concerning work or career issues. The Fijian teenage females indicated that an intergeneration gap about body ideals was developing with the introduction of television. For example, 31 percent of teenagers responded that their parents encouraged higher food consumption than they felt was necessary.

Even among adult participants, body image–related responses varied between 1989 and 1998. Fijian adults in 1998 reported that body shape can be changed. They also showed decreased body satisfaction and demonstrated higher social comparison with others and the desire to trade one's body for another. This body dissatisfaction or motivation to change one's body shape is often predictive of dieting, disordered eating, and eating disorders.

Eating Disorders and Fiji

There is no illness category in Fiji that corresponds to the eating disorders outlined by the DSM-IV-TR manual for mental health diagnoses. In fact, prior to the 1990s, anorexia nervosa and bulimia nervosa were thought to be nonexistent among ethnic Fijians. Conversely, Fijians have been more worried about *macake* (i.e., a cultural syndrome associated with appetite loss) and becoming too thin. Therefore, Westernized values of dieting and exercising for weight loss were not adopted by Fijian culture until the 1990s. When studying Fijian teenagers and adults in 1998, it was apparent that dieting behaviors had emerged since the introduction of television.

Binge Eating Disorder

When examining the presence of eating disorder symptoms, 10 percent of female participants reported symptoms consistent with binge eating and all of these individuals reported that binge episodes caused distress. Only 4 percent of the entire sample met the full DSM-IV-TR criteria for binge eating disorder (e.g., frequency requirements for binge episodes) which is consistent for a variety of Western populations. None of the participants reported purging behaviors associated with bulimia nervosa. One of the participants admitted to fasting behavior in which she neglected to eat anything for 24 hours. However, bulimia and anorexia rates for Fijian women overall appeared lower than for the other samples.

Obesity and Fiji

Although a more robust figure has been traditionally viewed as most aesthetically pleasing, obesity rates have been on the rise. In 1989, 60 percent of Fijian subjects were overweight or obese (i.e., Body Mass Index greater than or equal to 25) compared to 84 percent in 1998. In addition, the percentage of Fijian individuals with a Body Mass Index higher than 30 increased from 30 percent in 1989 to 44 percent in 1998.

Conclusion

The Fiji study has been an example of a culture affected by the media and the values associated with Western television. In a society that did not have a definition for eating disorders or body image, Fijian participants in 1998 showed significant increases in body dissatisfaction, desire to lose weight and change one's shape, dieting, and disordered eating behaviors. Likewise, overweight and obesity rates have risen between 1989 and 1998. When considering the powerful effect of the media, it is important to examine the health implications associated with these attitudes and behavioral shifts in Fiji.

JUSTINE J. REEL

Bibliography

Becker, Anne E. *Body, Self, and Society*. Philadelphia, PA: University of Pennsylvania, 1995.

Becker, Anne E. "Television, Disordered Eating, and Young Women in Fiji: Negotiating Body Image and Identity during Rapid Social Change." *Culture, Medicine and Psychiatry* 28 (2004): 2533–2559. doi: 10.1007/s11013-004-1067-5.

Becker, Anne E., Rebecca A. Burwell, David B. Herzog, Paul Hamburg, and Stephanie E. Gilman. "Eating Behaviors and Attitudes Following Prolonged Exposure to Television among Ethnic Fijian Adolescent Girls." *The British Journal of Psychiatry* 180 (2002): 509–514. doi: 10.1192/bjp.180.6.509.

Becker, Anne E., Rebecca A. Burwell, Kesaia Navara, and Stephen E. Gilman. "Binge Eating and Binge Eating Disorder in a Small-Scale, Indigenous Society: The View from Fiji." *International Journal of Eating Disorders* 34 (2003): 423–31. doi: 10.1002/eat.10225.

Becker, Anne E., Stephen E. Gilman, and Rebecca A. Burwell. "Changes in Prevalence of Overweight and in Body Image among Fijian Women between 1989 and 1998." *Obesity Research* 13, no. 1 (2005): 110–17.

Becker, Anne E., and Paul Hamburg. "Culture, the Media, and Eating Disorders." *Harvard Review of Psychiatry* 4, no. 3 (1996): 163–67.

FLIGHT ATTENDANTS

The original flight attendants, cabin boys or stewards in the 1920s, were all men. Ellen Church, the first female flight attendant, was a 25-year-old nurse hired by United Airlines in 1930. Female flight attendants were called stewardesses or air hostesses and the job represented one of the few positions available to women in the 1930s. In 1935, 2000 women applied to the Transcontinental and Western Airlines for roughly 35 spots. This represented the competitiveness present in acquiring a flight attendant's job for women. In 1936, flight attendant requirements were described as petite, low weight (between 100 to 118 pounds), single, and 20–26 years old. Flight attendants were subjected to firing if they got married, exceeded formal weight requirements during weight-checks set by the airlines, or turned 32 or 35 years old (depending on the airline). This age restriction was eliminated in the 1970s and flight attendants were able to get married in the 1980s; however, the weight restrictions have continued to persist for flight attendants (but not the pilots). In fact in 1993, United Airlines decided to reinstate weight requirements with the rationalization that such a measure would save costs for the company : http://articles.chicagotribune.com/1993-05-02/features/9305020252_1_flight-attendants-delta-air-lines-flight-united-flight.

Body Image and Flight Attendants

Once airlines began hiring females for flight attendant positions, women's bodies became scrutinized for recruitment and retention of the cabin crew. Females who were hired by the airline industry were required to complete beauty and etiquette-training, and were expected to smile at all times and retain composure under pressure. Flight attendants have been a metaphor for femininity and their bodies have been monitored formally and informally since their employment in the 1930s.

While there has been documented evidence of weight limits, weigh-ins, and firing based on weight, it appears that flight attendants also engage in self-monitoring to further the tendency for body dissatisfaction, body checking, and attempts to change undesirable aspects of one's body or appearance. Female flight attendants have acknowledged that their bodies are under constant surveillance and being scrutinized by the airlines, the other crew members, and the passengers. Female flight attendants have described the maintenance required to meet the aesthetic demands of the job including working out, expensive hair and nail treatments, makeup, and teeth straightening and whitening.

Beauty demands have historically been part of the recruitment and hiring process for female flight attendants. Applicants have been rejected for being too old, or for having blemished skin, short hair, messy hair, short or bitten nails, or poor posture; they have even been rejected for being out-of-proportion or otherwise unattractive with regard to a bodily feature. Interviews with flight attendants have revealed that female uniforms would be labeled a size larger to motivate flight attendants to be conscious of their weight and to create body concerns. While many of the formal weight requirements disappeared in the 1990s for the U.S. airlines, sociologists agree that flight attendants continue to engage in aesthetic competitions in which they compare themselves to one another and reap rewards for being the most slender, feminine, or beautiful.

Disordered Eating and Flight Attendants

It has been widely rumored that flight attendants have for several decades engaged in disordered eating, including restricting before weight-checks and flights, binge eating after flights, and purging behaviors. Their disordered eating behavior has been associated with airline weight requirements. A 1980s study of 466 flight attendants showed that 26 percent weighed five or more pounds over the airline's limit for height and age. Forty-eight percent of the "overweight" flight attendants reported purging by using self-induced vomiting and other methods. Over half of these individuals (62%) admitted that they began purging after they started working for the airline.

Current Events

In June 2010, 6000 male and female flight attendants of Thai Airways International were subjected to Body Mass Index (BMI) and waist circumference standards. Female flight attendants were expected to have a BMI of no more than 25 and a maximum waist measurement of 32 inches. Meanwhile, male flight attendants were restricted to a BMI of 27.5 or lower and a maximum 35-inch waist measurement. The flight attendants were notified of the policy and given six months to comply with the standards. The flight attendants who did not "make weight" were told that they could only fly on domestic flights, same day service. They were also expected to become ground crew within the year if they still failed to meet the weight and waist requirements. The following link describes the imposed weight standard for Thai Airways International: http://www.gadling.com/2011/03/02/flight-attendant-weight-restriction-causes-uproar/

Conclusion

Female flight attendants have represented poise, grace, and beauty since the 1930s. In addition to doing their job-related duties, flight attendants have experienced appearance demands as well as formal and informal weight expectations. While companies have justified that flight attendants represent the face of their airlines, few occupations have so blatantly used the guise of customer service to enforce body, weight, and appearance standards for women. Although many formal regulations have been lifted in the United States, female flight attendants recognize that they are being scrutinized and monitored informally by the airlines, themselves, and the passengers every day they report to work. Asian airlines continue to subject flight attendants to strict weight and size standards reflecting a traditional gender role expectation.

JUSTINE J. REEL

See also: Body Mass Index.

Bibliography

Dar, Reuven, Nurit Rosen-Korakin, Oren Shapira, Yair Gottlieb, and Hanan Frenk. "The Craving to Smoke in Flight Attendants: Relations with Smoking Deprivation, Anticipation of Smoking and Actual Smoking." *Journal of Abnormal Psychology* 119, no. 1 (2010): 248–53.

Delaney, Justin. "Flight Attendant Weight Restriction Causes Uproar." *Galding.* Last modified on March 2, 2011. http://www.gadling.com/2011/03/02/flight-attendant-weight-restriction-causes-uproar/

Graham, Frederick. "Winged Hostess: The Girl on the Plane May Also Be a Heroine." *The New York Times* (New York City, NY), January 7, 1940.

Hochschild, Arlie R. *The Managed Heart, 20th Anniversary Edition.* London: University of California Press, 2003.

Litvin, Michelle. "Flight Attendants' Weight Limit Brings On Turbulence." *Chicago Tribune.* Last modified on May 2, 1993. http://articles.chicagotribune.com/1993-05-02/features/9305020252_1_flight-attendants-delta-air-lines-flight-united-flight.

Porter, Nicole B. "Sex Plus Age Discrimination: Protecting Older Women Workers." *Denver University Law Review* 81, no. 1 (2003): 79–112.

Tyler, Melissa, and Pamela Abbott. "Chocs Away: Weight Watching in the Contemporary Airline Industry." *Sociology* 32 (1998): 433–50.

FOOD SECURITY

Eating disorder prevention programs have typically been implemented with individuals who face an overabundance of food, experience a dieting culture, and report the pressure to be thin. For lower-income populations the assumption is that food security issues would make eating disorders irrelevant. After all, food insecurity has been defined as limited or unpredictable and uncertain availability of nutritionally adequate and safe foods. Therefore, providing healthy and safe food sources to low-income Americans, and impoverished communities globally, has been the focus of health promotion initiatives. Although rates of anorexia nervosa and bulimia nervosa are suspected to be low to nonexistent in these food insecure individuals, food insecurity has been linked to increased overweight, obesity, and binge eating behaviors.

Food Insecurity and Obesity

Food insecurity can exist with or without feelings of hunger (i.e., the physiological sensation of being without food). Food insecurity has been associated with both overnutrition (overeating) and undernutrition (undereating). Limited food availability and the access to cheaper, less nutritious, and higher caloric foods can contribute to the link between food insecurity and obesity.

A pilot study conducted in Uganda determined that 31.2 percent of men and 66.3 percent of women who experienced food insecurity were overweight or obese. Food insecure females were less physically active and more likely to be overweight than the females in the food security group.

A separate study that examined food security issues in the United States found that food insecurity was related to a significant decrease in the frequency of fruit and vegetable consumption with 74.4 percent of food insecure individuals consuming two or fewer fruits and vegetables per day compared with 54.6 percent of individuals in the food secure group. Disordered eating patterns (e.g., binge eating behaviors) were also observed for food insecure participants who consumed less potassium, fiber, and vitamins than the food secure respondents. Similar findings have been revealed about food insecurity and poor nutritional habits across impoverished regions of the world.

Conclusion

Eating disorder prevention efforts are often targeted at middle and higher social economic status (SES) groups. Lower SES individuals are assumed to be immune from disordered eating concerns due to the more immediate food security issues they face. However, food insecurity has been linked to overweight, obesity, and binge eating behaviors. Particularly at risk were food insecure females who exercised less and were more overweight than their food secure counterparts. Therefore, it is important to promote healthy nutritional intake across income levels and to understand the risk for binge eating among food insecure participants.

JUSTINE J. REEL

Bibliography

Adams, Elizabeth J., Laurence Grummer-Strawn, and Gilberto Chavez. "Food Insecurity is Associated with Increased Risk of Obesity in California Women." *The Journal of Nutrition* 133 (2003): 1070–1074.

Carter, Kristie N., Kerri Kruse, Tony Blakely, and Sunny Collings. "The Association of Food Security with Psychological Distress in New Zealand and Any Gender Differences." *Social Sciences and Medicine* 72 (2011):1463–1471. doi: 10.1016/j.socscimed.2011.03.009.

Chaput, Jean-Philippe, Jo Anne Gilbert, and Angelo Tremblay. "Relationship between Food Insecurity and Body Composition in Ugandans Living in Urban Kampala." *Journal of the American Dietetic Association* 107 (2007): 1978–1982. doi: 10.1016/j.jada.2007. 08.005.

Kendall, Anne, Christine M. Olson, and Edward A. Frongillo. "Relationship of Hunger and Food Insecurity to Food Availability and Consumption." *Journal of the American Dietetic Association* 96 (1996): 1019–1024.

Murshed-e-Jahan, Khondker, Mahfuzuddin Ahmed, and Ben Belton. "The Impacts of Aquaculture Development on Food Security: Lessons from Bangladesh." *Aquaculture Research* 41 (2010): 481–95. doi: 10.1111/j.1365-2109.2009.02337.x.

FULL OF OURSELVES

Full of Ourselves (FOO) is an educational program designed for female adolescents that strives to promote mental, physical, and social health while reducing the likelihood of body preoccupation and eating disorders. FOO is a primary prevention program that targets the general population rather than eating disordered females. Although FOO was developed by Catherine Steiner-Adair and Lisa Sjostrom as a school-based program, FOO has been implemented in after-school programs, churches, and community settings (e.g., Boys and Girls Club) over the past decade.

Description of FOO Program

The program title, "Full of Ourselves" denotes the program's focus on building strength and confidence within females. Although FOO is an eating disorder prevention program, the program is framed in a positive light with the emphasis placed on power, health, and leadership. In fact, eating disorders are not mentioned as part of the lessons. Power is addressed by teaching female participants about body acceptance and assertiveness training. Using an interactive format, girls practice conflict resolution and standing up to teasing or bullying from their peers. In order to promote health, girls receive nutrition education and learn how to reject the popular diet mentality. To this end, FOO participants learn to replace the commonly held assumption of "good" versus "bad" foods with the idea of more or less "powerful" foods. Participants also practice mindful eating with raisins and candy kisses to fully use the senses. Finally, girls have the opportunity to develop leadership skills throughout the FOO program. Each lesson ends with a Call to Action that serves as a homework assignment geared toward practicing skills at home with family and friends.

The program is organized into two phases directed toward 6th, 7th, and 8th graders in the first phase (11- to 14-year-olds) and 4th and 5th graders (8- to 10-year-olds) in the second phase. The adolescent girls participate in eight FOO sessions that occur in a group setting once or twice weekly for 45–60 minutes. Group leaders consist of two women who may be school teachers, nurses, counselors, or after-school personnel. The second phase allows the girls who participated in the first phase to become group leaders for the younger girls.

Evaluation of FOO Program

The FOO program was tested with 500 seventh-grade girls and determined to be feasible and safe for participants. In addition, participants showed changes in knowledge about health, appearance, weightism, and media literacy (understanding media messages that contribute to body dissatisfaction). Participants also reported improvements in body esteem as a result of participating in the program. In another study using a community sample, participants reported program satisfaction, increased awareness about intuitive eating, and more positive body and confidence.

Conclusion

Although FOO has been designed for females with age-specific groups in mind, the program teaches important skills (e.g., assertiveness, health, confidence) for preventing eating disorders, negative body image, and body dissatisfaction. The program demonstrated positive outcomes of increased knowledge and body esteem in both school and community samples.

JUSTINE J. REEL

See also: Body Esteem; Intuitive Eating.

Bibliography

Reel, Justine J., Carlie Ashcraft, Rachel Lacy, Robert A. Bucciere, Sonya SooHoo, Donna Richards, and Nicole Mihalopoulos. "Full of Ourselves PLUS: Lessons Learned from an Obesity and Eating Disorder Intervention." *Journal of Sport Psychology in Action* 3, no. 1 (2011): 109–117.

Sjostrom, Lisa A., and Catherine Steiner-Adair. "Full of Ourselves: A Wellness Program to Advance Girl Power, Health and Leadership: An Eating Disorders Prevention Program That Works." *Journal of Nutrition Education and Behavior* 37, no. 2 (2005): S141–S144.

Steiner-Adair, Catherine, and Lisa Sjostrom. *Full of Ourselves: A Wellness Program to Advance Girl Power, Health and Leadership.* New York, NY: Teachers College Press, 2005.

Steiner-Adair, Catherine, Lisa Sjostrom, Debra L. Franko, Seeta Pai, Rochelle Tucker, Anne E. Becker, and David B. Herzog. "Primary Prevention of Risk Factors for Eating Disorders in Adolescent Girls: Learning from Practice." *International Journal of Eating Disorders* 32 (2002): 401–411. doi: 10.1002/eat.100089

G

GASTROINTESTINAL COMPLICATIONS ASSOCIATED WITH EATING DISORDERS

Gastrointestinal (GI) issues refer to common complications associated with all types of eating disorders. Complications may occur at any place along the GI tract from the mouth to the rectum. These complications may hinder progress in the treatment of eating disorders due to increased physical discomfort associated with eating. The most common GI problems associated with anorexia nervosa include constipation, gastroparesis, abnormal liver function tests, and acute gastric dilation. The GI complications associated with bulimia nervosa tend to have greater impact on the gastrointestinal tract. These complications include dental erosion and caries, parotid gland swelling, esophageal abnormalities, gastric dilation, and impaired colon function related to the use of laxatives and diuretics.

GI Complications Associated with Anorexia Nervosa

Constipation

Constipation is the most common GI complaint reported in anorexia nervosa. It is usually associated with a rapid decrease in food consumption and a decline in colon transit time. While constipation rarely leads to severe medical complications, it may hinder the treatment due to feelings of fullness and abdominal distention. Many individuals may rely on laxatives to treat constipation. However, that may lead to further complications manifested in electrolyte imbalances, pancreatic damage, and further delay in intestinal motility. Weight restoration, frequent feedings, gradual increase in fiber-rich foods, and adequate hydration may decrease symptoms associated with constipation.

Gastroparesis

Gastric emptying refers to the time it takes for the stomach to eliminate its contents into the duodenum. Gastroparesis is the term used to represent delayed gastric emptying. Gastroparesis has been associated with anorexia nervosa. While the exact mechanism remains uncertain, several mechanisms have been proposed. Such mechanisms include protein malnutrition leading to a decrease in the smooth muscle in the GI tract, adaptation to the stomach due to starvation and decreased food consumption, gastric dysrhythmias, and gastric adaptations associated with constipation. Weight restoration may improve gastric emptying, but it remains unknown if it is associated with nutrition rehabilitation, presence of food in the stomach, improved metabolic function, or the actual weight gain. An increased dietary intake is necessary to promote weight gain, but is often difficult due to increased feelings of early satiety, bloating, spontaneous vomiting, and abdominal discomfort with gastroparesis.

Abnormal Liver Enzymes

Liver function may be impacted in anorexia nervosa. Elevated liver enzymes (e.g., aspartate aminotransferase [AST], alanine aminotransferase [ALT], alkaline phosphatase [alk phos], and total bilirubin) may be identified in this population due to increased workload on the liver. Altered liver function abnormalities occur both in periods of weight loss and restricted food intake, and during the early stages of refeeding. The levels generally normalize with slow increases in caloric intake.

Acute Gastric Dilation

Acute gastric dilation occurs when one consumes an amount of food that is greater than what the stomach can hold. In anorexia nervosa, starvation causes the stomach to undergo muscular atrophy, and sudden consumption of food leads to gastric dilation. While gastric dilation is rare, it is a potential complication that could occur during refeeding in a starved state. It is characterized by a rapid onset of abdominal pain, vomiting, and distended abdomen. Gastric fluids need to be removed from the stomach to prevent rupturing of the stomach.

GI Complications Associated with Bulimia Nervosa

Dental Erosion

Dental erosion is a result of repetitive exposure to gastric acid caused by self-induced vomiting. The degree of damage varies depending on the length of time of the disorder, the degree and frequency of behaviors, and oral hygiene habits. The hydrochloric acid breaks down the enamel and dentin of the teeth. Eroded teeth appear worn, chipped, and discolored. While the elimination of vomiting will prevent further damage, dental erosion may require extensive dental treatments.

Dental caries, or cavities, are associated with both anorexia nervosa and bulimia nervosa. Diets high in carbohydrates have been associated with the development of dental caries. Sugar- and starch-containing foods are easily broken down by amylase and bacteria in the mouth, creating an environment for the production of acids. This acid demineralizes the tooth structure leading to dental caries.

Parotid Gland Swelling

The parotid glands are the largest of the salivary glands. These glands are responsible for the secretion of saliva into the oral cavity. Saliva then facilitates mastication (chewing) and begins the process of starch digestion. Enlargement of the parotid glands are a result of frequent binging and purging. This gives the appearance of "chipmunk-like cheeks." Parotid swelling tends to be soft to the touch and painless. It does not appear to alter salivary flow and is not infected. The onset of enlargement appears 3–6 days following a binge-purge cycle. The severity of the enlargement is associated with the frequency and duration of purging. Swelling generally decreases as the binge-purging episodes cease. However, in some cases, the enlargement may be permanent, causing an individual to seek cosmetic treatment.

Esophageal Complications

Complications associated with the esophagus can range from mild esophagitis to esophageal rupture. The esophageal mucosa is damaged from the acidic contents regurgitated from the stomach. This leads to esophagitis, esophageal erosions, ulcers, and bleeding.

Heartburn and acid-reflux symptoms are a common complaint from individuals with bulimia nervosa. Chronic emesis causes relaxation of the esophageal sphincter, resulting in increased reflux symptoms. Barrett's esophagus, which is an alteration in the lining of the esophagus potentially leading to precancerous cells, may result from recurrent vomiting. Mallory-Weiss tears occur due to the trauma associated with purging, and may lead to gastrointestinal bleeding.

Acute Gastric Dilation

Gastric dilation can also occur in bulimia nervosa. Unlike with anorexia nervosa, gastric dilation occurs as a result of binge eating. As with anorexia nervosa, if the excessive gastric fluid is not removed, stomach rupture can occur, leading to death. While gastric dilation is rare, it is a potential gastrointestinal complication seen as a result of binge eating.

Impaired Colon Function

Laxatives and diuretics are commonly used as a means to eliminate calories from the body. However, this is ineffective because the majority of nutrient absorption takes place in the small intestine, while the laxatives act in the large intestine and colon. There are five classes of laxatives grouped according to their mechanism of action: bulk laxatives, osmotic laxatives, surfactants, emollients, and stimulants. Stimulant laxatives are the primary class that is abused by individuals with bulimia nervosa. These laxatives have a mechanism of action that stimulates colon activity resulting in large amounts of watery diarrhea.

Cathartic colon occurs due to the decreased functioning of the colon nerves due to long-term stimulate-laxative abuse. Laxative stimulation prevents the colon from working properly causing impairment in normal colon function. Cathartic colon is characterized by bloating, abdominal pain, feelings of fullness, and inability to fully eliminate feces. Eliminating the use of laxatives may help, but full function of the colon may not return.

Hypovolemia and Electrolyte Disturbances

Vomiting, laxative, and diuretic abuse negatively impact electrolyte balance increase due to increased fluid elimination from the body which results in electrolyte (potassium, chloride, and bicarbonate) imbalances. Electrolyte imbalance, particularly potassium, impacts smooth and skeletal muscles, including the heart. The loss of electrolytes can lead to muscle weakness, acute renal failure, cardiac arrhythmias, convulsions, and even death.

GI Complications Associated with Eating Disorder Not Otherwise Specified

Eating Disorder Not Otherwise Specified (EDNOS) may lead to similar GI complications as anorexia nervosa and bulimia nervosa. Binge eating disorder may lead to similar complications as those resulting from the binging behavior in bulimia nervosa. These include heart burn, dental caries, and gastric dilation.

Conclusion

Eating disorders may result in a multitude of gastrointestinal complications. These complications can occur anywhere along the spectrum of the gastrointestinal tract—from the mouth to the rectum. It is necessary to address all complications to prevent irreversible damage to the gastrointestinal tract.

AMELIA MCBRIDE

Bibliography

Gurenlian, JoAnn R. "Eating Disorders." *The Journal of Dental Hygiene* 76 (2002): 219–34.

Hadley, Sallie J., and B. Timothy Walsh. "Gastrointestinal Disturbances in Anorexia Nervosa." *Current Drug Targets–CNS and Neurological Disorders* 2, no. 1 (2003): 1–9.

Mehler, Philip S. "Medical Complications of Bulimia Nervosa and Their Treatments." *International Journal of Eating Disorders* 44 (2011): 95–104.

Walsh, Judith M. E., Mary E. Wheat, and Karen Freund. "Detection, Evaluation, and Treatment of Eating Disorders–The Role of the Primary Care Physician." *Journal of General Internal Medicine* 15 (2000): 577–90.

Woolsey, Monika M. *Eating Disorder: A Clinical Guide to Counseling and Treatment.* Chicago: American Dietetic Association, 2002.

GENDER

Historically, body image concerns and eating disorders have been viewed as "women's diseases." Studies comparing the body dissatisfaction of males and females have consistently shown that as a group, girls and women report more negative body image and higher eating disorder rates than their male counterparts. However, the way eating disorders have been identified, assessed, and diagnosed has been highly gendered, with a clear bias toward females. Therefore, it is important to continue to refine assessment, treatment, and prevention efforts to develop a more accurate picture of males who struggle with body image disturbances and eating disorders.

Prevalence Rates by Gender

For several decades, males have reportedly represented 10 percent or 1 out of 10 of all eating disorder cases. Researchers and clinicians suspected that males might be suffering at higher rates but are more likely to go underdiagnosed and less likely to present for eating disorder treatment. Additionally, assessment tools have been less likely to detect male body image disturbances or eating disorders. When disregarding amenorrhea as part of the diagnostic criteria for anorexia nervosa, women were 3 to 12 times more likely to have anorexia, 3 to 18 times more likely to have bulimia, and 1.5 times more likely to have binge eating disorder (BED). Males were more likely to struggle with BED or Eating Disorder Not Otherwise Specified (EDNOS) than anorexia or bulimia. Prevalence rates for males range from 0–2.5 percent for anorexia, 0.13–6.8 percent for bulimia, and 5.0–40.8 percent for EDNOS (which includes BED).

Gender Differences in Eating Disorders and Body Image Disturbances

A meaningful finding from a 2011 study was that females perceived eating disorders to be a more serious condition than males. Males were less likely to present for treatment until symptoms had become severe and required medical attention. Males may receive less support from family members and friends who may also view eating disorders as primarily female disorders.

Males were more likely to report desiring a muscular and lean physique (i.e., reduction of body fat) whereas females often cited wanting to be "thinner" or "more slim." Males have reported wanting to increase the size of certain body parts (e.g., thighs, biceps) while still maintaining low body fat. Therefore, some of the traditional body image assessment questionnaires that contain items like, "I wish my thighs were smaller" may be inadequate for measuring male body image. Items regarding menstrual disturbances should be removed for male respondents. Notably, males are more likely to struggle with muscle dysmorphia (i.e., body distortion resulting in feeling too small) which is discussed in a separate entry. Certain males may be more at risk for developing disordered eating or clinical eating disorders including wrestlers, bodybuilders, and those engaged in sports that emphasize weight (e.g., rowers, jockeys).

Conclusion

Both females and males can be vulnerable to negative body image and the development of disordered eating. Although studies comparing males and females show that females report higher body dissatisfaction and more eating disorders, males are less likely to report a problem, strive for a different type of body ideal, and may have a higher tendency toward BED compared to the other eating disorder categories. Nonetheless, certain males are more "at risk" for engaging in disordered eating behaviors due to pressures within their environment.

JUSTINE J. REEL

See also: Binge Eating Disorder; Eating Disorder Not Otherwise Specified; Muscle Dysmorphia.

Bibliography

Culbert, Kristen M., Sarah E. Racine, and Kelly L. Klump. "The Influence of Gender and Puberty on the Heritability of Disordered Eating Symptoms." *Behavioral Neurobiology of Eating Disorders* 6 (2010): 177–85. doi: 10.1007/7854_2010_80.

Dissing, Agnete Skovlund, Nanna Hasle Bak, Laura Ern Toftegaard Pedersen, and Birgit H. Petersson. "Female Medical Students Are Estimated to Have a Higher Risk for Developing Eating Disorders than Male Medical Students." *Danish Medical Bulletin* 58, no.1 (2011): 1–5.

Koskina, Nefeli, and Theodoros Giovazolias. "The Effect of Attachment Insecurity in the Development of Eating Disturbances across Gender: The Role of Body Dissatisfaction." *The Journal of Psychology* 144, no. 5 (2010): 449–71.

Mond, Jonathan M., and Anais Arrighi. "Gender Differences in Perceptions of the Severity and Prevalence of Eating Disorders." *Early Intervention in Psychiatry* 5 (2011): 41–49. doi: 10.1111/j.1751.7893.2010.00257.x.

Sanftner, Jennifer L. "Quality of Life in Relation to Psychosocial Risk Variables for Eating Disorders in Women and Men." *Eating Behaviors* 12 (2011): 136–42. doi: 10.1016/j.eatbeh.2011.01.003.

Stoving, Rene Klinkby, Alin Andries, Kim Brixen, Niels Bilenberg, and Kirsten Horder. "Gender Differences in Outcome of Eating Disorders: A Retrospective Cohort Study." *Psychiatry Research* 186 (2011): 362–66. doi: 10/1016/j.psychres.2010.08.005.

GYMNASTICS

Gymnastics is a graceful and artistic sport that requires balance, coordination, strength, and agility. The sport of gymnastics has been around for over 2,000 years and dates back to ancient Greece. Gymnastics was used by the early Greeks and Romans to prepare for war and was a mandatory part of ancient Greek education. Although gymnastics was part of the ancient Olympic Games, modern gymnastics re-emerged in the late 18th and early 19th centuries as physical education for boys and young men. Friedrich Jahn, who is considered the "father of gymnastics," developed parallel bars, side horse with pommels, balance beam, ladder and vaulting horse to create exercises.

Men's gymnastics became popular as a competitive sport and appeared in the first modern Olympics in 1896. Women began to compete in gymnastics in the 1920s, with the first female Olympic competitors in the 1928 games and the first U.S. women's gymnastics team in 1936. By 1954, gymnastics was standardized to its current format which includes both individual and team competitions as well as the current point system from 1 to 10.

Female gymnasts have been associated with feminine grace of movement, beauty, and perfection. Nadia Comaneci became a societal sensation as a 14-year-old girl when she scored a perfect "10" in the 1976 Olympic Games. Nadia later admitted she suffered from an eating disorder. Additionally, U.S. gymnasts Cathy Rigby (a 1968 and 1972 Olympian) and Kathy Johnson (a 1984 silver medalist) publicly discussed their battles with eating disorders. Rigby, who helped popularize gymnastics in the United States, admitted that she struggled with bulimia nervosa for 12 years. She revealed that she engaged in binge episodes and vomiting and was hospitalized twice due to electrolyte imbalance. Christy Henrich, an aspiring competitive gymnast, died in 1994 from anorexia nervosa at age 22. She was purportedly informed by a judge at an international event in 1989 that she needed to lose weight to be competitive and was told by her coach that she looked like a "Pillsbury dough boy." This tragedy and the eating disorder reports by other competitive gymnasts underscore the risk of disordered eating and eating disorders in gymnastics.

Former gymnast Christy Henrich, is shown at a luncheon fundraiser on Friday, August 13, 1993, in Kansas City, Missouri, with her fiancé Bo Moreno. Henrich died July 26, 1994, at a Kansas City area hospital after a long battle with two eating disorders that had reduced her to just 60 pounds. The 4-foot, 10-inch Henrich, 22, weighed 93 pounds at the height of her competitive career. (Kansas City Star/Kelley Chin/AP/Wide World Photos)

Gymnastics and Eating Disorders

The prevalence of eating disorders and disordered eating has varied by the study. Most studies have found that gymnasts were actively dieting and using a variety of pathological methods to lose weight, such as restricting foods, self-induced vomiting, laxative abuse, fluid restriction, and diuretics. One study reported that up to 62 percent of gymnasts were engaging in pathogenic weight control methods. Another study using more sensitive assessment measures found that 22 percent of college gymnasts met criteria for a clinical eating disorder. Gymnastics is considered an aesthetic sport and has been associated with a sport environment that may have inherent risks for eating disorders and disordered eating.

Gymnastics as a Judged, Aesthetic Sport

Sports that are aesthetic in nature have been associated with higher drives for thinness and increased risk for eating disorders. Similar to figure skating and diving, gymnastics is based on a particular look that is judged using a subjective scoring system. Gymnastic stunts are scored higher when lines are more pronounced, which is often accomplished by a thinner, leaner physique and by reducing feminine curves. Gymnasts may feel the pressure to delay puberty and body-related changes due to the perception that they can remain more competitive at a smaller size.

Sources of Weight Pressures

Like other athletes from other aesthetic sports, gymnasts face sport-related weight pressures including form-fitting uniforms, coaching comments, comparison with peers, and judges. Gymnasts, like divers, have revealing team uniforms that show any perceived body imperfections and may increase feelings of body self-consciousness. The sport of gymnastics and its Olympic coaches were exposed in books like *Little Girls in Pretty Boxes* that showed daily weigh-ins and grueling physical training with restrictive food intake. Gymnasts have reported that coaches may comment about a gymnast's size, shape or weight and that the thinnest gymnasts may be the "coach's favorite." Gymnasts compete with other gymnasts in competitions and for spots in the competition and may use weight or size as a "controllable" factor. Finally, judges score gymnasts on their "aesthetic," with gymnasts who can perform with the longest, thinnest lines reaping the biggest rewards and highest scores.

Rhythmic Gymnastics

Rhythmic gymnastics was first recognized as a sport in 1962 by the International Gymnastics Federation. Participants in this form of gymnastics are expected to be feminine and graceful. A study conducted in Norway revealed that 8 of 12 rhythmic gymnasts had elevated drive for thinness and body dissatisfaction scores showing a risk for eating disorders, and that 33 percent of the gymnasts met the criteria for eating disorders. These researchers suggest that disordered eating may be normative in rhythmic gymnasts due to the perception that extreme thinness is a requirement for success in the sport. Even extremely thin rhythmic gymnasts reported dieting to fight their natural body weight. This sport should be explored further as rhythmic gymnastics includes similar weight pressures as the more familiar form of artistic gymnastics—such as pressure from coaches, judges, and parents.

Conclusion

Gymnastics has been categorized as an aesthetic sport and has been associated with risk for disordered eating and eating disorders. Dieting and pathological weight loss methods have been reported among youth and college gymnasts and seem to be normative for both artistic and rhythmic gymnastics. Many competitive gymnasts, such as Cathy Rigby, have admitted to battles with eating disorders and weight pressures associated with the sport.

JUSTINE J. REEL

See also: Aesthetic Sports; Puberty and Body Image.

Bibliography

Beals, Katherine A. *Disordered Eating among Athletes: A Comprehensive Guide for Health Professionals.* Champaign, IL: Human Kinetics, 2004.

Harris, Mary B., and Debbie Greco. "Weight Control and Weight Concern in Competitive Female Gymnasts." *Journal of Sport & Exercise Psychology* 12 (1990): 427–33.

Klinkowski, Nora, Alexander Korte, Ernst Pfeiffer, Ulrike Lehmkuhl, and Harriet Salbach-Andrae. "Psychopathology in Elite Rhythmic Gymnasts and Anorexia Nervosa Patients." *European Child and Adolescent Psychiatry* 17, no. 2 (2008): 108–113. doi: 10.1007/s00787-007-0643-y.

O'Connor, Patrick, Richard D. Lewis, Elisabeth M. Kirchener, and Dane B. Cook. "Eating Disorder Symptoms in Former Female College Gymnasts: Relations with Body Composition." *American Journal of Clinical Nutrition* 64 (1996): 840–43.

Petrie, Trent A. "Disordered Eating in Female Collegiate Gymnasts: Prevalence and Personality/Attitudinal Correlates." *Journal of Sport and Exercise Psychology* 15 (1993): 424–36.

Sundgot-Borgen, Jorunn. "Eating Disorders, Energy Intake, Training Volume and Menstrual Function in High-Level Modern Rhythmic Gymnasts." *International Journal of Sport Nutrition* 6 (1996): 100–109.

Thompson, Ron A., and Roberta Trattner Sherman. *Eating Disorders in Sport.* New York, NY: Routledge, 2010.

H

HATTOU SHIN IDEAL

The Hattou Shin Ideal refers to a socially constructed appearance ideal specific to Japanese culture and related to the head size and leg length of females. Although Japanese females are stereotyped in the United States as pale-skinned, dark-haired women who wear extravagant kimonos, Japanese attractiveness ideals more closely resemble Western appearance ideals than this stereotypical image. In fact, Asian women report a Westernized body ideal and includes being tall, blonde, buxom, and thin with European facial features. In 1989, 48 percent of male models and 42 percent of female models in Japanese magazines were Caucasian. In recent publications, 74 percent of the ads featured Western models.

Body Image and the Hattou Shin Ideal

A unique aspect of Japanese body image has been the development and reinforcement of the Hattou Shin Ideal (i.e., length of one's head should equal one-eighth of one's height) since World War II. This ideal translated into the glorification of females who had smaller heads and longer legs. Beginning in the early 1950s, Japanese magazine articles and advertisements began to actively promote the Hattou Shin Ideal by including models with unusually long legs that were digitally enhanced to meet this Japanese cultural ideal. This body ideal of long and thin legs has been tied to weight management techniques such as skipping meals, obsessive exercise, vomiting, and using laxatives or diuretics in attempts to slim down and strive toward the Japanese ideal. Additionally, Japanese females will dress in a way that accentuates thinness by wearing high heels to make their legs appear longer.

Conclusion

In Japan, a unique feature associated with having the ideal female body is largely based on genetics. Specifically, females in Japan have scrutinized their head and leg measurements by using tape measures to determine whether they fit the Hattou Shin Ideal (i.e., to see whether their head is one-eighth the length of the rest of their body). Interestingly, although models in magazines often depict this Hattou Shin Ideal, the standard is pretty unrealistic and represents a genetic anomaly.

HAILEY E. NIELSON

Bibliography

Chisuwa, Naomi, and Jennifer A. O'Dea. "Body Image and Eating Disorders amongst Japanese Adolescents. A Review of the Literature." *Appetite* 54 (2010): 5–15. doi: 10.1016/j. appet.2009.11.008.

Iwao, Shunichiro. "Nihon-jin no Tai-gaikoki-jin Taido (Attitudes of Japanese toward Foreigners)." *Financial Review* 12 (1989): 1–10.

Mormoto, Mariko, and Susan Chang. "Western and Asian Models in Japanese Fashion Magazine Ads: The Relationship with Brand Origins and International versus Domestic Magazines." *Journal of International Consumer Marketing* 21 (2009): 173–87. doi: 10.1080/08961530802202701.

Mukai, Takayo, Akiko Kambara, and Yuji Sasaki. "Body Dissatisfaction, Need for Social Approval and Eating Disturbances among Japanese and American College Women." *Sex Roles* 39 (1998): 751–63. doi: 0021–9630/94.

Nishizono-Maher, Aya, Yuko Miyake, and Akira Nakane. "The Prevalence of Eating Pathology and its Relationship to Knowledge of Eating Disorders among High School Girls in Japan." *European Eating Disorders Review* 12 (2004): 122–28.

Swami, Viren, Carolina Caprario, Martin J. Tovee, and Adrian Frunham. "Female Physical Attractiveness in Britain and Japan: A Cross-Cultural Study." *European Journal of Personality* 20, no. 1 (2006): 69–81.

HEALTH AT EVERY SIZE APPROACH

The U.S. obesity epidemic has placed size and weight at the center of attention. In attempts to combat the overweight and obesity problem, many researchers and practitioners have focused on using a weight loss approach that promotes dieting and, in some cases, can contribute to disordered eating and fear of fatness. Fat bias and weight discrimination (which are discussed in a separate entry) have served as a barrier for individuals who are overweight and obese, preventing them from receiving nonjudgmental and helpful treatment within the medical community. Like other "isms" (e.g., racism, sexism), being larger has been associated with stereotypes of being "lazy," "sloppy," and "unmotivated" by medical and health professionals. Therefore, a more long-term, health promotion approach that fosters self-acceptance as well as healthy eating and physical activity behaviors has been sorely needed.

Overview of the Health at Every Size (HAES) Approach

The Health at Every Size (HAES) approach, conceived by Linda Bacon in 2005, strives to counteract the negative effects of dieting and traditional weight management approaches that emphasize weight loss. When programs focus on losing body weight, many individuals may be triggered by the emotional baggage associated with the number on the scale rather than the idea of developing lifestyle changes that favor a moderation approach. Therefore, the HAES paradigm views dieting and obsession with weight as unhealthy, celebrates diversity in body size, and promotes overall health. Rather than encouraging dietary restraint, the HAES approach advocates eating in accordance with hunger and fullness cues (i.e., intuitive eating). It promotes physical activity for enjoyment rather than exercise solely for weight loss. Importantly, the HAES philosophy proposes to optimize psychological and physical health at any weight. The Association for Size Diversity and Health (ASDAH) is an international professional organization committed to HAES principles. Its mission is "to promote education, research and the provision of services which enhance health and well-being, and which are free from weight-based assumption and weight discrimination."

Health at Every Size and Body Image

The HAES approach was developed after the realization that traditional weight management approaches were associated with dieting behaviors, which in turn is associated with overeating, depression, low self-esteem, poor body image, weight cycling, and eating disorders. The HAES approach can promote health behaviors such as taking a balanced approach to eating and exercise while not compromising body image or creating an overemphasis on losing weight. HAES researchers have felt that overweight and obesity have been overemphasized. This view—which has been supported by recent research suggesting that health is not only about pounds—takes an unnecessary emphasis off of one's size, shape, or appearance: http://today.msnbc.msn.com/id/26184891/vp/44227119#44227119

Evaluation of the HAES Approach

A program evaluation using the HAES approach with 22 female participants showed significant improvement at 24 months for weight, exercise frequency, diastolic blood pressure, and systolic blood pressure. Interestingly, the participants continued to lose weight even after the program had finished, as they maintained their health lifestyle skills using a nondieting approach. In a separate study with 78 obese women, using the nondiet HAES approach yielded decreases in binge eating behaviors, depression, body dissatisfaction, and disordered eating. Initial findings for HAES studies show improvements in psychological and physical health, but more studies are needed with larger sample sizes.

Conclusion

Unfortunately, a disordered relationship with food and exercise can exist in people of all weights and sizes. Unlike traditional weight management approaches which focus on weight loss and can promote dieting, the HAES approach focuses on developing pleasurable physical activities and eating intuitively. Although some obesity researchers have been skeptical, HAES studies have produced significant health outcomes which are promising for a paradigm that celebrates self-acceptance and bodies of all sizes.

JUSTINE J. REEL

See also: Dietary Restraint; Intuitive Eating.

Bibliography

"Association for Size Diversity and Health." Sizediversityandhealth.org. Accessed August 22, 2011. http://www.sizediversityandhealth.org/index.asp.

Bacon, Linda, and Lucy Aphramor. "Weight Science: Evaluating the Evidence for a Paradigm Shift." *Nutrition Journal* 10, no. 9 (2011): 1–13. doi: 10.1186/1475-2891-10-9.

Bradshaw, Alison J., Caroline C. Horwath, Lisa Katzer, and Andrew Gray. "Non-dieting Group Interventions for Overweight and Obese Women: What Predicts Non-Completion and Does Completion Improve Outcomes?" *Public Health Nutrition* 13, no. 10 (2009): 1622–1628. doi: 10.1017/S1368980009992977.

Gagnon-Girouard, Marie-Pierre, Catherine Begin, Veronique Provencher, Angelo Tremblay, Lyne Mongeau, Sonia Boivin, and Simone Lemieux. "Psychological Impact of a 'Health at Every Size' Intervention on Weight Preoccupied Overweight/Obese Women." *Journal of Obesity* (2010): 1–12. doi: 10.1155/2010/928097

Hawley, Greer, Caroline Horwath, Andrew Gray, Alison Bradshaw, Lisa Katzer, Janine Joyce, and Sue O'Brien. "Sustainability of Health and Lifestyle Improvements Following a Non-Dieting Randomised Trial in Overweight Women." *Preventive Medicine* 47 (2008): 593–99. doi: 10.1016/j.ypmed2008.08.008.

King, Carrie. "Health at Every Size Approach to Health Management: The Evidence is Weighed." *Top Clinical Nutrition* 22, no. 3 (2007): 272–85.

Provencher, Veronique, Catherine Begin, Angelo Tremblay, Lyne Mongeau, Sonia Boivin, and Simone Lemieux. "Short-Term Effects of a 'Health At Every Size' Approach on Eating Behaviors and Appetite Ratings." *Obesity* 15, no. 4 (2007): 957–66.

Provencher, Veronique, Catherine Begin, Angelo Tremblay, Lyne Mongeau, Louise Corneau, Sylvie Dodin, Sonia Boivin, and Simone Lemieux. "Health at Every Size and Eating Behaviors: 1-Year Follow-up Results of a Size Acceptance Intervention." *Journal of American Dietetic Association* 109 (2009): 1854–1861. doi: 10.1016/j.jada.2009.08.017.

Reel, Justine J. and Allison R. Stuart. "Is the 'Health at Every Size' approach useful for addressing obesity prevention?"*Journal of Community Medicine & Health Education* 2, no. 4 (2012): 1–2.

"Today's Health: Why Health is Not Measured in Pounds." Today.com. Accessed August 22, 2011. http://today.msnbc.msn.com/id/26184891/vp/44227119#44227119.

IMPULSIVITY

Impulsivity has been defined as acting without thinking, having the perceived inability to delay gratification, or acting without considering the potential risks associated with one's behavior. Impulsive behaviors are thought to be performed without conscious decision-making or judgment and tend to be spontaneous actions that involve insufficient planning. Impulsivity has been linked with eating disorders and other pathological behaviors such as substance abuse, compulsive shopping, sexual promiscuity, and shoplifting. In fact, 37 percent of compulsive shoppers have eating disordered symptoms. Two factors, reward-sensitivity and rash, spontaneous impulsivity, have also been associated with the concept of impulsivity. Reward-sensitivity is the inability to delay reward and the tendency to choose small rewards over delayed ones, whereas rash spontaneous impulsivity refers to a person rapidly responding without adequately assessing the consequences of his or her action.

Eating Disorders and Impulsivity

One study found that 17 percent of individuals with a history of eating disorders suffered from impulse control problems. Typically, impulsivity has been associated with increased binge episodes for eating disordered individuals. For example, an individual who engages in uncontrollable eating patterns eats beyond the point of fullness despite the potential for weight gain, feelings of guilt, and negative health consequences. Most studies have found a higher prevalence of impulsivity among binge eaters who have been diagnosed with binge eating disorder or bulimia nervosa than those individuals with anorexia nervosa or nonclinical controls (i.e., people who do not have eating disorders). Therefore, impulsivity characteristics are thought to exist on a spectrum with binge eaters on one end and restrictive eaters on the other end who are less likely to engage in sensation-seeking or risk-taking behaviors. Higher impulsivity among individuals with eating disorders has also been associated with increased severity of eating disorder symptoms, higher incidence of personality disorders, and decreased psychological functioning and ability to cope.

Multi-Impulsivity versus Uni-Impulsivity

Researchers have distinguished between eating disordered individuals who exhibit several impulsive behaviors (i.e., multi-impulsivity) and those who have binge eating as their sole impulsive behavior (i.e., uni-impulsivity). Individuals who represent the subgroup of multi-impulsivity engage in at least three distinct behaviors (e.g., alcohol or drug abuse, suicide attempts, self-mutilation, sexual promiscuity, and stealing) in addition to the disordered eating behaviors. The multi-impulsive group has shown a stronger tendency to display comorbidity with other psychological disorders (e.g., substance abuse) and a higher drop-out rate for treatment than the uni-impulsivity group. Therefore, it is important to consider the role of impulsivity in treatment and recovery for eating disordered individuals.

Conclusion

Impulsivity has been widely linked to eating disorders. Although there is some confusion over whether being impulsive serves as a risk factor for the development of disordered eating and eating disorders, it is evident that impulsivity is more likely to be related to binge behavior. Impulsivity has also been related to increased eating disorder severity and decreased psychological functioning. Compared to individuals with binge eating disorder and bulimia nervosa, individuals who restrict food are less likely to engage in impulsive behaviors.

JUSTINE J. REEL

Bibliography

Boisseau, Christina L., Heather Thompson-Brenner, Kamryn T. Eddy, and Dana A. Satir. "Impulsivity and Personality Variables in Adolescents with Eating Disorders." *The Journal of Nervous and Mental Disease* 197, no. 4 (2009): 251–59.

Claes, Laurence, Patricia Bijttebier, James E. Mitchell, Martina de Zwaan, and Astrid Mueller. "The Relationship between Compulsive Buying, Eating Disorder Symptoms, and Temperament in a Sample of Female Students." *Comprehensive Psychiatry* 52 (2011): 50–55. doi: 10.1016/j.comppsych.2010.05.003.

Culbert, Kristen M., and Kelly L. Klump. "Impulsivity as an Underlying Factor in the Relationship between Disordered Eating and Sexual Behavior." *International Journal of Eating Disorders* 38, no. 4 (2005): 361–66. doi: 10.1002/eat.20188.

Fernandez-Aranda, Fernando, Susana Jimenez-Murcia, Eva M. Alvarez-Moya, Roser Granero, Julio Vallejo, and Cynthia M. Bulik. "Impulse Control Disorders in Eating Disorders: Clinical and Therapeutic Implications." *Comprehensive Psychiatry* 47 (2006): 482–88. doi: 10.106/j.comppsych.2006.03.002.

Fernandez-Aranda, Fernando, Andrea Poyastro Pinheiro, Laura M. Thornton, Wade H. Berrettini, Scott Crow, Manfred M. Fichter, Katherine A. Halmi, Allan S. Kaplan, Pamela Keel, James Mitchell, Alessandro Rotondo, Michael Strober, D. Blake Woodside, Walter H. Kaye, and Cynthia M. Bulik. "Impulse Control Disorders in Women with Eating Disorders." *Psychiatry Research* 157 (2008): 147–57. doi: 10.106/j/psychres.2007.02.011.

Rosval, Lindsay, Howard Steiger, Kenneth Bruce, Mimi Israel, Jodie Richardson, and Melanie Aubut. "Impulsivity in Women with Eating Disorders: Problem of Response, Inhibition, Planning or Attention?" *International Journal of Eating Disorders* 39, no. 7 (2006): 590–93. doi: 10.1002/eat.20296.

Waxman, Samantha E. "A Systematic Review of Impulsivity in Eating Disorders." *European Eating Disorders Review* 17 (2009): 408–425. doi: 10.1002/erv.952.

INFERTILITY

Infertility is defined as the inability to bear children despite refraining from contraception use for at least a year. Infertility affects 10–15 percent of married couples in the United States and has been linked to various psychological disorders including depression, obsessive-compulsive disorder, anxiety disorders, substance abuse, and eating disorders. Individuals with anorexia nervosa, bulimia nervosa, and binge eating disorder are more likely to experience infertility than the general female population due to extended menstrual cycle disturbances, hormonal imbalances, malnutrition, and vitamin deficiencies.

The pattern of higher proportion of eating disordered individuals suffering from infertility was noted by Canadian researchers. Specifically, investigators who were examining infertility clinics discovered that 1.5 percent of infertility patients had anorexia nervosa, 6 percent had bulimia nervosa, and another 9 percent had some other type of eating disorder (e.g., Eating Disorder Not Otherwise Specified) or disordered eating which would represent a higher proportion than would be expected in the community. The lack of fertility was attributed to lack of ovulation for all cases of infertility. In addition to infertility, eating disordered individuals may face problems with pregnancy and birth defects. Women with eating disorders may face greater risk for developing polycystic ovarian syndrome which is characterized by changes to the ovaries such that multiple follicles accumulate in the ovaries without ovulation. The risk of infertility as a health consequence from an eating disorder may serve as the sole motivation for some women to seek treatment or desire to restore menstruation.

Conclusion

There are numerous medical complications associated with anorexia nervosa, bulimia nervosa, and binge eating disorder. Coinciding with menstrual disturbances is the tendency for women to experience endocrine consequences that impact their reproductive system. In some cases, the risk of not being able to bear children can be a motivating factor to seek treatment and recover from an eating disorder. However, infertility may be the unfortunate consequence of a life-long struggle with an eating disorder that begins in adolescence.

JUSTINE J. REEL

Bibliography

Abraham, Suzanne, and Derek Llewellyn-Jones. *Eating Disorders: The Facts.* New York, NY: Oxford University Press, 1995.

Costin, Carolyn. *A Comprehensive Guide to the Causes, Treatments and Prevention of Eating Disorders, 3rd ed.,* New York, NY: McGraw-Hill, 2007.

Costin, Carolyn. *100 Questions & Answers about Eating Disorders.* Sudbury, MA: Jones and Bartlett, 2007.

Hall, Lindsey, and Leigh Cohn. *Bulimia: A Guide to Recovery.* Carlsbad, CA: Gurze, 2011.

Loucks, Anne B. "Energy Availability and Infertility." *Current Opinion in Endocrinology, Diabetes, and Obesity* 14, no. 6 (2007): 470–74.

Mehler, Philip S. "Bulimia Nervosa." *The New England Journal of Medicine* 349, no. 9 (2003): 875–82.

Mehler, Philip S., and Mori Krantz. "Anorexia Nervosa Medical Issues." *Journal of Women's Health* 12, no. 4 (2003): 331–40.

Practice Committee of the American Society for Reproductive Medicine. "Current Evaluation of Amenorrhea." *Fertility and Sterility* 82 (2004): 266–72.

Sharagli, Chiara, Giuseppe Morgante, Arianna Goracci, Tara Hofkens, Vincenzo De Leo, and Paolo Castrogiovanni. "Infertility and Psychiatric Morbidity." *Fertility and Sterility* 90, no. 6 (2008): 2107–2111.

INTEGRATIVE APPROACHES

Many Americans have never heard of integrative health, but the holistic movement has left its imprint on many of the nation's hospitals, universities, and medical schools. The goal is to treat the mind, body and spirit, all at the same time. Groundbreaking research has supported a strong interaction between the brain and the immune system, emotion and disease.

An integrative approach to eating disorders traditionally includes treatment by an interdisciplinary team of professionals, including but not limited to primary care doctors, cardiologists, dentists, dietitians, psychotherapists, recreational therapists, and art therapists. More recently, additional modalities of mind/body/spirit intervention have been utilized to promote whole person healing.

Meditation

Mindfulness meditation includes an abundance of techniques designed to bring awareness to every aspect of daily life. For example, the popular "raisin meditation" includes an experience of looking at and then eating a single raisin as mindfully as possible, as if a raisin has never been eaten before. This meditation takes only a few minutes, and many people report that it has a meaningful impact on their subsequent experiences with eating. Research based on sensory deprivation indicates that compulsive eaters and chronic dieters are often disconnected from internal self-regulatory methods of control over their eating, and are unduly influenced by external prompts, emotional signals, or belief systems. As such, the raisin meditation can be an appropriate introduction to increased self-awareness through meditation.

Other elements can also be used to increase mindfulness. Basic meditation techniques, such as *Transcendental Meditation,* involve a sitting or slightly reclined 20-minute meditation with repetition of a personal mantra. Focused breathing and simple yoga movements can also relax and re-engage the body. Often, those with eating disorders simultaneously feel disconnected from, yet completely defined by, their bodies. So, *meditative breathing* can be both a relaxation component as well as a powerful focusing technique. It works by balancing the autonomic nervous system and by drawing attention to physiological processes that can be directly experienced without being threatening. Additionally, *guided meditations* can be used in a safe place to help people address their fears and experiences with hunger and fullness. Also, *forgiveness meditation* can address anger and hurt that is directed toward the self and others, and can encourage nonjudgmental acceptance of feelings. A *spiritual wisdom* exercise can help people connect to values, strengths, and a higher life purpose through inner awareness and peace.

Therapeutic Massage/Touch (TT)

Therapeutic massage or therapeutic touch (TT) is an almost forgotten art of medicine, as many areas of the human body cannot be touched even by the physician without a specific reason for examination or biochemical treatment. Also, those who suffer from eating disorders often have a history of physical or sexual abuse, which indicates a need for caution when employing the use of this powerful technique. Manual medicine includes sensitive touch, and can be a much more powerful tool than many modern physicians assume. Pains and discomforts can be eased by just touching the sick area and assisting the person to be in better contact with the distressed area of the body. People who suffer from eating disorders often disengage from their bodies, and this lack of presence can be associated with many symptoms that can be reversed by sensitive healing touch. When touch is combined with emotional therapeutic work, holistic healing is enhanced and difficulties can be resolved in an effective way, often without the use of medication.

Acupuncture

In Oriental medicine, all illness is believed to be a result of mind-body-spirit energy imbalance. Acupuncture intends to restore health by readjusting and balancing energy. It is especially helpful for people with food allergies, digestive problems, and food cravings, often found in those with eating disorders. A recent study also indicates that acupuncture may provide benefits to eating disorder clients by improving their overall quality of life. The researchers found evidence of a lowering of anxiety and of perfectionism, which may help those with eating disorders succeed in learning healthy eating behaviors.

Energy Psychology

Energy psychology is based on the premise that painful emotional, spiritual, and physical symptoms are the consequence of disruption in the energy system. Correcting the disruption re-establishes the body's natural ability to heal itself. Energy psychology is practiced in many different forms beyond acupuncture, including meridian-tapping techniques, Thought Field Therapy, acupressure, Emotional Freedom Technique, and touch therapy. Traditional psychotherapy uses the influence of speech to transform or regulate emotions. By talking about feelings, one may come to a better understanding of the self and different ways to respond to old issues. For individuals with addictions, anxiety, phobias, PTSD, and eating disorders, energy psychology techniques can complement traditional psychotherapy to help release emotional blocks and promote healing. Specifically, meridian tapping involves repeating a neutral affirmation while rubbing a spot on the upper right or left chest, or tapping a karate chop point on the outside of either hand. Also, specific points on the face and body can be rubbed or tapped, depending on the symptoms. An affirmation could be, "even though I have this eating disorder, I deeply and completely accept myself." If an individual has significant trauma, the therapist may walk her or him through each traumatic event one step at a time, while tapping to relieve troubling emotions.

Conclusion

Therapeutic massage/touch, acupuncture, and energy psychology are three integrative approaches that are used in the treatment of eating disorders. Other integrative health approaches for eating disorders include, but are not limited to, adventure therapy, expressive arts therapy, EMDR, functional diagnostic medical testing, naturopathic medicine, neurofeedback, and yoga. Some of these topics are covered in detail within other entries.

JULIANN M. COOK

See also: EMDR; Mindfulness; Yoga.

Bibliography

Bono, Joseph. "Psychological Assessment of Transcendental Meditation." In *Meditation: Classic and Contemporary Perspectives,* edited by Deane Shapiro and Roger Walsh, 209–217. New York: Aldine, 1984.

"Holistic Treatment." Mirasol. Accessed October 4, 2011. http://www.mirasol.net/treatment-programs/holistic-treatment.php.

Marlatt, G., Alan L. Kristeller, and Jean L. Kristeller. "Mindfulness and Meditation." In *Integrating Spirituality in Treatment.* Washington, DC: American Psychological Association, 2000.

O'Connell, Daniel F., and Charles N. Alexander. *Self-Recovery: Treating Addictions Using Transcendental Meditation and Maharishi Ayur-Veda.* Binghamton, NY: Haworth Press, 1994.

Roucsh, Robert A. *Complementary and Alternative Medicine: Clinic Design.* New York: Haworth Integrative Healing Press, 2003.

Ventegodt, Soren, Niels Anderson, and Joav Merrick. "Holistic Medicine III: The Holistic Process of Healing." *The Scientific World Journal* 3 (2003): 1138–1146.

INTELLECTUAL DISABILITIES AND BODY IMAGE

People with intellectual disabilities have received little attention in the body image and eating disorder field, despite the fact that these individuals may face additional pressures related to body shape, size, and culturally constructed body ideals. This particular group has been the target of many stereotypes and faces stigma on a daily basis when interacting with others. Additionally, the terminology of individuals with intellectual disabilities (ID) versus those with mental retardation (MR) has been controversial over the past several years. According to the *Diagnostic Manual–Intellectual Disability: A Clinical Guide for Diagnosis of Mental Disorders in Persons with Intellectual Disability,* there has been a shift since 2003 to using the term intellectual disability.

Definition of Intellectual Disability

An intellectual disability, often referred to as developmentally delayed, is determined by three identifying criteria: (1) below average intellectual functioning (IQ < 70 or IQ-equivalent), (2) deficits in adaptive daily functioning, and (3) disability before the age of 18 years. Measurement of eating disorders and other mental disorders within this population can present some challenges as individuals with ID are a widely misunderstood and heterogeneous group. Persons with ID require just enough structure and cues to express their feelings in a spontaneous and unbiased fashion. Researchers have modified some surveys (e.g., Rosenberg's Self-Esteem Scale) that were developed for the general population to assess self-esteem and other psychological characteristics among individuals with ID.

Eating Disorders and Intellectual Disabilities

An individual who has an intellectual disability and has been diagnosed with an eating disorder may present with common stressors and indicators of an adult without an intellectual disability. For example, the individual with an intellectual disability may experience dysfunctional family dynamics, unhealthy eating habits, grief/loss issues, relationship issues, and other concerns that might complicate the eating disorder treatment. Poindexter and Loschen (2007) outlined the DSM-IV criteria for anorexia and bulimia nervosa and adapted it for people with severe to profound intellectual disabilities. Part of the criteria for anorexia nervosa is the refusal to gain weight and maintain age appropriate body weight. For example, a person with a severe/profound intellectual disability may exhibit a fear of gaining weight by avoiding food and restricting during meals.

Approximately 6–42 percent of adults with intellectual disabilities in a hospital setting met the criteria for a clinical eating disorder including anorexia nervosa, bulimia nervosa, and Eating Disorder Not Otherwise Specified (e.g., binge eating disorder). Another 19 percent in a community setting had a diagnosable eating disorder. However, these reported prevalence rates included individuals diagnosed with pica, severe/profound intellectual disabilities, autism, and other developmental diagnoses/genetic syndromes who would be unlikely to meet the full criteria for a clinical eating disorder (e.g., negative body image). Individuals who fit several of these diagnoses/syndromes tended to exhibit "eating disorder-like characteristics." However, the similar presentation of psychopathology within individuals with intellectual disabilities and eating disorders makes it challenging to distinguish an intellectual disability from an eating disorder. Additionally, the intellectual disability and eating disorder may co-exist; therefore, it is important to differentiate a person with a dual diagnosis from one with only an intellectual disability.

Body Image and Intellectual Disabilities

Few studies have examined body image among individuals with intellectual disabilities. However, some recent attention has been given to a higher proportionate obesity rate for this population. A rare study explored body image among 100 adult males and females with ID and found similar trends as the general population. For example, males with ID chose a larger body size for their ideal body than their female counterparts, and men were more satisfied with their bodies than women. Both males and females expressed a desire to have a thinner physique; however, males also reported wanting to increase muscle size. To allow for more in-depth body image responses, participants were asked this question: if they had a magic wand, what, if anything, would they change. The two most common themes were the desire to be more skinny or to have more muscles. Approximately 24 participants (23.3 percent) responded for open-ended items that they would like to lose weight or be skinnier. Although more females ($N = 15$) expressed an interest in losing weight, 9 males reported wanting to be thinner. One male athlete (age 23) with a body mass index (BMI) of 27.5 stated, "I want to lose some weight—that is why I do basketball." Another male (age 61) with a BMI of 41.1 indicated he would like to "lose a bunch of weight here" as he pointed to his midsection. However, many male athletes expressed a desire to build muscles for the open-ended item as shown by the following comment from a 21-year-old male with a BMI of 25.7, "I want to have a six pack. No, an eight pack. Big muscles like Hollywood Hulk Hogan. I need to go to the gym."

Study results of females with ID resembled findings from previous body image studies about females without intellectual disabilities. Female participants desired to be thinner or to lose weight. One female (age 38) with a BMI of 42.9 expressed her intense body dissatisfaction. "I am too fat, too ugly, and not pretty. I am not cute." Another female participant stated she would change "my body, from my neck down to my toes" and yet another female indicated she wanted to "lose weight and date boys." Interestingly, only two participants identified their disability as something they would want to change. One female with ID (age 55) who was a quadriplegic with cerebral palsy shared, "I wish I could walk. I wouldn't want to be in this chair." A male with ID (age 54) echoed her sentiment, "I don't want to be in this chair." However, the characteristics associated with ID (e.g., larger head) were never discussed.

Conclusion

In considering the full reach of eating disorders and body image disturbances, it is important to examine persons with intellectual disabilities. Although treatment is not usually readily available for individuals with decreased intellectual functioning within traditional eating disorder residential facilities, there is some evidence that these individuals may also suffer from clinical eating disorders, disordered eating, and poor body image. While much of the focus for this population has been on preventing obesity, healthy nutrition and physical activity can be promoted in a way that does not lead to dieting and unhealthy disordered eating behaviors.

JUSTINE J. REEL AND ROBERT A. BUCCIERE

See also: Pica.

Bibliography

Bucciere, Robert A., and Justine J. Reel. " 'Not So Different Than You': Body Image and Eating Disorders among Individuals with Disabilities." In *The Hidden Faces of Eating Disorders and Body Image,* edited by Justine J. Reel and Katherine A. Beals, 145–58. Reston, VA: AAHPERD, 2009.

Crabtree, Jason W., S. Alexander Haslam, Tom Postmes, and Catherine Haslam. "Mental Health Support Groups, Stigma, and Self-Esteem: Positive and Negative Implications of Group Identification." *Journal of Social Issues* 66, no. 3 (2010): 553–69.

Davis, Clare, Steven Kellett, Nigel Beail, and Jeremy Turk. "Utility of the Rosenberg Self-Esteem Scale." *American Journal on Intellectual and Developmental Disabilities* 114, no. 3 (2009): 172–78.

Dykens, E., K. Schwenk, M. Maxwell, and B. Myatt. "The Sentence Completion and Three Wishes Tasks: Windows into the Inner Lives of People with Intellectual Disabilities." *Journal of Intellectual Disability Research* 51, no. 8 (2007): 588–97.

Fletcher, Robert J., Earl Loschen, Chrissoula Stavrakaki, and Michael First. *Diagnostic Manual–Intellectual Disability: A Clinical Guide for Diagnosis of Mental Disorders in Persons with Intellectual Disability.* Kingston, NY: The NADD Press, 2007.

Gal, Eynat, Reem Hardal-Nasser, and Batya Engel-Yeger. "The Relationship between the Severity of Eating Problems and Intellectual Developmental Deficit Level." *Research in Developmental Disabilities* 32 (2011): 1464–1469.

Gravestock, Shaun. "Eating Disorders in Adults with Intellectual Disability." *Journal of Intellectual Disability Research* 44, no. 6 (2000): 625–37.

Gravestock, Shaun. "Diagnosis and Classification of Eating Disorders in Adults with Intellectual Disability: the Diagnostic Criteria for Psychiatric Disorders for Use with Adults with Learning Disabilities/Mental Retardation (DC-LD) Approach." *Journal of Intellectual Disability Research* 47 (2003): 72–83.

Howes, Hannah, Stephen Edwards, and David Benton. "Male Body Image Following Acquired Brain Injury." *Brain Injury* 19, no. 2 (2005): 135–47.

Howes, Hannah, Stephen Edwards, and David Benton. "Female Body Image Following Acquired Brain Injury." *Brain Injury* 19, no. 6 (2005): 403–415.

Keung Yuen, Hon, and Carolyn Hanson. "Body Image and Exercise in People with and without Acquired Mobility Disability." *Disability and Rehabilitation* 24, no. 6 (2002): 289–96.

Levi, Aurelia. "Orthopedic Disability as a Factor in Human-Figure Perception." *Journal of Consulting Psychology* 25, no. 3 (1961): 253–56.

MacMahon, Pamela, and Andrew Jahoda. "Social Comparison and Depression: People with Mild and Moderate Intellectual Disabilities." *American Journal on Mental Retardation* 113, no. 4 (2008): 307–318.

Murray, C. D., and J. Fox. "Body Image and Prosthesis Satisfaction in the Lower Limb Amputee." *Disability and Rehabilitation* 24, no. 17 (2002): 925–31.

Poindexter, Ann R., and Earl Loschen. "Eating Disorders." In *Diagnostic Manual–Intellectual Disability: A Clinical Guide for Diagnosis of Mental Disorders in Persons with Intellectual Disability,* edited by Robert J. Fletcher, Earl Loschen, Chrissoula Stavrakaki, and Michael First, 277–79. Kingston, NY: The NADD Press, 2007.

Potgieter, C., and G. Khan. "Sexual Self-Esteem and Body Image of South African Spinal Cord Injured Adolescents." *Sexuality and Disability* 23, no. 1 (2005): 1–20.

Reel, Justine J. "Tailoring Eating Disorder Treatment for Diverse Clients: How to Avoid a 'Cookie Cutter' Approach." In *The Hidden Faces of Eating Disorders and Body Image,* edited by Justine J. Reel and Katherine A. Beals, 193–207. Reston, VA: AAHPERD, 2009.

Reel, Justine J., Robert A. Bucciere. "Ableism and Body Image: Conceptualizing How Individuals with Disabilities are Marginalized." *Women in Sport & Physical Activity Journal: Moving toward Justice* 19, no. 1 (2010): 91–97.

Shapiro, Deborah R., and Jeffery J. Martin. "Athletic Identity, Affect, and Peer Relations in Youth Athletes with Physical Disabilities." *Disability and Health Journal* 3, no. 2 (2010): 79–85.

Stunkard, Albert J., Thorkild I. A. Sorenson, and F. Schulsinger. "Use of Danish Adoption Register for the Study of Obesity and Thinness." In *The Genetics of Neurological and Psychiatric Disorders,* edited by S. Kety, 115–120. New York: Raven, 1983.

Taub, Diane E., P. L. Fanflik, and Penelope A. McLorg. "Body Image among Women with Physical Disabilities: Internalization of Norms and Reactions to Nonconformity." *Sociological Focus* 36 (2003): 159–76.

INTERNATIONAL ASSOCIATION OF EATING DISORDER PROFESSIONALS

The International Association of Eating Disorder Professionals (IAEDP) is an organization that was formed in 1985 with the goal of providing quality training for eating disorder treatment providers from across the globe. Multidisciplinary professionals include physicians, psychiatrists, nurses, dietitians, psychologists, social workers, and other licensed health care providers who work with eating disorder clients in a variety of treatment settings. IAEDP has organized state and regional chapters to expand training opportunities at the local level in Arizona, California, Florida, New York, Utah, and Washington.

IAEDP offers the only recognized eating disorder treatment certification to professionals in the field with the goal of promoting high standards of care and continuing training and education. Professionals who treat eating disorders must meet requirements by taking educational classes and an examination. Mental health professionals (e.g., Licensed Professional Counselors [LPC], Psychologists, Licensed Clinical Social Workers [LCSW]) apply for certification to become a Certified Eating Disorder Specialist (CEDS) while registered dietitians are eligible to become a Certified Eating Disorders Registered Dietitian (CEDRD) if they meet the necessary requirements.

Conclusion

IAEDP offers a forum for professionals to receive advanced training related to the treatment of eating disorders. In addition to a national conference, state and regional chapters conduct training workshops and events. Certification is offered for mental health professionals and registered dietitians who specialize in eating disorder treatment.

JUSTINE J. REEL

Bibliography

"International Association of Eating Disorder Professionals." IAEDP. Accessed October 3, 2011. www.iaedp.com

INTUITIVE EATING

Intuitive eating refers to making decisions about eating based on biological cues of hunger and fullness rather than eating for emotional reasons. This popular approach has been defined as a nondiet, hunger-based approach to food and weight management. The overall goal of intuitive eating is to help individuals develop a healthy relationship with weight, self, and food and to reduce dysfunctional obsessive thought patterns related to food.

The basic premise of intuitive eating is that individuals are born with an innate ability to decipher the amount and kinds of food that are ideal for their development. Most children are naturally intuitive eaters and do not eat past the point of fullness even when their favorite foods are offered. However, many adults have become emotional eaters, and rarely respond exclusively to biologically based hunger cues. Learning intuitive eating allows an individual the ability to become reacquainted with the cues of hunger and satiety and encourages a response to these signals. Intuitive eating is part of the larger anti-diet movement with similar programs including normal eating, wisdom eating, conscious eating, and mindful eating. Intuitive eating is also a component of the *Health at Every Size* movement.

History of Intuitive Eating

The term "intuitive eating" was first coined by Evelyn Tribole and Elyse Resch in their book *Intuitive Eating,* first published in 1995. Tribole and Resch, registered dietitians working in California, began to recognize the ineffectiveness of traditional dieting and weight management approaches with their clients. Their clients would follow their elaborate meal plans to lose weight, only to regain the weight after leaving the program. The failure would cause the clients to blame themselves and feel tremendous amounts of guilt. Tribole and Resch concluded that traditional diet meal plans were ineffective and began looking to the existing anti-dieting movement for solutions. They felt the anti-dieting approach did not effectively address issues of basic nutrition and created intuitive eating in order to bridge that gap (www.intuitiveeating.org). Since the book's inception, the intuitive eating approach has been a popular method for teaching healthy nutritional habits to individuals with eating disorders, disordered eating, chronic dieting, or obesity. By honoring hunger and relinquishing the power of foods, many individuals find they are able to maintain a healthy weight rather than a continual yo-yo weight fluctuation. Although eating disordered individuals may take several months or more to use intuitive eating, they can begin by learning about the philosophy and 10 principles of intuitive eating.

Ten Principles of Intuitive Eating

Tribole and Resch outlined 10 principles of intuitive eating to describe the overriding philosophy of intuitive eating:

1. **Reject the diet mentality.** In order to become an intuitive eater, you must first reject the idea that diets work. Many people spend endless amounts of time and money on diets that promise to make them effortlessly thin. The commercial diet industry has a

failure rate of 95 percent; however, for most dieters, when they fail they blame them-selves and not the process of dieting. In order to fully embrace intuitive eating, you must get rid of the diet books and magazine articles that promote dieting.

2. **Honor your hunger.** Deprivation leads to overeating as the body tries to physically compensate for the lost nutrition. Many people have learned to silence hunger cues and often go long periods of time without eating, which is then followed by uncon-trolled overcompensation. Honoring your hunger involves learning to identify your body's unique hunger cues. When you feel slight hunger, you respond by eating. Intuitive eaters are encouraged to eat whenever they feel hungry, even if it is at non-meal times, as the body's hunger signals a physical need for nourishment.

3. **Make peace with food.** The dieting mentality promotes the idea that food is to be the enemy. In this step, work is done to undo that damage and begin relating to food in a healthy way. Part of making peace with food includes giving oneself uncondi-tional permission to eat. Dieting and deprivation lead to binging and guilt. By al-lowing yourself permission to eat, you end the feelings of deprivation and guilt that cause overeating.

4. **Challenge the food police.** Chronic dieters have trained themselves for years to de-cipher between good and bad foods. Often these dieters are able to recite calories, fat grams, points, or other numerical values when discussing food. Every food becomes good or bad in their minds, with the good foods being low-calorie, healthy options and the bad foods including anything calorie-laden or sweet. This leads people to have an internal voice which dictates whether they are good or bad based on the food choices they have made that day. Intuitive eaters challenge these voices, real-izing that these voices are sabotaging a healthy relationship with food and weight.

5. **Respect your fullness.** Even though eating beyond fullness is uncomfortable, it is a common behavior. In this step, you are encouraged to pay attention to your fullness signals and stop when you are satisfied, rather than stuffed. This is most effectively done when you are able to slow down and enjoy your food. Intuitive eaters are en-couraged to put their fork down throughout a meal and evaluate their fullness before continuing. They then stop when they feel satisfied, but give themselves permission to eat more if they become hungry again later.

6. **Discover the satisfaction factor.** In many cultures the eating process is slow and social. Interestingly, these cultures often have lower rates of obesity. There is wisdom in the advice to slow down and savor your food. If you eat slowly, in a comfortable environment, you are more likely to taste each bite of food and feel more satisfied after the meal.

7. **Honor your feelings without using food.** In this step, you are encouraged to iden-tify the emotional triggers that cause you to turn to food for support. It is important to understand that food will not fix these problems. Once you identify the emotional triggers, you can work to find different distracters and alternative ways of coping that do not involve food.

8. **Respect your body.** Understanding and appreciating body diversity, including your own, is critical in self-acceptance. Showing respect for your body includes doing nice things for yourself and not delaying enjoyable experiences such as swimming or va-cations because you are ashamed of how you look.

9. **Exercise—feel the difference.** Most dieters are either militant slaves of exercise, or have completely given up on exercise. This step encourages you to find a physical ac-tivity that you enjoy, such as walking, mountain biking, rollerblading, or rock climb-ing. The point of the activity is to make your body healthier and feel good about

yourself. Forget about calculating calories burned or trying to lose weight, just get active to feel better.

10. **Honor your health—gentle nutrition.** In this last step, the issue of nutrition is finally addressed. The key is to make food choices that honor your health, but are also appetizing to you. You want to eat what you love, but be mindful of health where you can. It is important to address your own feelings of deprivation. If you skip out on the chocolate chip cookies, will you feel deprived? If so, eat one when you are hungry. If not, choose something with more nutritional value.

Assessment of Intuitive Eating

In order to assess intuitive eating, the Hawks Intuitive Eating Scale (IES), a 30-item questionnaire, assesses one's relationship with exercise and eating using responses ranging from strongly agree to strongly disagree. For example, for relationship with food, one IES item states, "I seldom eat unless I notice I'm physically hungry." To address having a healthy relationship with exercise, another IES item is "One of my main reasons for exercising is to control my weight." This questionnaire has been used successfully with college students and is valid and reliable.

In 2006 another intuitive eating researcher, Dr. Tylka, developed a 21-item scale to measure the following components of intuitive eating: unconditional permission to eat, eating for physical reasons rather than emotional ones, and reliance on hunger and satiety cues. Sample items of this intuitive eating questionnaire include, "If I am craving a particular food, I let myself have it" and "I stop myself when I feel full (not overstuffed)." Item responses range from strongly agree to strongly disagree and the scale has been used with college students and women in their midlife successfully.

Overall, intuitive eating has been shown to be a promising approach to disordered eating prevention, as it can transition participants away from a dieting mentality. High levels of intuitive eating are correlated with lower body mass index, lower triglyceride levels, high levels of high-density lipoproteins, and improved cardiovascular risk. In addition, intuitive eaters have increased enjoyment and pleasure with food and fewer dieting behaviors and food anxieties.

Men have higher total intuitive eating levels, meaning they have more traits of an intuitive eater, when compared with women. Coercive feeding strategies from caregivers, association with individuals who are food/weight obsessed, and maladaptive personality characteristics negatively influence intuitive eating. Among obese women, intuitive eating was positively associated with self-esteem and negatively associated with uncontrolled emotional eating. Those higher in intuitive eating are less likely to report binge eating, and there is a marginal association between intuitive eating and reduced depression, anxiety, and stress.

Intuitive Eating and Health at Every Size Approach

Researcher Linda Bacon conducted a six-month randomized clinical trial with a two-year follow-up in which she had white, obese, female chronic dieters in either a "Health at Every Size (HAES)" intervention or a diet intervention. The HAES program included intuitive eating as a dietary approach. Dr. Bacon found more people dropped out of the diet group compared with the HAES group. The HAES group members maintained weight, improved on physical and psychological variables and sustained these improvements. The diet group participants lost weight and showed improvement in many variables at the one year mark, but the weight was regained and the variable improvement was not sustained after two years. From this study, she concluded that the HAES approach, including intuitive eating, enabled the participants to make long-term behavior change and resulted in improved health risks for obese women.

In the 2003 edition of the book *Intuitive Eating*, Tribole and Resch added a chapter entitled, "Intuitive Eating: The Ultimate Path toward Healing from Eating Disorders." In this chapter, they discuss the practical use of intuitive eating as a nutritional recovery plan for individuals suffering from various eating disorders. However, intuitive eating cannot be embraced in the beginning of a serious eating disorder recovery. It is important that biological restoration and balance be achieved before the client learns about intuitive eating. Since most eating disorders begin with a diet, the intuitive eating approach is ideal for eating disorder recovery as it encourages a healthy relationship with food and does not dictate specific amounts of foods that must be eaten. Many eating disorder facilities around the country exclusively use intuitive eating as their dietary approach with their clients.

Conclusion

Intuitive eating is a nutritional treatment approach that rejects the dieting mentality and promotes listening to biological cues for hunger and fullness. Because many individuals with eating disorders have been emotional eaters who have disregarded hunger and fullness signs for a long time, the first step is developing awareness about body signals. Once an individual learns an intuitive eating approach he or she can gauge hunger and fullness on a scale, with the intention of never becoming overly hungry or full. Intuitive eating has also been used in conjunction with the Health at Every Size approach for health promotion.

TeriSue Smith-Jackson

See also: Health at Every Size.

Bibliography

Augustus-Horvath, Casey L., and Tracy L. Tylka. "The Acceptance Model of Intuitive Eating: A Comparison of Women in Emerging Adulthood, Middle Adulthood, and Late Adulthood." *Journal of Counseling Psychology* 58, no. 1 (2011): 110–25.

Bacon, Linda. "Size Acceptance and Intuitive Eating Improve Health in Obese Female Chronic Dieters." *Journal of the American Dietetic Association* 105 (2005): 929–36.

Cole, Renee E., and Tanya Horacek. "Effectiveness of the 'My Body Knows When' Intuitive-eating Pilot Program." *American Journal of Health Behavior* (2010): 286–97.

Hawks, Steven R., Ray M. Merrill, and Hala N. Madanat. "The Intuitive Eating Validation Scale: Preliminary Validation." *American Journal of Health Education* 35 (2004): 26–35.

Hawks, Steven R., Hala Madanat, Jaylyn Hawks, and Ashley Harris. "Relationship between Intuitive Eating and Health Indicators among College Women." *American Journal of Health Education* 36, no. 6 (2005): 331–36.

Kroon Van Diest, Ashley, and Tracy Tylka. "Gender Differences in Intuitive Eating and Factors that Negatively Influence Intuitive Eating." Senior Honors Thesis, Ohio State University, 2008.

Smith, TeriSue, and Steven R. Hawks. "Intuitive Eating, Diet Composition, and the Meaning of Food in Healthy Weight Promotion." *American Journal of Health Education* 37, no. 3 (2006): 130–36.

Tribole, Evelyn, and Elyse Resch. *Intuitive Eating: A Revolutionary Program That Works.* New York: St. Martin's Griffin, 2003.

Tylka, Tracy L. "Development and Psychometric Evaluation of a Measure of Intuitive Eating." *Journal of Counseling Psychology* 53, no. 2 (2006): 226–40.

J

JOCKEYS

The word "jockey" refers to an athlete who competes in horseracing, which dates back to the ancient Greek Olympics around 648 BC. The first American race track was constructed in Long Island in 1665. This paved the way for organized horseracing which accelerated in the late 1800s, due to increased gambling interest. The sport has been associated with high injury rates and unhealthy weight control methods. Weight restrictions, rationalized by safety concerns for the horse, have been in place for professional horseracing since its inception. However, since 1979, the average weight of jockeys has increased by 37 percent. Therefore, jockeys have needed to engage in numerous weight reduction strategies and disordered eating. In 2005, Emanuel Jose Sanchez, a 22-year-old jockey, died from a suspected eating disorder.

Eating Disorders and Jockeys

Depending on the event or the type of horseracing, weight requirements may range from 110 pounds to 140 pounds. Weighing in occurs before and after the race and requires athletes to "make weight" in their clothing, shoes, helmet, and horse tack (i.e., saddle, saddle pad and crop). Generally this results in at least 3 additional pounds before meeting an already restrictive weight. In order to meet the weight requirements, many jockeys engage in similar weight loss methods as wrestlers. Jockeys may engage in fasting, deliberate dehydration, and "flipping" or "heaving," which refers to self-induced vomiting that often happens into "heave bowls." The most frequently reported weight loss method among jockeys at Delaware Park was the "Hot Box." Many jockeys admitted to sweating off pounds in rubber suits, steam rooms, and saunas. Every racecourse in the United Kingdom provides a sauna facility which is used heavily among jockeys to make riding weight.

In a separate study, 75 percent of jockeys regardless of gender reported skipping meals as a weight management strategy, and at least a third of them missed a meal per day. Over half of jockeys (60%) needed to lose weight in preparation for race day. Twenty interviews with jockeys revealed that 50 percent of jockeys consumed nothing but coffee or an energy drink (e.g., RedBull, Monster) before they rode in the morning. This is a noteworthy finding because jockeys exercise horses for long hours each day, representing strenuous physical activity and energy expenditure. Additionally, jockeys have identified smoking as an appetite suppressant, and reported using diet pills, diuretics, and laxatives to lose weight. Jockeys who engaged in wasting behaviors to meet a minimum weight tended to display more eating disorder symptoms, and 20 percent were considered to have eating disorders in one study. However, it is important to consider that like wrestlers, these unhealthy weight-related behaviors are normative for the jockey culture. Therefore, jockeys view flipping and hot boxes as part of the sport as described in the ESPN article: http://sports.espn.go.com/espn/wire?section=horse&id=3367868.

Equestrian Athletes

Horse-riding competitions are traditionally focused on show, beauty, and ceremony. Equestrian competitions, especially for Western riding, may emphasize the physical appearance of the rider. Specifically, equestrian athletes must control their horse while appearing aesthetically pleasing, similar to a gymnast or figure skater. Generally equestrian athletes with a lean physique are rewarded in the judging since scores are directly related to athletes' appearance. In a study of 138 college female equestrian athletes, 42 percent had eating disorders while 25 percent engaged in binge eating, 12 percent vomited to control weight or shape, and 15 percent abused laxatives, diet pills or diuretics.

Conclusion

Jockeys represent male and female athletes who are especially at risk for disordered eating and eating disorders. Because the weight expectation (e.g., 120 pounds) is extremely low for males, most jockeys must resort to pathological weight control methods such as self-induced vomiting, diet pills, and sweating in a sauna, steam room or rubber suit. To date, the health of the horse has been considered sometimes at the expense of the rider. Equestrian athletes may also experience pressure to change their weight, size, or appearance due to the focus on riders' appearance as part of the judging process in equestrian competitions.

JUSTINE J. REEL

See also: Weight Pressures in Sport.

Bibliography

Caulfield, Michael J., and Costas I. Karageorghis. "Psychological Effects of Rapid Weight Loss and Attitudes towards Eating among Professional Jockeys." *Journal of Sports Sciences* 26, no. 9 (2008): 877–83. doi: 10.1080/02640410701837349.

Cotugna, Nancy, O. Sue Snider, and Jennifer Windish. "Nutrition Assessment of Horse-Racing Athletes." *Journal of Community Health* 36 (2011): 261–64. doi: 10.1007/s10900-010-9306-x.

Graves, Will, and Jeff McMurray. "Jockeys Still Battle Weight Issues But Progress Being Made." *ESPN*. Last modified on April 26, 2008. http://sports.espn.go.com/espn/wire?section=horse&id=3367868.

Hughes, Mark. "Jockeys Run Risk of Eating Disorders in Bid to Stay Slim." *The Indepen-dent.* Last modified on March 11, 2008. http://www.independent.co.uk/sport/racing/jockeys-run-risk-of-eating-disorders-in-bid-to-stay-slim-793964.html.

Labadarios, Demetre, Juan Kotze, D. Momberg, and Theunis J. Kotze. "Jockeys and Their Practices in South Africa." *World Review of Nutrition and Dietetics* 71 (1993): 97–114.

Moore, Jan M., Anna F. Timperio, David A. Crawford, Cate M. Burns, and David Cameron-Smith. "Weight Management and Weight Loss Strategies of Professional Jockeys." *International Journal of Sport Nutrition and Exercise Metabolism* 12 (2002): 1–13.

Torres-McGehee, Toni M., Eva V. Monsma, Jennifer L. Gay, Dawn M. Minton, and Ashley N. Mady-Foster. "Prevalence of Eating Disorder Risk and Body Image Distortion among National Collegiate Athletic Association Division I Varsity Equestrian Athletes." *Journal of Athletic Training* 46, no. 4 (2011): 431–37.

JOURNALING

Journaling refers to self-reflection designed to elicit emotions or feelings through writing. Therapeutic writing and journaling exercises have been used as helpful interventions for a broad range of mental health conditions and have been recommended as a useful treatment strategy for eating disorders in inpatient and outpatient settings.

Uses of Journaling in Eating Disorder Treatment

Because many eating disordered individuals have difficulty identifying and expressing emotions, alternative therapies to talk therapy have been useful in getting out feelings. Journaling has been used with eating disordered clients as a way to freely express feelings without fear of judgment or negative consequences. Clients may use a traditional diary format to write down events and feelings surrounding situations encountered that can later be discussed in therapy. Journaling can also be more structured and may involve having the client self-report positive or negative behaviors. For example, a therapist may assign journaling as a way to track purging symptoms. The client and therapist can then analyze the patterns in precipitating events to purging as well as the specific times of the day when the client tends to be more susceptible to disordered eating thoughts and behaviors.

Recently some therapists have requested that clients email their journal entries between sessions, text feelings, or enter behaviors into a confidential website. By having a sense of the frequency of symptoms, triggers, or the client's response to situations, the therapist can gather information that can be used in treatment. In some cases, the clinician may be able to schedule an additional appointment to see the client sooner, if the client reports a marked increase in symptoms or reveals that he or she is struggling. Some clinicians use computer programs or apps that can tally behaviors and create bar graphs to show frequency of behaviors and change over time.

Barriers to Journaling in Eating Disorder Treatment

Although journaling can be an effective therapeutic tool for many clients, some individuals do not respond well to receiving journal-type assignments. Clients may resist keeping a journal if they dislike writing or feel that there is a risk of their written diary being read by family members. To protect privacy, clients can be encouraged to keep journal assignments on a password-protected computer rather than in a diary. Clients who have difficulty with writing may be encouraged to use a different forum for expressing themselves (e.g., drawing, pastels), or can be told to write more blog-style entries or tweets rather than use a formal writing style.

When clients are asked to self-report disordered eating behaviors, they realize there is increased accountability for one's actions. Therefore, clients who are less motivated to change or who are less ready for recovery may show resistance to documenting their symptoms. This resistance should be discussed in therapy.

Conclusion

Journaling may be an effective treatment tool for many eating disordered clients who struggle to identify and express emotions. Barriers to journaling (e.g., dislike for writing) should be recognized and addressed so that clients complete assignments in a way that is useful for the overall treatment process.

JUSTINE J. REEL

Bibliography

Wasson, Diane H., and Mary Jackson. "An Analysis of the Role of Overeaters Anonymous in Women's Recovery from Bulimia Nervosa." *Eating Disorders* 12 (2004): 337–56. doi: 10.1080/10640260490521442.

Wolf, Markus, Jan Sedway, Cynthia M. Bulik, and Hans Kordy. "Linguistic Analyses of Natural Written Language: Unobtrusive Assessment of Cognitive Style in Eating Disorders." *International Journal of Eating Disorders* 40, no. 8 (2007): 711–17. doi: 10.1002/eat.20445.

K

KETOACIDOSIS

Ketoacidosis is defined as a metabolic state marked by extreme and uncontrolled ketosis (elevated ketone levels in the body) and is found most commonly in individuals who have type 1 diabetes. According to *Medical-Surgical Nursing: Assessment and Management of Clinical Problems,* when insulin supply is insufficient, glucose cannot be used for energy. This condition causes the body to break down stored fats and proteins for energy. The liver metabolizes free fatty acids from stored triglycerides that are then released, which causes the formation of large quantities of ketones. Ketones alter the pH of the body and cause acidosis to develop. Loss of water occurs in an attempt to balance the pH, as ketones are excreted in the urine and blood glucose rises to dangerous levels.

Ketoacidosis in Eating Disordered Clients with Type 1 Diabetes

Binge eating disorder and bulimia nervosa are the most common types of eating disorders in individuals with type 1 diabetes. In an effort to control weight gain, an individual with an eating disorder may skip doses of insulin, which can lead to diabetic ketoacidosis.

Diabetic ketoacidosis can cause rapid weight loss, which is appealing to individuals with eating disorders. However, ketoacidosis is a life-threatening condition that can lead to coma and death. Some individuals with eating disorders may take just enough insulin to prevent ketoacidosis and avoid hospitalization.

Clinical Manifestation and Complications

Warning signs of ketoacidosis include deep, rapid breathing, dry skin and mouth, flushed face, nausea, vomiting, stomach pain, fatigue, frequent urination, and increased thirst. Acetone causes a fruity odor that can be smelled on the client's breath. Ketoacidosis can lead to serious diabetic complications, including eye disease, kidney failure, numbness and pain in the arms and legs, and vascular complications.

Treatment

According to an article in *Dimensions of Critical Care Nursing,* an individual who has ketoacidosis should be stabilized medically, which includes replacing fluid and electrolyte losses and initiating insulin therapy. Determining the degree of severity is done by assessing blood pH level, serum bicarbonate, and the degree of ketones present in the urine. During treatment the individual must also be monitored for hypokalemia (low serum potassium), high blood sugar, low blood sugar, overhydration, and cerebral edema. Frequent blood sugar assessment and supplemental doses of insulin may be needed to get the individual's blood sugar under control. Bicarbonate is frequently administered to those in severe ketoacidosis with a pH of less than 7.1 and bicarbonate less than 8 mEq/L. In addition, the eating disordered individual and his or her family members should receive education about nutrition and exercise, and psychotherapy is also recommended.

Ketoacidosis from Starvation

Chronic malnutrition, fasting, and starving can also induce ketoacidosis. Treatment includes correcting nutritional deficiencies and dehydration. According to an article in *Hospital Physician,* metabolic acidosis from starvation is mild and does not require treatment with bicarbonate.

Conclusion

Ketoacidosis is a medical complication that can occur when an individual who has type 1 diabetes neglects to take insulin or when an individual engages in fasting or severe restriction. Ketoacidosis results in elevated ketone levels in the body and can lead to numerous medical concerns including eye disease and kidney failure. While ketoacidosis should be avoided, treatment often includes fluid and insulin therapy.

SHELLY GUILLORY

Bibliography

Charles, Joseph C., and Raymond L. Heilman. "Metabolic Acidosis." *Hospital Physician* 41, no. 3 (2005): 37–42.

Lewis, Sharon M., Margaret Heitkemper, and Sharon Dirkson. "Patients with Diabetes Mellitus." In *Medical-Surgical Nursing: Assessment and Management of Clinical Problems, Fifth Edition,* edited by Sally Shrefer, 1393–1397. St. Louis: Mosby Inc., 2000.

Rodin, Gary, Marion P. Olmsted, Anne C. Rydall, Sherry I. Maharaj, Patricia A. Colton, Jennifer M. Jones, Lisa A. Biancucci, and Dennis Daneman. "Eating Disorder in Young Women with Type 1 Diabetes Mellitus." *Journal of Psychosomatic Research* 53 (2002): 943–49. PII: S0022-3999(02)00305-7.

Ruth-Sahd, Lisa A., Melissa Shneider, and Briggitte Haagen. "Diabulimia: What It Is and How to Recognize It in Critical Care." *Dimensions of Critical Care Nursing* 28, no. 4 (2009): 147–53. doi: 10.11097/01.CCN.0000384062.54832.89.

L

LANUGO

What Is Lanugo?

Lanugo hair refers to fine, downy soft hair that appears on the back, face and abdomen of individuals who have eating disorders as the result of inadequate protein intake. Lanugo hair is normal for infants, but for adults lanugo represents a red flag that an individual is struggling with an eating disorder and is in a severe state of malnutrition. Lanugo is usually of a pale and light color; however, it may be darker in individuals who have a darker complexion.

Lanugo and Eating Disorders

Lanugo develops in response to loss of body fat resulting from severe restriction that mimics starvation. In an effort to keep the body warm and prevent hypothermia, lanugo grows to help prevent heat loss from the body. According to the *Medical Management of Eating Disorders*, lanugo hair does not grow in individuals suffering from starvation due to causes other than the protein-calorie nutrition of anorexia nervosa. Other eating disorders, such as bulimia nervosa and binge eating disorder, do not exhibit this symptom. Lanugo, along with other clinical signs and a detailed health history, can help aid the physician in the diagnosis of anorexia nervosa. Lanugo hair begins to disappear naturally once an individual with anorexia nervosa restores weight, body fat, and starts consuming adequate calories.

Conclusion

Lanugo grows on individuals with eating disorders in response to a lack of adequate body fat. While lanugo hair is not dangerous in itself and there is no specific treatment for it, the appearance of lanugo usually signals that the individual is not consuming enough protein and calories to maintain an appropriate body weight. Once an individual begins eating disorder treatment and increases his or her food intake, lanugo begins to disappear from the body.

SHELLY GUILLORY

Bibliography

Birmingham, C. Laird, and Janet Treasure. "Complications by System." *Medical Management of Eating Disorders, 2nd ed.,* 32. New York: Cambridge University Press, 2010.

"Health Consequences of Eating Disorders." National Eating Disorders Association. Accessed August 13, 2011. http://www.nationaleatingdisorders.org/nedaDir/files/documents/handouts/HlthCons.pdf.

Nicholls, Dasha, and Russell Viner. "ABC of Adolescence: Eating Disorders and Weight Problems." *British Medical Journal* 330 (2005): 950–53.

Pritts, Sarah D., and Jeffrey Susman. "Diagnosis of Eating Disorders in Primary Care." *American Family Physician* 67, no. 2 (2003): 297–304.

Walsh, Judith M., Mary E. Wheat, and Karen Freund. "Detection, Evaluation, and Treatment of Eating Disorders." *Journal of General Internal Medicine* 15, no. 8 (2000): 577–90.

LATE LIFE AND LATE-ONSET EATING DISORDERS

It is becoming clear that women are developing and suffering from eating disorders later in life. One study examined body image and eating behaviors in women between the ages of 55 and 65 years (middle-aged) and in women who were 66 years and older (elderly); not surprisingly, it found that all women regardless of age desired a smaller ideal figure. More recently, Mangweth-Matzek and colleagues (2006) found that 56 percent of the women (60–70 years) stated that they restrict their food consumption to prevent weight gain and 86 percent of the women engaged in unhealthy weight loss methods such as fasting, vomiting, taking laxatives and diuretics, and spitting out food. Alarmingly, 18 women (3.8%) met the criteria for an eating disorder with the majority of them having Eating Disorder Not Otherwise Specified (EDNOS) based on the Structured Clinical Interview for the *Diagnostic and Statistical Manual of Mental Disorders-IV-TR* (American Psychiatric Association, 2000) and 21 women (4.4%) reported single symptoms of eating disorders. A Canadian sample of women revealed that symptoms of disordered eating were present in 1.8 percent of women aged 65 and older and 2.6 percent of women in the age group 50–64 years. A rare study with males demonstrated that 11–19 percent of elderly males had abnormal eating attitudes and negative body image. Deaths due to anorexia nervosa among the elderly were 10 percent in the 55–64 years age group, 12 percent in the 65–74 years age group and 28 percent in the 85 and older group.

Late-Onset Eating Disorders

Eating disorders among the elderly population can be separated in terms of early onset and late onset. While early-onset eating disorders represent eating disorders that begin in the younger years and may persist into late life, it is also possible for the disorder to recur after an individual has been free from eating disorder symptoms. By contrast, late-onset eating disorders, sometimes referred to as "tardive anorexia," develop for the first time after an individual reaches the age of 50 years. A contributing factor for late-onset eating disorders is having a history of trauma, which can include flashbacks to emotional connections to mealtimes earlier in life. Having a sexual abuse history was more common among women with late-onset eating disorders than the general population. Another factor associated with late-onset eating disorders is depression, which has been linked to eating disorders as a comorbid condition. Interestingly, substance abuse was less common among late-onset eating disordered clients than in their young adult counterparts.

Conclusion

Although eating disorders have been associated with adolescent and college-aged individuals, it is becoming evident that individuals are also struggling with disordered eating into their mid-life and late-life. Body image issues associated with developmental changes can trigger disordered eating thoughts and behaviors. Therefore, it is important to monitor body dissatisfaction and dieting behaviors regardless of the age of an individual.

JUSTINE J. REEL

Bibliography

American Psychiatric Association. *Diagnostic and Statistical Manual of Mental Disorders, 4th ed., text revision.* Washington, DC: American Psychiatric Association, 2000.

Brandsma, Lynn. "Eating Disorders across the Life Span." *Journal of Women & Aging* 19 (2007): 155–72. doi: 10.1300/J074v19n01_10

Cumella, Edward J., and Zina Kally. "Profile of 50 Women with Midlife-onset Eating Disorders." *Eating Disorders* 16 (2008): 193–203. doi: 10.1080/10640260802016670

Lapid, Maria I., Maria C. Prom, M. Caroline Burton, Donald E. McAlpine, Bruce Sutor, and Teresa A. Rummans. "Eating Disorders in the Elderly." *International Psychogeriatrics* 22, no. 4 (2010): 523–36.

Lewis, Diane M., and Fary M. Cachelin. "Body Image, Body Dissatisfaction, and Eating Attitudes in Midlife and Elderly Women." *Eating Disorders* 9 (2001): 29–39.

Mangweth-Matzek, Barbara, Claudia I. Rupp, Armand Hausmann, Karin Assmayr, Edith Mariacher, Georg Kemmler, Alexandra B. Whitworth, and Wilfried Biebl. "Never Too Late for Eating Disorders or Body Dissatisfaction: A Community Study of Elderly Women." *International Journal of Eating Disorders* 39 (2006): 583–86.

Midlarsky, Elizabeth, and George Nitzburg. "Eating Disorders in Middle-aged Women." *The Journal of General Psychology* 135, no. 4 (2008): 393–407.

Patrick, Julie H., and Sarah T. Stahl. "Understanding Disordered Eating at Midlife and Late Life." *The Journal of General Psychology* 136, no. 1 (2008): 5–20.

Peat, Christine M., Naomi L. Peyerl, and Jennifer J. Muehlenkamp. "Body Image and Eating Disorders in Older Adults: A Review." *The Journal of General Psychology* 135, no. 4 (2008): 343–58.

Scholtz, Samantha, Laura S. Hill, and Hubert Lacy. "Eating Disorders in Older Women: Does Late-onset Anorexia Nervosa Exist?" *International Journal of Eating Disorders* 43, no. 5 (2010): 393–97.

Zerbe, Kathryn J. "Eating Disorders in Middle and Late Life: A Neglected Problem." *Primary Psychiatry* 10 (2003): 80–82.

LAXATIVE ABUSE

Common purging methods for individuals with bulimia nervosa include self-induced vomiting and laxative abuse. Laxatives can be purchased over the counter and should only be used in the short term for the treatment of constipation; however, individuals with anorexia nervosa or bulimia nervosa may take laxatives in large quantities in order to control their weight. According to a study in *The International Journal of Eating Disorders,* inducing diarrhea is a purging method used when an individual feels desperate, and many individuals report that emptying themselves is associated with gratifying weight loss and a sense of purification. The study further states that it is questionable as to whether or not the weight lost from purging through laxatives is an effective form of weight control because most of the weight loss is from fluid loss. But individuals with eating disorders feel rewarded on seeing a lower number on the scale, and this is likely to cause them to continue using the laxatives.

Types of Laxatives

According to The Mayo Clinic, there are five different types of laxatives. The Mayo Clinic explains that oral bulk formers such as Metamucil and Citrucil increase the bulk of stool by absorbing water, which causes normal contraction of the intestinal muscles. Oral osmotics, such as Milk of Magnesia, magnesium citrate, sodium phosphate, and Miralax, pull water into the colon from the body's tissues to allow for easier passage of stool. Oral and rectal stimulant laxatives, including senna, Ex-Lax and suppositories, cause the colon to contract and stool is eliminated. Stool softeners such as Colace, and lubricants including mineral oil, help an individual strain less during the elimination of stool by providing moisture.

Medical Complications

In addition to diarrhea, laxatives taken in large quantities can cause cramping, nausea and vomiting. When an individual with an eating disorder takes more than recommended doses she can place herself at risk for life-threatening medical complications, including gastrointestinal bleeding which can cause anemia, dehydration and electrolyte imbalances. Symptoms of dehydration include tachycardia (increased heart rate), fainting, and dizziness upon standing. Long-term use of laxatives can cause tolerance, especially to stimulant laxatives. Higher doses of laxatives are needed to produce a bowel movement.

Electrolyte loss can be severe in individuals who abuse laxatives. Loss of potassium (hypokalemia) can cause cardiac arrhythmias and renal damage. Large amounts of sodium may be lost, but because of water loss, hyponatremia (low sodium) is rare. Hypocalcemia (low calcium) and hypomagnesemia (low magnesium) can also occur.

In addition to the above health consequences, individuals with eating disorders who abuse laxatives for years may develop impairment in the functioning of the colon. In these clients, X-ray examination shows changes in the lining of the colon and the colon may appear shortened. These changes in the colon are often permanent.

Treatment Considerations for Laxative Abuse

Treatment of an individual with an eating disorder should include a detailed health history. If laxative abuse is suspected after conducting an initial assessment, physical and laboratory tests will be necessary to rule out medical complications. Because withdrawal from laxatives can cause constipation and fluid retention, some individuals may feel heavier from the bloating and constipation that can result. This may make it hard for some individuals to cease using laxatives.

Individuals withdrawing from laxatives should consume a high-fiber diet and drink plenty of water. Some individuals with eating disorders restrict the amount of water they consume to minimize fluid retention, but fluid restriction can cause dehydration and increase the risk of further constipation. In some cases, doctors prescribe psyllium-containing laxatives or osmotic-type laxatives for short-term use in individuals with severe constipation at risk for a bowel obstruction.

Electrolyte imbalances should be corrected, and vitamins and minerals lost through laxative purging should also be replaced. It is important to explain to an individual undergoing treatment for laxative abuse that with continued treatment, constipation and bloating should resolve.

Conclusion

Severe laxative abuse can cause life-threatening complications and an individual without treatment can develop electrolyte imbalances that cause cardiac arrhythmias and kidney problems. Long-term laxative abuse can also cause the lining of the intestine to change, which is often irreversible. Despite knowing the dangers of continual laxative abuse, discontinuing laxatives may be frightening for an individual with an eating disorder due to the resulting edema and constipation, which may be interpreted as weight gain. It is important for treatment professionals to reassure individuals in treatment for laxative abuse that with continued treatment, bowel habits will usually return to normal and bloating and constipation will disappear.

SHELLY GUILLORY

Bibliography

Baker, E. H., and G. I. Sandle. "Complications of Laxative Abuse." *Annual Review of Medicine* 47, no.1 (1996): 127–33. doi: 10.1146/annurev.med.47.1.127.

Kovacs, Dora, and Robert L. Palmer. "The Associations between Laxative Abuse and Other Symptoms among Adults with Anorexia Nervosa." *International Journal of Eating Disorders* 36, no. 2 (2004): 224–28. doi: 10.1002/eat.20024.

Mitchell, James E., and Lana Boutacoff. "Laxative Abuse Complicating Bulimia: Medical and Treatment Complications." *International Journal of Eating Disorders* 5, no. 2 (1986): 325–34. doi: 10.1002/1098-108X(198602)5:2 325::AID-EAT2260050211 3.0.CO;2-Z.

Mitchell, James E., Dorothy Hatsukami, Richard Pyle, Elke D. Eckert, and Lana L. Boutacoff. "Metabolic Acidosis as a Marker for Laxative Abuse in Patients with Bulimia." *International Journal of Eating Disorders* 6, no. 4 (1987): 557–60. doi: 10.1002/1098-108X (198707)6:4<557::AID-EAT2260060413>3.0.CO;2-Z.

"Over-the-counter Laxatives for Constipation: Use with Caution." MayoClinic.com. Last Modified April 23, 2011. Accessed August 25, 2011. http://www.mayoclinic.com/health/laxatives/HQ00088.

Pryor, Tamara, Michael W. Wiederman, and Beth McGilley. "Laxative Abuse among Women with Eating Disorders: An Indication of Psychopathology?" *International Journal of Eating Disorders* 20, no. 1 (1996): 13–18.

Roering, James L., Kristine J. Steffan, James E. Mitchell, and Christi Zunker. "Laxative Abuse: Epidemiology, Diagnosis and Management." *Drugs* 70, no. 12 (2010): 1487–1503. doi: 10.2165/10898640-000000000-00000.

LEPTIN

What Is Leptin?

Leptin is a protein hormone found primarily in white adipose tissues. It can also be produced in the tissue of the stomach, skeletal muscle, hypothalamus, pituitary gland, bone marrow, and mammary gland. Leptin functions as part of the endocrine system and is involved in the regulation of appetite, energy expenditure, and body weight.

The hypothalamus is involved in appetite regulation by detecting leptin levels in the blood. Leptin acts as a sign to indicate satiety and regulate metabolism. As weight is gained the body releases additional leptin, which binds to receptors in the hypothalamus resulting in a suppression of appetite and an increase in metabolic rate. In theory, this would lead an individual to consume less food in an effort to return to a set weight point. When weight loss occurs, the reverse occurs as well. The body reduces the amount of leptin released into the blood, resulting in an increase in appetite and reduction in metabolism as a means to conserve energy, thus increasing body weight.

Leptin and Eating Disorders

Leptin and Anorexia Nervosa

Serum concentration levels of leptin have been found to be low in individuals with anorexia nervosa. The decreases in leptin levels appear to be an endocrine adaption to prevent further weight loss. The body decreases its release of leptin from the adipose cells in an attempt to increase appetite and decrease metabolic rate. Weight restoration appears to increase serum leptin levels; however, there is some evidence that leptin levels may reach elevated levels when recovering from a malnourished state. This may increase the difficulty with weight restoration due to an increase in the metabolic rate of an individual. Decreased serum leptin levels have been linked to exercise-induced amenorrhea as well as hypothalamic amenorrhea, suggesting that low levels of leptin may be involved in amenorrhea in anorexia nervosa. Without increasing leptin levels through weight restoration, further complications associated with amenorrhea (i.e. bone loss and impaired fertility) may occur.

Leptin and Bulimia Nervosa

Serum leptin levels have been reported to be decreased, normal, or elevated in bulimia nervosa. Low serum leptin levels have been seen in normal weight individuals with bulimia nervosa, indicating that leptin is not solely influenced by weight, but is also impacted by eating patterns. A longer duration of illness and frequency of binge/purge episodes appear to lead to decreased levels of leptin. Decreased leptin levels may result in menstrual irregularities in individuals with bulimia nervosa.

Leptin and Binge Eating Disorder

Research is limited on the effects of leptin levels in binge eating disorder. It appears that leptin levels are increased in individuals with binge eating disorder, but it remains unknown if the increased levels are related to the binge episodes, obesity and/or weight fluctuations. Chronic elevations in leptin have been associated with obesity and may lead to the development of diseases such as hypertension, metabolic syndrome, and cardiovascular disease.

Conclusion

Leptin levels are impacted across the spectrum of eating disorders. Low weight is known to contribute to decreased leptin levels; however, the mechanism behind the decreased levels in those with bulimia nervosa remains unknown. Erratic eating behaviors may also lead to alterations in leptin levels.

AMELIA MCBRIDE

Bibliography

Bluher, Susann, and Christos S. Mantzoros. "The Role of Leptin in Regulating Neuroendocrine Function in Humans." *The Journal of Nutrition* 134 (2004): 2469S–2474S.

Chan, Jean L., and Chritos S. Montzoros. "Role of Leptin in Energy-deprivation States: Normal Human Physiology and Clinical Implications for Hypothalamic Amenorrhea and Anorexia Nervosa." *Lancet* 366 (2005): 74–85.

Eckert, Elake D., Claire Pomeroy, Nancy Raymond, Peter F. Kohler, Paul Thuras, and Cyril Y. Bowers. "Leptin in Anorexia Nervosa." *Journal of Clinical Endocrinology Metabolism* 83 (1998): 791–95.

Haas, Verena, Simone Onur, Thomas Paul, Detlev O. Nutzinger, Anja Bosy-Westphal, Maren Hauer, Georg Brabant, Harald Klein, and Manfred J. Muller. "Leptin and Body Weight Regulation in Patients with Anorexia Before and During Weight Recovery." *American Journal of Clinical Nutrition* 81 (2005): 889–96.

Mitchell, James E., and Scott Crow. "Medical Complications of Anorexia Nervosa and Bulimia Nervosa." *Current Opinions of Psychiatry* 19 (2006): 438–43.

Monteleone, Pamiero, Vassilis Martiadis, Barbara Colurgio, and Mario Maj. "Leptin Secretion is Related to Chronicity and Severity of the Illness in Bulimia Nervosa." *Psychosomatic Medicine* 64 (2002): 874–79.

Monteleone, Pamiero, Antonio DiLieto, Eloisa Castaldo, and Mario Maj. "Leptin Functioning in Eating Disorders." *CNS Spectrums* 9 (2004): 523–29.

LET'S MOVE!

"Let's Move! America's Move to Raise a Healthier Generation of Kids" refers to an initiative designed to fight the childhood obesity problem in the United States. The campaign was introduced by First Lady Michelle Obama on February 9, 2010. The program has been touted as a comprehensive, collaborative, and community-based effort to address contributing factors of obesity and to promote healthy lifestyles among children and their families.

Five Pillars of the Let's Move! Initiative

Coinciding with the launch of the Let's Move! Campaign, President Barack Obama signed a Presidential Memorandum charging a new Task Force on Childhood Obesity with the project of reviewing current nutrition and physical activity programs and identifying relevant goals and objectives. As an outgrowth of their efforts, the Task Force recommended the following five pillars: (1) create a healthy start for children; (2) empower parents and caregivers; (3) provide healthy foods in schools; (4) improve access to healthy, affordable foods; and (5) increase physical activity. These pillars have been addressed by efforts to increase physical education, eliminate "food deserts" (i.e., areas in the industrialized world that have barriers to providing healthful and affordable foods), and provide healthier school lunches with the support of chefs.

Taking Action

The Let's Move! campaign has used technology (e.g., website, YouTube videos) to promote messages and to provide resources on various topics including healthy eating and movement. Additionally, "taking 5 steps to success" targets kids and parents as well as schools, community leaders, chefs, elected officials, and health care providers. Finally, the Let's Move website offers an opportunity for citizens to take a pledge for health. At the time of this publication, 312 cities across the United States had organized and posted "Let's Move" face-to-face meetings to address childhood obesity at a community level. To personalize the obesity issue, Michelle Obama created a video to address the need to make behavioral changes and launch this initiative: www.letsmove.gov/videos-and-photos.

Conclusion

The Let's Move! campaign represents a nation-wide initiative to address childhood obesity. This collaborative initiative brings a variety of professionals together to improve school lunches, provide physical education, and improve nutrition across communities. Additionally, efforts have been made to educate parents about how to access healthier and more affordable meals.

JUSTINE J. REEL

Bibliography

"Let's Move." www.letsmove.gov/. Accessed November 1, 2011.

LEVELS OF CARE

"Levels of care" refers to the levels of treatment that vary in intensity and the amount of structure provided to the individual who has an eating disorder. The five main levels of treatment include inpatient hospitalization, residential, partial hospitalization (PHP), intensive outpatient (IOP), and outpatient. A number of factors are taken into consideration when an individual is being assessed to determine the appropriate level of care such as the medical status of the client, level of motivation to recover, amount of family support for treatment, and how much weight is needed to be restored. Generally treatment facilities (e.g., Center for Change, an eating disorder treatment center in Orem, Utah) provide a complimentary in-depth clinical interview/assessment prior to admission to fully understand the client's needs.

Types of Treatment

The most intensive level of care, inpatient hospitalization, is recommended when an individual requires medical stabilization, 24-hour supervision and support, or medical refeeding and meal supervision. This setting resembles a hospital setting and the client who has often shown severe restricting prior to intake is typically placed on bed rest or prescribed minimal movement beyond stretching. Medications are monitored carefully and the client may be monitored for risk of suicide or self-harm behaviors.

Residential treatment is a step down from inpatient hospitalization and is similar to a dorm setting. Clients live at the treatment facility and actively participate in comprehensive treatment including therapeutic meals, and group and individual therapy. Some eating disorder treatment facilities also provide yoga, nia, or other exercise classes to address exercise dependence issues. Although the client in residential treatment requires structure and is provided support round-the-clock, he or she is not medically compromised or actively suicidal.

Partial hospitalization (PHP) is often a step down or a transition from the residential level of care. Clients may live in a home environment or housing associated with a treatment center that involves less structure and supervision than a residential facility. Generally PHP clients will have one to two meals while in treatment and will participate in groups and individual treatment. Clients will be responsible for monitoring their outside meals and bathroom policies for PHP level of care.

Intensive Outpatient (IOP) and outpatient levels of care represent the least restrictive levels of care. While IOP programs may include some of the group and individual approaches found in PHP, less support is provided throughout the week and on the weekends. Outpatient is the least intensive level of care and can include weekly visits to one's therapist as well as regular check-ups with a physician and dietitian who serve on a client's multidisciplinary treatment team.

Conclusion

Once an individual is diagnosed with an eating disorder it is important to assess for the appropriate level of treatment. Levels of care from most to least intensive include inpatient hospitalization, residential, partial hospitalization, intensive outpatient, and outpatient. A client who initially requires more medical stabilization may begin at a higher level of care, whereas some individuals only need an outpatient setting to focus on eating disorder treatment and recovery.

JUSTINE J. REEL

Bibliography

American Psychiatric Association. *Practice Guideline for the Treatment of Patients with Eating Disorders, Third Edition.* Arlington, VA: American Psychiatric Association, 2006.

Committee on Adolescence. "Identifying and Treating Eating Disorders." *Pediatrics* 111, no. 1 (2003): 204–211. doi: 10.1542/peds.111.1.204.

Stewart, Tiffany M., and Donald A. Williamson. "Multidisciplinary Treatment of Eating Disorders–Part 1: Structure and Costs of Treatment." *Behavior Modification* 28, no. 6 (2004): 812–30. doi: 10.1177/0145445503259855.

Turner, Hannah, Rachel Bryant-Waugh, and Robert Peveler. "A New Approach to Clustering Eating Disorder Patients: Assessing External Validity and Comparisons with DSM-IV Diagnoses." *Eating Behaviors* 11 (2010): 99–106. doi: 10.1016/j.eatbeh.2009.10.005.

Wilson, G. Terence, Kelly M. Vitousek, and Katharine L. Loeb. "Stepped Care Treatment for Eating Disorders." *Journal of Consulting and Clinical Psychology* 68, no. 4 (2000): 564-72. doi: 10.1037//0022-006X.68.4.564.

MASCULINITY IDEALS

There has been a growing focus on body image over the last several decades. The male physique, in particular, has become a means of differentiating gender and emphasizing masculinity. Western society has transformed the way gender roles and gender identity are portrayed and interpreted. Typically research in gender roles has focused on the female and the body image concerns associated with a thin ideal. Similarly, men can have body dissatisfaction concerns. This increase in dissatisfaction in both males and females is evidenced by the billions spent annually by Americans on gym memberships, exercise equipment, and cosmetic surgery.

Traditional Role Changes

The role of men in society, or the definition of manhood, is created by culture. The perfect man in the 18th century was expected to be a father, a gentleman, a model of virtue, refined, and classy. His identity was represented by strictly male occupations such as the work of frontiersmen, policemen, doctors, businessmen, or soldiers. By 2011, masculinity based on one's occupation has largely evaporated. Consequently, many men may struggle to find their identity and to understand what qualities distinguish them from women.

This gender transformation, which should be distinguished from the biological term "sex," is a change defined by culture. It has required males to seek identities that are separate from earlier norms. One identity that has been embraced by the male gender is sexually based—muscularity. Current societal expectations encourage a male to develop a lean, muscular, mesomorphic body type.

The word "muscle" originates from the French word *mus,* meaning mouse. Its original meaning implied that a woman during that period was to swoon when seeing either muscle or mouse. The symbolism of muscle and its interpretation as a highly male characteristic lingers, and the size of muscles has traditionally symbolized the difference between the sexes.

Gender Differentiation

This distinct sexual difference between the genders allows a man to portray his physique as more powerful and thereby underscore perceived feminine weaknesses. Gerzon cites five traditional archetypes that depict masculinity: frontiersman,

In earlier decades men, such as this pilot photographed in 1926, were more sure of their roles in society. (National Archives and Records Administration)

soldier, expert, breadwinner, and lord. Today, the archetypes of frontiersman and lord no longer exist whereas the breadwinner and expert are shared by both males and females. Indeed, while a soldier may also be a female, the role remains as a viable male archetype expressing an image of a strong, muscle-bound body.

Women may also possess a muscular body, which men may view as a threat to how they perceive their own masculinities. After all, masculinity is driven by a fear of being feminine or less than what a man should be, and a female intruding in a male domain threatens to abolish the physical distinction between the sexes. A muscular woman can threaten a male's perceived dominance in the areas of sexuality, sex, gender, the workplace, and social power. Thus, men are searching for a feature that distinguishes them from the opposite sex. Klein describes it best in *Muscles and Men:* "The path taken by those wishing to accrue flesh has much more to do with gender insecurities. To be male has, in our culture, been linked with dangerous and demanding occupations and roles, such as frontiersman, soldier, policeman and doctor. But the golden era when 'men were men' has passed, and the powerful roles traditionally the exclusive province of men have vanished, weakened or are no longer gender-specific. Accordingly, many bodybuilding men have clutched to themselves the only trait that gives them hegemony over women; their size."

Klein's insight is supported through the increasing muscularity of men over the last 50 years. For males, having a more muscular physique and lower body fat has been referred to as a drive for muscularity. Men's bodies are judged by the size of their muscles. A muscular physique can depict traits that include power, dominance, strength, sexual virility, and self-esteem.

Implications for Body Image

While it is generally understood that the ideal human form is a representative consensus of what is dictated by society, these ideals change over time and vary across cultures. Therefore, if a perceived self-image does not equal the ideal as defined by a culture, a distorted view of one's body may develop. With men, there is a risk of developing dangerous attitudes and behaviors (e.g., obsession about size) that are associated with one's physique. Specifically, there is an increased risk of taking unhealthy measures (e.g., extreme dieting, overtraining) to attain a muscular and lean physique. Unfortunately, an individual with an intense drive for muscularity who attempts to rapidly reduce his or her body fat and becomes pathologically body conscious may be at risk for developing muscle dysmorphia. Muscle dysmorphia is discussed in a separate entry.

Conclusion

Society is largely blamed for reinforcing masculinity ideas, gender roles, and gendered body expectations. Parents, toys, peers, and the media have all been identified as contributing to masculinity ideals. Research is underway to highlight the cultural expectations of today's man, but his physique remains the one feature that can distinguish him from being a woman. Being obsessed with the hypermasculine ideal, boys and men may become more vulnerable for developing a strong drive for muscularity or muscle dysmorphia.

TIMOTHY M. BAGHURST

See also: Body Image in Males; Dolls; Drive for Muscularity; Muscle Dysmorphia.

Bibliography

Alexander, Susan M. "Stylish Hard Bodies: Branded Masculinity in *Men's Health* Magazine." *Sociological Perspectives* 46 (2003): 535–54.

Baghurst, Timothy M., David Carlston, Julie Wood, and Frank Wyatt. "Preadolescent Male Perceptions of Action Figure Physiques." *Journal of Adolescent Health* 41 (2007): 613–15.

Gerzon, Mark. *A Choice of Heroes: The Changing Faces of American Manhood.* Boston, MA: Houghton Mifflin, 1982.

Goldberg, Jonathan. "Recalling Totalities: The Mirrored Stages of Arnold Schwarzenegger." In *Building Bodies,* edited by Pamela L. Moore, 217–49. London: Rutgers University Press, 1997.

Klein, Alan M. "Of Muscles and Men." *The Sciences* (1993): 32–37.

Peoples, James G. "The Cultural Construction of Gender and Manhood." In *Men and Masculinity,* edited by Theodore Cohen, 9–19. Stamford, CT: Thomson Learning, 2001.

Pope, Harrison G. Jr., Katharine A. Phillips, and Roberto Olivardia. *The Adonis Complex: The Secret Crisis of Male Body Obsession.* New York: The Free Press, 2000.

Wesely, Jennifer K. "Negotiating Gender: Bodybuilding and the Natural/Unnatural Continuum." *Sociology of Sport Journal* 18 (2001): 162–80.

MAUDSLEY FAMILY THERAPY

Maudsley Family Therapy (Family-Based Treatment [FBT]) is a family therapy that was introduced by Christopher Dare and his team in 1985 at the Maudsley Hospital in London. This approach was originally aimed at treating adolescents with anorexia nervosa, in the home environment with therapeutic oversight by a trained professional. The Maudsley Approach was later adapted for use in the treatment of bulimia nervosa. A study that compared individual therapy and family therapy found that family therapy was the most useful approach for patients under 18 of age and if undertaken within 3 years of the onset of their illness, as determined by a decrease in eating disorder symptoms. In this study, individual therapy was found to be more effective for clients over 18. However, the Maudsley Approach has since been adapted for use with adults and with other eating disorders, including those behaviors that lead to obesity.

Phases of Treatment

The Maudsley Approach involves three phases which together span more than a year, typically, and include 15 to 20 sessions in the home. The three phases include weight restoration, returning control of eating to the child, and helping the adolescent establish an identity separate from the eating disorder.

Phase I: Weight Restoration

In the first phase, the therapist addresses the dangers of malnutrition that are associated with anorexia nervosa. Dangers include hypothermia, growth hormone changes, cardiac dysfunction, and cognitive/emotional changes. The family's routine eating habits and interaction patterns are assessed and the therapist assists the parents in refeeding their daughter or son. Every effort is made by the treatment team to help the parents in a joint attempt to restore their adolescent's weight. At the same time, the therapist will attempt to align the client with his or her siblings to provide positive peer support. A family meal is used to assess the family's interaction patterns around eating and to educate parents about how to support the adolescent. During this phase, the therapist models for the parents an uncritical stance toward the child. The Maudsley Approach maintains the philosophy that the child is not at fault for distorted attitudes and behaviors, but rather, the symptoms are usually outside of the child's control. The therapist confronts any criticism or hostility from the parents.

Phase II: Returning Control to the Child over Eating

The adolescent's acceptance of parents' demands for increasing the intake of food, along with a steady weight gain and a change in the family's mood are all signals of Phase II. Phase II focuses on helping the parents to empower the child to assume increasing control over his or her own eating. The therapist continues to keep the family focused on weight gain with minimal tension. Other familial relationship difficulties that have been postponed can now be addressed in the counseling sessions. The child's symptoms also remain central in the discussions between the therapist and the family.

Phase III: Establishing Healthy Adolescent Identity

Phase III starts when the adolescent can independently maintain weight above 95 percent of ideal weight, and no longer engages in self-starvation. The focus shifts to the impact anorexia nervosa has had on the individual's ability to establish a healthy adolescent identity. Key issues of adolescence are addressed along with an increase in support of autonomy for the adolescent. In addition, parents are encouraged to develop healthy boundaries, and a strong couple's relationship.

Conclusion

The Maudsley Approach holds great promise for adolescents who have been struggled with an eating disorder for a relatively short period of time (i.e., less than three years). This family-based treatment can prevent hospitalization and assist the adolescent in her or his recovery, provided that parents are encouraged to play an active role in treatment and recovery. The Maudsley Approach provides a positive role for parents to play in their child's recovery. Drs. Le Grange and Lock have founded the Training Institute for Child and Adolescent Eating Disorders as a vehicle to conduct regular workshops for clinicians who wish to become certified FBT therapists (www.train2treat4ed.com). For more information on the Maudsley Approach, visit www.maudsleyparents.org.

JULIANN M. COOK

Bibliography

Alexander, June, and Daniel Le Grange. "My Kid Is Back." *Empowering Parents to Beat Anorexia Nervosa.* Melbourne: Melbourne University Press, 2009.

Eisler, Ivan, Christopher Dare, Matthew Hodges, Gerald Russell, Elizabeth Dodge, and Daniel Le Grange. "Family Therapy for Adolescent Anorexia Nervosa: The Results of a Controlled Comparison of Two Family Interventions." *Journal of Child Psychology and Psychiatry* 41 (2000): 727–36.

"Google Privacy Policy." http://www.maudsleyparents.org.

"Google Privacy Policy." http://www.train2treat4ed.com.

Lock, James, Daniel Le Grange, W. Stewart Agras, and Christopher Dare. *Treatment Manual for Anorexia Nervosa: A Family-Based Approach.* New York: Guilford Publications, Inc., 2001.

Lock, James, and Daniel Le Grange. *Help Your Teenager Beat an Eating Disorder.* New York: Guilford Press, 2005.

Russell, Gerald, George Szmukler, Christopher Dare, and Ivan Eisler. "Family Therapy versus Individual Therapy for Adolescent Females with Anorexia Nervosa and Bulimia Nervosa." *Archives of General Psychiatry* 44 (1987): 1047–1056.

MEDIA

Media consists of television, print (e.g., magazines) and now the Internet and serves as a vehicle for promoting advertisements, conveying information and news, providing entertainment, and exposing individuals to visual images. Due to the constant exposure to pictures that emphasize perfect skin, flawless appearance, and bodies sculpted to optimal fitness, the media has often been blamed for being a primary cause of body image disturbances and eating disorders. Although cultural ideals have changed over time, what has remained constant is the tendency to promote a particular *type* or *look* that represents beauty and serves as a marker for others (especially women) to try to emulate. Women in the 1950s favored a curvaceous, feminine body ideal represented by the likes of Marilyn Monroe. By contrast, women in the 1960s were inundated by ultrathin models such as Twiggy who were on display exposing gaunt body frames with sharp lines. The media goes a step further by showing solutions to beauty problems and flaws by educating society about products that can change body and appearance imperfections.

Body Dissatisfaction and the Media

Margaret Carlisle Duncan, a sociologist who studies sport, has used the metaphor that the media serves as a prison guard tower that provides a constant gaze over societal members and monitors bodily flaws. Individuals in society internalize their appearance imperfections thus reinforcing body dissatisfaction and the tendency to engage in dieting and other behaviors geared toward changing one's appearance closer to the unattainable ideal. Many studies have supported the contention that the media contributes to negative body image. For example, studies have found that females who read a fashion magazine or watched a commercial were more likely to report feelings of body dissatisfaction, decreased self-esteem, and negative mood following the media exposure. In a separate study, researchers confirmed that trying to look like same-sex persons in the media was a stronger risk factor for females than males. However, for both males and females, the media promotes highly unrealistic and unattainable images that represent either highly masculine or feminine qualities. The models in advertisements possess unusual genetic attributes, such as being above average height, being well-proportioned, and having a naturally thin waist; these attributes are accentuated in the media images. It is unlikely that these genetically gifted models need or could benefit from the products (e.g., cellulite cream, anti-wrinkle eye cream, fat burning supplements) they are promoting. However, it is not uncommon for even these genetic masterpieces to be airbrushed or digitally altered in the photographs. For example, as seen in this video clip, waist sizes may be decreased, moles may be removed, and skin blemishes may be eliminated: https://www.youtube.com/watch?v=YP31r70_QNM&feature=player_embedded.

Television and Body Image

Considering that in Western societies television is viewed daily for 7 hours on average, with an average exposure of 35,000 television commercials per year, it is noteworthy that television commercials that promote women as young, thin and attractive have been shown to have a stronger effect on negative body image than static images in fashion magazines. Alarmingly, similar negative impacts on body image have been observed among females in Fiji with the introduction of the Western media. Television advertisements display stimuli associated with eating and certain foods including trigger foods or binge foods (e.g., desserts); it also includes dieting messages that are found in many ads (e.g., Yoplait yogurt): http://youtu.be/3wzkKs0TOTs. Last year, there was a commercial for Sketcher shoes promoting shape-up and tone-up properties that was targeted toward 7- and 8-year-old females: http://today.msnbc.msn.com/id/26184891/vp/43045515#43045515. In addition to commercials, television actresses and actors in weekly shows are most likely to fit the socially constructed body ideal and are less likely to be older, overweight, or unattractive.

Internet and Body Image

Although magazines and television have been powerful forces influencing body image, the Internet provides a new wave of exposure to messages and images. Ads serve as banners for websites and flash in the margins of social networking sites (e.g., Facebook). In addition, a number of Pro-Ana websites have popped up that encourage, promote and reinforce dieting and pathological weight control methods and overtly champion eating disorders. Photos are posted that promote ultrathin images (e.g., protruding collar bones and rib cages) to encourage thinness and discipline. "Thinspirations" including poems and messages about staying on course with one's eating disorders are often used to motivate visitors to engage in disordered eating; there are also forums that allow individuals to post their struggles associated with restricting and maintaining discipline for anorexia nervosa.

Conclusion

In considering the causes of eating disorders and negative body image, the media is often mentioned as a culprit. Media can serve to expose children and adults to messages about beauty and attractiveness as well as advertisements promoting antiaging and dieting products. Furthermore, the Internet provides constant exposure to additional ads and messages beyond television and print media. Although the cultural body ideal has changed over time, it is unlikely that the presence of the media will evaporate. Therefore, it is important that eating disorder prevention programs contain media literacy lessons that teach individuals to cope with triggering images and messages.

JUSTINE J. REEL

See also: Pro-Ana.

Bibliography

Becker, Anne E., Kristen E. Fay, Jessica Agnew-Blais, A. Nisha Khan, Ruth H. Striegel-Moore, and Stephen E. Gilman. "Social Network Media Exposure and Adolescent Eating Pathology in Fiji." *British Journal of Psychiatry* 198, no. 1 (2011): 43–50. doi: 10.1192/bjp.198.1.50.

Carper, Teresa L. Marino, Charles Negy, and Stacey Tantleff-Dunn. "Relations among Media Influence, Body Image, Eating Concerns, and Sexual Orientation in Men: A Preliminary Investigation." *Body Image* 7 (2010): 301–309. doi: 10.1016/j.bodyim.2010.07.002.

"Do 7-Year-Olds Really Need 'Shape-Ups?'" Today.msnbc.msn.com. Accessed November 22, 2011. http://today.msnbc.msn.com/id/26184891/vp/43045515#43045515.

Field, Alison E., Kristin M. Javaras, Parul Aneja, Nicole Kitos, Carlos A. Camargo, C. Barr Taylor, and Nan M. Laird. "Family, Peer and Media Predictors of Becoming Eating Disordered." *Archives of Pediatric Medicine* 162, no. 6 (2008): 574–79.

Legenbauer, Tanja, Ilka Ruhl, and Silja Vocks. "Influence of Appearance-Related TV Commercials on Body Image State." *Behavior Modification* 32 (2008): 352–71. doi: 10.1177/0145445507309027.

Mazzeo, Suzanne E., Sara E. Trace, Karen S. Mitchell, and Rachel Walker Gow. "Effects of a Reality TV Cosmetic Surgery Makeover Program on Eating Disordered Attitudes and Behaviors." *Eating Behaviors* 8 (2007): 390–97. doi: 10.1016/j.eatbeh.2006.11.016.

Mousa, Tamara Y., Rima H. Mashal, Hayder A. Al-Domi, and Musa A. Jibril. "Body Dissatisfaction among Adolescent Schoolgirls in Jordan." *Body Image* 7 (2010): 46–50. doi: 10.1016/j.bodyim.2009.10.002.

Spettigue, Wendy, and Katherine A. Henderson. "Eating Disorders and the Role of the Media." *The Canadian Child and Adolescent Psychiatry Review* 13, no. 1 (2004): 16–19.

"The Photoshop Effect." YouTube.com. Accessed November 22, 2011. https://www.youtube.com/watch?v=YP31r70_QNM&feature=player_embedded.

Van den Berg, Patricia, Susan J. Paxton, Helene Keery, Melanie Wall, Jia Guo, and Dianne Neumark-Sztainer. "Body Dissatisfaction and Body Comparison with Media Images in Males and Females." *Body Image* 4 (2007): 257–68. doi: 10.1016/j.bodyim.2007.04.003.

"Yoplait Commercial." YouTube.com. Last modified July 3, 2010. http://youtube/3wzkKs0TOTs.

MEDICAL AND HEALTH CONSEQUENCES

Eating disorders can lead to a wide array of medical complications affecting many systems within the body. These complications result from the stress exerted on the body due to the effects of malnutrition brought about by nutrient deficiencies and starvation; they could also be the result of binge episodes and purging behaviors. It is crucial that all bodily systems (e.g., cardiovascular system) are reviewed as part of the treatment of eating disorders to ensure that any complications are addressed.

Cardiovascular Complications

Cardiovascular complications resulting from eating disorders can be seen in either the short term or the long term duration of the illness. These complications generally result from electrolyte imbalances, dehydration associated with persistent purging, or a weakened heart due to muscular adaptations associated with malnutrition. The cardiac muscle adapts both structurally and functionally in efforts to preserve the body. Weight restoration and/or the elimination of compensatory (purging) behaviors allows for the reversal of these complications. However, extensive damage to the heart may lead to irreversible or life-threatening complications such as heart failure. Common cardiovascular complications include electrocardiogram (EKG) abnormalities, bradycardia, mitral valve prolapse, hypotension, and congestive heart failure.

Electrocardiogram Abnormalities

Electrocardiogram abnormalities are commonly seen in both anorexia nervosa and bulimia nervosa. Anorexia nervosa and bulimia nervosa may result in prolonged QT intervals—the time it takes for the heart to contract, and subsequently refill with blood in preparation for the next contraction—due to low levels of serum electrolytes (sodium, potassium, calcium, and bicarbonate), phosphorus and/or magnesium deficiencies, dehydration, and low body weight. Low serum potassium is commonly a cause of prolonged QT intervals in individuals with bulimia nervosa. The QT interval is generally normalized with the correction of the cause.

Mitral Valve Prolapse

The mitral valve is involved in the blood flow in the cardiac muscle. In normal physiology the mitral valve opens to allow blood to flow from the left atrium into the left ventricle. Anorexia nervosa may result in a change in the size of the cardiac muscle, without changing the size of the supporting tissue. Consequently, the mitral valve bulges slightly upward into the left atrium, rather than closing smoothly. Mitral valve prolapse is characterized by a clicking sound after the contraction of the ventricle. Individuals with a mitral valve prolapse may experience chest palpitations or pain, dizziness, fainting, and fatigue. Mitral valve prolapse is generally not life-threatening. Weight restoration will typically allow the heart to repair itself, thereby resolving mitral valve prolapse.

Bradycardia

Bradycardia (slowed heart rate) is defined as a resting heart rate of less than 60 beats per minute. This condition is generally seen in individuals with anorexia nervosa and is a physiological adaptation associated with a hypometabolic state. Heart rates as low as 30 beats per minute may be seen in this population. Generally, there are no additional symptoms directly associated with bradycardia; however, it is often seen in conjunction with hypotension. As malnutrition is resolved and weight is restored bradycardia improves.

Hypotension

Hypotension is characterized by decreased blood pressure resulting from a decrease in cardiac output, arterial tone, and effective arterial blood volume. It is defined by a systolic blood pressure of less than 90 mm Hg and diastolic blood pressure of less than 50 mm Hg. Orthostatic hypotension results when blood pressure decreases by values greater than 20/10 mm Hg when going from a supine to upright position. This is detected by measuring blood pressure in different positions (supine, sitting, and standing). Common symptoms associated with orthostatic hypotension include dizziness or fainting when changing positions (laying/sitting to standing). Malnutrition, dehydration (associated with inadequate fluid intake or excessive loss of fluids through vomiting and/or diarrhea), and cardiac problems are the most common causes of hypotension in eating disorders.

Congestive Heart Failure

Congestive heart failure results when the body is unable to effectively pump blood into the body. It occurs as a result of fluid overload on a weakened heart or in the final stages of starvation. It is primarily a concern during the refeeding process due to rapid increase in intake either orally or enterally. Congestive heart failure has also been associated with severe hypokalemia or B-vitamin deficiencies. Symptoms of congestive heart failure should be monitored in the early stages of refeeding.

Anorexia nervosa may result in various cardiac complications which can generally be reversed with weight restoration and nutrition rehabilitation. Cardiac complications of normal-weight individuals with bulimia nervosa are typically limited to electrolyte imbalances associated with frequent purging.

Gastrointestinal Complications

Gastrointestinal complaints are common in both anorexia nervosa and bulimia nervosa. These complications can occur at any point along the gastrointestinal tract. Many of the complications are linked to compensatory behaviors such as self-induced vomiting, laxative abuse, and diuretic abuse. Prolonged use of compensatory behaviors may result in irreversible damage to the gastrointestinal tract.

Anorexia nervosa may lead to complications such as constipation, bloating, gastroparesis (increased gastric emptying time), and abnormal liver function tests. A decrease in food intake results in physiological adaptations of the gastrointestinal tract. Consequently, as increased amounts of food are reintroduced into the body, it leads to gastrointestinal discomfort including constipation, bloating, and gastroparesis. While these symptoms may impact an individuals' ability to tolerate foods, symptoms generally improve as food intake normalizes and the gastrointestinal tract readapts to the presence of food in the system.

Abnormal liver function tests may be seen as a result of weight loss and in the early stages of weight restoration. Frequent abnormalities include elevated levels of aspartate aminotransferase (AST), alanine aminotransferase (ALT), alkaline phosphatase, and total bilirubin. Levels generally normalize as increases in caloric intake stabilize and body weight improves.

Bulimia nervosa has greater impact on the gastrointestinal tract than anorexia nervosa. Complications include disruptions in the esophagus, stomach, small and large bowel, and rectum. Damages can be reversed if addressed, but long term abuse of purging behaviors may result in irreversible consequences.

Chronic vomiting leads to repetitive exposure of the esophagus to the acid components of gastric content. The esophageal sphincter valve is weakened, leading to increases in heartburn and gastrointestinal reflux symptoms. Alterations along the esophagus may result in cellular changes leading to Barrett's esophagus. Mallory-Weiss tears may be seen in the esophagus due to the trauma of vomiting. These tears may lead to internal bleeding. Although rare, esophageal ruptures could occur in bulimia nervosa.

The chronic use of laxatives impairs the function of the colon. Laxatives disrupt the normal peristaltic function of the colon, decreasing mobility. Symptoms of constipation may increase as the body adapts to long-term use of laxatives. Normal bowel function can return if laxative intake is stopped, although it takes time for the body to readapt.

Gastrointestinal complaints are common in both anorexia nervosa and bulimia nervosa. Constipation, bloating, gastroparesis, and abnormal liver function tests are often seen in anorexia nervosa. These are a result of the reintroduction of foods into the gastrointestinal tract and will improve with continual intake. Bulimia nervosa may alter the lining of the esophagus and function of the colon depending on the method of purging.

Renal Complications

Kidneys are involved in the elimination of waste and urine from the body. Chronic dehydration and compensatory behaviors may lead to kidney and electrolyte imbalances. Electrolytes are involved in cell communication and muscle contraction, and alterations in serum electrolyte disrupt these processes. The electrolytes include sodium, potassium, chloride, and bicarbonate.

Vomiting causes the body to lose hydrochloric acid from the stomach leading to metabolic acidosis (elevated serum bicarbonate levels). Hypokalemia (low serum potassium levels) and hypochloremia (low chloride levels) are related to the frequency of purging behaviors. Metabolic alkalosis (low serum bicarbonate levels) results from the loss of alkaline fluids from the bowel due to laxative abuse. Hyponatremia (low serum sodium levels) may occur as a result of consuming large amounts of fluids. Hypernatremia (elevated serum sodium levels) is a result of inadequate fluid intake or excessive fluid loss via diarrhea and/or vomiting. Mixed compensatory behaviors may lead to multiple electrolyte imbalances. Electrolyte imbalances are seen less frequently in restricting behavior and are primarily associated with dehydration.

Endocrine Complications

The endocrine system is comprised of glands which produce and secrete hormones. These hormones are involved in metabolism, growth and development, and in sexual development and function. Endocrine abnormalities in eating disorders primarily result from states of prolonged starvation.

Thyroid
The thyroid hormone is primarily responsible for regulation of metabolic processes and thermoregulation of body temperature. It is also involved in the cardiovascular system, central nervous system, and the reproductive system. The body adapts to starvation by lowering thyroid hormone production leading to decreased

metabolic rate, increased cold intolerance, slowed heart rate, constipation, and fatigue. Weight restoration generally allows these symptoms to resolve.

Growth

Growth retardation has been associated with anorexia nervosa in children and adolescents. Inadequate energy intake leads to a reduction in the production of thyroxine and triiodothyronine, and sex hormones. Additionally, an elevation in cortisol levels and changes in growth hormones are commonly reported. These hormones are involved in growth, and alterations may impact linear growth during this critical time of growth and development. Anorexia nervosa in children and adolescents may prevent them from reaching their full height potential.

Amenorrhea

The presence of amenorrhea is a diagnostic criterion in anorexia nervosa. However, irregular menstrual function has also been observed in bulimia nervosa and Eating Disorder Not Otherwise Specified (EDNOS). Amenorrhea results from a physiological adaptation to starvation. Starvation leads the pituitary gland to decrease the production of follicle-stimulating hormone and luteinizing hormone resulting in a decrease in production of estrogen and progesterone. The decreased levels of these hormones results in the absence of menstruation. While amenorrhea may impact fertility, it does not always cause anovulation; therefore it cannot be seen as an assurance that pregnancy will not occur. Weight restoration appears to stimulate the production of estrogen and progesterone leading to restoration of menstruation.

Reduced Bone Density

A reduction in bone density is commonly associated with anorexia nervosa and may lead to osteopenia or osteoporosis. There are multiple factors that are believed to be related to low bone density including low estrogen levels, increased cortisol levels, poor nutrition, low calcium and vitamin D intake, and low body mass. Because amenorrhea reduces the estrogen levels, there is a greater risk of decreased bone density. Targeting the cause of reduced bone density is essential, but it should be noted that complete bone density may never be fully restored. Bone mineral density does not seem to be impacted as greatly in bulimia nervosa.

Hypercholesterolemia

Hypercholesterolemia, or elevated cholesterol, is commonly identified in individuals with anorexia nervosa. High density lipoprotein (HDL) concentrations are likely to be elevated because of high levels of exercise and weight loss. Elevations in low density lipoprotein (LDL) concentrations have also been identified. Probable mechanisms include acceleration in cholesterol metabolism and abnormalities in estrogen, thyroid hormone, and glucocorticoids. Nutrition and weight restoration generally result in the normalization of cholesterol levels.

Cortisol

Elevated cortisol levels have been identified in anorexia nervosa. Other symptoms such as hyperglycemia, hypotension, and skin atrophy associated with elevated cortisol levels are not present. This indicates that anorexia nervosa leads to a resistance of the tissues to glucocorticoids.

Endocrine abnormalities are associated with starvation. Individuals with anorexia nervosa may exhibit various endocrine complications. Early detection, monitoring, and evaluation of any endocrine irregularities may prevent long-term complications.

Neurological Complications

Eating disorders affect both the central and peripheral nervous systems. Complications associated with the central nervous system stem from structural and functional adaptations. The most common peripheral abnormality seen in eating disorders involves muscle weakness.

Images of the brain indicate eating disorders may impact its overall structure and function. Individuals with anorexia nervosa exhibit pseudoatrophy of the brain characterized by enlarged ventricles and external cerebrospinal fluid spaces. The mechanism behind this abnormality remains unknown, but it appears to reverse with weight restoration. Seizures, headaches, and syncope have been reported in eating disorders. These complications are thought to be associated with malnutrition and decrease as nutrition is improved.

Muscle weakness is common in anorexia nervosa and bulimia nervosa. Nutrient deficiencies, dehydration, and electrolyte imbalances appear to have the greatest impact on muscular weakness. As these issues are addressed muscular weakness improves.

Hematological Complications

Hematological complications have been identified in anorexia nervosa. Bone marrow hypoplasia has been associated with states of malnutrition leading to an increased presence of anemia, leukoneutropenia, and thrombocytopenia. A low body mass has also been correlated with lower hemoglobin, leukocyte, red blood cell, and neutrophil counts. Anemia can also be related to various factors including the state of starvation, increased blood loss through the gastrointestinal tract due to purging behaviors, and/or nutrient deficiencies (iron, vitamin B12, and folic acid). The improvement in dietary status will generally reverse the effects of anemia. Leukopenia (low white blood cell count) can be seen due to protein energy malnutrition. This does not appear to impact the immune system and improves as nutritional status recovers.

Dermatological Complications

Anorexia nervosa and bulimia nervosa both impact dermatological health. Dermatological symptoms may overlap between anorexia nervosa and bulimia nervosa. Common dermatological manifestations include acne, xerosis, lanugo, carotenderma, hair and nail fragility, acrocyanosis, peripheral edema, and Russell's Sign.

Dermatological complications are mainly aggravated by poor nutritional intake. Acne, both facial and back, is commonly seen during the weight restoration process. Weight loss results in the body reverting to a prepubescent state, including a decrease in hormone production. As weight is restored the body is adapting to hormonal shifts resulting in the development of acne.

Xerosis (dry skin) develops as a result of vitamin deficiency and trace elements. Lotions and creams may help alleviate symptoms associated with dry skin; improved nutrition will resolve the condition.

Lanugo is fine, downy, pale hair that grows on the body in attempts to provide insulation for a malnourished individual. It is generally found on the face, chest, arms, legs, and back. The body will rid itself of the hair as improved thermoregulation is achieved.

Carotenderma results in an abnormal yellow-orange hue on the skin, primarily on the ears, palms, and soles. It is a result of an accumulation of serum carotene. Carotenderma is thought to be associated with a high intake of carotene-rich foods and/or an alteration in the hepatic breakdown of carotene. This will resolve with improved nutrition status allowing for the normalization of liver function.

Hair and nails may be brittle due to protein-energy malnutrition as well as a deficiency of vitamins and minerals. Increased hair loss may also occur. Restoration of nutrition leads to improved health of hair and nails.

Acrocyanosis results from a disruption in the circulatory system. This is often seen in anorexia nervosa as the body decreases blood circulation to the periphery as it attempts to conserve blood flow for the vital organs. It is characterized by cold hands and feet resulting in a bluish-purple coloring of the finger and toe nails. Weight restoration appears to improve circulation, thus reducing symptoms of acrocyanosis.

Peripheral edema is observed in anorexia nervosa and bulimia nervosa. Fluid retention occurs in the refeeding phase of anorexia nervosa as a result of the low basal metabolic rate and fluid shifts in the body. Binge episodes and purging (through self-induced vomiting, diuretics, and laxatives) interrupt the fluid balance in the body. The elimination of these behaviors will cause the body to initially retain fluids, resulting in peripheral edema. Fluid retention is typically improved as the body adapts to increased intake and the cessation of purging behaviors.

Russell's Sign is a distinguishing characteristic of using one's hand to force vomiting. It is identified by calluses or abrasions along the knuckles of the hands due to contact with the teeth. The abrasions may lead to permanent scarring.

Oral Complications

Oral complications are primarily seen as a result of repetitive vomiting. Common oral complications include angular cheilosis, dental caries, dental erosion, and parotid gland swelling.

Angular cheilosis is characterized by dry, painful fissures along the corners of the mouth. It results from repetitive exposure of the mouth to the acidic content of the vomitus. It is not permanent, and like other wounds, will heal on its own, although it may leave scarring. Angular cheilosis is also associated with riboflavin deficiency. A correction of the deficiency may be necessary.

Dental caries is a potential result of both anorexia nervosa and bulimia nervosa. High intake of carbohydrate-rich foods provides a breeding ground for bacterial growth in the mouth. The increase in bacteria leads to a greater risk of developing dental caries.

Dental erosion is frequently associated with bulimia nervosa due to the long-term contact with gastric acid. This leads to the decay in dental and tooth enamel. This is likely to occur after two years of frequent excessive vomiting. Treatment includes eliminating vomiting behaviors and being diligent about dental hygiene.

Parotid gland swelling is characterized by chipmunk-like cheeks. It occurs as a result of recurrent binging and purging. It has been attributed to an increase in cholinergic nerve stimulation, repetitive stimulation of the gland due to binging behaviors, chronic elevated bicarbonate, and/or increased autonomic stimulation resulting from the stimulation of lingual taste receptors. Parotid gland swelling generally occurs two to three days after a purging episode. While it may be cosmetically unappealing, it is generally painless. A reduction in the frequency of purging behaviors leads to a reduction in the swelling of the glands.

Conclusion

There are numerous possible medical complications associated with anorexia nervosa and bulimia nervosa. Every system in the body may be impacted and it is essential that a complete medical check-up is conducted to ensure that all medical complications are addressed. In general, complications are more severe in individuals who are more malnourished, have a greater frequency of purging behaviors, or exhibit both conditions. If complications are addressed early, nutrition is restored, and purging behaviors are stopped, many of the medical concerns can be reversed.

AMELIA MCBRIDE

See also: Amenorrhea; Dehydration; Diuretics; Edema; Electrocardiogram; Gastrointestinal Complications Associated with Eating Disorders; Lanugo; Laxative Abuse.

Bibliography

Birmingham, C. Laird, and Janet Treasure. *Medical Management of Eating Disorders, 2nd ed.,* Cambridge: Cambridge University Press, 2010.

Katzman, Debra K. "Medical Complications in Adolescents with Anorexia Nervosa: A Review of the Literature." *International Journal of Eating Disorders* 37 (2005): S52–59.

Lamber, Michel, Catherine Hubert, Benevieve Depresseux, Bruno Vande Berg, Jean-Paul Thissen, Charles Nagant de Deuxchaisnes, and Jean-Pierre Devogelaer. "Hematological

Changes in Anorexia Nervosa are Correlated with Total Body Fat Mass Depletion." *International Journal of Eating Disorders.* 21 (1997): 329–34.

Mehler, Philip S. "Medical Complications of Bulimia Nervosa and Their Treatments." *International Journal of Eating Disorders* 44 (2011): 95–104.

Mehler, Philip S., and Arnold E. Anderson. *Eating Disorders: A Guide to Medical Care and Complications, 2nd ed.* Baltimore: The Johns Hopkins University Press, 2009.

Mitchell, James E., and Scott Crow. "Medical Complications of Anorexia Nervosa and Bulimia Nervosa." *Current Opinions of Psychiatry* 19 (2006): 438–43.

Reiff, Dan W., and Kathleen Kim Lampson Reiff. *Eating Disorders Nutrition Therapy in the Recovery Process, 2nd ed.* Mercer Island: Life Enterprises, 2007.

Rushing, Jona M., Laura E. Jones, and Caroline P. Carney. "Bulimia Nervosa: A Primary Care Review." *Primary Care Companion Journal of Clinical Psychiatry* 5 (2003): 217–24.

Walsh, Judith M., Mary E. Wheat, and Karen Freund. "Detection, Evaluation, and Treatment of Eating Disorders: The Role of the Primary Care Physician." *Journal of General Internal Medicine* 15 (2000): 577–90.

MENOPAUSE

Menopause refers to a developmental milestone that occurs naturally as women age. Females during their midlife stop having their period for at least 12 consecutive months and their lack of menses cannot be explained by other reasons (e.g., oral contraceptives). Women usually experience menopause between 45 and 55 years of age and can expect to encounter some biological changes that parallel pubertal changes in adolescence. These physical changes in the body (e.g., body weight and shape) for menopausal women include increased body mass index (BMI) and evidence of adipose (fat) tissue gathered around the abdominal region. Physiological changes such as decreased metabolic rate and changes in hormone levels also contribute to weight gain during menopause.

Women tend to gain 5 to 10 pounds per decade of life until the age of 60, and double the percent of fat in their bodies once they reach 50 years of age. Although menopause is associated with changes in body weight and shape, the understanding of women's perceptions of body image during menopause is limited. As a result of decreased estrogen production, hot flashes, sweats, and sleep disturbances are common and symptoms may linger for 5 or more years. Generally menopausal women report feeling less attractive, worry more about being fat, and diet more to lose weight than premenopausal women, supporting the contention that physiological symptoms such as hot flashes have an impact on a woman's body image and make her feel like her body is out of control. Media often reinforces stereotypes about menopausal women being emotionally unstable, out of control, and "crazy," leading many women to fear and fight this natural part of the aging process. Case studies of women in their fifties show that eating disordered behaviors may be triggered among midlife women in response to menopausal weight gain.

Conclusion

Although much attention has been given to eating disorders and body image disturbances among adolescent females, women in their midlife have shown signs of continued body dissatisfaction. It is expected that developmental milestones such as menopause, which contribute to weight gain, trigger increased body consciousness and negative body image.

JUSTINE J. REEL

Bibliography

Cumella, Edward J., and Zina Kally. "Profile of 50 Women with Midlife-onset Eating Disorders." *Eating Disorders* 16 (2008): 193–203. doi: 10.1080/10640260802016670

Deeks, Amanda A., and Marita P. McCabe. "Menopausal Stage and Age and Perceptions of Body Image." *Psychology and Health* 16 (2001): 367–79.

Kearney-Cooke, Ann, and Florence Isaacs. *Change Your Mind, Change Your Body: Feeling Good about Your Body and Self after 40.* New York: Atria, 2004.

Maine, Margo, and Joe Kelly. *The Body Myth: Adult Women and the Pressure to Be Perfect.* Hoboken, NJ: John Wiley & Sons, 2005.

North American Menopause Society (NAMS). "Basic Facts about Menopause." Retrieved June 8, 2011 from: http://www.menopause.org/

Peat, Christine M., Naomi L. Peyerl, and Jennifer J. Muehlenkamp. "Body Image and Eating Disorders in Older Adults: A Review." *The Journal of General Psychology* 135, no. 4 (2008): 343–58.

SooHoo, Sonya, Justine J. Reel, and Judy Van Raalte. "Chasing the 'Fountain of Youth': Body Image and Eating Disorders among 'Older' Women." In *The Hidden Faces of Eating Disorders and Body Image,* edited by Justine J. Reel and Katherine A. Beals. Reston, VA: NAGWS/AAHPERD, 2009.

Zerbe, Kathryn J. "Eating Disorders in Middle and Late Life: A Neglected Problem." *Primary Psychiatry* 10 (2003): 80–82.

MINDFULNESS

Mindfulness is defined as a process of bringing increased attention and nonjudgmental awareness to the present moment experience. Mindfulness has been linked with positive psychological health and has been used as a skill for decreasing depressed mood, anxiety, and other negative emotions. Mindfulness has gained recognition recently as a way to address and treat eating disorders including anorexia nervosa, bulimia nervosa, and binge eating disorder. Mindfulness (i.e., focus on the present) as emphasized through meditation and other modalities is also taught to the general population as a way to deal with stress, improve one's quality of life, and experience more personal life enjoyment.

Mindfulness and Eating

A mindfulness practice that the general population and individuals with eating disorders can benefit from is mindful eating. It is common in the United States to engage in distracted eating that involves eating while standing up, driving, or watching television. However, distracted eating negatively impacts one's dining experience; it results in the person not tasting the flavors of food and being disconnected with hunger and fullness cues. By not being mindful, individuals may eat more or less than the body needs and can trigger binge eating episodes.

By contrast, mindful eating encourages the use of all senses to experience the food. In addition to eating slowly and noticing the flavors of the food, an eater who is mindful does not eat in front of a television or at the desk at work. Mindful eating results in being more in touch with one's hunger and being able to avoid overeating.

Mindfulness and Exercise

Eating disordered individuals who engage in obligatory exercise are usually mindless exercisers. Similar to mindless eaters, mindless exercisers often engage in distracted exercise that is disconnected from how the body is feeling. As a result, the mindless exerciser may exercise through pain, increasing risk for injuries or soreness. Mindless exercisers may use external cues (e.g., calorie counters on exercise machines) to determine duration of work-out rather than how the body feels; therefore they are likely to experience more boredom during exercise and less exercise enjoyment than mindful exercisers.

Exercise interventions that include mindfulness encourage participants to attend to the senses and the outside environment. A meditative walk or mindful walking may involve smelling, seeing, and listening to one's surroundings while moving at a more controlled pace. Mindful exercise also involves retraining oneself to listen to body cues to determine when to exercise and when to stop.

Mindfulness and Eating Disorders Treatment

Mindfulness has been shown to be a useful adjunct in eating disorder treatment for addressing distorted cognitions. For example, having a mindful outlook may help to cope with distressing cognitions (e.g., irrational thoughts or rigid thinking about a "bad food") and feelings (e.g., desire to purge); it helps one view these cognitions and feelings as temporary events that will pass. Mindfulness has been directly incorporated into Dialectical Behavior Therapy (DBT) to increase awareness and promote self-acceptance.

Similarly, mindfulness can be applied to experiences with body image. Mindfulness teaches a person to observe his or her body without judgment and emotional reaction in order to decrease the likelihood of impulsive and self-destructive reactions and behaviors. Furthermore, the individual is forced to become more mindful about the ways in which negative body image thoughts occur in an automatic or mindless fashion. Body image disturbances represent a type of mindlessness (i.e., rigid, inflexible, and unwilling to adapt to an ever-changing bodily form) that should be viewed from multiple perspectives without judgment.

Conclusion

The state of mindfulness is a sense of being in the present moment with attention and lack of judgment. Mindfulness training has been applied to a diverse range of psychological disorders and has shown initial promise as an adjunct to eating disorder treatment. There is direct application for eating disordered individuals who often engage in both mindless eating and exercise and must relearn mindful eating and exercise practices. Additionally, mindfulness can be used to address negative cognitions related to eating and body image so that an individual can develop increased attention and acceptance.

JUSTINE J. REEL

See also: Dialectical Behavior Therapy.

Bibliography

Boudette, Robin. "Integrating Mindfulness into the Therapy Hour." *Eating Disorders: The Journal of Treatment & Prevention* 19 (2011): 108–115. doi: 10.1080/10640266.2011.533610.

Hepworth, Natasha S. "A Mindful Eating Group as an Adjunct to Individual Treatment for Eating Disorders: A Pilot Study." *Eating Disorders: The Journal of Treatment & Prevention* 19 (2011): 6–16. doi: 10.1080/10640266.2011.533610.

Lavender, Jason M., Bianca F. Jardin, and Drew A. Anderson. "Bulimic Symptoms in Undergraduate Men and Women: Contributions of Mindfulness and Thought Suppression." *Eating Behaviors* 10 (2009): 228–31. doi: 10.1016/j.eatbeh.2009.07.002.

Masuda, Akihiko, and Johanna W. Wendell. "Mindfulness Mediates the Relation Between Disordered Eating-Related Cognitions and Psychological Distress." *Eating Behaviors* 11 (2010): 293–96. doi: 10.1016/j.eatbeh.2010.07.001.

Stewart, Tiffany M. "Light on Body Image Treatment: Acceptance through Mindfulness." *Behavior Modification* 28, no. 6 (2004): 783–811. doi: 10.1177/0145445503259862.

Wanden-Berghe, Rocio Guardiola, Javier Sanz-Valero, and Carmina Wanden-Berghe. "The Application of Mindfulness to Eating Disorders Treatment: A Systematic Review." *Eating Disorders: The Journal of Treatment & Prevention* 19 (2011): 34–48. doi: 10.1080/10640266.2011.533604.

MORTALITY RATES

Mortality is defined as fatality or death. Since Karen Carpenter's death in 1983, eating disorders have been increasingly recognized as severe illnesses with a mortality risk. Individuals with anorexia nervosa, bulimia nervosa, and Eating Disorder Not Otherwise Specified (EDNOS) may be at increased risk for premature death due to medical complications (e.g., cardiovascular problems) as well as self-harm behaviors and suicide. Mortality rates vary across studies; however, it is known that eating disorders represent the highest mortality rate among psychiatric disorders.

Anorexia Nervosa and Mortality

Mortality has most commonly been associated with anorexia nervosa with one study showing the mortality rate for this disorder as 0.56 percent per year or approximately 5.6 percent per decade. Another study reported a 4.0 percent mortality rate across anorexia nervosa cases. The combination of low body weight, potential use of purging behaviors, severe restriction, and mental health issues (e.g., self-harm and suicide) predicts a higher mortality rate among individuals with anorexia nervosa. Research has shown that only 46 percent of individuals fully recover from anorexia nervosa, and 20 percent suffer from anorexia nervosa chronically leading to increased risk for death. These findings have been a matter of great concern.

A 10-year mortality study conducted in France showed that mortality risk for anorexic inpatients was 10 times higher than the mortality risk for the general female French population. During the study, 40 deaths were recorded and half of these deaths occurred in the three years following hospitalization. Interestingly, several characteristics were found to predict mortality among anorexia nervosa clients: older age, longer eating disorder duration, history of suicide attempt, and diuretic use. Additionally, French researchers found that the lower the desired body mass index and the more severe the eating disorder symptoms, the higher the risk for death.

Other Eating Disorders and Mortality Risk

Although most attention has been given to mortality risk associated with anorexia nervosa, bulimia nervosa and EDNOS also present serious concerns. In one study, crude mortality rates were 3.9 percent for bulimia nervosa and 5.2 percent for EDNOS, compared with 4.0 percent for anorexia nervosa. It is well-recognized that substantial medical complications (e.g., electrolyte disturbances) are associated with purging behaviors (e.g., vomiting, laxatives, diuretics) that can pose severe medical risk. Moreover, individuals with bulimia nervosa and EDNOS may exhibit impulsivity which has been associated with substance abuse and higher suicide risk.

Conclusion

Most studies conclude that anorexia nervosa yields the highest mortality rate due to medical complications and increased suicide rates. However, it is important not to discount the severity of bulimia nervosa and Eating Disorder Not Otherwise Specified when considering risk for mortality. Predictors for mortality include longer duration of eating disorder, older age, purging behaviors, and suicide attempts.

JUSTINE J. REEL

See also: Carpenter, Karen; Medical and Health Consequences.

Bibliography

Arcelus, Jon, Alex J. Mitchell, Jackie Wales, and Soren Nielsen. "Mortality Rates in Patients with Anorexia Nervosa and Other Eating Disorders." *Archives of General Psychiatry* 68, no. 7 (2011): 724–31.

Huas C., A. Caille, N. Godart, C. Foulon, A. Pham-Scottez, S. Divac, A. Deschartres, G. Lavoisy, J. D. Guelfi, F. Rouillon, and B. Falissard. "Factors Predictive of Ten-Year

Mortality in Severe Anorexia Nervosa Patients." *Acta Psychiatrica Scandinavica* 123 (2011): 62–70. doi: 10.111/j.1600–0447.2010.01627.x.

Kaye, Walter. "Eating Disorders: Hope Despite Mortal Risk." *American Journal of Psychiatry* 166, no. 12 (2009): 1309–1311.

Preti, A., M.B.L. Rocchi, D. Sisti, M. V. Camboni, and P. Miotto. "A Comprehensive Meta-Analysis of the Risk of Suicide in Eating Disorders." *Acta Psychiatrica Scandinavica* 124 (2011): 6–17. doi: 10.1111/j.1600–0447.2010.01641.x.

Rosling, Agneta, Par Sparen, Claes Norring, and Anne-Liis von Knorring. "Mortality of Eating Disorders: A Follow-up Study of Treatment in a Specialist Unit 1974–2000." *International Journal of Eating Disorders* 44, no. 4 (2011): 304–310. doi: 10.1002/eat.20827.

Suzuki, Kenji, Aya Takeda, and Aihide Yoshino. "Mortality 6 Years after Inpatient Treatment of Female Japanese Patients with Eating Disorders Associated with Alcoholism." *Psychiatry and Clinical Neurosciences* 65 (2011): 326–32. doi: 10.1111/j.1440–1819.2011.02217.x.

MOTIVATIONAL INTERVIEWING

Motivational interviewing refers to a therapeutic approach used to help people work through barriers, commit to change, and enhance intrinsic motivation. This client-centered approach assesses the individual's readiness for change as represented by his or her stage of change for an addictive disorder or health behavior.

Stages of Change Model

The Stages of Change model, which is also known as the Transtheoretical model, was first developed by Prochaska to promote smoking cessation. Clients were moved through the stages of change beginning with working with individuals who were highly resistant to treatment and moving toward actively maintaining a smoke-free lifestyle. The treatment is tailored to the client's particular stage of change which could include precontemplation, contemplation, preparation, action, or maintenance. Precontemplation refers to a stage in which an individual is not consciously aware that there is a problem or concern. Contemplation, on the other hand, represents a stage when an individual begins to think about change but has not taken action. Preparation indicates a stage in which an individual begins taking steps to change behavior (e.g., purchases a gym membership). When the individual is exercising more consistently he or she is classified as being in the action and maintenance stages.

The Stages of Change model has been used as the guiding framework for motivational interviewing techniques with a variety of target populations (e.g., those with exercise, gambling, substance abuse problems). Motivational interviewing combines a supportive and empathic counseling style with a directive method for decreasing client ambivalence and helping the client focus on a direction for change. Clients are encouraged to form their own arguments for change (i.e., "change talk") to represent their desire, ability, and need to change. As a result, clients engaging in motivational interviewing show a greater commitment to the process of change.

Motivational Interviewing and Eating Disorder Treatment

Because eating disordered individuals are notoriously resistant to change and difficult to treat, motivational interviewing has shown much promise as a treatment approach for this population. Researchers and clinicians view motivational interviewing as a natural fit in helping with addictive aspects of eating disorders while helping to reinforce and enhance the client's motivation to change. Motivational interviewing has been used as a stand-alone intervention or in combination with other forms of treatment (e.g., cognitive behavioral therapy) for anorexia nervosa, bulimia nervosa, and binge eating disorder.

A noteworthy study involved 108 women who had binge eating disorder and were assigned to either the motivational interviewing treatment group or a control group. The participants who received motivational interviewing were more confident in their ability to change binge eating patterns and tended to abstain from binge eating episodes at a higher rate compared to the control group (27.8% versus 11.1%).

Conclusion

Although more outcome studies are needed that use motivational interviewing to treat eating disorders, initial findings show that this approach can be helpful in addressing clients who are resistant to change. Motivational interviewing has been used successfully with substance abuse and other addiction populations and can be used to assess an eating disordered individual's stage of change so that the intervention can be matched with his or her readiness for change.

JUSTINE J. REEL

See also: Cognitive Behavioral Therapy.

Bibliography

Brennan, Leah, Jeff Walkley, Steve F. Fraser, Kate Greenway, and Ray Wilks. "Motivational Interviewing and Cognitive Behavior Therapy in the Treatment of Adolescent Overweight and Obesity: Study Design and Methodology." *Contemporary Clinical Trials* 29 (2008): 359–75. doi: 10.1016/j.cct.2007.09.001.

Cassin, Stephanie E., Kristin M. von Ranson, Kenneth Heng, Joti Brar, and Amy E. Wojtowicz. "Adapted Motivational Interviewing for Women with Binge Eating Disorder: A Randomized Controlled Trial." *Psychology of Addictive Behaviors* 22, no. 3 (2008): 417–25. doi: 10.1037/0893–164X.22.3.417.

Hettema, Jennifer, Julie Steele, and William R. Miller. "Motivational Interviewing." *Annual Review of Clinical Psychology* 1 (2005): 91–111. doi: 10.1146/annurev.clinpsy.1.102803.143833.

Towell, Down Baker, Sally Woodford, Steven Reid, Barbara Rooney, and Anthony Towell. "Compliance and Outcome in Treatment-resistant Anorexia and Bulimia: A Retrospective Study." *British Journal of Clinical Psychology* 40 (2001): 189–95.

Wade, Tracey D., Anna Frayne, Sally-Anne Edwards, Therese Robertson, and Peter Gilchrist. "Motivational Change in an Inpatient Anorexia Nervosa Population and Implications for Treatment." *Australian and New Zealand Journal of Psychiatry* 43 (2009): 235–43.

Wilson, G. Terence, and Tanya R. Schlam. "The Transtheoretical Model and Motivational Interviewing in the Treatment of Eating and Weight Disorders." *Clinical Psychology Review* 24 (2004): 361–78. doi: 10.1016/j.cpr.2004.03.003.

MUSCLE DYSMORPHIA

Originally called "reverse anorexia" or "bigorexia," muscle dysmorphia is a proposed psychiatric disorder that is characterized by an intense desire to gain muscle mass while simultaneously reducing one's body fat. Muscle dysmorphia is not exclusive to males; however, muscle dysmorphia among females is rare. Its prevalence is unknown although it has been suggested that up to 90,000 men may meet the criteria for this disorder. It is difficult to estimate an accurate number since men are unlikely to admit that they are struggling due to embarrassment or shame. The millions of gym memberships sold to males each year in the United States could be associated with the desire of males to change their bodies. Furthermore, there is evidence to suggest that male adolescent use of steroids is often to improve athletic performance, but many use steroids for the sole purpose of enhancing appearance.

Muscle Dysmorphia and Body Image

It should be noted that while many men may be unhappy with their lack of muscularity, it does not always mean that they struggle with muscle dysmorphia. However, a problem may occur when a discrepancy exists between what someone perceives as an ideal physique and one's actual physique. This perception must be combined with the belief that coming closer to this proposed ideal will generate some kind of reward.

Male body image satisfaction exists on a continuum with one extreme representing men who have no interest in or care little about their physiques. The middle of the continuum represents men who may be somewhat dissatisfied with their physiques, but are not at the pathological level for concern. However, a male who falls on the opposite extreme of the continuum is highly preoccupied with his physique and is willing to take extreme actions to change his appearance and muscularity.

Classification of Muscle Dysmorphia

Muscle dysmorphia is not included in the *Diagnostic and Statistical Manual of Mental Disorders 4th Edition* (DSM-IV-TR). This is primarily because its classification has yet to be established. This condition includes traits that are characteristic of other disorders such as anorexia nervosa. It remains unclear whether it is a spectrum disorder of obsessive-compulsive disorder or a somatoform disorder. Some researchers argue that muscle dysmorphia should fit under obsessive-compulsive disorder and subsequently, a type of body dysmorphic disorder. Body dysmorphic disorder is defined as a preoccupation with an imagined or slight physical defect concerning a particular body part (e.g., nose). The individual believes that this supposed flaw is unappealing or ugly even though in reality the flaw is negligible or even nonexistent to others.

Some researchers believe that muscle dysmorphia should be categorized as an eating disorder diagnosis because the condition has characteristics similar to those of anorexia nervosa. Currently, many individuals with muscle dysmorphia are being diagnosed as having Eating Disorder Not Otherwise Specified (EDNOS). Thus, muscle dysmorphia is and remains a proposed psychiatric disorder. Research about muscle dysmorphia is in its infancy, and more research is needed before a clear understanding of its traits and characteristics can be obtained.

Etiology of Muscle Dysmorphia

What causes muscle dysmorphia or where it comes from is not entirely clear. In fact, attributing it to a single factor is shortsighted and it is likely to be caused by a combination of factors. While most research would suggest that muscle dysmorphia begins in teenage or early adulthood, an understanding of physique may begin much earlier.

Various models have been proposed to explain the etiology of muscle dysmorphia and similar factors appear in them. Poor self-esteem, body dissatisfaction, and distortion play a significant role whereby poor self-perception leads to steps to alter physique. The media is also a frequently cited source. Seemingly perfect images of muscular, toned males portrayed in the media allow for comparison between those images and the self. As a consequence, a negative or upward social comparison may occur wherein a comparison against a seemingly superior physique can lead to decreased self-esteem and negative effect.

Peer experiences and the effect of parents is another contributor to muscle dysmorphia. Parents appear to exert more influence than peers, particularly the father figure. Other influences during youth can include action figures and dolls which are discussed in a separate entry.

Perhaps a key element to be considered in relation to muscle dysmorphia is the gender transformation that has occurred over the past several decades. Men have traditionally attained their masculinity from their work, and they have enjoyed dominance in certain vocations such as business and security forces. However, these vocations are no longer exclusive to males, thereby leaving males to seek their identity through alternate means. Muscularity is a visible entity where differentiation clearly remains.

Consequences of Muscle Dysmorphia

For those with muscle dysmorphia, there are potentially very serious physical, psychological, and environmental risks; these are in addition to other negative attitudes and behaviors associated with an extreme desire for muscle mass. Examples of physical consequences include heart failure, renal failure, dehydration, and sometimes death. In part, these effects can be caused by the abuse of illegal substances such as anabolic steroids; they can also be caused by extreme dieting, overtraining, and exercise addiction.

An individual may also experience negative social, recreational, and occupational hazards including depression, social physique anxiety, low self-esteem, neuroticism, and perfectionism as a result of muscle dysmorphia. It is interesting that men with muscle dysmorphia are often highly muscular and lean, and yet they exhibit intense vulnerability with respect to their body image leading them to continually build their bodies in pursuit of an unattainable goal.

Perhaps some of the least discussed aspects of muscle dysmorphia are the social and recreational effects. Someone seeking an ideal body expects rewards such as a fuller life, happiness, and successful relationships with the opposite gender. However, these rewards are seldom realized, as muscle dysmorphia creates a preoccupation that supersedes other responsibilities and desires. For example, sexual activity may be impaired due to fears that one's small physique will be exposed or because of the perception that sex wastes energy needed for working out. Because of the strict diets required to achieve muscularity with low body fat, eating out socially can be difficult. Exposing one's physique at a doctor's office or a beach may cause extreme discomfort. A sufferer may become so preoccupied with working out that he could give up jobs or careers to spend more time in the gym. Or he may build a gym in his home so that he can work out continually without fear of physique comparisons that might occur in a gym setting.

Measurement of Muscle Dysmorphia

Measurement tools for muscle dysmorphia are quite varied primarily because there has been little agreement regarding the diagnostic criteria for the condition. Although each measure has issues, there have been several attempts to measure muscle dysmorphia or the drive for muscularity. These include the Swansea Muscularity Attitudes Questionnaire, Muscle Appearance Satisfaction Scale, Bodybuilder Image Grid, Drive for Muscularity Scale, Somatomorphic Matrix, and Muscle Dysmorphia Inventory.

The Swansea Muscularity Attitudes Questionnaire assesses the perceived positive attributes of being muscular and the desire to be muscular, but it has not been well tested. The Muscle Appearance Satisfaction Scale (MASS) is a 19-item measure that assesses the symptoms of muscle dysmorphia. The self-report measure includes five factors: bodybuilding dependence, muscle checking, substance use, injury, and muscle satisfaction. The MASS includes injury-related statements which are not part of general characteristics of muscle dysmorphia. The Bodybuilder Image Grid (BIG) uses a series of two-dimensional pictures on a grid that vary in muscularity and body fat. Again, the BIG has been little used in empirical research.

One of the most commonly used assessment methods is the Drive for Muscularity Scale, a 15-question survey assessing drive for muscularity traits. Although initially designed and tested with adolescents, it has been widely used in subsequent research and has been well tested for reliability and validity.

The Somatomorphic Matrix includes 100 images which are placed in a 10 x 10 matrix database computer program that allows the user to increase or decrease the fat-free mass index or body fat percentage of the image that is being shown. Participants only see one image at a time. The advantage of the Somatomorphic Matrix is that both muscularity and body fat are assessed as determinants of body image. Although the scale has good construct validity, it is not adequately reliable and further testing is needed.

The Muscle Dysmorphia Inventory (MDI) aims to identify characteristics associated with muscle dysmorphia. It uses 27 questions on a Likert scale to assess characteristics associated with muscle dysmorphia that are then broken down into subscales of size/symmetry, physique protection, exercise dependence, supplement use, dietary behavior, and pharmacological use. Subscales are measured separately, as each is designed to measure conceptually independent traits. Although the MDI appears to be a valid and reliable method for assessing traits associated with muscle dysmorphia, the inventory should not be employed as a diagnostic tool.

Future Directions

The challenge for researchers is to assess and treat muscle dysmorphia. The term is barely a decade old, and the field remains fertile for research. Perhaps the most important need is a clear understanding of where the condition fits within the spectrum of other mental disorders. Furthermore, there is no consistent method for identifying someone with muscle dysmorphia. Thus, one cannot be categorically identified with muscle dysmorphia, but one can exhibit characteristics associated with the proposed condition.

While the general definition of muscle dysmorphia has been relatively consistent, what traits or characteristics the definition includes is still debatable. For example, while steroid use is a commonly assumed characteristic, there is research to suggest individuals may not necessarily use steroids, and yet they can still be excessively concerned about their physiques. Physique protection is also a characteristic that needs further research. For example, why do some individuals exhibit extreme preoccupation with displaying their physique while others appear to seek affirmation as much as possible through the praise of others or through mirror checking.

Conclusion

In sum, the initial groundwork for understanding muscle dysmorphia has begun, but there are many unanswered questions that remain. Only when the proposed condition is defined, is measureable, and clear methods for treatment are available will those struggling with this condition receive the full support that they need.

TIMOTHY M. BAGHURST

See also: Bigorexia; Body Image in Males; Bodybuilding; Dolls; Drive for Muscularity; Eating Disorder Not Otherwise Specified; Masculinity Ideals.

Bibliography

Baghurst, Timothy M., and Cathy Lirgg. "Characteristics of Muscle Dysmorphia in Male Football, Weight Training, and Competitive Natural and Non-natural Bodybuilding Samples." *Body Image* 6 (2009): 221–27.

Baghurst, Timothy M., and Dan B. Kissinger. "Perspectives on Muscle Dysmorphia." *International Journal of Men's Health* 8 (2009): 82–89.

Bahrke, Michael S., Charles E. Yesalis, Andrea N. Kopstein, and Jason A. Stephens. "Risk Factors Associated with Anabolic-Androgenic Steroid Use among Adolescents." *Sports Medicine* 29 (2000): 397–406.

Davies, Rebecca, and Dave Smith. "Muscle Dysmorphia among Current and Former Steroid Users." *Journal of Clinical Sport Psychology* 5 (2011): 77–94.

Lantz, Christopher D., Deborah J. Rhea, and J. L. Mayhew. "The Drive for Size: A Psycho-behavioral Model of Muscle Dysmorphia." *International Sports Journal* 5 (2001): 71–86.

Leit, Richard A., James J. Gray, and Harrison G. Pope, Jr. "The Media's Representation of the Ideal Male Body: A Cause for Muscle Dysmorphia?" *International Journal of Eating Disorders* 31 (2002): 334–38.

Leone, James E., Edward J. Sedory, and Kimberly A. Gray. "Recognition and Treatment of Muscle Dysmorphia and Related Body Image Disorders." *Journal of Athletic Training* 40 (2005): 352–59.

McCreary, Donald R., and Doris K. Sasse. "An Exploration of the Drive for Muscularity in Adolescent Boys and Girls." *Journal of American College Health* 48 (2000): 297–304.

Morgan, John F. "From Charles Atlas to Adonis Complex: Fat Is More Than a Feminist Issue." *Lancet* 356 (2000): 1372–1374.

Murray, Stewart B., Elizabeth Rieger, Stephen W. Touyz, and Yolanda L. De La Garza Garcia. "Muscle Dysmorphia and the SDM-V Conundrum: Where Does It Belong? A Review Paper." *International Journal of Eating Disorders* 43 (2010): 483–91.

Olivardia, Roberto. "Mirror, Mirror on the Wall, Who's the Largest of Them All? The Features and Phenomenology of Muscle Dysmorphia." *Harvard Rev Psychiatry* 9 (2001): 254–59.

Olivardia, Roberto. "Body Image Obsession in Men." *Healthy Weight Journal* 16 (2002): 59–64.

Olivardia, Roberto, Harrison G. Pope Jr., John J. Borowiecki III, and Geoffrey H. Cohane. "Biceps and Body Image: The Relationship between Muscularity and Self-esteem, Depression, and Eating Disorder Symptoms." *Psychology of Men and Masculinity* 5 (2004): 112–20.

Pope, Harrison G. Jr., A. J. Gruber, Precilla Choi, Roberto Olivardia, and Katharine A. Phillips. "Muscle Dysmorphia: An Unrecognized Form of Body Dysmorphic Disorder." *Psychosomatics* 38 (1997): 548–57.

Pope, Harrison G. Jr., Katharine A. Phillips, and Roberto Olivardia. *The Adonis Complex: The Secret Crisis of Male Body Obsession.* New York: The Free Press, 2000.

Tucker, Readdy, Patti L. Watkins, and Bradley J. Cardinal. "Muscle Dysmorphia, Gender Role Stress, and Sociocultural Influences: An Exploratory Study." *Research Quarterly for Exercise and Sport* 82 (2011): 310–19.

MYTH OF THE "FRESHMAN 15"

The "Freshman 15" refers to the common catchphrase related to gaining 15 pounds during the freshman year of college. This phenomenon has been popularized in the media and is frequently discussed by college students, but appears to be more of a myth than based in evidence. A few freshmen do gain weight, but studies have found that only about half of students gain any weight during their freshman year, and the average weight gain is around five pounds.

The concept of the Freshman 15 first appeared in an academic journal article in 1985 but was not popularized until the late 1990s. Since that time the Freshman 15 has been used as a marketing tool for gyms, grocery stores, and restaurants trying to appeal to customers who are interested in seeking a healthy lifestyle. As a result of the media exposure and marketing, the Freshman 15 has become a topic of conversation among students. The vast majority of college students are able to accurately define the Freshman 15 and up to 60 percent are at least moderately concerned that they will gain weight. This concern can turn into a self-fulfilling prophecy when college students sabotage their health behaviors by eating unhealthy foods and not exercising because they feel the Freshman 15 is inevitable. Even though the Freshman 15 concept has been exaggerated, the concern about weight gain appears to negatively affect some students by distorting the way they think about weight, leading to an increasingly negative body image.

Although gaining 15 pounds during the freshman year is often a gross overestimation of actual weight gain, many students do gain at least some weight in their first year of college. In fact, studies have shown that college students gain weight between 6 to 36 times faster than the general population. Although both genders are affected, women gain slightly more weight than men. Almost all college women have an ideal weight that is less than their current weight and roughly half are currently dieting. Ironically, dieting during the freshman year often contributes to weight gain rather than weight loss for most college students. This is due to a decrease in metabolism because of the diet, combined with a greater likelihood of overeating post-diet. There are a number of environmental and social reasons for weight gain during the freshman year of college, including changes in eating habits, physical activity, stress, and societal pressure.

Eating Habits

Dietary Freedom
For many students, going to college is the first time they have total freedom to make their own dietary choices. This freedom may result in students opting for their favorite tasting foods, which can be less nutritious, high-calorie options. Many students are initially attracted to the unhealthy foods because they can eat them without parental restraints. Parents are no longer there to encourage fruits and vegetables and discourage excessive fried foods and sweets. Students must learn to self-regulate their eating to match their calorie output.

Dining Halls
Many universities offer on-campus dormitory housing and some require the purchase of a meal plan that allows students to eat at cafeterias with buffet style, "all-you-can-eat menus." These buffets can be problematic for both nutritional quality and portion control. At some universities, these meal plans can also be

used to purchase items from snack carts, fast food kiosks, or vending machines. One study found that students who ate in a dining hall felt they ate more and left with a greater sense of fullness. This communal eating may encourage constant overeating.

As students adjust to a new living situation, they must also learn to balance obligations at school, work, and with their families and friends. With the chaos of their lives, convenience may be the single most important factor in food choices. Students report eating fewer meals per day while in college than they did previously in high school. They may opt for quick, processed meals, fast food, or vending machine snacks. Many college campuses are surrounded by fast-food restaurants, making fast foods a quick and easy option for meals. Not only are these foods high in fat and low in vitamins and minerals, but the serving sizes have also gotten increasingly bigger each year. Research has found that the larger the serving, the more the individual will eat. The accessibility of vending machines at schools as well as in some dormitory halls may contribute to weight gain, as individuals who snack more often are more likely to gain weight. Late-night parties and pulling "all-nighters" to study for exams may also contribute to excessive snacking for college students. Most people do not appear to compensate for the food they eat while snacking by lowering their calorie content at meals.

Alcohol Consumption

Another common health problem tied to weight gain among college freshmen is the consumption of large quantities of calorically-dense alcohol. The use of alcohol becomes more prevalent during the early college years, and college students are more likely to engage in binge drinking. Though not extensively studied, it is hypothesized that the additional calories consumed from alcohol use may contribute to weight gain for some people. Increased alcohol use during the freshman year has also been linked to disordered eating and alcohol abuse. The effects of smoking and illicit drug use on weight gain during the freshman year require further study.

Contradictory Evidence

While most studies support the common causes of freshman weight gain, there are some contradictory findings. For example, a few studies have found that living in residential halls where food is provided is not related to weight gain; the amount of fruits and vegetables and high-fat fast foods consumed does not change; and, the transition to college does not significantly change eating patterns. This contradictory evidence is likely to be due to the complex nature of weight gain and the varying experiences at individual universities.

Calorie Intake

Given the dietary freedom, dining halls, hectic lifestyle, and alcohol consumption, it is assumed that a college student's caloric intake would be considerably higher than high school. However, research suggests that the average calorie intake usually remains constant or decreases during the first year of college. The decrease in caloric intake and increase in body weight suggests that a change in physical activity may be primarily responsible for freshman weight gain.

Physical Activity

College students vary in the amount of physical activity levels and lack of activity can contribute to weight gain. Many students report that the busier schedule allows less time for recreational and organized sports. Fewer students have the opportunity to play collegiate sports than high school sports. In addition, having more hectic schedules makes it more difficult to make exercise a priority. Those who were relatively inactive in high school may find that their activity levels actually increase as they walk around campus and no longer rely on a car for daily transportation. One research study found that all students dramatically decreased their exercise during the beginning of the school year, but many students returned to their previous level of exercise after the initial college transition. However, the participants in the study who gained weight during their freshman year had decreased physical activity levels when compared to high school. Another study found participation in exercise to be stable throughout the school year, although aerobic exercise was declining.

Stress

Many students encounter stress as they transition away from home and to a university setting. This stress may be short-lived, lasting only till the student adjusts to college life, or it may be chronic as the academic pressures are continual. Those students who fail to adjust may start indulging in unhealthy behaviors and experience negative physical and psychological health. Universities typically are a more competitive academic setting, so while a student may have performed well in high school, he or she may struggle at the university level. Some students reported that an increased workload, more rigorous class schedules, and less lenient grading contributed to stress for new university students. The severity and frequency of stress has been associated with weight gain or weight loss. Students who are stressed may turn to food in order to unwind and feel better, thus increasing their emotional eating. People who eat emotionally are more likely to have trouble managing their weight, as they may eat unneeded calories throughout the day. Stress is also more likely to affect an individual when he or she is sleep deprived. Research has found that freshmen sleep far less on average than they did during their high school days.

Societal Pressure

The societal pressure to be thin for women and to be muscular for men may contribute to weight dissatisfaction for this population. Freshmen are bombarded by the media, peers, and family members outlining an ideal that is nearly impossible to achieve. Students feel the university setting intensifies the comparison between peers and perpetuates weight dissatisfaction. The effect of weight dissatisfaction during the freshman year has been primarily researched in women, though it is postulated that men would have similar experiences. For freshman women, weight dissatisfaction intensifies as actual weight increases. Those with greater weight dissatisfaction are more likely to develop worsening symptoms and further eating pathology during the college years. Weight dissatisfaction is related to dieting, which is related to weight gain for freshman women.

Eating Disorders and Obesity

Research has found that a higher weight was significantly positively correlated to concern about the Freshman 15. Those who weighed more upon entering college were more worried about gaining additional weight. The more overweight the individual, the less likely he or she is to have healthy eating habits and exercise. The overweight college freshman is more likely to eat more and be more dissatisfied with additional weight gain.

The overall prevalence of clinical eating disorders does not appear to increase during the freshman year; however, disordered eating and eating disorder symptoms do increase in those without clinical eating disorders. This means that more individuals have behaviors that could be symptoms of eating disorders, while not having a full diagnosable case. Researchers speculate that for most women, eating disorders are established before college, but self-image, dieting behaviors and eating disorder symptoms are common during college. In one study, about a fourth of the freshman class started a diet for the first time during their freshman year. Similarly, for females, about 15 percent began binge eating for the first time during their freshman year.

Prevention of the Freshman 15

Health professionals fear that the unhealthy habits that cause freshman weight gain may persist throughout adulthood, continually adding extra weight to these individuals, thus putting them at risk of obesity, heart disease, and diabetes. Given the threefold increase in the prevalence of overweight and obesity when comparing adolescent and adult age groups, the college years appear to be an appropriate time for prevention programs. Many universities are working to prevent the Freshman 15 by making modifications at the university level. Helping freshmen to understand the facts, along with some of the possible causes of the Freshman 15, through presentations during courses or at orientation can help address some of the underlying emotions that may perpetuate the problem. Universities can also offer healthier eating options in dining rooms and in vending machines. Access to equipment for exercise can also decrease the likelihood of gaining weight during the first year of college. In addition, universities can offer nutrition and/or physical education courses to support students to make better food choices and increase physical activity.

Conclusion

Although the concept of Freshman 15 has been a popular way to label weight gain associated with the college years, the amount of weight gain (i.e., 15 pounds) has not been consistently documented. Many researchers in the field suggest changing the term "Freshman 15" to "Freshman 5" to more accurately explain the weight gain of first-year college students. This transition may help eliminate the irrational fear and concern among many students, which leads to unhealthy dietary attitudes and behaviors. A better approach to prevent the Freshman 15 weight gain is to promote healthful eating and exercise habits by providing access to nutritional foods and exercise classes.

TERISUE SMITH-JACKSON

Bibliography

Brown, Cecelia. "The Information Trail of the 'Freshman 15'—A Systematic Review of A Health Myth Within the Research and Popular Literature." *Health Information and Libraries Journal* 25, no. 1 (2008):1–12.

Butler, Scott M., David R. Black, Carolyn L. Blue, and Randall J. Gretebeck. "Changes in Diet, Physical Activity and Body Weight in Female College Freshman." *American Journal of Health Behavior* 28, no. 1 (2004): 24–32.

Cooley, Eric, and Tamina Toray. "Body Image and Personality Predictors of Eating Disorder Symptoms during the College Years." *International Journal of Eating Disorders* 30, no. 1 (2001): 28–36.

Cooley, Eric, and Tamina Toray. "Disordered Eating in College Freshman Women: A Prospective Study." *Journal of American College Health* 49, no. 5 (2001): 229–35.

Delinsky, Sherrie S., and Terence G. Wilson. "Weight Gain, Dietary Restraint, and Disordered Eating in the Freshman Year of College." *Eating Behaviors* 9, no. 1 (2008): 82–90.

Graham, Melody A., and Amy L. Jones. "Freshman 15: Valid Theory or Harmful Myth?" *Journal of American College Health* 50, no. 4 (2002): 171–73.

Hajhosseini, Laleh, Tawni Holmes, Parinez Mohamadi, Vida Goudarzi, Lucy McProud, and Clarie B. Hollenbeck. "Changes in Body Weight, Body Composition and Resting Metabolic Rate (RMR) in Freshmen Students First-year University." *Journal of the American College of Nutrition* 25, no. 2 (2006): 123–27.

Hoffman, Daniel J., Peggy Policastro, Virginia Quick, and Soo-Kyung Lee. "Changes in Body Weight and Fat Mass of Men and Women in the First Year of College: A Study of the 'Freshman 15'." *Journal of American College Health* 55, no. 1 (2006): 41–45.

Holm-Denoma, Jill M., Thomas E. Joiner, Kathleen D. Vohs, and Todd F. Heatherton. "The 'Freshman Fifteen' (the 'Freshman Five' Actually): Predictors and Possible Explanations." *Health Psychology* 27, no. 1 (2008): S3–9.

Jung, Mary Elizabeth, Steven Russell Bray, and Kathleen Anne Martin Ginis. "Behavior Change and the Freshman 15: Tracking Physical Activity and Dietary Patterns in 1st-year University Women." *Journal of American College Health* 56, no. 5 (2008): 523–30.

Lowe, Michael R., Rachel A. Annunziato, Jessica Tuttman Markowitz, Elizabeth Didie, Dara L. Bellace, Lynn Riddell, Caralynn Maille, Shortie McKinney, and Eric Stice. "Multiple Types of Dieting Prospectively Predict Weight Gain during the Freshman Year of College." *Appetite* 47, no. 1 (2006): 83–90.

Mihalopoulos, Nicole L., Peggy Auinger, and Jonathon D. Klein. "The Freshman 15: Is it Real?" *Journal of American College Health* 56, no. 5 (2008): 531–33.

Rozin, Paul, Jordana Riklis, and Lara Margolis. "Mutual Exposure or Close Peer Relationships Do Not Seem to Foster Increased Similarity in Food, Music or Television Program Preferences." *Appetite* 42, no. 1 (2004): 41–48.

Serlachius, Anna, Mark Hamer, and Jane Wardle. "Stress and Weight Change in University Students in the United Kingdom." *Physiology & Behavior* 92, no. 4 (2007): 548–53.

Smith, TeriSue, Justine J. Reel, and Rosemary Thackeray. "Coping with 'Bad Body Image Days': Strategies from Freshmen College Women." *Body Image: An International Journal of Research* 8, no. 4 (2011): 335–42. doi: 10.1016/j.bodyim.2011.05.002

Vohs, Kathleen D., Todd F. Heatherton, and Marcia Herrin. "Disordered Eating and the Transition to College: A Prospective Study." *International Journal of Eating Disorders* 29, no. 3 (2001): 280–88.

Zielke, Judi. "Just for Teens. Mood Swings. Not the Freshman 15." *Diabetes Forecast* 56, no. 11 (2003): 47–48.

N

NATIONAL EATING DISORDERS ASSOCIATION

The National Eating Disorders Association (NEDA) is a nonprofit organization that was created to expand eating disorder prevention efforts and access to quality eating disorder treatment. The mission of NEDA is to support individuals and families affected by eating disorders and to stimulate initiatives to treat and prevent eating disorders. Every year, NEDA hosts an annual convention to bring in professional speakers who address treatment professionals, families, and individuals recovering from eating disorders. NEDA also offers research grants to young investigators who desire to advance the field and explore innovative topics related to eating disorders.

History of National Eating Disorders Association

NEDA was formed in 2001 when two existing organizations, Eating Disorders Awareness and Prevention (EDAP) and the American Anorexia Bulimia Association (AABA), merged into one association. A national toll-free helpline has been provided since 1999 to help individuals find eating disorder treatment. NEDA's vision is as follows: "NEDA envisions a world without eating disorders."

National Eating Disorders Awareness Week

On an annual basis, NEDA promotes a nationwide Eating Disorders Awareness Week every February to raise awareness about eating disorders. Each year has a theme and includes a variety of activities to mark the event, including walks to represent the awareness week. Groups around the country at universities, high schools, and treatment centers organize local and regional events to honor the week. For example, the University of Utah hosts a "Love Your Body Week" to promote positive body image and raise eating disorder awareness during the national eating disorders awareness week. Purple ribbons may be worn as a symbol of eating disorders awareness and memorials are held to honor those lost to eating disorders. During this week, many individuals and families are able to identify there is a problem, seek support for struggles with eating disorders, and find appropriate treatment.

Conclusion

Compared to organizations like the Academy for Eating Disorders and the International Association of Eating Disorder Professionals that are geared toward treatment professionals and researchers, NEDA strives to help individuals and families with eating disorders. NEDA has a distinct outreach focus as marked by a national effort to host an eating disorders awareness week and other prevention efforts. Additionally, NEDA serves as a unique resource for families, friends, coaches, treatment professionals, and educators with articles, videos, and toolkits.

JUSTINE J. REEL

See also: Academy for Eating Disorders; Eating Disorders Anonymous; International Association of Eating Disorder Professionals.

Bibliography

"NEDA." National Eating Disorders Association. Accessed November 23, 2011. www.nationaleatingdisorders.org.

NEUROFEEDBACK

Neurofeedback—also called EEG biofeedback, neurotherapy, or neurobiofeedback—is a method of biofeedback that utilizes real-time displays of electroencephalography to show brain wave activity. The goal of neurofeedback is to train people to gain self-control over electro-physiological processes in the human brain. Neurofeedback utilizes sensors that are placed on the scalp to measure activity, with measurements displayed using video displays or sound. The trainee (person receiving the neurofeedback) uses the signals from the displays to obtain information about his or her brain wave activity. When brain wave activity changes in the direction desired by the trainer who is directing the training, a positive reward feedback is given to the trainee. If the change is in the opposite direction from what was intended, then either different feedback is given or the provision of otherwise attained positive feedback is inhibited or blocked. Rewards and reinforcements can be as simple as a change in the pitch of a tone or as complex as a certain type of movement of a character in a video game.

Before an individual begins neurofeedback, a diagnostic test called a multi-site quantitative electroencephalogram (QEEG) can be performed to measure and identify abnormal patterns of cortical activity since many neurological and medical disorders are accompanied by such abnormalities. Clinical training with EEG feedback can then enable the individual to modify those patterns, which normalizes brain activity. Neurofeedback practice is growing rapidly with wide acceptance for application in a variety of medical, neurological, and emotional disorders.

History of Neurofeedback

In 1924, Hans Berger, a German psychiatrist, connected two small round disks of metal to his client's scalp and monitored a small current by using a ballistic galvanometer. From 1929 through 1938, Dr. Berger published several reports about his studies of EEGs. Much of the modern knowledge regarding neurofeedback is due to his research.

Berger analyzed EEGs through descriptive rather than numerical values. In 1932, Dr. Dietsch analyzed seven records of EEG and became the first researcher of quantitative (numerical analysis) EEG (QEEG), which is widely used today to measure abnormal brain patterns. In 1968, Joseph Kamiya published his groundbreaking alpha brain wave experiments in Psychology Today. Specifically, Kamiya found that alpha brain states were related to relaxation, which meant that alpha brain wave training showed potential for alleviating stress and stress-related conditions.

During the late 1960s and early 1970s, Barbara Brown authored several books on biofeedback, which increased public awareness about neurofeedback. Brown likened brain wave self-regulation to switching on an electric train. Within the past 10 years, neurofeedback has emphasized the significance of deep-state, or alpha-theta, training (predominantly nonintellectual, nonverbal, and not available to analysis in one's awakened state). Alpha-theta (deep-state) training has been used in the treatment of various addictions and anxiety. This low frequency training involves accessing painful or repressed memories through the alpha-theta state by tapping in to nonverbal, nonintellectual material.

Complementary Therapy

Neurofeedback and biofeedback are attractive approaches for individuals who are seeking alternatives to traditional psychotherapy; they allow the client to have a more active role in his or her health care. Secondly, neurofeedback represents a holistic emphasis on body, mind and spirit and provides noninvasive treatment. Finally, neurofeedback engages the body in the healing process by training the brain to send corrective messages to the body. Therefore, neurofeedback can be useful in the treatment of eating disorders and related concerns as an adjunct to other traditional or alternative therapies. Mirasol Eating Disorder Treatment Center in Tucson, Arizona, employs individual neurofeedback sessions at least three times weekly as part of its holistic treatment protocol with the belief that changes in the mind and emotions affect the body and changes in the body also influence the mind and emotions. NFB emphasizes on training individuals to self-regulate, gain awareness, increase control over their bodies, brains and nervous systems, and improve flexibility in physiological response. The positive effects of feedback training enhance health, learning, and performance. In clinical settings, neurofeedback and biofeedback are often combined with a wide variety of adjunctive therapies, including relaxation training, visualization, behavior therapies, client education, and other strategies.

Neurofeedback in Practice

A typical neurofeedback therapy session today may be as follows:

1. In a 90-minute intake, the client will complete a questionnaire that identifies the complaints. In some cases, a full EEG will be performed and recorded.
2. If a full EEG is advised, the recording is usually conducted on 19–21 sites on the scalp, which results in a brain map (QEEG). The brain map is compared to a

database to establish areas of over- and under-activity based on averages in brain maps of other individuals in the same age and gender brackets. Several commercial providers construct the databases.

3. The neurofeedback session involves placing sensors on the head. Feedback may include a certain tone, light, or game that will move and play when particular brain activity is detected by the system. For other brain activity, the tone, light or game is taken away.

4. A usual course of sessions entails 20–40 visits. At the beginning of each session, the client reports complaints and other mental effects. On the basis of this report, the therapy may be adjusted. In some cases, a client takes a feedback machine home for self-administered sessions.

Professional Standards and Neurofeedback

Neurofeedback and biofeedback rely on well-developed professional guidelines and standards for competent practice. A national certification organization, the Biofeedback Certification Institute of America, has established a blueprint of necessary knowledge and skills, and conducts examinations to qualify individuals for certification in general biofeedback and neurofeedback. For more information, please visit www.bcia.org.

Conclusion

Neurofeedback (neurotherapy, neurobiofeedback, or EEG biofeedback) is a type of biofeedback that uses real-time displays of electroencephalography to illustrate brain wave activity in order to train people to gain self-control over electro-physiological processes in the human brain. Within the past 10 years, neurofeedback has emphasized the significance of deep-state training that is predominantly nonintellectual, nonverbal, and not available to analysis in one's awakened state. Deep-state training has been used in the treatment of various addictions and anxiety and is now being used as an adjunct to traditional and alternative therapies in the treatment of eating disorders. Neurofeedback holds promise for individuals who suffer from eating disorders by providing an alternative method of accessing painful or repressed memories that are often correlated with eating disorder symptoms.

JULIANN M. COOK

Bibliography

Evans, James, and Andrew Abarbanel. *Introduction to Quantitative EEG and Neurofeedback.* San Diego: Academic Press, 1999.

Freeman, Lyn. *Mosby's Complementary & Alternative Medicine: A Research-Based Approach.* Philadelphia: Elsevier Science, 2008.

"Google Privacy Policy." http://mirasol.net/treatment-programs/holistic-treatment

Kaiser, David. "Basic Principles of Quantitative EEG." *Journal of Adult Development* 12 (2005): 2–3.

Yucha, Carolyn, and Doil Montgomery. *Evidenced-Based Practice in Biofeedback and Neurofeedback.* Las Vegas: University of Nevada, 2008.

NIA

Neuromuscular Integrative Action (Nia) is an expressive movement created in 1983 by Debbie and Carlos Rosas. According to the Californian founders, Nia is "a sensory-based movement practice that leads to health, wellness and fitness." The original principles of Nia promote the ability of a diverse population for individuals of all shapes and sizes to connect with the body, mind, emotions, and spirit. Nia instructors are trained to design classes for all age groups, individual needs, and abilities.

The movements of Nia are composed of 9 forms and 52 principles of the martial arts, dance arts, and healing arts. Each category delivers unique components of the original movements. From dance arts, participants experience components of jazz, modern, and Duncan dance. The movements from the healing arts incorporate yoga, Feldenkrais, and Alexander techniques. From the martial arts, participants learn elements of Tai Chi, Tae Kwon Do, and Aikido. Nia movements have been known to soothe and ease the 13 principal joints. The sensations from Nia also stimulate tendons, ligaments, and all 20 digits of the toes and fingers. Additionally, Nia massages internal organs. Through practicing Nia, individuals can improve overall balance and physical strength.

Nia and Eating Disorder Treatment

Nia has been widely adopted as an effective therapeutic tool in the comprehensive treatment of eating disorders. Nia gently provides body-mind awareness and an understanding of the whole body. Through Nia movements, clients are encouraged to observe their thoughts, emotions, and the body. The purpose of Nia in eating disorder treatment is to provide a nonjudgmental world in which to evaluate sensations of pleasure, listen to body cues, and trust the function of body movements. Typically, Nia classes for eating disorder treatment need to be modified based on the clients' medical conditions—blood pressure, electrolyte concentrations, EKG, body weight, and bone density. In order to provide a safe and enjoyable experience in eating disorder treatment, Nia instructors are highly encouraged to complete training in eating disorders.

Conclusion

Nia has been used as a form of fitness and movement for many populations. It has been shown to be beneficial for eating disorder clients, especially as a group therapy option within a structured residential setting. Nia can be modified and individualized for persons of all ages, body shapes and fitness levels, and even for those in differing phases of treatment and recovery.

MAYA MIYAIRI

Bibliography

Lowry, Anne. "Nia: The Fountain of Youth?" *New Life Journal* (2007): 20

Mearder, Lori L. "The Nia Technique: Through Movement We Find Health." The Psychotherapy and Training Collective of New York (2008). http://www.psychotherapistsnyc.com/20090818.asp

Oberliesen, Elise. "Freshness Factor Breathes Life into Nia Routine." *American Fitness* 3 (2009): 38–39

NIGHT EATING SYNDROME

Night Eating Syndrome (NES) refers to dysfunctional eating patterns that occur relative to the time of the day and have been linked to obesity in some studies. NES was first described by Stunkard in 1955 as an eating disorder characterized by consumption of foods with low caloric intake in the earlier part of the day (morning anorexia), night eating or "evening hyperphagia," and sleep disturbances. The definition of NES has since been expanded to include another characteristic—awakening from sleep to eat (nocturnal ingestions). Sleep disruptions and mood disturbances have both been associated with these disordered eating behaviors. Although NES has not received a separate diagnosis in the eating disorder section of the *Diagnostic and Statistical Manual of Mental Disorders IV-TR,* individuals with NES typically receive the diagnosis of Eating Disorder Not Otherwise Specified. Diagnostic criteria that should be used to distinguish NES from other eating disorders are discussed below.

Proposed Diagnostic Criteria for NES

During the First International Night Eating Symposium (April 26, 2008) held in Minneapolis, doctors and other experts developed a set of provisional research diagnostic criteria for NES. As originally conceived, NES is characterized by "significantly higher food intake in the evening or during night." This is measured using the following criteria: at least 25 percent of food intake should have been consumed after the evening meal; at least two episodes of nocturnal eating (awakening from sleep to eat) should have occurred per week; awareness of the nocturnal eating episodes should be present; and, at least three of the following features should be reported: (1) Lack of desire to eat in the morning, or having no breakfast on four or more mornings per week; (2) Having a strong urge to eat between dinner and sleep onset and/or during the night; (3) Insomnia (difficulty getting to sleep or staying asleep) at least four nights per week; (4) Having the belief that one must eat in order to return to sleep; and (5) Depressed mood or mood deterioration in the evening hours. To meet the research diagnostic criteria for NES an individual must maintain these dysfunctional patterns of eating for at least three months, and report difficulty participating in daily life activities; moreover, the individual's behavior should not be attributable to other issues (e.g., substance abuse, medications). It is the hope of these researchers that by having a set of clearly defined criteria, NES can receive more recognition and can be understood as a separate eating disorder from anorexia nervosa, bulimia nervosa, and binge eating disorder.

Prevalence of NES

The prevalence of NES in the general population appears to be lower (1.5%) than for obesity clinic patients (6–14%). Among individuals undergoing bariatric surgery the prevalence of NES ranges from 8 percent to 42 percent. In examining prevalence data, trends have been found for: (1) obesity status; (2) age; (3) gender; (4) ethnicity; and (5) day of the week. Although NES is much more common among obese individuals, NES does occur in individuals who are not necessarily overweight or obese. Adolescents were most likely to meet NES criteria and the elderly were least likely to exhibit NES symptoms. NES was more common among males than females and black Americans were more likely to experience NES than other ethnicities. Interestingly, survey research determined that night eating occurs more often on weekends than weekdays.

Assessing Night Eating Syndrome

The Night Eating Questionnaire (NEQ) is a 14-item survey designed to assess behavioral and psychological symptoms of NES using a 5-point Likert scale with responses ranging from "not at all likely" to "very likely." Current items of NEQ measure the presence of morning hunger, the times when food consumption occurs, food cravings, and control over food consumption after dinner and throughout the night. Items also assess mood disturbances and night eating.

Conclusion

Night eating syndrome is a less well-known condition associated with eating disorders. Individuals with NES consume vastly different amounts of food from day to night. Although NES is not a current diagnostic category in the DSM-IV-TR, the syndrome is expected to receive increased attention in future versions of the clinician's manual.

JUSTINE J. REEL

Bibliography

Allison, Kelly C., Scott J. Crow, Rebecca R. Reeves, Della Smith West, John P. Foreyt, Vicki G. DiLillo, Thomas A. Wadden, Robert W. Jeffery, Brent Van Dorsten, and Albert J. Stunkard. "Binge Eating Disorder and Night Eating Syndrome in Adults with Type 2 Diabetes." *Obesity* 15(5) (2007): 1–12.

Allison, Kelly C., Jennifer D. Lundgren, John P. O'Reardon, Nicole S. Martino, David B. Sarwer, Thomas A. Wadden, Ross D. Crosby, Scott G. Engel, and Albert J. Stunkard. "The Night Eating Questionnaire (NEQ): Psychometric Properties of a Measure of Severity of the Night Eating Syndrome." *Eating Behaviors* 9 (2008): 62–72.

Allison, Kelly C., Jennifer D. Lundgren, John P. O'Reardon, Allan Geliebter, Marci E. Gluck, Piergiuseppe Vinai, James E. Mitchell, Carlos H. Schenck, Michael J. Howell, Scott J. Crow, Scott Engel, Yael Latzer, Orna Tzischinsky, Mark W. Mahowald, and Albert J. Stunkard. "Proposed Diagnostic Criteria for Night Eating Syndrome." *International Journal of Eating Disorders* 43 (2010): 241–47.

Grave, Riccardo Dalle, Simona Calugi, Antonella Ruocco, and Giulio Marchesini. "Night Eating Syndrome and Weight Loss Outcome in Obese Patients." *International Journal of Eating Disorders* 44 (2011): 150–56.

Striegel-Moore, Ruth H., Debra L. Franko, Douglas Thompson, Sandra Affenito, Alexis May, and Helena C. Kraemer. "Exploring the Typology of Night Eating Syndrome." *International Journal of Eating Disorders* 41 (2008): 411–18.

Townsend, Ann B. "Night Eating Syndrome." *Holistic Nursing Practice* (2007): 217–21.

NUTRITION TREATMENT APPROACHES

Nutrition therapy is provided for a variety of individuals with medical or mental health issues. Nutritional support and treatment is often provided by various health care workers; however, a registered dietitian is uniquely trained to provide nutrition therapy and education for diverse populations. A registered dietitian conducts nutrition assessments, identifies and implements nutrition interventions, helps the individual normalize eating behaviors, supports the individual through his or her concerns associated with food and weight-related behavioral change, and provides nutrition education.

Nutrition and Eating Disorder Clients

A registered dietitian (RD) is naturally a key component of a comprehensive eating disorder treatment program. It is necessary for the RD to understand the medical and psychological aspects of eating disorders, as she or he is part of a collaborative multidisciplinary treatment team along with other treatment professionals who typically include a psychologist and physician. The specific goals for nutrition therapy can vary depending on the individual and eating disorder, but the ultimate goals are as follows: (1) To resolve nutrition-related complications, (2) To normalize eating behaviors, (3) To decrease fears and anxieties associated with food, and (4) To provide education to dispel inaccurate beliefs related to food and weight. Treating eating disorder clients involves conducting a nutritional assessment, setting nutritional goals, implementing meal planning, and providing support for the client's nutritional changes. In addition, the RD will also help to identify and monitor a healthy target weight range with frequent weight checks. Although ideally a separate exercise expert (e.g., exercise therapist, physical therapist, personal trainer) would manage exercise behaviors as part of a comprehensive treatment team, the RD often performs this function.

Nutrition Assessment for Eating Disorder Clients

A comprehensive nutrition assessment includes conducting a detailed medical, dietary, weight, and eating disorder history. Additionally, the RD should inquire about any prescription medication, dietary supplements, or other over-the-counter medications which may interfere with nutrition status. The assessment allows the RD to evaluate an individual's current dietary intake (including food preferences and allergies), assess nutritional status, determine a target weight goal for optimal health, and assess nutrition knowledge and beliefs. The RD uses the information gathered from the assessment to determine the appropriate nutritional treatment for the individual.

Nutrition Goals Specific to Anorexia Nervosa

Because a primary characteristic of anorexia nervosa is the refusal to maintain one's body weight at a minimally normal weight for age and height, the initial step for treatment involves addressing acute medical complications and the reversal of weight loss. An individual in the early stages of the refeeding process needs to be monitored for possible complications (e.g., arrhythmia) associated with refeeding syndrome.

There is a risk for refeeding syndrome during the early phases of the reintroduction of food, specifically carbohydrates, into the body of a significantly malnourished individual. Refeeding syndrome results as the body adjusts from a catabolic to anabolic state. As carbohydrates are introduced into the body, the pancreas releases insulin resulting in the cellular uptake of magnesium, potassium, and phosphorus. The sudden drop in the serum concentration of these electrolytes can lead to cardiac complications such as arrhythmias. It is essential that individuals who are greater than 30 percent below their ideal body weight or who have rapidly lost weight are closely monitored for symptoms of refeeding syndrome. The initial caloric intake for anorexia nervosa treatment may start as low as 30–40 calories/kilogram/day. Once medical stability is established, caloric intake can safely be increased, by gradual increments of 200–300 calories every 3 to 4 days, to promote a weight gain of 1–3 pounds per week.

Nutrition Goals Specific to Bulimia Nervosa

Bulimia nervosa is characterized by chaotic eating behaviors with episodes of binge eating followed by compensatory behaviors such as self-induced vomiting, excessive exercise, starvation, or use of laxatives/diuretics. Initially, nutrition treatment should focus on developing a meal plan to help reduce episodes of binge eating and purging, balance intake of carbohydrates, proteins, and fats, and normalize biochemical abnormalities. Nutrition education is essential to help an individual with bulimia nervosa understand the concepts of normal eating and nutritional requirements, as well as the physical and psychological consequences associated with binge eating and compensatory behaviors.

Nutrition Goals for Binge Eating Disorder

Binge eating disorder is characterized by repeated episodes of binge eating, without the compensatory behaviors seen in bulimia nervosa. As in the case of bulimia nervosa, nutrition treatment begins with reducing binge eating episodes as well as following a balanced diet. Chronic dieting is often documented among binge eaters, and therefore, the negative aspects of chronic dieting need to be discussed. Any medical complications associated with binge eating disorder—such as obesity, heart disease, hypertension, type 2 diabetes, hyperlipidemia—must be addressed as part of treatment.

Meal Planning for Eating Disorder Clients

The early stages of nutrition therapy involve stabilizing acute medical complications, stopping and preventing further weight loss, and starting the process of increasing food intake or decreasing binge eating and/or purging behaviors. Regardless of the eating disorder diagnosis, the purpose of meal planning remains to assist the individual in developing the ability to select a well-balanced diet, in a carefree manner, while incorporating a variety of foods. This may be anxiety-provoking for many individuals; feeling a loss of control and a fear of excessive weight gain is common. Meal planning is not intended to be a permanent solution, but it provides a way to guide the individual away from disordered eating behaviors.

Meal plans should be tailored to meet an individual's specific requirements as well as his or her food preferences. Meal plans should have a balance of carbohydrates, proteins, and fats as well as vitamins and minerals. Nutrition status, medical conditions, current dietary intake, growth, and physical activity need to be taken into account when determining one's overall nutritional needs.

Exchange List for Meal Planning

The exchange list for meal planning was initially developed to help individuals with diabetes mellitus manage their intake of carbohydrates and fats. The exchange system organizes foods based on the proportions of carbohydrates, proteins, and fats they contain. Portion sizes are determined to allow for the food on each list to have similar energy values. Foods found on the same list can be interchanged without affecting the total calories and balance of carbohydrates, proteins, and fats.

The exchange list has become a popular approach for the treatment of eating disorders; it is a way to encourage clients to eat a balanced meal. Specifically, the eating disorder client is prescribed a meal plan indicating how many exchanges he or she needs from each food list. The client is allowed more flexibility in making food choices as compared to a rigid meal plan with pre-set foods; at the same time, adequate nutritional intake is also ensured.

Food Guide Pyramid (MyPyramid)

The Food Guide Pyramid was initially developed to help teach nutrition guidelines to the general population. Foods were categorized into six basic groups and recommendations for the number of servings from each food group were determined. The traditional Food Guide Pyramid was updated in 2005 in order to individualize the recommended caloric intake for an individual and include physical activity. In 2011, the Food Guide Pyramid/MyPyramid, was replaced with MyPlate. MyPlate is a visual depiction of the 2010 Dietary Guidelines for America and is used as a means to represent how to incorporate all of the food groups into a meal using the visual of a plate to replace the pyramid. A meal plan constructed from emphasizing categories of food groups can be useful in the treatment of eating disorders and in recovery. Developing healthy meal patterns, while ensuring a proper distribution of the essential nutrients, can support a sustained healthy lifestyle beyond the eating disorder.

Calorie Counting

Individuals with eating disorders often enter the treatment process compulsively tracking their calorie, fat, or carbohydrate intake. Eating disorder clients are often resistant to relinquishing control over monitoring the precise nutrient breakdown in the foods they are consuming. Calorie counting as a nutritional treatment approach may need to be used initially, until the individual is willing to use another method such as the exchange list, as a meal plan. The sole or continued use of calorie counting may lead to a poor distribution of nutrients in the diet and will not address underlying emotional issues with food. Therefore, other approaches (e.g., intuitive eating) should be the ultimate goal in nutrition therapy with eating disordered individuals.

Intuitive Eating

Intuitive eating refers to a nutritional philosophy built on the concept of recognizing and listening to one's biological cues with regard to making food choices. Intuitive eating allows an individual to rely on his or her internal signals to make food selections without guilt or ethical dilemma. It is important to recognize that intuitive eating is not likely to be successful during the weight restoration process and it may take several months for individuals with anorexia and bulimia nervosa to detect hunger and fullness cues. However, nutrition therapy allows these individuals to work through the process of becoming comfortable with eating.

Nutrition therapy is not limited to increasing caloric intake and weight restoration. Eating disordered individuals have a variety of disordered food beliefs and behaviors. It is essential that individuals are challenged to evaluate their food rules and behaviors. Individuals will often use their eating disorder to avoid certain foods or food groups. Food challenges are used to allow the individual an opportunity to confront his or her distorted thoughts associated with all foods.

Determining Target Weight Range

Numerous formulas and charts are available to determine an ideal body weight. In calculating an individual's target weight range, it is important for the treatment provider to consider weight history, body composition, genetics, growth state, and physiological state. The Body Mass Index (BMI) is a simple calculation to assess the adiposity based on height and weight. BMI has been criticized as a physical marker because it does not differentiate between fat mass and lean body mass and does not consider body frame while making the calculations. BMI is calculated by dividing weight (kg) by height (m²). These standards indicate that an individual is considered to be underweight at a BMI of less than 18.5 kg/m2. In adults, a BMI of 17.5 kg/m2 is generally accepted as 85 percent of ideal body weight.

The Hamwi equation, developed by Dr. George Hamwi, is another method which can be used to calculate an ideal body weight. Height and frame structure are accounted for in this measurement. The formula used for men is 106 pounds for the first five feet plus 6 pounds for every inch over five feet. For women, 100 pounds for the first five feet plus 5 pounds for every inch over five feet. Ten percent is added or subtracted for a large and small frame, respectively.

The Metropolitan Life Insurance weight charts were developed to determine a desirable weight for a decreased risk of mortality. However, the purpose of these weight charts has shifted to identifying an ideal weight for height and frame size. The height value is based on height with shoes (1-inch heels) and indoor clothing (5 pounds for men and 3 pounds for women). Additionally, it is not appropriate for use in children and adolescents.

Ideal weight charts, formulas, and absolute BMI values need to be used with caution in children and adolescents. They are going through periods of growth, resulting in changes in BMI. Target weight ranges need to be adjusted as growth occurs. Pre-illness growth charts can be used as a guide in determining appropriate BMI and weight percentile goals. Target body weight ranges should not be determined using a single formula or chart. Multiple factors need to be considered including weight history, familial weight history, body composition, and physiological and cognitive functionality. Due to natural fluctuations in weight, it is best to recommend a target weight range, rather than an absolute weight.

Weight Restoration Techniques

Complete weight restoration to a healthy weight for one's frame is essential in the treatment of an eating disorder. Maintaining a below-normal weight inhibits psychotherapy, prevents an individual from fully addressing body image concerns, and potentially increases the risk of adverse health effects. Due to the increased caloric requirement for weight restoration, it may be difficult for an individual to rely solely on solid foods. While using solid foods is most ideal, liquid nutrition support may be necessary in conditions such as (1) persistent failure to gain weight despite oral intake; (2) life-threatening weight loss; (3) worsening psychological state; or (4) individual is unwilling to cooperate with oral feedings.

Liquid nutrition supplementation can be utilized orally or enterally (feeding tube). There are several liquid nutrition supplemental drinks that can be consumed orally in conjunction with solid foods. These drinks allow for a balanced source of carbohydrates, proteins, and fats in addition to vitamins and minerals. Oral liquid nutrition supplements should be used when an individual is unable to consume his or her caloric goal due to physical and/or psychological issues. Ultimately, supplemental drinks should be weaned as intake of solid foods allows for appropriate weight gain and weight stabilization at target weight range.

In some circumstances, enteral nutrition is necessary to either complement oral feedings or provide 100 percent of nutritional needs. Enteral nutrition support allows for the delivery of liquid nutrition via a tube entering the body (through the nasal cavity or the stomach) into the gastrointestinal tract. Nutrition can be delivered to the body continuously through the day and/or night or via bolus feedings (infusion of a larger volume of liquid nutrition supplement—up to 500 mL—into the stomach in a time span of less than 30 minutes) several times during the day. Continuous feeds may inhibit appetite, which can undermine oral intake.

In extreme cases of malnutrition or gastrointestinal disturbances, parental nutrition (PN) may be used. PN allows for the delivery of nutrients intravenously rather than through the gastrointestinal tract. This method of feeding is more invasive and consequently leads to a greater risk of infection and complications. Therefore, PN should be reserved for cases in which oral or enteral feeds are not practical.

Exercise

Individuals with eating disorders commonly engage in physical activity which can undermine nutritional goals. Once an individual is medically cleared to participate in physical activity, the RD needs to ensure caloric recommendations are increased according to the level of activity. Nutrition therapy should include education on the importance of nutrition in activity performance. Nutrition rehabilitation is not limited to achieving full weight restoration and consuming an appropriate caloric amount. Ultimately the goal of nutrition therapy is to assist an individual to reach the point where he or she can eat without following a meal plan or engaging in compensatory behaviors; all this while maintaining optimal medical and weight status.

Conclusion

Nutrition counseling is an integral component in the treatment of eating disorders. Nutrition treatment is not limited to weight restoration and compliance with a meal plan, but also includes education. The ultimate goal is to aid an individual to follow flexible eating patterns to support growth, physical activity, and overall well-being.

AMELIA MCBRIDE

See also: Body Mass Index; Intuitive Eating.

Bibliography

Henry, Beverly W., and Amy D. Ozier. "Position of the American Dietetic Associate: Nutrition Intervention in the Treatment of Anorexia Nervosa, Bulimia Nervosa, and Other Eating Disorders." *Journal of American Dietetic Association* 106 (2006): 2073–2082.
Reiff, Dan W., and Kathleen Kim Lampson Reiff. *Eating Disorders: Nutrition Therapy in the Recovery Process, 2nd ed.* Mercer Island: Life Enterprises, 2007.

Reiter, Christina Scribner, and Leah Graves. "Nutrition Therapy for Eating Disorders." *Nutrition in Clinical Practice* 25 (2010): 122–36.

Setnick, Jessica. *The Eating Disorder Clinical Pocket Guide: Quick Reference for Health Care Providers.* Dallas: Snack Time Press, 2005.

Tribole, Evelyn, and Elyse Resch. *Intuitive Eating: A Revolutionary Program That Works.* New York: St. Martin's Griffin, 2003.

Woolsey, Monika M. *Eating Disorders: A Clinical Guide to Counseling and Treatment.* Chicago: American Dietetic Association, 2002.

NUTRITIONAL DEFICIENCIES

Vitamins and minerals are micronutrients that the body requires to function correctly. Food choices and disordered eating behaviors vary among individuals with eating disorders; therefore, the types of nutrient deficiencies that exist among these clients vary. For example, those who avoid dairy products may have inadequate calcium and vitamin D intake. In addition, many eating disorder clients restrict their dietary fat intake. Fat soluble vitamins, which include vitamins A, D, E, and K, are absorbed in conjunction with fat; thus, inadequate fat in the diet may lead to deficiencies in these nutrients. Nutritional deficiencies can also result from inadequate dietary intake or from increased losses via fluids (i.e., as an effect of vomiting, laxative abuse, or diuretic abuse). Some of the most common nutrient deficiencies are summarized below.

Electrolytes

Electrolytes, such as sodium, potassium, chloride, magnesium, and phosphorus, can be impacted by many different types of weight control methods, including laxative or diuretic abuse, vomiting, excessive exercise, and dietary restriction. Electrolytes must be balanced outside and inside of the cells in order for muscles and nerves to function properly and to maintain acid-base balance. Electrolyte imbalances can cause muscle weakness or cramping, fatigue, irregular heartbeat, dizziness, confusion, and even death if not treated. Electrolyte levels are closely monitored and replenished when nutrition is re-introduced and gradually increased in the malnourished client to assess for refeeding syndrome, in which an influx of electrolytes into cells leads to dangerously low levels of potassium, phosphorus, or magnesium outside of the cells.

Thiamine

Thiamine (Vitamin B1) is required for the metabolism of carbohydrate. Although thiamine is found in a wide variety of foods, low overall energy intake may lead to deficiency of this nutrient. Because there is an increased demand for thiamine when nutrition is re-introduced to the malnourished client, nutrition support protocols generally recommend thiamine supplementation upon initiating a refeeding regimen to avoid acute thiamine deficiency. Deficiency in thiamine can lead to a syndrome called Wernicke's Encephalopathy, which is characterized by neurological symptoms such as confusion, lack of muscle coordination, involuntary eye movements, and short term memory loss. One study found that 38 percent of anorexia nervosa clients had laboratory values indicative of thiamine deficiency, and there have been several case reports regarding the diagnosis of Wernicke's Encephalopathy in anorexia nervosa clients.

Calcium and Vitamin D

Calcium is a mineral that is predominantly stored in the bones and teeth to support their function. When blood calcium levels are low, calcium is released from the bone to increase blood levels; therefore, the assessment of serum calcium levels may not accurately indicate calcium status. Because bones break down when stored calcium is leached into the blood, bone mineral density may be a better marker of calcium deficiency over the long term; calcium intake analysis based on food records could be used for a short-term indication. It is recommended that eating disordered clients who are not consuming adequate calcium, and those who are amenorrheic, should consume 1500 milligrams per day. Calcium supplementation is often required until dietary intake is sufficient.

Similarly, vitamin D also plays a role in bone health by promoting calcium absorption from the gut, reabsorption of calcium by the kidneys, and the maintenance of blood calcium levels. It also supports immune function, and is currently being studied for its role in decreasing the risk for autoimmune diseases (e.g., type 1 diabetes, multiple sclerosis, rheumatoid arthritis) and certain types of cancer. Sunlight is the main natural source of vitamin D as it activates vitamin D synthesis in the body. There are very few natural food sources of vitamin D, but many dairy products are fortified with vitamin D. Those individuals who avoid dairy products, include very little fat in their diet, and receive very little sunlight exposure are at high risk for vitamin D deficiency. Many calcium supplements also contain vitamin D, but additional supplementation should be provided if vitamin D laboratory values are low.

Zinc

Zinc is a mineral that has numerous physiological functions, including growth and development, immunity, neurological function, taste perception and appetite, and reproduction. Symptoms of zinc deficiency include stunted growth, weight loss, increased infection risk, poor wound healing, menstrual dysfunction, poor appetite, altered taste, and mood disturbances. One study found that 40 percent of bulimia nervosa clients and 54 percent of anorexia nervosa clients had poor zinc status. In addition, vegetarian clients with anorexia nervosa, which describes approximately half of this population, have been found to have lower dietary intake of zinc than non-vegetarian anorexia nervosa clients, as red meat and certain types of seafood are rich in this mineral. Zinc is also not absorbed as well from meatless sources, such as whole grains, nuts, vegetables, and legumes, due to the high fiber content; thus, zinc requirements may be higher for those who do not consume meat products. The body can also lose significant amounts of zinc with high stool output and other fluid losses as described above. Some research has shown that anorexia nervosa clients who receive zinc supplementation have a higher rate of weight gain than clients who do not receive supplementation.

Iron

Iron is found in red blood cells, which transport oxygen to different parts of the body. Iron consumption may be lacking in eating disordered individuals who follow vegetarian or vegan diets, as iron from plant sources is not absorbed as well as iron from meat sources. However, vitamin C enhances iron absorption; thus, it is beneficial to eat iron-containing foods with foods or beverages that have high vitamin C content. Iron deficiency can lead to fatigue, difficulty in concentration, and increased risk for illnesses or infections. It is unclear as to whether eating disorder clients are at a higher risk for iron deficiency as research results have varied and it has been suggested that amenorrhea may protect against iron deficiency anemia due to reduced blood loss. During nutritional recovery, however, iron needs may increase as tissues are rebuilding and more red blood cells are being produced.

Conclusion

Micronutrient status varies among individuals with eating disorders and may be an ongoing process to optimize nutritional status. Thus, it is important for clinicians to routinely assess food/beverage consumption and dietary supplement use for adequacy of intake and monitor biochemical indices of deficiency during treatment.

HOLLY E. DOETSCH

See also: Refeeding Syndrome; Zinc.

Bibliography

Bakan, Rita, Carl L. Birmingham, Laurel Aeberhardt, and Elliot M. Goldner. "Dietary Zinc Intake of Vegetarian and Nonvegetarian Patients with Anorexia Nervosa." *International Journal of Eating Disorders* 13, no. 2 (1993): 229–33.

Birmingham, Carl L., Elliot M. Goldner, and Rita Bakan. "Controlled Trial of Zinc Supplementation in Anorexia Nervosa." *International Journal of Eating Disorders* 15, no. 3 (1994): 251–55.

Humphries, Laurie, Beverly Vivian, Mary A. Stuart, and Craig J. McClain. "Zinc Deficiency and Eating Disorders." *Journal of Clinical Psychiatry* 50, no. 12 (1989): 456–59.

Kennedy, Andrew, Michael Kohn, Ahti Lammi, and Simon Clarke. "Iron Status and Haematological Changes in Adolescent Female Inpatients with Anorexia Nervosa." *Journal of Paediatrics and Child Health* 40, no. 8 (2004): 430–32.

Khan, Laeeq U. R., Jamil Ahmed, Shakeeb Khan, and John MacFie. "Refeeding Syndrome: A Literature Review." *Gastroenterology Research and Practice* 2011 (2011): 1–6. Accessed June 28, 2011. http://www.hindawi.com/journals/grp/.

Misra, Madhusmita, Patrika Tsai, Ellen J. Anderson, Jane L. Hubbard, Katie Gallagher, Leslie A. Soyka, Karen K. Miller, David B. Herzog, and Anne Klibanski. "Nutrient Intake in Community-Dwelling Adolescent Girls with Anorexia Nervosa and in Healthy Controls." *American Journal of Clinical Nutrition* 84, no. 4 (2006): 698–706.

Nova, Esther, Irene Lopez-Vidriero, Pilar Varela, Olga Toro, Jose Casas, and Ascension Marcos. "Indicators of Nutritional Status in Restricting-Type Anorexia Nervosa Patients: A 1-Year Follow-Up Study." *Clinical Nutrition* 23 (2004): 1353–1359.

Peters, Todd E., Matthew Parvin, Christopher Petersen, Vivian C. Faircloth, and Richard L. Levine. "A Case Report of Wernicke's Encephalopathy in a Pediatric Patient with Anorexia Nervosa—Restricting Type." *Journal of Adolescent Health* 40, no. 4 (2007): 376–83.

Setnick, Jessica. "Micronutrient Deficiencies and Supplementation in Anorexia and Bulimia Nervosa: A Review of the Literature." *Nutrition in Clinical Practice* 25, no. 2 (2010): 137–42.

Winston, Anthony P., C. P. Jamieson, Webster Madira, Nicholas M. Gatward, and Robert L. Palmer. "Prevalence of Thiamine Deficiency in Anorexia Nervosa." *International Journal of Eating Disorders* 28, no. 4 (2000): 451–54.

O

OBESITY

Obesity refers to a medical condition wherein a person has a Body Mass Index (BMI) equal to or greater than 30, which puts him or her at risk for numerous health conditions including type 2 diabetes, cardiovascular disease, stroke, and some cancers. The prevalence of obesity among children, adolescents, and adults has increased rapidly over the past 30 years. In fact, some researchers predict that this obesity epidemic will contribute to a decline in life expectancy among Americans in the 21st century.

Prevalence of Obesity

Among adults, the obesity prevalence doubled between 1980 and 2004 with recent reports showing that two-thirds of adults are overweight (i.e., have a BMI of 25.0–29.9) or obese. In the United States, 28 percent of men, 34 percent of women, and almost 50 percent of non-Hispanic black women are reported to be obese. Obesity trends affect all racial and ethnic groups, all states and socioeconomic strata. However, the largest increases in obesity have been observed among children and minority populations. Approximately 2 million U.S. children are estimated to be obese, with a recent study suggesting that 36 percent of the pediatric population is overweight or obese.

Causes of Obesity

The causes of obesity are many; they include genetic, biological, and lifestyle factors related to one's environment. Genetic factors, associated with having a family history of particular body types and shapes, can be passed down to future generations. Biological factors represent a variety of factors that contribute to a body's ability to regulate hunger and fullness and digest food efficiently. However, lifestyle factors are modifiable. At the most basic level, weight gain that leads to obesity corresponds to an energy imbalance (i.e., more energy or food intake than what is required for energy expenditure needs). Furthermore, U.S. adults and their children have been shown to eat fast and convenient foods that are high in fat, sugar, and caloric content while being relatively inactive. Both children and adults fail to meet recommended quantities of fruits and vegetables or levels of physical activity required to remain at optimal health. Physical education classes have been decreased nationally and this has removed a structured opportunity for physical activity.

Screen time (i.e., amount of time spent watching television and viewing other electronic media) has often been blamed for increased inactivity among children and adults. For example, it has been reported that children who watch more than two hours of television per day consume less fruits and vegetables and more of high energy drinks and energy-dense foods; they also engage in more snacking behavior. An Australian study found that use of electronic media by parents, siblings, and friends led to increased sedentary behavior and more screen time.

Treatment of Obesity

Traditional treatment of obesity has included weight management approaches designed to change nutritional habits and reduce food intake while increasing activity levels with weight loss as the primary goal. However, obesity treatment professionals are recognizing the need to provide family-based treatment interventions (e.g., BodyWorks) that involve shaping the family environment to encourage healthy habits and education among parents and siblings. Additionally, the importance of acknowledging the psychological relationship with food and emotional eating has been noted and is slowly being incorporated into treatment programs. There have been divergent viewpoints related to whether obesity treatment should be based on weight management (i.e., monitoring weight loss and gain) or a "Health at Every Size" approach to address health and obesity.

Prevention of Obesity

Obesity prevention has been a major focus for local, state, and national efforts in attempts to reverse the trend of the obesity epidemic among youth and their parents. Prevention programs include school-based and community-based programs using a variety of approaches to improve nutritional habits and increase physical activity. School-based programs may include efforts to reinstate physical education classes or to implement after-school programming that includes more movement rather than screen time. Nutritional changes may be addressed in a variety of ways including policy-related moves to remove vending machines, change nutrient contents of school lunches, and/or provide educational classes about healthy eating. Community-based programs aim to address nutrition and physical activity recommendations as well, but may be implemented with children, adolescents or adults in a community setting (e.g., Boys and Girls Club, recreation center, or Head-Start program). Recently, the First Lady of the United States, Michelle Obama, has placed much attention on the need to address childhood obesity with her Let's Move campaign. Additionally, community-based efforts may target community weight loss goals, neighborhood walkabouts, and trail building to improve built environments for health.

Obesity and Eating Disorders

The focus on the rising obesity rates among children and adults has minimized the severity of the eating disorder problem in this country. In some cases, obesity

prevention efforts have actively promoted weight loss while inadvertently pushing a dieting mentality. This dieting mentality has led to restricting, fear of weight
gain, and fasting among adolescents and children and can contribute to disordered
eating behaviors. Therefore, researchers are slowly realizing the need to integrate
obesity and eating disorder prevention efforts so that individuals can learn how
to develop healthier behaviors that result in a positive relationship with food, exercise, and body. The Planet Health program discussed in a separate entry shows
promise for reducing both obesity and eating disorder outcomes.

It is expected that as many as one-third to one-half of overweight and obese individuals meet the criteria for binge eating disorder. Therefore, it is important that
when obesity is addressed, emotional eating and disordered eating characteristics
are also recognized. For example, individuals can move along the spectrum from
one eating disorder (e.g., binge eating disorder) and develop new disordered behaviors which lead to a different eating disorder (e.g., anorexia nervosa). It is critical that underlying psychological and emotional issues be treated for individuals
who are overweight and obese. This relationship between obesity and binge eating disorder is illustrated by the following video: http://youtu.be/zrYANKK0p2A.

Conclusion

Obesity rates have skyrocketed in the United States and globally, and this has contributed to the inflation of type 2 diabetes and other medical conditions. Identified
causes of obesity have included lack of physical activity, poor diet, and frequent
screen time in addition to genetic and biological factors. Obesity treatment and
prevention programs are implemented in schools and communities and may incorporate parent education to influence changes within the family environment. It
is important to recognize the link between obesity and eating disorders so that a
dieting mentality does not emerge from obesity prevention efforts. Additionally,
binge eating disorder is common among individuals who are overweight and
obese, which underscores the importance of addressing emotional eating and psychological factors of obesity.

JUSTINE J. REEL

See also: Body Mass Index; BodyWorks; Health at Every Size Approach; Let's Move; Planet
Health.

Bibliography

Boutelle, Kerri N., Robyn W. Birkeland, Peter J. Hannan, Mary Story, and Dianne Neumark-
    Sztainer. "Associations between Maternal Concern for Healthful Eating and Maternal
    Eating Behaviors, Home Food Availability, and Adolescent Eating Behaviors." *Journal
    of Nutrition Education Behavior* 39 (2007): 248–56. doi: 10/1016/j.jneb.2007.04.179.
Brown, Judith E., Dorothy H. Broom, Jan M. Nicholson, and Michael Bittman. "Do Work-
    ing Mothers Raise Couch Potato Kids? Maternal Employment and Children's Life-
    style Behaviours and Weight in Early Childhood." *Social Science & Medicine* 70 (2010):
    1816–1824. doi: 10.1016/j.socscimed.2010.01.040.
"Chevese Turner Educates about Binge Eating Disorder and Obesity." YouTube.com. Last
    modified November 11, 2010. http://youtu.be/zrYANKK0p2A.

Granich, Joanna, Michael Rosenberg, Matthew Knuiman, and Anna Timperio. "Understanding Children's Sedentary Behaviour: A Qualitative Study of the Family Home Environment." *Health Education Research* 25, no. 2 (2010): 199–210. doi: 10.1093/her/cyn025.

Isnard, Pascale, Gregory Michel, Marie Laure Frelut, Gilbert Vila, Bruno Falissard, Wadih Naja, Jean Navarro, and Marie Christine Mouren Simeoni. "Binge Eating and Psychopathology in Severely Obese Adolescents." *International Journal of Eating Disorders* 34 (2003): 235–43. doi: 10.1002/eat.10178.

Kalarchain, Melissa A., Michele D. Levine, Silva A. Arslanian, Linda J. Ewing, Patricia R. Houch, Yu Cheng, Rebecaa M. Ringham, Carrie A. Sheets, and Marsha D. Marcus. "Family-Based Treatment of Severe Pediatric Obesity: Randomized, Controlled Trial." *Pediatrics* 124 (2009): 1060–1068. doi: 10.1542/peds.2008–3727.

Khan, Laura Kettel, Kathleen Sobush, Dana Keener, Kenneth Goodman, Amy Lowry, Jakub Kakietek, and Susan Zaro. "Recommended Community Strategies and Measurements to Prevent Obesity in the United States." *Morbidity and Mortality Weekly Reports* 58, no. 7 (2009): 1–29.

Mckee, M. Diane, Stacia Maber, Darwin Deen, and Arthur E. Blank. "Counseling to Prevent Obesity among Preschool Children: Acceptability of a Pilot Urban Primary Care Intervention." *Annals of Family Medicine* 8, no. 3 (2010): 249–55.

Neumark-Sztainer, Dianne, Jess Haines, Ramona Robinson O'Brien, Peter J. Hannan, Michael Robins, Bonnie Morris, and Christine A. Petrich. "Ready. Set. ACTION! A Theater-Based Obesity Prevention Program for Children: A Feasibility Study." *Health Education Research* 24, no. 3 (2009): 407–420. doi: 10.1093/her/cyn036.

Pott, Wilfried, Ozgur Albayrak, Johannes Hebebrand, and Ursula Pauli-Pott. "Treating Childhood Obesity: Family Background Variables and the Child's Success in a Weight Control Intervention." *International Journal of Eating Disorders* 42 (2009): 284–89. doi: 10.1002/eat.20655 .

Zenzen, Wandy, and Suha Kridli. "Integrative Review of School-Based Childhood Obesity Prevention Programs." *Journal of Pediatric Health Care* 23, no. 4 (2009): 242–58. doi: 10.1016/j.pedhc.2008.04.008.

OBJECTIFICATION THEORY

Objectification theory is a conceptual framework that "places female bodies in a sociocultural context with the aim of illuminating lived experiences and mental health risks of girls and women who encounter sexual objectification." Women and girls are often portrayed as sexual objects in American culture. Thus, Fredrickson and Roberts, in 1997, proposed the objectification theory to understand how women are socialized to be sexual objects. This theory explains why women and girls develop mental health problems (i.e., eating disorders, depression, and sexual dysfunction) associated with being objectified.

Objectification of the Body

Sexualization of the body is represented in different forms such as sexual violence and sexualized evaluation of the body. A subtle way of sexualized evaluation of the body is through external gaze or visually inspecting the body. Sexual objectification occurs when the woman's body is considered separate from her person and treated merely as an object for the use and pleasure of others. This sexual objectification can occur in interpersonal and social situations (e.g., workplace, parties) and in media representation (e.g., television shows, magazines, advertisements, Internet) where women's bodies are depicted as sexual objects. Women report being sexually watched and evaluated more often than men.

Self-Objectification

According to the theory, sexual objectification experiences socialize girls and women to treat themselves as objects and to believe that they are evaluated based on their physical appearance. This internalization of an observer's perspective is called self-objectification. Self-objectification can lead to self-consciousness that is characterized by habitual monitoring of the appearance of the body (i.e., body surveillance). Individuals could internalize the objectification at varying degrees ranging from daily gazes from passersby to a single occurrence while walking by a group of the opposite sex. Nonetheless, this internalization of the observer's perspective on the physical self could lead to psychological consequences (i.e., body shame, anxiety, internal bodily awareness, and flow experiences).

Media and Self-Objectification

Fredrickson and Roberts (1997) suggest that one of the most common ways of sexually objectifying women is through the visual media, and viewing these sexualized bodies and images may increase self-objectification. The use of thin-idealized women in the media is ubiquitous; therefore, it is likely that women will experience self-objectification several times per day. Women who watched video clips of women playing sports that emphasize leanness had more elevated scores on self-objectification than those who did not watch these video clips. In a more recent study, women who viewed thin-idealized magazine advertisements of other women reported higher levels of self-objectification than women who only viewed magazine advertisements of products without people. As predicted by the objectification theory, the process of viewing thin-idealized images can encourage a woman to think about her own physical appearance as if she is looking at it as a critical observer, by adopting a third-person perspective. Increased exposure to these images will elevate the level of self-objectification, and in turn, place women at risk of experiencing the psychological consequences of self-objectification.

Consequences of Self-Objectification

The psychological consequences of self-objectification are increased body shame and anxiety, and reduction in awareness of internal bodily states and flow experiences. Body shame is the emotion that a woman could feel when she is comparing herself to an internalized or cultural standard and perceiving that she is failing to obtain that standard. Anxiety occurs when a woman feels threatened or fearful about when and how her body will be evaluated. Awareness of internal bodily states is the ability to accurately detect and interpret physiological sensations such as physiological sexual arousal. Peak motivational states or flow experiences, according to Csikszentmihalyi, are "rare moments during which we feel we are truly living, uncontrolled by others, creative and joyful" that improve the quality of life.

Objectification theory states that sexual objectification experiences promote self-objectification and body surveillance, which in turn, promote body shame and anxiety and reduce or disrupt the flow and awareness of internal bodily states. Increased body shame and anxiety, and decreased flow and awareness of internal bodily states, can lead women to develop depression, eating disorders, and sexual dysfunction.

Self-Objectification among Women

Studies reveal that women with heightened self-objectification experienced more body shame and anxiety than women who reported lower self-objectification. In addition, women with higher levels of self-objectification were more likely to restrain from eating cookies and chocolates among ethnically diverse groups of women. Women with more body shame tended to want to change their bodies through weight loss or cosmetic surgery. In a longitudinal study, college women's levels of body surveillance and body shame persisted over time but the same did not hold true for middle-aged women, indicating that body surveillance and body shame is stable for young women. In a different study, women smokers who monitor their bodies have higher body shame, body dissatisfaction, and eating disorder symptoms. Women with higher appearance anxiety had higher eating disorder symptoms among an ethnically diverse sample, but this was not the case among adolescents, adults, and college women who were white.

Self-Objectification among Men

Researchers have also examined the application of objectification theory for men and boys. In general, men and boys reported lower self-objectification, body surveillance, and body shame than women and girls. However, African American women and men do not differ in levels of body shame, and Asian American men reported higher self-objectification than Asian American women. Although there are gender differences in levels of self-objectification, there are gender similarities in self-objectification and mental health consequences. Similar to findings for women and girls, men and boys who have higher self-objectification, body surveillance, and body shame have lower body-esteem, self-esteem, and health-promoting behaviors. Also consistent with findings for women, body surveillance leads to body shame and appearance anxiety, and in turn, leads to eating disorder symptoms.

Self-objectification is related to body shame in men, but the type of situation that enhances self-objectification may differ for women and men. Women who are exposed to beauty magazines internalize the cultural standards of attractiveness, which leads to body dissatisfaction and eating disorder symptoms. Men who were exposed to fitness magazines had higher internalization, which leads to body dissatisfaction, than those who were not exposed to the fitness magazines. Therefore, beauty magazines send messages of cultural body ideals to women, whereas fitness magazines communicate such standards to men. These different types of standards may promote different ways of body surveillance and body shame—women worry about being thin while men worry about building muscles. For example, men who were bodybuilders reported higher self-objectification and eating disorder symptoms than non-bodybuilders.

Conclusion

Objectification theory asserts that women are often sexualized, inspected, evaluated, and treated as objects for the value of others. Media exposure of sexualized and thin-ideal bodies can socialize women to adopt an observer's perspective (self-objectification). When engaged in self-objectification, attention is directed at monitoring and assessing observable body characteristics. Consequently, self-objectification can lead to body shame, anxiety, internal bodily awareness, disruption of flow experiences, and mental health disorders (i.e., depression, eating disorders). Although the majority of studies using objectification theory have focused on women and girls, research findings have shown that men and boys also experience self-objectification and body shame.

SONYA SOOHOO

Bibliography

Bartky, Sandra L. *Femininity and Domination: Studies in the Phenomenology of Oppression.* New York: Routledge, 1990

Csikszentmihalyi, Mihaly. *Flow: The Psychology of Optimal Experience.* New York: Harper Perennial, 1990.

Fredrickson, Barbara L., and Tomi-Ann Roberts. "Objectification Theory: Toward Understanding Women's Lived Experiences and Mental Health Risks." *Psychology of Women Quarterly* 21 (1997): 173–206.

Fredrickson, Barbara L., Tomi-Ann Roberts, Stephanie M. Noll, Diane M. Quinn, and Jean M. Twenge. "That Swimsuit Becomes You: Sex Differences in Self-Objectification, Retrained Eating, and Math Performance." *Journal of Personality and Social Psychology* 75 (1998): 269–84.

Hallsworth, Lisa, Tracey Wade, and Marika Tiggemann. "Individual Differences in Male Body-Image: An Examination of Self-Objectification in Recreational Body Builders." *British Journal of Health Psychology* 10 (2005): 453–65.

Harrell, Zaje A.T., Barbara L. Fredrickson, Cynthia S. Pomerleau, and Susan Nolen-Hoeksema. "The Role of Trait Self-Objectification in Smoking among College Women." *Sex Roles* 54 (2006): 735–43.

McKinley, Nita M. "Longitudinal Gender Differences in Objectified Body Consciousness and Weight-Related Attitudes and Behaviors: Cultural and Developmental Contexts in the Transition from College." *Sex Roles* 54 (2006): 159–73.

Moradi, B. "Addressing Gender and Cultural Diversity in Body Image: Objectification Theory as a Framework for Integrating Theories and Grounding Research." *Sex Roles* 63 (2010): 138–48.

Moradi, Bonnie, and Yu-Ping Huang. "Objectification Theory and Psychology of Women: A Decade of Advances and Future Directions." *Psychology of Women Quarterly* 32 (2008): 377–98.

Noll, Stephanie M., and Barbara L. Fredrickson. "Mediational Model Linking Self-Objectification, Body Shame, and Disordered Eating." *Psychology of Women Quarterly* 22 (1998): 623–36.

OBLIGATORY EXERCISE

Definition of Obligatory Exercise

Obligatory exercise is a term used to refer to individuals who continue to exercise despite pain, allow exercise to interfere with significant relationships or work, lack time for other leisure pursuits, obsess with the activity (exercise), and show other psychological problems. Characteristics of obligatory exercise include: (1) maintaining a rigorous schedule of vigorous exercise; (2) resisting the urge to cut exercise routines; (3) feelings of guilt and anxiety when the practice plan is violated; (4) pushing oneself even when tired, ill, in pain, or injured; (5) mental obsession with exercise; (6) keeping accurate records on exercise; and (7) outrageous compensatory increase in exercise to make up for lapses.

Obligatory Exercise and Eating Disorders

Obligatory exercisers tend to feel compelled to engage in intense exercise, past the point of enjoyment or what would be considered mentally or physically healthy. Their attitudes toward exercise can be harmful to their physical and psychological well-being. Previous studies have revealed that obligatory exercise is associated with drive for thinness in obligatory weight-lifters and runners, eating and body image attitudes in appearance-motivated exercisers, and eating disordered behaviors in a community sample. Moreover, a number of studies have shown significant associations between the characteristics of obligatory runners and women with eating disorders. Examples of overlapping characteristics between obligatory exercisers and women with eating disorders include family backgrounds, socio-economic status, certain personality characteristics (e.g., anger, perfectionism and high self-expectations), a tendency for social isolation, high tolerance of pain and physical discomfort, and a tendency toward depression.

Characteristics of Obligatory Exercise

Distinguishable characteristics of obligatory exercise are elevated concerns over mistakes, the pursuit of high personal standards, and extreme doubts about the quality of actions. The motivational drive of obligatory exercise behavior tends to be a combination of outcome after overstriving, a pervasive sense of anxiety about personal adequacy, and the consequences of failure to maintain desired standards. One explanation about the reason behind the particular drive among obligatory exercisers describes a culture that encourages people to strive toward the optimal body composition (lean body mass to body fat ratio). In this competitive society, obligatory exercise behaviors may be linked to the establishment of strict dietary guidelines. This explanation has been consistent with other studies in obligatory exercise.

Psychological Characteristics of Obligatory Exercisers

Much like individuals who suffer from eating disorders, obligatory exercisers use strenuous exercise sessions and routines to feel a sense of control in order to cope with low self-esteem and related psychological issues. Similar to anorexia athletica or exercise dependence, obligatory exercise behaviors (also called overtraining) may serve as a way to reassure individuals, especially athletes, by nurturing confidence and self-worth as athletes prepare for performance. Although the rigorous training sessions may be associated with performance enhancement in sports, they bear some resemblance to the features of eating disorders. This comparison may foster additional correlation with other psychological traits such as negative body image, low self-esteem, anxiety, depression, and a preoccupation with weight that are observed in certain eating disorders.

Conclusion

Although there are many comparable features between obligatory exercise and eating disorders, there is some controversy related to labeling this behavior as an addiction. Specifically, many obligatory exercisers who participated in past research failed to meet the requisite criteria for clinical dependence as outlined by the American Psychology Association in the *Diagnostic and Statistics Manual for Mental Disorders (DSM-IV-TR)*. However, the psychological features of obligatory exercise are clearly pathological and eating disorder clients should be assessed for dysfunctional exercise-related thoughts and behaviors.

Maya Miyairi

Bibliography

American Psychiatric Association. *Diagnostic and Statistical Manual of Mental Disorders, 4th Edition, Text Revised*. Washington, DC: American Psychiatric Association, 2000.

De Young, Kyle P., and Drew A. Anderson. "The Importance of the Function of Exercise in the Relationship between Obligatory Exercise and Eating and Body Image Concerns." *Eating Behaviors* 11 (2010): 62–64.

Hall, Howard K., Alistair W. Kerr, Stephen A. Kozub, and Steven B. Finnie. "Motivational Antecedents of Obligatory Exercise: The Influence of Achievement Goals and Multidimensional Perfectionism." *Psychology of Sport and Exercise* 8 (2007): 297–316.

Hall, Howard K., Andrew P. Hill, Paul R. Appleton, and Stephen A. Kozub. "The Mediating Influence of Unconditional Self-Acceptance and Labile Self-Esteem on the Relationship between Multidimensional Perfectionism and Exercise Dependence." *Psychology of Sport and Exercise* 10 (2009): 35–44.

Krejci, Richard C., Roger Sargent, Kenneth J. Forand, John R. Ureda, Ruth P. Saunders, and J. Larry Durstine. "Psychological and Behavioral Differences among Females Classified as Bulimic, Obligatory Exerciser and Normal Control." *Psychiatry* 55 (1992): 185–93.

Matheson, Hilary, and Anne Crawford-Wright. "An Examination of Eating Disorder Profiles in Student Obligatory and Non-Obligatory Exercisers." *Journal of Sport Behavior* 23, no. 1 (2000): 42–50.

Pasman, Larry, and J. Kevin Thompson. "Body Image and Eating Disturbance in Obligatory Runners, Obligatory Weightlifters, and Sedentary Individuals." *International Journal of Eating Disorders* 7, no. 6 (1988): 759–69.

Reel, Justine J., and Katherine A. Beals, eds. *The Hidden Faces of Eating Disorders and Body Image*. Reston, VA: AAHPERD/NAGWS, 2009.

Steffen, John J., and Bonnie J. Brehm. "The Dimensions of Obligatory Exercise." *Eating Disorders* 7 (1999): 219–26.

Yates, Alayne, Kevin Leehey, and Catherine M. Shisslak. "Running—An Analogue of Anorexia." *The New England Journal of Medicine* 308 (1983): 251–55.

OBSESSIVE-COMPULSIVE DISORDER

Obsessive-Compulsive Disorder (OCD) is an anxiety disorder characterized by unwanted and repeated thoughts (obsessions) and/or repetitive behaviors that an individual feels driven to perform (compulsions). Repetitive behaviors, such as hand washing, checking, or cleaning, are used to reduce anxiety by making the obsessions go away. Engaging in the behaviors, however, provides only temporary relief and attempting to reduce behaviors can cause increased anxiety.

Comorbidity of OCD and Eating Disorders

Research studies demonstrate a frequent co-occurrence of eating disorders and OCD. While all types of anxiety disorders co-occur with eating disorders frequently, OCD has one of the highest comorbidities (along with social phobia) of all the anxiety disorders. Studies show that the lifetime prevalence of OCD in clients with anorexia nervosa is 10–15 percent and the lifetime prevalence of OCD in clients with bulimia nervosa is up to 43 percent. Individuals who are primarily diagnosed with OCD have shown a lifetime prevalence of eating disorders ranging from 5 percent to 17 percent.

The relationship between OCD and eating disorders is not straightforward; some researchers argue that OCD is a risk factor for developing an eating disorder while other researchers argue that eating disorders trigger OCD tendencies. Interestingly, some researchers and clinicians have claimed that eating disorders are a form of OCD while most experts maintain that OCD and eating disorders are clearly two distinct conditions and should receive separate diagnoses. Experts have reported that for eating disordered individuals diagnosed with OCD, OCD usually precedes eating disorder onset, suggesting that OCD might be a risk factor for eating disorders. Conversely, Yaryura-Tobias has argued that eating disorders lead to OCD symptoms. In 1986, Rothenberg suggested that eating disorders were a symptom of OCD. However, most eating disorder experts agree that while OCD and eating disorders share similar features, they are in fact different disorders and should receive separate classifications.

For eating disordered individuals who suffer from OCD, the impact of OCD on treatment responses is inconclusive. It has been suggested that co-occurring OCD has little effect on eating disorder treatment. In fact, one study argues that eating disorder clients with co-occurring OCD in an inpatient setting seem to have the same treatment prognosis as those who do not have the OCD diagnosis, if the co-occurring OCD is treated using evidence-based practices. However, another study found that OCD symptoms were significantly associated with poor treatment outcomes in anorexia nervosa clients. A separate study indicated that greater severity in OCD symptomology at discharge was linked with a higher probability of eating disorder relapse. Researchers have also found that eating disorder clients also diagnosed with OCD had significantly longer duration of eating disorders, which suggests that OCD might be a factor in maintaining eating disorders. Interestingly, clients with both OCD and eating disorders have been reported to be more likely to refuse treatment than those with only OCD.

Severity and Comorbidity

Researchers agree that eating disorder clients diagnosed with comorbid OCD exhibit a greater severity in their illness and an increase in other mental health diagnoses such as major depressive disorder, bipolar disorder, post-traumatic stress disorder, and generalized anxiety disorder, as compared to eating disorder clients without OCD. Clients with comorbid eating disorders and OCD tend to develop their eating disorder at an earlier age, have longer eating disorder durations, are admitted to treatment with a lower body mass index (BMI), and report more prior inpatient treatment episodes for eating disorders. Some researchers have found evidence that these clients have a worse prognosis than eating disorder clients without OCD.

Similarities between Eating Disorders and OCD

Eating disorders and OCD have considerable overlap with regard to shared neurological, genetic, and psychological elements. Shared characteristics between the disorders suggest an association. The disorders share psychopathological similarities, such as obsessions or compulsions related to food (i.e., eating foods in a particular order), or overeating or restricting food. People with eating disorders and OCD also share personality traits, such as perfectionism, rigidity, and preoccupations with cleanliness. Eating disorders and OCD have similar epidemiological data including their prevalence, age of onset, course of the illness, and genetic predisposition. Both disorders show similar responses to the same pharmacological and psychotherapeutic approaches.

While the disorders share many features, it is important to recognize that they are distinct illnesses and be able to separate obsessions and compulsions stemming from the eating disorder from those that may be linked to a direct diagnosis of OCD. A client who reports obsessions and compulsions around food, weight, appearance, and/or exercise—such as obsessive calorie counting—should not be given a diagnosis of OCD. If, however, the individual reports additional obsessions and compulsions beyond obsessions and/or compulsions related to food, weight, appearance, or exercise—such as counting—he or she should receive a secondary OCD diagnosis.

Researchers have expressed concerns specifically with regard to being able to differentiate between obsessions and compulsions linked to eating disorders and obsessions and compulsions due to OCD, in the case of persons with anorexia nervosa. Malnutrition and starvation can create obsessive-compulsive symptoms. As a result, in the case of people with anorexia nervosa who display obsessive-compulsive symptoms, the experts question whether the symptoms are in fact a direct result of starvation as opposed to true OCD symptoms. Another key difference between the disorders is that OCD is an ego-dystonic disorder whereas anorexia nervosa is an ego-syntonic disorder. In other words, obsessions and compulsions in a person diagnosed with OCD are seen by the person as being inconsistent with her beliefs and personality while those of a person diagnosed with anorexia nervosa are viewed by the person as consistent with her beliefs and personality.

Conclusion

Eating disorders and OCD often co-occur. Much research has been conducted in the area, but the relationship remains unclear. There is a significant indication that eating disorder clients with OCD have a greater severity of symptoms, both with regard to the eating disorder itself and with regard to other diagnoses, such as depression. Research does support the idea that there are similarities between the disorders and that for individuals who do present with both disorders, treatment of both is essential for recovery.

JESSICA GUENTHER

Bibliography

Carter, J. C., E. Blackmore, K. Sutandar-Pinnock, and D. B. Woodside. "Relapse in Anorexia Nervosa: A Survival Analysis." *Psychological Medicine* 34 (2004): 671–79.

Cumella, Edward J., Zina Kally, A. David Wall. "Treatment Responses of Inpatient Eating Disorder Women with and without Co-occurring Obsessive-compulsive Disorder." *Eating Disorders* 15, no. 2 (2007): 111–124.

Fahy, Thomas A., Autor Osacar, Isaac Marks. "History of Eating Disorders in Female Patients with Obsessive-compulsive Disorder." *International Journal of Eating Disorders* 14, no. 4 (1993): 439–43.

Halmi, Katharine A., Federica Tozzi, Laura M. Thornton, Scott Crow, , Manfred Fichter, , M. Kaplan, Allan S. Keel, Pamela Klump, Kelly L. Lilenfield, Lisa R. Mitchell, James E. Plotnicov, Katherine H. Pollice, Christine Rotondo, Alessondro Strober, Michael Woodside, D. Blake, Wade H. Berretini, Walter Kaye, Cynthia M. Bulik. "The Relationship among Perfectionism, Obsessive-Compulsive Personality Disorder, and Obsessive-Compulsive Disorder in Individuals with Eating Disorders." *International Journal of Eating Disorders* 38, no. 4 (2005): 371–74.

Hsu, L. K. George, Walter Kaye, and Theodore Weltzin. "Are the Eating Disorders Related to Obsessive Compulsive Disorder?" *International Journal of Eating Disorders* 14, no. 3 (1993): 305–318.

Kaye, Walter H., Cynthia M. Bulik, Laura Thornton, Nicole Barbarich, Kim Masters, and The Price Foundation Collaborative Group. "Co-morbidity of Anxiety Disorders with Anorexia and Bulimia Nervosa." *The American Journal of Psychiatry* 161 (2004): 2215–2221.

Milos, Gabriella, Anja Spindler, Giovanni Ruggiero, Richard Klaghofer, and Ulrich Schnyder. "Co-morbidity of Obsessive-compulsive Disorders and Duration of Eating Disorders." *International Journal of Eating Disorders* 31, no. 3 (2002): 284–89.

Roncero, Maria, Conxa Perpina, and Gemma Garcia-Soriano. "Study of Obsessive Compulsive Beliefs: Relationship with Eating Disorders." *Behavioural and Cognitive Psychotherapy* 39 (2011): 457–70.

Sallet, Paulo C., Pedro Gomes de Alvarenga, Ygor Ferrao, Maria Alice de Mathis,Albina R. Torres, Andrea Marques, Ana G. Hounie, Victor Fossaluza, Maria Conceicao do Rosario, Leonardo F. Fontenelle, Katia Petribu, and Bacy Fleitlich-Bilyk. "Eating Disorders in Patients with Obsessive-compulsive Disorder: Prevalence and Clinical Correlates." *International Journal of Eating Disorders* 43, no. 4 (2010): 315–25.

Yaryura-Tobias, Jose A., Fugen A. Neziroglu, and Steven Kaplan. "Self-mutilation, Anorexia, and Dysmenorrhea in Obsessive Compulsive Disorder." *International Journal of Eating Disorders* 17, no. 1 (1995): 33–38.

OFF THE C.U.F.F.

Off the C.U.F.F. (Calm, Unwavering, Firm and Funny) refers to a skills training program created for parents who have children who struggle with eating disorders by Dr. Nancy Zucker at Duke University Medical Center. The program aims to open the lines of communication between parents and their daughters with the goal of building a healthy relationship that allows for an environment that nurtures treatment of and recovery from an eating disorder.

Description of the Program

Off the C.U.F.F. is implemented in group settings to build skills among parents. The impetus for the program's development came from the realization that insurance support for inpatient eating disorder treatment was inadequate to meet the enormous needs of adolescents with eating disorders. The program provides parents with knowledge, skills, and the opportunity to practice these skills, in order to extend support to adolescents who require weight restoration and positive eating disorder recovery in the home environment.

The Off the C.U.F.F. group uses a process-focused approach rather than an outcome-oriented approach. In contrast to other eating disorder support groups for parents, Off the C.U.F.F. provides a structured agenda for teaching parenting skills related to eating. Parents are taught to avoid power struggles and conflicts over food while remaining calm and patient.

The three barriers to successful meals including negative perfectionism, expressed negative emotion, and poor self-efficacy are identified and addressed in the program. Parents learn to foster a home environment that promotes acceptance while working on their own emotional regulation. For example, parent participants are assigned an eating disorder behavior to target as well as an adaptive coping skill for modeling purposes.

The group also provides emotional support for parents who are experiencing extreme stress related to their daughters' eating disorders. Parents become more attuned to their own eating issues and commentary related to their body image. Ultimately parents are encouraged to serve as healthy role models for their daughters.

Evaluation of Off the C.U.F.F.

Although more outreach research is needed to evaluate this program, preliminary findings demonstrated successful outcomes for parent satisfaction and client (daughter) improvement. Among parents who participated in Off the C.U.F.F., 91 percent strongly agreed that the group was essential for their children's improvement and 82 percent of parents believed that their children would not be doing well if they had not participated in the group. All of the parents reported that the program helped them become better parents and that they would recommend the group. The majority of parents felt that the group helped them to reduce stress, take better care of the self, better handle stressful situations, and become more confident in parenting skills. For eating disorder clients, scores on weight concerns, shape concerns, and restraint decreased after the program, while Body Mass Index scores improved for the underweight clients.

Conclusion

Off the C.U.F.F. represents a unique training program for parents. The program is implemented in a group setting with the support of other parents who have daughters with eating disorders. Parents are taught to be role models for their children and to foster a supportive and healthful environment ripe for positive recovery from eating disorders. Initial results show that this program has much promise for educating parents with daughters who have eating disorders.

JUSTINE J. REEL

Bibliography

Sullivan, Michele G. "Parents Enlisted to Fight Teens' Eating Disorders: Skills-training Program Gives Families the Tools and the Support They Need to Address Behavior at Home." *Family Practice News* (2001): 39.

Sullivan, Michele G. "Parents of Eating Disorder Patients Join Forces: Group Training Program Aims to Give Families the Skills to Reinforce Positive Eating Habits in Adolescents." *Child/Adolescent Psychiatry* (2003): 42.

Zucker, Nancy. *Off the C.U.F.F.!!!! A Parents Skills Book for the Management of Eating Disorders.* Durham, NC: Duke University Medical Center, 2004.

OLIGOMENORRHEA

Oligomenorrhea is defined as a condition in which a female's menstrual cycles last longer than 35 days after the onset of menses, resulting in fewer than 10 menstrual periods per year. The average menstrual cycle is 25–35 days long. The primary cause of oligomenorrhea in individuals with eating disorders is presumed to be low energy availability (energy availability is the amount of dietary energy remaining for other physiological functions after exercise). Oligomenorrhea can occur in many types of eating disturbances that result in energy deficiency, either from inadequate energy intake, too much exercise, or a combination of both.

Health Consequences

Infrequent menstrual periods are associated with decreased bone mineral density, increased frequency of stress fractures and other musculoskeletal injuries in athletes, longer interruption of sports training from injuries, and impaired dilation of blood vessels (i.e., premature cardiovascular disease). It is possible that these adverse effects occur based on the severity of the menstrual cycle disturbance. For example, individuals with oligomenorrhea have been found to have lower bone mineral density and more vascular dysfunction than regularly menstruating women; however, individuals with amenorrhea (i.e., lack of any menstrual periods) have been found to have lower bone mass and greater impairment of vascular function than oligomenorrheic women.

Management

Increasing energy intake and/or reducing exercise energy expenditure is recommended to meet the energy demands of the reproductive system and restore regular menstrual cycles. Improvement in nutritional status and hormone levels has been shown to positively impact bone health as well as vascular function.

Conclusion

Oligomenorrhea, or infrequent menstrual cycles, may lead to stress fractures, decreased bone mineral density, and impaired cardiovascular function. The longer the menstrual irregularities persist, the further the decline in bone health; therefore, early intervention is important to decrease long-term complications.

HOLLY E. DOETSCH

Bibliography

Beckvid Henriksson, Gabriella, Cathy Schnell, and Angelica Linden Hirschberg. "Women Endurance Runners with Menstrual Dysfunction have Prolonged Interruption of Training due to Injury." *Gynecologic and Obstetric Investigation* 49 (2000): 41–46.

Bennell, Kim L, Susan A. Malcolm, Shane A. Thomas, Sally J. Reid, Peter D. Brukner, Peter R. Ebeling, and John D. Wark. "Risk Factors for Stress Fractures in Track and Field

Athletes: A Twelve-Month Prospective Study." *American Journal of Sports Medicine* 24, no. 6 (1996): 810–18.

Drinkwater, Barbara L., Barbara Bruemner, and Charles H. Chesnut III. "Menstrual History as a Determinant of Current Bone Density in Young Athletes." *Journal of the American Medical Association* 263 (1990): 545–48.

Nattiv, Aurelia, Anne B. Loucks, Melinda M. Manore, Charlotte F. Sanborn, Jorunn Sundgot-Borgen, and Michelle P. Warren. "American College of Sports Medicine Position Stand. The Female Athlete Triad." *Medicine and Science in Sports and Exercise* 39, no. 10 (2007): 1867–1882.

Ouyang, Fengxiu, Xiaobin Wang, Lester Arguelles, Linda L. Rosul, Scott A. Venners, Changzhong Chen, Yi-Hsiang Hsu, Henry A. Terwedow, Di Wu, Genfu Tang, Jianhua Yang, Houxun Xing, Tonghua Zang, Binyan Wang, and Xiping Xu. "Menstrual Cycle Lengths and Bone Mineral Density: A Cross-Sectional, Population-Based Study in Rural Chinese Women Ages 30–49 Years." *Osteoporosis International* 18, no. 2 (2007): 221–33.

Rauh, Mitchell J., Jeanne F. Nichols, and Michelle T. Barrack. "Relationships among Injury and Disordered Eating, Menstrual Dysfunction, and Low Bone Mineral Density in High School Athletes: A Prospective Study." *Journal of Athletic Training* 45, no. 3 (2010): 243–52.

Rickenlund, Anette, Maria J. Eriksson, Karin Schenck-Gustafsson, and Angelica Linden Hirschberg. "Amenorrhea in Female Athletes is Associated with Endothelial Dysfunction and Unfavorable Lipid Profile." *Journal of Clinical Endocrinology and Metabolism* 90, no. 3 (2005): 1354–1359.

Tomten, S. E., J. A. Falch, K.I. Birkeland, P. Hemmersbach, and A.T. Høstmark. "Bone Mineral Density and Menstrual Irregularities. A Comparative Study on Cortical and Trabecular Bone Structures in Runners with Alleged Normal Eating Behavior." *International Journal of Sports Medicine* 19, no. 2 (1998): 92–97.

OPERATION BEAUTIFUL

Operation Beautiful strives to promote self-acceptance by using post-it notes to spread positive, uplifting messages. The mission of Operation Beautiful is to make the statement "You are beautiful just the way you are." Operation Beautiful has combated "fat talk" (negative thoughts and criticisms about weight and size) by sticking post-it notes on scales in public places that read, "You have no hold on my mood, my day or my life. I am MORE than just a number."

Operation Beautiful started in 2009 as a spontaneous act by a community college student, Caitlin Boyle. Caitlin had been attempting to use positive self-affirmations in her own life to fight perfectionist tendencies and negative self-talk. On a particularly stressful day, Boyle decided to make a strong statement by writing "You are beautiful" on a scrap sheet of paper and sticking it to a public bathroom mirror. She realized that she actually felt better as a result of looking at the positive message on the note. She took a photograph of the note and posted it on her blog to start a mission she called "Operation Beautiful." Boyle urged other females to participate by posting positive notes in public places (e.g., mirrors, magazines, gym scales). Her appeal went viral almost immediately and Boyle's inbox was filled with emails from women across the world.

What started as a simple act in a private moment has spread to post-it note campaigns across the globe. Many universities (e.g., Michigan State University,

University of Utah) have incorporated post-it note campaigns into their national eating disorder awareness week events. Other women and men have been motivated to spontaneously post positive messages in retail stores, schools, and in their homes. An unexpected benefit of Operation Beautiful has been the response from individuals who find the post-it notes and feel uplifted as a result. Boyle's *Today* show interview about Operation Beautiful can be found at: http://today.msnbc.msn.com/id/26184891/vp/38573588#38573588. Suggestions for creative and uplifting post-it note messages can be found at her website: www.operationbeautiful.com.

Conclusion

Many attempts have been made to promote positive body image messages. However, Operation Beautiful has been a successful campaign for spreading the word using a universal approach and has generated enormous publicity. By using post-it notes in public places, self-acceptance can be reinforced with positive affirmations.

JUSTINE J. REEL

Bibliography

Boyle, Caitlin. *Operation Beautiful: Transforming the Way You See Yourself One Post-it Note at a Time.* New York: Gotham Books, 2010

Boyle, Caitlin. "Operation Beautiful." *Operation Beautiful.* Retrieved June 13, 2011. www.operationbeautiful.com

Today Show (2010). Blogger Caitlin Boyle is trying to start a revolution to spread positive body image one Post-it note at a time. Retrieved June 13, 2011. http://today.msnbc.msn.com/id/26184891/vp/38573588#38573588

ORTHOREXIA NERVOSA

Orthorexia nervosa is a term that has been used to describe eating behavior that is characterized by a pathological obsession for biologically pure foods that are free of herbicides, pesticides, and other artificial substances. Although orthorexia nervosa is not a separate eating disorder diagnostic category, there are overlaps between orthorexia nervosa and other disordered eating behaviors. Although consuming natural and organic foods is not pathological in itself, orthorexia nervosa is marked by the excessive preoccupation or concern associated with consuming healthy foods.

History of Orthorexia

The term "orthorexia" was coined by Steven Bratman in 1997 to describe eating disordered behaviors related to excessive worry about the techniques and materials used in food preparation. The term "orthorexia" was created from the Latin word, "orthos," which means accurate or correct. The Latin word, "orexsis," means hunger and orthorexia translates to "obsession of healthy and proper nutrition." Individuals with orthorexia nervosa have been found to experience obsessive thoughts about foods, loss of social relationships, and mood swings.

Differences between Orthorexia and Other Eating Disorders

Orthorexia nervosa is not included in the current edition of the *Diagnostic and Statistical Manual of Mental Disorders*. Therefore, an individual with orthorexia nervosa may be classified as Eating Disorder Not Otherwise Specified for treatment and insurance reimbursement purposes. However, it is important to distinguish between orthorexia nervosa and other eating disorders (i.e., anorexia nervosa, bulimia nervosa, binge eating disorder). Although individuals with orthorexia nervosa exhibit features similar to those of anorexic individuals—such as being careful, detailed, and preoccupied with food—they have no fear associated with gaining weight or changing one's body shape. Individuals with orthorexia nervosa are concerned with certain foods being impure or toxic, but they are not motivated by weight loss. Orthorexia nervosa has been found to differ from anorexia nervosa and bulimia nervosa as individuals with orthorexia nervosa are concerned with quality of food versus quantity of food for other eating disorders. Orthorexia nervosa may lead to strict diets with a shortage of essential nutrients that result in a modification of social behaviors (e.g., eating out) related to food consumption.

Prevalence of Orthorexia

Although orthorexia nervosa has not been recognized as a disorder for as long as other eating disorders have been, several researchers have examined the frequency of orthorexia nervosa. Certain groups are considered more at risk for orthorexia nervosa including women, adolescents, athletes, physicians, and medical students. In one study, 43.6 percent of medical students in Erzurum, Turkey, met the criteria for orthorexia nervosa; and male students who were younger showed a stronger orthorexic tendency. A separate study with dietitians found that although 52.3 percent did not exhibit orthorexia nervosa, 34.9 percent of dietitians showed some orthorexic behavior and 12.8 percent exhibited orthorexia. These dietitians showed some behaviors associated with orthorexia nervosa including: avoidance of eating away from home for fear of unhealthy food, bringing one's own food when eating away from home, and experiencing guilt or self-loathing when straying away from one's eating plan.

Conclusion

A term, orthorexia nervosa, has been coined to describe the excessive preoccupation with eating pure foods. Although individuals with orthorexia nervosa are not concerned with weight loss, they experience negative moods associated with eating foods not considered healthy. Orthorexia nervosa can result in impaired social relationships, mood swings, and obsessive thoughts related to healthy food consumption. Currently there is no psychiatric diagnosis to represent this eating behavior disorder.

JUSTINE J. REEL

Bibliography

Bosi, A. Tulay Bagci, Derya Camur, and Cagatay Guler. "Prevalence of Orthorexia Nervosa in Resident Medical Doctors in the Faculty of Medicine (Ankara, Turkey)." *Appetite* 49 (2007): 661–66. doi: 10.1016/j.appet.2007.04.007.

Eriksson, L., A. Baigi, B. Marklund, and E. C. Lindgren. "Social Physique Anxiety and Sociocultural Attitudes toward Appearance Impact on Orthorexia Test in Fitness Participants." *Scandinavian Journal of Medicine & Science in Sports* 18 (2008): 389–94. doi: 10.1111/j.1600–0838.2007.00723.x.

Fidan, Tulin, Vildan Ertekin, Sedat Isikay, and Ismet Kirpinar. "Prevalence of Orthorexia among Medical Students in Erzurum, Turkey." *Comprehensive Psychiatry* 51 (2010): 49–54. doi: 10.1016/j.comppsych.2009.03.001.

Kimmer, A., M. V. Dias, A. L. Teixeira. "On the Concept of Orthorexia Nervosa." *Scandinavian Journal of Medicine & Science in Sports* 18 (2008): 395–96. doi: 10.1111/j.1600-0838.2008.00809.x.

Kinzi, Johann F., Katharina Hauer, Christian Traweger, and Ingrid Kiefer. "Orthorexia Nervosa in Dieticians." *Psychotherapy and Psychosomatics* 75 (2006): 395–96. doi: 10.11 59/000095447.

Korinth, Anne, Sonja Schiess, and Joachim Westenhoefer. "Eating Behavior and Eating Disorders in Students of Nutrition Sciences." *Public Health Nutrition* 13, no. 1 (2009): 32–37. doi: 10.1017/S1368980009005709.

Vandereycken, Walter. "Media Hype, Diagnostic Fad or Genuine Disorder? Professionals' Opinions about Night Eating Syndrome, Orthrexia, Muscle Dysmorpia and Emetophobia." *Eating Disorders: Journal of Treatment and Prevention* 19 (2011): 145–55. doi: 10.1080/10640266.2011.551634.

OSTEOPOROSIS

Osteoporosis refers to a bone disease associated with low bone mineral density and is represented by bone density loss of more than 2.5 standard deviations from what is considered normal for one's age. Osteoporosis and low bone density have been associated with advanced age, amenorrhea, and anorexia nervosa. Males and females with eating disorders have been found to experience bone density loss at higher rates than the general population. Therefore, bone density loss (previously osteoporosis) has been identified as a component of the female athlete triad that intersects with menstrual disturbance and energy availability to represent the triad.

Prevalence of Osteoporosis in Eating Disordered Individuals

Bone density has been found to be reduced at either the spine or the hip by more than 2.5 standard deviations (i.e., osteoporosis) in almost 40 percent of eating disordered clients. Alarmingly, 92 percent of eating disordered clients had bone density reduced by more than one standard deviation showing the presence of osteopenia in this group.

Although adolescents with anorexia nervosa have typically experienced a shorter duration of illness than older clients, in one study, 41 percent of adolescents with anorexia nervosa had osteopenia and 11 percent met the criteria for osteoporosis. Because optimization of bone growth and achievement of peak bone mass occurs during adolescence, anorexia nervosa contributes to a long-term risk of stress fractures and irreversible skeletal damage.

Treatment Implications and Bone Health

Because of the risk of osteopenia and osteoporosis among individuals with anorexia nervosa, it is important to address bone health as part of comprehensive eating disorder treatment.

Hormonal Therapy

Once individuals have been assessed for bone health, it is common for physicians to prescribe supplemental estrogen as a form of hormonal replacement therapy or as an oral contraceptive for clients with anorexia nervosa to minimize osteopenia or osteoporosis. However, although 75–80 percent of physicians may use hormonal therapy to address bone health concerns, results have been mixed regarding the efficacy of estrogens in reversing bone loss.

Weight Restoration

Weight restoration is another common treatment method for clients with anorexia nervosa. Although weight restoration is important to restore bodily functions and avoid further medical complications, the direct effect of weight gain on bone health is unknown. As with hormonal therapy, conflicting results have been found in relation to the benefits of weight restoration in preventing bone density loss associated with anorexia nervosa.

Calcium Supplementation

Calcium may also be prescribed for individuals diagnosed with anorexia nervosa. The American Academy of Pediatrics recommends that adolescents should consume 1,200 to 1,500 mg of calcium daily to meet bone health requirements. Although calcium supplementation is often encouraged in eating disordered populations, calcium may be insufficient by itself to prevent osteopenia and osteoporosis among individuals with anorexia nervosa.

Exercise

Weight-bearing exercise has been used to prevent osteoporosis and improve bone health in the general population. Exercise as an adjunct treatment may be beneficial for individuals with eating disorders if menstruation has been restored. However, eating disordered individuals will not be medically cleared to exercise until they have experienced adequate weight restoration and are no longer medically compromised. It is critical that once individuals are able to exercise, they gradually incorporate light physical activity to avoid the potential for stress fractures. Individuals must monitor the potential to abuse exercise which can lead to overtraining injuries and mental fatigue.

Conclusion

Osteoporosis is a debilitating bone disease that has usually been associated with older women. However, substantial evidence exists to show that individuals with anorexia nervosa are much more likely to experience bone density loss that can lead to osteopenia and osteoporosis. Therefore, individuals who demonstrate disordered eating and/or menstrual disturbances should be assessed for bone health. Unfortunately, the most common forms of treatment to prevent bone density loss have been inconclusive in showing the benefits of reversing bone damage.

JUSTINE J. REEL

Bibliography

Drinkwater, Barbara L., Barbara Bruemner, and Charles H. Chesnut III. "Menstrual History as a Determinant of Current Bone Density in Young Athletes." *Journal of the American Medical Association* 263 (1990): 545–48.

Mehler, Philip S. "Osteoporosis in Anorexia Nervosa: Prevention and Treatment." *International Journal of Eating Disorders* 33 (2003): 113–26.

Mehler, Philip S., and Thomas D. MacKenzie. "Treatment of Osteopenia and Osteoporosis in Anorexia Nervosa: A Systematic Review of the Literature." *International Journal of Eating Disorders* 42 (2009): 195–201.

Nichols, David L., Charlotte F. Sanborn, and Eve V. Essery. "Bone Density and Young Athletic Women." *Sports Medicine* 37, no. 11 (2007): 1001–1014.

Rauh, Mitchell J., Jeanne F. Nichols, and Michelle T. Barrack. "Relationships among Injury and Disordered Eating, Menstrual Dysfunction, and Low Bone Mineral Density in High School Athletes: A Prospective Study." *Journal of Athletic Training* 45, no. 3 (2010): 243–52.

OVEREATERS ANONYMOUS

Overeaters Anonymous (OA) refers to a twelve-step program for people who struggle with a dysfunctional relationship with food. Members include individuals who have been diagnosed with anorexia nervosa, bulimia nervosa, and binge eating disorder, as well as others who are compulsive eaters or who have a problem with food. OA hosts worldwide meetings that offer a "fellowship of experience, strength and hope."

OA is funded through member contributions and does not charge fees or dues. Although OA is not a religious organization, like other twelve-step groups, OA promotes gaining strength from a higher power. OA provides emotional support to members and does not promote any specific diet or meal plan. On its website OA provides tools including a daily meditation for visitors.

History of OA

OA was founded in 1960 by Rozanne S. and two other women to address compulsive overeating as a form of addiction. Rozanne S. conceived the idea of OA after attending a Gamblers Anonymous meeting with a friend two years earlier. Today, OA's headquarters are located in Rio Rancho, New Mexico, and OA's membership has been estimated to be over 54,000 people and 6,500 groups across 75 countries. OA has modified program materials from Alcoholics Anonymous to apply the twelve-step tradition to compulsive overeating by helping individuals to admit their powerlessness over food and to begin to experience physical, emotional, and spiritual healing.

Conclusion

In addition to other support groups, Overeaters Anonymous provides free weekly meetings to individuals who are suffering from a poor relationship with food. Although the focus of OA meetings tends to be compulsive overeating, in smaller communities that do not have active Eating Disorder Anonymous groups, OA can provide an alternative. OA follows the twelve traditions and provides numerous resources related to problems with food.

JUSTINE J. REEL

See also: Eating Disorders Anonymous; Twelve-Step Programs.

Bibliography

"Overeaters Anonymous." Oa.org. Accessed November 23, 2011. www.oa.org.

Stefano, S. C., J. Bacaltchuk, S. L. Blay, and P. Hay. "Self-help Treatments for Disorders in Recurrent Binge Eating: A Systematic Review." *Acta Psychiatrica Scandinavica* 113 (2006): 452–59. doi: 10.1111/j.1600–0447.2005.00735.x

Wasson, Diane H., and Mary Jackson. "An Analysis of the Role of Overeaters Anonymous in Women's Recovery from Bulimia Nervosa." *Eating Disorders: Journal of Treatment and Prevention* 12 (2004): 337–56. doi: 10.1080/10640260490521442

P

PARENTS

Parental eating behaviors and body image have been linked to the tendency of disordered eating practices, dietary restraint, and negative body image among young children and adolescents. For example, mothers who display symptoms of pathological eating behaviors were found to be more intrusive and controlling of their children's mealtimes and reported using more restrictive feeding practices. Fathers' eating attitudes and behaviors were also important determinants of children's eating attitudes and behaviors. Similarly, parents who express dissatisfaction with their bodies model body shame and disgust which is often internalized by younger children. This entry will discuss research related to eating disorder symptoms and parental styles, weight-related talk, and how parents can receive education about promoting healthy approaches to nutrition and physical activity that will build positive body esteem and self-perceptions among children and adolescents.

Eating Disorder Symptoms and Parenting Styles

In addition to mothers with eating disorder symptoms showing a higher tendency to be more controlling about children's feeding practices characteristic of an authoritative parental style, these mothers may also withdraw from conflict arising from stressful eating interactions with their children. This withdrawal may be associated with a more permissive or neglectful parenting style. In one study of 105 mothers with young children, higher levels of eating disorder symptoms among mothers were associated with authoritarian and permissive parenting styles.

Once children or adolescents display pathological eating behaviors, it is not uncommon for parents to begin to oversee meals and encourage food consumption with a "finish your plate" mentality. Unfortunately, this type of encouragement around meals has not been found to be successful in curbing disordered eating behaviors. In fact, many treatment professionals caution parents to avoid becoming the food police so that food does not become the object of a control issue. One exception is the Maudsley treatment approach which encourages parents to take on an active role in the treatment team for eating disorders.

Influence of Mother Weight Talk and Dieting

Studies have found that parental comments about weight and encouragement of dieting behaviors have adverse effects on the health of adolescents. For example, parent weight talk and weight-teasing were linked to decreased body satisfaction and led to eating disorder behaviors (e.g., fasting, restricting, skipping meals, purging).

Interestingly, one study found that two-thirds of adolescent girls reported that their mothers dieted or talked about their own weight, and nearly half of the girls reported that their mothers encouraged them to diet. In this same study, maternal dieting was associated with greater use of unhealthy and extreme weight control behaviors among the adolescent females. Mothers who talked about their weight predicted weight control behaviors and binge eating behaviors among daughters. Over a quarter (26%) of girls who were encouraged to diet by their mothers used extreme weight control behaviors, which was much higher than girls whose mothers did not encouraging dieting behavior.

Influence of Father Dieting and Weight Talk

Forty percent of adolescent girls reported that their father was on a diet, talked about his weight, or encouraged them to diet. Interestingly, father dieting was less associated with the negative outcomes that were observed for mother dieting. However, 22.2 percent of girls who reported that their father talked about his weight admitted using extreme weight control behaviors, which was higher than for girls whose fathers did not discuss weight. Furthermore, girls' use of unhealthy weight control behaviors was associated with being encouraged by their fathers to go on a diet.

Family Weight-Teasing

Alarmingly, one study found that 60 percent of girls reported weight-related teasing by family members over the past year. Weight-related teasing by family members was associated with higher body mass index, body dissatisfaction, unhealthy weight control methods, and binge eating behaviors. The higher the frequency of weight-related teasing, the stronger the tendency to use more extreme weight control methods. Most researchers concur that family members innocently tease their adolescent children about weight and that more education is needed about the influence this behavior can have in triggering disordered eating and eating disorders.

Impact of Eating Disorders on Caregivers

Regardless of which treatment approach is used, it is important for parents to receive support and education during eating disorder treatment and recovery. Having a daughter, son, or loved one with an eating disorder can contribute to stress, guilt, and shame. One study found that 27 percent of caregivers suffered from anxiety while 10.3 percent of caregivers reported depressive symptoms. Some of the significant stressors reported for mothers of eating disordered individuals included the financial burden of treatment, having inadequate health insurance (100%), changing family dynamics (70%), difficulty finding and navigating treatment (50%), and personal sacrifice (50%).

Identifying financial concerns related to treatment is not surprising given the expensive nature of eating disorder care. For instance, some residential eating disorder facilities charge $1,500 or more per day of treatment despite the need for more than 90 days of minimum treatment before discharge. Because it is unlikely that an insurance company will pay for the recommended amount of treatment, the family must often pay out of its own pocket to fill the gap. Families reported using retirement funds or mortgaging their house to cover the costs in the desperation to save their son or daughter from an eating disorder.

Family dynamics are affected by the eating disorder and undergoing treatment. When a child is struggling with disordered eating, many family members report "walking on egg shells." Once the problem is addressed, the family faces a long road of treatment and recovery. Parents note the effect this has on the siblings, who may receive less attention and who may need to sacrifice their activities for time or finances required for eating disorder treatment. The dynamics of the family are often scrutinized in the treatment setting and certain family members may feel like they have been put under a microscope. Once the contributing factors are identified, parents may be asked to change attitudes, communication patterns, and behaviors.

Unfortunately, parents have also expressed frustration over the lack of a clear path for eating disorder treatment. Because there was no single option provided on how to treat the daughter or son, parents have felt that they did not receive adequate guidance from treatment professionals (e.g., physicians). In some cases, options for specialized eating disorder treatment are scarce within a particular city or state, and providing care could require sending one's son or daughter to another state with no guarantee of recovery. Some parents have also reported having negative experiences with treatment providers or a lack of support upon discharge from an eating disorder–specific program into an outpatient setting.

Personal sacrifices have also been cited by parents as a necessary outgrowth of providing treatment to a daughter or son with an eating disorder. Both parents reported the need to miss work to provide transportation or to attend appointments; they also reported other financial sacrifices associated with the cost of treatment. Parents have expressed frustration over having their routines disrupted by treatment (e.g., meal plans) that may involve careful planning for family grocery shopping and meal preparations.

Parent Education

Although there are many factors contributing to disordered eating and eating disorders, parent dieting, talk about weight and weight-related teasing can all influence eating behaviors of children and adolescents. Therefore, it is necessary to provide parent education surrounding the issues of nutrition, physical activity, and body image. The BodyWorks program addresses the question of how to promote healthy eating and increased activity in the home while reducing "fat talk." Another program, Off the C.U.F.F, teaches healthy communication skills which can set the stage for stronger relationships between parents and adolescents. Ultimately, it is important that parents receive support while their children and adolescents are receiving treatment for eating disorders. Parents may find comfort by securing their own therapist or attend a parent support group for family members of individuals with eating disorders.

Conclusion

Parental behaviors associated with dieting and talking about weight can influence the behaviors of children and adolescents. Parents with eating disorders were found to have more controlling tendencies around feeding practices or may withdraw to avoid stress and conflict. Additionally, the maternal dieting behaviors, talking about weight and encouraging the daughter to diet were all related to a higher tendency in the daughter to use extreme weight control methods, experience more negative body image, and engage in binge eating episodes. Fathers' weight talk and encouraging of dieting were also associated with a higher tendency to develop disordered eating.

Daughters with higher BMI face more weight-related teasing, which is associated with increased use of unhealthy and extreme weight control methods, negative body image, and binge eating risk. Therefore, families can benefit from increased education on how to discuss food and bodies for prevention and treatment of eating disorders. Parents should and can be a part of the solution for decreasing the rate of disordered eating practices. Family members of individuals with eating disorders should receive necessary support.

JUSTINE J. REEL

See also: BodyWorks; Off the C.U.F.F.

Bibliography

Blissett, Jackie, and Emma Haycraft. "Parental Eating Disorder Symptoms and Observations of Mealtime Interactions with Children." *Journal of Psychosomatic Research* 70 (2011): 368–71. doi: 10.1016/j.jpsychores.2010.07.006.

Haycraft, Emma, and Jackie Blissett. "Eating Disorder Symptoms and Parenting Styles." *Appetite* 54 (2010): 221–24. doi: 10/1016/j.appet.2009.11.009.

Keitel, Merle A., Melinda Parisi, Jessica L. Whitney, and Lauren F. Stack. "Salient Stressors for Mothers of Children and Adolescents with Anorexia Nervosa." *Eating Disorders: The Journal of Treatment and Prevention* 18 (2010): 435–44. doi: 10.1080/10640266.2010.511937.

Lock, James, and Daniel Le Grange. *Help Your Teenager Beat an Eating Disorder.* New York, NY: Guilford Press, 2005.

Martin, Josune, Angel Padierna, Urko Aguirre, Jose M. Quintana, Carlota Las Hayas, and Pedro Munoz. "Quality of Life among Caregivers of Patients with Eating Disorders." *Quality of Life Research* 20, no. 9 (2011): 1359–1369. doi: 10/1007/s11136-011-9873-z.

Neumark-Sztainer, Dianne, Katherine W. Bauer, Sarah Friend, Peter J. Hannan, Mary Story, and Jerica M. Berge. "Family Weight Talk and Dieting: How Much Do They Matter for Body Dissatisfaction and Disordered Eating Behaviors in Adolescent Girls." *Journal of Adolescent Health* 47 (2010): 270–76. doi: 10.1016/j.jadohealth.2010.02.001.

Reba-Harreleson, Lauren, Ann Von Holle, Robert M. Hamer, Leila Torgersen, Ted Rich-born-Kjennerud, and Cynthia M. Bulik. "Patterns of Maternal Feeding and Child Eating Associated with Eating Disorders in the Norwegian Mother and Child Cohort Study (MoBa)." *Eating Behaviors* 11, no. 1 (2010): 54–61. doi: 10.1016/j.eatbeh.2009.09.004.

Rortveit, Kristine, Sture Astrom, and Elisabeth Sevrinsson. "The Meaning of Guilt and Shame: A Qualitative Study of Mothers Who Suffer from Eating Difficulties." *International Journal of Mental Health Nursing* 19 (2010): 231–39. doi: 10.1111/j.1447-0349.2010.00672.x.

PERSONALITY CHARACTERISTICS

The causes of eating disorders include biological, psychological, and environmental factors. Psychological factors refer to personality characteristics that have been commonly observed across individuals with eating disorders. Personality characteristics associated with eating disorders include perfectionism, impulsivity, being achievement-oriented, and exhibiting dichotomous thinking. It should be noted that, according to Podar, Hannus, and Allik (1999), these characteristics may "either play a causal role in the development of eating disorders or at least modify the course of their expression without having a direct etiological role" (p. 134.)

Perfectionism

Perfectionism refers to a personality trait characterized by high personal standards and subsequent self-criticism, concern over and intolerance of mistakes, and extreme organization and need for order. According to Josefina Castro-Fornieles and colleagues (2007), perfectionism is "a personality characteristic involving a tendency to place excessive emphasis on precision and organization, the setting of and striving for unrealistic personal standards, critical self-evaluation if these standards are not reached, excessive concern over mistakes, and doubts about the quality of personal achievements" (p. 562). One could imagine that everyone experiences varying degrees of perfectionism during chance encounters on a daily basis. In the world of eating disorders, having high standards for the self and a need for order are similar to the traits of other individuals without eating disorder diagnosis. On the other hand, perfectionism that results in a preoccupation with mistakes and performance anxiety has been shown to be higher in individuals diagnosed with eating disorders. Individuals with eating disorders have also been shown to have a tendency to set unrealistic personal standards and believe they are evaluated harshly by others. Additionally, research has indicated that perfectionism does not operate differently by gender in individuals with eating disorders and is predictive of eating disorders 5 to 10 years down the road.

Research indicates that perfectionism is strongly related to eating disordered behaviors and highly perfectionistic individuals exhibit greater body dissatisfaction, dietary restraint, and purging behaviors. In one study, 17.6 percent of individuals with anorexia nervosa or bulimia nervosa demonstrated high self-oriented perfectionism and 10.2 percent of clinically eating disordered participants had high socially-prescribed perfectionism. Statistically, the percentage of individuals with either type of perfectionism was significantly different from participants who were not eating-disordered. Of the two types of perfectionism, self-oriented perfectionism was shown to predict eating disorders. Another study found that 93 percent of the variance in body dissatisfaction, dietary restraint, and purging behaviors in women aged 18–31 years was explained by perfectionism. It has been suggested that perfectionism may be related to other personality characteristics that may increase the risk of eating disordered behaviors (e.g., perfectionism is related to low self-esteem), exacerbating the influence of either characteristic on its own.

Impulsivity

Impulsiveness has been defined as a lack of forethought; it involves doing things with little regard for risks and consequences. Impulsiveness has been linked to substance abuse and to bulimic symptoms. What is surprising is that impulsiveness is more strongly related to purging behavior than to binge eating behavior. It is unknown as to whether impulsiveness as a personality trait precedes bulimic symptomology or if the erratic mood changes result from dietary inconsistencies and emotional instability associated with bulimia nervosa. Additionally, individuals who exhibit more disordered eating behaviors also tend to demonstrate more sensation-seeking tendencies (e.g., outdoor activities that involve speed or danger, or trying novel experiences for the sake of experiencing new things). Sensation-seeking individuals are often more willing to take risks and ignore physical or social consequences while searching for new and exciting experiences and sensations.

Interoceptive Awareness

Interoceptive awareness refers to clearly identifying one's emotions and accepting those emotions. Individuals with eating disorders typically display poor interoceptive awareness. That is, they are often unclear about the type of physical or emotional response they are experiencing (e.g., knotted stomach) and tend to experience fear or guilt as a result of the experience. The second component, how one appraises or accepts the physical or emotional experience, has been shown to be more predictive of dietary restraint in individuals with eating disorders. The non-acceptance of emotional/physical experience explained 27 percent of the differences in dietary restraint in a sample of 50 women with eating disorders attending an outpatient treatment program at the time of the study. In another sample of 49 adolescents with eating disorders four years after attending an inpatient treatment program, interoceptive awareness was moderately negatively related to bulimic tendencies ($r=-.62$, $p < .01$). If one conceptualizes eating disorders on a continuum ranging from normal, asymptomatic eating behavior to eating disordered behavior, individuals with low emotional awareness tend to be placed toward the symptomatic and eating disordered end of the continuum.

Maturity Fears

Maturity fears represent the desire to return to preadolescent years when faced with the responsibilities of adulthood. A four-year longitudinal study with eating disordered females demonstrated that maturity fears predicted poor outcomes in patients with anorexia. In that sample, maturity fears explained 62 percent of the differences in individuals with anorexia nervosa, restrictive type. With adults, maturity fears were revealed in 88.3 percent of individuals with anorexia nervosa.

Achievement-Orientation

Achievement-orientation is defined by the need to succeed, in comparison to others. That is, whereas some individuals may be motivated to improve their own personal ability beyond its previous measurement (e.g., marathon split times), individuals who are highly achievement-oriented are motivated to achieve in comparison to their competition (e.g., placing first in the marathon). According to researchers, individuals with unresolved body image issues (i.e., overestimation of body shape and weight) tended to excessively control their diet and exercise habits in an attempt to minimize their body dissatisfaction. Additionally, hypercompetitiveness, or the need to be successful at all costs, has been documented in college students with eating disorders. As appearance has been identified as one domain of competition, it has been theorized that hypercompetitiveness is used by eating disordered individuals as a means to gain or regain control or to offset low self-esteem temporarily by being better than someone else. It is related to other personality traits common in individuals with eating disorders such as neuroticism and low self-esteem. As a result, hypercompetitiveness and the motivation to achieve in the domain of appearance (demonstrating achievement-orientation) predicted disordered eating behaviors in female college students.

Dichotomous Thinking

Dichotomous thinking refers to the need to see things as one way or another, as black or white or as right or wrong. Individuals who think in such extreme terms have reported more disordered eating behaviors than those who exhibit no eating disordered symptoms and those who exhibit fewer disordered eating behaviors. Although some research has indicated that dichotomous thinking does not increase at the same rate that disordered eating behaviors increase, individuals with eating disordered behaviors have reported more dichotomous thinking than individuals who do not exhibit eating disordered behaviors.

Neuroticism

Heightened levels of neuroticism, or a propensity toward negative emotions like worry, anxiety, hypersensitivity, depression, guilt, fear, and disgust, have been observed in individuals with disordered eating behaviors. Individuals who exhibit more neurotic tendencies also have a tendency to have more intense mood swings. This may interact with other personality traits present in individuals with disordered eating behaviors. Neuroticism has been more evident among individuals who have binge tendencies. It may be that individuals with binge tendencies exhibit more neurotic tendencies because individuals with more binge tendencies also have a tendency to be more obsessive. That is, individuals with higher binge tendencies are also more likely to express feelings of worry, anxiety, depression, guilt, and fear than anorexic clients.

Approval from Others (Low Self-Esteem)

Although most individuals seek approval from others, research indicates that the need to gain approval from others is higher among individuals with eating disorders. This need to obtain others' approval to be happy and impress others tends to increase as disordered eating symptomology intensifies. As some researchers have suggested, gaining approval from others is based upon perceived worth (i.e., self-esteem) in the form of attractiveness. Therefore, if an individual requires approval from others to feel happy, that individual must be viewed as attractive. This may be exacerbated in individuals who may be more preoccupied with physical appearance, may be more sensitive to interpersonal relationships, or have more fragile self-esteem (i.e., narcissistic tendencies). Additionally, because individuals with eating disordered symptomology often think in terms of black and white, they may believe the only way to gain approval is to lose weight and be perceived as attractive.

Researchers have found that 20.8 percent of females in Spain in the age group of 12–21 years who exhibited higher scores on the EAT-40 had low self-esteem. As one might imagine, self-esteem is directly related to body dissatisfaction such that individuals with lower self-esteem also have greater body dissatisfaction. Moreover, individuals with lower self-esteem and greater body dissatisfaction tend to exhibit more disordered eating behaviors. It seems that low self-esteem, paired with high levels of perfectionism, may be a predisposing factor to eating disorder pathology.

Conclusion

A number of personality traits have been shown to be associated with eating disordered behaviors. Low self-esteem, body dissatisfaction, ineffectiveness, interpersonal distrust, low interoceptive awareness, maturity fears, impulse regulation, and social insecurity predicted nearly 46 percent of college women with eating disorders. Gaining an understanding of which psychological characteristics are associated with eating disorders is a good start to understanding these disorders. However, eating disorders are complex and personality factors can interact with each other as well as with social and biological influences.

ASHLEY M. COKER-CRANNEY

Bibliography

Borda Mas, Mercedes, Maria Luisa Avargues Navarro, Ana Maria Lopez Jimenez, Inmaculada Torres Perez, Carmen del Rio Sanchez, and Maria Angeles Perez San Gregorio. "Personality Traits and Eating Disorders: Mediating Effects of Self-Esteem and Perfectionism." *International Journal of Clinical and Health Psychology* 11 (2011): 205-227.

Burckle, Michelle A., Richard M. Ryckman, Joel A. Gold, Bill Thorton, and Roberta J. Audesse. "Forms of Competitive Attitude and Achievement Orientation in Relation to Disordered Eating." *Sex Roles* 40 (1999): 853–70.

Cassin, Stephanie E., and Kristin M. von Ranson. "Personality and Eating Disorders: A Decade in Review." *Clinical Psychology Review* 25 (2005): 895–916.

Castro-Fornieles, Josefina, Pilar Gual, Fransisca Lahortiga, Araceli Gila, Vanesa Casula, Cynthia Fuhrmann, Milagros Imirizaldu, Begona Saura, Esteve Martinez, and Josep Toro. "Self-Oriented Perfectionism in Eating Disorders." *International Journal of Eating Disorders* 40 (2007): 562–68.

Cohen, Diane L., and Trent A. Petrie. "An Examination of Psychological Correlates of Disordered Eating among Undergraduate Women." *Sex Roles* 52 (2005): 29–42.

Garner, David M., Marion P. Olmsted, and Janet Polivy. "Development and Validation of a Multidimensional Eating Disorder Inventory for Anorexia Nervosa and Bulimia." *International Journal of Eating Disorders* 2 (1983): 15–34.

Merwin, Rhonda M., Nancy L. Zucker, Jennie L. Lacy, and Camden A. Elliott. "Interoceptive Awareness in Eating Disorders: Distinguishing Lack of Clarity from Non-acceptance of Internal Experience." *Cognition and Emotion* 24 (2010): 892–902.

Peck, Lisa D., and Owen Richard Lightsey, Jr. "The Eating Disorders Continuum, Self-Esteem, and Perfectionism." *Journal of Counseling and Development* 86 (2008): 184–92.

Podar, Iris, Aave Hannus, and Juri Allik. "Personality and Affectivity Characteristics Associated with Eating Disorders: A Comparison of Eating Disordered, Weight-Preoccupied, and Normal Samples." *Journal of Personality Assessment* 73 (1999): 133–47.

Rossier, Valerie, Monique Bolognini, Bernard Plancherel, and Olivier Halfon. "Sensation Seeking: A Personality Trait Characteristic of Adolescent Girls and Young Women with Eating Disorders?" *European Eating Disorders Review* 8 (2000): 245–52.

Stice, Eric. "Risk and Maintenance Factors for Eating Pathology: A Meta-Analytic Review." *Psychological Bulletin* 128 (2002): 825–48.

van der Ham, T., D. C. van Stien, and H. van Engeland. "Personality Characteristics Predict Outcome of Eating Disorders in Adolescents: A 4-year Prospective Study." *European Child & Adolescent Psychiatry* 7 (1998): 79–84.

von Ransen, Kristin M. "Personality and Eating Disorders." In *Annual Review of Eating Disorders Part 2 — 2008,* edited by Stephen Wonderlich, James E. Mitchell, Martina de Zwaan, and Howard Steiger, 84–96. New York: Radcliff Publishing, 2008.

PERSONALITY DISORDERS

Personality disorders represent a category of mental health diagnoses from the *Diagnostic and Statistical Manual of Mental Disorders* that covers a pattern of personality traits that are inflexible and maladaptive. Certain enduring personality traits are displayed across social and personal contexts. An individual with a personality disorder often experiences subjective distress, problems with impulse control, and difficulty with interpersonal difficulties. Although personality disorders typically begin in adolescence or early adulthood, characteristics are often enduring and tied to long-term issues. When personality disorders are coupled with other mental disorders (e.g., eating disorders), the prognosis (i.e., likelihood of recovery) is generally poorer than if there was a sole diagnosis. Therefore, it is important that assessment for comorbid conditions (e.g., personality disorders) occur early in the treatment process with eating disorder clients.

Types of Personality Disorders

Ten specific types of personality disorders were identified in the *DSM-IV* to include Paranoid Personality Disorder, Schizoid Personality Disorder, Schizotypal Personality Disorder, Antisocial Personality Disorder, Borderline Personality Disorder, Histrionic Personality Disorder, Narcissistic Personality Disorder, Avoidant Personality Disorder, Dependent Personality Disorder, Obsessive-Compulsive Personality Disorder, and Personality Disorder Not Otherwise Specified. Although all personality disorder diagnoses have been identified among eating disordered clients, according to some studies the most common comorbid personality disorders with eating disorders are borderline personality disorder and obsessive-compulsive disorder. Borderline personality disorder is characterized by a pervasive pattern of instability in interpersonal relationships, self-image, and mood. Impulsivity is often observed by early adulthood and is present across contexts. Individuals with borderline personality disorder experience intense abandonment issues and have a pattern of intense and unstable relationships. It is common for these individuals to report love-hate relationships with others in their lives. Borderline personality disorder was the most commonly diagnosed personality disorder among individuals with an eating disorder diagnosis. In fact, borderline personality occurred among 28 percent of individuals with bulimia nervosa and among 25 percent of individuals who had anorexia nervosa with purging symptoms.

Obsessive-Compulsive Personality Disorder was the second most common personality disorder within individuals who had eating disorders. Obsessive-Compulsive Personality Disorder, which is a separate diagnosis from Obsessive-Compulsive Disorder (OCD), represents a personality trait of having a preoccupation with orderliness, perfectionism, and mental and interpersonal control. Individuals with Obsessive-Compulsive Personality Disorder struggle with flexibility, openness, and efficiency. Behaviors such as painstaking attention to rules, trivial details, lists and schedules appear in early adulthood. Individuals with anorexia nervosa (restricting type) show a 22 percent prevalence rate of Obsessive-Compulsive Personality Disorder. These rates of personality disorders were higher than the estimated rates of 5–10 percent within the general population.

Treatment Implications of Personality Disorders and Eating Disorders

It is important to address rigid personality patterns and impulse control issues within treatment to prevent relapse among eating disorder clients who have personality disorders. Therefore, Dialectical Behavior Therapy (DBT), which was originally developed for individuals with personality disorders, is commonly used as part of a comprehensive treatment program in both individual and group settings. Individuals are challenged to be mindful and notice when they are experiencing emotional dysregulation so that they can use effective and adaptive coping skills rather than revert back to their eating disordered behaviors. Unfortunately, personality disorders have often been associated with a lower recovery rate and higher rates of relapse within residential and inpatient populations. Therefore, clinicians with strong boundaries who are trained in DBT are most ideal for addressing the complexity of comorbid eating disorder and personality disorders.

Conclusion

Personality disorders occur at higher rates among the eating disorder population than in the general population. Although 10 personality disorders have been identified in the *Diagnostic and Statistical Manual of Mental Disorders, Fourth Edition,* borderline personality disorder and obsessive-compulsive personality disorder are observed most frequently among eating disordered clients. A comprehensive treatment plan should assess for and address personality disorders. Because of the high rate of personality disorders within residential and inpatient populations, many eating disorder treatment facilities include DBT groups as part of standard care. Unfortunately, if not addressed, personality disorders can represent long-term patterns of interpersonal difficulty that can contribute to poorer prognosis among eating disordered individuals.

JUSTINE J. REEL

Bibliography

American Psychiatric Association. *Diagnostic and Statistical Manual of Mental Disorders, 4th Edition, Text Revision.* Washington, DC: American Psychiatric Association, 2000.

Chen, Eunice Yu, Milton Zebediah Brown, Melanie Susanna Harned, and Marsha Marie Linehan. "A Comparison of Borderline Personality Disorder with and without Eating Disorders." *Psychiatry Research* 170, no. 1 (2009): 86–90. doi: 10.1016/j.psychres. 2009.03.006.

Chen, Eunice Yu, Michael Sean McCloskey, Sara Michelson, Kathryn Hope Gordon, and Emil Coccaro. "Characterizing Eating Disorders in a Personality Disorders Sample." *Psychiatry Research* 185 (2011): 427–32. doi: 10.1016/j.psychres.2010.07.002.

Courbasson, Christine, and Jacqueline M. Brunshaw. "The Relationship between Concurrent Substance Use Disorders and Eating Disorders with Personality Disorders." *International Journal of Environmental Research and Public Health* 6 (2009): 2076–2089. doi: 10.3390/ijerph6072076.

De Bolle, Marleen, Barbara De Clercq, Alexandra Pham-Scottez, Saskia Meis, Jean-Pierre Rolland, Julien Daniel Guelfi, Caroline Braet, and Filip De Fruyt. "Personality Pathology Comorbidity in Adult Females with Eating Disorders." *Journal of Health Psychology* 16 (2011): 303–313. doi: 10.1177/1359105310374780.

Diaz-Marsa, Marina, Jose L. Carrasco, Laura de Anta, Rosa Molina, Jeronimo Saiz, Jesus Cesar, and Juan J. Lopez-Ibor. "Psychobiology of Borderline Personality Traits Related to Subtypes of Eating Disorders: A Study of Platelet MAO Activity." *Psychiatry Research* 190, no. 2–3 (2011): 287–90. doi: 10.1016.j.psychres.2011.04.035.

Lilenfeld, Lisa Rachelle Riso, Carli Heather Jacobs, Amanda Michelle Woods, and Angela Katherine Picot. "A Prospective Study of Obsessive-Compulsive and Borderline Personality Traits, Race and Disordered Eating." *European Eating Disorders Review* 16 (2008): 124–32. doi: 10.1002/erv.842.

Rowe, Sarah L., Jenny Jordan, Virginia V. W. McIntosh, Frances A. Carter, Chris Frampton, Cynthia M. Bulik, and Peter R. Joyce. "Complex Personality Disorder in Bulimia Nervosa." *Comprehensive Psychiatry* 51 (2010): 592–98. doi: 10.1016/j.comppsych.2010.02.012.

Sansone, Randy A., Jamie W. Chu, and Michael W. Wiederman. "Body Image and Borderline Personality Disorder among Psychiatric Inpatients." *Comprehensive Psychiatry* 51 (2010): 579–84. doi: 10.1016/j.comppsych.2010.04.001.

Sansone, Randy A., and Lori A. Sansone. "Personality Pathology and Its Influence on Eating Disorders." *Innovations in Clinical Neuroscience* 8, no. 3 (2011): 14–18.

PHYSICAL SELF-PERCEPTIONS

Physical self-perceptions, considered part of an individual's overall self-concept, are specifically associated with how a person perceives his or her physical appearance, attractiveness, condition, strength, and competence. In other words, physical self-perceptions include an individual's evaluation of his or her physical appearance as well as physical abilities. Physical self-perceptions are strongly related to general self-concept and self-esteem.

Perceived Physical Attractiveness

Perceptions of physical appearance seem to be particularly important in influencing how individuals feel about themselves overall. This is not too surprising given the social influences of mass media and the value placed upon having an attractive and sexually appealing physique. In cultures where physical beauty is desired and socially and economically rewarded, it is logical that appearance would play a central role in how individuals evaluate themselves. Physical self-perceptions appear to have a strong impact on girls and women, who generally rate their perceived appearance and attractiveness lower than boys and men. Strong cultural pressures to attain and maintain a socially and sexually desirable physique, directed toward females, probably contribute to this gender-related pattern.

Perceived Physical Competence

Perceived physical competence is another important aspect of physical self-concept and is moderately related to overall self-esteem. Individuals who believe that they have strong physical skills and abilities are likely to have positive feelings about themselves in general. Men and boys, compared to women and girls, tend to have more positive evaluations of their physical skills and competence. Males are socialized to participate in sports and athletics from young ages, which may influence perceptions of athletic and physical ability and skills. Early experiences and social reinforcement send clear and consistent messages to boys that excelling in sports is a sign of masculinity, which is highly valued in society. Although it is now more socially acceptable for girls and women to participate in sports and be competent athletes, the expectation is still stronger for boys and men. Thus, gender differences in perceptions of physical and athletic competence still exist.

Physical Self-Perceptions and Physique Control and Eating Behaviors

Positive perceptions of one's physical self are associated with a number of healthy physical behaviors and psychological characteristics. Individuals who feel good about their bodies, both in terms of appearance and competence, are more likely to be physically active and engage in healthful eating. Similarly, positive psychological characteristics such as confidence and assertiveness are generally higher among individuals who have positive self-evaluations of their bodies. Unfortunately, negative perceptions of one's physical self are related to unhealthy behaviors and psychological characteristics. Specifically, individuals who have poor views of their bodies are more likely to engage in body control and eating behaviors that are damaging to their health.

Some individuals, unhappy with their physical appearance and competence, engage in behaviors intended to move their bodies toward what they perceive as a more desirable and attractive shape. Whereas girls and women often desire a thinner, leaner body shape, boys and men often want a more muscular and defined physique. Thus, the types of body control behaviors most commonly used vary. Both males and females report restricting their eating and increasing their physical activity. However, males are more likely to restrict their eating to high-protein foods and to increase their strength training with the goal of developing musculature and losing body fat whereas females are more likely to restrict their caloric intake and to increase their aerobic activity in order to lose weight and attain a thinner physique. More extreme physique and weight and body control behaviors include self-induced vomiting and use of diuretics and laxatives. Such behaviors can be quite dangerous and damaging to one's physical health.

Negative perceptions of one's appearance and attractiveness are also associated with disordered eating attitudes and behaviors. Individuals who are unhappy and dissatisfied with how their bodies look and feel anxious about how others perceive and evaluate their physiques (e.g., social physique anxiety) and have higher incidences of disordered eating. For example, negative perceptions of physical attractiveness are related to binge eating and bulimic symptoms, body dissatisfaction, and a strong desire to be thin. Additionally, individuals diagnosed with eating disorders report more negative physical appearance perceptions compared to individuals without eating disorders. It may be the case that dissatisfaction with one's body promotes unhealthy eating behaviors, thus poor physical self-concept can be an early sign of potentially problematic eating.

Assessment of Physical Self-Perceptions

One of the most commonly used assessments of physical self-perception is the Physical Self-Perception Profile (PSPP), originally developed by Fox and Corbin (1989). The PSPP includes five 6-item subscales including perceived sport competence, body attractiveness, physical conditioning, physical strength, and general self-worth. Items are presented in a structured alternative format; that is, individuals select one of two options presented (e.g., "Some people are fit" but "Other people are not fit") and then identify how true the statement is for them (i.e., very like me or somewhat like me). Items are scored and then summed for each subscale for a subscale score and all items are summed for a total test score. Low scores indicate poor self-perceptions and high scores indicate positive self-perceptions. The PSPP is appropriate for adults and has demonstrated evidence of cross-cultural validity (i.e., the measurement is appropriate for use even with individuals outside of the United States). Additionally, there is a separate version of the PSPP that is appropriate for use with children and youth.

Strategies for Enhancing Physical Self-Perceptions

Although some individuals may engage in excessive exercise or obligatory exercise in order to cope with negative physical self-perceptions which can be associated with disordered eating, in general, physical activity improves perceived physical self-concept. In a review of research studies that implemented an exercise intervention, Fox (2000) found that 78 percent of the studies demonstrated improved physical self-perceptions. There are several possible explanations for these findings. Actual improvements in physical fitness and changes in one's physique resulting from exercise may result in improved self-perceptions. As individuals engage in physical activity, their bodies may start to more closely approximate socially idealized bodies which, in turn, may lead to more positive evaluations of appearance and attractiveness. Additionally, individuals may experience enhanced self-confidence and perceptions of competence associated with physical activity. Improvements in mood and reductions in negative affect resulting from exercise may also contribute to the psychological benefit of physical activity and exercise, which may have positive effects on how individuals evaluate themselves and their bodies.

There seems to be a reciprocal relationship (i.e., a two-way relationship) between physical self-concept and physical activity; physical self-concept influences physical activity and physical activity influences physical self-concept. In other words, (a) interventions targeting improved physical self-concept may be effective in leading to increased physical activity, and (b) interventions targeting increased physical activity may result in increases in positive perceptions of the physical self. Thus, health professionals have multiple options for effectively intervening to improve the psychological and physical health of individuals.

Conclusion

Physical self-perceptions are an important part of one's overall self-concept, playing a central role in how an individual feels about himself or herself. Perceptions of appearance and attractiveness seem to be strongly tied to self-evaluations, with positive perceptions being associated with healthy behaviors and negative perceptions being associated with unhealthy body and eating attitudes and behaviors. Individuals can improve their physical self-perceptions through moderate physical activity.

CHRISTY GREENLEAF

Bibliography

Bardone-Cone, Anna M., Lauren M. Schaefer, Christine R. Maldonado, Ellen E. Fitzsimmons, Megan B. Harney, Melissa A. Lawson, D. Paul Robinson, Aneesh Tosh, and Roma Smith. "Aspects of Self-Concept and Eating Disorder Recovery: What Does The Sense of Self Look Like When An Individual Recovers From An Eating Disorder?" *Journal of Social and Clinical Psychology* 29 (2010): 821–46.

Fox, Kenneth R. "The Effects of Exercise on Self-Perceptions and Self-Esteem." In *Physical Activity and Psychological Well-Being,* edited by Stuart J.H. Biddle, Kenneth R. Fox, and Steve H. Boutcher, 88–117. London: Routledge, 2000.

Fox, Kenneth R., and Charles B. Corbin. "The Physical Self-Perception Profile: Development and Preliminary Validation." *Journal of Sport & Exercise Psychology* 11 (1989): 408–430.

Gentile, Brittany, Shelly Grabe, Brenda Dolan-Pascoe, Jean M. Twenge, and Brooke E. Wells. "Gender Differences in Domain-Specific Self-Esteem: A Meta-Analysis." *Review of General Psychology* 13 (2009): 34–45.

Hagger, Martin S., Stuart J.H. Biddle, Edward W. Chow, Natalia Stambulova, and Maria Kavussanu. "Physical Self-Perceptions in Adolescence: Generalizability of a Hierarchical Multidimensional Model across Three Cultures." *Journal of Cross-Cultural Psychology* 34 (2003): 611–28.

Hagger, Martin S., and Andy Stevenson. "Social Physique Anxiety and Physical Self-Esteem: Gender and Age Effects." *Psychology and Health* 25 (2010): 89–110.

Kerremans, Anneleen, Laurence Claes, and Patricia Bijttebier. "Disordered Eating in Adolescent Males and Females: Associations with Temperament, Emotional and Behavioral Problems and Perceived Self-Competence." *Personality and Individual Differences* 49 (2010): 955–60.

Marsh, Herbert W., Athanasious Papaioannou, and Yannis Theodorakis. "Causal Ordering of Physical Self-Concept and Exercise Behavior: Reciprocal Effects Model and the Influence of Physical Education Teachers." *Health Psychology* 25 (2006): 316–28.

Mehlenbeck, Robyn S., Elissa Jelalian, Elizabeth E. Lloyd-Richardson, and Chantelle N. Hart. "Effects of Behavioral Weight Control Intervention on Binge Eating Symptoms of Overweight Adolescents." *Psychology in the Schools* 46 (2009): 776–86.

Taylor, Adrian E., and Ken R. Fox. "Effectiveness of a Primary Care Exercise Referral Intervention for Changing Physical Self-Perceptions Over 9 Months." *Health Psychology* 24 (2005): 11–21.

Welk, Gregory J., and Bob Eklund. "Validation of the Children and Youth Physical Self-Perceptions Profile for Young Children." *Psychology of Sport & Exercise* 6 (2005): 51–65.

PICA

Pica is a feeding disorder that is characterized by the persistent eating of nonnutritive substances for at least one month when this behavior is developmentally inappropriate (i.e., > 18 to 24 months). The type of substance ingested tends to vary by age with infants and younger children eating paint, plaster, string, hair, or cloth. Older children with pica have been observed eating animal droppings, sand, insects, leaves, or pebbles. Adolescents and adults with pica often consume clay or soil. Other nonfood substances ingested by individuals with pica include laundry starch, vinyl gloves, plastic, pencil erasers, ice, fingernails, coal, chalk, light bulbs, needles, cigarette butts, and burnt matches. Pica does not represent a food aversion, fear of gaining weight, or body image disturbance. Therefore, pica is not classified in the main eating disorder section of the *Diagnostic and Statistical Manual of Mental Disorders* with other eating disorders (e.g., Anorexia Nervosa, Bulimia Nervosa). Rather, it is categorized within feeding and eating disorders of infancy or early childhood due to the fact that its highest frequency of occurrence is among children.

Frequency of Pica

The exact prevalence of pica is unknown since the disorder is often unrecognized and underreported. Pica is observed more commonly during the second and third years of life. Pica occurs in 25–33 percent of young children and in 20 percent of children who are seen in mental health clinics. Children who are developmentally delayed (i.e., intellectual disabilities) and those suffering from autism are affected more often than children without intellectual disabilities. The risk for the development of pica and the severity of pica increases with increasing severity of the intellectual disability. In fact, pica represents the most prevalent type of eating-related diagnosis among individuals who have an intellectual disability. In one study, pica was observed in 25.8 percent of persons with intellectual disabilities residing at a mental health institution.

It is rare for an adult to have pica unless he or she has an intellectual disability, with a few exceptions cited for pregnant women. In terms of gender, pica typically occurs in equal numbers among boys and girls. It is considered rare for pica to occur among adolescent males of average intelligence who live in developed countries. Risk factors for pica include poverty, neglect, lack of parental supervision, and being developmental delayed.

Treatment for Pica

Treatment is indicated for persons with pica and has typically involved behavioral approaches that use reinforcers and punishers to shape behaviors. Although behavioral approaches have shown moderate improvement, social interaction has been found to lower rates of pica. The more an individual with an intellectual ability had the opportunity to have social contact, the more pica-related behaviors were reduced or went away. Treatment has often involved introducing a new task to replace pica behavior. Because pica can include ingesting toxic substances, it has been found to be more deadly than other forms of self-injurious behavior.

Conclusion

Although pica has been labeled a feeding disorder, it is often quite separate from other types of eating disorders. Pica typically occurs in young children and individuals with intellectual disabilities. Pica decreases with age and with higher intelligence levels among individuals from developed countries. The form of nonfood substances ingested can vary, but treatment is critical since many of the items can be toxic. Treatment is difficult, but social interaction has been related to decreases in pica behavior.

JUSTINE J. REEL

Bibliography

American Psychiatric Association. *Diagnostic and Statistical Manual of Mental Disorders, 4th Edition, Text Revision.* Washington, DC: American Psychiatric Association, 2000.

Ammaniti, Massimo, Loredana Lucarelli, Silvia Cimino, Francesca D'Olimpio, and Irene Chatoor. "Feeding Disorders of Infancy: A Longitudinal Study to Middle Childhood." *International Journal of Eating Disorders* 4 (2011): 1–9. doi: 10.1002/eat.20925.

Fotoulaki, Maria, Paraskevi Panagopoulou, Ioannis Efstration, and Sanda Nousia-Arvanitakis. "Pitfalls in the Approach to Pica." *European Journal of Pediatrics* 166 (2007): 623–24. doi: 10.1007/s00431-006-0282-1.

Maslinski, Pantcho G., and Jeffrey A. Loeb. "Pica-associated Cerebral Edema in an Adult." *Journal of the Neurological Sciences* 225 (2004): 149–51. doi: 10.1016/j.jns.2004.07.016.

Piazza, Cathleen C., Wayne W. Fisher, Gregory P. Hanley, Linda A. LeBlanc, April S. Worsdell, Steven E. Lindauer, and Kris M. Keeney. "Treatment of Pica through Multiple Analyses of its Reinforcing Functions." *Journal of Applied Behavior Analysis* 31 (1998): 165–89.

Wasano, Lauren C., John C. Borrero, and Carolynn S. Kohn. "Brief Report: A Comparison of Indirect Versus Experimental Strategies for the Assessment of Pica." *Journal of Autism Developmental Disorders* 39 (2009): 1582–1586. doi: 10.1007/s10803-009-0766-8.

PLANET HEALTH

Planet Health is an interdisciplinary middle school health curriculum designed to address low activity levels among adolescents that can contribute to the development of obesity and diabetes. The goal of Planet Health is to improve the fitness level and nutritional habits of students by providing classroom and physical education activities across the school curricula for existing math, science, social studies, language arts, health, and physical education classes.

History of Planet Health

The Planet Health curriculum was originally developed and refined over a seven-year period with the first edition of the program published in 2001. A team of researchers developed the Planet Health program and the accompanying micro-units with funding from the National Institutes of Health. The curriculum was tested by more than 100 teachers with 2,000 students in four Boston-area school districts. During the two-year filed testing period, teachers helped to revise the curriculum and develop the eventual Planet Health program. The second edition updated materials to incorporate new lessons—including decreasing sugar-sweetened beverages—and provides CD-ROM materials to teachers.

Evaluation of Planet Health

The effectiveness of Planet Health was evaluated using 10 schools with half being assigned to receive the curriculum and half serving as a control group. Planet Health was found to reduce obesity among female participants over a two-year period with a noteworthy decrease in screen time. This decrease in television viewing was found for both male and female participants. Additionally, an increase in knowledge about nutrition and physical activity and improved consumption of fruits and vegetables was reported for participants in Planet Health.

An unintended consequence of the program was a decrease in pathological eating behaviors observed among teen girls. In order to assess the impact of Planet Health on disordered eating behaviors of middle school students, 480 girls in the age group of 10–14 years were assigned to either an intervention or a control condition. After the intervention, girls in the group that received Planet Health were less than half as likely to report purging or using diet pills at follow-up compared with girls in control groups.

Conclusion

The Planet Health curriculum has been in existence for over a decade; it aims to address poor nutritional habits and lack of physical activity among middle school students. In addition to providing classroom lectures to disseminate knowledge about leading a healthy lifestyle, the curriculum includes physical education activities that can be integrated into an existing school curriculum. Although many obesity prevention programs have been implemented in health and physical education classes, Planet Health's curriculum is unique in its ability to fit into math, social studies, science, and language arts classes as well. Evaluation of Planet Health found that students who participated in it reduced screen time, increased consumption of fruits and vegetables, and increased their knowledge about healthy diet and exercise. The program showed decreased obesity rates and screen time for female participants. An unintended benefit of the Planet Health curriculum was reduced dieting and disordered eating (e.g., purging behaviors). Therefore, Planet Health shows promise as a prevention program that can effectively address both obesity and eating disorders through a single intervention.

JUSTINE J. REEL

Bibliography

Austin, S. Bryn, Alison E. Field, Jean L. Wiecha, Karen E. Peterson, and Steven L. Gortmaker. "The Impact of a School-Based Obesity Prevention Trial on Disordered Weight-Control Behaviors in Early Adolescent Girls." *Archives of Pediatric Adolescent Medicine* 159 (2005): 225–30.

Carter, Jill, Jean L. Wiecha, Karen E. Peterson, Suzanne Nobrega, and Steven L. Gortmaker. *Planet Health: an Interdisciplinary Curriculum for Teaching Middle School Nutrition and Physical Activity, Second Edition.* Champaign, IL: Human Kinetics, 2007.

Gortmaker, Steven L., Karen E. Peterson, Jean L. Wiecha, Arthur M. Sobol, Sujata Dixit, Mary K. Fox, and Nan Laird. "Reducing Obesity via a School-Based Interdisciplinary Intervention among Youth: Planet Health." *Archives of Pediatric Adolescent Medicine* 153 (1999): 409–418.

PREGNANCY

Women often strive to be skinny while pregnant and then attempt to lose weight quickly after giving birth. This obsession of wanting to stay thin during pregnancy, a natural course in a woman's life cycle, has many professionals concerned about the health of the mother and the baby. According to a recent poll on NBC's TODAY Moms website, approximately 49 percent of the readers selected "Why doesn't she eat more?" when asked, "When you see someone who is skinny while pregnant, are you. . . . " However, 27 percent of the people chose "How does she do it?" and 24 percent selected "Wow, she looks great." In other words, 51 percent or over 4,600 people envy or are impressed by a woman who is skinny while she is pregnant. This type of mentality is driven by celebrities' fixation for the ideal body even during pregnancy (e.g., Rachel Zoe, Nicole Richie, Victoria Beckham, Bethenny Frankel), but striving for perfection can have psychological and physical consequences. According to the TODAY NBC chief medical consultant, Dr. Nancy Snyderman, overeating and undereating are bad for pregnant women because "you're starving the fetus." http://moms.today.com/_news/2011/07/28/7184564-is-skinny-while-pregnant-a-goal-or-unrealistic-trend.

Physiological Changes during Pregnancy

A multitude of physiological changes occur during pregnancy, which constitutes alterations in the human body and function. During the first trimester, a woman's body undergoes many changes. Hormonal changes affect every organ, with the stopping of the menstrual cycle serving as a clear sign of being pregnant. Other changes during the first trimester include extreme tiredness, tender or swollen breasts, upset stomach (morning sickness), craving or distaste for certain foods, mood swings, constipation, higher frequency of urination, headaches, heartburn, and weight gain. During the second trimester, the abdomen stretches and expands as the baby continues to grow. Some women may also experience body aches (e.g., back, abdomen, groin, thigh), stretch marks on the stomach, breasts, thighs, and buttocks, patches of darker skin on the cheeks, forehead, nose or upper lid, tingling hands, and swelling of the ankles, fingers, and face. Some of the same discomforts experienced during the second trimester may persist in the third trimester. In addition, many women will notice shortness of breath, heartburn, belly button sticking out, baby "dropping" or moving lower in the abdomen, and contractions.

Maternal blood supply increases by 20–50 percent during pregnancy, and cardiac output increases by 30–40 percent, which makes it one of the most important changes of pregnancy. During pregnancy heart rate increases by 10 to 15 beats per minute (bpm) around 28 to 32 weeks. The increase in blood volume helps to provide the fetus with oxygenated blood and nutrients. Changes in ventilation also occur as early as the fourth week of gestation. Minute ventilation increases by approximately 50 percent. This is caused by an increase in tidal volume (40%) and respiratory rate (15%). In addition, many hormones are being secreted during pregnancy. The hormone relaxin is responsible for relaxing the ligaments as well as softening the collagenous tissues. Thus, relaxin is also responsible for lordosis (inward curvature of the spine) during pregnancy. All of these bodily changes can overwhelm the expecting mother, especially when she is experiencing these changes for the first time.

Pregnancy and Body Image

As a woman experiences her pregnancy, she becomes increasingly aware of her bodily changes with each trimester. Pregnant women are likely to re-evaluate their body image over time as they gain weight and as they experience changes in body size and shape. The resulting body dissatisfaction that accompanies these changes during pregnancy can lead to unhealthy eating and weight loss behaviors (e.g., restricting food intake). Restrictive eating leads to complications (e.g., hypertension, premature delivery, low birth weight) for the mother and unborn child.

Researchers have been examining women's changing body image throughout pregnancy for over 40 years. Early studies have indicated that body dissatisfaction increases over the course of pregnancy. However, more recent studies have reported that there were no significant changes in body dissatisfaction from early to middle pregnancy, but body dissatisfaction was greater at early pregnancy compared to pre-pregnancy. Other researchers have found that women reported higher body dissatisfaction during early- and mid-second trimester. Similar to body image research with nonpregnant women, 77 percent of pregnant women indicated that they would like their bodies to be smaller. Despite feeling dissatisfied with their bodies, women reported feeling more fit and strong during the pregnancy than before the pregnancy, and they felt more attractive prior to pregnancy than they did during the early, middle, and late trimesters.

Body image prior to pregnancy was also a strong predictor of negative body image in late pregnancy. Other factors that influenced women to feel less attractive and strong were depression (in late pregnancy) and comparing one's body to other people's bodies (in early pregnancy). Body comparison tendencies in early pregnancy predicted women viewing weight and shape and feeling fat as important factors during late pregnancy. This body comparison could lead to more body dissatisfaction and weight concerns.

Body Image and Weight Gain during Pregnancy

The relationship between body image and weight-related concerns prior to pregnancy suggests that body image may be related to women gaining weight during pregnancy. For example, a 2007 study found that women who were obese before they were pregnant had greater weight and body shape concerns before and during pregnancy than non-obese women. In a 2011 study, researchers at the University of North Carolina, Chapel Hill, conducted a study interviewing 1,192 women during pregnancy at 15 to 20 weeks, 17 to 22 weeks, 24 to 29 weeks, 27 to 30 weeks, and in-hospital following delivery about their health behaviors, diet, physical activity, and body image. They found that approximately 50 percent of the women preferred a small body size, and most women who preferred the small body size were between the ages of 25 and 34, were Caucasian, had normal BMI before pregnancy, were married, highly educated, and of high income. In addition, the researchers identified at-risk women (i.e., women with body dissatisfaction, women who had a thin ideal body size, lower education level, and lower income) who had gained excessive weight outside of the recommended guidelines from the Institute of Medicine. Gaining excessive weight outside of the recommended ranges can result in poorer birth outcomes due to increased maternal and fetal complications such as increased risk of cesarean section and macrosomia (baby weighing more than 8 pounds and 13 ounces), whereas inadequate weight gain can lead to premature birth.

Effects of Pregnancy on Eating Disorders

Approximately 5–7 percent of pregnant women suffer from eating disorders. Previous studies have investigated the impact of pregnancy on eating disorder symptoms, but the results remain unclear. Most studies evaluating the course of eating disorder symptoms during pregnancy have reported improvement, a return to prepregnancy symptom levels, or even worse symptoms in the postpartum period. Rocco and colleagues investigated the effects of pregnancy on eating attitudes and disorders in 97 women who were either pregnant with a positive history of dieting, pregnant with a clinical diagnosis of an eating disorder, or no history of an eating disorder. They found that eating attitudes and body satisfaction improved in the clinical and subclinical eating disorder groups of pregnant women during the middle phase of the pregnancy. This improvement could be due to an increase in the quality of life, but the benefits were short-lived, with the women returning to previous levels after delivery.

On the other hand, weight gain during pregnancy may exacerbate or reignite weight and shape concerns, which may lead to a relapse of the eating disorder in the postpartum period. For example, researchers examined the presence of eating disordered behaviors, body and weight concerns among women with a recent episode of eating disorder and women with a past history of eating disorder. They found that about 10 percent of the women with recent eating disorders reported dieting for weight loss at 32 weeks, a third of the women purged during pregnancy, and they had high rates of concern about weight gain during the third trimester of pregnancy. Similarly, 10 percent of women with a past history of eating disorder had purged in the first 18 weeks of pregnancy and 15 percent vomited at least once daily during pregnancy.

Effects of Eating Disorders on Pregnancy

Although there is a lack of information on the effects of eating disorders on pregnancy, the limited information does suggest that there are many potential negative consequences for the mother and the baby. Eating disorders, such as anorexia nervosa and bulimia nervosa, are associated with negative consequences during pregnancy such as higher rates of miscarriage, low birth weight, obstetric complications, and postpartum depression. Eating disorders are associated with nutritional, metabolic, and psychological changes that can have negative effects on the development of the fetus. The most cited complications in anorexic and bulimic pregnant women include not gaining enough weight, miscarriage, and hyperemesis gravidarum during pregnancy; birth complications include low birth rate, preterm delivery, stillbirth, breech delivery, and fetal abnormality.

It has been reported that women with eating disorders gain less weight and have smaller infants than healthy women. Researchers have investigated the relationship between pregnancy outcomes and eating behaviors in women who delivered low body weight infants. Women who delivered small-for-gestational-age (SGA) infants at term reported unhealthier eating behaviors before, during, and after the pregnancy than women who delivered preterm infants (before 37 weeks). In addition, women who had low prepregnancy weight, smoked, and had bulimic tendencies tended to have a SGA infant. Factors that predicted preterm births were vomiting during pregnancy and lower dietary restraint. Furthermore, miscarriage rate seemed to be higher in women with eating disorders than in women without eating disorders.

Hyperemesis gravidarum or persistent nausea or vomiting is more common in women with eating disorders than in women without eating disorders. Researchers have reported that 10 percent of the 25 women who were actively engaging in bulimic behaviors had persistent nausea or vomiting during their pregnancies.

One reason for higher frequency of hyperemesis gravidarum in women with bulimia is that it might be a way to rationalize the negative behaviors with more typical consequences of pregnancy. This may actually allow the women with bulimia to hide the bulimic behaviors behind the medical-related consequences of being pregnant.

Although there is not enough evidence to conclude why cesareans are more common in women with eating disorders, researchers have shown that the rate of cesarean delivery was higher in women with eating disorders (16%) than women without eating disorders (3%). Women with eating disorders might be viewed as higher-risk cases by physicians, which might increase the probability that physicians will perform cesareans. Moreover, the behaviors of women with anorexia and bulimia might lead to more complicated labors and deliveries.

Women with eating disorders also reported having higher postpartum depression than women without eating disorders. These women have concerns that healthy women might not have—such as body image concerns, weight concerns, anxiety, and disordered eating behaviors. These concerns could make them more vulnerable to developing postpartum depression. Investigators have reported that 40 percent of women with eating disorders have a history of affective disorders, which places them at a higher risk for postpartum depression.

Postpartum and Body Image

Researchers have found that postpartum women express body image concerns and feel compelled to rapidly return to their prepregnancy weight. Body dissatisfaction may be of particular concern among postpartum women because it can lead to unhealthy dieting, which may result in impaired milk production, milk contamination, and energy deficiency. One study reported that 75 percent of women were concerned about their weight in the first weeks of postpartum. Other researchers revealed that women were still dissatisfied with their weight four months post partum, six months post partum, and a year post partum, and engaged in weight loss methods (e.g., exercise) to lose the weight gained from pregnancy. However, some postpartum women were less dissatisfied with their bodies post partum than during pregnancy.

One noteworthy factor to examine among body dissatisfied postpartum women is weight gain. According to the Institute of Medicine, excessive gestational weight gain (i.e., over 35 pounds for normal weight women, over 25 pounds for overweight women, and over 20 pounds for the obese women) can be associated with long-term weight retention or obesity, which could lead to more body dissatisfaction. However, it is unclear as to which weight factor (e.g., prenatal weight, postpartum weight, or prepregnancy to postpartum weight gain) is most important in predicting body dissatisfaction. Gjerdingen and colleagues in 2009 surveyed over 500 postpartum women at the beginning of postpartum (0-1 month) and 9 months later on weight, body dissatisfaction, and mental health and revealed that body dissatisfaction increased over time, supporting previous research showing that body image concerns become more negative postpartum. In addition, Gjerdingen and colleagues found that mothers' body dissatisfaction at 9 months postpartum was associated with increased weight gain and poorer mental health. The combination of body dissatisfaction and poorer mental health may put mothers at higher risk for developing an eating disorder post partum.

Because postpartum women are dissatisfied with their bodies, a growing number of them are undergoing cosmetic surgery. "Mommy makeover," a term coined by plastic surgeons, is aimed at mothers and usually involves a breast lift with or without breast implants, a tummy tuck, and some liposuction to restore or improve their postpregnancy bodies. According to the American Society of Plastic Surgery, 36 percent (n=107,638) of women between the ages of 30 and 39 underwent breast augmentation and 35 percent of women (n=40,706) in this age group underwent a tummy tuck in 2010. The marketing of the mommy makeover is making women believe that their bodies are worse after giving birth, and that they can easily fix their bodies and problems with cosmetic surgery.

Conclusion

During pregnancy, women experience significant physical changes to the body. Differences in eating, weight, and body shape are significant changes that could influence how women think and feel about their bodies. Some women are dissatisfied with their bodies and desire to be thin because of internal pressures or media portrayals of "skinny while pregnant" celebrities, who they want to emulate and quickly bounce back to their pre-pregnancy weight. Therefore, the desire to have the ideal body while pregnant can have detrimental physical, emotional, and psychological consequences for the mother and baby, including inadequate nutritional intake and eating disorders.

SONYA SOOHOO

Bibliography

Crowell, Debra Tooke. "Weight Change in the Postpartum Period: A Review of Literature." *Journal of Nurse-Midwifery* 40 (1995): 418–23.

Fairburn, Christopher G., and Sarah L. Welch. "The Impact of Pregnancy on Eating Habits and Attitudes to Shape and Weight." *International Journal of Eating Disorders* 9 (1990): 153–60.

Franko, Debra, and Emily B. Spurrell. "Detection and Management of Eating Disorders during Pregnancy." *Obstetrics & Gynecology* 6 (2000): 942–46.

Gjerdingen, Dwenda, Patricia Fontaine, Scott Crow, Patricia McGovern, Bruce Center, and Michael Miner. "Predictors of Mothers' Postpartum Body Dissatisfaction." *Women's Health* 49 (2009): 491–504.

Mehta, Ushma, Anna Maria Siega-Riz, and Amy H. Herring. "Effects of Body Image on Pregnancy Weight Gain." *Maternal and Child Health Journal* 15 (2011): 324–32.

Micali, Nadia, Janet Treasure, and Emily Simonoff. "Eating Disorders Symptoms in Pregnancy: A Longitudinal Study of Women with Recent and Past Eating Disorders and Obesity." *Journal of Psychosomatic Research* 63 (2007): 297–303.

Rocoo, Pier Luigi, Barbara Orbitello, Laura Perini, Valentina Pera, Rossana P. Ciano, and Matteo Balestrieri. "Effects of Pregnancy on Eating Attitudes and Disorders: A Prospective Study." *Journal of Psychosomatic Research* 59 (2005): 175–79.

Skouteris, Helen, Roxane Carr, Eleanor H. Wertheim, Susan J. Paxton, and Dianne Duncombe. "A Prospective Study of Factors That Lead to Body Dissatisfaction during Pregnancy." *Body Image* 2 (2005): 347–61.

TODAY Moms. "Is skinny-while-pregnant a trend?" Accessed August 13, 2011. http://moms.today.com/_news/2011/07/28/7184564-is-skinny-while-pregnant-a-goal-or-unrealistic-trend

U.S. Department of Health and Human Services Office on Women's Health. "Pregnancy." Accessed August 13, 2011. http://www.womenshealth.gov/pregnancy/you-are-pregnant/stages-of-pregnancy.cfm

PREVENTION

Prevention broadly refers to stopping a problem before it occurs by providing health promotion programs or education. There are several types of prevention—including primary and secondary—that are used in efforts to decrease unwanted behaviors and reduce diseases. Although national attention has been placed on the obesity epidemic with less funding available for eating disorder prevention efforts, it is important to consider that weight-related problems exist along a continuum and that binge eating behaviors are often present among overweight and obese individuals.

Types of Prevention

Primary prevention refers to the reduction of the prevalence of a disease mainly by preventing new cases from occurring. For eating disorders, primary prevention efforts can be aimed to address risk factors (e.g., dieting, body dissatisfaction) while strengthening resilience by developing protective factors (e.g., high self-esteem). Universal primary prevention refers to a program that is given to everyone regardless of their risk for developing an eating disorder. For example, National Eating Disorder Awareness Week represents community-wide campaigns that attempt to raise consciousness among diverse individuals about eating disorders. Universal prevention approaches would also include policy changes or laws that are designed to fight a particular problem. Universal prevention is often the easiest type of prevention to execute because programs can be conducted in large groups (e.g., school assemblies). However, research indicates that universal prevention programs are less effective than other types of prevention approaches.

Selective primary prevention is geared toward individuals who may be more at risk for developing eating disorder symptoms. Females have been identified as having higher body dissatisfaction and a stronger likelihood of engaging in disordered eating. Therefore, all-female prevention programs (e.g., Full of Ourselves) are targeted at and implemented with these higher risk groups.

Secondary prevention refers to identifying and working with individuals who show signs of being in the early stages of disordered eating. This type of prevention is used to screen college athletes who are starting their freshman year for any eating issues. Athletes who are red-flagged can get necessary support and treatment (e.g., dietitian) and receive continued monitoring throughout their athletic careers. Another example of secondary prevention is the Identity Intervention Program (IIP) which includes individual and group therapies geared to decrease eating disorder symptoms, improve health, and facilitate a more positive sense of self.

Lack of Prevention Programs

One study determined that 41 percent of male and 61 percent of female undergraduate students felt that eating disorder prevention was very important. Although many schools and students are interested in having eating disorder prevention programs, very few schools offer ongoing eating disorder interventions that are incorporated into required curricula. Instead, schools tend to provide a single lesson about eating disorders in health classes; this involves lecturing about definitions or types of eating disorders and/or showing a movie about an individual (e.g., Tracey Gold) who has suffered from an eating disorder. Unfortunately, these lessons can backfire, as students receive information about pathogenic weight control methods and may be triggered to engage in disordered eating. In fact, using scare tactics such as showing movies or horrifying photos (e.g., protruding rib cages and collar bones) seemed to produce an opposite of the intended effect for students. The most important consideration for any prevention effort is to avoid doing any harm to participants.

History of Prevention Programs

The first generation of primary prevention programs was universally available to all participants and tended to educate them about the adverse effects of eating disorders through the use of psychoeducation materials. As with antidrug campaigns that use scare tactics (e.g., "this is your brain on drugs") to increase one's awareness, it was assumed that any efforts to provide knowledge would be useful in preventing disordered eating behaviors.

A second generation of prevention programs utilized a universal and didactic format that went beyond scare tactics by adding an educational component about sociocultural pressures (e.g., influence of media) to be thin and lose weight. These early programs were provided to everyone regardless of their gender, race, and whether they were considered to be at risk for developing an eating disorder. In addition, the format was didactic and tended to promote an increase of knowledge without any accompanying behavioral change.

More recently, primary prevention programs (e.g., Healthy Buddies) have attempted to target high-risk individuals using an interactive format that goes beyond lecture. Full of Ourselves, which was designed for female adolescents, uses a school-based curriculum that focuses on building self-esteem, girls' leadership, and peer relationships through interactive discussions and activities. Participants have the opportunity to practice skills and receive feedback from peers in the group.

Effectiveness of Eating Disorder Prevention Programs

A recent review of published prevention programs determined that 51 percent of eating disorder prevention programs decreased eating disorder risk factors and that 29 percent of programs decreased current or future disordered eating. Programs that used selected approaches targeted at high-risk individuals were more effective than universal approaches disseminated to everyone. Only selected programs were able to prevent future increases in eating pathology observed in control samples. Alarmingly, other studies have found that universal programs were associated with increased dietary restraint and increased awareness about available eating disorder techniques that can be used to lose weight. Examples of selected prevention efforts include eating disorder prevention programs for dancers, sorority sisters, and teenage females.

According to the same review, the most effective prevention programs were interactive rather than following a lecture-only format and used multiple sessions within the same program rather than a single session. This finding about the need for repeated exposure may explain why universal prevention programs have been largely unsuccessful. Prevention programs that separate females from males seem to produce stronger positive results than programs that keep both sexes in the same group. Eating disorder prevention programs that had participants over the age of 15 were also more effective than programs with younger participants.

Prevention programs that included body acceptance and cognitive behavioral skills training were found to be more successful than psychoeducation programs: however, other researchers indicated that psychoeducation programs were equally effective. Generally, the content of the program curriculum seemed to be less important than the characteristics of the group participants (e.g., female, over 15 years). Furthermore, prevention programs that used trained interventionists who were eating disorder experts were more successful than programs that used teachers who had diverse responsibilities.

Limitations of Prevention Programs

Although selected prevention efforts were found to be significantly more effective in promoting behavior change than universal prevention programs, it is important to ensure that diverse individuals are not excluded from prevention efforts. Most prevention programs rely on risk factor studies rather than on context-specific approaches to eating disorder prevention. By employing a context-specific emphasis one can avoid ignoring variables like race, social class, and gender. Interestingly, gender and other variables have been considered salient in other health promotion efforts (e.g., smoking and AIDS) but have been left out of many eating disorder prevention studies.

For example, it is important for males to have specific prevention programs to address their body image disturbances and the tendency to be at increased risk for abusing steroids and other supplements associated with a stronger drive for muscularity. Interventions should be sensitive to cultural norms and beliefs of the population being served. To avoid oversimplification, it is also important to modify programs for the target population (e.g., males) with the understanding that the needs may be different for preventing anorexia nervosa compared to bulimia nervosa or binge eating disorder. These trends should be taken into consideration rather than creating a one-size-fits-all program.

A limitation for providing eating disorder prevention programs could be access and transportation issues. Individuals who live in rural geographical areas may not be able to participate in prevention programs or may attend schools that lack the resources or diminish the importance of eating disorder prevention. Fortunately, an alternative to providing school-based prevention programs is using an internet-based prevention platform. For example, Student Bodies was developed to provide a forum for support and psycho education to individuals across the country. This 8–10 week program utilizes message boards to allow for discussion about body image concerns. A clear advantage is that computerized formats could provide support to individuals and may be more cost effective than face-to-face programs if the individual has internet access. However, it cannot be taken for granted that every individual will have access to online prevention efforts (e.g., lower socioeconomic status individuals) or will have the technology expertise (e.g., older adults) to utilize a computerized intervention.

Family-Based Prevention Efforts

The importance of involving parents and family cannot be stressed enough and obesity programs have begun to recognize the need to change the entire family system rather than merely focusing on the individual who is identified to be most at risk. In one study, 66 percent of male and 72 percent of female participants felt that parents should be included in eating disorder prevention efforts.

For obesity interventions, family members are used to model healthy (but not excessive) physical activity and nutritional eating. The BodyWorks program provides skills to parents who learn to cook healthy snacks and meals while moving with their kids to increase physical activity. In the Health at Every Size approach obesity prevention programs, the emphasis is on healthy behaviors rather than on losing weight. Obesity prevention efforts need not be separate from eating disorder prevention programs, and recently, integrative approaches have successfully combined eating disorder and obesity prevention programs.

In addition to being positive role models, parents influence the body image of children and adolescents through their use of subtle and overt messages related to size, shape, and appearance. Teasing and negative comments are triggers that are consistently reported by individuals with body image and eating disturbances. Therefore, programs like BodyWorks teach parents to become more aware of "fat talk" and how to replace statements that encourage a diet mentality with more positive statements about health. Interestingly, few eating disorder prevention programs designed for families are available. A rare exception is Off the C.U.F.F., a parent skills program designed to help parents manage eating disorder symptoms in the home. Parents are taught about perfectionism and self-esteem to create an environment of self-acceptance.

Conclusion

Prevention efforts are generally aimed at stopping a behavior or reducing the likelihood that a problem will occur. The different types of prevention include primary and secondary prevention as well as selected and universal prevention. Prevention programs that use an interactive format, have multiple sessions, separate the sexes, and use participants over 15 years of age appear to be the most effective. Eating disorder prevention efforts have been overshadowed by the attention given to obesity interventions. However, integrative programs for eating disorders and obesity are promising. Family-based prevention programs are encouraged to educate all members of the family system about the dangers of dieting and "fat talk."

JUSTINE J. REEL

See also: BodyWorks; Full of Ourselves; Health at Every Size Approach; Off the C.U.F.F.; Parents.

Bibliography

Becker, Carolyn Black, Anna C. Ciao, and Lisa M. Smith. "Moving from Efficacy to Effectiveness in Eating Disorders Prevention: The Sorority Body Image Program." *Cognitive and Behavioral Practice* 15 (2008): 18–27.

Berg, Francie, Jennifer Buechner, Ellen Parham, and Weight Realities Division of the Society for Nutrition Education. "Guidelines for Childhood Obesity Prevention Programs: Promoting Healthy Weight in Children." *Journal of Nutrition Education and Behavior* 35, no. 1 (2003): 1–4.

Costin, Carolyn. *A Comprehensive Guide to the Causes, Treatments and Prevention of Eating Disorders: The Eating Disorder Sourcebook, 3rd Edition.* New York, NY: McGraw-Hill, 2007.

Fingeret, Michelle Cororve, Cortney S. Warren, Antonio Cepeda-Benito, and David H. Gleaves. "Eating Disorder Prevention Research: A Meta-Analysis." *Eating Disorders: A Journal of Treatment and Prevention* 14 (2006): 191–213. doi: 10.1080/10640260600638899.

Levine, Michael P., and Linda Smolak. *The Prevention of Eating Problems and Eating Disorders: Theory, Research, and Practice.* Mahwah, NJ: Lawrence Erlbaum Associates, 2005.

Lindenberg, Katajun, Markus Moessner, Joanna Harney, Orla McLaughlin, and Stephanie Bauer. "E-Health for Individualized Prevention of Eating Disorders." *Clinical Practice & Epidemiology in Mental Health* 7 (2011): 74–83.

McMillan, Whitney, Eric Stice, and Paul Ronde. "High- and Low-Level Dissonance-Based Eating Disorder Prevention Programs with Young Women with Body Image Concerns: An

Experimental Trial." *Journal of Consulting and Clinical Psychology* 79, no. 1 (2011): 129–34.

Neumark-Sztainer, Dianne. "Preventing the Broad Spectrum of Weight-Related Problems: Working with Parents to Help Teens Achieve a Healthy Weight and a Positive Body Image." *Journal of Nutrition Education and Behavior* 37 (2005): S133-S139.

Reel, Justine J., and Joseph Halowich. "Do's and Don'ts for Eating Disorder and Obesity Prevention in Community Settings." *Utah's Health: An Annual Review* 15 (2010): 58–61.

Steiner-Adair, Catherine, Lisa Sjostrom, Debra L. Franko, Seeta Pai, Rochelle Tucker, Anne E. Becker, and David B. Herzog. "Primary Prevention of Risk Factors for Eating Disorders in Adolescent Girls: Learning from Practice." *International Journal of Eating Disorders* 32, no. 4 (2002): 401–411.

Stice, Eric, and Heather Shaw. "Eating Disorder Prevention Programs: A Meta-Analytic Review." *Psychological Bulletin* 130, no. 2 (2004): 206–227.

Stice, Eric, Heather Shaw, and C. Nathan Marti. "A Meta-Analytic Review of Eating Disorder Prevention Programs: Encouraging Findings." *Annual Review of Clinical Psychology* 3 (2007): 207–231.

Wick, Katharina, Christina Brix, Bianca Bormann, Melanie Sowa, Bernhard Strauss, and Uwe Berger. "Real-world Effectiveness of a German School-based Intervention for Primary Prevention of Anorexia Nervosa in Preadolescent Girls." *Preventive Medicine* 52 (2011): 152–58. doi: 10.1016/j.ypmed.2010.11.022.

Zucker, Nancy. *Off the C.U.F.F.!!!! A Parents Skills Book for the Management of Eating Disorders.* Durham, NC: Duke University Medical Center, 2004.

PRO-ANA

Pro-ana refers to the promotion of anorexia nervosa while Pro-mia is the celebration of bulimia nervosa. Both groups are considered to be in direct opposition to a pro-recovery stance; they offer encouragement for individuals to engage in and continue disordered eating behaviors (e.g., fasting, restricting). Pro-ana and the celebration of anorexia nervosa has been symbolized by wearing red bracelets and pro-mia has been represented by blue bracelets. Pro-ana and Pro-mia organizations have emerged with the opportunity to have a web presence.

Pro–Eating Disorder Websites

Pro–eating disorder websites, which claim to be "free of judgment for one's eating disorder lifestyle," have proliferated since the late 1990s and provide online forums for discussion boards, "tips and tricks" as well as "thinspirations" (i.e., pictures, quotes and lyrics designed to inspire individuals to stay committed to the maintenance of anorexic behaviors). Photos on these websites portray ultrathin models with protruding collar bones and rib cages. It is also common for pro–eating disorder websites to post an "Ana Creed" that includes statements such as "I must weigh myself first thing every morning, and keep that number in mind throughout the remainder of that day." "Thin Commandments" consist of 10 pro-ana "truths" related to the celebration of thinness and the reinforcement of all or nothing thinking (e.g., "Losing weight is good/gaining weight is bad").

Pro–eating disorder websites are not regulated and do not represent the views of trained eating disorder professionals. Unfortunately, the content on these websites can be damaging to the treatment progress of individuals suffering from eating disorders and can be triggering for disordered eating behaviors.

The Impact of Pro–Eating Disorder Websites

Pro-ana websites have created controversy due to their support for resistance against eating disorder treatment and recovery with an already difficult treatment population. Additionally, these pro–eating disorder websites have been found to trigger disordered eating behaviors and to contribute to relapses among individuals with an eating disorder history.

College females who were exposed to a pro-anorexia website reported decreased self-esteem and perceived unattractiveness, feeling overweight, and more negative mood than when they viewed a generic home décor website. In a separate investigation of 1575 women, researchers found that females who viewed pro–eating disorder sites had higher body dissatisfaction and dysfunctional eating patterns than the control group which was not exposed to such sites. Alarmingly, a more recent 2010 study found that college students who were exposed to pro–eating disorder websites for 1.5 hours reduced weekly caloric intake from 12,167 calories to 9697 calories following exposure. These changes in energy intake persisted for three weeks following exposure to the sites.

Parent Education about Pro–Eating Disorder Websites

Although the results of being exposed to pro-ana websites have been staggering, only 52.8 percent of parents reported being aware of pro–eating disorder sites. Many parents did not know whether their children visited pro-ana websites and 62.5 percent of parents were unaware of pro-recovery sites. However, in this same study, 96 percent of adolescents who viewed pro–eating disorder websites reported learning new techniques for weight loss.

Conclusion

Pro-ana and pro-mia represent the promotion of eating disorders as a choice rather than a serious disease. In fact, the celebration of anorexia nervosa and thinness has led to pro-ana support groups and bracelets as symbols of the ana lifestyle. Pro-eating disorder websites offer forums for discussion boards about how to stay disordered, thinspirations, and techniques related to unhealthy weight loss. Although research over the past decade has clearly documented the damaging effects of exposure to pro–eating disorder websites, websites are difficult to regulate and have a large group of pro-ana followers. Parents need to receive education about the triggering nature of pro–eating disorder websites.

JUSTINE J. REEL

Bibliography

Bardone-Cone, Anna M., and Kamila M. Cass. "Investigating the Impact of Pro-Anorexia Websites: A Pilot Study." *European Eating Disorders Review* 14 (2006): 256-62. doi: 10.1002/ERV.714.

Bardone-Cone, Anna M., and Kamila M. Cass. "What Does Viewing a Pro-Anorexia Website Do? An Experimental Examination of Website Exposure and Moderating Effects." *International Journal of Eating Disorders* 40, no. 6 (2007): 537–48. doi: 10.1002/eat.20396.

Giles, David. "Constructing Identities in Cyberspace: The Case of Eating Disorders." *British Journal of Social Psychology* 45 (2006): 463–77. doi: 10/1348/014466605X53596.

Harper, Kelley, Steffanie Sperry, and J. Kevin Thompson. "Viewership of Pro–Eating Disorder Websites: Association with Body Image and Eating Disturbances." *International Journal of Eating Disorders* 41 (2008): 92–95. doi: 10.1002/eat.20408

Jett, Scarlett, David J. LaPorte, and Jill Wanchisn. "Impact of Exposure to Pro–Eating Disorder Websites on Eating Behaviour in College Women." *European Eating Disorders Review* 18 (2010): 410–16. doi: 10.1002/erv.1009

Lyons, Elizabeth J., Matthias R. Mehl, and James W. Pennebaker. "Pro-anorexics and Recovering Anorexics Differ in their Linguistic Internet Self-presentation." *Journal of Psychosomatic Research* 60 (2006): 253–56. doi: 10.1016/j.psychores.2005.07.017

Ransom, Danielle C., Jennifer G. La Guardia, Erik Z. Woody, and Jennifer L. Boyd. "Interpersonal Interactions on Online Forums Addressing Eating Concerns." *International Journal of Eating Disorders* 43 (2010): 161–70.

Wilson, Jenny L., Rebecka Peebles, Kristina K. Hardy, and Iris F. Litt. "Surfing for Thinness: A Pilot Study of Pro–Eating Disorder Web Site Usage in Adolescents with Eating Disorders." *Pediatrics* 118 (2006): 1635–1643. doi: 10.1542/peds.2006-1133

PROGNOSIS

Prognosis refers to one's potential to improve from a particular condition and demonstrate favorable treatment outcomes. It has been difficult to pinpoint an exact prognosis rate for eating disorders due to the complexity and range of the types of disorders represented. However, preliminary findings from outcome studies provide prognosis estimates for Anorexia Nervosa, Bulimia Nervosa, and Eating Disorder Not Otherwise Specified (EDNOS).

Prognosis Rates for Anorexia Nervosa

Anorexia nervosa is marked by frequent relapses and has the highest mortality rate of all mental disorders. Approximately 20 percent of individuals with anorexia nervosa continue to present with eating disorder symptoms. The proportion of deaths ranges from 5 percent to 16 percent across longitudinal studies. However, women with anorexia nervosa are 12 times more likely to experience mortality than women of the same age in the general population. Fifty-four percent of anorexia nervosa deaths were linked to eating disorder–related medical complications, 27 percent was suicide, and 19 percent represented deaths from unknown or other causes.

The prognosis for adolescents is more optimistic than for adults with anorexia nervosa. In contrast to the 30–50 percent of adults who fully recover from anorexia nervosa, approximately 76 percent of adolescents achieved full recovery. It is expected that this improved anorexia nervosa prognosis among adolescents can be attributed to a shorter duration of symptoms before receiving treatment.

Prognosis Rates for Bulimia Nervosa

The prognosis for bulimia nervosa appears to be more favorable than for anorexia nervosa. In one study, almost 60 percent of bulimia nervosa clients achieved a good outcome, 29 percent of clients realized an intermediate outcome, and 10 percent reported a poor outcome. Bulimia nervosa clients in this study had a 1.1 percent mortality rate, which was more than five times lower than anorexia nervosa clients. In a separate study, 74 percent of bulimia nervosa clients achieved full recovery compared with one-third of anorexia nervosa clients. Partial recovery was actualized by 99 percent of bulimia nervosa clients. It is estimated that one-third of individuals can expect to relapse.

Prognosis Rates for EDNOS

More research is needed to better understand the prognosis and treatment outcomes for the diverse category of EDNOS. However, in a rare study, 83 percent of individuals with EDNOS achieved recovery and the relapse rate was estimated to be 42 percent for this group. One challenge in identifying treatment outcomes has been that individuals may shift from EDNOS to another diagnosis category representing diagnostic crossover.

Conclusion

The prognosis for clients with eating disorders is better for younger individuals than adults. Generally, individuals with bulimia nervosa or EDNOS have stronger treatment outcomes and lower mortality rates than individuals with anorexia nervosa.

JUSTINE J. REEL

Bibliography

Goldstein, Mandy, Lorna Peters, Andrew Baillie, Patricia McVeagh, Gerri Minshall, and Dianne Fitzjames. "The Effectiveness of a Day Program for the Treatment of Adolescent Anorexia Nervosa." *International Journal of Eating Disorders* 44, no. 1 (2011): 29–38. doi: 10.1002/eat.20789.

Keel, Pamela K., and Tiffany A. Brown. "Update on Course and Outcome in Eating Disorders." *International Journal of Eating Disorders* 43 (2010): 195–204.

Miller, Catherine A., and Neville H. Golden. "An Introduction to Eating Disorders: Clinical Presentation, Epidemiology and Prognosis." *Nutrition in Clinical Practice* 25 (2010): 110–15. doi: 10.1177/0884533609357566.

Zeeck, Almut, Stephanie Weber, Angelika Sandholz, Andreas Joos, and Armin Hartmann. "Stability of Long-term Outcome in Bulimia Nervosa: A 3-Year Follow-up." *Journal of Clinical Psychology* 67, no. 3 (2011): 318–27. doi: 10.1002/jclp.20766.

PROTECTIVE FACTORS

In health and medicine, the term protective factor is used to describe a behavior or event that reduces one's vulnerability to developing a specific disease or condition. A protective factor is often seen as the opposite of a risk factor, as protective factors lessen the likelihood of disease and risk factors increase the likelihood of disease. Thus, eating disorder protective factors reduce the likelihood of an individual developing an eating disorder.

Eating disorders and body image and weight issues have many of the same protective factors. This is partly because having a positive body image and following healthy weight management practices serve as protective factors for eating disorders. Thus, the factors that protect against having a negative body image would also protect against an eating disorder through a chain reaction. If a person does not develop a negative body image, they will most likely not develop an eating disorder. The list of protective factors for eating disorders is quite lengthy. Most individuals who avoid developing an eating disorder have a few of these factors. It would be extremely rare for an individual to possess all of the factors. Increasing the number of protective factors will decrease the likelihood of developing an eating disorder. While there are many protective factors for eating disorders, they primarily fall into the broader categories of media exposure, psychosocial functioning, physical health, positive spirituality, and the influence of family and friends.

Media Exposure

The media perpetuates the ideal image and reinforces stereotypes about body size and weight. Magazines, television shows, and movies all display images of perfect physical appearances. Individuals who have lower exposure to the media are less likely to develop negative body image or eating disorders, making it a protective factor.

Psychosocial Functioning

While lessened exposure to the media is ideal, it is nearly impossible to completely eliminate the media. In order for an individual to maintain a positive body image, he or she must be able to effectively cope with the pressures of society with regard to beauty and weight. Coping, or resiliency, is an especially important skill when it comes to eating disorder prevention. Beyond coping with body image challenges, an individual must be able to cope with daily tasks and challenges, negative emotion, sadness, grief, and pain. Individuals with a high level of resiliency are able to find purpose and meaning in suffering, use appropriate coping methods, and avoid using eating disorder behaviors to mask underlying unresolved issues.

Similarly, effective stress management is a protective factor for eating disorders. Individuals who are able to appropriately handle the stressful demands of life are less likely to develop eating disorders. Appropriate stress management is also a protective factor for obesity, as individuals who are unable to find healthy outlets for stress more often turn to food for comfort and support.

Being able to effectively solve problems and resolve conflicts is also a protective factor for eating disorders. Self-esteem may be a confounding factor as individuals with higher self-esteem may have the internal confidence to stand up for themselves and address conflicts in an assertive manner. Individuals who lack the ability to resolve interpersonal problems are more likely to turn to dieting and weight loss.

Individual psychosocial characteristics that are protective against eating disorders include low levels of depression, high self-esteem, low levels of self-criticism, and low levels of perfectionism. An individual's ability to identify and express emotions and feelings is also correlated with fewer eating disorders. Better emotional regulation is a protective factor suggesting that being able to process and cope with negative emotions can predict resistance to eating disorders. Individuals who are unable to cope effectively may be more at risk for an eating disorder as they attempt to block or numb painful or unpleasant thoughts and emotions through eating disorder behaviors and rituals. Similarly, a childhood free from abuse and/or neglect serves as a protective factor for eating disorders.

The social abilities of an individual may make him or her more or less likely to develop an eating disorder. Individuals who have better social skills are less likely to have a negative body image, diet, and/or develop an eating disorder. Additionally, individuals who feel socially connected to others are less likely to turn to food for an emotional release. In a common fashion, individuals with strong social support are less likely to develop an eating disorder. Individuals who have a lot of close friends and family who they can turn to during difficult trials are less likely to turn to negative coping methods to deal with painful emotions.

Physical Health

Being physically healthy may be a protective factor for eating disorders. Those with active lifestyles, including appropriate amounts of exercise, healthy eating and abstinence from cigarettes and drugs, are less likely to develop an eating disorder. While physical health is a protective factor for some, increased concern with weight and shape, dieting, and excessive levels of exercise put an individual at greater risk for an eating disorder. The protective value of physical health comes only at a level where the individual feels good about herself and her body, but is not obsessively trying to alter or change it.

Positive Spirituality

For some individuals, a high level of religion and/or spirituality is a protective factor for eating disorders. Individuals who gain acceptance and reassurance about their physical bodies from religious teachings may be less affected by media influences. This protective factor, however, is not true for all religious individuals.

Influence of Family and Friends

A positive home environment that protects children from eating disorders is one in which parents are highly connected to their children and are able to discuss issues related to appearance, body image, and weight. Parents may be needed to mediate teasing or bullying about appearance and provide a safe haven where children can be free from social pressures. Connectedness with at least one parent is a protective factor for eating disorders.

Having a family that eats meals together is a protective factor for eating disorders. The process of eating together as a family has positive effects on weight, eating habits, and body image. The interaction between family members builds social bonds and helps establish a connected relationship. Children are often able to discuss problems or issues they are having, along with chatter about their friends and school responsibilities. The conversations at the dinner table allow parents to get to know their children, which is important because parents who are connected with their children are more likely to have a positive influence when giving counsel about weight or body image issues. Furthermore, adolescents who ate frequently with their families reported less use of alcohol, tobacco, and marijuana and were also more likely to get higher grades and have lower risk of depression and suicide. In addition, the typical family meal can be healthier which can contribute to lower body mass index among adolescents. For adolescent females, eating with the family most nights of the week protects against extreme weight loss behaviors and disordered eating.

A parent with an authoritative parenting style is also a protective factor for teens. Kids who have parents who establish rules but allow for circumstantial changes to be made to those rules are less likely to have children with eating disorders. The increased connectedness and authoritative parenting may go together. Parents who are able to identify initial signs of disordered eating have an increased chance of preventing the emergence of a serious eating disorder.

The social group that an adolescent associates with may have a large influence on his or her eating disorder risk. Peer protective factors include having friends who have good self-esteem, are not interested in dieting or weight loss, and refrain from appearance-related teasing. If one peer in the group exhibits dieting or eating disorder behavior, it puts the additional members of the group at risk for initiating the same behavior. Adolescents need friends who are supportive, can identify potential eating problems, and are willing to take necessary action to ensure their friends do not engage in dangerous eating behaviors. Friends who are worried about dieting, weight, body image, and beauty put a girl at risk for an eating disorder. Similarly for males, having friends who are overly concerned with body shape and size, muscle mass and/or weight may put them at additional risk. Ideally, adolescents need friends who have a positive body image, are not interested in dieting or losing weight, but participate in healthy eating and exercise behaviors. Research has found that girls who mature early are more likely to develop eating problems. Early breast development and menarche may place a girl at risk as she might appear or feel different from her peers.

Having positive role models is one of the most critical protective factors for eating disorder prevention. Children and adolescents frequently look up to and admire peers and adults. They may emulate the behavior of their parents or older siblings. In this way, parents may have a very direct role in the prevention of eating disorders. Many research articles have stated the influence of comments made by a mother to her daughter. Negative comments about weight and body result in an increased risk for eating disorders. Similarly, comments made by a girl's father or brothers may also be dangerous.

Parents should serve as positive role models to the children and teens around them by practicing healthy nutrition and engaging in appropriate amounts of exercise. Parents should also talk openly about the media's effect on women and the unrealistic images that are being portrayed. Teaching children about media literacy from a young age may decrease the likelihood of them internalizing these ideals. Parents need to promote self-worth and compliment their children on things that are unconnected to body shape or size. They must discourage dieting behavior and weight-related teasing in the home. They need to resist the urge to make derogatory statements about their own body shape, weight, beauty, or size. If a parent is overly concerned with weight and seems upset by fluctuations, a child is more likely to mimic that behavior. Thus, a protective factor is having parents who accept their own bodies and do not make negative comments about themselves.

Conclusion

Protective factors are positive behaviors, traits, or experiences which decrease the likelihood of developing an eating disorder. There are many factors that positively influence body image and prevent dieting and eating disorders. These factors include: a lack of media exposure, a personal emphasis on healthy eating and exercise, positive spirituality, personal attributes of resiliency and coping, and a healthy relationship with parents and peers. While it is not necessary to have all of the protective factors in order to prevent an eating disorder, the increased amount of protective factors decreases the risk of eating disorders.

TeriSue Smith-Jackson

See also: Media; Parents.

Bibliography

Aime, Annie, Wendy M. Craig, Debra Pepler, Depeng Jiang, and Jennifer Connolly. "Developmental Pathways of Eating Problems in Adolescents." *Eating Disorders* 41 (2008): 686–96.

Bardone-Cone, Anna M., Kamila M. Cass, and Jennifer A. Ford. "Examining Body Dissatisfaction in Young Men within a Biopsychosocial Framework." *Body Image* 5, no. 2 (2008): 183–94.

Cain, Angela S., Anna M. Bardone-Cone, Lyn Y. Abramson, Kathleen D. Vohs, and Thomas E. Joiner. "Refining the Relationships of Perfectionism, Self-efficacy, and Stress to Dieting and Binge Eating: Examining the Appearance, Interpersonal, and Academic Domains." *International Journal of Eating Disorders* 41 (2008): 713–72

Cordero, Elizabeth, and Tania Israel. "Parents as Protective Factors in Eating Problems of College Women." *Eating Disorders* 17 (2009): 146–61.

Crago, Marjorie, Catherine M. Shisslak, and Anne Ruble. "Protective Factors in the Development of Eating Disorders." In *Eating Disorders: Innovative Directions in Research and Practice,* edited by R. H. Striegel-Moore and L. Smolak, 75–89. Washington, DC: American Psychological Association, 2001.

Fennig, Silvana, Arie Hadas, Liat Itzhaky, David Roe, Alan Apter, and Golan Shahar. "Self-criticism is a Key Predictor of Eating Disorder Dimensions among Inpatient Adolescent Females." *International Journal of Eating Disorders* 41 (2008): 762–65.

Gustafsson, Sanna Aila, Birgitta Edlund, Lars Kjellin, and Claes Norring. "Risk and Protective Factors for Disturbed Eating in Adolescent Girls—Aspects of Perfectionism and Attitudes of Eating and Weight." *European Eating Disorders Review* 17 (2009): 380–89.

Levine, Michael. "10 Things Parents Can Do to Help Prevent Eating Disorders." *National Eating Disorders Association.* Accessed June 2011. http://www.nationaleatingdisorders.org/nedaDir/files/documents/handouts/10Parent.pdf

Neumark-Sztainer, Dianne. *"I'm, Like, SO Fat!" Helping Your Teen Make Healthy Choices about Eating and Exercise in a Weight-Obsessed World.* New York: The Guilford Press, 2005.

Patrick, Heather. "The Benefits of Authoritative Feeding Style: Caregiver Feeding Styles and Children's Food Consumption Patterns." *Appetite* 44 (2005): 243–49.

PSYCHODRAMA

Psychodrama refers to a form of psychotherapy that utilizes a large variety of dramatic action methods, such as role playing and spontaneous dramatization, to examine the problems or issues of an individual or group, and to encourage healthy change through the development of new perceptions, behaviors, and a connection with others. Psychodrama focuses on interactive role play as the therapeutic medium is usually within a group setting. Typically, the role-playing involves using a scenario to enact scenes from a client's life. By participating in active role plays during group therapy, an individual can begin to process a painful issue within a safe environment.

History of Psychodrama

Psychodrama was developed by Jacob Levy Moreno in Vienna during the early part of the 20th century to address the health of individuals and of humanity as a whole. Moreno introduced psychodrama to the United States in 1925. Moreno reported that his hope for humanity was the transformation of consciousness through the integration of creative play, spontaneity, and psychological theory. Psychodrama is the vessel that he developed to facilitate this transformative process.

Description of Psychodrama in Therapy

Psychodrama sessions can last up to two or three hours and are facilitated by a trained psychotherapist who acts as the director. The psychotherapist guides the participants through each phase of the session while providing therapeutic support. Other key players in psychodrama sessions include the protagonist, the auxiliary egos, the audience, and the stage. The protagonist is played by a group member selected to represent the theme of the group in the drama. A real life, emotionally charged issue is enacted in the session's role-play. The auxiliary egos consist of group members who play the roles that represent significant others in the drama. The audience is made up of group members who witness the drama and represent the world at large; they typically do not provide feedback until the sharing phase of the session, at which time they speak of their own individual experience. The stage is the actual physical space in which the drama is conducted.

Each session consists of three phases: the warm-up phase, the action phase, and the sharing phase. The warm-up phase is when the group theme is identified and a protagonist is selected. It is also a time in which people in the group connect so that they can work better together. The scene is set in the action stage as the protagonist determines the issue she wants to act out and selects group members in the room to play the other roles in the scene. In the action phase the problem/painful issue is dramatized and the protagonist examines new methods of working through it. The sharing phase is when group members are invited to express how they related to or connected with the protagonist's work.

Psychodrama and Eating Disorders

Psychodrama is a useful adjunct therapy for eating disorders. Persons with eating disorders often accommodate the wishes, demands, wants, or needs of others at the cost of developing a sense of self. Psychodrama can help individuals to begin to develop a stronger identity with role play as psychodrama works with the idea that one's true self develops from the role one plays. Persons with eating disorders may tend to dissociate from their bodies as well as from intense memories and experiences. Psychodrama can be especially helpful in enabling individuals to assume roles without necessarily experiencing them as a part of the self. Examples of this experience include enabling the protagonist to step out of the scene and watch others act out the scene or to switch her role with another, such as her sibling, to gain a different viewpoint.

Psychodrama and Bulimia Nervosa

Monica Callahan has examined the ways in which psychodrama is helpful for persons with bulimia nervosa and the techniques to use within psychodrama to specifically adapt to the needs of persons with bulimia. She has argued that psychodrama techniques are especially useful for helping this population "to overcome blocks to emotional experience and to gain access to hidden parts of the self." She further reports that psychodrama "provides opportunities to experience, practice, and strengthen the healthier aspects of the self, and sharing such intense experiences with others can help counteract the isolation so characteristic of people with bulimia."

She has suggested three ways in which psychodrama can be adapted for people with bulimia nervosa. One modification of psychodrama involves allowing group members to work on their own issues indirectly by playing roles in others' dramas. Another strategy is to capitalize on the playfulness of some psychodrama techniques. A specific example of this would be the personification of a binge food. Finally, Callahan recommends altering some techniques so they are less threatening in respect to the sensitivity bulimics have about their body. An example would be utilizing techniques that require limited physical movement.

Psychodrama and Anorexia Nervosa

M. Katherine Hudgins has studied the use of psychodrama with persons who have anorexia nervosa. She identified three concepts that should guide the clinical treatment of anorexia within psychodrama: active experiencing, surplus reality, and empathetic bonding. Active experiencing is a term used in drama that indicates that the person is putting herself into the role of the character she is playing. In the case of psychodrama, this occurs when auxiliary egos act out roles from the protagonist's painful issue or memory. Active experiencing helps persons with anorexia form "an experiential sense of self that can be trusted." Surplus reality is described as an intervention with the goal of "making the patient's internal reality overtly visible between the therapist and patient." Surplus reality enables the person with anorexia to move past rigid control and rejection of sensation by enacting images in a way that appears larger than life. Hudgins reports that empathic bonding is the first step in effective treatment of anorexia nervosa. Empathic bonding within therapy includes establishing a trusting relationship with the client and a therapeutic alliance. People suffering with anorexia often have developmental arrest and struggle to establish a working relationship in therapy. For this reason, empathic bonding often needs to occur more actively, such as by mirroring nonverbal communication, with clients with anorexia.

Conclusion

Psychodrama is a form of therapy that aids persons in developing new perceptions, changing behaviors, and fostering deeper connections with others. It is gaining greater momentum as an adjunct therapy in the treatment of eating disorders. Persons with eating disorders can benefit from psychodrama by acting out difficult life situations. They can work through emotional experiences and develop a stronger sense of self. Psychodrama provides a less intimidating approach to addressing eating disorder issues than traditional therapies and has been shown to be an effective adjunct.

JESSICA GUENTHER

Bibliography

American Society of Group Psychotherapy and Psychodrama. "General Information about Psychodrama." Accessed September 8, 2011 from http://www.asgpp.org/html/psycho drama.html.

Callahan, Monica Leonie. "Pyschodrama and the Treatment of Bulimia." In *Experiential Therapies for Eating Disorders,* edited by Lynne M. Hornyak and Ellen K. Baker, 101–120. New York: The Guilford Press, 1989.

Davis, Leslie. "Acting Out Your Issues through Psychodrama." Retrieved on September 6, 2011, from http://www.sierratucson.com/sierratucson_articles/acting-out-your-issues-through-psychodrama.php.

Dayton, Tian. *The Living Stage.* Deerfield Beach: Health Communications, Inc., 2005.

Hudgins, M. Katherine. "Experiencing the Self through Psychodrama and Gestalt Therapy in Anorexia Nervosa." In *Experiential Therapies for Eating Disorders,* edited by Lynne M. Hornyak and Ellen K. Baker, 234–51. New York: The Guilford Press, 1989.

PSYCHODYNAMIC PSYCHOTHERAPY APPROACHES

Brief History of Psychodynamic Psychotherapy

Psychodynamic psychotherapy refers to a group of treatment approaches and techniques that have their foundation in psychoanalytic psychotherapy—the theory proposed by Sigmund Freud. Current understanding and application of Freud's ideas frequently differ from that which was prevalent in the late 1800s and the early 1900s. Additionally, many psychodynamic and psychoanalytic principles (e.g., establishing a working alliance, bringing into awareness that of which the client was previously unaware) are often found in other treatment approaches.

Elements of Psychodynamic Psychotherapy

There are several different theoretical approaches to psychodynamic psychotherapy including self psychology, object relations, and attachment theory. Although these approaches may differ in the specific focus of treatment or the language used to describe the issues faced by clients, there is considerable overlap of the main features of these approaches. Shelder captured this when he stated that what psychodynamic psychotherapists do is to help clients explore parts of themselves that they may not be fully aware of, and that psychodynamic psychotherapists do this in the context of the relationship between the psychotherapist and the client. The elements of psychodynamic psychotherapy described below represent features that generally differentiate psychodynamic psychotherapy from other forms of counseling and psychotherapy.

A focus on the quality of how people relate to one another is an important aspect in psychodynamic psychotherapies. Helping clients figure out why they interact with others the way they do is paramount in these approaches because clients' relationships with others can be beneficial or harmful. Figuring out how and why certain relationships work and contribute to the clients' overall happiness will allow clients to better identify and nurture future relationships that will also be satisfactory. Conversely, identifying how and why some relationships do not work (i.e., are harmful or distressing for the client) can allow clients to avoid developing such relationships with others. One of the ways by which a psychodynamic psychotherapist can help clients navigate interpersonal concerns is by using the relationship that exists between client and psychotherapist. Focusing on how the client and the psychotherapist interact with one another can provide useful information or *insight* into what works and what does not work for the client interpersonally. This is often referred to as work in the "here-and-now." Working with interpersonal exchanges in the moment rather than working with information about relationships outside of psychotherapy can help clients work through recurring themes and patterns that are apparent in every aspect of their lives (e.g., thoughts, feelings, view of themselves).

Examining how a client relates to others often means addressing past experiences with others. A common misconception about psychodynamic psychotherapy is that the past is an area of focus purely for the sake of figuring out what occurred during the client's childhood years. Knowing about past experiences, however, can help clients develop a better understanding of what is going on in their daily lives. Clients can then identify dysfunctional behavioral patterns (e.g., repeatedly dating the same type of person).

Finally, psychodynamic psychotherapists focus on clients' emotions. For some clients, this may mean that they are helped to simply identify feelings when they occur. For others, focusing on emotions may mean that they are helped to make sense of emotions that seem to conflict with one another (e.g., "How can I feel angry and sad at the same time?"). Work on emotions often leads to exploration of the ways in which clients try to avoid experiencing distressing feelings.

Clients who participate in psychodynamic psychotherapy will often benefit in ways beyond symptoms remission (e.g., no longer feeling depressed, improved relationships, decrease in intense feelings of anxiety). As a result of engaging in psychodynamic psychotherapy, many clients will also develop and expand the resources they have to cope with life-related struggles with the goal of experiencing a greater sense of satisfaction.

Evidence for the Effectiveness of Psychodynamic Psychotherapy

Research on the effectiveness of psychodynamic psychotherapy suggests that this form of treatment is effective; however, the quantity of research is significantly less than for other forms of therapy such as cognitive-behavioral therapy (CBT). Likewise, the evidence for the effectiveness of psychodynamic psychotherapy in the treatment of eating disorders is significantly less than for other forms of therapy. The evidence that does exist, however, suggests that psychodynamic psychotherapy is effective in helping clients and that the benefits seen at the end of the treatment seem to grow as time passes. This means that clients continue to get better even after treatment has stopped. In studies specifically examining the use of psychodynamic psychotherapy with clients having eating disorders, results show that this form of treatment is at least as good as other forms of therapy in addressing eating disorders. Individuals who write about the evidence for psychodynamic psychotherapy recognize that more studies are needed to adequately compete with the vast amount of research conducted on other forms of therapy. The existing evidence, however, indicates that psychodynamic psychotherapy is an empirically supported therapy that performs as well as or better than other forms of therapy and the benefits clients experience as a result are likely to grow beyond the end of treatment.

The Application of Psychodynamic Psychotherapy for Eating Disorders

Available evidence on how and why eating disorders develop indicates that there is no single cause and that what may have caused an eating disorder for one person may not be the cause for another. Potential causes can include genetics, personality factors, the client's family and developmental history, co-occurring disorders, and sociocultural factors. Given the complexity and seriousness of eating disorders, attention to a client's eating-related behaviors must be a primary focus of treatment; however, due to the array of possible causes of eating disorders, attention to symptoms alone is not likely to result in long-term results. Clients with eating disorders not only require assistance with managing their eating behaviors but also require help in finding other ways to manage distressing emotions, in improving their interpersonal relationships which can contribute to distressing emotions, and in coming to terms with past experiences (traumatic or nontraumatic) that may continue to affect them. Psychodynamic psychotherapy—or at minimum, psychodynamic techniques—is perhaps best suited to address these deep and often long-standing concerns. Clients struggling with eating disorders often struggle to manage their relationships with others and the emotions that accompany those relationships—issues for which psychodynamic psychotherapists are specifically trained. The emphasis on the relationship between the therapist and the client as well as the attention given to identifying and managing emotions can make psychodynamic psychotherapy an ideal form of treatment for many clients with eating disorders.

Conclusion

Psychodynamic psychotherapies have strength in their focus on the relationship between the client and psychotherapist. Addressing the quality of this relationship directly assists clients in learning how to interact more effectively with others in their everyday lives, which in turn can lead to greater life satisfaction. Psychodynamic psychotherapies have been demonstrated to be effective in the treatment of many different disorders and the benefits are often found to increase far beyond the end of treatment. The current evidence on the effectiveness of psychodynamic psychotherapies in the treatment of eating disorders indicates that they are, at minimum, as good as other forms of counseling and psychotherapy.

CHRISTINE L. B. SELBY

Bibliography

Casper, Regina C. "Integration of Psychodynamic Concepts into Psychotherapy." In *Psychobiology and Treatment of Anorexia Nervosa and Bulimia Nervosa,* edited by Katherine A. Halmi, 287–305. Washington, DC: American Psychiatric Association, 1992.

Shedler, Jonathan. "The Efficacy of Psychodynamic Psychotherapy." *American Psychologist* 65, no. 2 (2010): 98–109.

Thompson-Brenner, Heather, Jolie Weingeroff, and Drew Westen. "Empirical Support for Psychodynamic Psychotherapy for Eating Disorders." In *Handbook of Evidence-Based Psychodynamic Psychotherapy,* edited by Raymond A. Levy and Stuart J. Ablon, 67–92. New York, NY: Humana Press, 2010.

Zerbe, Kathryn J. "Psychodynamic Management of Eating Disorders." In *Clinical Manual of Eating Disorders,* edited by Joel Yager and Pauline S. Powers, 307–334. Arlington, VA: American Psychiatric Publishing, 2007.

Zerbe, Kathryn J. "Psychodynamic Therapy for Eating Disorders." In *The Treatment of Eating Disorders: A Clinical Handbook,* edited by Carlos M. Grilo and James E. Mitchell, 339–58. New York, NY: The Guilford Press, 2010.

PUBERTY

Puberty refers to the maturation process of the reproductive system that occurs naturally during adolescence and leads to physical, sexual, and psychosocial maturation. Physical and sexual changes that emerge during puberty include physical growth, onset of menstruation, and development and appearance of organs and sexual characteristics (e.g., breasts and pubic hair). Among American girls, the majority of pubertal changes occur during early adolescence. The average age of menarche (i.e., first period) is 13 years, which coincides with an increase in the amount of body fat on a girl's body. Typically, boys tend to have 1.5 times the lean body mass and bone mass of girls, while girls have twice as much body fat as boys. This significant amount of weight gain coupled with other pubertal changes has been shown to both positively and negatively influence the body image of adolescents.

Pubertal Changes and Body Image

During puberty, physical appearance and body shape changes for girls and boys, and this can influence how they think and feel about their bodies. Most girls accept pubertal changes like developing breasts and getting taller; however, some girls are distressed about gaining weight and fat during normal development. Pubertal weight gain occurs during a time when girls want to be popular and attractive to the opposite sex and are extremely self-conscious about their appearance, weight, and body shape. During early and middle adolescence, girls are more likely to judge their own attractiveness based on attention from boys. This emphasis on attractiveness and popularity with the opposite sex along with normative development of fat during puberty heightens the girls' awareness of their bodies and leads to increased body dissatisfaction. For example, according to a recent study, 56 percent of 9-year-olds and 43 percent of girls in the age group of 13–16 years were dissatisfied with their bodies.

Early Maturation and Stress

Adolescents may be self-critical and embarrassed about their bodies because they are maturing too early or too late, or because they are not developing according to society's expectations or meeting the prescribed standard of beauty. Early onset or precocious puberty is defined as the beginning of the physical maturation process before the age of eight for girls and before nine for boys. This condition is occurring more often in girls and boys in industrialized societies. Although early physical development could occur in both girls and boys, girls are 10 times more likely to experience early onset puberty. Young girls who experience precocious puberty report struggling with identity confusion and psychological distress at higher levels than girls who experience puberty on schedule. This overall distress can result in negative body image and self-worth due to not feeling emotionally and cognitively ready to handle the implications associated with early physical development.

For girls, researchers have reported that early maturation is a risk factor for body dissatisfaction because the physical changes (e.g., weight gain, menarche) associated with puberty deviates from the Western culture's belief that the thin ideal body type is attractive and beautiful. Early maturing girls indicated a stronger desire to be thin than average or late maturing girls. In addition, early maturers reported a preference for a more slender ideal figure than the average or late maturers when they were asked to choose the ideal figure that they desired. Diamond recently stated that girls who have larger breasts and hips are sexualized in our society. Because young girls are not mature enough to cope with this attention, they develop negative feelings toward their own bodies well into adulthood.

Obesity and Puberty

Researchers have also found that obesity tends to increase in early maturers during puberty. Females who perceived that they were overweight prior to puberty reported more body dissatisfaction, desire to be thin, and eating disorder tendencies compared to girls who perceived their prepubertal weight as average or underweight. In a different study, a researcher interviewed adolescent girls about their body image and one adolescent girl's quote illustrates this point:

> I was kind of chubby when I was little . . . I hated it and so in like 9th grade, I think it was, I decided to eat more healthy and like watch what I eat because I really

wanted to make the high school squad [cheerleading] really bad . . . it was really hard though because you obviously feel really awkward with yourself because you're going through puberty and you don't know what's going on with your body and so I was really insecure in junior high. It was just awkward and I just hated it.

Males and Puberty

For boys, the ideal image is a muscular body with a large chest and shoulders and a slim waist. In contrast to early maturing girls, early maturing boys typically experience a developmental advantage related to societal standards for an ideal body compared to late maturing boys. Late maturing boys may appear to have a greater risk of developing body dissatisfaction and unhealthy eating and exercise behaviors. Unlike the girls, early maturing boys are viewed as more attractive and self-confident, have more positive body image, and are more popular with their peers compared to late maturing boys. A reason for this is that boys gain muscle mass and definition and their shoulder width increases, which places a majority of the boys closer to the societal standard of the ideal body shape for a man. Researchers have examined pubertal timing and body image among adolescent boys and found that late maturing boys reported more body dissatisfaction than early maturers. However, the research on the developmental trajectory of boys' body image into adulthood remains unclear.

Conclusion

Puberty is the maturation process of the reproductive system that leads to a multitude of physical and psychosocial changes. Physical appearance and body shape changes for girls and boys during puberty can influence how they feel and think about their bodies. Research has shown that the influence of timing of maturation on body image is different for girls and boys. Girls with early onset of puberty are more likely to experience poor body image and self-worth, whereas early maturing boys have positive body image and confidence.

SONYA SOOHOO

Bibliography

Ackard, Diann, and Carol B. Peterson. "Association between Puberty and Disordered Eating, Body Image, and Other Psychological Variables." *International Journal of Eating Disorders* 29 (2001): 187–94.

Bradley University. "Precocious Puberty and Body Image." Accessed August 5, 2011, http://thebodyproject.bradley.edu/sex/puberty.shtml.

McCabe, Marita P., and Lina A. Ricciardelli. "A Longitudinal Study of Pubertal Timing and Extreme Body Change Behaviors among Adolescent Boys and Girls." *Adolescence* 39 (2004): 145–66.

Mendle, Jane, Eric Turkheimer, and Robert E. Emery. "Detrimental Psychological Outcomes Associated with Early Puberty Timing in Adolescent Girls." *Developmental Review* 27 (2007): 151–71.

Pineyerd, Belinda, and William B. Zipf. "Puberty—Timing Is Everything!" *Journal of Pediatric Nursing* 20 (2005): 75–82.

Tremblay, Line, and Jean-Yves Frigon. "Precocious Puberty in Adolescent Girls: A Biomarker of Later Psychosocial Adjustment Problems." *Child Psychiatry and Human Development* 36 (2005): 73–91.

Williams, Joanne M., and Candace Currie. "Self-Esteem and Physical Development in Early Adolescence: Pubertal Timing and Body Image." *Journal of Early Adolescence* 20 (2000): 129–49.

PURGING

Purging refers to the purposive elimination of food and liquids using a variety of methods including self-induced vomiting, use of laxatives, diuretics, or enemas, and exercising excessively. Purging may occur as a way to compensate for the consumption of trigger foods (e.g., chocolate cake), as a way to compensate for a binge eating episode, or as a continuous weight control behavior. Purging behaviors may occur among the general population as well as among individuals with disordered eating or clinical eating disorders. Generally, purging behaviors are quite secretive and individuals attempt to hide evidence (e.g., laxative boxes).

Prevalence of Purging Behaviors

Both males and females report using purging methods to control weight. In a U.S. sample, 1.9 percent of women and 1.4 percent of men reported diuretic use whereas 0.4 percent of women and 0.3 percent of men took laxatives. Approximately 0.1 percent of males and females admitted to self-induced vomiting to control weight. In a separate Australian study, adult women reported self-induced vomiting (1.4%) and use of laxatives (1.0%) or diuretics (0.3%) on a weekly basis. Prevalence rates of purging behaviors were even higher for adolescent boys and girls with 27.1 percent of girls and 6.5 percent of boys reporting use of purging methods (i.e., vomiting, laxatives, diet pills, diuretics) in order to lose weight or prevent weight gain.

Alarmingly, prevalence rates for diuretic use have climbed from 0.5 percent in 1990 to 2.1 percent in 2004 as evidenced by a longitudinal investigation of female college students. Three percent of college women reported self-induced vomiting while 2.7 percent of college women misused laxatives. Meanwhile, an increase in disordered eating behaviors has been documented among both males and females in Australia over a 10 year period.

Disordered Eating and Purging Behaviors

Purging behaviors may begin as a strategy to avoid weight gain or as a supplement to dieting with the goal of weight loss. Unfortunately, these disordered eating patterns can lead to full-fledged eating disorders. Across studies, the prevalence of laxative abuse has been estimated to range from 10 percent to 60 percent for eating disordered individuals. However, a more recent study showed that 67 percent of eating disordered clients had used laxatives at some point to control weight or compensate for food intake. Purging behaviors are exhibited among individuals diagnosed with anorexia nervosa with binge eating/purging subtype and among those diagnosed with bulimia nervosa. The current diagnostic criteria for anorexia nervosa binge eating/purging subtype is purging through self-induced vomiting or the misuse of laxatives, diuretics, or enemas at least weekly. The anorexia nervosa subtypes will be eliminated from the fifth edition of the *Diagnostic and Statistical Manual of Mental Disorders*.

The bulimia nervosa diagnosis describes purging as compensatory behavior to prevent weight gain, including self-induced vomiting, laxatives, diuretics, enemas, as well as medications, fasting, or excessive exercise. Individuals with Eating Disorder Not Otherwise Specified (EDNOS) who do not meet the full criteria for anorexia nervosa or bulimia nervosa may also exhibit purging behaviors. A study that compared purging behaviors between bulimia nervosa and EDNOS groups found that laxative use was higher among EDNOS (62%) than bulimia nervosa (27%) groups whereas self-induced vomiting was more frequently used by individuals with bulimia nervosa (86%) than EDNOS (38%).

Purging behaviors are important to address during treatment due to the numerous health consequences that can result after continued use (e.g., gum erosion, dehydration, electrolyte imbalances). Additionally, outcome studies have shown that individuals who continue to purge during treatment have a poorer prognosis for full recovery from eating disorders.

Prevention of Purging Behaviors

Of particular concern is the fact that many purging products (e.g., laxatives, diuretics, diet pills) are readily available over the counter. While it is difficult to regulate whether an individual is abusing laxatives that may have initially been prescribed for a legitimate medical concern (e.g., constipation), it is recommended that physicians attempt to provide natural solutions that do not require diuretic or laxative use. Another challenge associated with purging behaviors is the tendency for eating disorder education to center around a discussion of types of eating disorders. Inadvertently, lectures that discuss behaviors may provide purging ideas to vulnerable students who then begin to initiate pathogenic weight control behaviors.

Conclusion

Purging behaviors include self-induced vomiting and misuse of laxatives, diuretics, enemas, or diet pills for weight control. Excessive exercise may also be considered a type of purging when movement is used to compensate for food consumption. Purging behaviors may be used by the general population and may also be part of formal eating disorder diagnoses (e.g., anorexia nervosa binge eating/purging type, bulimia nervosa). Prevention efforts are indicated as purging can lead to poorer treatment outcomes among eating disordered individuals.

JUSTINE J. REEL

See also: Diuretics; Laxative Abuse.

Bibliography

Ackard, Diann M., Catherine L. Cronemeyer, Lisa M. Franzen, Sara A. Richter, and Jane Norstrom. "Number of Different Purging Behaviors Used Among Women with Eating Disorders: Psychological, Behavioral, Self-Efficacy and Quality of Life Outcomes." *Eating Disorders: Journal of Treatment and Prevention* 19 (2011): 156–74. doi: 10.1080/10640 266.2010.511909.

American Psychiatric Association. *Diagnostic and Statistical Manual of Mental Disorders, Revised 4th Edition.* Washington, DC: Author, 2000.

Liechty, Janet M. "Body Image Distortion and Three Types of Weight Loss Behaviors among Nonoverweight Girls in the United States." *Journal of Adolescent Health* 47 (2010): 176–82. doi: 10.1016/j.jadohealth.2010.01.004.

Lock, James. "Treatment of Adolescent Eating Disorders: Progress and Challenges." *Minerva Psichiatrica* 51, no. 3 (2010): 207–216.

Roerig, James L., Kristine J. Steffen, James E. Mitchell, and Christie Zunker. "Laxative Abuse: Epidemiology, Diagnosis and Management." *Drugs* 70, no. 12 (2010): 1487–1503.

R

RECOVERY

Recovery from an eating disorder has been broadly defined as the complete absence of symptoms so that an individual with an eating disorder history is indistinguishable from individuals who do not have a history. Specifically, in order to be "fully recovered" individuals should possess the following characteristics: (1) no longer meet diagnostic criteria for an eating disorder; (2) have not engaged in any disordered eating behaviors (e.g., vomiting, binge eating) for three months; (3) have a body mass index (BMI) of 18.5 or more; and (4) score within age-matched norms on eating disorder screening instruments.

An individual who is considered fully recovered from an eating disorder represents minimal risk for relapse. In contrast, "partial recovery" refers to refraining from disordered eating behaviors and having acceptable BMI scores while not meeting the psychological criteria necessary for full recovery. Individuals who are in partial recovery often admit that they continue to experience negative body image and eating disorder triggers.

Is Recovery from an Eating Disorder Possible?

A common belief related to addiction is that an individual who has a history of addiction will always be an "addict" and will remain in "recovery," and that recovery represents a life-long process. Eating disorders differ from other addictions in that it is impossible to abstain from eating. Therefore, individuals with eating disorders must develop a healthier and more positive relationship with food in order to recover from an eating disorder.

Eating disorder clinicians and researchers promote the philosophy that individuals can be "recovered from" an eating disorder rather than "in recovery." Being recovered represents past tense which is more empowering for individuals and encourages the disengagement from one's eating disorder identity. Furthermore, working toward full recovery or being recovered denotes optimism and the ability to improve one's condition.

It is estimated that around half of all individuals with eating disorders are able to recover. Among individuals with anorexia nervosa, 46 percent recover, 33 percent improve symptoms, and 20 percent remain disordered. Meanwhile half of individuals with bulimia nervosa recover, 30 percent improve symptoms, and 20 percent continue to meet bulimia nervosa criteria.

Conclusion

A common question is whether individuals with eating disorders can ever fully recover. Although being in recovery is the common language within addiction populations, eating disorder clinicians actively promote "being recovered" from an eating disorder and individuals who are fully recovered are indistinguishable from the general non-disordered population.

JUSTINE J. REEL

Bibliography

Bardone-Cone, Anna M., Megan B. Harney, Christine R. Maidonado, Melissa A. Lawson, D. Paul Robinson, Roma Smith, and Aneesh Tosh. "Defining Recovery from an Eating Disorder: Conceptualization, Validation, and Examination of Psychosocial Functioning and Psychiatric Comorbidity." *Behavioral Research Therapy* 48, no. 3 (2010): 194–202. doi: 10.1016/j.brat.2009.11.001.

Darcy, Alison M., Shaina Katz, Kathleen Kara Fitzpatrick, Sarah Forsberg, Linsey Utzinger, and James Lock. "All Better? How Former Anorexia Nervosa Patients Define Recovery and Engaged in Treatment." *European Eating Disorders Review* 18, no. 4 (201): 260–70. doi: 10.1002/erv.1020

Gisladottir, M., and E. K. Svavarsdottir. "Educational and Support Intervention to Help Families Assist in the Recovery of Relatives with Eating Disorders." *Journal of Psychiatric and Mental Health Nursing* 18 (2011): 122–30. doi: 10.1111/j.1365-2850.2010.01637.x.

Keifer, Ekaterina, Kevin Duff, Leigh J. Beglinger, Erin Barstow, Arnold Andersen, and David J. Moser. "Predictors of Neuropsychological Recovery in Treatment for Anorexia Nervosa." *Eating Disorders: Journal of Treatment and Prevention* 18 (2010): 302–317. doi: 10.1080/10640266.2010/490120.

Turton, Penelope, Alexia Demetriou, William Boland, Stephen Gillard, Michael Kavuma, Gillian Mezey, Victoria Mountford, Kati Turner, Sarah White, Ewa Zadeh, and Christine Wright. "One Size Fits All: Or Horses for Courses? Recovery-based Care in Specialist Mental Health Services." *Social Psychiatry and Psychiatric Epidemiology* 46 (2011): 127–36. doi: 10.1007/s00127-009-0174-6.

Vanderlinden, J., H. Buis, G. Pieters, and M. Probst. "Which Elements in the Treatment of Eating Disorders Are Necessary 'Ingredients' in the Recovery Process? A Comparison between the Patient's and Therapist's View." *European Eating Disorders Review* 15, no. 5 (2007): 357–65. doi: 10.1002/erv.768.

REFEEDING SYNDROME

Refeeding syndrome refers to severe electrolyte and fluid shifts that may occur when nutrition is reinstituted in a malnourished individual too rapidly, irrespective of whether it is provided orally, enterally (i.e., tube feeding), or parenterally (i.e., intravenously). During starvation the body becomes catabolic, a state in which the intracellular stores of phosphorus, potassium, and magnesium become depleted, insulin secretion decreases, and the body relies heavily on breaking down fat for energy. During refeeding, the body shifts to an anabolic state in which insulin levels are increased to promote the synthesis of glycogen, protein, and fat. The cells require phosphorus, potassium, and magnesium for this process and these extracellular electrolytes shift into the cell, lowering serum levels. Refeeding syndrome can cause serious consequences, including pulmonary, muscular, cardiovascular, hematological, gastrointestinal, and neurological complications, which can lead to death. The prevalence of refeeding among individuals with eating disorders is currently unknown and may be difficult to assess as it is multifactorial and may be underdiagnosed.

History of Refeeding Syndrome

Historically, cardiac dysfunction, edema, and other neurological conditions were observed in groups of malnourished refugees before refeeding syndrome was officially recognized. A 1940s study examined the effects of starvation and refeeding on a group of previously healthy volunteers. After a period of severe food restriction, several subjects within this study experienced cardiac problems once a normal intake of food resumed, and two study participants died due to complications associated with refeeding syndrome. An article published in the *British Medical Journal* in 2004 noted that refeeding syndrome was first identified when the condition was observed among numerous prisoners of war after World War II, which further linked refeeding syndrome to starvation and prolonged fasting. Interestingly, numerous studies were conducted on people who were released from concentration camps after World War II in which documented cases of refeeding resulted in gastrointestinal problems (e.g., diarrhea), neurological complications (e.g., coma, convulsions), and heart failure symptoms.

The Minnesota Starvation Experiment

Ancel Keys, the lead investigator of the Minnesota Starvation Experiment, conducted his well-known research at the University of Minnesota beginning in 1944 to better understand the physiological and psychological effects of prolonged starvation and subsequent refeeding. The initial study participants included 36 male volunteers in the age group of 20–33 years who were subjected to a semistarvation diet and lost approximately 25 percent of their body weight after 24 weeks on the diet. Next, the participants underwent a 24-week period of nutritional rehabilitation. After nearly three months of controlled rehabilitation from September through October of 1945, the experiment ended. Interestingly, study participants experienced physical changes including a 24 percent reduction in body weight on average as well as hair loss and edema in the knees, ankles, and face. Participants suffered complications from refeeding, including muscle cramps and soreness, increased heat tolerance, reduced tolerance to cold, episodes of vertigo, giddiness, and momentary blackouts when they stood up from a sitting position. Participants also reported decreased libido, and feeling unfocused, fatigued, weak, depressed, and apathetic.

Signs, Symptoms, and Risk Factors

Factors that place clients at a high risk for developing refeeding syndrome include little or no nutritional intake for greater than 7–10 days, greater than 10–15 percent weight loss within a short period of time, body mass index of less than 16, and a history of chronic malnutrition. Common signs and symptoms indicating that a client may be developing refeeding syndrome consist of electrolyte abnormalities, particularly decreases in potassium, magnesium, and phosphorus, sharp increases in blood glucose, peripheral edema, rapid weight gain of greater than 0.5 lb per day, abnormal lung sounds, changes in pulse rate, and neurological issues such as confusion, muscle weakness, tremors, and seizures. Thus, clinical and biochemical indices must be monitored frequently for early recognition and intervention to prevent complications from progressing.

Complications associated with refeeding-induced hypophosphatemia include respiratory issues, complications within the cardiovascular system, skeletal problems, neurological problems, issues with the endocrine system, and hematological complications. According to McCray's (2005) work, clients suffering from hypokalemia-induced refeeding syndrome usually experience cardiac dysfunction, neurological problems, metabolic complications, and gastrointestinal disorders. Clients with signs or symptoms related to hypomagnesemia-induced refeeding syndrome show signs of cardiac abnormalities, neurological issues, gastrointestinal disorders, electrolyte issues, as well as hematological complications.

Prevalence of Refeeding Syndrome

According to research, hypokalemia (which is associated with refeeding syndrome) has been reported in approximately 14 percent of clients suffering from bulimia nervosa. However, based on a separate report, McCray suggested that the incidence rates regarding cases of refeeding syndrome are unknown. According to a report from North Bristol NHS Trust in the United Kingdom, the general incidence rate for hospital patients who have hypophosphatemia ranges from 0.2 percent to 5 percent. Refeeding syndrome has been reported in as much as 25 percent of cancer patients, due to numerous surgical procedures. Incidence rates of hypophosphatemia have ranged from 30 percent to 38 percent in studies of patients already receiving treatment through intravenous total parenteral nutrition (TPN) when phosphate was introduced. The refeeding syndrome incidence rate went up to 100 percent when parenteral nutrition was introduced to the patients in the absence of phosphate.

Management of the Client at Risk for Refeeding Syndrome

Identification of at-risk clients, close monitoring, and implementing an appropriate feeding regimen are three critical factors to consider in the prevention of refeeding syndrome. Nutritional rehabilitation should be advanced gradually so that signs and symptoms of refeeding syndrome may be recognized early on and treated to avoid further complications. Many hospitals and eating disorder units follow strict guidelines when refeeding a malnourished patient; the guidelines generally include the following: (1) obtaining electrolyte and blood glucose levels at regular intervals, (2) assessing fluid status and body weight daily, and (3) monitoring cardiac function and blood pressure frequently. Thiamine, which is required for carbohydrate metabolism, is often supplemented during the initial stages of refeeding due to increased demand for this nutrient. Deficiency of thiamine may result in Wernicke's Encephalopathy, a neurological disorder. Initial caloric intake may be started at as little as 10 kcal/kg/day, depending on the extent of malnourishment, and increased gradually. If phosphorus, magnesium, and/or potassium levels fall, they should be corrected immediately and caloric intake should not be advanced until electrolytes are stable. Labs may be monitored at longer intervals if they have been stable for several days.

Intravenous fluids may help clients restore nutrients and hydration, but should be used with caution to decrease the risk of fluid overload. It may take a few days for clients to advance to 100 percent of energy requirements, depending on biochemical stability and feeding tolerance.

Conclusion

Although weight restoration is a key component of any comprehensive eating disorder program, it is important to avoid introducing food and fluid too quickly. Malnourished individuals who receive tube feedings or begin to consume food too quickly may be particularly at risk for developing refeeding syndrome. Identification of high-risk individuals and close monitoring are important in preventing refeeding syndrome. If not treated promptly, complications of refeeding syndrome can be severe and even lead to death.

JUSTINE J. REEL, HOLLY E. DOETSCH,
AND SHELLY GUILLORY

Bibliography

Brynes, Matthew C., and Jessica Stangenes. "Refeeding in the ICU: An Adult and Pediatric Problem." *Current Opinion in Clinical Nutrition and Metabolic Care* 14 (2011): 186–92. doi: 10.1097/MCO.ob013e328341ed93.

Cantani, Marco, and Roger Howells. "Risks and Pitfalls for the Management of Refeeding Syndrome in Psychiatric Patients." *The Psychiatrist* 31 (2007): 209–211. doi: 10.1192/pb.bp.106.009878.

"Eating Disorders: Nutritional Considerations." NutritionMD.org. Accessed December 12, 2011 http://www.supportiveoncology.net/jso/journal/articles/0701020.pdf.

Fotheringham, J., K. Jackson, R. Kersh, and S. E. Gariballa. "Refeeding Syndrome: Life-Threatening, Underdiagnosed, but Treatable." *Oxford Journals, QJM: An International Journal of Medicine* 98, no. 4 (2005): 318–19.

Hearing, Stephen D. "Refeeding Syndrome is Underdiagnosed, Undertreated, but Treatable." *British Medical Journal* 328 (2004): 908–909.

McCray, Stacey, Sherrie Walker, and Carol Rees Parrish. "Much Ado about Refeeding: Nutrition Issues in Gastroenterology, Series #23." *Practical Gastroenterology* (2005): 26–44. Accessed December 12, 2011. http://www.medicine.virginia.edu/clinical/departments/medicine/divisions/digestive-health/nutrition-support-team/copy_of_nutritionarticles/McCrayArticle.pdf.

Parrish, Carol Rees. "The Refeeding Syndrome in 2009: Prevention is the Key to Treatment." *The Journal of Supportive Oncology* 7, no. 1 (2009): 20–21. Accessed December 12, 2011. http://www.supportiveoncology.net/jso/journal/articles/0701020.pdf.

Prickett, Joanna. "Refeeding Syndrome." Powerpoint Presentation, North Bristol NHS Trust. Accessed December 12, 2011 www.peng.org.uk/presentations/presentations06/JoPrickett.ppt.

Skibsted, Ashley. "Starvation and Refeeding Syndrome." Powerpoint Presentation, Concordia College, MN. Accessed December 12, 2011. www.win.cord.edu/fnd/ . . . /RFS%20FINAL%20PROJECT%5B1%5D.pptx.

Warren, Mark. "Living with Food: The Science Supporting Eating Disorder Treatment. Medical Complications of Eating Disorders-Refeeding Syndrome." Eatingdisorders cleveland.org. Last modified June 25, 2010. http://www.eatingdisorderscleveland.org/blog/bid/34100/Medical-Complications-of-Eating-Disorders-Refeeding-Syndrome.

Whitelaw, Melissa, Heather Gilbertson, Pei-Yoong Lam, and Susan M. Sawyer. "Does Aggressive Refeeding in Hospitalized Adolescents with Anorexia Nervosa Result in Increased Hypophosphatemia? *Journal of Adolescent Health* 46 (2010): 577–82. doi: 10.1016/j.jadohealth.2009.11.207.

REFERRING SOMEONE FOR EATING DISORDER TREATMENT

Anyone who suspects that a friend or family member has a problem faces the dilemma of how to approach that individual. Because professional help is often required, it is important to be able to refer the family member or friend for help. Understanding and implementing strategies for increasing the potential likelihood of having a successful interaction are important for secretive disorders like eating disorders. Additionally, finding resources in the local community and having them available during the meeting is critical to ensure follow-through for treatment.

Denial and Eating Disorders

As with other types of addictions, individuals who suffer from disordered eating and eating disorders usually deny that there is a problem. Common responses to being confronted about symptoms (e.g., restricting, weight loss) include making excuses (e.g., "I've had the stomach flu"), expressing anger, and adamantly denying that a problem exists. Therefore, it is important to carefully consider who will approach the person suspected of having a problem; it is also important to have that individual engage in several strategies throughout the communication process. Furthermore, this initial meeting should be viewed as an opportunity to express concern and a way to plant the seed for support. In the event that the individual suspected of having a problem is open to seeking help, it is critical to locate local support networks and professional help available.

By identifying treatment resources in advance of the meeting, one can direct a friend or family member to specific treatment professionals or groups and can assist in making an appointment. National eating disorder resources can be found at www.edreferral.com or http://www.something-fishy.org/.

Strategies for Referring Someone for Eating Disorder Treatment

Ideally, the individual who has the strongest rapport and relationship history should approach the person who has the suspected eating disorder. In some cases, a sibling or friend has fewer power dynamics, is closer in age, and can be more effective than a parent or coach. However, in other instances, a concerned and respected teacher may have a significant influence and it should not be assumed that someone else has already expressed concern. The individual who approaches someone suspected of having an eating disorder should show genuine concern for the well-being of the individual while identifying tangible observations (e.g., "You seem tired and sad lately.")

To avoid putting the individual on the defense it is recommended that the person use "I" statements rather than "you" to keep lines of communication open. As mentioned in the previous section, it should be assumed that the person will respond with denial. The purpose of this meeting should be to identify that there is a problem and to extend support when the individual is ready to seek assistance. If the person does agree to get help for the eating disorder, the friend or family member can help locate resources, make appointments, and help with transportation to treatment.

Voluntary versus Involuntary Treatment

It is important to note that regardless of the severity of the eating disorder, treatment has been found to be more beneficial when the client has been admitted on a voluntary basis. Although parents may admit an individual under 18 years of age and this is sometimes required out of medical necessity, it is important for a client to also develop intrinsic motivation for recovery to ensure long-term success. The parallel to involuntary eating disorder treatment is court-ordered treatment associated with breaking the law. Although an individual receives treatment, he or she may only do the bare minimum of what is required instead of making meaningful changes in cognitions or behaviors.

However, one of the advantages of getting a professional involved is that the psychologist/therapist will probably address both the benefits and drawbacks of the eating disorder, illuminating some of the consequences of the eating disorder. The client will be forced to examine his or her readiness to address the problem and will be in a position to identify barriers to fully engaging in the treatment process.

Conclusion

Referring someone for eating disorder treatment can be an important influence on an individual's path to treatment and recovery. It should be recognized that the decision to seek treatment should be voluntary and friends and family members can provide support by identifying resources and helping with transportation to appointments.

JUSTINE J. REEL

Bibliography

Costin, Carolyn. *100 Questions & Answers about Eating Disorders.* Boston, MA: Jones and Bartlett, 2007.
Costin, Carolyn. *A Comprehensive Guide to the Causes, Treatments and Prevention of Eating Disorders: The Eating Disorder Sourcebook, 3rd Edition.* New York, NY: McGraw-Hill, 2007.
"Eating Disorder Referral and Information Center." EDREFERRAL.com. Accessed December 29, 2011. http://www.edreferral.com/.
"Something Fishy Website on Eating Disorders." Eating Disorders Anorexia, Bulimia & Compulsive Eating. Accessed December 29, 2011. http://www.something-fishy.org/.

REFLECTIONS

Reflections or the Sorority Body Image Program (SBIP) refers to a body image program that was developed for and implemented with sorority women at universities. The Reflections initiative began in 2001 at Trinity University when a research team collaborated with an on-campus sorority group to create a program based on Dr. Eric Stice's 4-session cognitive dissonance intervention (i.e., targeting the internalization of the thin-ideal standard of beauty for females).

Description of Reflections Program

Reflections or SBIP is implemented over two sessions that are facilitated by trained peer leaders who are active sorority members. Peer leaders receive nine hours of training before leading two 2-hour sessions. Participants engage in activities geared to promote positive body image and acceptance related to finding ways for sororities to change. In the initial session, participants are asked to describe the thin ideal, factors that reinforce this standard, and the costs of striving for the thin ideal. As a homework assignment, participants are asked to stand in front of a mirror and to record positive qualities about themselves including physical, emotional, and intellectual characteristics. In the second session participants share positive attributes and engage in role plays to challenge the thin ideal. Participants are encouraged to think about changes that can occur within each sorority (e.g., policy changes) to challenge the thin ideal.

Although researchers reported challenges associated with funding and time, preliminary findings showed decreases in dietary restraint, bulimic tendencies, body dissatisfaction, and thin-ideal internalization among the peer leaders for Reflections. More evaluation is needed to determine the effectiveness of the Reflections program.

Conclusion

The Reflections prevention program is a body image program designed for sorority women on college campuses. The curriculum has been adapted from an original cognitive dissonance program and incorporates messages about how to change the sorority structure to resist thin-ideal messages.

JUSTINE J. REEL

See also: Sorority Women.

Bibliography

Becker, Carolyn Black, Stephanie Bull, Lisa M. Smith, and Anna C. Ciao. "Effects of Being a Peer-Leader in an Eating Disorder Prevention Program: Can We Further Reduce Eating Disorder Risk Factors?" *Eating Disorders: Journal of Treatment and Prevention* 16 (2008): 444–59. doi: 10.1080/10640260802371596.

Becker, Carolyn Black, Anna C. Ciao, and Lisa M. Smith. "Moving from Efficacy to Effectiveness in Eating Disorders Prevention: The Sorority Body Image Program." *Cognitive and Behavioral Practices* 15 (2008): 18–27.

Becker, Carolyn Black, Eric Stice, Heather Shaw, and Susan Woda. "Use of Empirically-supported Interventions for Psychopathology: Can the Participatory Approach Move Us beyond the Research to Practice Gap?" *Behavioral Research Therapy* 47, no. 4 (2009): 265–74. doi: 10.1016/j.brat.2009.02.007.

RELAPSE

Relapse refers to the resumption of disordered eating behaviors (e.g., purging) after completing treatment and being symptom-free for a significant period of time. Relapse rates vary from 22 percent to 63 percent for anorexia nervosa, bulimia nervosa, and EDNOS depending on the definition of relapse and the timing of follow-up. Relapse or sliding back into disordered behaviors is often associated with feelings of shame similar to being discovered with an eating disorder in the first place, and clients may feel they have failed their treatment team, family members, and other clients in their support group.

Predictors of Relapse for Eating Disorders

Several factors have been consistently associated with a greater risk for relapse, including greater body image disturbances, poor psychosocial functioning, history of suicidal ideations, higher severity of eating disorder before treatment, and comorbidity with other mental disorders (e.g., personality disorders). Furthermore, individuals who had a tendency to excessively exercise toward the end of treatment were more likely to relapse. By contrast, individuals who had the ability to abstain from disordered behaviors throughout treatment seemed to be more likely to report a full recovery regardless of the client's initial diagnosis, suggesting that clinicians should help clients avoid slip-ups during the course of treatment.

In a unique study, eating disordered clients were interviewed about relapse and recovery. Participants who relapsed admitted to being more ambivalent about their recovery, less confident about their ability to maintain change, and more likely to seek treatment in order to satisfy a family member. Another finding was that participants who relapsed reported dissatisfaction with their treatment experience. For example, individuals expressed feeling overconfident about recovery and felt that the difficult work was behind them when they discharged. Other individuals felt that behavioral goals (e.g., weight restoration) were emphasized at the expense of dealing with emotional and psychological issues during treatment.

Relapse Prevention

Knowledge about predictors of relapse for eating disorders is needed to develop effective treatments and relapse-prevention strategies. A study of 51 first-admission clients with anorexia nervosa who were weight-restored when they discharged from inpatient treatment revealed that the overall rate of relapse was 35 percent and the highest risk period was from 6 to 17 months after discharge. This finding suggests that some clients relapsed after remaining weight-restored for the first year which suggests that clients should receive long-term follow-up care aimed at preventing relapse after being hospitalized. This study also found excessive exercise and residential concern about body shape and weight to be predictive of relapse, suggesting that treatment should incorporate skills for gradually increasing physical activity and coping skills for body image disturbances.

A separate study with 140 clients who were treated for bulimia nervosa using cognitive-behavioral therapy (CBT) found that 30 clients relapsed during follow-up. Specifically, 37 percent of the clients reported binge or purge episodes within 17 weeks of the follow-up period and an additional 16 percent engaged in behaviors in the year following treatment. None of the relapsed clients sought additional treatments, which suggests that telling clients who appear to have been successfully treated to come back if they have problems is an ineffectual relapse prevention strategy. More innovative outreach such as phone and text message follow-ups and regularly scheduled visits are warranted for relapse prevention.

Conclusion

Eating disorders are complicated and the course to recovery is difficult. With some studies reporting that a majority of eating disordered individuals will relapse, it is important to understand some of the factors related to falling off the wagon. Consistently, poor social support, negative body image, and comorbidity (e.g., depression, anxiety) have been predictive of relapse. In addition, having a history of suicide, a more severe eating disorder case, and more ambivalence toward recovery were related to relapse of eating disordered clients.

JUSTINE J. REEL

Bibliography

Bardone-Cone, Anna M., Megan B. Harney, Christine R. Maidonado, Melissa A Lawson, D. Paul Robinson, Roma Smith, and Aneesh Tosh. "Defining Recovery from an Eating Disorder: Conceptualization, Validation, and Examination of Psychosocial Functioning and Psychiatric Comorbidity." *Behavioral Research Therapy* 48, no. 3 (2010): 194–202. doi: 10.1016/j.brat.2009.11.001.

Carter, J. C., E. Blackmore, K. Sutandar-Pinnock, and D. B. Woodside. "Relapse in Anorexia Nervosa: A Survival Analysis." *Psychological Medicine* 34 (2004): 671–79. doi: 10.1017/S0033291703001168.

Federici, Anita, and Allan S. Kaplan. "The Patient's Account of Relapse and Recovery in Anorexia Nervosa: A Qualitative Study." *European Eating Disorders Review* 16 (2008): 1–10.

Keel, Pamela K., David J. Dorer, Debra L. Franko, Safia C. Jackson, and David B. Herzog. "Postremission Predictors of Relapse in Women with Eating Disorders." *American Journal of Psychiatry* 162 (2005): 2263–2268.

McFarlane, Traci, Marion P. Olmsted, and Kathryn Trottier. "Timing and Prediction of Relapse in a Transdiagnostic Eating Disorder Sample." *International Journal of Eating Disorders* 41 (2008): 587–93. doi: 10.1002/eat.20550.

Mitchell, James E., W. Stewart Agras, G. Terence Wilson, Katherine Halmi, Helena Kraemer, and Scott Crow. "A Trial of Relapse Prevention Strategy in Women with Bulimia Nervosa who Respond to Cognitive-Behavior Therapy." *International Journal of Eating Disorders* 35 (2004): 549–55.

Vanderlinden, J., H. Buis, G. Pieters, and M. Probst. "Which Elements in the Treatment of Eating Disorders are Necessary 'Ingredients' in the Recovery Process? A Comparison between the Patient's and Therapist's View." *European Eating Disorders Review* 15, no. 5 (2007): 357–65. doi: 10.1002/erv.768.

RELIGION

The influence of religion on eating attitudes and body image can be highly individualized and important to understand. The influence of religion on an individual's eating disorder may be affected by personality differences, differences in religious beliefs, rigidity of religious beliefs, personal spirituality levels, and cultural religious values. Therefore, religion may play a positive or negative role in eating disorder treatment and recovery or may have no effect on one's eating disorder.

Positive Influence on Body Image and Eating Behaviors

As an unhealthily thin body ideal is normative for women, turning to religion to help fill voids in self-esteem and body image may have a protective factor against eating disorders. Religious systems that teach its adherents that their bodies are acceptable regardless of size or shape may give purpose and direction to individuals. For example, many Christian sects view the body as a divine gift from God. One experimental study found that women who read religious affirmations had better body esteem after exposure to a thin ideal, when compared with those who read spiritual (but not religious) affirmation, or read information about campus issues. In clinical practice, many therapists have found religion to be a useful tool to help with eating disorder recovery, as it helps provide a social network and positive emotion. Additionally, residential eating disorder treatment groups may incorporate spirituality groups as part of comprehensive treatment to address the whole person. Twelve step groups (e.g., Eating Disorder Anonymous) exemplify the use of a higher power to provide clients with strength and draw upon faith to conquer addictions and recover from one's eating disorder.

Negative Influence on Body Image and Eating Behaviors

For some, religious practices or rituals may become a justification for eating disorder behaviors. Many religions speak of holy fasting, or label gluttony as a sin. Throughout history, religious figures in various belief systems have often fasted or refrained from food for religious quests and spiritual connectedness. A well-known example of this in Western culture is Jesus, who Christians believe fasted for 40 days. Furthermore, other faiths also encourage their adherents to fast—such as Islam during the month of Ramadan. Fasting behavior can be viewed as holy or righteous, as the individual is able to conquer the desires of the human body and rise to a more spiritual state. Similarly, for some, gluttony is judged to be sinful and unrighteous behavior to be avoided at all costs. Unsurprisingly, individuals with eating disorders may use religious beliefs to justify their disordered thoughts and behaviors as a spiritual quest. They may even feel a spiritual righteousness in deprivation, and justify that they are removing gluttony by purging.

By contrast, other individuals may view their eating disorder as wrong, selfish and sinful, causing them to feel unrighteous and guilty for the behaviors. These negative emotions may further perpetuate eating disorder behaviors as they feel unholy, sinful, and worthless. Individuals may continue to participate in eating disorder behaviors as a punishment for their unrighteousness.

When Religion Does Not Influence Body Image

Religious women may identify an element of personal strength gained by their beliefs. Regardless, their body image may suffer when exposed to cultural stereotypes of thin ideals. Even though their religion tells them they are worthwhile and valued, they may feel inferior when bombarded by negative images from the media. This may be due to the saturation of the message and the individual's exposure to it. For example, a religious woman may spend time each day praying, reading scripture, or attending religious services, but the amount of time she spends watching television shows which perpetuate a thin ideal is likely to be greater than the time spent on spiritual efforts. The religious convictions may not be strong enough to undo the damage from constant media exposure. Thus, the religion may appear to have no effect on a woman's body image.

Conclusion

For many people, religion and/or spirituality has influenced their self perceptions and eating behaviors. The degree to which this influence is positive or negative is highly variable and unique to the individual. When helping individuals with body image and eating disorder problems, it is important to consider the religious influences that the individual may have had and how these influences may be helping, or contributing, to the negative behaviors.

TeriSue Smith-Jackson

Bibliography

Baxter, Helen. "Religion and Eating Disorders." *European Eating Disorders Review* 9 (2001): 137–39.

Boyatzis, Chris J., Sarah Kline, and Stephanie Backof. "Experimental Evidence that Theistic-religious Body Affirmations Improve Women's Body Image." *Journal for the Scientific Study of Religion* 49, no. 4 (2007): 553–64.

Boyatzis, Chris J., and Katherine B. Quinlan. "Women's Body Image, Disordered Eating, and Religion: A Critical Review of the Literature." *Research in the Social Scientific Study of Religion* 19 (2008): 183–208.

Grenfell, Joanne Woolway. "Religion and Eating Disorders: Towards Understanding a Neglected Perspective." *Feminist Theology* 14, no. 3 (2006): 367–87.

Latzer, Yael, Faisal Azaiza, and Orna Tzischinsky. "Eating Attitudes and Dieting Behaviors among Religious Subgroups of Israeli-Arab Adolescent Females." *Journal of Religious Health* 48 (2009): 189–99.

Pinhas, Leorna, Margus Heinmaa, Pier Bryden, Susan Bradley, and Brenda Toner. "Disordered Eating in Jewish Adolescent Girls." *The Canadian Journal of Psychiatry* 53, no. 9 (2008): 601–608.

Smith-Jackson, TeriSue, Justine J. Reel, and Rosemary Thackeray. "Coping with 'Bad Body Image Days': Strategies from First-year Young Adult College Women." *Body Image* (2011).

RESILIENCY

Resiliency refers to the ability of individuals to positively adapt to difficult circumstances. The concept of resiliency is of particular interest to child and developmental psychologists engaged in understanding how some individuals are able to achieve life success despite adverse childhood conditions such as poverty, abuse, and broken families. Interest in resiliency has blossomed over the past 20 years, as researchers, practitioners, and self-help authors alike have taken an interest in the qualities that allow people to be resilient to trauma and life obstacles. Although the increased attention to resiliency has stimulated awareness of its importance, it has also caused some confusion regarding what it actually means to be resilient. Most definitions of resiliency imply the action of overcoming adversity, but fail to account for the underlying factors that result in resilient outcomes. To clarify the meaning of resiliency, professionals have generally adopted one of two views: (a) the trait view, or (b) the process view.

The Trait View: Resiliency as Something You "Have"

Resiliency is generally considered to be a trait or a set of traits possessed by certain individuals. In fact, much of the early research on resiliency adopted a trait approach. Although a few experts still believe in a singular resilient personality trait, most trait resiliency research has instead focused on resilient qualities, which are a type of protective factor. Protective factors are those qualities and/or environmental conditions that are conducive to positive adaptation to stress. In a 30-year study of at-risk children born on the Hawaiian island of Kauai, it was found that those children who achieved life competence (i.e., had loving relationships, a career, enjoyed a healthy amount of recreation, and were optimistic about their future) possessed several common personality characteristics that aided them in overcoming their life obstacles. Specifically, the at-risk children who grew to be competent adults were more self-confident, autonomous, affectionate, outgoing, and intelligent than the children who failed to achieve competence as adults. Many researchers and practitioners have proposed their version of the trait profile that makes a resilient personality. However, some experts caution against a solely trait view of resiliency, as this may encourage those who work with at-risk individuals to conclude that resiliency is something individuals either have or don't, and curb efforts to teach resiliency.

The Process View: Resiliency as a Constant Evolution

Resilience has also been described as a process. Specifically, Luthar, Cicchetti, and Becker defined resiliency in *Child Development* as "a dynamic process encompassing adaptation in the context of significant adversity." A process view forms a more holistic view of resiliency by encompassing traits, environmental influences (e.g., family support, socioeconomic status), and outcomes. From the process perspective, resiliency is comprised of four interrelated components: (a) risk factors, (b) protective factors, (c) vulnerability factors, and (d) positive adaptation. Risk factors are circumstances or triggering events that have been shown to lead to adverse outcomes. For example, participating in a sport that emphasizes being extremely lean and includes weekly weigh-ins might be a risk factor for unhealthy eating or eating disorders. Protective factors, as defined above, are factors that may buffer individuals from risk, and account for positive responses. By contrast, vulnerability factors are those factors that serve to intensify the effects of risk. Depending on the context, the same factor may be considered either as a protective factor or as a vulnerability factor. For example, having positive self-esteem might protect individuals from risk, whereas having negative self-esteem might make individuals more likely to succumb to risk. Finally, positive adaptation is an outcome that is much better than would be expected given the presence of a certain risk factor. Although the idea of positive adaptation may seem simple, it varies depending on the social context. For example, dropping out of school to help support one's family may be viewed as a negative outcome in some cultures, but is seen as a positive outcome in others. Individuals typically experience a number of risk, protective, and vulnerability factors simultaneously. Positive adaptation to one risk may change how they handle future risks. Thus, the process view presents resiliency as a capacity that develops over time in the context of multiple and simultaneous life events. Researchers have proposed process views of resiliency for specific groups such as bereaved spouses, military families, couples affected by HIV/AIDS, and older adults. Some research has also been conducted examining resiliency and eating disorders.

Applying the Process View of Resiliency to Eating Disorders: A Case Example

The following case example will illustrate how a process view of resiliency can be applied to the development of an eating disorder. When considering a 12-year-old girl's (Jacky) risk for, and possible resiliency to an eating disorder, each type of factor previously discussed would be considered. Jacky might possess several risk factors, such as a history of abuse, a family history of eating disorders, and pressure from friends to lose weight. Further, a number of vulnerability factors may exacerbate her risk, including low self-esteem and high perfectionism. However, a number of protective factors may buffer Jacky from developing an eating disorder, including strong social support and a deep sense of spirituality. The interaction of all factors would determine whether Jackie develops an eating disorder (i.e., negative adaptation), or does not develop an eating disorder (i.e., positive adaptation).

Body Image as a Protective/Vulnerability Factor for Eating Disorders

One of the most important protective/vulnerability factors to consider in eating disorder prevention is body image. Individuals who place high importance on body appearance and evaluate their bodies negatively are more likely to engage in unhealthy body-related change behaviors such as restricting, purging, or binge eating. On the other hand, body image satisfaction can serve as a protective factor against the development of eating disorders. Individuals who are less invested in and/or have a positive evaluation of their bodies are more likely to be accepting of the size and shape of their bodies, and less likely to take drastic measures to alter their weight.

Resiliency and Body Image Dissatisfaction

Because body image dissatisfaction is a critical factor in the development of eating disorders, it can and should be approached as an important outcome in its own right. In addition to enhanced risk for eating disorders, individuals who have poor body image are also likely to suffer from a variety of other mental health issues such as low self-esteem, social anxiety, and sexual inhibition. From a resiliency process perspective, viewing body image dissatisfaction as an outcome means that research and practice are aimed at identifying the risk, protective, and vulnerability factors associated with poor body image.

Risk Factors for Body Image Dissatisfaction

Perhaps the most pervasive risk factor for body image dissatisfaction in Western societies is sociocultural pressure to achieve an ideal body. Both women and men are strongly influenced by the images of ultrathin women and hypermuscular men depicted in the media through television, magazines, billboards, and the World Wide Web. Indeed, numerous studies have revealed that media exposure to idealized bodies triggers body dissatisfaction for both men and women. Friends and family, who represent another source of sociocultural body image pressure, engage in teasing about body weight, shape, and size which can have a profoundly negative effect on a child's body image. Parents and family members also model body dissatisfaction by making self-deprecating comments about their bodies or by dieting. Peers may serve as an additional risk factor due to the social comparison effect with same-aged peers who model negative body image and can participate in teasing which is equally harmful.

Protective Factors for Body Image Dissatisfaction

Compared to risk factors, protective factors for body image dissatisfaction have received far less attention. One protective factor that has been studied in relation to body image is the quality of parental relationships. Having supportive parents has been shown to increase body image satisfaction in girls. For girls in particular, parental encouragement to be strong, assertive, and independent may buffer them from sociocultural pressure to be thin. In addition to parental relationships, experts have suggested several other factors as potentially protecting individuals from body image dissatisfaction. First, individuals who believe that they have control and can effect change over their body weight, shape, and size may be less likely to feel dissatisfied with their appearance. Second, having a flexible conception of the ideal body may protect individuals from body image dissatisfaction. For example, black women have historically reported less body image dissatisfaction than white women partially due to the fact that they often endorse a larger ideal body type. Finally, having a more holistic view of beauty that extends beyond body size may guard women from body image dissatisfaction.

A Model of Body Image Resiliency for Women

In the *Journal of Counseling and Development*, Choate contended that researchers and practitioners can learn a great deal from girls and women who possess positive body image. Specifically, Choate proposed a model of body image resilience for females included five interrelated protective factors: (a) family-of-origin support, (b) gender role satisfaction, (c) positive physical self-concept, (d) effective coping strategies, and (e) sense of holistic balance and wellness.

Factor (a), family-of-origin support, refers to parental modeling of eating behaviors and attitudes toward food that are important predictors of body image in their children. According to Choate, family-of-origin support is essential for the development of the other four protective factors, as it leads directly to factors (b), (c), and (d) in the model. Factor (b), gender role satisfaction, deals with the conflict faced by women in trying to both meet the demands placed on them by society to be physically attractive, nurturing, and passive, while at the same time fulfilling their own personal, social, and occupational needs. Women who internalize conflicting gender role pressures are likely to succumb to body image dissatisfaction, while women who are supported are better able to acknowledge these pressures and create their own definition of what it means to be a woman. Family support is also directly related to factor (c), positive physical self-concept. Women with a positive physical self-concept are more likely to engage in and enjoy sports, exercise, and physical activity than women with a poor physical self-concept. Although women may adopt exercise to alter their physical appearance, they often continue exercising for the psychosocial benefits such as increased awareness of their physical strength, lowered anxiety, and increased body image satisfaction. Finally, women with strong family-of-origin support develop coping strategies to ward off the negative effects of sociocultural pressure; these coping strategies include critical thinking, stress management, and assertiveness. Gender role satisfaction, positive physical self-concept, and effective coping strategies work together such that changes in one influence changes in the other. For example, being satisfied with one's gender role might contribute to positive physical self-concept, which in turn may be related to more effective coping strategies such as using physical activity to manage stress. In addition to working together, factors (b), (c), and (d) combine to result in factor (e), holistic balance and wellness. Women who have achieved physical, social, emotional, intellectual, and spiritual wellness have a diverse view of their self-worth and place less emphasis on the importance of their physical appearance.

Strategies for Promoting Body Image Resilience

Based on Choate's model, several recommendations can be made for parents and school counselors regarding enhancement of body image resiliency in boys and girls. With regard to the influence of family and friends, parents should be educated about the strong effect their own eating attitudes and behaviors have on the attitudes and behaviors of their children. Further, parents and school staff should have a no-tolerance policy for weight teasing or bullying. To increase gender role satisfaction, parents and counselors should normalize the physical changes occurring with puberty, discourage comparisons to the bodies of others, and promote acceptance of multiple body types by encouraging children to identify role models of varying shapes and sizes. To enhance physical self-concept, children should be encouraged to participate in a variety of physical activities, with an emphasis on enjoyment and health benefits rather than weight loss and aesthetic changes. Parents and counselors play an important role in teaching children effective coping strategies. Perhaps the most important strategy to promote positive body image is media literacy. Boys and girls should be taught to be critical of dominant media portrayals of the ideal male and female body. One way to promote critical thinking is by asking children to review popular magazines and to identify both helpful and harmful body messages. Although all of the previously discussed strategies emphasize holistic wellness, other strategies include keeping a gratitude journal, serving as a peer mentor, and embracing their spiritual beliefs. By adopting some or all of these strategies, youth can learn to have a more broad and balanced conception of health, an increased acceptance of their bodies, and resilience to risk factors related to body image dissatisfaction.

NICK GALLI

Bibliography

Choate, Lauren H. "Toward a Theoretical Model of Women's Body Image Resilience." *The Journal of Counseling & Development* 83 (2005): 320–30.

Choate, Lauren H. "Counseling Adolescent Girls for Body Image Resilience: Strategies for School Counselors." *Professional School Counseling* 10 (2007): 317–26.

Luthar, Suniya S., Dante Cicchetti, & Bronwyn Becker, "The Construct of Resilience: A Critical Evaluation and Guidelines for Future Work." *Child Development* 71 (2000): 543–62.

Presnell, Katherine, Sarah Kate Bearman, and Mary Clare Madeley, "Body Dissatisfaction in Adolescent Females and Males: Risk and Resilience." *Prevention Researcher* 14 (2007): 3–6.

Stice, Eric, and Heather E. Shaw, "Role of Body Dissatisfaction in the Onset and Maintenance of Eating Pathology: A Synthesis of Research Findings." *Journal of Psychosomatic Research* 53 (2002): 985–93.

Werner, Emmy E, "Vulnerable but Invincible: High Risk Children from Birth to Adulthood." *European Child & Adolescent Psychiatry* 5 (1996): 47–51.

RISK FACTORS

Risk factor refers to the concept that someone who is exposed to a particular element will be more likely to develop a particular condition (e.g., eating disorders). Therefore, it is reasonable to conclude that intervening with a risk factor in some way (e.g., reducing its intensity or duration, or changing when it appears in one's developmental trajectory) should result in a reduced rate of the condition. Although seemingly straightforward, researchers warn that identifying risk factors in the field of eating disorders is not clear cut.

Alternatives to Risk Factors

The term "risk factor" has been identified by researchers as being potentially problematic as it is not consistently defined across studies. Variants of this term used in the eating disorders field have included "variable risk factor," "causal risk factor," "proxy risk factor," "fixed marker," and "variable marker." Additionally, less precise terms such as "contributor" have been used interchangeably with the term "risk factor." Regardless of the actual term being used, what distinguishes a "risk" factor from any other factor is that a risk factor must *precede* the condition in question; otherwise the factor simply co-occurs with or is a correlate of the condition. Therefore, a risk factor is one that reliably relates to the onset of a particular pathology.

In addition to how the term risk factor is defined, others have noted that simply identifying a risk factor as such may not be sufficiently helpful. It is likely that the mere presence of a single risk factor may not be enough to increase the incidence of a condition. Duration, intensity, and timing of the risk factor may determine the extent to which someone is "at risk" for a particular condition. The importance of properly identifying risk factors in the field of eating disorders can potentially aid professionals and paraprofessionals in preventing the development of eating disorders, and identifying and treating those who already have an eating disorder or who, at the very least, are "at risk" for developing an eating disorder.

As noted above, a true risk factor for an eating disorder must precede the onset of the disorder; however, some researchers have noted that distinguishing between risk factors for eating disorders and symptoms of the disorders themselves is not always clear. For example, risk factor constructs such as perfectionism, the need for control, and low self-esteem have previously been considered to be symptoms of eating disorders suggesting that these constructs may not precede onset but may be a part of the disorders themselves.

An additional problem in the identification of risk factors for eating disorders is that such factors do not consistently differentiate between the types of eating disorders. For example, a factor that is considered a risk factor for bulimia nervosa may not be a risk factor for anorexia nervosa. Additionally, identification of risk factors that may distinguish between the various subtypes of eating disorders has been largely unsuccessful. Despite these apparent shortcomings, various lists of factors have been generated pointing to the types of factors, controllable and uncontrollable, that can put someone at risk for an eating disorder. These factors can be broadly classified as biological factors, sociocultural factors, and psychological factors.

Examples of Risk Factors

Specific factors nominated as putting an individual at risk for developing an eating disorder have included gender, age, ethnicity, family history, sexual abuse, life stressors, genetics, neurochemical levels, perfectionism, low self-esteem, pubertal timing, negative affect, body image dissatisfaction, internalization of the thin ideal, pregnancy complications, concern with weight and shape, and dieting. Some of these factors are regularly identified as being risk factors for eating disorders. For example, dieting is sometimes referred to as a gateway behavior to eating disorders. Individuals may begin a diet innocently enough only to find themselves engaged in a full-blown eating disorder very quickly. Researchers have questioned whether dieting itself can truly be considered a risk factor when such a large percentage of people in Western cultures engage in dieting but so few ultimately develop an eating disorder. This begs the question: If dieting was a true risk factor, wouldn't the incidence of eating disorders be a lot higher? Indeed, this is often the question posed in response to many proposed risk factors.

Other risk factors such as low self-esteem are consistently identified in individuals with eating disorders; however, as noted above, a problem with identifying risk factors accurately is that it is not always clear whether or not the risk factor in question preceded the eating disorder or whether it is a result of the eating disorder itself. In the case of low self-esteem, it is conceivable that low self-esteem could either precede or be a consequence of an eating disorder. Moreover, low self-esteem may not necessarily be a unique risk factor for eating disorders, but may contribute to the development of psychopathology in general. Low self-esteem has been found to relate to other mental disorders such as depression and anxiety.

Research with Risk Factors

Studies conducted to date do not use the term "risk factor" consistently. Jacobi and colleagues identified that the "most potent risk factor" was having a high degree of weight and shape concerns. These researchers also concluded that some previously identified risk factors (e.g., family interaction styles, perfectionism) should no longer be considered risk factors for eating disorders based on more recent findings in the literature. An area of exploration that has received considerable attention by researchers is in the broad area of biological factors (e.g., genetics, how pregnancy and the birth process unfold, and the timing of biological developmental events). However, researchers indicated that results of twin studies suggest that genetics seems to be an important factor for the development of eating disorders, but other proposed biological factors simply co-occur with eating disorders and cannot yet be reliably classified as risk factors for eating disorders.

Conclusion

Although "risk factor" has been commonly used in connection with various psychological constructs, some of the so-called risk factors (e.g., perfectionism, low self-esteem) may more accurately reflect symptoms of an eating disorder or co-existing conditions. The appropriate and accurate classification of particular factors as being risk factors, symptoms, or otherwise has a direct impact on how these disorders are prevented, identified, and treated. Moreover, having a clear understanding of what factors are malleable and which ones are unchangeable also affects the decision regarding where our energies ought to be directed. Although many lists of risk factors for eating disorders exist, it is important to remember that the presence of any one or more of those factors in an individual does not necessarily mean that she has or will develop an eating disorder. Therefore, it is important that anyone suspected of being at risk for or of having an eating disorder is evaluated by a qualified medical or mental health professional.

CHRISTINE L. B. SELBY

Bibliography

Jacobi, Corinna, and Eike Fittig. "Psychosocial Risk Factors for Eating Disorders." In *The Oxford Handbook of Eating Disorders,* edited by Stewart W. Agras, 123–36. New York, NY: Oxford University Press, 2010.

Jacobi, Corinna, Chris Hayward, Martina de Zwaan, Helena C. Kraemer, and W. Stewart Agras. "Coming to Terms with Risk Factors for Eating Disorders: Application of Risk Terminology and Suggestions for a General Taxonomy." *Psychological Bulletin* 130, no. 1 (2004): 19–65.

Keel, Pamela K., Kamryn T. Eddy, Jennifer J. Thomas, and Marlene B. Schwartz. "Vulnerability to Eating Disorders across the Lifespan." In *Vulnerability to Psychopathology,* edited by Rick E. Ingram and Joseph M. Price, 489–94. New York, NY: Guilford Press, 2010.

Polivy, Janet, and C. Peter Herman. "Distinguishing Risk Factors from Symptoms: Are Eating Disorders Simply Disordered Eating?" In *Behavioral Mechanisms and Psychopathology: Advancing the Explanation of Its Nature, Cause and Treatment,* edited by Kurt Salzinger and Mark R. Serper, 175–98. Washington, DC: American Psychological Association, 2009.

Stice, Eric. "Risk and Maintenance Factors for Eating Pathology: A Meta-Analytic Review." *Psychological Bulletin* 128, no. 5 (2002): 825–48.

ROWING

Rowing has experienced popularity as an Olympic sport and as a college sport within certain geographical areas. Like judo, wrestling, and horseracing, rowing has been classified as a weight-dependent sport due to the existence of weight classes (i.e., lightweight and heavyweight) that require athletes to "make weight" for competition. Although male rowing has a strong tradition in elite Ivy League schools, female rowing has only recently been made available for college athletes. It is expected that rowers could experience similar pressures to lose weight as wrestlers and that could promote disordered eating and clinical eating disorders.

Eating Disorders and Male Rowers

One 1993 study found an equal prevalence of body image disturbances among male rowers and wrestlers, with 8 percent of rowers exhibiting clinical eating disorders. Rowers may engage in unhealthy weight loss methods such as fasting, restricting, purging, and dehydration strategies (e.g., saunas). However, rowing differs from other weight class sports in that the performance success is based on strength and power once the rower has achieved necessary weight requirements. Male lightweight rowers have been found to have significantly higher restrained eating behaviors and stronger body dissatisfaction than heavyweight rowers. In a separate study, male lightweight rowers were shown to have greater weight fluctuations throughout the season; they also gained more weight in the off-season. Therefore, male lightweight rowers should be considered an at-risk group for developing seasonal disordered eating patterns.

Eating Disorders and Female Rowers

Lightweight rowing for women is a more recent sport and requires college female athletes to meet a single weight class of 130 pounds. In one study comparing female and male rowers of both heavyweight and lightweight classes, female rowers displayed more disturbed eating practices and weight control methods than their male counterparts. In another study that compared lightweight female rowers to female distance runners, rowers were found to have significantly more eating restraint and higher diuretic use than runners. However, female rowers in this study seemed to have fewer body image concerns than either runners or the control group. Because female lightweight rowing is a relatively new sport, more research is needed that focuses on this potentially at-risk group of athletes.

Conclusion

Rowing is considered a weight class sport like wrestling and horseracing. As expected, lightweight rowers tend to show a stronger tendency toward eating restraint and unhealthy weight loss methods than heavyweight rowers. For male rowers, weight loss appeared to be related to being in-season or off-season, as weight gain tended to occur when athletes were not actively competing. As with other athletes who compete in weight-dependent sports, it is important to assess rowers for eating disturbances. Female lightweight rowers who must make weight may also become a vulnerable group for developing pathogenic weight control behaviors.

JUSTINE J. REEL

See also: Jockeys; Weight Class Sports; Weight Pressures in Sport; Wrestling.

Bibliography

Karlson, Kristine A., Carolyn Black Becker, and Amanda Merkur. "Prevalence of Eating Disordered Behavior in Collegiate Lightweight Women Rowers and Distance Runners." *Clinical Journal of Sport Medicine* 11 (2001): 32–37.

Nichols, David L., Charlotte F. Sanborn, and Eve V. Essery. "Bone Density and Young Athletic Women." *Sports Medicine* 37, no. 11 (2007): 1001–1014.

Sykora, Cahrlotte, Carlos M. Grilo, Denise E. Wilfley, and Kelly D. Brownell. "Eating, Weight, and Dieting Disturbances in Male and Female Lightweight and Heavyweight Rowers." *International Journal of Eating Disorders* 14, no. 2 (1993): 203–211.

Thiel, Andreas, H. Gottfired, and F. W. Hesse. "Subclinical Eating Disorders in Male Athletes: A Study of the Low Weight Category in Rowers and Wrestlers." *Acta Psychiatrica Scandinavia* 88 (1993): 259–65.

Thompson, Ron A., and Roberta Trattner Sherman. *Eating Disorders in Sport.* New York, NY: Routledge, 2010.

SELECTIVE EATING DISORDER

Selective Eating Disorder (SED) is often referred to as picky eating or fussy eating that prevents the consumption of certain foods. More recently, SED has been recognized by the medical community as an eating disorder; however, SED is not categorized as a clinical eating disorder diagnosis in the current version of the *Diagnostic and Statistical Manual of Mental Disorders.*

Symptoms of Selective Eating Disorder

Children are often identified as picky eaters, but selective eating patterns may persist throughout adulthood. Individuals with SED avoid certain foods based on their color, texture, or smell. In some cases, individuals with SED may be unable to eat an entire food group (e.g., fruits, vegetables). Individuals with SED may also limit consumption of foods to certain brands. Individuals with SED may prefer products that are more bland or lighter in color (e.g., plain pasta, cheese pizza). SED should be distinguished from other eating disorders such as anorexia nervosa because in SED picky eating occurs without the accompanying body image disturbance and food preferences are not based on calorie content. Although similar to orthorexia, SED is a distinct condition because the food preferences are not necessarily healthy. For example, adult picky eaters have identified french fries and bacon as common food preferences.

Prevalence of Selective Eating Disorder

SED has been understudied and the exact prevalence is unknown. However, SED in toddlers may be identified as an unwillingness to try new foods which can continue into adolescence and adulthood. SED occurs more often in boys than girls and is thought to be more common among children who have autistic spectrum disorders. One online support group for adult picky eaters has 1,400 active members.

Consequences of Selective Eating Disorder

Individuals who suffer from SED may face consequences such as developmental delays, problems in growth and weight gain, and malnutrition. Individuals with SED may fail to meet the body's nutrient needs due to cutting out certain types of foods or entire food groups. Psychological and emotional consequences include anxiety, social avoidance, and conflict. Adults with SED may report challenges associated with food preferences that can interfere with social and professional relationships.

Conclusion

Selective eating disorder refers to an understudied and less well-known eating disorder that is characterized by picky eating behaviors related to the color, texture, and smell of foods. Although SED is frequently recognized in childhood, disordered eating patterns can continue throughout one's life resulting in challenges during social and professional situations that revolve around meals. Because individuals with SED have narrow food preferences, having inadequate nutrition to support body functions is a concern. Therefore, individuals with SED should seek help just like individuals with any other type of eating disorder.

JUSTINE J. REEL

Bibliography

American Psychiatric Association. *Diagnostic and Statistical Manual of Mental Disorders.* Washington, DC: Author, 2000.

Skarda, Erin. "Does Extremely Picky Eating in Adulthood Signal a Mental Disorder?" *TIME.* Last modified December 10, 2010. http://healthland.time.com/2010/12/03/does-extremely-picky-eating-in-adulthood-signal-a-mental-disorder/.

"The Food F.A.D. Study (Finicky Eating in Adults)." Dukehealth.org. Accessed December 27, 2011. http://www.dukehealth.org/clinicaltrials/the_food_fad_study_finicky_eating_in_adults.

Wang, Shirley S. "No Age Limit on Picky Eating." *The Wall Street Journal.* Last modified July 5, 2010. http://online.wsj.com/article/SB10001424052748704699604575343130457388718.html.

SELF-INJURY

Self-injurious behavior or "cutting" refers to the deliberate infliction of self-harm and direct physical injury to one's body. In contrast to suicide, self-injury behaviors have no lethal intent and can include both compulsive and impulsive acts of self-harm. Compulsive forms of self-injury such as hair pulling and skin picking tend to be repetitive and habitual. Impulsive self-harm is also triggered by stressful events and can include skin cutting, bruising, and burning.

Prevalence of Deliberate Self-Harm

Deliberate self-harm has often been considered an adolescent phenomenon, but self-injurious behaviors can continue into adulthood. Among U.S. adolescents, cutting was estimated to range from 26 percent to 37 percent of 9th to 12th graders with over half (51.2%) of cutters being female. A similar study in Canada revealed that 17 percent of individuals in the age group of 14–21 years reported self-harm behaviors and the most common behaviors were cutting, scratching, or self-hitting. An Irish study with 3,881 teens found that females (13.9%) engaged in more deliberate harm than males (4.3%) and that self-cutting was more common than overdose. A separate study of Japanese adolescents in a juvenile detention center found that 16.4 percent of participants had engaged in cutting and 35 percent of participants had burned themselves. Deliberate self-harm has been associated with personality disorders as well as schizophrenia, major depression, substance abuse disorders, and eating disorders.

Deliberate Self-Harm and Eating Disorders

Although deliberate self-harm behaviors are considered socially unacceptable, nonsuicidal self-injury rates were highest among eating disordered individuals who engaged in purging behaviors (e.g., self-induced vomiting). One review showed that nonsuicidal self-injury occurred in 13.6–42.1 percent of individuals with anorexia nervosa restricting subtype, 27.8–68.1 percent of individuals with anorexia nervosa binge eating/purging subtype, and 26.0–55.2 percent of individuals with bulimia nervosa. Self-harm behaviors are associated with the attempt to deal with negative mood states (e.g., anger, depression) and 69.2 percent of eating disordered individuals reported feeling better immediately after self-injurious behavior. A couple of hours after self-injurious behavior, only one-third of eating disordered individuals felt better and the other one-third felt worse. It is common for feelings of guilt and shame to follow the self-harm incident. Clients have reported using self-injurious behaviors to punish themselves and to feel physical rather than emotional pain.

Conclusion

Self-injurious behaviors are behaviors involving direct and deliberate destruction of one's own body without suicidal intent. Self-injurious behaviors can include cutting, scratching, burning, and bruising and can inflict visible wounds and burns. Although considered an adolescent behavior, adults can engage in self-harm and individuals with psychiatric disorders are at increased risk for deliberate self-harm. Eating disordered individuals who purge are more likely to engage in self-injurious behaviors than individuals who restrict. Deliberate self-harm is generally associated with mood disturbances and an attempt to cope with negative emotions.

JUSTINE J. REEL

Bibliography

Claes, Laurence, E. David Klonsky, Jennifer Muehlenkamp, Peter Kuppens, and Walter Vandereycken. "The Affect-Regulation Function of Nonsuicidal Self-Injury in Eating

Disordered Patients: Which Affect States Are Regulated?" *Comprehensive Psychiatry* 51 (2010): 386–92. doi: 10.1016/j.comppsych.2009.09.001.

Claes, Laurence, Walter Vandereycken, and Hans Vertommen. "Therapy-Related Assessment of Self-Harming Behaviors in Eating Disordered Patients: A Case Illustration." *Eating Disorders: Journal of Treatment and Prevention* 10 (2002): 269–79. doi: 10.1080/10640260290081858.

Favaro, Angela, and Paolo Santonastaso. "Different Types of Self-Injurious Behavior in Bulimia Nervosa." *Comprehensive Psychiatry* 40, no. 1 (1999): 57–60.

Franko, Debra L., and Pamela K. Keel. "Suicidality in Eating Disorders: Occurrence, Correlates and Clinical Implications." *Clinical Psychology Review* 26, no. 6 (2006): 769–82. doi: 10.1016/j.cpr.2006.04.001.

Franko, Debra L., Pamela K. Keel, D. J. Dover, S. S. Delinsky, K. T. Eddy, V. Charat, R. Renn, and David B. Herzog. "What Predicts Suicide Attempts in Women with Eating Disorders?" *Psychological Medicine* 34 (2004): 843–53.

Greydanus, Donald E., and Daniel Shek. "Deliberate Self-Harm and Suicide in Adolescents." *Keio Journal of Medicine* 58, no. 3 (2009): 144–51.

Hintikka, Jukka, Tommi Tolmunen, Marja-Liisa Rissanen, Kirsi Honkalampi, Jari Kylma, and Eila Laukkanen. "Mental Disorders in Self-Cutting Adolescents." *Journal of Adolescent Health* 44 (2009): 464–67. doi: 10.1016/j.jadohealth.2008.10.003.

Kerr, Patrick L., Jennifer J. Muehlenkamp, and James M. Turner. "Nonsuicidal Self-Injury: A Review of Current Research for Family Medicine and Primary Care Physicians." *Journal of the American Board of Family Medicine* 23, no. 2 (2010): 240–59.

Milos, Gabriella, Anja Spindler, Urs Hepp, and Ulrich Schnyder. "Suicide Attempts and Suicidal Ideation: Links with Psychiatric Comorbidity in Eating Disorder Subjects." *General Hospital Psychiatry* 26, no. 2 (2004): 129–35. doi: 10.1016/j.genhosppsych.2003.10.005.

Pompili, Maurizio, Paolo Girardi, Giulia Tatarelli, Amedeo Ruberto, and Roberto Tatarelli. "Suicide and Attempted Suicide in Eating Disorders, Obesity, and Weight Image." *Eating Behaviors* 7, no. 4 (2006): 384–94. doi: 10.1016/j.eatbeh.2005.12.004.

SKI JUMPING

Ski jumping refers to an antigravitation Olympic sport that involves flying through the air on skis to achieve the greatest distance. Ski jumping is considered a leanness-demand sport because of the focus on weight and the perception that performance will improve with decreased weight (i.e., lighter will fly further). Historically ski jumping has been limited to male athletes, but female ski jumpers have been training and competing outside the Olympics. It is expected that eventually women's ski jumping will become an Olympic sport.

Weight Pressures in Ski Jumping

Because of the noted advantage among the lightest ski jumpers, ski jumping has resembled other weight class sports in which athletes "make weight" to improve their performance. Ski jumpers may restrict certain foods, engage in fasting, purging, or excessive exercise prior to competitions. Ski jumpers tend to have petite physiques, similar to that of a jockey, and athletes are expected to remain light for competitions. Although ski jumpers wear revealing and form-fitting training and competition attire, to date no studies have explored body image concerns among these athletes.

World Cup and Olympic competitions discovered that the body mass index of ski jumpers had dropped drastically during the period of events between 1970 and 1995. Therefore, the Federation Internationale de Ski (FIS), the governing body for ski jumping, created regulations regarding the weight of competitors; this was dubbed the "anorexic rule" for male ski jumpers.

Anorexic Rule for Male Ski Jumpers

Prior to the 2006 Olympics, the FIS established a weight penalty for underweight ski jumpers that would result in shortening of skis. Because ski length affects flight, having the ski length shortened creates a competitive disadvantage for underweight ski jumpers. Generally, skis can be as long as 146 percent of a ski jumper's height. Ski jumpers who are weighed in the nude and in gear must meet minimum body mass index requirements of 18.5 and 20 respectively. When a skier drops below the minimum, his skis are shortened by 2 percent for each kilogram of weight below the standard. In the 2006 Olympics, only 4 of the top 50 competitors in the individual event did not make weight, suggesting that the anorexic rule has been an effective tool for preventing excessive weight loss. However, sports professionals have suggested that athletes use the weight limit as a guide for where their weight should be, and reportedly, ski jumpers lose weight down to the minimum requirement.

Conclusion

Ski jumping is an antigravitation, leanness-demand sport in which there is a performance advantage associated with being lighter. The governing body has taken proactive measures to prevent extreme weight loss among ski jumpers by instituting the anorexic rule (i.e., penalizing ski jumpers who do not weigh in with a body mass index of 18.5). Although only male ski jumpers compete in the Olympics, female ski jumpers are preparing for their entrance into the games.

JUSTINE J. REEL

See also: Jockeys; Weight Class Sports; Weight Pressures in Sport.

Bibliography

Muller, W. "Determinants of Ski Jump Performance and Implications for Health, Safety and Fairness." *Sports Medicine* 39 (2009): 85–106.

Reel, Justine J., and Katherine A. Beals, eds. *The Hidden Faces of Eating Disorders and Body Image.* Reston, VA: AAHPERD/NAGWS, 2009.

Reel, Justine J., and Holly M. Estes. "Treatment Considerations for Athletes with Disordered Eating." In *Disordered Eating among Athletes: A Comprehensive Guide for Health*

Professionals, edited by Katherine A. Beals, 131–58. Champaign, IL: Human Kinetics, 2004.

Sherman, Roberta T. "Protecting the Health of Athletes: Possible Changes." Paper presented at the meeting of the International Olympic Committee Medical Commission. Monte Carlo, Monaco, 2007.

Thompson, Ron A., and Roberta Trattner Sherman. *Eating Disorders in Sport.* New York, NY: Routledge, 2010.

SKIN TONE

Skin tone can represent a significant component of a person's body image. In the United States having a tan may be associated with a youthful glow, in contrast to other cultures that value lighter tones. Changing one's skin tone to make it lighter or darker has occurred throughout the years. The desire to change one's appearance is closely correlated with body dissatisfaction which is the strongest predictor of eating disorders.

Cultural Influences on Skin Tone

Many cultures desire lighter skin color, as pale skin is associated with beauty and wealth. For example, Japanese culture values white (or light) skin color, because this skin tone is believed to reflect spiritual refinement, femininity, purity, and goodness. Historically, this light skin color preference was grounded in class distinctions. Dark skin tones have been linked to the assumption that the individuals concerned were from a low social class that was involved in performing intense outdoor labor. By contrast, upper-class Japanese women who commonly applied white powder to their face to lighten the appearance were viewed by others as being wealthy enough to protect their skin from the sun. Currently, the desire for white skin among Japanese women still exists, as white skin is considered beautiful. There are many cosmetic companies selling non-bleach skin creams; the advertisements for these products claim that they whiten the skin. While it is unclear if these products actually lighten the skin, they generally do not contain chemicals associated with skin cancer.

Skin Bleaching

Throughout Asia, Latin America, and Africa, skin bleaching has become increasingly popular—particularly in areas colonized by Europe, such as Ghana, Kenya, Tanzania, Senegal, Mali, South Africa, and Nigeria—as being white equals a high social and economic status. While both men and women report desiring a lighter skin shade, women generally have higher rates of skin bleaching than their male counterparts. Furthermore, women sometimes apply skin bleaching products to their children in attempts to meet the socially desirable skin tone standard.

Individuals from Africa may choose to apply skin bleaching creams to cover their naturally black skin tones. Researchers suggest that this practice could reflect

In this 2011 photo, roadside vendor Sophia McLennan displays her selection of skin bleaching agents near a pharmacy in downtown Kingston, Jamaica. People around the world often try to alter their skin color, using tanning salons or dyes to darken it or other chemicals to lighten it. In the slums of Jamaica, doctors say the skin lightening phenomenon has reached dangerous proportions. (AP/Wide World Photos)

an internalization of the discrimination experienced. Furthermore, researchers suggest that descendants of enslaved Africans have not only developed negative attitudes about themselves, but have also turned to skin bleaching to erase the past.

The largest impact of Western cultural values of lighter skin has been observed in Senegal and extends to other parts of Africa. In fact, the desire for lighter skin and the corresponding chemical skin bleaching behavior has resulted in skin cancer. In addition to these severe health implications, the cost of a bottle of skin bleach is $5.00, which is highly unattainable by the majority of the population which lives on less than $2.00 per day. Although expensive, some women in Senegal choose to spend scarce resources on potentially dangerous skin bleaching products rather than on necessary living expenses (e.g., food and clothing).

Skin Lightening Products

Skin lightening products are widely available for purchase by the general public, for both clinical treatment of skin disorders and cosmetic reasons. Hydroquinone has been the standard for 40 years in treating hyperpigmentation and unaffected skin in vitiligo patients. This chemical can be found in tea, wheat, berries, beer, and coffee. Flavanoids like licorice and naturally occurring Kojic acid have also been used to lighten skin.

Advertisers tend to sell their skin lightening products to consumers by getting popular light-skinned women of color to appear in advertisements within their country of origin. For example, Halle Berry of the United States, Aishwarya Rai of India (L'Oreal), Genevieve Nnaji of Nigeria (Lux soap), and Terry Pheto of South Africa (L'Oreal) have been depicted in the ads. The first skin lightening cream to be targeted at men, Fair and Handsome, was created by the British company Unilever; its advertisement featured India's Bollywood celebrity Shah Rukh Khan. The advertisement led men to believe that they would be more masculine if they lightened their skin. Organizers of the "Miss Authentica Pageant"—a beauty pageant— in Africa's Ivory Coast are aware of the dangers of skin bleaching and require that pageant participants do not bleach their skin to qualify. This requirement is intended to raise awareness of the dangers of skin bleaching throughout the country. Similarly, the Jamaican government launched a campaign called "Don't Kill the Skin" to raise awareness about the irreversible dangers of skin bleaching.

Conclusion

In conclusion, while tanned skin is often considered desirable in the United States, a lighter skin tone is preferred in many other countries throughout the world. In Japan, Africa, Latin America, and other Asian countries, light skin tone is associated with beauty and wealth. As a result, dangerous skin bleaching practices have been used in some countries to change one's skin tone; in other countries, false advertisements regarding nondangerous skin lightening creams that do not deliver a lighter skin tone can be seen in the media.

HAILEY E. NIELSON

Bibliography

Charles, Christopher A. D. "Skin Bleaching, Self-Hate, and Black Identity in Jamaica." *Journal of Black Studies* 33, no. 6 (2003): 711–28.

Gillbro, J. M., and M. J. Olsson. "The Melanogenesis and Mechanisms of Skin-Lightening Agents—Existing and New Approaches." *International Journal of Cosmetic Science* 33 (2010): 210–21.

Hall-Iijima, Christine. "Asian Eyes: Body Image and Eating Disorders of Asian and Asian American Women." *Eating Disorders* 3 (1995): 5–19.

Hunter, Margaret L. "Buying Racial Capital: Skin Bleaching and Cosmetic Surgery in a Globalized World." *The Journal of Pan African Studies* 4, no. 4 (2011).

Mahe, Antoine, Fatimata Ly, Guy Aymard, and Jean Marie Dangou. "Skin Diseases Associated with the Cosmetic Use of Bleaching Products in Women from Dakar, Senegal." *British Journal of Dermatology* 148, no. 3 (2003): 493–500. doi: 10.1046/j.1365–2133. 2003.05161.x.

SOCIAL COMPARISON THEORY

Social comparison theory is a theory that was originally developed by Festinger in 1954 to explain how individuals are driven by the desire for self-evaluation of their abilities. According to Festinger, when individuals do not have objective means to evaluate themselves, they compare their own attributes and abilities with those of other people. Comparing themselves to others who are better or worse in terms of certain characteristics can strongly influence how they think and feel about themselves, and thus lead them to engage in positive or negative behaviors.

Upward and Downward Comparisons

Unfavorable comparisons (the other person is evaluated more positively for a particular attribute than oneself) are called upward comparisons. Individuals often make upward comparisons to improve themselves. For example, a woman may compare herself to someone more accomplished in school as a source of inspiration. However, the risk of upward comparison is that it may bring attention to her own flaws (e.g., body fat) and threaten her self-esteem. Research on upward comparisons indicates that people with a strong tendency to make physical appearance–related comparisons that are typical of societal ideals (i.e., thin ideal) experience more body dissatisfaction and disordered eating.

In contrast to upward comparisons, downward comparisons or favorable comparisons (the other person is evaluated more negatively for a particular attribute than oneself) may serve as an attempt to build confidence by comparing oneself with someone who is perceived to be inferior on a certain attribute. Researchers suggest that people experiencing negative emotions or cognitions about themselves (e.g., low self-esteem) often try to enhance their self-regard by engaging in downward comparisons.

Social Comparison among Girls and Women

In the body image and weight control context, there are numerous studies that show that girls and women frequently engage in social comparisons when evaluating their own bodies. Social comparison theory suggests that individuals may also use media images and toys as inspirational standards or models of societal attractiveness. Warren and colleagues (2010) found that adolescent girls made more social comparisons with media models (e.g., actresses) than boys, and girls who scored higher on the social comparison tendency also exhibited greater eating pathology. In another recent study, investigators examined the effects of playing with thin dolls (e.g., Barbie) compared to playing with more realistic-sized dolls on the consumption of sweet snacks among girls in the age group of 6–10 years. Approximately half of the girls in the study wanted to be thin, and the girls who played with the thin dolls consumed fewer snacks than those who played with realistic-sized dolls, suggesting that exposing real-life environmental cues that relate to body size can have a powerful influence on girls' eating behaviors.

Prior research has found that girls gather information on peer values, ideals, and behaviors which they then use to judge their bodies and engage in weight control behaviors. Recently, researchers examined the social contexts in schools to understand what influences girls' decisions to practice weight control. They found that girls are less likely to try to lose weight in schools where there are many overweight girls or where the average female BMI is high, and more likely to lose weight in schools where there are many underweight girls. However, schoolmates with a similar body size had the most powerful impact on individual girls' weight loss behaviors. This research suggests that weight loss is motivated by normative standards of beauty as well as the ideals of those most similar to an individual.

Women who were exposed to images of ultrathin females as beautiful compared their own bodies to the media images, and as a result of this comparison, these women reported more negative mood and body dissatisfaction. Researchers have shown that women who view images of thin women in print ads, television commercials, and music videos experience lower self-esteem and higher body dissatisfaction than women who view neutral images. Even a brief exposure to media images of the thin ideal can have a negative impact on women's body image. For women, appearance comparison was one of the strongest predictors of body dysmorphic disorder.

Social Comparison among Boys and Men

Over the past 30 years, content analyses of male media images indicate that media images of men have become increasingly more muscular and less realistic. Because there are more media images of what men should look like, boys and men are prone to comparing themselves to the ideal images. Studies have shown that adolescent boys engage in social comparison regarding their bodies, and this is related to negative body image and disordered eating. A recent study found that social body comparison in adolescent boys predicted the use of media and muscle building behaviors; other researchers found that social body comparison is associated with eating pathology among adolescent boys. These recent studies support previous research indicating that boys made upward comparisons of their bodies with those of their friends as early as eight years of age.

Karazsia and Crowther (2010) examined social comparison among adult men and found that social comparisons influence body dissatisfaction indirectly through internalization (i.e., the individual buys into socially defined ideals of attractiveness). In a separate study, researchers exposed some men to television commercials with the muscular ideal and found that these men felt less physically attractive and less satisfied with their muscle shape and size than men who did not watch these commercials. The frequency of comparisons did not predict body dissatisfaction in men. It appears that men engage in less social comparison to idealized media images than women. However, the direction of comparison (upward versus downward) was an important factor in influencing body dissatisfaction.

The more the upward social comparison after watching commercials with images of the muscular ideal, the greater the decrease in feeling strong, weight satisfaction, and muscle satisfaction.

Conclusion

Individuals, regardless of age and gender, engage in social comparison to measure attributes, capabilities, and characteristics (e.g., appearance) to others. Exposure to media-presented images of thinness and attractiveness serve as unrealistic objects for obsessive comparison. When individuals compare themselves to others who they think are better (e.g., models, celebrities, actors), this upward comparison often leads to body dissatisfaction and unhealthy eating.

SONYA SOOHOO

See also: Body Image; Body Image in Males; Dolls; Media.

Bibliography

Anschutz, Doeschka J., and Rutger C.M.E. Engels. "The Effects of Playing with Thin Dolls on Body Image and Food Intake in Young Girls." *Sex Roles* 63 (2010): 621–30.

Boroughs, Michael S., Ross Krawezyk, and J. Kevin Thompson. "Body Dysmorphic Disorder among Diverse Racial/Ethnic and Sexual Orientation Groups: Prevalence Estimates and Associated Factors." *Sex Roles* 63 (2010): 725–37.

Festinger, Leon. "A Theory of Social Comparison Processes." *Human Relations* 7 (1954): 117–40.

Hargreaves, Duane, and Marika Tiggerman. "Muscular Ideal Media Images and Men's Body Image: Social Comparison Processing and Individual Vulnerability." *Psychology of Men and Muscularity* 10 (2009): 109–19.

Karazsia, Bryan T., and Janis Crowther. "Sociocultural and Psychological Links to Men's Engagement in Risky Body Change Behaviors." *Sex Roles* 63 (2010): 747–56.

Smolak, Linda, and Jonathan A. Stein. "A Longitudinal Investigation of Gender Role and Muscle Building in Adolescent Boys." *Sex Roles* 63 (2010): 738–46.

Tantleff-Dunn, Stacey, and Jessica L. Gokee. "Interpersonal Influences on Body Image Development." In *Body Image: A Handbook of Theory, Research, and Clinical Practice,* edited by Thomas Cash. New York: The Guilford Press, 2002.

Warren, Cortney S., Andrea Schoen, and Kerri J. Schafer. "Media Internalization and Social Comparison as Predictors of Eating Pathology among Latino Adolescents: The Moderating Effect of Gender and Generational Status." *Sex Roles* 63 (2010): 712–24.

SOCIAL PHYSIQUE ANXIETY

Social physique anxiety refers to worry associated with having one's body evaluated by others. The term "social physique anxiety" (SPA) was coined in the late 1980s by researchers at Wake Forest University to conceptualize body-related anxiety as a perceptual, cognitive, and behavioral component of body image. Individuals with higher SPA perceive negative evaluations by others in social situations and engage in strong impression management related to their presentation of self. For example, individuals with high SPA have a stronger tendency to hide perceived bodily flaws and to avoid social situations in which their body may be evaluated (e.g., fitness centers, pool parties).

Self-Presentation and Social Physique Anxiety

"Self-presentation" refers to the ways in which people seek to present themselves favorably to others in attempts to make a positive impression and avoid scrutiny. Individuals experience intense social anxiety when they perceive unfavorable reactions from others. This negative evaluation specific to one's body is social physique anxiety.

SPA and self-presentation are especially relevant for exercise settings in which bodies are on display and evaluation by social others is likely. Individuals who have high SPA may avoid exercise settings that promote social interactions (e.g., "meat markets"), may seek gyms with modest clothing policies, or may exercise in private. Individuals with high SPA tend to cover their bodies with loose fitting clothing when they are exposed in public. A study revealed that adult women expressed more favorable opinions of a particular exercise class when participants wore less form-fitting clothing than when participants wore revealing attire. Furthermore, high SPA exercisers tended to position themselves at the back of a group exercise class. The presence of SPA can serve as a barrier to certain types of activities that promote bodies on display (e.g., swimming, yoga).

Social physique anxiety has also been explored among different types of athletes. Gymnasts with higher SPA tended to have lower confidence about sport performance and lower physical self-perceptions. Dancers and cheerleaders in aesthetic activities had higher SPA scores than swimmers. Although all of the participants (i.e., dancers, cheerleaders, swimmers) wore revealing team uniforms, the participants in dance and cheerleading perceived the appearance of their bodies as having a direct impact on their performance.

Assessment of Social Physique Anxiety

Researchers developed a survey to measure SPA among males and females of diverse ages and abilities. The original scale (i.e., the Social Physique Anxiety Scale [SPAS]) was published in 1989 with 12 items to assess the level of anxiety surrounding the evaluation of one's body. More recently, researchers have advocated using a 9-item version of SPAS, but both versions of the measure are widely used with athletes, exercisers of all ages, and persons with disabilities. An example of an item from the SPA is, "In the presence of others, I feel apprehensive about my physique or figure."

Conclusion

Social physique anxiety is a type of body image that specifically refers to the anxiety associated with having one's body evaluated negatively by others in public.

Individuals with higher SPA actively work to disguise their bodies or to avoid social situations that can increase body self-consciousness. The Social Physique Anxiety Scale can assess one's degree of SPA to serve as a tool for self-awareness.

JUSTINE J. REEL

Bibliography

Bratrud, Sharon, Marissa M. Parmer, James R. Whitehead, and Robert C. Eklund. "Social Physique Anxiety, Physical Self-Perceptions and Eating Disorder Risk: A Two-Sample Study." *Pamukkale Journal of Sport Sciences* 1, no. 3 (2010): 1–10.

Hart, Elizabeth, Mark R. Leary, and W. Jack Rejeski. "The Measurement of Social Physique Anxiety." *Journal of Sport and Exercise Psychology* 11 (1989): 94–104.

Kowalski, Kent C., Diane E. Mack, Peter R.E. Crocker, Cory B. Niefer, and Tara-Leigh Fleming. "Coping with Social Physique Anxiety in Adolescence." *Journal of Adolescent Health* 39, no. 2 (2006): 275e9–275e16.

Leary, Mark R. *Self-presentation: Impression Management and Interpersonal Behavior.* Boulder, Colorado: Westview Press, 1996.

Martin, Jeffrey J. "Predictors of Social Physique Anxiety in Adolescent Swimmers with Physical Disabilities." *Adapted Physical Activity Quarterly* 16 (1999): 75–85.

Martin, Jeffrey J. "Social Physical Anxiety, Body Image, Disability, and Physical Activity." In *Social Anxiety: Symptoms, Causes and Techniques,* edited by Theresa M. Robinson, 29–46. London, England: Nova Science, 2010.

Martin, Jeffrey J., Amy Kliber, Pamela Hodges Kulinna, and Marianne Fahlman. "Social Physique Anxiety and Muscularity and Appearance Cognitions in College Men." *Sex Roles* 55, no. 3–4 (2006): 151–58. doi: 10.1007/s11199-006-9069-0.

Reel, Justine J., and Diane L. Gill. "Psychosocial Factors Related to Eating Disorders among High School and College Female Cheerleaders." *The Sport Psychologist* 10, no. 2 (1996): 195–206.

Reel, Justine J., Sonya SooHoo, Diane L. Gill, and Kathie M. Jamieson. "Femininity to the Extreme: Body Image Concerns among College Female Dancers." *Women in Sport and Physical Activity Journal* 14, no. 1 (2005): 39–51.

SORORITY WOMEN

Sororities are college organizations for female college students that provide a group identity, a social outlet, as well as leadership and philanthropic opportunities to its members. Sororities have been stereotyped as breeding grounds for eating disorders with suspicion that binge and purge behaviors are rampant among sisters.

Disordered Eating and Sororities

Earlier studies provided evidence that joining a sorority can contribute to eating disordered behavior. For example, one researcher found that when certain eating behaviors were modeled within peer groups (i.e., sorority friends) the behaviors became normalized and accepted over time. Although binge eating frequency was dissimilar among friends at the beginning of the semester, binge frequency was highly related by the end of the year.

A separate study found that sorority sisters tended to be more attractive, had higher family incomes, and were more willing to attempt to fit in than non-sorority college females. Specifically, sorority sisters were found to have higher alcohol use and more body dissatisfaction and fears of fatness than a non-sorority comparison group. In another study, disordered eating, body mass index, and ideal weight did not differ between sorority and non-sorority women at baseline before women joined sororities. Interestingly, by the third year, sorority women reported significantly higher levels of dieting and concern for weight than non-sorority women who showed a gradual decrease in the preoccupation with thinness throughout their college years.

Conclusion

Sorority groups foster social interaction and connectedness throughout a female's college experience. However, a group's focus on appearance or modeling of disordered eating behaviors (e.g., binge eating) can contribute to dysfunctional eating patterns, dieting, and body dissatisfaction among its members. Therefore, eating disorder prevention programs—such as Reflections— which are peer-led by other sorority sisters have been created for and implemented with sorority groups.

JUSTINE J. REEL

See also: Reflections.

Bibliography

Allison, Kelly C., and Crystal L. Park. "A Prospective Study of Disordered Eating among Sorority and Nonsorority Women." *International Journal of Eating Disorders* 35 (2004): 354–58. doi: 10.1002/eat.10255.

Becker, Carolyn Black, Anna C. Ciao, and Lisa M. Smith. "Moving from Efficacy to Effectiveness in Eating Disorders Prevention: The Sorority Body Image Program." *Cognitive and Behavioral Practice* 15 (2008): 18–27.

Becker, Carolyn Black, Eric Stice, Heather Shaw, and Susan Woda. "Use of Empirically-supported Interventions for Psychopathology: Can the Participatory Approach Move Us beyond the Research to Practice Gap?" *Behavioral Research Therapy* 47, no. 4 (2009): 265–74. doi: 10.1016/j.brat.2009.02.007.

Hoerr, Sharon L., Ronda Bokram, Brenda Lugo, Tanya Bivins, and Debra R. Keast. "Risk for Disordered Eating Relates to Both Gender and Ethnicity for College Students." *Journal of American College of Nutrition* 21, no. 4 (2002): 307–314.

Piquero, Nicole Leeper, Kristan Fox, Alex R. Piquero, George Capowich, and Paul Mazerolle. "Gender, General Strain Theory, Negative Emotions and Disordered Eating." *Journal of Youth Adolescence* 39 (2010): 380–92. doi: 10.1007/s10964-009-9466-0.

Scott-Sheldon Lori A. J., Kate B. Carey, and Michael P. Carey. "Health Behavior and College Students: Does Greek Affiliation Matter?" *Journal of Behavioral Medicine* 31, no. 1 (2008): 61–70.

SPORTS

For anyone who has ever played or coached sports, unhealthy eating patterns are not a foreign subject—whether it is working to gain weight or to lose it, when healthy methods are not effective or fast enough, some athletes resort to unhealthy methods. Although the reasons behind these unhealthy eating behaviors are still being studied, given the complex nature of eating disorders and disordered eating behaviors, research and practical experience have combined to shed light on the nature of eating disorders in athletes.

Prevalence of Eating Disorders in Athletes

Prevalence rates of disordered eating among athletes vary from 0 to 62 percent across studies (i.e., 1-62% for female athletes and 0-57% for male athletes) depending on measures used, competitive levels of athletes and types of sports studied. In a recent prevalence study, 2.0 percent of female college athletes were classified as having a clinical eating disorder and an additional 25.5 percent of athletes exhibited disordered eating patterns. Furthermore, it has been estimated that approximately 0.9 percent of female athletes and 0.3 percent of male athletes suffer from anorexia nervosa and approximately 1.5 percent of females and 0.5 percent of males suffer from bulimia nervosa.

Athletes versus Nonathletes

The question of whether athletes are more at risk for developing eating disorders than nonathletes is complicated. Some studies have demonstrated that athletes exhibit less preoccupation with weight and lower body dissatisfaction than nonathletes. Other researchers suggest that athletes have greater perceptions of self-efficacy, or self-confidence in one's ability to succeed.

However, some studies indicate that athletes are actually at greater risk for eating disorders than nonathletes. It has been argued that athletes not only experience the same weight pressures nonathletes experience (e.g., pressure from family, friends, media), but they may also experience weight pressures unique to sport participation (e.g., pressure from coaches, subjective evaluation by judges, uniform pressures). Regardless, when reviewing numerous studies with athletes, the differences of disordered eating rates between athletes and nonathletes are found to be small. Results indicate that athletes, especially athletes in lean sports (e.g., gymnastics, wrestling, distance running), are at a greater risk for disordered eating behaviors than athletes in nonlean sports (e.g., soccer, basketball, swimming) or nonathletes.

Lean versus Nonlean Sports

Classifying sports as either lean (e.g., diving, gymnastics, dance) or nonlean sports (e.g., ball sports, track and field, swimming) has been a popular way to categorize athletes and identify the potential risk for disordered eating and eating disorders. In a recent study on eating disorders in elite athletes, researchers found that approximately 45 percent of lean sport athletes and less than 20 percent of nonlean sport athletes reported disordered eating behaviors.

Because sports are diverse in type, generalizing prevalence rates by sport is difficult and lean versus nonlean is not always an accurate portrayal of the prevalence rates in every sport. Therefore, some research has been done to expand sport categories (i.e., weight-class, aesthetic, endurance, and team sports) and to investigate weight-related pressures in specific sports. For instance, weight-class athletes such as wrestlers and body builders exhibit a disordered eating prevalence between 15 percent and 17 percent. Aesthetic sports, including sports like diving, gymnastics, and figure skating, had a prevalence rate of approximately 18 percent for anorexia nervosa, bulimia nervosa, and Eating Disorder Not Otherwise Specified. This group of sports has also been associated with additional sport-specific concerns such as subjective judging and revealing attire, which may increase their risk over other sport categories. A third category of lean sports includes endurance sports (e.g., distance running, cycling). Athletes in endurance sports have reported prevalence rates of nearly 10 percent for males and 25 percent for females at the elite level. Participants in anti-gravitational sports (e.g., ski jumping) have also experienced increased pressure to maintain a low body weight. Ski jumpers have traditionally maintained a low body weight because lower body weight increases the distance jumped. However, because athletes were using unhealthy means to maintain that low body weight, the International Ski Federation developed rules and procedures to guard against competing at too low a BMI (e.g., ski length deductions based on weight in kilograms, minimum BMI of 18.5). Finally, one must not forget that nonlean sport athletes are also at risk for developing eating disorders. In a study on youth swimmers, 15 percent of female swimmers and 4 percent of male swimmers exhibited disordered eating behaviors.

Competitive Levels

For girls and women, the prevalence of athletes with the female athlete triad—low energy availability, changes in menstrual function, and low bone mineral density—increases as competitive levels increase. Among high school female athletes, the prevalence rate for the female athlete triad has been estimated to be 18.2 percent, compared with 26.1 percent in college athletes and 46.2 percent for elite female athletes. Nonetheless, a clear relationship between the level of competition and eating disorders has yet to be established and results are mixed. Although competitive level may not necessarily be a risk factor or a protective factor, it may work in concert with other factors in the athlete's life to either prevent or exacerbate disordered eating behaviors.

Weight Loss Methods

Methods for attempted weight loss vary across athletes. For instance, in a study of the prevalence of eating disorders in male collegiate athletes, although none were classified as eating   disordered, of the 20 percent who exhibited symptoms of eating disorders, 32 percent excessively exercised to lose weight while 14.2 percent dieted and approximately 10 percent used laxatives, diuretics, or self-induced vomiting. For female athletes, exercise for at least two hours a day specifically to burn calories was the most frequently reported method (25.5%). Another 15.7 percent of athletes admitted to dieting and less than 6 percent of female athletes reported using laxatives, diuretics, or vomiting to control weight. A less commonly reported method for weight loss involves using heat to sweat out water weight (e.g., the use of saunas or heavy layering of clothing while running). The use of thermal methods to lose weight is found more often in weight-dependent sports where weight-cycling is fairly typical (e.g., wrestling).

Sport-Specific Considerations

Weight and Performance

To understand the nature of eating disorders in athletes, it is important to consider perceptions related to how weight affects performance. At present, many athletes and coaches believe that reduced weight helps performance. Improved physical ability (e.g., being lighter requires less energy while running long distances) or achieving an aesthetic based on long and thin lines are among the reported benefits of lower body weight. Consequently, athletes and coaches who believe that reduced weight improves performance tend to hold rigid beliefs that weight gain will always negatively impact performance. Therefore, the goal becomes to keep weight down and attempt to lose as much weight as possible to gain a performance advantage.

Research demonstrates that body weight and performance are represented by a curvilinear relationship. Therefore, while initial weight reductions yield short-term performance improvements when that athlete "feels" lighter or experiences a brief increase in VO2 max (i.e., improved cardiovascular fitness by improved processing of oxygen in the body), in the long term and with continued weight loss, performance tends to drop sharply. By reducing the amount of energy consumed by the body, the athlete experiences physical (e.g., dehydration) and psychological (e.g., irritability) detriments. Other physical detriments include loss of lean body mass, fatigue, cardiovascular damage, and bone damage, whereas another psychological effect is decreased concentration. In combination, physical and psychological detriments may increase the risk of acute injury in athletes. More long-term consequences of continued weight loss include the risk of hypertension (i.e., high blood pressure) later in life, poor basal metabolism due to the body's response of protecting food stores, damage to the reproductive system, and increased risk of coronary heart disease, renal disease and failure, and irreversible bone damage.

Personality Characteristics of Athletes

Given the complex nature of eating disorders, one cannot discount the influence of individual differences on eating disorders in athletes. One study compared the personality characteristics of individuals with eating disorders and athletes and found similar personality characteristics. This is not to say that all athletes with these characteristics are guaranteed to develop an eating disorder; rather, the same characteristics that help athletes succeed in sport are also evident in nonathletes with eating disorders.

Research on the similarities between good athletes and eating disordered non-athletes included drive for perfection, desire for control, extreme self-discipline, detachment from feelings (such as pain), and the desire to please others. For instance, good athletes are able to make sacrifices, ignoring stress and sensations of pain, in the pursuit of success. Similarly, individuals with anorexia nervosa are able to ignore sensations of pain and hunger in their pursuit of continued weight loss. Additionally, good athletes exhibit a strong drive for perfectionism when they continually strive for improvement, are not satisfied with their current level of success, and are driven to be the best. Individuals with anorexia nervosa exhibit similar perfectionistic tendencies when they continually strive for thinness, do not accept their current body weight, and continue to use unhealthy weight loss methods in order to lose weight.

Subculture of Sport

The belief that weight loss can improve performance has resulted in specific sport subcultures and weight-related traditions. For example, some sport subcultures may require rookies to carry equipment or have team sweat sessions in which wrestlers exercise together in rubber suits. If sport subculture encourages unhealthy weight loss methods, disordered eating may become normalized within a particular team sport. Specifically, if a sport finds pathogenic weight loss methods acceptable (e.g., weight cycling in wrestling, overtraining in gymnastics), athletes may assume that coaches and other sport professionals condone these unhealthy practices as part of the sport.

Additionally, some athletes may understand that unhealthy weight loss methods are not acceptable to the general public. However, if athletes see that unhealthy practices are accepted in the sport, have benefited other athletes, will help them to win, and are necessary to maintain team membership, those athletes may be motivated to engage in unhealthy weight loss methods regardless of the lack of acceptance of such practices outside of sport. Athletes learn about weight loss methods from their teammates, practice them, and share them with other teammates. Eventually, teams may have the majority of team members using similar weight loss strategies. Then, if the team is successful, athletes may feel reinforced in their efforts to continue to lose weight.

Other Sport Considerations

Athletes are not immune to stressors experienced by the general population. Interestingly, magazine covers and television shows are fraught with images of thinner-than-average women and more-muscular-than-average men that contradict with body expectations for sport. For example, female track and field throwers are expected to be muscular and athletic in order to succeed and long distance male runners are encouraged to be lean and light to conserve energy while running.

Additionally, some athletes are required to meet weight-related guidelines. These may be in the form of weight limits at tryout, periodic weigh-ins throughout the season, and body fat percentage monitoring. The introduction of these more rigid weight ideals may serve to encourage athletes to lose more weight in an effort to maintain their position on the team.

The very nature of sport has also been shown to influence unhealthy eating behaviors. To excel in sport, athletes have to be competitive. But for some athletes, it is not enough to be as powerful, as attractive, or as successful as other athletes; they want to be the best. Because competitiveness has been found to be related to body dissatisfaction and body dissatisfaction is related to characteristics of eating disorders, competitiveness may actually be a risk factor for eating disorders in athletes.

Conclusion

The prevalence of athletes who exhibit disordered eating behaviors varies widely across studies. Given the complex nature of eating disorders, however, a black-and-white explanation of how and why eating disorders develop among athletes should be avoided. Key factors to consider are the gender of the athlete, the type of sport, competitive level, beliefs about weight and performance, personality characteristics, and the subculture of sport. It is important to educate sport professionals about the identification, referral, and prevention of eating disorders in athletes.

ASHLEY M. COKER-CRANNEY

See also: Aerobics; Aesthetic Sports; Athletic Trainers; Ballet; Bodybuilding; Cheerleading; Coaches; Dancers; Distance Running; Drill Team/Dance Team; Endurance Sports; Figure Skating; Gymnastics; Jockeys; Rowing; Ski Jumping; Swimming and Synchronized Swimming; Team Sports; Weight Class Sports; Weight Pressures in Sport; Yoga.

Bibliography

Beals, Katherine A. *Disordered Eating among Athletes: A Comprehensive Guide for Health Professionals.* Champaign, IL: Human Kinetics, 2004

Brownell, Kelly D., Suzan Nelson Steen, and Jack H. Wilmore. "Weight Regulation Practices in Athletes: Analysis of Metabolic and Health Effects." *Medicine and Science in Sports and Exercise* 19 (1987): 546–56.

Dosil, Joaquin. *Eating Disorders in Athletes.* Hoboken, NJ: John Wiley & Sons, Inc., 2008.

Galli, Nick, and Justine J. Reel. "Adonis or Hephaestus? Exploring Body Image in Male Athletes." *Psychology of Men & Masculinity* 10 (2009): 95–108.

Greenleaf, Christy, Trent A. Petrie, Jennifer Carter, and Justine J. Reel. "Female Collegiate Athletes: Prevalence of Eating Disorders and Disordered Eating Behaviors." *Journal of American College Health* 57 (2009): 489–95.

Johns, David P. "Fasting and Feasting: Paradoxes of the Sport Ethic." *Sociology of Sport Journal* 15 (1998): 41–63.

Peden, Jamie, Beverly L. Stiles, Michael Vandehey, George Diekhoff. "The Effects of External Pressures and Competitiveness on Characteristics of Eating Disorders and Body Dissatisfaction." *Journal of Sport & Social Issues* 32 (2008): 415–29.

Petrie, Trent A. "Differences between Male and Female College Lean Sport Athletes, Non-lean Sport Athletes, and Nonathletes on Behavioral and Psychological Indices of Eating Disorders." *Journal of Applied Sport Psychology* 8 (1996): 218–30.

Petrie, Trent A., Christy Greenleaf, Justine J. Reel, and Jennifer Carter. "Prevalence of Eating Disorders and Disordered Eating Behaviors among Male Collegiate Athletes." *Psychology of Men & Masculinity* 9 (2008): 267–77.

Smolak, Linda, Sarah K. Murnen, and Anne E. Ruble. "Female Athletes and Eating Problems: A Meta-Analysis." *International Journal of Eating Disorders* 27 (2000): 371–80.

Sundgot-Borgen, Jorunn, and Monica Klungland Torstveit. "Prevalence of Eating Disorders in Elite Athletes Is Higher than in the General Population." *Clinical Journal of Sports Medicine* 14 (2004): 25–31.

Thompson, Ron A., and Roberta Trattner Sherman. "'Good Athlete' Traits and Characteristics of Anorexia Nervosa: Are They Similar?" *Eating Disorders* 7 (1999): 181–90.

Thompson, Ron A., and Roberta Trattner Sherman. *Eating Disorders in Sport.* New York: Routledge, 2010.

Torstveit, M. K., J. H. Rosenvinge, and J. Sundgot-Borgen. "Prevalence of Eating Disorders and the Predictive Power of Risk Models in Female Elite Athletes: A Controlled Study." *Scandinavian Journal of Medicine and Science in Sports* 18 (2008): 108–118.

STUDENTS PROMOTING EATING DISORDER AWARENESS AND KNOWLEDGE (SPEAK)

What Is SPEAK?

SPEAK, which stands for "Students Promoting Eating Disorder Awareness and Knowledge," is a student organization at the University of Utah. The group was founded by the author in 2002 as a research team when several students approached her about learning the research process while expressing an interest in body image and eating disorders. Currently, the organization has over 85 active members who include undergraduate and graduate students at the University of Utah and other universities, alumni, and professional members in the community. From its inception, SPEAK has focused on both research and outreach and SPEAK's mission as stated on www.utah.edu/speak/ is to "promote awareness of eating disorders and body image issues through educating diverse populations, developing strategies for prevention, providing resources for treatment and conducting relevant research."

Outreach Projects

SPEAK has delivered presentations designed to prevent eating disorders and promote health in elementary, middle and high schools, as well as college classes, church groups, and community groups (e.g., Boys and Girls Clubs). SPEAK receives requests to conduct workshops for women in substance abuse centers and midlife clinics about body image and building body confidence. In addition to providing outreach presentations and health fairs, SPEAK organizes an annual Love Your Body Week in conjunction with the National Eating Disorder Awareness Week (NEDAW). The week-long event typically includes a recovery panel (SPEAK members share their eating disorder recovery stories), a film screening about body image issues, Love Your Body yoga, and other professional speakers. Purple ribbons are worn to raise awareness about eating disorders and in 2011, SPEAK initiated its "post-it for better body image" campaign (see Operation Beautiful for full description). For the Maximum Impact theme of 2011 LYBW, SPEAK filmed a YouTube video entitled "What do you LOVE about your body?" to encourage appreciation of one's body and to spread a positive body image message: http://youtu.be/ehnftl0QDJ8.

In 2009, SPEAK partnered with *Wasatch Woman* magazine to organize a Love Your Body 5K/10K walk/run event to honor the late Tiffany Cupit who died from an eating disorder. Over 800 walkers and runners donned purple ribbons and participated in a health fair about healthy body image.

Research Efforts

SPEAK expanded internationally in 2010 to host several hundred professionals at the "Treating Bodies across the Globe" event that drew doctors, nurses, social workers, psychologists, and dietitians from as far as Japan to cover the latest research about eating disorders and body image. Beginning in 2009, SPEAK began offering the SPEAK Tiffany Cupit Research Award to annually support student projects about body image and eating disorders. To date, seven SPEAK members have received this award.

Future of SPEAK

Dr. Justine Reel continues to serve as the faculty advisor for SPEAK. The team is currently supporting other schools (George Washington University, SUNY-Brockport, California State University at Channel Islands, Brigham Young University, Xavier University, and Utah Valley University) to begin their own SPEAK chapters. SPEAK is partnering with professionals in the community to offer ongoing education programs to parents, youth, and professionals as well as to continue to provide a yearly Love Your Body Week. SPEAK will continue to provide outreach and offer treatment referrals and resources to the community.

JUSTINE J. REEL

Bibliography

"Students Promoting Eating Disorder Awareness and Knowledge." Accessed June 13, 2011. www.utah.edu/speak.

"What do you LOVE about your body?" Accessed June 13, 2011. http://youtube/ehnftl0QDJ8.

SUBSTANCE ABUSE

Substance abuse refers to an unhealthy pattern of drug or alcohol use that results in significant life problems, such as failure to take care of one's responsibilities at work or home, or legal problems. Eating disorders and substance use disorders commonly co-occur. Up to 35 percent of persons who have substance abuse disorders have eating disorders and up to 50 percent of persons with eating disorders have a problem with drug or alcohol abuse. This is a substantial rate as only 9 percent of the general population abuse alcohol or illicit drugs. Persons with eating disorders are up to five times likelier than persons in the general population to abuse alcohol or illegal drugs and persons who abuse alcohol or drugs are up to 11 times likelier to have an eating disorder.

Risk Factors for Substance Abuse and Eating Disorders

Eating disorders and substance use disorders share many risk factors. These include: occurrence in times of transition or stress; common brain chemistry; common family histories; low self-esteem, depression, anxiety, and impulsivity; history of sexual or physical abuse; unhealthy parental behaviors and low monitoring of children's activities; unhealthy peer norms and social pressures; and susceptibility to messages from advertising, entertainment, and other media.

Eating disorders and substance abuse also have many characteristics in common. Both disorders include a component of obsessive preoccupation with substances, food, or behaviors, and cravings for these substances, food, or behaviors. Individuals with eating disorders and individuals with substance abuse issues engage in compulsive behaviors, secretiveness about their behaviors, and rituals. Individuals in both of these groups often present with a denial of the presence and severity of the disorder. Both disorders are difficult to treat, require intensive therapy, and have a high rate of comorbidity with other psychiatric disorders. They are both life threatening and are chronic diseases with high relapse rates.

Bulimia Nervosa and Substance Abuse

Of the types of eating disorders, bulimia nervosa has the highest overlap with substance abuse. Researchers estimate that 30–70 percent of individuals with bulimia nervosa abuse alcohol, tobacco, or drugs. One study found that individuals with substance use disorders and bulimia displayed lower impulse control, greater affective lability, more stimulus seeking behavior, a higher degree of self-harm, more anxiety and conduct disorders, and more borderline or antisocial personality disorder diagnoses than persons diagnosed with bulimia nervosa alone.

Anorexia Nervosa and Substance Abuse

Research suggests that 12–18 percent of individuals with anorexia nervosa also abuse drugs or alcohol. Within that group, the majority with substance abuse disorders have anorexia binge/purge type as opposed to anorexia/restricting type.

This is probably due to a greater link to impulsive behaviors and a novelty-seeking temperament in persons with purging subtypes of eating disorders and in persons with substance abuse histories.

Addictive Characteristics

Some researchers have claimed that the comorbidity of these disorders is part of an overall addictive dimension of personality. Many researchers have argued that bulimia nervosa and substance use disorder represent different manifestations of an underlying predisposition to addiction. For example, Ram et al advised that bulimia nervosa and substance use disorders are separate disorders and stated that "applying an addictive model to BN [bulimia nervosa] should be done with caution, because it does not address various personality correlates that have been found as characterizing BN." They do, however, report that the disorders share a similarity in their motivational structure and clinicians should be aware that shifting between the disorders is to be expected.

Individuals with bulimia nervosa and substance use disorders have higher rates of other co-occurring psychiatric disorders, including depression, anxiety, post-traumatic stress (PTSD), and personality disorders, than persons with bulimia nervosa alone. There are higher rates of sexual abuse history among persons with bulimia nervosa and persons with substance abuse disorders than the general population. Persons with bulimia nervosa and substance abuse disorders are more likely to report a history of sexual abuse than persons with bulimia nervosa alone.

The high rate of comorbidity between eating disorders and substance abuse is an area of clinical concern. Clinicians should take a careful history of substance use when clients seek treatment for eating disorders. Piran and Gadalla suggest that there is a need for development and utilization of short screening instruments for adult women with eating disorders and substance abuse. Some researchers have asserted that the risk for drug abuse in clients with eating disorders continues over time and should be continually monitored throughout the treatment process.

Treatment Approaches for Comorbid Substance Abuse and Eating Disorders

Treatment approaches that address both conditions may be more effective than approaches that focus exclusively or specifically on the disorder for which a person sought treatment. Research is needed to develop strategies that address the co-occurrence of substance use and eating disorders. Clients with a dual diagnosis of a substance use disorder and an eating disorder present with somewhat unique and difficult challenges. They often have a willingness to examine only certain behaviors while they deny the existence or severity of other problematic behaviors. For example, a client may be willing to examine her binge and purge behaviors while denying that her alcohol use is problematic. Clients with this dual diagnosis are often resistant to letting go of unhealthy, maladaptive coping strategies such as disordered eating, purging, excessive exercise, or substance abuse. Unfortunately, there is some evidence that substance abuse is correlated with worse outcomes from eating disorder recovery.

Conclusion

There is a high comorbidity between eating disorders and substance abuse. Research indicates a higher correlation with bulimic type eating disorders than with solely restrictive type disorders. Individuals who have comorbid eating disorders and substance abuse disorders often present with greater rates and higher severity of other mental health disorders such as depression, anxiety, and personality disorders. Treatment approaches that address both substance abuse and eating disorders conjointly are indicated.

JESSICA GUENTHER

See also: Comorbidity.

Bibliography

Herzog, David B., Debra L. Franko, David J. Dorer, Pamela K. Keel, Safi Jackson, and Mary Pat Manzo. "Drug Abuse in Women with Eating Disorders." *International Journal of Eating Disorders* 39, no. 5 (2006): 364–68.

Killeen, Therese K., Shelly F. Greenfield, Brian E. Bride, Lisa Cohen, Susan Merle Gordon, and Paul M. Roman. "Assessment and Treatment of Co-Occurring Eating Disorders in Privately Funded Addiction Treatment Programs." *The American Journal on Addictions* 20 (2011): 205–211.

Krug, Isabel, Andrea Poyastro Pinheiro, Cynthia Bulik, Susana Jimenez-Murcia, Roser Granero, Eva Penelo, Cristina Masuet, Zaida Aguera, and Fernando Fernandez-Aranda. "Lifetime Substance Abuse, Family History of Alcohol Abuse/Dependence and Novelty Seeking in Eating Disorders: Comparison Study of Eating Disorder Subgroups." *Psychiatry and Clinical Neurosciences* 63 (2009): 82–87.

Piran, Niva, and Tahany Gadalla. "Eating Disorders and Substance Abuse in Canadian Women: A National Study." *Addiction* 102, no. 1 (2007): 105–113.

Piran, Niva, Shannon R. Robinson, and Holly C. Cormier. "Disordered Eating Behaviors and Substance Use in Women: A Comparison of Perceived Adverse Consequences." *Eating Disorders* 15 (2007): 391–403.

Ram, A., D. Stein, S. Sofer, and S. Kreitler. "Bulimia Nervosa and Substance Use Disorder: Similarities and Differences." *Eating Disorders* 16 (2008): 224–40.

Sinha, Rajita, and Stephanie S. O'Malley. "Alcohol and Eating Disorders: Implications for Alcohol Treatment and Health Services Research." *Alcoholism: Clinical and Emotional Research* 24, no. 8 (2000): 1312–1319.

Varner, Lisa M. "Dual Diagnosis: Patients with Eating and Substance-Related Disorders." *Journal of the American Dietetic Association* 95, no. 2 (1995): 224–25.

SUICIDE

Suicide is a major cause of death in individuals with anorexia nervosa and bulimia nervosa. Suicide and eating disorders have shown varying levels of comorbidity across studies, but present a concern due to risk for fatality.

Prevalence of Suicide

Suicide among adolescents has received increased attention as the link to bullying and other mental disorders has been identified. It has been estimated that 2 million people die as a result of homicide or suicide. Of 877,000 suicides across the world in 2002 alone, 200,000 suicides involved adolescents. Suicide is one of the leading causes of death for adolescents in the world and rates are increasing faster among teens than in other age categories. Of 4 million suicide attempts annually, approximately 90,000 adolescents complete the suicide, which works out to one suicide every five minutes. Causes of suicide include mental health disorders such as depression, substance abuse, and eating disorders. Other triggers like loss of friends, weight-related teasing or bullying, social isolation, and academic failure have been identified as links to suicidal attempts and suicide. Self-harm behaviors have also been associated with suicidal attempts and suicide.

Relationship between Self-Injurious Behavior and Suicide

Deliberate self-harm or self-injurious behavior refers to an act of hurting oneself intentionally. The most common self-harm methods have included overdosing, self-poisoning, and self-cutting. Cutting among U.S. adolescents was estimated to range from 26 percent to 37 percent of 9th to 12th graders. Self-harm behaviors can become repetitive and can be associated with increased depression, suicidal ideation, and suicide attempts. Suicide can result from either chronic issues surrounding self-harm behaviors or by accident, if self-harm behavior (e.g., overdose) turns fatal. Specifically, the overall risk of suicide increases if self-harm persists, with a 1.7 percent increase after 5 years, 2.4 percent increase after 10 years, and 3.0 percent increase after 15 years. Five percent of self-harm clients who are hospitalized or require emergency care commit suicide within 9 years of the self-harm incident. Youth who cut their wrists have higher suicide risks than individuals who cut their arms.

Anorexia Nervosa, Bulimia Nervosa, and Suicide

Eating disorders have been associated with cutting and other self-harm behaviors. Eating disordered individuals describe self-injurious behavior as a way to cope with intense feelings or to "experience the pain." Children who suffer from sexual abuse were at increased risk for developing self-cutting behavior, which is related to eating disorders and suicidal ideation. Bulimia nervosa compared to other types of eating disorders has been most clearly associated with self-harm and suicide risk with one study demonstrating that a history of suicide attempts was prevalent among 16.6 percent of bulimic subjects. In fact, suicide is one of the most frequently reported causes of death among bulimic clients. Approximately 25 percent of bulimic individuals who attempted suicide reported more than one suicide attempt with repeaters being at greater risk of death than nonrepeaters. Another study found that 22.1 percent of anorexia nervosa clients and 10.9 percent of bulimia nervosa clients had at least one suicidal attempt. Males with bulimia have been found to be especially at risk for suicide attempts and suicide; however, both males and females and individuals who have been diagnosed with an eating disorder present a risk for comorbidity with suicide.

Conclusion

Suicide rates among adolescents are alarming and have been increasing globally. Certain risk factors, such as self-harm and mental disorders, can lead to suicide attempts or suicide. Eating disordered individuals should be assessed for self-harm and suicidal ideations. Especially at risk for suicide are males with bulimia nervosa.

JUSTINE J. REEL

Bibliography

Favaro, Angela, and Paolo Santonastaso. "Different Types of Self-Injurious Behavior in Bulimia Nervosa." *Comprehensive Psychiatry* 40, no. 1 (1999): 57–60.

Franko, Debra L., and Pamela K. Keel. "Suicidality in Eating Disorders: Occurrence, Correlates and Clinical Implications." *Clinical Psychology Review* 26, no. 6 (2006): 769–82. doi: 10.1016/j.cpr.2006.04.001.

Franko, Debra L., Pamela K. Keel, D. J. Dover, S. S. Delinsky, K. T. Eddy, V. Charat, R. Renn, and David B. Herzog. "What Predicts Suicide Attempts in Women with Eating Disorders?" *Psychological Medicine* 34 (2004): 843–53.

Greydanus, Donald E., and Daniel Shek. "Deliberate Self-Harm and Suicide in Adolescents." *Keio Journal of Medicine* 58, no. 3 (2009): 144–51.

Milos, Gabriella, Anja Spindler, Urs Hepp, and Ulrich Schnyder. "Suicide Attempts and Suicidal Ideation: Links with Psychiatric Comorbidity in Eating Disorder Subjects." *General Hospital Psychiatry* 26, no. 2 (2004): 129–35. doi: 10.1016/j.genhosppsych.2003.10.005.

Pompili, Maurizio, Paolo Girardi, Giulia Tatarelli, Amedeo Ruberto, and Roberto Tatarelli. "Suicide and Attempted Suicide in Eating Disorders, Obesity, and Weight Image." *Eating Behaviors* 7, no. 4 (2006): 384–94. doi: 10.1016/j.eatbeh.2005.12.004.

SWIMMING AND SYNCHRONIZED SWIMMING

Swimming is a popular sport in the United States for both males and females who compete in summer leagues, year-round programs, high schools, and colleges. Swimming events in the Summer Olympics have brought faces to the sport along with increased media attention. For example Amanda Beard, a breaststroke champion, posed for Playboy magazine, representing the growing trend of sexualizing athletes and rewarding them for appearance attributes that go beyond sport prowess. Synchronized swimming represents a unique water sport that requires

U.S. Olympic swimmer Amanda Beard attends the BCBG Max Azria Fall 2009 fashion show at Bryant Park in New York. Beard, a teen sensation at the 1996 summer Olympics and a gold medalist in 1996 and 2004, was working on a memoir that tells of her "secret life" away from the pool, a "harrowing journey" through drugs, alcohol and eating disorders. (AP/Wide World Photos)

flexibility, strength, power, grace, and control. Although this sport has received less attention than other water sports (e.g., competitive swimming, diving), synchronized swimming has characteristics that are similar to those of other aesthetic and leanness-demand sports like figure skating, gymnastics, and diving. For example, competitors in synchronized swimming wear revealing team uniforms and are judged based upon an artistic aesthetic.

History of Synchronized Swimming

Synchronized swimming became an Olympic sport at the 1984 Los Angeles Summer Games. Initially, both solo and duet events were included in the Olympics; however, in 2000 at the Sydney Olympic Games, the solo event was eliminated and the team event was added. Historically, men have not competed in synchronized swimming and feminine qualities have been valued and emphasized in the sport. Males are beginning to participate in certain geographic areas at lower levels.

Body Image and Disordered Eating in Synchronized Swimming

As a judged sport that emphasizes a particular aesthetic, synchronized swimming athletes face pressure to be thin and change their appearance. For duet and team competitions, synchronized swimming athletes are rewarded for symmetry and for appearing identical in shape with limbs of a similar length and size. A rare study that investigated the body esteem of 42 elite synchronized swimming athletes found that synchronized swimmers reported greater negative feelings about their appearance and had lower body mass index scores (19.2) than nonleanness demand sport participants (21.2) or female nonathletes (19.9).

Body Image and Disordered Eating among Swimmers

Swimming has been classified as a nonlean or endurance sport in eating disorder studies. In early 1987, a study found that 15 percent of female and 3.6 percent of male swimmers admitted to using pathogenic weight control methods. A separate Spanish study reported that 10 percent of swimmers vomited to lose weight, which was a higher prevalence than any of the other 17 women's sports in the sample. A Brazilian study found that 45 percent of swimmers engaged in disordered eating behaviors.

Swimmers have been found to report stronger body satisfaction and less social physique anxiety than athletes from other sports (e.g., aesthetic sports). However, 45 percent of Division II and III female swimmers felt that the swimsuit increased body consciousness. Furthermore, swimmers wore racing suits that were a couple of sizes smaller to gain a perceived competitive advantage and reduce drag. Motivation to lose body weight was related to the perception that performance would improve or attempts to meet societal ideals of beauty beyond the sport.

Conclusion

Swimming has been classified as an endurance sport in some studies and considered a nonlean sport in other research. However, swimmers report disordered eating patterns and weight pressures consistent with athletes from leanness-demand activities. By contrast, synchronized swimming represents an aesthetic and judged sport that possesses an emphasis on thinness and appearance. Although more research is needed about this unique group of athletes, preliminary work suggests that synchronized swimming athletes have lower body esteem and BMI than other athletes. However, for both water sports, the revealing competitive swimsuit can make athletes more conscious of their appearance.

JUSTINE J. REEL

See also: Aesthetic Sports; Endurance Sports; Weight Pressures in Sport.

Bibliography

Ferrand, Claude, Claire Magnan, and Roberta Antonini Philippe. "Body Esteem, Body Mass Index and Risk for Disordered Eating among Adolescents in Synchronized Swimming." *Perceptual and Motor Skills* 101 (2005): 877–84.

Mountjoy, Margo. "Injuries and Medical Issues in Synchronized Olympic Sports." *Current Sports Medicine Reports* 8, no. 5 (2009): 255–61.

People for the Ethical Treatment of Animals (PETA). "Amanda Beard Poses Nude to Help Save Animals on Fur Farms." Accessed December 20, 2011. https://secure.peta.org/site/Advocacy?cmd=display&page=UserAction&id=1989.

Reel, Justine J., and Diane L. Gill. "Slim Enough to Swim? Weight Pressures for Competitive Swimmers and Coaching Implications." *The Sport Journal* 4 (2001): 1–5.

Reel, Justine J., and Katherine A. Beals, eds. *The Hidden Faces of Eating Disorders and Body Image.* Reston, VA: AAHPERD/NAGWS, 2009.

Schtscherbyna, Annie, Eliane Abreu Soares, Fatima Plaha de Oliveira, and Beatriz Goncalves Ribeiro. "Female Athlete Triad in Elite Swimmers of the City of Rio de Janeiro, Brazil." *Nutrition* 25 (2009): 634–39. doi: 10.1016/j.nut.2008.11.029.

Thompson, Ron A., and Roberta Trattner Sherman. *Eating Disorders in Sport.* New York, NY: Routledge, 2010.

T

TANNING BEHAVIORS AND BODY IMAGE

Tanning behaviors involve exposing oneself to ultraviolet radiation (UV) from sun, sunlamps, tanning beds, or tanning booths for cosmetic purposes. According to the Skin Cancer Foundation, the majority (70%) of the 1 million people who visit tanning salons are Caucasian females who are 16 to 49 years of age. Significantly, use of indoor tanning (e.g., tanning beds) among Caucasian female teenagers was at 30–40 percent, and in a separate study it was estimated that 2.3 million teens tan indoors using tanning salons and sunlamps. Furthermore, students 14 years and younger were significantly more likely to wear sunscreen than older high school students. Females were more likely to use sunscreen than males; however, females felt that it was worth having a sunburn to achieve a tan and reported having at least three sunburns the previous summer.

Body Image and Tanning Practices

Although people seem to understand the risks associated with UV exposure and skin cancer, they still choose to engage in tanning behaviors when they feel that having a suntan will enhance their physical appearance. In fact, tanning was cited as one of the most commonly used methods to improve physical beauty along with clothing, exercise, dieting, and personality. Although other cultures (e.g., Japan) have traditionally viewed pale skin as the symbol of beauty and wealth, the U.S. culture supports the notion that tanned skin represents a healthy, youthful glow.

In a rare investigation of tanning behaviors and body image among gay males, of 215 respondents, 52 participated in sun tanning, 34 frequented tanning salons, and 26 used cosmetic tanning (i.e., liquids, gels, and powders to change the color of one's skin). Tanning behaviors in this study were most associated with the desire to look attractive. In a separate study of male and female college students, females reported higher appearance motives to engage in tanning practices.

"Tanorexia" refers to a tanning addiction, labeling individuals who engage in excessive tanning behaviors (e.g., sunbathing, use of tanning beds to the extreme, usually for the cosmetic purpose of achieving a tanned appearance). This addiction, which has not been formally identified in the *Diagnostic and Statistical Manual of Mental Disorders,* parallels eating disorders due to the tendency to be obsessive in behaviors (e.g., tanning beds) related to body image concerns. Much media attention has been given to the case of a mother who took her 5-year-old daughter into a tanning booth with her: http://www.huffingtonpost.com/2012/05/03/patricia-krentcil-tanning-mom-tanorexia_n_1475138.html. Because unhealthy

Patricia Krentcil, 44, waits to be arraigned at the Essex County Superior Court, Wednesday, May 2, 2012 in Newark, New Jersey where she appeared on charges of endangering her five-year-old child by taking her into a tanning salon. Krentcil maintains that her daughter got her sunburn from being outside on a recent warm day. New Jersey state law prohibits anyone under 14 from using tanning salons. (Julio Cortez/AP/Wide World Photos)

tanning practices are often linked to appearance demands, it is recommended that programming for eating disorder prevention and skin cancer prevention be combined to address both skin health and body image issues.

Conclusion

Despite the skin cancer risk, millions of individuals choose to expose their skin to sun, tanning beds, and sunlamps in the quest for beauty. Because having a tan is associated with attractiveness, teenagers reported beliefs that having a sunburn was worth the risk and individuals engaged in high-risk tanning practices including visiting tanning beds and neglecting to wear sunscreen. It is important for skin cancer prevention specialists to consider the appearance motives behind tanning practices when developing and implementing interventions.

JUSTINE J. REEL

Bibliography

Cafri, Guy, J. Kevin Thompson, Paul B. Jacobsen, and Joel Hillhouse. "Investigating the Role of Appearance-based Factors in Predicting Sunbathing and Tanning Salon Use." *Journal of Behavioral Medicine* 32 (2009): 532–44. doi: 10.1007/s10865-009-9224-5.

Cafri, Guy, J. Kevin Thompson, Megan Roehrig, Ariz Rojas, Steffanie Sperry, Paul B. Jacobsen, and Joel Hillhouse. "Appearance Motives to Tan and Not Tan: Evidence for Validity and Reliability for a New Scale." *Annuals of Behavioral Medicine* 35 (2008): 209–220. doi: 10.1007/s12160-008-9022-2.

Dixon, Helen G., Charles D. Warne, Maree L. Sully, Melanie A. Wakefield, and Suzzane J. Dobbinson. "Does the Portrayal of Tanning in Australian Women's Magazines Relate to Real Women's Tanning Beliefs and Behavior? *Health Education and Behavior* 38, no. 2 (2011): 132–42.

Mahler, Heike I. M., James A. Kulik, Fredrick X. Gibbons, Megan Gerrard, and Jody Harrell. "Effects of Appearance-based Interventions on Sun Protection Intentions and Self-Reported Behaviors. *Health Psychology* 22, no. 2 (2003): 199–209.

Pettijohn II, Terry F., Terry F. Pettijohn, and Kaela S. Geschke. "Changes in Sun Tanning Attitudes and Behaviors of U.S. College Students from 1995 to 2005." *College Student Journal* 43, no. 1 (2009): 161–65.

Reilly, Andrew, and Nancy A. Rudd. "Sun, Salon, and Cosmetic Tanning: Predictors and Motives." *International Journal of Humanities and Social Sciences* 2, no. 3 (2008): 170–76.

Reynolds, Diane. "Literature Review of Theory-based Empirical Studies Examining Adolescent Tanning Practices." *Dermatology Nursing* 19, no. 5 (2007): 440–47.

TEAM SPORTS

Teams have been defined as groups of individuals who interact and mutually influence one another to achieve a specific objective. Teams or groups share a collective sense of identity and defined roles and responsibilities. Most sports are played using teams rather than individual participation (e.g., diving or figure skating). Team sports have sometimes been defined by researchers as those requiring anaerobic training (i.e., short duration and high intensity activities) and the use of a ball. However, many team sports involve a variety of both aerobic and anaerobic training regimens and a range of sports equipment. Team sports can include basketball, soccer, field hockey, ice hockey, lacrosse, baseball, softball, football, and volleyball.

Team Sports, Disordered Eating, and Body Image

Some research suggests that fewer team sport athletes experience clinical eating disorders as compared to athletes in other types of sports. One study revealed that only 1 percent of team sport athletes reported a current or previous diagnosis of anorexia nervosa as compared to 3.5 percent of endurance sport athletes and 5.6 percent of aesthetic sport athletes. Similarly, 2.1 percent of team sport athletes reported a current or previous diagnosis of bulimia nervosa as compared to 1.6 percent and 5.6 percent of endurance and aesthetic sport athletes, respectively. In addition, preliminary research suggests that individual sport athletes exhibit greater self-consciousness of their physique and engage in more dieting and bulimic behavior than team sport athletes. It may be argued that there is far less social evaluation and exposure of one's physique in team-based athletics because performances are carried out in groups rather than in isolation. However, it is also plausible that those involved in team sports may already focus less on weight and self-select into a team sport environment that does not emphasize weight, body shape, and appearance.

Despite some evidence suggesting that team sport athletes are less at risk for clinical eating disorders than other sport types, this does not mean that disordered eating is not evident among these athletes. One study suggests that although aesthetic sport athletes may be at greatest risk for body dissatisfaction (41.6%) and disordered eating (27.7%), the incidence of such attitudes and behaviors in team sport athletes (41.7%; 14.6%) may be similar to those in endurance sports (32.2%; 13.6%). Research also shows that the prevalence of eating disorders in ball game sports alone, like handball, volleyball, basketball, and soccer, is 5 percent for male participants and 16 percent for female participants. Although ball-game sports have not traditionally been considered high-risk sports for the development of eating disorders, prevalence rates in female ball-game participants have increased from 11 percent in 1990 to 16 percent in 1997. Researchers postulate that such increases may be due to a greater emphasis on appearance and body composition assessments, particularly at the elite levels.

Weight Pressures

Pressures to lose or maintain weight are evident in some team sports and come from a variety of sources. In a study of 204 collegiate female athletes, the most frequently cited sources of weight pressures were teammates (36.8%), the team uniform (34.3%), and the coach (33.8%). More specifically, athletes may fear that their teammates will notice weight gain, become self-conscious wearing the form-fitting or revealing uniforms required by their sport (e.g., tight spandex shorts in volleyball), or engage in unhealthy weight loss techniques because of a body-related comment made by a coach.

Other sources of body-related pressure may include team weigh-ins. Although weigh-ins may be used to ensure that a healthy weight is maintained and to avoid dehydration, performing routine weigh-ins in public can be psychologically harmful to the athlete and may lead to the adoption of a number of pathogenic eating behaviors, such as self-induced vomiting, fasting, or the abuse of laxatives, diet pills, and diuretics.

Media exposure of team sport athletes is also a noted source of pressure to lose or maintain weight. For example, the swimsuit edition of *Sports Illustrated* issues photos of female athletes across the globe in suggestive positions and barely-there clothing. Hundreds of magazines and other media forums publish lists of the most attractive, beautiful, or "hottest" female athletes of the year with little, if any, acknowledgment of their athletic accomplishments. Some female athletes, such as world-renowned soccer player Brandi Chastain, have explained that they posed nude as a means of empowerment rather than to project sexual appeal. Other athletes have reported that they wanted to assert their femininity. Many scholars argue that such behavior only further belittles women's athleticism and promotes patriarchal power. Research has shown that the type of female athlete images displayed may have a negative impact on young girls. More specifically, exposure to images of female athletes performing their sport triggers a focus on what their own bodies can do, while exposure to sexualized images of female athletes triggers negative statements about their bodies.

Revealing photos of female athletes also promotes the notion that fitness and athletic success is equated with thinness when fitness and athletic performance cannot be determined by appearance alone. Organizations like the Women's Sports Foundation have published a number of resources aimed at promoting female athletes in positive ways and preventing the objectification of female athletes through the media and other social forums.

Team Sport Subculture

Teams may be vulnerable to contagion or spreading of disordered eating behaviors among athletes based on the norms developed by the team and the coaches. For example, some teams may develop a subculture that supports weight loss, and teammates may exchange strategies on how to alter their weight, shape, or appearance (e.g., how to purge). Teammates may also engage in size and shape comparisons because they often shower and dress together. Because athletes are generally competitive to start with, team sport athletes may compete with their peers on the parameter of thinness as well. This may be especially true in aesthetic sport teams, such as collegiate gymnastics, where athletes on the same team must compete with one another for spots on a line-up that will ultimately be judged based on both performance and appearance standards. The revealing uniforms required in some team sports like volleyball may also increase size and shape comparisons between teammates because of the desire to look good while on the court. Some scholars believe that female athletes may also strive to meet thin ideal standards in order to attract fans and encourage game attendance.

Although not often studied specifically in sports, peer influence is indeed predictive of disordered eating in nonathlete populations. Given the quantity and quality of time spent on a team, it can be anticipated that a similar relationship exists between peer influence and disordered eating in the context of sports. However, while the attitudes and behaviors of teammates may create a subculture that promotes thinness and unhealthy weight loss techniques, teammates may just as easily promote an environment that supports healthy nutrition and body image with the right education and modeling from supportive adults, including the coaches, as well as the captains of the team. In addition, when a member of a team is struggling with or receiving treatment for an eating disorder, teammates can play an important role in providing the necessary support for that athlete. The team atmosphere, although potentially detrimental in some cases, may therefore be quite useful in preventing disordered eating and body image concerns among athletes.

Benefits of Team Sport Participation

Team sport participation is linked to a range of benefits. For example, findings from one study suggested that the time spent on the team—but not individual

sports—is associated with enhanced sport self-concept (i.e., improved perceptions of one's sport abilities) and therefore, greater self-esteem. Another study revealed that mothers of kindergarten through third grade children perceived that
the greatest number of benefits come from team sport participation as compared
to involvement in individual sports, the performing arts, and community recreational activities. These benefits can include character development, improved academic achievement, and the acquisition of important social skills. Other research
suggests that youth sport coaches both expect and believe that youth athletes have
fun, learn important life skills, and build confidence through their sport participation. This is especially true when coaches promote physically and psychologically safe sport environments and use teachable moments to purposefully build
character and life skills in their athletes. In sum, team sports have been identified
as an important avenue for building positive developmental outcomes in youth
participants.

Conclusion

Team sports have not traditionally been considered "high risk" for the development of eating disorders. However, body dissatisfaction and disordered eating
have been reported among this population of athletes. Most concerning is the pressure to lose or maintain weight stemming from teammates, coaches, the team uniform, and media exposure to sexualized images of team sport athletes. Some teams
are also prone to developing a negative team subculture that promotes unhealthy
body image and eating habits to improve appearance or performance. Avoiding
team weigh-ins, allowing athletes to choose their athletic attire when possible,
avoiding exposure to sexualized images of athletes, and promoting healthy team
norms for eating and exercise are a few of the ways by which body image disturbances and disordered eating may be prevented in team sports. Making these
concerted efforts will increase the likelihood that athletes will reap the benefits of
team sport participation, including enhanced self-concept and the development of
important life skills.

DANA K. VOELKER

Bibliography

Beals, Katherine A., and Melinda M. Manore. "Disorders of the Female Athlete Triad among
    Collegiate Athletes." *International Journal of Sport Nutrition and Exercise Metabolism* 12
    (2002): 281–93.
Daniels, Elizabeth. "Sex Objects, Athletes, and Sexy Athletes: How Media Representations
    of Women Athletes Can Impact Adolescent Girls and College Women." *Journal of Ado-
    lescent Research* 24 (2009): 399–422. doi: 10.1177/0743558409336748.
Gould, Daniel, and Sarah Carson. "Life Skills Development through Sport: Current Status and
    Future Directions." *International Review of Sport and Exercise Psychology* 1 (2008): 58–78.
Haase, Anne M. "Physique Anxiety and Disordered Eating Correlates in Female Athletes:
    Differences in Team and Individual Sports." *Journal of Clinical Sports Psychology* 2 (2009):
    218–31.

Reel, Justine J., Sonya SooHoo, Trent A. Petrie, Christy Greenleaf, and Jennifer E. Carter. "Slimming Down for Sport: Development of Weight Pressures in Sport Measure for Female Athletes." *Journal of Clinical Sport Psychology* 4 (2010): 99–111.

Sundgot-Borgen, Jorunn, and Monica Klungland Torstveit. "Prevalence of Eating Disorders in Elite Athletes is Higher Than in the General Population." *Clinical Journal of Sports Medicine* 14 (2004): 25–32.

Thompson, Ron A., and Roberta Trattner Sherman. "Athletes, Athletic Performance, and Eating Disorders: Healthier Alternatives." *Journal of Social Issues* 55 (1999): 317–77.

TEASING

Teasing refers to negative commentary, such as joking and name calling, which can happen between siblings within family units and between peers in school environments. Teasing or emotional bullying is reported by one in four children and often includes social exclusion, being singled out, and humiliated by others. Teasing related to one's weight is particularly common and can even involve parents making weight-related comments.

Weight-Related Teasing among Adolescents

Weight-related teasing is reported by 26 percent of female and 22 percent of male adolescents. Adolescents who are overweight have a greater likelihood of receiving weight-related comments and teasing from peers and family members than adolescents of an average weight. For example, one study reported that 45 percent of overweight adolescent girls and 50 percent of overweight adolescent boys experienced frequent weight-related teasing compared with only 19 percent of girls and 13 percent of boys who were of an average weight. In addition to teasing, overweight adolescents have also been found to be at increased risk for disordered eating behaviors have lower self esteem, and report higher rates of depression.

Weight-Related Teasing and Disordered Eating

In one study, 46 male and 84 female adolescents were surveyed. Findings indicated that frequent teasing by family and peers was associated with increased disordered eating thoughts and behaviors, depression, anxiety, anger, and decreased self-esteem. Adolescents who experienced more weight-related teasing also placed a higher value on thinness and evaluated self based on shape and weight. High rates of teasing were predictive of severe binge eating behaviors.

Gender Differences in Teasing

Generally, female adolescents have reported being teased more often than their male counterparts. In an Australian study that examined teasing within sport and exercise contexts, females participated in organized sports less often than boys. However, adolescent girls were still teased more frequently than boys. Both girls and boys were teased by same-sex peers; however, girls were also teased by their opposite-sex peers. Teasing was associated with negative body image which may have contributed to decreased rates of sport and exercise participation for female participants.

Prevention of Teasing Behaviors

With increased awareness about the potential harms of bullying (e.g., suicide), efforts have been made to implement antibullying campaigns. While it is important to teach healthy peer relationships and coping skills to adolescents, it is equally important to educate adults who may also participate in teasing behaviors. Interventions aimed to reduce weight-related teasing should take place within both family and school settings in order to prevent disordered eating and other negative consequences of teasing.

Conclusion

Teasing includes both joking and name calling that can be focused on one's size, shape, or appearance. It appears that females experience slightly more teasing than their male counterparts and family members and peers are frequently responsible for teasing behaviors. Unfortunately, weight-related teasing can result in a higher drive for thinness as well as increased depression, disordered eating behaviors (e.g., binge eating episodes), and lowered self-esteem. Given the high occurrence of teasing and the devastating consequences, it is important to support preventive efforts in schools.

JUSTINE J. REEL

Bibliography

Benas, Jessica S., Dorothy J. Uhrlass, and Brandon E. Gibb. "Body Dissatisfaction and Weight-Related Teasing: A Model of Cognitive Vulnerability to Depression among Women." *Journal of Behavioral Therapy and Experimental Psychiatry* 41 (2010): 352–56. doi: 10.1016/j.jbtep.2010.03.006.

Buhlmann, Ulrike, Laura M. Cook, Jeanne M. Fama, and Sabine Wilhelm. "Perceived Teasing Experiences in Body Dysmorphic Disorder." *Body Image* 4 (2007): 381–85. doi: 10.1016/j.bodyim.2007.06.004.

Eisenberg, Maria E., Jerica M. Berge, Jayne A. Fulkerson, and Dianne Neumark-Sztainer. "Weight Comments By Family and Significant Others in Young Adulthood." *Body Image* 8 (2011): 12–19. doi: 10.1016/j.bodyim.2010.11.002.

Libbey, Heather P., Mary T. Story, Dianne R. Neumark-Sztainer, and Kerri N. Boutelle. "Teasing, Disordered Eating Behaviors and Psychological Morbidities among Overweight Adolescents." *Obesity* 16, no. 2 (2008): S24–S29.

Menzel, Jessie E., Lauren M. Schaefer, Natasha L. Burke, Laura L. Mayhew, Michael T. Brannick, and J. Kevin Thompson. "Appearance-related Teasing, Body Dissatisfaction, and Disordered Eating: A Meta-analysis." *Body Image* 7 (2010): 261–70. doi: 10.1016/j.bodyim.2010.05.004.

Slater, Amy, and Marika Tiggemann. "Gender Differences in Adolescent Sport Participation, Teasing, Self-objectification and Body Image Concerns." *Journal of Adolescence* 34 (2011): 453–63. doi: 10.1016/j.adolescence. 2010.06.007.

Spresser, Carrie D., Kristen M. Keune, Diane L. Filion, and Jennifer D. Lundgren. "Startle as an Objective Measure of Distress Related to Teasing and Body Image." *International Journal of Eating Disorders* 44, no. 1 (2011): 58–64. doi: 10.1002/eat.20774.

THERAPEUTIC RECREATION

Therapeutic recreation refers to a field that views leisure as an important contributor to one's quality of life. Recreational therapists and occupational therapists work with populations, such as individuals with disabilities or psychiatric clients, to foster the development of a healthy leisure lifestyle. Therapeutic recreation is frequently incorporated into comprehensive treatment programs at eating disorder facilities in order to provide clients with the opportunity to engage in a variety of normal activities while they are in a residential setting.

Therapeutic Recreation for Eating Disordered Individuals

Therapeutic recreation as part of eating disorder treatment is especially important given that in many cases eating disordered individuals are no longer able to experience leisure activities without feeling strong emotions. For example, eating disordered individuals have often abandoned leisure physical activity (e.g., climbing) for enjoyment's sake for activities (e.g., running) that are more cardiovascular in nature and burn more calories. Furthermore, individuals with eating disorders have difficulty sitting with their emotions and handling stress. Recreational therapists can teach stress management techniques using group activities such as deep breathing, muscle relaxation, and meditation. In order to help eating disorder clients develop social skills and enjoy the natural environment, recreational therapists may bring groups of eating disordered clients hiking, canoeing, fishing, and gardening. Metaphors can be used to reflect the healing process and recovery while individuals are engaging in outdoor activities.

Some recreational therapy activities may involve using crafts, arts, and games to help clients gain personal satisfaction and achievement. An outing, such as going to a park or a museum, can be a useful tool to promote group cohesiveness among clients and staff as well as to provide a real world experience.

Conclusion

Therapeutic recreation is an important part of comprehensive eating disorder treatment. Recreational therapists can work with eating disordered individuals to teach leisure skills and stress management and to practice social interaction through group activities. Therapeutic recreation may involve activities like meditation, nature walks, or attending a concert.

JUSTINE J. REEL

Bibliography

Gardiner, Clare, and Naomi Brown. "Is there a Role for Occupational Therapy within a Specialist Child and Adolescent Mental Health Eating Disorder Service?" *British Journal of Occupational Therapy* 73, no. 1 (2010): 38–43. doi: 10.4276/030802210X1262954 8272745.

Nowell, Rhonda. "The Role of Therapeutic Recreation with Eating Disorder Patients." *Psychiatric Medicine* 7, no. 4 (1989): 285–92.

Schaffner, Angela D., and Linda P. Buchanan. "Integrating Evidence-Based Treatments with Individual Needs in an Outpatient Facility for Eating Disorders." *Eating Disorders: Journal of Treatment and Prevention* 16 (2008): 378–92.

TRAUMA

Trauma refers to a single event, repeating events, enduring events, or multiple events that overwhelm an individual's ability to cope with and/or make sense of the event. Traumatic events include, but are not limited to: childhood emotional, physical, and sexual abuse; adult emotional, physical, and sexual abuse; natural disasters (i.e., hurricanes, tornados); and man-made disasters (i.e., automobile accidents, bombings). Many persons with eating disorders endorse histories of trauma. Researchers point to a comorbidity between eating disorders, traumatic events, and posttraumatic stress disorder (PTSD). Childhood sexual abuse is the trauma most commonly linked to later eating disorders, though certainly other forms of trauma, such as childhood or adulthood physical or verbal abuse or neglect, are also aligned with eating disorders. Studies indicate that bulimia is the eating disorder most associated to trauma, but trauma histories are found in persons with other eating disorder diagnoses as well.

Brewerton asserts that in individuals with eating disorders, comorbidity is "the rule rather than the exception." Eating disorders have a high comorbidity with mood disorders, anxiety disorders, somatoform disorders, personality disorders, and posttraumatic stress disorder. In one study of 101 individuals with eating disorders, 63.3 percent of the individuals with anorexia and 57.7 percent of the individuals with bulimia had experienced at least one trauma in their life. These percentages differ from the majority of research which shows a higher correlation between bulimia nervosa and trauma than anorexia nervosa and trauma, but nonetheless exemplifies the high rate of trauma histories in eating disorder clients.

Sexual Abuse and Eating Disorders

As noted above, childhood sexual abuse is the type of trauma most correlated with eating disorders. Researchers indicate that between 30 percent and 48 percent of eating disorder clients reveal a history of childhood sexual abuse. A longitudinal study that was conducted over an 18-year period found that sexual abuse was a significant predictor of bulimia nervosa and other purging disorders (i.e., anorexia, binge/purge subtype). Consistent with findings on trauma as a whole, the strongest associations between sexual abuse and eating disorders have been found in individuals with bulimia nervosa. One study found that specific types of disordered eating, such as compensatory behaviors in bulimia, are associated with higher rates of sexual abuse victimization. This study reported higher rates of sexual assault and aggravated assault among individuals with bulimia nervosa than among individuals without this diagnosis, suggesting that sexual and aggravated assault may contribute to the development and/or maintenance of bulimia nervosa. Furthermore, when bulimia is combined with other psychiatric comorbidity, especially substance abuse, there is a link to higher frequency and greater severity of sexual abuse.

Several researchers have found a link between sexual abuse and impulsivity and perfectionism—traits also found to be linked to eating disorders. Wonderlich found that clients who have eating disorders and a past history of sexual abuse report engaging in self-destructive behaviors and other impulsive behaviors. Particular circumstances concerning sexual abuse have been connected to heightened eating disorder symptoms, including if the sexual trauma involved parents or if it was recurring. Researchers have found that individuals with eating disorders and sexual trauma history often have issues of body dissatisfaction and struggle to accept their own sexuality. It has been suggested that eating disorders may be a way to deny sexuality and avoid painful memories and feelings associated with sexual trauma.

Childhood Abuse

Many other forms of trauma have been found in persons with eating disorders. Persons with eating disorders report a high amount of childhood emotional abuse. Physical child abuse as well as childhood neglect have also been found to be strong predictors of eating disorders later in life. Research indicates that any type of childhood trauma may lead to a more complex clinical presentation in an individual with an eating disorder than might otherwise be the case. Effects of childhood abuse in eating disorder clients may include low self-esteem, shame, and a negatively distorted body image. The risk of developing psychopathology including eating disorders heightens when exposure to abusive experiences is repetitive. Other traumas that are linked to eating disorders include adult sexual victimization, prisoner-of-war experiences, and exposure to violent environments.

PTSD and Eating Disorders

Posttraumatic stress disorder (PTSD) has a high comorbidity with eating disorders. It is important to note that not every individual who has undergone trauma develops PTSD. While researchers in one study found that over half of the individuals with eating disorders in the study had experienced trauma, only 12.9 percent met the criteria for diagnosis of PTSD. This is significant and of clinical concern as the lifetime prevalence of PTSD in the adult general population is

6.8 percent. PTSD has three major categories of symptoms: reliving the event, avoidance, and hyperarousal. Reliving the event disturbs day-to-day living and includes flashbacks, nightmares, and intrusive memories. Avoidance symptoms include avoiding people, places, and situations that remind the person of the trauma. Hyperarousal symptoms include a heightened startle response, hyper alertness, and sleep disturbances. Somatization in persons with comorbid eating disorders and PTSD is likely and reported more frequently than in eating disorder clients without PTSD. Most researchers agree that PTSD is more common in bulimic type eating disorders than in anorexia restricting type eating disorders.

Conclusion

There is a strong correlation between trauma and eating disorders. Childhood abuse has been linked to eating disorders with childhood sexual abuse being the most prevalent comorbidity. Bulimia nervosa and purging behaviors are more strongly linked to trauma than other eating disorders. Not all trauma presents as posttraumatic stress disorder, but there is a high correlation between PTSD and eating disorders. Therefore, it is important for clinicians and researchers to understand the potential effects of trauma on the development and maintenance of one's eating disorder.

JESSICA GUENTHER

See also: Comorbidity.

Bibliography

Brewerton, Timothy D. "Eating Disorders, Trauma, and Comorbidity: Focus on PTSD." *Eating Disorders* 15 (2007): 285–304.

Briere, John, and Catherine Scott. "Assessment of Trauma Symptoms in Eating-Disordered Populations." *Eating Disorders* 15 (2007): 347–58.

Johnson, Jeffrey G., Patricia Cohen, Stephanie Kasen, Judith S. Brook. "Childhood Adversities Associated with Risk for Eating Disorders or Weight Problems during Adolescence or Early Adulthood." *American Journal of Psychiatry* 159 (2002): 394–400.

Sansone, Randy A., and Lori A. Sansone. "Childhood Trauma, Borderline Personality, and Eating Disorders: A Developmental Cascade." *Eating Disorders* 15 (2007): 333–46.

Smyth, Joshua M., Kristin E. Heron, Stephen A. Wonderlich, Ross D. Crosby, Kevin M. Thompson. "The Influence of Reported Trauma and Adverse Events on Eating Disturbance in Young Adults." *International Journal of Eating Disorders* 41, no. 3 (2008): 195–202.

Tagay, Sefik, Sandra Schlegl, and Wolfgang Senf. "Traumatic Events Post-Traumatic Stress Symptomatology and Somatoform Symptoms in Eating Disorder Patients." *European Eating Disorder Review* 18, no. 2 (2010): 124–52.

Wonderlich, Stephen A., Ross D. Crosby, James E. Mitchell, Kevin M. Thompson, Jennifer Redlin, Gail Demuth, Joshua Smyth, and Beth Haseltine. "Eating Disturbance and Sexual Trauma in Childhood and Adulthood." *International Journal of Eating Disorders* 30, no. 4 (2001): 401–412.

TREATMENT

Treatment refers to a licensed professional providing care and support for a mental health concern. An exhaustive list of eating disorder treatment providers can be found at www.edreferral.com, including medical, nutrition, and mental health professionals who specialize in treating eating disorders. Generally, eating disorder treatment should be comprehensive so that all issues (e.g., meal plan, weight stabilization, etc) are addressed; treatment should also be individualized to the level of care (e.g., inpatient) that is needed by the disordered eating individual. Eating disorder mental health treatment may include individual therapy, group therapy, family therapy, and couples counseling.

Individual Therapy

Because eating disorders are a mental health concern, it is important to address psychological and emotional issues with a trained psychotherapist who may be a Licensed Clinical Social Worker (LCSW), a Licensed Professional Counselor (LPC), or a Licensed Psychologist (LP). In individual therapy, disordered eating clients can reveal their deepest concerns without fear or feeling self-conscious. Individuals may receive individual counseling in a school setting in a more generalized counseling center or from a private practice clinician who specializes in eating disorder treatment.

Individual counseling usually involves exploring triggers and contributing factors related to one's eating disorder. The client is encouraged to adopt coping strategies to address stressors and to replace disordered eating behaviors. Generally, the eating disorder client needs to work on setting personal boundaries in relationships and to become more assertive across situations (e.g., family, work).

Group Counseling

Group counseling provides advantages over individual therapy in that individuals with similar issues can provide support to one another. An eating disordered individual may feel validated when hearing similar concerns from other group members rather than feeling socially isolated. Group therapy for eating disordered individuals may focus on Dialectical Behavior Therapy (DBT) skills and body image or body politics groups. Eating disorder treatment facilities may provide additional groups such as spirituality, assertiveness, or twelve-step groups. Group therapy is facilitated by at least one licensed professional. By contrast, support groups (e.g., Eating Disorders Anonymous, Overeaters Anonymous) provide a peer-led group environment to discuss one's concerns.

Family and Couples Counseling

Family and couples counseling may be offered in both outpatient and inpatient settings. Family therapy helps identify the family system issues that contribute to eating disorder patterns and is particularly indicated for child and adolescent clients. Family therapy is also intended to act as a vehicle for educating parents and significant others about how to support the eating disordered individual in a healthy way. For example, the role of a family member in an individual's treatment and recovery is negotiated in therapy. Some family therapy approaches (e.g., Maudsley) encourage parents to act as co-therapists and to closely monitor meal planning efforts. In other cases, family members will be advised to serve solely as emotional support.

In couples counseling it may be important to address co-parenting issues—such as differing parenting styles—or to work on communication skills. Couples may also need to identify how the eating disorder has affected the relationship and repair hurt feelings. Anger management and assertiveness training are commonly provided for couples as an adjunct for eating disorder treatment. The level of family involvement may depend on several factors such as family history, potential for family support, timing related to the client's treatment progress, and level of care (e.g., outpatient, residential).

Levels of Care for Eating Disorder Treatment

The type of treatment a client should pursue is determined by the severity and duration of the eating disorder. The American Psychiatric Association has identified five levels of care for clients with eating disorders. These include Level 1 (Outpatient Treatment), Level 2 (Intensive Outpatient Treatment), Level 3 (Partial Hospitalization), Level 4 (Residential Treatment), and Level 5 (Inpatient Hospitalization). The level of care that a client should receive is based on the following criteria: medical complications, suicidal tendencies, body weight (i.e., Body Mass Index), motivation to recover, environmental stress, purging behavior, comorbidities, treatment availability, and structure needed for eating and weight management. For example, Level 1 (Outpatient Treatment) involves clients who are medically stable, have no suicidal ideations, have good motivation to recover, and are self-sufficient. The most intensive level of care (i.e., Level 5, Inpatient Hospitalization) is recommended for individuals who are suffering from medical complications (e.g., low heart rate), severe electrolyte imbalances (e.g., low potassium levels), and suicidal ideations, as well as for individuals who need refeeding to help with weight restoration. It has been suggested that anorexic individuals who are 25 percent or more below their expected weight for height should be treated on an in-patient basis. Inpatient treatment should also be provided if the disordered eating patients are at risk of engaging in self-destructive behaviors (e.g., self-mutilation) or if they have identified suicidal intent and plan. Motivation to recover for individuals requiring inpatient treatment is generally poor to very poor and there is a strong need for a structured environment with full supervision. In the hospital setting, vital signs can be monitored, physical activity can be limited, and gradual weight gain can be encouraged.

Residential eating disorder treatment facilities can provide a less intensive and less expensive alternative to an inpatient level of care. Many eating disorder treatment centers provide residential level of care within a campus-like atmosphere. Residential clients need to be medically stable and present with stronger motivation for recovery or have stronger social support. Residential programs often include a variety of treatment approaches including individual therapy, group therapy, family and couples counseling, and nutritional support. A nursing staff is available to help with medication management and to police disordered eating behaviors (e.g., purging).

Partial Hospitalization or day treatment is a step down from the highly structured residential and inpatient treatment facilities; however, support is still provided during meals. Clients generally receive group, family, and individual therapy and focus on practicing coping skills with support and monitoring from a multidisciplinary team. Intensive Outpatient (Level 2) provides a half-day version of the partial hospitalization and can represent a gradual transition to traditional outpatient therapy. An eating disordered individual should be medically stable to be appropriate for partial hospitalization or intensive outpatient levels of care.

Outpatient Treatment, or traditional psychotherapy, is considered appropriate when the disordered eating client is not medically compromised. Historically, individuals with bulimia nervosa have been treated on an outpatient basis more frequently than individuals with anorexia nervosa. Outpatient therapists who specialize in eating disorder treatment can address underlying emotional issues such as feelings of inadequacy, lack of control, and perfectionistic tendencies. Typically, outpatient sessions last for 50 minutes once or twice weekly and most commonly involve individual therapy.

Counseling Approaches for Eating Disorders

Various theoretical frameworks have been forwarded for the treatment of anorexia nervosa and bulimia nervosa, including cognitive-behavioral, motivational interviewing, acceptance and commitment therapy (ACT) and behavioral approaches. While each approach varies, all counseling approaches are designed to address and reduce disordered eating symptoms.

For example, highly regarded, evidence-based cognitive-behavioral approaches involve identifying dysfunctional thought patterns that trigger negative eating patterns and developing functional coping strategies that do not involve disordered eating. In Cognitive Behavioral Therapy (CBT), the therapist helps individuals identify cognitive distortions related to body image and eating disturbances. Dialectical Behavior Therapy (DBT), developed by Marsha Linehan, is a type of CBT that was designed to help individuals regulate and tolerate strong emotions. A skills-based approach, DBT focuses on helping the client to increase mindfulness, improve distress tolerance, re-establish healthy interpersonal skills and relationships, and regulate emotions appropriately.

Counselors can use motivational interviewing or motivational enhancement to help clients explore their own motivation for and resistance to recovery using the Stages of Change model. Using this approach, a counselor can avoid labeling or judging and can help the client build self-efficacy and relevant goals according to his or her stage of change. The potential advantage in using this approach with diverse clients is that it empowers the individual to increase his or her self-awareness and to take responsibility for behaviors rather than using a formulaic approach to treatment.

Acceptance and commitment therapy (ACT) incorporates both the present (i.e., "here and now") with the past contexts in which behaviors occur into psychotherapy. The acceptance component of ACT is associated with being more mindful and encouraging clients to accept thoughts and feelings without judgment. The commitment component of ACT is closely tied to behavioral therapy with the goal of helping clients identify and alter specific behaviors. ACT is showing promise as a therapeutic approach for eating disordered populations and has been adopted as an approach by many eating disorder treatment facilities (e.g., Avalon Hills Residential Eating Disorders Program).

In an intensive treatment setting, a variety of treatment modalities may be employed. The challenge of eating disorder treatment parallels court-ordered counseling cases in that the client's motivation to change impacts treatment efficacy. Therefore, finding a therapeutic approach that most closely fits the needs of the individual is a critical aspect of the recovery process. A therapeutic approach that shows promise in dealing with eating disorders and body image disturbances among diverse individuals is the relational perspective. This perspective allows for the individual to be considered within the context of his or her relationships and was originally created to empower women to see their focus on connections with others as a personal strength rather than a deficit. This approach coupled with a person-centered or client-centered approach will allow the counselor to listen attentively to the client's view of his or her universe without reacting too quickly. These counseling approaches (e.g., CBT, psychodynamic) are discussed in more detail in separate entries.

Multidisciplinary Team Approach to Treatment

The advantage of residential and inpatient eating disorder–specific programs is that medical professionals (i.e., physicians, nursing staff), dietitians, and mental health counselors are offered within a comprehensive treatment package. Because these facilities specialize in treating clients with eating disorders, they are acquainted with the complexities of dealing with this population. These professionals are able to distinguish between overeating at Thanksgiving and displaying actual disordered eating patterns. When a multidisciplinary team approach is implemented, it is important for team members to exhibit the following: strong communication, a willingness to meet regularly, self-awareness to avoid splitting by providing consistent messages to the client and monitoring treatment progress.

Eating Disorder Treatment for Athletes

Researchers emphasize the importance of determining the athlete's motivation to change in order to increase treatment efficacy. Denial by the athlete is especially likely if the athlete is receiving positive reinforcement for disordered eating behaviors in his or her sport and the behaviors are perceived as necessary and normal to compete. It is recommended that the counselor have a specialization in eating disorder treatment and have an understanding of the competitive athletic environment in order to build trust and create a strong athlete-counselor relationship. The focus should be on gradually helping the athlete increase weight and decrease eating disorder behaviors within the context of sport and on working toward relapse prevention. If the eating disorder symptoms are severe and the athlete's weight loss becomes a medical concern, he or she may need to be benched. The athlete will benefit most from learning adaptive coping skills and relaxation techniques irrespective of whether he or she continues to participate in the sport, needs to take a break, or needs to ultimately leave the sport to pursue eating disorder recovery. Ideas for sequencing athlete-specific treatment sessions have been outlined.

Eating Disorder Treatment for Males

It is anticipated that approximately one million males in the United States suffer from eating disorders. Unfortunately, most eating disorder facilities are geared toward female adolescents and young adults. Two exceptions, Rosewood and Remuda Ranch, located in Wickenburg, Arizona, treat male clients in a residential setting. Barriers involved in admitting males into an eating disorder facility relate to: (1) having a separation of males and females on the unit, (2) having male and female clients receive adequate privacy, (3) gender-identity and sexuality concerns of males, and (4) males and females have different issues related to body image and disordered eating behaviors.

Another exception, the Sante Center for Healing program (www.santecenter. com), treats males and females together using an addictions approach within a residential setting. Sante therapists find it useful to have both genders merged together in body image and eating disorder group therapy so that unique perspectives can be offered to the opposite sex. A rare outcome study compared males and females one year post discharge from a residential facility and discovered that while males averaged a longer length of stay (mean = 84 days; range = 25–226 days) than females (mean = 72 days; range = 23–156 days), males reported more improvement during follow-up. Differences in body image concerns were noted for the male clients at Rogers Memorial Hospital, including a focus on increasing muscle rather than trying to lose weight or become thinner. Males tended to gain more weight (mean = 19 lbs) from discharge to follow-up when compared with females (mean = 7 lbs). Using a person-centered approach and motivational interviewing has been recommended for treating males with eating disorders.

Treatment Considerations for Adult Women

The number of women over the age of 30 years who are seeking treatment has increased by 400 percent and demonstrates that eating disorders should not be considered a young or adolescent illness. Unfortunately, adults in midlife may be reluctant to seek treatment due to home and work responsibilities or may go underdiagnosed (e.g., it can be difficult to diagnose anorexia in postmenopausal women due to the absence of their menstrual cycle). In addition, insurance companies can be less supportive of adults in midlife than of adolescents because they sometimes take the disorder less seriously or consider it a chronic condition.

Renfrew Center in Philadelphia (www.renfrewcenter.com) provides a "30-something and beyond" track for women over the age of 35 years who are seeking eating disorder treatment. This unique track allows older clients to have five groups as well as coffee outings together. Unique issues relevant to this population can be addressed, including menopause, empty nest syndrome, facing the meaning of age in a youth-obsessed society, and guilt related to leaving children at home while in treatment. These women may benefit greatly from individual therapy and will probably need to educate their spouses and partners about how to support their treatment and recovery.

Cost of Treatment

Unfortunately eating disorder treatment is costly. Inpatient hospitalization or residential treatment is similar in price to in-patient psychiatric stays ($1000–2000/day and up), and usually a 30–90 day minimum stay is required for eating disorder programs. Insurance companies vary widely in their willingness to cover eating disorder treatment and residential stays. Insurance companies will sometimes cover a portion of the stay and then pressure the program to transition the client to a less expensive and less intensive level of care (i.e., outpatient). Another challenge is that for many clients a return visit is clinically indicated to continue the process of recovery as the step down from residential care is a difficult transition.

When one considers the comprehensive nature of treatment required for eating disorders (i.e., psychiatrist, dietician, and counselor), it is not surprising that even in an outpatient setting clients and their families struggle to meet the financial demands for care. Although some outpatient services (e.g., physician, counselor) may be covered by insurance and only require the copayment, dietitians are unlikely to be covered by insurance and may become an out-of-pocket expense. In addition, many eating disorder specialists have decided against getting on insurance panels to avoid paperwork or having to accept a lower fee than what one may charge per session. Low cost alternatives include twelve-step support groups and online message boards. However, these groups are not typically run by a trained counselor and fail to provide individualized and comprehensive treatment.

Conclusion

Eating disorder treatment should be comprehensive and individualized; it would ideally involve a multidisciplinary team approach. Individuals with eating disorders may require treatment covering a spectrum of levels of care ranging from most structured (i.e., inpatient) to least intensive (i.e., outpatient). Types of treatment may include individual therapy, group therapy, family and couples counseling as well as nutrition and medical monitoring.

JUSTINE J. REEL

See also: Cognitive Behavioral Therapy; Dialectical Behavior Therapy; Eating Disorders Anonymous; Levels of Care; Maudsley Family Therapy; Overeaters Anonymous.

Bibliography

American Psychiatric Association. *Practice Guideline for the Treatment of Patients with Eating Disorders, 3rd Edition.* Arlington, VA: American Psychiatric Association, 2006.

Calegoro, Rachel M., and Kelly N. Pedrotty. "The Practice and Process of Healthy Exercise: An Investigation of the Treatment of Exercise Abuse in Women with Eating Disorders." *Eating Disorders* 12 (2004): 273–91.

Costin, Carolyn. *100 Questions & Answers about Eating Disorders.* Boston, MA: Jones and Bartlett, 2007.

Costin, Carolyn. *A Comprehensive Guide to the Causes, Treatments and Prevention of Eating Disorders: The Eating Disorder Sourcebook, 3rd Edition.* New York, NY: McGraw-Hill, 2007.

"Eating Disorder Referral and Information Center." EDREFERRAL.com. Accessed December 29, 2011. http://www.edreferral.com/.

Johnson, Craig J. "Current Challenges in Recognizing and Treating Eating Disorders." *Minnesota Medicine* 86, no. 11 (2003): 34–39.

Joy, Elizabeth A., Claudia Wilson, and Steve Varochok. "The Multidisciplinary Team Approach to the Outpatient Treatment of Disordered Eating." *Current Sports Medicine Reports* 2 (2003): 331–36.

Lock, James, and Daniel Le Grange. *Help Your Teenager Beat an Eating Disorder.* New York, NY: Guilford, 2005.

Lock, James, Daniel Le Grange, W. Stewart Agras, and Christopher Dare. *Treatment Manual for Anorexia Nervosa: A Family-Based Approach.* New York, NY: Guilford, 2001.

Reel, Justine J., and Katherine A. Beals, eds. *The Hidden Faces of Eating Disorders and Body Image.* Reston, VA: AAHPERD/NAGWS, 2009.

Reel, Justine J., and Holly M. Estes. "Treatment Considerations for Athletes with Disordered Eating." In *Disordered Eating among Athletes: A Comprehensive Guide for Health Professionals,* edited by Katherine A. Beals, 131–58. Champaign, IL: Human Kinetics, 2004.

Renfrew Center. "Anorexia Bulimia Eating Disorder Treatment." Accessed December 29, 2011. http://www.renfrewcenter.com/.

Richards, P. Scott, Randy K. Hardman, and Michael E. Berrett. *Spiritual Approaches in the Treatment of Women with Eating Disorders.* Washington, DC: American Psychological Association, 2007.

Santé Center. "Santé Center for Healing." Accessed December 29, 2011. http://www.santecenter.com/.

Stewart, Tiffany M., and Donald A. Williamson. "Multidisciplinary Treatment of Eating Disorders–Part 1: Structure and Costs of Treatment." *Behavior Modification* 28, no. 6 (2004): 812–30. doi: 10.1177/0145445503259855.

Thompson, J. K., L. J. Heinberg, M. Altabe, and S. Tantleff-Dunn. *Exacting Beauty: Theory, Assessment, and Treatment of Body Image Disturbance.* Washington, DC: American Psychological Association. 1999.

TWELVE-STEP PROGRAMS

Twelve-step programs are self-help programs designed to aid individuals in recovery from addictions, compulsions, and other behavioral problems such as relationship issues related to addictions. Twelve-step programs originated with Alcoholics Anonymous (AA), which was founded in 1935 by Bill Wilson and Dr. Bob Smith. "Bill W." and "Dr. Bob," were two "recovering" alcoholics (i.e., sober and living a lifestyle that promoted and maintained their sobriety). They developed the AA program to assist individuals working toward recovery, with the basic premise that alcoholics needed to connect to other alcoholics and to a spiritual source to obtain and sustain recovery. The Twelve Steps utilized as the guiding principles to gaining and maintaining recovery were first published in 1939 in the book *Alcoholics Anonymous: The Story of How More than One Hundred Men Have Recovered from Alcoholism* (referred to by many members of twelve-step programs as the "Big Book"). The steps as adapted for any addiction can be found at the following website: www.12step.org.

Since their origin, the Twelve Steps have been adapted for many other compulsive and other behavioral problems, such as Narcotics Anonymous, Gamblers Anonymous, and Debtors Anonymous. Currently, over 200 self-help programs, often referred to as fellowships, exist worldwide. Twelve-step groups developed specifically for eating disorders and for persons struggling with disordered eating include Overeaters Anonymous, Eating Disorders Anonymous, and Anorexics and Bulimics Anonymous.

Overeaters Anonymous

Overeaters Anonymous (OA) was founded in 1960 and now has fellowship groups in more than 20 countries. The premise of OA is that members have a disease of compulsive overeating and an addiction to particular foods or to the way that they eat. While the fellowship group is designed for persons struggling with compulsive eating, members also include those with other eating-related problems, including anorexia nervosa, bulimia nervosa, and Eating Disorder Not Otherwise Specified (EDNOS). The framework for recovery is the same for all members of OA regardless of symptomology.

Eating Disorders Anonymous

Eating Disorders Anonymous (EDA) was founded in 2000 by members of AA in Phoenix, Arizona. The EDA's website states, "Our primary purpose is to recover from our eating disorders and to carry this message of recovery to others with eating disorders." The fellowship reports that its goal is balance as opposed to abstinence.

Anorexics and Bulimics Anonymous

Anorexics and Bulimics Anonymous (ABA) is a twelve-step group established in 1992, adapting the Twelve Steps and program of AA specifically for persons with anorexia nervosa and bulimia nervosa. According to the ABA website, the only requirement for membership is "a desire to stop unhealthy eating practices." ABA is modeled after Alcoholics Anonymous (AA) and originally utilized AA's text *Alcoholics Anonymous,* also referred to as the "Big Book," for its text. In 2002 ABA published its own text, *Anorexics and Bulimics Anonymous,* with the intention of it being a text that the group could use to supplement the material in the "Big Book." ABA's program is intended for people with anorexia or bulimia to gain support from a community of others struggling with the same disorders. ABA is clear that the program is not intended as a substitute for professional treatment for an eating disorder, but rather is a resource to complement treatment by professional health care providers.

Conclusion

Research on the efficacy of twelve-step programs in dealing with eating disorders has been inconclusive, but some common themes regarding the benefits obtained from the programs are reported by their members. Members have found comfort in the unified language of twelve-step programs and the shared conceptualization of their problem in a way that reflects their life experiences. A key focal point of the groups is emotional and spiritual healing as being vital to recovery, and many members report that this makes the program effective for them.

Although research on twelve-step programs has yet to produce any evidence regarding their effectiveness, the model has been shown to have had a profound effect on many of the participants in the various twelve-step programs. The fundamental objectives of these programs are to provide individuals with a strong support network through emotional and spiritual connections. In addition, the fellowships encourage their participants to take accountability for their behaviors and to construct a plan for their recovery.

JESSICA GUENTHER

See also: Eating Disorders Anonymous; Overeaters Anonymous.

Bibliography

Alcoholics Anonymous. *Alcoholics Anonymous, 4th Edition.* New York: A.A. World Services, 2001.
Anorexics and Bulimics Anonymous (ABA). "Anorexics and Bulimics Anonymous (ABA) Welcome." Aba12steps.org. Last modified September 18, 2011. http://aba12steps.org/.
Carter, Bobbi L., P. Scott Richards, Randy K. Hardman, and Michael E. Berrett. "Twelve-Step Groups for Patients with Eating Disorders." In *Spiritual Approaches in the Treatment of Women with Eating Disorders,* edited by P. Scott Richards, Randy K. Hardman, and Michael E. Berrett, 187–203. Washington, D.C.: American Psychological Association, 2007.
Eating Disorders Anonymous. "Eating Disorders Anonymous About." *Eating Disorders Anonymous.org.* Accessed August 16, 2011. http://www.eatingdisordersanonymous.org/about.html.

Johnson, Craig L., and Randy A. Sansone. "Integrating the Twelve-step Approach with Traditional Psychotherapy for the Treatment of Eating Disorders." *International Journal of Eating Disorders* 14, no. 2 (1993): 121–34.

McAleavey, Kristen. "Short-Term Outcomes of a 12-Step Program among Women with Anorexia, Bulimia, and Eating Disorders." *Journal of Children and Family Studies* 19 (2010): 728–37.

Russell-Mayhew, Shelly, Kristin M. von Ranson, and Philip C. Masson. "How Does Over-eaters Anonymous Help Its Members? A Qualitative Analysis." *European Eating Disorders Review* 18 (2010): 33–42.

V

VEGETARIANISM

Vegetarianism refers to restricting meat and animal products. Vegan-type vegetarianism involves restricting all animal products (i.e., meat, fish, dairy and eggs), whereas other forms of vegetarian diets may include dairy and eggs or fish. Strict vegetarian diets usually consist of foods low in fat, but can result in deficiencies in protein, calcium, and vitamins D and B12. Therefore, vegetarians must be careful to reach the nutritional value of a well-balanced meal plan without meat products. Vegetarian diets are often associated with moral and ethical beliefs related to animal welfare; however, health reasons and the desire to lose weight may also serve as motives for adopting vegetarianism.

Eating Disorders and Vegetarian Diets

Vegetarianism has been linked with disordered eating attitudes and behaviors and having a stronger desire for thinness. In a study conducted in Minnesota, adolescents who were self-reported vegetarians were significantly more likely to report bulimic behaviors than nonvegetarian adolescents. In a separate Australian study, vegetarian teenagers expressed more concerns with being slim and higher restriction of food intake than nonvegetarian teenagers. This higher tendency for dietary restraint was also observed among college students who were vegetarians. In the same study, 37 percent of college-aged vegetarians were found to report disordered eating patterns compared to only 8 percent of nonvegetarian college peers.

In a larger study with 2,516 males and females between the ages of 15 and 23 years, researchers revealed that adolescent and young adult current vegetarians were more likely to report binge eating with loss of control than nonvegetarian participants. Former vegetarians were more likely to engage in extreme unhealthful weight control behaviors than current vegetarians and nonvegetarian participants. Because of the confirmed link between vegetarian practices and disordered eating, self-identified vegetarianism has been used as a marker for the early detection of eating disorders.

Treatment Implications of Self-Identified Vegetarians with Eating Disorders

Because vegetarian behaviors can be related to the onset of disordered eating and eating disorders, it is important for treatment professionals to assess the timing and role of vegetarianism as it relates to the development of eating disorder symptomatology. For example, vegetarian diets may represent one way that an individual's food consumption has become more restrictive in response to a desire to lose weight. Many eating disorder treatment facilities do not accommodate vegetarian-diets as such food preferences are considered to be part of one's eating disorder. However, it is possible in the outpatient setting for dietitians to develop meal plans that limit animal product intake or replace protein with more vegetarian-friendly choices (e.g., legumes, tofu) if it is determined that vegetarianism reflects a moral or spiritual belief rather than a weight control strategy.

Conclusion

Vegetarianism refers to avoiding meat and other animal products. Historically, vegetarian diets stemmed from beliefs regarding animal welfare and spiritual opposition to consuming sacred animals. More recently, vegetarianism has been viewed as a healthy lifestyle decision which may be associated with a desire to lose weight and thinness. Studies with adolescents and adults have found a conclusive link between self-identified vegetarians and increased binge eating, bulimic behaviors, and restricting compared with nonvegetarians. Therefore, assessing for vegetarian practices can be a vital marker in the early detection of disordered eating and eating disorders.

JUSTINE J. REEL

Bibliography

Amit, M. "Vegetarian Diets in Children and Adolescents." *Pediatric Child Health* 15, no. 5 (2010): 303–308.

Barnard, Neal D., and Susan Levin. "Vegetarian Diets and Disordered Eating." *Journal of the American Dietetic Association* 109, no. 9 (2009): 1523. doi: 10.1016/j.jada.2009.07.037.

Bas, Murat, Efsun Karabudak, and Gul Kiziltan. "Vegetarianism and Eating Disorders: Association between Eating Attitudes and Other Psychological Factors among Turkish Adolescents." *Appetite* 44 (2005): 309–315. doi: 10.1016/j.appet.2005.02.002.

Klopp, Sherre A., Cynthia J. Heiss, and Heather S. Smith. "Self-reported Vegetarianism May be a Marker for College Women at Risk for Disordered Eating." *Journal of the American Dietetic Association* 103 (2003): 745–47. doi: 10.1053/jada.2003.50139.

Robinson-O'Brien, Ramona, Cheryl L. Perry, Melanie M. Wall, Mary Story, and Dianne Neumark-Sztainer. "Adolescent and Young Adult Vegetarianism: Better Dietary Intake and Weight Outcomes but Increased Risk of Disordered Eating Behaviors." *Journal of the American Dietetic Association* 109 (2009): 648–55. doi: 10.1016/jada.2008.12.014.

Yackobovitch-Gavan, Michal, Moria Golan, Avi Valevski, Shulamit Kreitler, Eytan Bachar, Amia Lieblich, Edith Mitrani, Abraham Weizman, and Daniel Stein. "An Integrative Quantitative Model of Factors Influencing the Course of Anorexia Nervosa Over Time." *International Journal of Eating Disorders* 42 (2009): 306–317. doi: 10.1002/eat.20624.

VIRTUAL REALITY

Introduction

Virtual reality (VR) is a relatively new technology that creates human and computer interaction to allow individuals to experience sensations as a result of becoming immersed in lifelike virtual worlds. Although VR was initially used for play and computer games intended to stimulate real-life situations (e.g., racing cars on a track), the potential for use of VR as an educational and treatment tool has recently been identified by researchers and clinicians. VR has been proposed as an innovative form of exposure therapy for individuals suffering from a variety of psychological disorders (e.g., anxiety) to assist in the practice of coping skills relative to a specific triggering setting (e.g., social party). VR has effectively been used to understand and treat addictions. VR has helped demonstrate that people with addiction respond with strong cravings to specific cues (e.g., cigarette packs, liquor bottles) and social settings (e.g., party) associated with use. Using VR, these same people can learn and practice relapse prevention skills while getting experience in a lifelike but safe environment.

VR and Eating Disorder Treatment

VR is ideal for simulating food cues and environmental settings to determine an individual's emotional response and self-reported cravings/hunger. By interviewing the eating disordered individual to understand triggering environments, a VR high-risk eating context (e.g., restaurant) can be configured with the click of a mouse. By building upon commonly cited triggering situations for individuals with eating disorders, VR can be used as an assessment tool that goes beyond the standard clinical interview.

In the treatment setting, clinicians can address both negative eating behaviors and body image with the help of VR technology. Currently, many eating disorder residential treatment facilities often offer various challenges to provide exposure to triggering situations out in the community. One's primary therapist will accompany the client to a clothing store, restaurant, or fitness center to experience exposure and practice skills. Because this is highly impractical to do on a frequent basis, most clients will only have one or two challenges throughout their treatment program. However, VR not only offers the opportunity to customize the setting to the client's actual home, gym, favorite restaurant, grocery or clothing store, but also ensures that he or she is exposed to triggering situations and is able to practice skills on a regular basis during treatment and upon discharge from a residential facility.

Body image concerns may be addressed using VR by presenting situations known to produce body dissatisfaction and body distortion. Eating disordered individuals have the opportunity to experience these negative feelings during the counseling session and can process the emotions in the moment. VR is a relatively new tool that shows great promise for use in the assessment and treatment of eating disorders.

JUSTINE J. REEL

Bibliography

Bordnick, Patrick S., Brian L. Carter, and Amy C. Traylor. "What Virtual Reality Research in Addictions Can Tell Us about the Future of Obesity Assessment and Treatment." *Journal of Diabetes Science and Technology* 5, no. 2 (2011): 265–71.

Gorini, Alessandra, Eric Griez, Anna Petrova, and Giuseppe Riva. "Assessment of the Emotional Responses Produced by Exposure to Real Food, Virtual Food and Photographs of Food in Patients Affected by Eating Disorders." *Annals of General Psychiatry* 9 (2010): 30–41.

Gutiérrez-Maidonado, José, Marta Ferrer-Garcia, Alejandra Caqueo-Urizar, and Elena Moreno. "Body Image in Eating Disorders: The Influence of Exposure to Virtual-Reality Environments." *Cyberpsychology, Behavior, and Social Networking* 13, no. 5 (2010): 521–31.

Plante, Thomas G., Cara Cage, Sara Clements, and Allison Stover. "Psychological Benefits of Exercise Paired with Virtual Reality: Outdoor Exercise Energizes Whereas Indoor Virtual Exercise Relaxes." *International Journal of Stress Management* 13, no. 1 (2006): 108–117. doi: 10.10137/1072-5245.13.1.108

Riva, Giuseppe. "The Key to Unlocking the Virtual Body: Virtual Reality in the Treatment of Obesity and Eating Disorders." *Journal of Diabetes Science and Technology* 5, no. 2 (2011): 283–92.

W

WANNAREXIA

"Wannarexia" refers to a slang term used to depict an eating disorder "wannabe"—someone who visits pro-ana and pro-mia websites, participates in community forum discussions and diets occasionally, but is not considered to be dedicated to an eating disordered lifestyle. In a question of authenticity, wannarexic individuals are sometimes called "fake anorexics" or "wannabes" by the pro-ana community which believes that wannabes undermine the credibility of the anorexia nervosa cause. Derogatory comments about wannarexics plague pro-ana discussion boards as participants attempt to weed out the posers in the community.

Wannarexia as a Warning Sign for Eating Disorders

Posts on pro–eating disorder websites are generally made by females younger than 20 years of age. Wannarexia has often been used as a label for preteen and teenage females who claim to have anorexia nervosa and view anorexia as a quick fix to lose weight and gain popularity. Although wannarexic individuals do not meet the diagnostic criteria for anorexia nervosa or other clinical eating disorders and may in fact be overweight, visiting pro–eating disorder websites should be viewed as a warning sign for a harmful dieting mentality that usually precipitates disordered eating behaviors. Wannabes may receive direct advice from online communities about how to develop anorexia nervosa and techniques for losing weight in an unhealthy way. Furthermore, what begins as a naïve curiosity about eating disorders and a desire to become popular can lead to a genuine problem.

Conclusion

Wannarexia is a term that has emerged to describe individuals who visit pro–eating disorder sites regularly but do not yet meet the criteria for eating disorders. Wannabes are viewed as threatening by the pro-ana community due to feelings that wannarexia undermines the credibility of anorexia nervosa. Although wannabe anorexics may not meet the diagnostic criteria for clinical eating disorders and may be overweight, wannarexia should be identified as a warning sign. Exposure to pro–eating disorder websites can lead to active engagement in disordered eating behaviors and the development of a more serious problem.

JUSTINE J. REEL

See also: Pro-Ana.

Bibliography

Bardone-Cone, Anna M., and Kamila M. Cass. "What Does Viewing a Pro-Anorexia Website Do? An Experimental Examination of Website Exposure and Moderating Effects." *International Journal of Eating Disorders* 40, no. 6 (2007): 537–48. doi: 10.1002/eat.20396.

Giles, David. "Constructing Identities in Cyberspace: The Case of Eating Disorders." *British Journal of Social Psychology* 45 (2006): 463–77. doi: 10/1348/014466605X53596.

Hardin, Pamela K. "Shape-shifting Discourses of Anorexia Nervosa: Reconstituting Psychopathology." *Nursing Inquiry* 10, no. 4 (2003): 209–217.

Harper, Kelley, Steffanie Sperry, and J. Kevin Thompson. "Viewership of Pro-Eating Disorder Websites: Association with Body Image and Eating Disturbances." *International Journal of Eating Disorders* 41 (2008): 92–95. doi: 10.1002/eat.20408.

Jett, Scarlett, David J. LaPorte, and Jill Wanchisn. "Impact of Exposure to Pro–Eating Disorder Websites on Eating Behaviour in College Women." *European Eating Disorders Review* 18 (2010): 410–16. doi: 10.1002/erv.1009

Ransom, Danielle C., Jennifer G. La Guardia, Erik Z. Woody, and Jennifer L. Boyd. "Interpersonal Interactions on Online Forums Addressing Eating Concerns." *International Journal of Eating Disorders* 43 (2010): 161–70.

Wilson, Jenny L., Rebecka Peebles, Kristina K. Hardy, and Iris F. Litt. "Surfing for Thinness: A Pilot Study of Pro-Eating Disorder Web Site Usage in Adolescents with Eating Disorders." *Pediatrics* 118 (2006): 1635–1643. doi: 10.1542/peds.2006-1133

WEIGHT CLASS SPORTS

Weight class sports include sports that have divisions or categories by weight such as wrestling, boxing, martial arts, weight lifting, power lifting, bodybuilding, and rowing. Not only is a particular weight range required per category, but athletes are also expected to weigh in to ensure that they are eligible to compete. Historically, categories based on weight were created in order to equalize the playing field. Before weight classes were introduced, the stronger and larger athletes would dominate competitions.

For weight class sports, categories vary based on weight and not appearance or muscularity. Categories are often named featherweight, lightweight, or middleweight. If a competitor does not make weight prior to his or her competition, he or she is barred from competing. The timing of when a competitor is weighed in prior to competition varies by sport, and may even occur prior to the season's start.

Training for Weight

In general, weight-focused sports will provide a weight range for the athlete to compete within a particular category. Typically, the athlete gains a competitive advantage by weighing as close to the maximum limit of the range as possible without exceeding his or her class. Two methods are most commonly used to achieve and maintain an athlete's ideal weight for his or her weight class. The first strategy is to gain as much muscle mass and strength as possible in the off-season before radically cutting weight prior to the start of the season or weigh-in. The intent behind this training approach is to attempt to retain the strength and power acquired during the off-season and effectively compete with strength above that weight limit. Although not a strength-based sport, bodybuilders follow this protocol by amassing as much muscle and weight as possible in the off-season before cutting back to reduce as much body fat as possible while retaining the muscle mass. A second training method which requires less weight change involves having the athlete seek to attain and maintain maximum strength and fitness while maintaining a competitive body weight throughout the off-season and during the regular season.

Pathogenic Weight Control Methods

Unfortunately, because athletes need to adhere to a specific weight—the heavyweight category is usually the exception—they may take unhealthy risks in order to cut weight for a perceived competitive edge. Such risks may include caloric and fluid restriction, self-induced vomiting, excessive exercise, exercising in a sweat suit, using saunas, diet pills, and laxatives. Therefore, athletes in weight class sports (e.g., bodybuilding, wrestling) are more likely to exhibit disordered eating behaviors than athletes in sports that are not weight-dependent.

It is important to recognize that efforts to meet weight expectations for one's sport tend to be more heavily influenced by coaches and other teammates than by socially constructed appearance standards. Thus, there is less concern about how a weight class athlete looks than about the pressure from significant others to do what it takes in order to be successful. As a consequence, an athlete may take unhealthy risks to achieve that perceived performance advantage. In addition, any sport in which physique evaluation may be made or in which aesthetics is judged may also experience such pressures.

Conclusion

Because weight class sports have been criticized in the past due to the rules that seemed to encourage pathogenic weight loss methods, some sports and their respective organizations have taken steps to encourage long-term evaluations of weight as opposed to a single weigh-in. These efforts appear to have been successful in reducing the extreme cases associated with rapid weight loss, as is in the case of competitive wrestling. However, given that the emphasis on body weight remains, there is conflicting evidence that these revised weight class guidelines can adequately discourage disordered eating behaviors in weight class sports.

TIMOTHY M. BAGHURST

See also: Bodybuilding; Rowing; Wrestling.

Bibliography

Galli, Nick, Justine J. Reel, Trent Petrie, Christy Greenleaf, and Jennifer Carter. "Preliminary Development of the Weight Pressures in Sport Scale for Male Athletes." *Journal of Sport Behavior* 34 (2011): 47–68.

Lambert, Charles P., Laura L. Frank, and William J. Evans. "Macronutrient Considerations for the Sport of Bodybuilding." *Sports Medicine* 34 (2004): 317–27.

Morton, James P., Colin Robertson, Laura Sutton, and Don P. M. MacLaren. "Making the Weight: A Case Study from Professional Boxing." *International Journal of Sport Nutrition and Exercise Metabolism* 20 (2010): 80–95.

Reel, Justine, Sonya SooHoo, Trent A. Petrie, Christy Greenleaf, and Jennifer E. Carter. "Slimming Down for Sport: Developing a Weight Pressures in Sport Measure for Female Athletes." *Journal of Clinical Sport Psychology* 4 (2010): 99–111.

Shriver, Lenka H., Nance M. Betts, and Mark E. Payton. "Changes in Body Weight, Body Composition, and Eating Attitudes in High School Wrestlers." *International Journal of Sport Nutrition and Exercise Metabolism* 19 (2009): 424–32.

Thompson, Ron A., and Roberta Trattner Sherman. *Eating Disorders in Sport.* New York, NY: Routledge, 2010.

WEIGHT PRESSURES IN SPORT

Sport involves pressure from many sources to change one's body shape, size, or appearance. The pressure to lose or gain weight comes from the media, family, friends outside of sport, and personal factors, as well as teammates, coaches, judges, uniforms, and the sport-related norms associated with the sport culture. As a result, athletes are not immune to developing eating disorders. The media has sensationalized cases like Christy Heinrich, the gymnast who weighed 47 pounds when she died from an eating disorder that she developed after hearing from a judge that she was too fat to excel, and Heidi Guenther, a ballerina who died at 22 years of age after she developed anorexia because she was told to lose five pounds in order to land the best role.

Prevalence

Lifetime prevalence estimates of clinical eating disorders are 5–10 percent in females and approximately 1 percent in males. Research indicates that as many as 1–64 percent of female athletes and 0–53 percent of males report disordered eating behaviors, placing them at risk of developing clinical eating disorders. The discrepancy in lifetime prevalence rates based on gender has been observed in the athletic population as well. Collegiate female athletes, specifically, reported clinical eating disorder and subclinical eating disorder occurrence rates of 2 percent and 25.5 percent, respectively. Fewer collegiate males have reported clinical eating disorders (0–1.8%), but nearly 20 percent were categorized as having subclinical eating disorders in one study. As a result, research has sought to identify the pressures athletes experience with regard to weight management.

Weight Pressures Outside of Sport

Athletes perform in an environment full of pressure to lose weight or maintain a low body weight in the quest for achievement. However, they do not take on this quest in a vacuum; therefore, they are vulnerable to pressures typical of the general public in addition to various weight-related sport pressures. Although the focus of this chapter is on sport-specific weight pressures, it is important to remember that athletes still experience general social pressure from the media, family, friends, and other sources.

Media

Athletes who are successful in their sport and represent the ideal body size and shape in everyday society are often the ones who are written and reported about the most. As a result, other athletes who strive for distinction may feel pressure to conform to society's idea of beauty while trying to maintain athletic excellence. These conflicting appearance ideals in greater society and in the sports world may contribute to the athletes' willingness to resort to unhealthy eating behaviors in an effort to gain recognition.

Family

Researchers have suggested that because many individuals with disordered eating behaviors seek approval from others, critical comments in the absence of praise from family members increase perceptions of weight-related pressure. Critical comments include remarks that focus on physical appearance, stress on weight loss, and reinforce the thin ideal. Consequently, some athletes have indicated that negative weight-related comments from their family were pivotal events in the development of their eating disorders.

The criteria by which comments are identified as critical are dependent upon the comment's purpose (i.e., weight loss for health versus weight loss for appearance versus weight loss for performance), the setting in which the comment was made (e.g., public versus private), and the direction of the comment (i.e., weight loss versus weight gain). Athletes most frequently tend to recall negative comments on the basis of appearance and weight loss/gain when they are communicated in a public setting. For instance, athletes have reported being affected by a family member who focuses on the amount of food consumed by an athlete, being told by a family member to eat less, or being given something different than others around her.

Moreover, athletes who receive inconsistent praise for their accomplishments are more likely to develop perfectionistic tendencies similar to those evident in individuals who exhibit disordered eating behaviors. Subsequently, athletes may be willing to do whatever it takes, however harmful that may be, to either avoid criticism or receive praise in their pursuit of success.

Self-Pressure

Although many athletes report external pressure to lose weight or maintain a low body weight, some pressure comes from internal sources. When asked if they would like to lose weight, 92 percent of figure skaters said that body weight and appearance are important to them and 94 percent said they noticed if they gained weight. It may be that body weight and appearance are important to athletes because of influences outside of sport that emphasize the thin ideal or it might be that sport-related weight pressures contribute to the internalization of the ideal sport body type.

Sport-Specific Weight Pressures

Because athletes live in a world where they succeed or fail based on physical ability, their bodies take center stage. As such, they experience weight-related pressures in addition to those of the general public. Specifically, external pressure has been elevated in athletes who recalled more external weight-related pressure than athletes who recalled less external weight-related pressure. Sport-specific external pressure includes perceptions of weight-related pressure from coaches, teammates, judges, uniforms, and the sport subculture. It is perhaps not surprising then that many athletes report a desire to lose weight (e.g., 72% of figure skaters expressed a desire to lose weight).

Significant Others

Although athletes are influenced by others in their nonsport lives, they are also influenced on a daily basis by a number of significant others in their sport lives. Researchers have suggested that the weight-related pressure athletes feel from coaches, judges, and teammates is related to the disordered eating behaviors those athletes adopt. Thus, a growing body of research has been dedicated to investigating this relationship in athletes.

Researchers have suggested that coaches' weight expectations and/or weight-related comments influence athletes' disordered eating behaviors. Coaches play a big role in the professional development of athletes. In some cases, they are inclined to advise their athletes on weight and appearance. Gymnastics coaches (54%) in one study reported determining an athlete's need for weight loss based solely on her appearance. Whereas 61 percent of competitive cheerleaders reported active dieting, 56 percent reported being told by a coach to lose weight. Likewise, 57 percent of synchronized skaters—synchronized skating is a type of figure skating—reported that weight and appearance were important to their coach.

These results, and others, indicate that coaches probably contribute to the adoption of disordered eating behaviors. In a 1991 study of female athletes diagnosed with clinical eating disorders, five contributing factors directly related to their coaches were identified including direct remarks, public weigh-ins, regular posting of weigh-in results, feelings of being required to lose weight to fit the coach's ideal, and fear of losing the team position following failure to lose weight. More recently, 8.3 percent to 33.8 percent of female collegiate athletes felt pressure from coaches to lose weight or maintain a low body weight often, usually, or always. Additionally, male athletes are not exempt from these findings. In fact, 70 percent of male collegiate athletes reported pressure from their coaches to either lose or gain weight. Although the coach is not likely to be the only reason athletes adopt unhealthy weight loss behaviors, one can assume that weight-related coach pressure probably contributes to dieting behaviors.

Whether athletes participate in individual or team sports, they can be and are influenced by their teammates. That is, even though athletes in individual sports do not compete with their teammates per se, they do practice together and compete at the same competitions. This puts them in direct proximity with each other, increasing the flow of weight management information between team members. In a study of female athletes from a multitude of sports, 17–26.8 percent reported pressure from teammates and 5.4 percent believed their team/sport should have a weight limit. In more specific sport contexts, researchers found that nearly 55 percent of synchronized skaters and 16 percent of swimmers thought that weight and appearance were important to their teammates.

For male athletes, the pressure from teammates related to weight may be more closely linked to increasing size and power. Regardless, 20 percent of a collegiate male athletic sample mentioned that their teammates were important in motivating them to improve their fitness. However, another sample indicated that weight pressure from teammates/coaches was related to higher drive for muscularity ($r = .43$) and bulimic symptomology ($r = .25$) in male athletes. This finding highlights the importance of teammate influence, regardless of weight-loss intention.

Judges are often a critical part of the sport environment. Specifically, in some sports, athletes are subjectively judged on their performance by a panel of judges. Subjective judging, then, has led some coaches and athletes to believe that low body weight produces more appealing lines, which in turn results in higher subjective scores from judges. Divers, figure skaters, gymnasts, and the like are judged not only by their skill, but also by their ability to demonstrate grace, strength, agility, and attractiveness. Therefore, it is not surprising that athletes in similar sports believed that their weight was important to judges (e.g., 64% of synchronized skaters).

Uniforms

Uniforms are the most frequently reported weight pressure in many sports. Uniforms include tight swimsuits, dance attire, gymnastic leotards, volleyball shorts, or track and field spandex. Tight-fitting, revealing attire has resulted in feelings of self-consciousness and the awareness that perceived bodily flaws are readily apparent. In some studies, swimmers and dancers have reported that uniforms were often ordered two or more sizes smaller than an athlete's typical size. Conversely, some athletes reported that uniforms were ordered first and the athlete was selected to fit into whatever sizes were left.

For swimmers, one study indicated that the most salient weight pressure was team uniform (45.2%), followed by teammates (16.1%), the crowd (12.9%), and perceived performance advantage (9.7%). More than half of college (53.5%) and high school (60.7%) cheerleaders reported that their uniforms represented a weight-related pressure in their sport. Although elite divers did not report increased disordered eating behaviors due to uniform pressure, some researchers have suggested that individuals more susceptible to these pressures retire from the sport prior to reaching the elite level, alleviating the weight-related pressure uniforms may represent.

A related pressure worth mentioning here is the presence of full-length mirrors reported by dancers. While full-length wall-to-wall mirrors give dancers the opportunity for immediate feedback about lines and body position, they may also act as a constant reminder of body size/shape. Utilized on a consistent basis, the constant feedback may become distressing to many dancers.

Weight Requirements

Although some researchers have suggested that weigh-ins are detrimental to athletes' health, they do continue to occur. In fact, one study indicated that cheerleaders had a weight limit of 120 pounds and were required to have a body fat percentage between 9 percent and 17 percent at the college level. Furthermore, nearly 50 percent of college cheerleaders reported having a weight limit at tryouts and almost 40 percent indicated that they experienced periodic weigh-ins throughout the season.

Although more recent research indicates that collegiate athletes do not experience regular weigh-ins by their coaches, they do still occur in some cases. For instance, weigh-in sessions commonly occur in sports like wrestling that have specific weight classes. As successful attempts to compete at a lower weight class help the wrestler to gain a performance advantage, many wrestlers experience weight cycling. On average, wrestlers lose 13 pounds during a one-week weight-cutting period with some wrestlers reporting losing 9–11 pounds directly before a match using typical weight loss methods of dehydration, chronic dieting, fasting, and overtraining.

However, given the adverse effects of weight-cutting, the National Wrestling Coaches Association and National Federation of State High School Associations introduced a new rule that set minimum weight class opportunities based on the body composition of wrestlers prior to the start of the season. This rule stipulated that wrestlers could not compete if they lost more than 1.5 percent of their body weight per week. Although it is a step in the right direction, as of 2009, this rule did not positively influence high school wrestlers' attitudes toward eating and weight loss. Instead, 20 percent more wrestlers reported thinking about losing weight while exercising more than when they were in-season.

Beliefs about Weight and Performance

Although several external factors associated with sports have contributed to athletes' experiences of weight-related pressure, the internalization of that pressure may also contribute to eating disorders and disordered eating behaviors. That is, in a recent study, 15.7 percent of athletes believed that their performance would improve if they lost five pounds. Whether they developed this belief from others or their own experience in sport has yet to be explored, but they are probably unknowingly placing pressure on themselves to lose weight in the pursuit of athletic achievement. As de Bruin and colleagues explained in their work on body image and dieting in female gymnasts and nonlean athletes, "Whereas [nonlean athletes] believe that 'thin is beautiful,' gymnasts seem more convinced that 'thin is going to win'" (p. 507).

Conclusion

Regardless of the source, athletes have reported weight-related pressure on a consistent basis in studies over the years. Although early studies looked specifically at lean sports, using different measures and making comparisons among different populations is difficult. Therefore, the field of study has recently expanded to include athletes from all sports and genders. The overwhelming consensus is that athletes do feel pressure to lose weight or maintain a low body weight as 20–80 percent of athletes have reported pressures associated with their sport to lose weight or maintain a low body weight. Moreover, research has indicated that higher levels of competition, and subsequent perceptions of greater external pressures, are predictors of increased disordered eating behaviors.

ASHLEY M. COKER-CRANNEY

See also: Ballet; Cheerleading; Coaches; Dancing; Figure Skating; Gymnastics; Media; Parents; Swimming and Synchronized Swimming; Weight Class Sports; Wrestling.

Bibliography

Beals, Katherine A. *Disordered Eating among Athletes: A Comprehensive Guide for Health Professionals.* Champaign, IL: Human Kinetics, 2004.

Casa Palmera. "Top 20 Famous Athletes with Eating Disorders." Casapalmera.com, 2009. Accessed December 2, 2008.

de Bruin, A. P. (Karin), Raoul R. D. Oudejans, and Frank C. Bakker. "Dieting and Body Image in Aesthetic Sports: A Comparison of Dutch Female Gymnasts and Non-Aesthetic Sport Athletes." *Psychology of Sport and Exercise* 8 (2007): 507–520.

Galli, Nick, and Justine J. Reel. "Adonis or Hephaestus? Exploring Body Image in Male Athletes." *Psychology of Men & Masculinity* 10 (2009): 95–108.

Greenleaf, Christy. "Weight Pressures and Social Physique Anxiety among Collegiate Synchronized Skaters." *Journal of Sport Behavior* 27 (2004): 260–76.

Greenleaf, Christy, Trent A. Petrie, Jennifer Carter, and Justine J. Reel. "Female Collegiate Athletes: Prevalence of Eating Disorders and Disordered Eating Behavior." *Journal of American College Health* 57 (2009): 489–95.

Harris, M. B., and D. Greco. "Weight Control and Weight Concern in Competitive Female Gymnasts." *Journal of Sport & Exercise Psychology* 12 (1990): 427–33.

Hausenblas, Heather A., and Diane E. Mack. "Social Physique Anxiety and Eating Disorder Correlates among Female Athletic and Nonathletic Populations." *Journal of Sport Behavior* 22 (1999): 502–512.

Kerr, Gretchen, Erica Berman, and Mary Jane De Souza. "Disordered Eating in Women's Gymnastics: Perspectives of Athletes, Coaches, Parents, and Judges." *Journal of Applied Sport Psychology* 18 (2006): 28–43.

Muscat, Anne C., and Bonita C. Long. "Critical Comments about Body Shape and Weight: Disordered Eating of Female Athletes and Sport Participants." *Journal of Applied Sport Psychology* 20 (2008): 1–24.

Peden, Jamie, Beverly L. Stiles, Michael Vandehey, and George Diekhoff. "The Effects of External Pressures and Competitiveness on Characteristics of Eating Disorders and Body Dissatisfaction." *Journal of Sport & Social Issues* 32 (2008): 415–29.

Petrie, Trent A. "Differences between Male and Female College Lean Sport Athletes, Non-lean Sport Athletes, and Nonathletes on Behavioral and Psychological Indices of Eating Disorders." *Journal of Applied Sport Psychology* 8 (1996): 218–30.

Petrie, Trent A., Christy Greenleaf, Justine Reel, and Jennifer Carter. "Prevalence of Eating Disorders and Disordered Eating Behaviors among Male Collegiate Athletes." *Psychology of Men & Masculinity* 9 (2008): 267–77.

Reel, Justine J., and Nick A. Galli. "Should Coaches Serve as the 'Weight Police' for Athletes?" *Journal of Physical Education Recreation and Dance* 77 (2006): 6–7.

Reel, Justine J., and Diane L. Gill. "Psychosocial Factors Related to Eating Disorders among High School and College Female Cheerleaders." *The Sport Psychologist* 10 (1996): 195–206.

Reel, Justine J., and Diane L. Gill. "Slim Enough to Swim? Weight Pressures for Competitive Swimmers and Coaching Implications." *The Sport Journal* 4 (2001): 1–5.

Reel, Justine J., Sonya Soohoo, Katherine M. Jamieson, and Diane L. Gill. "Femininity to the Extreme: Body Image Concerns among College Female Dancers." *Women in Sport and Physical Activity Journal* 14 (2005): 39–51.

Reel, Justine J., Sonya Soohoo, Trent A. Petrie, Christy Greenleaf, and Jennifer E. Carter. "Slimming Down for Sport: Developing a Weight Pressures in Sport Measure for Female Athletes." *Journal of Clinical Sport Psychology* 4 (2010): 99–111.

Shriver, Lenka Humenikova, Nancy Mulhollen Betts, and Mark Edward Payton. "Changes in Body Weight, Body Composition, and Eating Attitudes in High School Wrestlers." *International Journal of Sport Nutrition and Exercise Metabolism* 19 (2009): 424–32.

WRESTLING

Competitive wrestling requires a fine balance between strength and weight. Wrestlers must be as strong and agile as they possibly can, while remaining within the weight limits of their chosen category. This is a fine line, and as a consequence, some athletes have taken extreme measures to "make the weight." Studies investigating rapid weight loss among wrestlers began in the 1970s. Early studies found that up to 80 percent of competitors engaged in some form of weight loss procedure. The methods used were varied and included saunas, exercising in rubberized suits, and severely curtailing caloric and fluid intake. In addition, the use of diuretics, laxatives, diet pills, self-induced vomiting, and "spit cups" were common methods for rapid weight loss.

History of Wrestling and Eating Disorders

In 1997, three collegiate wrestlers died from weight-related causes which helped prompt the National Collegiate Athletic Association (NCAA) to implement a program designed to control rapid weight loss among athletes. Robert Oppliger and colleagues (2003) investigated whether the stricter guidelines worked and found that 40 percent of the 741 wrestlers reported that the new rules deterred extreme weight loss behaviors. However, over half of the wrestlers continued to fast to lose weight or maintain low weight, and 25 percent of wrestlers used saunas and rubberized suits to lose water weight at least once a month. Dieting behaviors among college wrestlers were more extreme than methods reported by high school wrestlers, but there was a clear reduction in overall pathological weight control methods compared to the 1980s. In addition, although many wrestlers admitted engaging in occasional pathogenic weight management behaviors, only 5 (of 741) met the clinical criteria for bulimia nervosa.

In 2006, the National Wrestling Coaches Association (NWCA) designed and implemented a weight management program for high school wrestlers requiring a minimum weight to be set at the beginning of each season. Under the guidelines, wrestlers are not permitted to compete under their minimum weight limits and cannot lose more than 1.5 percent of their body weight per week. Shriver and colleagues (2009) evaluated the efficacy of the NWCA guidelines and found that although body weight and body fat did not appear to fluctuate as widely as might be expected before these rules were introduced, wrestlers continued to report weight concerns and caloric expenditure. Thus, even though body weight and fat were more monitored using the new regulations, wrestlers were not deterred from obsessing about body weight.

Future of Wrestling

Although measures have been taken to reduce the extreme weight loss during season, fluctuations in weight have been reported between in-season and off-season. Typically, wrestlers experience significant weight gain during the off-season which may indicate that they are not competing at a typical or ideal body weight.

It appears that wrestlers are less likely to fit the clinical eating disorder criteria than disordered eating which is characterized by a focus on losing weight for short-term performance improvements. There is evidence to suggest that wrestlers do exhibit characteristics of anorexia nervosa (e.g., restricting food intake) or bulimia nervosa (e.g., excessive exercise). Reports of extreme dieting and use of diuretics, even with the changes implemented by the NCAA and NWCA, are still being identified. However, not all wrestlers exhibit the same eating disorder characteristics and as a group they may be similar to bodybuilders who undergo severe caloric restriction in order to reduce body fat prior to a competition.

Conclusion

Because wrestling is a weight category sport, an athlete's concern regarding his or her weight is likely to continue. Regulations enforced over the last 15 years in both high school and collegiate wrestling appear to have reduced the incidence of weight-related deaths. However, thoughts and some practices involving weight control and weight loss in wrestling continue.

TIMOTHY M. BAGHURST

See also: Bodybuilding; Weight Class Sports; Weight Pressures in Sport.

Bibliography

Buford, Thomas A., Stephen J. Rossi, Douglas B. Smith, Matthew S. O'Brien, and Chris Pickering. "The Effect of a Competitive Wrestling Season on Body Weight, Hydration, and Muscular Performance in Collegiate Wrestlers." *Journal of Strength and Conditioning Research* 20 (2006): 689–92.

Oppliger, Robert A., Suzanne A. N. Steen, and James R. Scott. "Weight Loss Practices of College Wrestlers." *International Journal of Sport Nutrition and Exercise Metabolism* 13 (2003): 29–46.

Shriver, Lenka H., Nance M. Betts, and Mark E. Payton. "Changes in Body Weight, Body Composition, and Eating Attitudes in High School Wrestlers." *International Journal of Sport Nutrition and Exercise Metabolism* 19 (2009): 424–32.

Steen, Suzanne N., and Kelly D. Brownell. "Patterns of Weight Loss and Regain in Wrestlers." *Medicine & Science in Sport & Exercise* 22 (1990): 762–68.

Weissinger, Ellen, Terry J. Housh, and Glen O. Johnson. "Coaches' Attitudes, Knowledge, and Practices Concerning Weight Loss Behaviors in High School Wrestling." *Pediatric Exercise Science* 5 (1993): 145–50.

Y

YOGA

Yoga is referred to as an integration of the body, mind, and spirit. The origins of yoga date back several thousand years in India. Yoga was created as the art, science, and philosophy of life. It is believed that the vast body of knowledge, when practiced through the system of yoga, can lead to greater health, mental control, and ultimately, self-realization.

When the body is out of alignment, the mind is rarely in control or balance. Yoga movement acts to stimulate stretching, purifying, and healing of the body. Yoga movements bring balance, peace, and harmony to the mind, thus creating health, happiness, and fulfillment. Moreover, yoga helps us practice readjusting negative thoughts. The emotional content of current thoughts affects future reality. By creating a conscious mind through yoga, negative conditioning of the past can be let go. This concept is especially critical for individuals with poor self-image and low self-esteem.

In the American culture, yoga is also interpreted as "a means of gaining a sense of physical and mental well-being." Thus, yoga can deliver beneficial effects for a variety of medical conditions such as blood pressure, cancer, depression, anxiety, and eating disorders. By practicing yoga regularly, the mind and body can be balanced and deep relaxation can be achieved. Once the balance and relaxation techniques are mastered, a sense of accomplishment can be experienced along with an inner peace that may help our mind release daily worries. This mechanism may result in greater self-esteem, which is identified as a protective factor for individuals suffering from eating disorders.

Neurotransmitter Effects from Yoga

It has been scientifically explained as to why yoga movement stimulates neurophysiological activities, proven to improve the following human functions, in the brain. First, the neurotransmitter melatonin is released through yoga movement and circadian rhythms are normalized, thus improving sleep and mood. Second, yoga promotes increased γ-aminobutyric acid (GABA) levels, thereby having a positive impact on depression and anxiety. Third, yoga increases dopamine levels in the brain, leading to improvements in cognition, motor behavior, motivation, reward, sleep, mood, attention, and learning. Next, increased levels of serotonins help regulate anger, aggression, mood, body temperature, sleep, sexuality, metabolism, and appetite. Lastly, numerous studies have shown consistent evidence of the fact that positive relationships between mindfulness movements such as yoga and

Yoga has become a popular intervention for eating-disordered clients. (Hongqi Zhang/Dreamstime.com)

reduced cortisol (also known as stress hormone) levels decrease stress.

Benefits of Yoga for Eating Disorder Treatments

In the past decade, clinicians and clients have embraced the benefits of yoga for treating eating disorders. Although few studies related to eating disorders have shown the effectiveness of yoga therapy in inpatient and outpatient settings, a study conducted by Carei and colleagues demonstrated greater decreases in eating disorder symptoms and food preoccupation. Another study reported that yoga helped decrease impulsivity among clients with bulimia.

One significant benefit of practicing yoga during the recovery process of eating disorders is an increased level of body awareness. Clients with eating disorders are often preoccupied with food, body shape, calories, and weight. As such, yoga group therapy, through mindfulness, promotes positive thoughts, self-image, and self-talk and helps the participant stay in the present moment instead of getting preoccupied with negative thoughts and poor self-image. Yoga also initiates slow movements with attention, compassion, and awareness. This integrated approach increases one's sense of well-being and calmness which results in less reactivity and increased self-care. Learning to sense the body, mind and spirit is a powerful means to overcome personal battles with eating disorders.

Treatment Challenges Associated with Yoga

Yoga is an effective way to create a state of reflection and increased awareness for individuals experiencing intense self-hatred and suffering. Because of the nature of the disease, however, the quality of the yoga group may be dismissed if health care providers and yoga instructors are not aware of certain behaviors that are contributing factors for eating disorders. Examples of common behaviors observed among individuals with eating disorders are the comparison of one's body to those of peers and the yoga instructor, body checking by looking in the mirrors or by touching one's body, wearing extremely baggy or tight clothing, and excessively repeating yoga poses to burn extra calories. The intensity level or the types of yoga movements may trigger poor self-image and negative thoughts because of feeling a lack of physical strength, feeling fat, or feeling the urge to overexercise. The other caution is the language used during the yoga group. The yoga instructor should be mindful while selecting terminologies of physical movements and functions (e.g., "getting toned") and should use the yoga philosophy as a means of spiritual guidance instead of integrating religious views so as to create a safe and nonjudgmental atmosphere in the yoga group.

Moreover, feeling fat, ugly, shamed, and disgusted is described as a typical emotional state in eating disorders, and facing the challenge of experiencing body awareness through yoga movements may require much effort among those with extremely distorted self-image. Thus, some clients in inpatient or residential settings may avoid any activities guiding them to connect with their sensations, such as a yoga group. Health care providers and yoga instructors must set clear boundaries with clients who refuse or avoid yoga groups by educating them about the benefits of yoga and also helping them to understand the yoga experience as a part of recovery.

Considerations for Yoga Group/Therapy as Treatment for Eating Disorders

Yoga group or therapy can be an effective treatment for eating disorders. The most significant element is to select yoga instructors who are knowledgeable about eating disorders or have a strong willingness to learn about and understand eating disorders. Based on the clients' medical level, trained yoga instructors should have a clear understanding of how to design modified poses and levels of yoga movements (i.e., Power or Hot Yoga vs. Fundamental Yoga) for populations with eating disorders. When they notice common behaviors such body-checking, comparisons, or overexercise during the group, they must feel comfortable redirecting the actions assertively. Lastly, it is strongly desirable to include yoga instructors as part of the treatment team. The most crucial element of success in the treatment of eating disorders is to provide consistent messages to clients. In order to maintain the quality of treatment, yoga instructors and health care providers should exchange necessary client information related to the yoga group.

Conclusion

Yoga can bring various benefits not only to eating disorder recovery but also to the new journey undertaken after recovering from eating disorders. To contribute to positive outcomes in the treatment of eating disorders, health care providers must make efforts to search for influential yoga instructors who can provide safe, peaceful, and enjoyable yoga groups. Lastly, more studies examining the effectiveness of yoga are necessary to support yoga groups or therapy in the treatment of eating disorders.

MAYA MIYAIRI

See also: Body Checking; Treatment.

Bibliography

Bai, Bath. *Complete Guide to Pilates, Yoga, Medication, and Stress Relief.* New York: Sterling Publisher, 2006.

Carei, T. Rain, Amber L. Fyfe-Johnson, Cora C. Breuner, and Margaret A. Brown. "Randomized Controlled Clinical Trial of Yoga in the Treatment of Eating Disorders." *Journal of Adolescent Health* 46 (2010): 346–51.

Douglass, Laura. "Yoga as an Intervention in the Treatment of Eating Disorders: Does It Help?" *Eating Disorders* 17 (2009): 126–39.

Douglass, Laura. "Thinking Through the Body: The Conceptualization of Yoga as Therapy for Individuals with Eating Disorders." *Eating Disorders* 19 (2011): 83–96.

McIver, Shane, Paul O'Halloran, and Michael McGartland. "Yoga as a Treatment for Binge Eating Disorder: A Preliminary Study." *Complementary Therapies in Medicine* 17 (2009): 196–202

Price, Beverly. "Yoga as the Missing Link in Eating Disorder Recovery." *Yoga Therapy Today* 6, no. 1 (2010): 15–18.

Reel, Justine J., and Katherine A. Beals, eds. *The Hidden Faces of Eating Disorders and Body Image.* Reston, VA: AAHPERD, 2009.

Z

ZINC

Zinc Deficiencies among Eating Disordered Individuals

Eating disorders contribute to numerous vitamin and mineral deficiencies including deficiencies in zinc. In one study, 40 percent of individuals with bulimia nervosa and 54 percent of individuals with anorexia nervosa presented with zinc deficiencies. These deficiencies could be caused by lower dietary intake of zinc, impaired zinc absorption, vomiting, diarrhea, and binge episodes with low-zinc foods. Having a zinc deficiency is important for individuals who are at risk for eating disorders because lack of zinc contributes to decreased appetite and a loss of one's ability to taste foods. Therefore, restrictive behavior associated with a diet can lead to a physiological response that causes a lack of desire to eat and perpetuates anorexia nervosa.

Zinc Taste Test

The Zinc Taste Test (ZTT) can be administered to assess for zinc deficiency among eating disordered individuals in a noninvasive way. To follow the ZTT protocol, an individual is asked to refrain from eating, drinking, or smoking for at least 30 minutes. The client is then asked to place 1–2 teaspoons of Aqueous Zinc in his or her mouth, swirl for 10 seconds and spit out the solution. The client is asked to describe the taste of the solution to test for physiological zinc status. Optimal zinc levels are represented by reports of an extremely unpleasant taste usually accompanied by a nonverbal grimace while tasting the solution whereas individuals who are deficient in zinc tend to describe the solution as tasteless or tasting like water.

Because most individuals with anorexia nervosa and bulimia nervosa are deficient in zinc, individuals can be given a supplement with liquid zinc in order to detect the presence of eating disordered symptoms. This is particularly useful since eating disorders are such secretive disorders and other assessment tools (e.g., questionnaires) are typically based on an individual's self-report of his or her symptoms.

Nutritional Supplementation as Treatment

In addition to showing promise for the detection of eating disorders, zinc supplementation should be considered for the treatment of eating disorders. Specifically, preliminary studies have shown that zinc supplementation leads to increased appetite, eating, and weight gain. In a frequently cited 1994 study, anorexia nervosa clients who received zinc supplementation achieved a 10 percent increase in body mass index and increased their body mass index at twice the rate of the control group.

Conclusion

Zinc deficiency represents one of many health consequences resulting from restrictive behavior and having an inadequate nutritional intake. A zinc test can be administered to detect the presence of eating disorder symptoms, providing a more objective assessment tool than traditional self-report measures (e.g., clinical interview). Additionally, as part of nutritional treatment, zinc supplementation has been recommended to help individuals experience improved taste acuity and stronger appetite.

JUSTINE J. REEL

Bibliography

Birmingham, Carl L., Elliott M. Goldner, and Rita Bakan. "Controlled Trial of Zinc Supplementation in Anorexia Nervosa." *International Journal of Eating Disorders* 15, no. 3 (1994): 251–55. doi: 10.1002/1098-108X.

Costin, Carolyn. *The Eating Disorder Sourcebook: A Comprehensive Guide to the Causes, Treatments and Prevention of Eating Disorders, Third Edition.* New York, NY: McGraw-Hill, 2007.

Costin, Carolyn. *100 Questions & Answers about Eating Disorders.* Boston, MA: Jones and Bartlett, 2007.

Humphries, Laurie, Beverly Vivian, Mary Stuart, and Craig J. McClain. "Zinc Deficiency and Eating Disorders." *Journal of Clinical Psychiatry* 50, no. 12 (1989): 456–59.

Appendix: Case Illustrations

Case Number 1: Brittany

Background

Brittany is 17 years old and is an academically gifted high school student. She is slated to be the valedictorian for her class and she has been applying to top universities across the country. She does not drink or use drugs, but her boyfriend of one year has been pressuring her to have sex. Pressure from the boyfriend coupled with the uncertainty of where she will go to school has created immense stress. Everyone keeps telling her how "together" she is, but she feels pretty scattered and confused on the inside.

Presenting Problem

Brittany has felt out of control lately and has been restricting her food intake. She finds that eating is the one aspect of her life that can be structured. Brittany has a calorie counter on her iPhone that helps her calculate and track the energy intake of each meal and snack. She avoids foods that have high fat content and has become a vegetarian. She has lost 20 pounds in several months and her clothes are loose. She is surprised that despite her weight loss, she feels more concerned about food and gaining weight than before she began restricting her food.

Diagnosis

Although Brittany is showing some early signs of anorexia nervosa, she would most likely be diagnosed as Eating Disorder Not Otherwise Specified unless she reported amenorrhea and continued weight loss. Her behaviors and psychological features are consistent with disordered eating and should be a cause for concern.

Treatment Recommendation

Brittany would probably be a good candidate for outpatient counseling since she is not presenting with comorbid conditions (e.g., substance abuse, self-harm). The goal of counseling would be to allow Brittany to discuss the stressors in her life. She can work with a treatment professional to develop healthier coping skills to replace her dysfunctional eating behaviors. She may also need to process feelings of having to be "perfect" and "together" so that she can allow herself to be human. Her prognosis is likely to be very good if she receives treatment and support.

Case Number 2: Cara

Background

Cara is 14 years old and has wanted to be a model for her whole life. From the time she was a toddler she took ballet and baton twirling lessons and participated in gymnastics. While in 3rd grade, she was recruited by a modeling agency and she began doing fashion shows for local department stores. Cara has always felt comfort in taking care of her appearance, even when her parents went through a nasty divorce. She has hair extensions, eyelash extensions, regularly goes to a tanning salon, and gets a manicure weekly. She is of normal weight for her height, but she is shorter than many models which leads her to wear three-inch platform heels.

Problem

Despite Cara's attention toward making herself look more beautiful, she has a terrible secret. She constantly diets but sometimes "goes wild" when she gets hungry and binges on ice cream or Kettle chips. She is usually able to make herself vomit to get up some of the food, but she feels shameful and often cuts her arms as a punishment. She also engages in self-harming to experience pain on days when she feels "blah." Cara also is obsessed with pro-ana websites and spends several hours a day blogging and gazing at "thinspo" photos, dreaming that one day she will have her photo posted by an admiring fan. Cara has been purging for over two years and has had secret binges for over four years. She has been on a diet since 1st grade when she started giving away her brown bag lunch. Cara sees her eating disorder as part of her identity and a necessary evil.

Diagnosis

Cara meets the diagnostic criteria for bulimia nervosa since the behaviors have been present for over six months. She has both binge episodes and purging symptoms and admits being a "yo-yo" dieter. She also reports extreme body image dissatisfaction which is a salient feature for eating disorder identification.

Treatment

Cara is relatively young and has been experiencing symptoms for most of her short life. The eating disordered behavior appears to be fairly entrenched and she displays body dissatisfaction. Therefore, it is important that Cara receive eating disorder–specific treatment and be assessed for the level of care for admission to an eating disorder treatment facility. Her self-harm behaviors should be considered along with her lack of family support and motivation to justify a higher level of care. A residential level of care would afford Cara the structure required to eliminate purging and self-harm behaviors while addressing body image concerns, low self-esteem, and development of more positive coping skills. In this environment Cara could engage in Dialectical Behavior Therapy (DBT) groups, individual therapy, and nutritional support.

About the Editor and Contributors

The Editor

Justine J. Reel, PhD, LPC, CC-AASP is an Assistant Professor in the Department of Health Promotion and Education at the University of Utah, a Licensed Professional Counselor, and a certified sport psychology consultant. She received her Bachelor's degree from North Carolina State University and completed her doctoral and master's degrees from the University of North Carolina at Greensboro. She has treated eating disorder clients across inpatient, residential, partial, intensive outpatient, and outpatient settings. She has conducted research about body image and eating disorders for the past 19 years. She currently focuses on integrating eating disorder and obesity prevention approaches among adolescents and their families.

Dr. Reel, the editor of *The Hidden Faces of Eating Disorders and Body Image,* has published over 60 papers, and has delivered over 200 presentations about body image and eating disorders. She has founded the SPEAK (Students Promoting Eating Disorder Awareness and Knowledge) organization at the University of Utah to promote positive body image, health and to raise eating disorder awareness. She is a founding board member for the Utah Chapter of International Association of Eating Disorder Professionals.

The Contributors

Timothy M. Baghurst, PhD is an Assistant Professor in the department of Health and Human Performance at Oklahoma State University. He has published research articles on male body image and muscle dysmorphia.

Robert A. Bucciere, MSW, LCSW is the Lead Licensed Clinical Social Worker at the University of Utah Health Care: Neurobehavior HOME Program. He graduated from the University of Maryland at Baltimore and the University of North Carolina at Greensboro. He has published and presented on the body image concerns of persons with intellectual disabilities while providing individual, couples, and group psychotherapy to thousands of individuals in a variety of populations across the life span.

Ashley M. Coker-Cranney, MS is a doctoral student at West Virginia University. She received her master's degree in the Department of Exercise and Sport Science at the University of Utah. She previously served as the Head Coach for the University of Idaho cheerleading squad.

Juliann M. Cook, LCSW is a Licensed Clinical Social Worker and PhD student at the University of Utah. She is advanced-trained and certified in EMDR (Eye Movement Desensitization and Reprocessing) and maintains a part-time private practice in Salt Lake City while she completes her doctoral studies in Health Promotion and Education.

Holly E. Doetsch, MS, RD is a Clinical Dietitian at Primary Children's Medical Center in Salt Lake City, Utah, where she assists with the inpatient management of eating disorders. She holds master's degrees in Exercise and Sport Science and Nutrition from the University of Utah. Her presentations and publications have addressed such topics as nutrition therapy for eating disorders, the female athlete triad, and disordered eating among the diabetes population.

Nick Galli, PhD is an Assistant Professor in Sport Studies at California State University at Northridge. He received his doctoral degree in the Department of Exercise and Sport Science from the University of Utah.

Christy Greenleaf, PhD is an Associate Professor in the Department of Kinesiology at the University of Wisconsin - Milwaukee. She received her Bachelor of Arts degree in Psychology from Bowling Green State University, her Master of Science degree in Sport Studies from Miami University (Ohio), and her Doctor of Philosophy degree in Exercise and Sport Science from the University of North Carolina–Greensboro. Dr. Greenleaf's research focuses on psychosocial aspects of weight, physical activity, body image, and disordered eating.

Jessica Guenther, MSW is a Primary Therapist who works with eating disordered clients at the Eating Recovery Center in Denver, Colorado. She holds a bachelor's degree in Science with majors in Addiction Counseling and Social Work from the University of Mary in Bismarck, North Dakota, and a Master's of Social Work with a certificate in Women's Health from the University of Utah.

Shelly Guillory, RN, BSN earned bachelor's degrees in nursing and journalism from the University of Utah. She is the Director of Nursing at a nonprofit substance abuse treatment center, Odyssey House, located in Salt Lake City.

Amelia McBride, MS, RD, CD practices as an Outpatient Dietitian at Primary Children's Medical Center in Salt Lake City, Utah. She received a Bachelors of Science in Dietetics from the University of Arizona, and a Master of Science in Nutrition from the University of Utah.

Maya Miyairi, MS is currently a College Instructor in the Department of Health Promotion and Education at the University of Utah while completing her doctoral studies. She earned Bachelor's and Master's degrees in Exercise and Sports Science from the University of Utah. She served as the Exercise Director for Avalon Hills, a residential eating disorder facility, and Resident Manager for New Life Centers.

Hailey E. Nielson, MS, CHES is a Certified Health Education Specialist and received her Master's degree from the University of Utah in Health Promotion and Education with an Emphasis in Weight Management, Body Image, and Eating Disorders in addition to a Graduate Certificate in Global Health and a minor in Nutrition. She has conducted research related to nutrition globally. Currently, she works for the International Rescue Committee addressing nutrition with refugees.

Christine L. B. Selby, PhD, CC-AASP is an Assistant Professor of Psychology at Husson University in Bangor, Maine. She also maintains a limited private practice as a licensed psychologist, sport psychologist, and eating disorder specialist. Dr. Selby is active in a number of professional organizations including the Academy for Eating Disorders where she serves on the Fitness Industry Guidelines Task Force and the Association for Applied Sport Psychology where she co-founded and co-chairs the Eating Disorder Special Interest Group.

TeriSue Smith-Jackson, PhD, MPH is an Assistant Professor at Utah Valley University in Orem, Utah. She received her doctoral degree in the Department of Health Promotion and Education from the University of Utah. Her primary research interests are body image, the "freshmen 15" and intuitive eating.

Sonya SooHoo, PhD received her doctorate in the Department of Exercise and Sport Science from the University of Utah. She currently serves as a research analyst and consultant for grant projects. She has published numerous scholarly articles on body image and eating disorders among diverse populations.

Dana K. Voelker, PhD is an Assistant Professor in the Department of Kinesiology, Sports Studies, and Physical Education at The College at Brockport, State University of New York. Prior to her position at Brockport, she was a doctoral student and university fellow at the Institute for the Study of Youth Sports, Michigan State University. She teaches sport sociology and sport psychology, studies eating and exercise behaviors in athletes, and works as a consultant assisting athletes at all levels to develop to their fullest both as athletes and people.

Index

221–22; with bulimia nervosa, 222–24;
with eating disorder not otherwise specified, 224

Ghana, 80, 413

Gender, 39–40, 47, 66, 76, 86, 145,
152–53, 193, 203, **224–26**, 249,
265–66, 288–89, 292, 301, 304, 320,
341, 348–49, 352, 362–63, 402, 404,
443, 453, 466; differences in eating
disorders and body image disturbances,
225; prevalence rates by, 225

Generalized Anxiety Disorder (GAD). *See*
Anxiety Disorders

Gonadarche, 2

Group Counseling, *See* Treatment

Guenther, Heidi, 48, 466

Gull, Sir William, 27, 30

Gymnastics, 11, 25, 107–8, 199,
226–29, 422–23, 425, 434, 441, 468,
482; and eating disorders, 227; as a
judged, aesthetic sport, 228; rhythmic,
228; sources of weight pressures,
228

HAES. *See* Health at Every Size Approach

Hattou Shin Ideal, **230–31**; body
image and the, 230

Health at Every Size Approach (HAES),
231–33, 244, 246–47, 316, 364; and
body image, 232; evaluation of the, 232;
overview of the, 231–32

Heinrich, Christy, 13, 466

IAEDP. *See* International Association of
Eating Disorder Professionals

Impulsivity, 134, **234–35**, 284,
341–42, 346, 429, 447, 476; eating
disorders and, 234; multi-impulsivity
versus uni-impulsivity, 234–35

Individual Therapy. *See* Treatment

Infertility, 23, 30, 41, **236–37**

Integrative Approaches, **237–39**,
364; acupuncture, 238; energy psychology, 238–39; mediation, 237–38;
therapeutic massage/touch (TT),
238

Intellectual Disabilities and Body Image,
239–43, 352; body image

and, 240–41; eating disorders,
240

International Association of Eating
Disorder Professionals (IAEDP),
243

Intuitive Eating, 169, 220, 232,
244–48, 308; and Health at Every Size
Approach (HAES), 246–47; assessment
of, 246; history of, 244; ten principles
of, 244–46

Italy, 47, 77, 121

Japan, 77–79, 91, 230, 410, 413, 428,
437

Jazzercise, 9

Jockeys, 30, 225, **249–51**, 411; eating
disorders and, 249–50; equestrian athletes, 250–51

Journaling, 117, **251–52**; barriers to,
252; uses of journaling in eating disorder treatment, 251

Ketoacidosis, 129, **253–54**; clinical
manifestation and complications,
253; from starvation, 254; in eating disordered patients with Type 1 Diabetes,
253; treatment, 253–54

Lanugo, 30, **255–56**, 277–78; and
eating disorders, 255; what is,
255

Late Life and Late-Onset Eating Disorders,
17, **256–57**

Laxative Abuse, 54, 97, 127, 144, 150,
163–64, 223, 227, **257–60**, 274, 275,
311, 383; medical complications, 258;
treatment considerations, 258–59; types
of 258

Leptin, **260–61**; and anorexia nervosa,
260; and binge eating disorder, 261;
and bulimia nervosa; and eating
disorders, 260–61; what is,
260

Let's Move!, **261–62**, 316; five pillars
of, 262; taking action, 262

Levels of Care, 38, **262–64**, 450–51;
types of treatment, 263

Liposuction, 16, 72, 81, 360